COMMERCIAL LAW AND PRACTICE

Judith Embley, Keir Bamford and Martin Smith

Published by

College of Law Publishing,
Braboeuf Manor, Portsmouth Road, St Catherines, Guildford GU3 1HA

British Library Cataloguing-in-Publication Data

A catalogue record for this book is available from the British Library.

ISBN 978 1 907624 22 3

Typeset by Style Photosetting Ltd, Mayfield, East Sussex

Printed in Great Britain by Ashford Colour Press Ltd, Gosport, Hampshire

COMMERCIAL LAW AND PRACTICE

Preface

All parts of the work are being substantially rewritten, on an ongoing basis, to reflect the changes in modern vocational training practice. It is hoped that the level of detail and analysis of the cases and statutes will be suited to both vocational study and to the early years of practice. Clearly, with such a diverse range of discrete topics, many limitations are imposed upon such a work, but it is intended that the reader should be assisted in gaining a firm grasp of the general principles and a flavour of the current state of legislation and case law.

Judith Embley would like to thank her colleagues at Bloomsbury, Susan Sang, Alex Laski and Mary Medyckyj, who reviewed and contributed invaluable suggestions to the Sale of Goods and Marketing chapters.

JUDITH EMBLEY
KEIR BAMFORD
MARTIN SMITH
The College of Law

Further Study

The following books may be of interest to readers wishing to pursue a particular topic further. In addition, there are some references to Internet sources in the text, as well as the obvious ones such as the European Commission sites and the UK legislation ones.

Sale of Goods

Adams and MacQueen, *Atiyah's Sale of Goods* (12th rev edn, Pearson Education, 2010)

Bridge, *Benjamin's Sale of Goods* (8th rev edn, Sweet & Maxwell, 2010)

Encyclopedia of Forms and Precedents (5th edn, LexisNexis Butterworths), vol 34 on Sale of Goods (2002 Reissue)

Rosenberg, *Practical Commercial Precedents* (Sweet & Maxwell), section on Sale of Goods: Precedent L1.

(The above works have useful sections on exclusion of liability.)

Drafting

Beale, *Chitty on Contracts* (30th edn, Sweet & Maxwell, 2009)

Christou, *Drafting Commercial Agreements* (4th edn, Sweet & Maxwell, 2009)

Christou, *Boilerplate: Practical Clauses* (5th edn, Sweet & Maxwell, 2009)

Marketing Agreements

Practical Commercial Precedents and the *Encyclopedia of Forms and Precedents* have useful sections on agency distribution and other types of marketing agreement. See also:

Christou, *International Agency, Distribution and Licensing Agreements* (5th edn, Sweet & Maxwell, 2008)

Goyder, *EU Distribution Law* (4th edn, Hart Publishing, 2005)

Commercial Law

Bradgate, *Commercial Law* (3rd edn, Oxford University Press, 2005)

Byles on Bills of Exchange and Cheques (28th edn, Sweet & Maxwell, 2007)

Christou, *Drafting Commercial Agreements* (4th edn, Sweet & Maxwell, 2009)

Goode, *Commercial Law* (4th edn, LexisNexis Butterworths, 2009)

International Chambers of Commerce, *Incoterms 2010* (ICC Publishing, 2010)

Malek and Quest, *Jack: Documentary Credits* (4th edn, Bloomsbury Professional, 2009)

Murray, *Schmitthoff's Export Trade* (11th edn, Sweet & Maxwell, 2007)

Sealy and Hooly, *Commercial Law* (4th edn, Oxford University Press, 2008)

Wilson, *Carriage of Goods by Sea* (7th edn, Pearson Educational, 2010)

Competition Law

Lindrup, *Butterworths Competition Law Handbook* (15th edn, LexisNexis Butterworths, 2009)

Whish, *Competition Law* (6th edn, Oxford University Press, 2008)

Goyder, *EC Competition Law* (5th edn, Oxford University Press, 2009)

Bellamy and Child, *EC Law of Competition* (6th edn, Oxford University Press, 2009)

A number of works have been written specifically on the Competition Act 1998, including:

Coleman and Grenfell, *The Competition Act 1998: Law and Practice* (Oxford University Press, 1999)

Frazer and Hornsby, *The Competition Act 1998: A Practical Guide* (Jordans, 1999)

Intellectual Property

Cornish and Llewelyn, *Intellectual Property* (7th edn, Sweet & Maxwell, 2010)

CIPA Guide to the Patents Acts (6th edn, Sweet & Maxwell, 2009)

Phillips and Firth, *Introduction to Intellectual Property Law* (4th edn, Oxford University Press, 2001)

(For works which consider the relationship of competition law and intellectual property, in particular in relation to licensing, see the list under 'Marketing Agreements' above.)

Information Technology

Reed and Angel, *Computer Law* (6th edn, Oxford University Press, 2007)

Susskind, *Transforming the Law* (Oxford University Press, 2004)

Todd, *E-Commerce Law* (Routledge-Cavendish, 2005)

Contents

Table of Cases

C

D

E

J

K

L

M

N

O

P

Q

R

S

T

U

V

W

Z

U

V

W

Z

Table of Primary Legislation

EU primary legislation

International conventions

Treaty on the Functioning of the European Union [illegible]

[illegible]

International conventions

[illegible]

Trade Union and Labour Relations (Consolidation) Act 1992 [illegible]

[illegible]

EU primary legislation

[illegible]

Table of Secondary Legislation

Codes

EU secondary legislation

Commission Notices

Directives

Table of Abbreviations

ADR	alternative dispute resolution
ALCS	Authors' Licensing and Collecting Society
BEA 1882	Bills of Exchange Act 1882
BIS	Department for Business, Innovation and Skills
CA 1957	Cheques Act 1957
CA 1998	Competition Act 1998
CDPA 1988	Copyright, Designs and Patents Act 1988
CFR	Cost and Freight
CIF	Cost, Insurance and Freight
CIP	Carriage and Insurance Paid To
CJJA 1982	Civil Jurisdiction and Judgments Act 1982
CLA	Copyright Licensing Agency Ltd
CPT	Carriage Paid To
CTM	Community Trade Mark
DAF	Delivered at Frontier
DAP	Delivered at Place
DAT	Delivered at Terminal
DC	debtor-creditor
DCS	debtor-creditor-supplier
DDP	Delivered Duty Paid
DTI	Department of Trade and Industry
ECB	extortionate credit bargain
ECJ	European Court of Justice
EDI	Electronic Data Interchange
EEA	European Economic Area
EFTA	European Free Trade Area
EPC 1973	European Patent Convention 1973
EPO	European Patents Office
EXW	Ex Works
FAS	Free Alongside
FCA	Free Carrier
FOB	Free On Board
FSR	*Fleet Street Reports*
ICANN	Internet Corporation for Assigned Names and Numbers
ICC	International Chamber of Commerce
IP	intellectual property
IT	information technology
MCPS	Mechanical Copyright Protection Society
NLA	Newspaper Licensing Agency Ltd
OFT	Office of Fair Trading
PA 1977	Patents Act 1977
PCP	Rosenberg, *Practical Commercial Precedents* (Sweet & Maxwell)
PCT	Patent Co-operation Treaty
PLS	Publishers Licensing Society
PPL	Phonographic Performance Ltd
RDA 1949	Registered Designs Act 1949
RPA 1976	Resale Prices Act 1976
RPC	*Reports of Patent, Design and Trade Mark Cases*

RTPA 1976	Restrictive Trade Practices Act 1976
RUC	restricted-use credit
SGA 1979	Sale of Goods Act 1979
SGSA 1982	Supply of Goods and Services Act 1982
TFEU	Treaty on the Functioning of the European Union
UCP	Uniform Customs and Practice for Documentary Credits
UCTA 1977	Unfair Contract Terms Act 1977
ULIS	Uniform Law on the International Sale of Goods
UNCITRAL	UN Commission on International Trade Law
VPL	Video Performance Ltd
WIPO	World Intellectual Property Organisation

Part I

COMMERCIAL AGREEMENTS

Chapter 1
Introduction to Commercial Contracts

1.1 Introduction

This book will deal with some of the legal issues that arise in relation to commercial transactions which govern everyday business activity. The term 'commercial law' covers a large number of interconnecting areas of law and practice (both domestic and international), including the sale of goods, marketing agreements, transport, finance and credit arrangements, competition law, intellectual property, insurance and related areas, such as banking or tax law. Clearly it will not be possible to cover all aspects of commercial law. However, the thread which links together all of these interconnecting areas of law is the use of commercial contracts. All of the topic areas which will be considered are in some way related to commercial contracts, either very obviously, for example the drafting of standard terms and conditions for the supply of goods, or indirectly, for example the application of competition law to distribution agreements or the exploitation of intellectual property rights by the use of licensing agreements. This reflects the realities of commercial practice.

It is extremely difficult to generalise on the role of a commercial solicitor which will, inevitably, be varied and depend on the type of firm in which he practises. In smaller firms, combined company/commercial departments (so-called 'CoCo' departments) may deal with a range of matters, from the setting up of companies and partnerships to consumer issues. In a large corporate firm, there will be a far higher degree of specialisation within discrete areas, for example shipping law or the competition aspects of distribution agreements. However, any commercial lawyer will be routinely involved with either the drafting or interpretation of contracts. **Figure 1.1** below illustrates the main types of commercial contract that will be covered in this book.

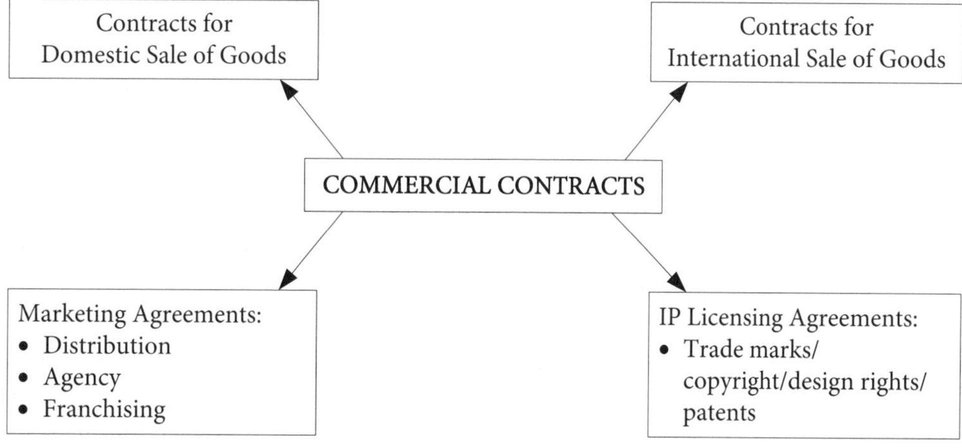

Figure 1.1 Commercial contracts

Part I on Commercial Contracts will cover the content and drafting of contracts for the sale of goods and marketing agreements within the UK. It will also consider briefly other types of contract under which goods may pass, such as hire purchase and leasing. It is designed to bring together most of the basic legal considerations that must be addressed in order to understand the nature of these types of commercial contracts. Part II will go on to deal with the extra considerations required where such contracts involve international aspects.

The emphasis throughout this book will be on business-to-business contracts (B2B contracts) focusing on the position and protection of the commercial supplier. Most manufacturers do not themselves sell directly to end users, so contracts which govern the supply of goods to consumers (B2C contracts) are outside the scope of this book, although there are some areas of overlap, for example the drafting of exclusion clauses, and the chapter on e-commerce (**Chapter 25**) will touch on some aspects of consumer protection.

1.2 Sources of commercial law

Where do you look to find the legal principles on which commercial law is based? The main sources of commercial law are:

(a) the law of contract;

(b) established custom and usage of the trade;

(c) national legislation;

(d) European Union law; and

(e) international conventions.

If you are dealing with a commercial contract matter in practice, the sources which are likely to cause the most difficulty are custom and usage of the trade and international conventions. Legal databases are ideal for sourcing legislation, but the 'soft' material can be harder to track down. Indeed, half the problem is knowing that it exists in the first place. As regards the custom and usage of the trade, a lawyer will be often be reliant on the client for information on this aspect, as the client's knowledge of the market will often be far greater.

1.3 The supply chain

The fundamental concern of a commercial supplier is how to get his goods to the ultimate consumer in the most efficient and cost-effective manner. Most of the contracts that are covered in this book are designed to achieve this goal, so it is important to understand the steps in the supply chain. This is illustrated in **Figure 1.2** below.

One possibility is for a manufacturer (Manufacturer 1) to sell his goods direct to retailers, who will sell on to other retailers or direct to the end user. This is, however, not the most usual arrangement, and often a 'middle man' in the form of either a distributor (see Manufacturer 2) or an agent (see Manufacturer 3) will be involved.

The choice of marketing arrangement will be dictated by commercial factors, and the appropriate form of contract must be drafted. This will be considered in **Chapter 9**.

A manufacturer will also be concerned with producing the goods as efficiently and cheaply as possible. One aspect of the manufacturing process is the sourcing of the raw materials, goods, services and utilities necessary to produce the goods and enable the business to function effectively. (This is referred to as 'supply chain procurement'.) Commercial contracts are sometimes classified into two types: 'upstream' and 'downstream' contracts.

(a) Upstream contracts are typically those which provide the client with the resources needed in order to carry on his business, for example contracts for the supply of goods or services to the business, the supply of funds through loan agreements, permission to manufacture through intellectual property licences and the variety of contracts that come under the heading 'overheads', such as utilities, employees, IT, maintenance, security etc – in other words, contracts which require some sort of financial outlay by the business. These are outside the scope of this book, but a commercial lawyer will need to be aware of their existence.

(b) Downstream contracts are those under which the client passes on and exploits the fruits of his labour, contracts for the supply of goods and services by the business – in other words, contracts which generate income for the business. It is these contracts which will be considered in this book.

When acting for a manufacturer, it is important to remember that the client's objectives, and thus the drafting considerations, will be very different depending on whether it is buying or selling.

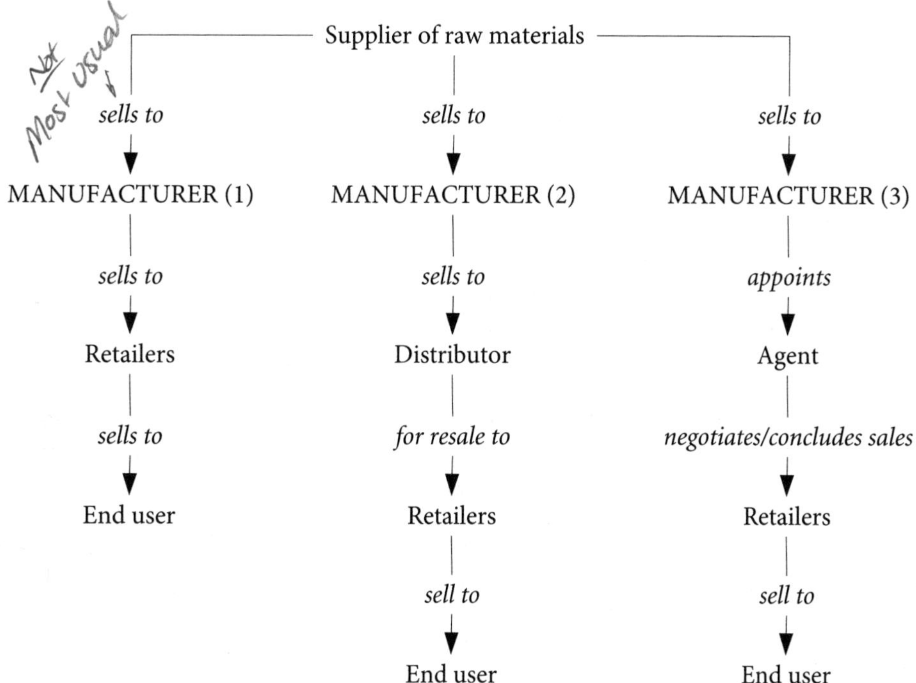

Figure 1.2 Steps in the supply chain

1.4 Standard terms and conditions

An important consideration for the client will be whether to use standard terms and conditions or individually negotiated contracts. In practice, it is very common for a set of terms to be put into a standard contract which a business will use for all transactions. Whether the contract between the buyer and seller is based on the seller's standard terms and conditions or the buyer's will depend on the relative bargaining positions of the parties.

There are advantages and disadvantages to the use of standard terms and conditions (see the table below).

In any transaction for the sale of goods, the seller and buyer have very different agendas. At the very least, the buyer:

(a) will want the goods to be delivered on time, preferably to its own premises; and

(b) will want the seller to be liable for any defects.

The seller:

(a) will want flexibility for late delivery if it is let down by its own suppliers;

(b) will want the buyer preferably to collect the goods from its factory; and

(c) whilst it might be willing to accept some liability for defects, will not want to be liable for every trivial problem.

The use of standard terms ensures that the final contract suits the needs of whichever party has been able to insist on their use. Not all transactions are the same, and standard terms are never going to be suitable for every occasion. However, they can provide a useful starting point for negotiation, and differences may be resolved without the need for major revision. Standard terms and conditions have the added advantage of ensuring commercial certainty.

A commercial contract is a long and complex document, and so the cost of drafting individual contracts will be high. Although some transactions may require individually negotiated contracts to be drafted, generally the parties will want to avoid incurring these costs for each sale. Such costs would have an impact throughout the supply chain. A seller will invariably try to pass the additional cost on to a buyer, and this will eventually impact on the ultimate consumer.

In addition, there are practical and administrative considerations in the use of standard terms and conditions. They create standardised procedures which enable sales or purchasing representatives or junior staff, with proper training and instruction, to safely use the standard terms and conditions to enter into contracts without having to refer back to managers or solicitors every time. It is, however, essential that clients understand the need for proper training and procedures to ensure that staff do not use standard terms inappropriately. One major practical difficulty is the need to ensure that the terms are properly incorporated into the sales contract, and the so-called 'battle of the forms'. Staff must be trained to ensure that their company's terms are the ones that are incorporated into the contract (see **2.3.3**).

It is important that standard terms and conditions are reviewed regularly to ensure that they take account of any legislative changes or new case law, and that they reflect any changes in the way that the client does business.

Standard terms and conditions are subject to greater regulation than individually negotiated contracts. Most importantly, s 3 of the Unfair Contracts Terms Act 1977 (UCTA 1977) subjects any exclusion of liability contained in standard terms to the test of reasonableness. The implications of this will be considered in **Chapter 7**.

Standard Terms and Conditions	
Advantages	**Disadvantages**
Contract on terms favourable to client	Lack of flexibility
Standardised procedures	Effective training and procedures essential
Commercial certainty	Incorporation difficulties/'battle of the forms'
Cheaper	Need for regular review
Starting point for negotiation	Legal constraints, eg UCTA 1977

1.5 Drafting and content of a commercial contract

1.5.1 The structure of a commercial agreement

The choice of commercial agreement dictates the type of contract. However, most commercial contracts, whether on standard terms or individually negotiated, follow the same basic structure. It is the specific provisions which differ, according to the type of agreement reached and the underlying commercial factors.

Key factors in drafting a commercial agreement are:

(a) analysis of the client's instructions;

(b) establishing the client's objectives;

(c) not losing sight of the client's commercial aims;

(d) adapting precedents to fit the client's instructions, and not adapting the client's instructions to fit the precedents.

In practice, this is easier said than done.

A basic checklist for a commercial agreement will be as follows:

(a) commencement and date;
(b) the parties;
(c) the recitals, if any;
(d) definitions and interpretation;
(e) conditions precedent, if any;
(f) agreements;
(g) representations and warranties; } 'operative part'
(h) indemnities;
(i) limitations and exclusions;
(j) 'boiler-plate' clauses;
(k) execution clause and signature; and
(l) schedules.

1.5.1.1 Recitals

Recitals are not essential, but can be useful to help put a contract in context or explain the reason for a contract being entered into. Alternatively, recitals may set out the factual background to an exclusion clause by explaining the decision of the parties to impose the risk of loss on one party rather than the other, for example because it is more economical from an insurance point of view. This may help the party excluding liability to establish that it was reasonable to do so. However, recitals must be used with care to ensure that they do not introduce ambiguity into a document.

1.5.1.2 Definitions clause

There are a few basic rules to follow when drafting a definitions clause:

(a) A definitions clause should do no more than give a clear meaning to defined terms. A definition should not be operative, ie impose obligations on the parties, as this may lead to ambiguity.

(b) All defined terms should start with a capital letter. If the same word or phrase is used in the agreement without being capitalised then the inference is that something different from the defined term is intended.

(c) Defined terms should be listed alphabetically for ease of reference.

(d) Defined terms should be used only where they are recurrent in the body of the agreement, or where there is a danger of ambiguity if no clear definition is given.

(e) All defined terms in the agreement should be defined in the definitions section. (In some complex agreements, the entry in the definitions section will merely be a cross-reference, possibly to an appendix or other part of the agreement.)

(f) The definitions must meet the requirements of the agreement, for example, should the definition of 'Territory' include the whole of the UK or just England and Wales? As the agreement progresses through negotiations with the other side and a number of drafts are drawn up, continual checks should be made to ensure the definitions still work satisfactorily and reflect any changes to the agreement. (In practice, changes will be 'tracked' on the document, so it should be clear where such changes have been made.)

(g) Care should be taken in defining things which might be subject to change during the contract, such as 'the Contract Goods'. This definition would need to cover different goods at different periods under the contract, and would need to be expressed accordingly.

1.5.1.3 Interpretation clause

This section should be non-controversial. It covers the basics of interpretation, for example by providing that the headings do not form part of the agreement (as if they did, lawyers would feel the need to draft them more comprehensively, which would detract from their usefulness).

1.5.1.4 The operative part

Conditions precedent

Conditions precedent are conditions that have to be satisfied before the agreement comes into effect. For example, in an international sale of goods contract, the contract may specify that the supply of the goods is conditional on the buyer obtaining a letter of credit. If the condition is not satisfied, there will be no binding contract.

Agreements

Agreements define the rights and obligations of the parties. In a sale of goods contract, the seller will be promising to sell and deliver goods of a certain description and quality. The buyer will be promising to pay the price. In addition, there will be provisions covering what happens if the seller fails to deliver or the buyer fails to pay, and exclusions of one or other party's rights or liability in these circumstances.

This part of the contract is the key section of a commercial agreement. Most of the key operative provisions will be considered throughout Part I of this book.

Representations and warranties

These are statements of factual and legal matters which one of the parties requires to be made to it in a legally binding way. Warranties are promises that a given statement or fact is true. They tend to be of less importance in sale of goods contracts, where any specification or description of the goods is a condition of the contract, than in contracts for the sale of businesses, where the buyer will want some assurance that, for example, profit figures are accurate. However, the warranties section can provide for remedies in addition to the usual remedy of contract damages, for example, they may make provision for repair or replacement. Representations and remedies for misrepresentation will be covered in **Chapter 2**.

Indemnities

Indemnities are different from warranties in that here one party promises to make good another's loss. The contract may provide that if one party (A) incurs loss as a result of the happening of a particular event, then the other (B) will indemnify A. They can be used where the parties have done a risk assessment and decided that should that event occur, one party should bear the cost. In sale of goods contracts, for example, an indemnity for intellectual property infringement claims relating to the goods may be included.

Limitation and exclusion of liability in contracts

This is an important area of commercial contracts and is dealt with in **Chapter** 7. An important aspect of limitation, exclusion and transfer of liability clauses in commercial contracts is the question whether the clause is liable to come within the scope and effect of the Unfair Contract Terms Act 1977 (UCTA 1977), and this is also dealt with in **Chapter 8**.

1.5.2 Introduction to boiler-plate clauses

So-called 'boiler-plate' clauses (often simply referred to as the 'boiler-plate') are standard clauses which are included as a matter of course into all agreements of a certain type. They often remain as drafted in the precedent which is being used. They are not usually individually negotiated, as they are relatively uncontroversial. Nevertheless, you must of course check that they are not contrary to your client's interests when negotiating an agreement. It can be a bad mistake to assume that boiler-plate clauses can just be copied out of a precedent. For example, in *Oxonica Energy Ltd v Neuftec Ltd* [2008] EWHC 2127 the High Court attacked an agreement where standard paragraphs had been bolted together to make a 'nonsensical agreement'. Mr Peter Prescott QC, sitting as a Deputy High Court Judge, stated that 'Bits of legal phraseology have been lifted from I know not what precedents and assembled in a strange way'.

There is no precise definition of 'boiler-plate clauses', nor do they have to appear at a given point in the agreement. However, it is common to have a group of boiler-plate clauses at or towards the end of an agreement. Typical boiler-plate clauses are as follows:

1.5.2.1 Prevail clauses

A prevail clause states that, in the event of a dispute, one party's (eg the seller's) terms will prevail.

1.5.2.2 Entire or whole agreement clauses

An entire or whole agreement clause provides that all of the obligations of the parties are recorded in one document. They seek to avoid the evidential difficulties associated with oral representations and discussions.

1.5.2.3 'No authority' clauses

A 'no authority' clause states that variation of the contract will be effective only if made by certain people (eg directors) or in a certain way (eg evidenced in writing). It makes clear which terms certain employees, eg sales staff, have no authority to agree on behalf of the company. Sometimes, a seller will want to give other employees, for example sales representatives, limited discretion (eg to agree discounts) and, if so, the clause will need to be amended appropriately.

Prevail, whole agreement and 'no authority' clauses are attempts to keep out extraneous terms and to prevent unauthorised variation of the terms of the contract. Their effectiveness will be dealt with in **Chapter 2**.

1.5.2.4 Waiver

There may also be a clause trying to prevent any waiver arising as a result of one party agreeing to a relaxation of a contractual provision, for example an express delivery date. Again, these clauses will be considered in **Chapter 2**.

1.5.2.5 Buyer becoming insolvent

This is a standard provision relating to the operation of the agreement. It makes provision for what happens if one of the parties becomes insolvent. This clause is often linked to the retention of title clause in a sale of goods agreement, as retention of title clauses are typically used when the buyer is going insolvent (see **Chapter 5**). It will normally make payment obligations immediate, or allow for termination.

1.5.2.6 Choice of law and jurisdiction

It is important that the contract includes an express choice of the law and the jurisdiction which will govern the contract in the event of a dispute. This will normally be the law of England and Wales and the jurisdiction of the English courts. If for any reason this clause had been omitted then the courts of all EU Member States will apply Regulation 593/2009 ('Rome I') in relation to law, and Regulation 44/2001 ('Brussels I') in relation to jurisdiction (see **Chapter 13**).

1.5.2.7 Service of notices

A notice clause has to provide for the places where notice is to be served, the method of service and the time at which the notice is deemed to be served. Such clauses have become more complex with the increase in the number of ways in which notice could be given (eg, fax and email). Most notice clauses will not permit oral notice but rather will require it to be in writing. They will specify the address(es) to which, and the person (eg, the company secretary for a corporate party to the contract) to whom, notice is to be sent.

Notice clauses will typically require notice to be served during business hours if served in person. If notice is permitted to be sent by fax or email then it could be deemed served when received. If sent by post then it could be deemed served two days after posting. It will all depend on the wording agreed by the parties.

1.5.2.8 Force majeure

A force majeure clause is intended to suspend or terminate the contractual obligations in the event of an occurrence outside the control of the parties (eg fire, flood, storm etc). A force majeure clause is usually for the benefit of the seller or deliverer of the goods, as it is the party obliged to supply and/or deliver the goods.

If one or more of the specified events occurs then contractual performance will be suspended for a specified period. If the event is still continuing at the end of that period then the contract will be considered to be terminated. Whether one or both parties will have the right to terminate the contract will depend on the bargaining strength of the parties.

The force majeure events must be defined in the contract. The list of events can cause some discussion. The usual ones are so-called Acts of God, adverse weather such as floods or snow, war, riot, government action and embargoes or strikes by third parties.

The effectiveness of force majeure clauses will be discussed in **Chapter 8**.

1.5.2.9 'No partnership' clauses

This type of clause seeks to ensure that the agreement cannot be construed as a partnership between the parties to the agreement. There are obvious disadvantages to partnership law, such as being liable for a partner's debts. However, the factor that determines whether or not a partnership is in existence is the definition of 'partnership' in the Partnership Act 1890, s 1, not the wording of a 'no partnership' clause.

1.5.2.10 'No assignment, no subcontracting' clauses

If a buyer has selected a specific supplier, it will not want that supplier to subcontract the work to an unknown third party. Similarly, the buyer may not want the contract to be assigned to another supplier. Thus, a clause to cover both these possibilities is often included in commercial contracts.

1.5.3 Schedules

Schedules are a way of removing unnecessary detail from the body of an agreement and thereby improving its readability. In a large agreement, representations and warranties would also be removed to the schedules. Schedules can also be used to annex other documents to the contract.

Chapter 2

Negotiation, Contract Formation and Post-contractual Considerations

2.1 Introduction

From the list of sources of law in **1.2** above, it is clear that a basic understanding of the law of contract is essential for a commercial lawyer. In addition, where sales of goods are involved, s 62(2) of the Sale of Goods Act 1979 (SGA 1979) states:

> The rules of common law, including the law merchant, except in so far as they are inconsistent with the provisions of this Act, and in particular the rules relating to the law of principal and agent and the effect of fraud, misrepresentation, duress or coercion, mistake, or other invalidating cause, apply to contracts for the sale of goods.

This chapter considers the underlying principles of contract law as they affect a contract from the negotiation stage to the conclusion and discharge of the contract. The 'lifespan' of a contract can be broken down into distinct phases:

(a) negotiation;

(b) entry into the contract;

(c) performance;

(d) discharge.

Each phase raises different issues and problems, as illustrated in **Figure 2.1** below.

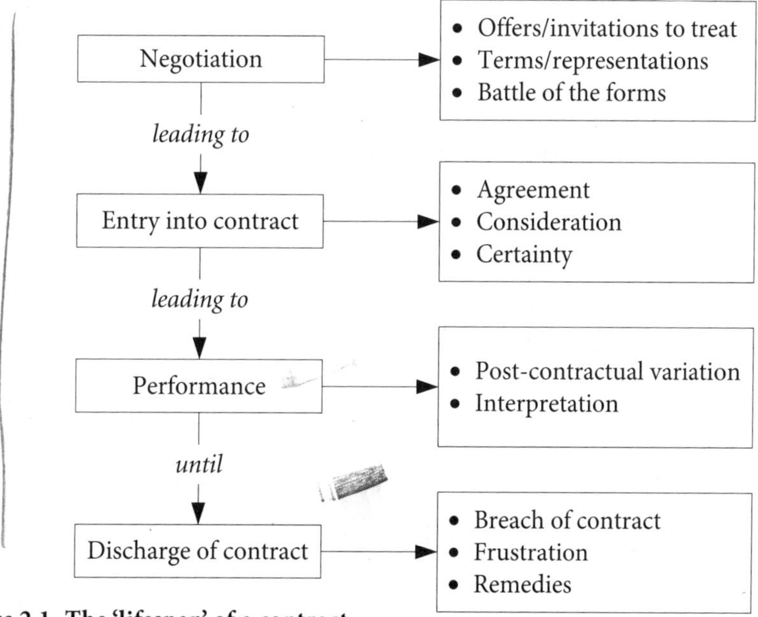

Figure 2.1 The 'lifespan' of a contract

2.2 Formation of the contract

Before there can be a contract, one party (the offeror) must make an identifiable offer on certain terms, showing intention to be bound, and the other party (the offeree) must accept those terms unconditionally. This agreement must be supported by consideration, and there must be intention to be legally bound by the terms of the contract. At that point the contract comes into existence. Where the contract is in writing and signed by the parties, it will be obvious when this occurs. However, it may not always be clear exactly when the contract was made, especially if the parties did not sign any form of written document.

2.3 The negotiation phase

In all but the simplest of commercial contracts, the entry into the contract will be preceded by a period of negotiation, either oral or written. The length and complexity of the negotiations (and the resulting documentation) will depend on a number of factors, for example whether this is the first time the parties have dealt with each other, the subject matter of the contract, and whether or not the parties are using standard terms and conditions. In a simple sale of goods contract, the only negotiations may be a discussion of the quantity and the price, but in many contracts the negotiations will be more complex. However long or short the negotiations, some of the same issues and problems can arise.

Where several offers have been made and refused, or met with counter-offers, it can be difficult to decide exactly when the parties have moved from negotiation to conclusion of the contract and whether or not unwanted terms have been 'accidentally' included in the contract. All documentation should be carefully monitored throughout the negotiating process to prevent this from happening. Factors to consider include the following.

2.3.1 Offers

An offer must be distinguished from an invitation to treat, where there is no intention to be legally bound. Generally, the following will not be offers:

(a) advertisements;

(b) estimates;

(c) brochures;

(d) price lists;

(e) enquiries or requests for information;

(f) letters of intent/heads of terms/memoranda of understanding (these are documents which outline the terms on which the parties intend to contract with each other in the future).

However, these are general rules, and whether a communication is an offer or an invitation to treat will always depend on the facts of each case. Particular issues can arise, for example, with letters of intent/heads of terms. If the intended terms of the contract are set out in too much detail or, in a goods and services contract, include requests for work to commence, then they may be construed as an offer.

In practice, the words 'subject to contract' indicate that the parties do not intend to be bound by the terms of any informal agreement or pre-contractual negotiations, and this qualification will usually rebut the usual presumption that, in commercial contracts, the parties do intend to be legally bound. However, the courts will look at the conduct of the parties during negotiations, so, to be absolutely certain, the parties should also include an express statement to the effect that they do not intend to be legally bound.

Throughout the negotiation process, it is important to ensure that any offer remains on the table. An offer can be ended by rejection, counter-offer, lapse of time, death of the other party or by revocation before it has been accepted. If any of these has occurred, then there will be no offer capable of acceptance.

2.3.2 Terms and representations

Pre-contractual statements can cause difficulties between the parties, particularly if they subsequently turn out to be untrue. There are three types of pre-contractual statement:

(a) terms;

(b) representations; and

(c) mere advertising puff.

The last will never have an effect on the contract, but the first two may. It is important to distinguish between terms and representations, as the remedies where problems arise are different for each.

A pre-contractual statement which amounts to a term will form part of the contract, and breach will give the injured party the usual contractual remedies, including the right to terminate the contract and sue for damages as of right, depending on the status of the term. To decide whether a statement amounts to a term or not, the courts will look at the common intention of the parties and, in the absence of clear intent, will apply various guidelines, looking at, for example, the importance of the statement to the contract and the skill and knowledge of the party making it.

Not all pre-contractual statements made during negotiations will end up as terms of the contract: some may be representations. A representation is a statement of fact made by one party to the contract to the other which induces the contract (although it need not be the sole inducement). If it turns out to be untrue it will be a misrepresentation. There are three types of misrepresentation: fraudulent, negligent and innocent. The primary remedy for misrepresentation is rescission, although it may be possible to claim damages under s 2(1) of the Misrepresentation Act 1967. However, if the maker of the statement can show that he honestly believed that the statement was true at the time that it was made, and that he had reasonable grounds for that belief, then the innocent party may lose his right to damages. The right to rescission may be lost where one of the equitable bars, such as delay or affirmation, applies.

Depending on its bargaining strength, the buyer may insist that any pre-contractual representations form part of the express terms of the contract, and they may be included as warranties (see **1.5.1.4**). A warranty is a promise given by one or other party to the contract that a given statement or set of facts is true, for example that a business makes a specified annual profit. In the event of a breach, the buyer would then be entitled to contractual damages as of right. The only time when a claim for damages for misrepresentation may be appropriate is if there is a problem with remoteness (see **2.7.3.1**). However the parties describe them, the test as to whether a statement is a term or a representation is objective.

2.3.3 Battle of the forms

Where both parties seek to impose their own terms on the other, it may not be clear whose standard terms apply. A battle of the forms may occur, for example where the seller provides the buyer with an invitation to treat, containing the seller's standard terms and conditions, and the buyer then makes an offer, introducing his own terms. If the seller does not accept the buyer's terms, and insists instead on reinstating its own terms, the seller has made a counter-offer. Another possibility is that the seller makes the original offer, which the buyer purports to 'accept' but with the introduction of new terms, thereby itself making a counter-offer.

If the contract is dealt with by the seller's sales representatives or untrained administrative staff, who may not be aware of the rules relating to offer and acceptance, there is always a possibility that the wrong set of terms may be accepted by accident. The offer may be accepted by the conduct of the parties, eg by the seller delivering the goods or the buyer accepting delivery. In *Butler Machine Tool Co Ltd v Ex-Cell-O Corporation (England) Ltd* [1979] 1 WLR 401, CA, the return of a signed acknowledgement slip amounted to acceptance of the buyer's terms. Where negotiations are protracted, there may be several sets of terms and conditions put forward. In the event of a dispute, the court will consider whose terms and conditions were on the table at the time of acceptance, and apply 'the last shot wins' doctrine. In *Tekdata Interconnections Ltd v Amphenol Ltd* [2009] EWCA Civ 1209 the Court of Appeal confirmed that the courts should use the traditional offer and acceptance analysis to decide on a battle of forms dispute, rather the relationship and conduct of the parties.

2.3.4 Prevention

As discussed in **1.5.2**, the parties may attempt to keep out extraneous terms, eg statements by sales representatives in relation to the goods which may amount to terms of the contract. The problem is that these attempts are not always effective.

2.3.4.1 Prevail clauses

A prevail clause provides in effect that if there is a battle of the forms then the seller's terms will prevail. Legally, the clause is ineffective, as any later set of terms which is introduced will act as a counter-offer and override an earlier set. However, a prevail clause is often included for bluff value.

2.3.4.2 Entire or whole agreement clauses

The seller may include an 'entire' or 'whole agreement' clause. This is intended to prevent any statements made by sales representatives, or statements included in sales literature, brochures and the like, forming terms of the contract. The clause will state that the seller's terms and conditions form the whole agreement between the seller and the buyer and cannot be varied in any way. It will also usually include a statement that no other express terms, written or oral, shall be included as part of the contract, thus avoiding the evidential difficulties associated with oral representations and discussions.

In the absence of a whole agreement clause, the parties would have to rely on the parol evidence rule which provides that outside, or extrinsic, evidence should not be adduced to vary the written contract. However, it may be possible for a contract to be part written and part oral, if this is what the parties intended. A whole agreement clause avoids oral terms being included in the contract.

Although the inclusion of an entire agreement clause may solve the problem of extrinsic evidence, as far as the battle of the forms is concerned, it is open to the same objections as a prevail clause. If the buyer makes an offer or counter-offer on different terms, this clause will be destroyed along with all the seller's other terms.

A further danger of a whole agreement clause is that it might exclude other documents which the parties do wish to have taken into account, for example a price list.

Where the clause attempts also to exclude liability for misrepresentation, it can also be seen as an exclusion clause. To be effective, it must be reasonable under s 3 of the Misrepresentation Act 1967. In *Thomas Witter v TBP Industries* [1996] 2 All ER 573, such a clause was held to have excluded liability for fraudulent misrepresentation and was therefore void. One way around this is for the clause also to include a statement of non-reliance, with an express carve-out for fraudulent misrepresentation.

2.3.4.3 'No authority' clauses

These are attempts by the seller:

(a) to put a limit on the extent to which its sales representatives, or other employees, are permitted to negotiate individual terms with the buyer; and

(b) to exclude any extravagant claims made by the sales representatives to induce the buyer to enter into the contract.

To some extent there is an overlap with whole agreement clauses, and they are subject to the same difficulties.

2.3.4.4 Importance of staff training

The best way to avoid a battle of the forms problem is to ensure that all staff are effectively trained so that they know what they may and may not say in negotiations. Administrative staff should be warned not to send anything to the other side which could be interpreted as acceptance of an offer, without referring the matter on to managers or higher authority.

2.4 Entry into the contract

The essence of a contract, therefore, is that there should be valid agreement between the parties. All parties must have been agreeing to the same thing, and must not have been talking at cross-purposes. The existence, or otherwise, of agreement is judged objectively. We have already seen that there must be a genuine offer, as opposed to an invitation to treat, which has been accepted in its entirety. Usually, an identifiable offer and acceptance have to be made and communicated to the other party and, generally, actual communication is needed. However, a contract can come into existence by means of performance, although this must be clear from the conduct of the parties.

2.4.1 Consideration

There has to be consideration for the contract (or it has to be drafted as a deed). The courts will not look at the value of the consideration, which in a commercial contract will usually be money, goods or services, or the promise of these. However, some types of act or promise are not regarded by law as being valid consideration, for example past consideration or performance of an existing duty. In commercial contracts, consideration will not generally be a problem when the contract is entered into, as there is usually the exchange of goods for payment, or the promise of payment of the price. Problems tend to arise when there is a variation of the terms of the contract, which will be dealt with at **2.5.1** below.

2.4.2 Certainty

One of the key concepts in the law of contract is that there must be contractual certainty, that is the parties must be specific about the terms of the contract. An agreement which fails to address a key area, for example the price, will be void for uncertainty unless it can be saved by using a statutory provision such as s 8 of the SGA 1979 (see **4.2**). The general approach adopted by the courts is that it is the responsibility of the parties to make their agreement, and if they do so incompetently then that is their problem. However, the courts can fix a badly drafted contract if there is other evidence of the intent of the parties which can be used to plug the gaps, or the court may agree to sever an irrelevant or badly drafted clause, provided that the rest of the contract is still commercially workable.

2.4.2.1 Agreements to agree

The courts will not enforce an 'agreement to agree'. So an agreement to enter into a contract at a later date, or an agreement that a certain provision will be agreed between the parties after the commencement of the contract would be void for uncertainty. These are both fairly obvious examples of uncertainty, but there are provisions where the position is less clear (see, eg, *Courtney & Fairbairn Ltd v Tolaini Bros (Hotels) Ltd* [1975] 1 WLR 297; cf the older case of *Foley v Classique Coaches Ltd* [1934] 2 KB 1, where there was an arbitration clause if the parties could not agree on the price and the contract was upheld).

exception

In *Cable & Wireless plc v IBM United Kingdom Ltd* [2002] EWHC 2059 (Comm), it was held that although the law did not generally recognise agreements to agree, the situation here was different. The fact that the agreement prescribed the means by which dispute negotiation should take place, by the identification of a specific recognised procedure, meant that the requirement for contractual certainty was fulfilled and the agreement was thus enforceable. In *Balfour Beatty Northern Ltd v Modus Corovest (Blackpool) Ltd* [2008] EWHC 3029 (TCC), a mediation agreement was held to be a simple 'agreement to agree' and was too uncertain to be enforced.

2.4.2.2 Lock-out and lock-in agreements

A lock-out agreement is one in which one party, for example a manufacturer (A), agrees with another, a distributor (B), not to negotiate with anyone other than B. It is essentially a negative promise. From a commercial point of view, if a manufacturer approaches a potential distributor, the distributor may not want to commit to the arrangement until he has carried out some market research to establish whether there is a viable market. In the meantime, he wants to be sure that the manufacturer will not enter into negotiations with anyone else. Such agreements may be enforceable provided that B gives consideration for the promise not to negotiate with anyone else.

A lock-in agreement, where one party agrees to negotiate with another, is different from a lock-out agreement. In a lock-out agreement, A is not obliged to negotiate with B; A simply agrees not to negotiate with anyone else. In a lock-in agreement, there is such an obligation. Such agreements are too uncertain and therefore unenforceable. In *Walford v Miles* [1992] 1 All ER 453, HL, Lord Ackner thought that such agreements would be 'unworkable in practice'.

2.4.2.3 Cancellation clauses

Both the buyer and the seller might want to have a let-out clause, allowing them to withdraw from the contract without liability in certain circumstances, particularly during periods of economic uncertainty where it may be uneconomic to continue with the contract. The parties may therefore include a cancellation clause in the contract. The content of the clause will depend on the bargaining strength of the parties, but typically a clause may provide that one or other party (often the seller) can cancel in a wide variety of circumstances.

However, if the cancellation clause is too wide, it may have the effect of invalidating the contract altogether, as it may mean that the seller is simply making mere statements of intention to perform but is not, in effect, under any obligation to perform its obligations under the contract.

A further possibility is that the clause will provide that the buyer can cancel only with the seller's written consent and must pay a percentage of the purchase price (eg 10% of the contract price). Here the parties must be careful to ensure that the clause does not amount to a penalty clause or it will be unenforceable.

2.4.3 Mistake

A mistake may mean that the parties have failed to reach agreement, because, for example, unknown to the parties, the subject matter of the contract does not exist or has perished. To have an effect on the contract, the mistake must have occurred before the contract was made. In practice, the doctrine of mistake is quite narrow and very few mistakes will affect the validity of a contract, but where they do, the effect is to render the contract void. Innocent third parties may find themselves out of pocket as a result. Note that in the case of sale of goods contracts, where there is a contract for the sale of specific goods, if the goods have perished before the contract is made, s 6 of the SGA 1979 provides that the contract is void and there is no need to rely on the common law doctrine of mistake.

2.5 Performance of the contract

2.5.1 Post-contractual variation

Once the contract is in existence, it is important that the terms of the contract are not inadvertently varied by sales representatives or other staff. An example would be where the parties have contracted on standard terms and conditions which state that all delivery dates are approximate, thus avoiding liability for late delivery, but, after the contract is entered into, a sales representative agrees that the goods will be delivered on a particular date. There are two problems here: the general principle that any variation of the contract must be supported by consideration and the sales representative's authority to bind the seller.

Where one party agrees to do something over and above the terms of an existing contract, the other party must provide consideration for that promise, either by providing something extra over and above his existing contractual duty, as in *Hartley v Ponsonby* (1857) 7 EB 872, or by conferring a benefit on the promisor, as in *Williams v Roffey Bros* [1990] 1 All ER 512, CA. However, such a promise might be enforceable even though no consideration has been provided for it in the two following situations.

2.5.1.1 The doctrine of waiver

Where the promise in question is a promise not to enforce the other party's obligations under the contract (ie a negative promise), the courts of equity may give limited effect to the promise. An example would be where a delivery date has been agreed, but the seller finds that he is unable to deliver. Normally the buyer can refuse to accept late delivery, but if the buyer agrees to it, the court will usually decide that the buyer has waived its right to terminate the contract for late delivery.

However, the limit on this exception is that the buyer always has the right to reinstate the original terms by reasonable notice. So if the original delivery date was 22 June, but the buyer has agreed to accept delivery on 31 July, if nothing more is said, the buyer will be unable to refuse delivery on that date. If, however, the buyer contacts the seller in the first week of July and says that he now wants delivery, say within 7 days, the seller will have to deliver within that 7-day period or the buyer's right to termination will be reinstated (provided that the 7-day notice period is reasonable in the circumstances).

2.5.1.2 Promissory estoppel

The doctrine of promissory estoppel applies to promises not to claim sums of money which would otherwise be due under a contract. This is of limited application in practice, and its scope is unclear. The main application of the doctrine has been in relation to contracts where there are continuing obligations, for example as in the leading case of *Central London Property Trust v High Trees House* [1947] KB 130, where the obligation concerned payments of rent during the Second World War. How far the doctrine applies to one-off payments under a contract is unclear. In a sale of goods context, if a buyer agrees to buy goods for £10,000 but then tells the seller that it cannot afford the full price and the seller agrees to accept £8,000, it seems that the seller can change its mind and, on reasonable notice, sue for the outstanding £2,000.

2.5.1.3 Prevention

In the same way that the parties can attempt to draft the contract to solve 'battle of the forms' problems, they may also attempt to prevent unauthorised variation of the terms of the contract, by extending the no-authority clause (see **2.3.4.3**) into the contract to restrict the grant of variations or waivers to senior staff (eg, providing that a variation or waiver will only be valid if agreed in writing by a director of the company). Alternatively, a statement may be included that any variation or waiver does not affect the seller's strict rights under the contract, or that sales representatives and other staff have no authority to vary the contract.

The effectiveness of such a clause is arguable. The whole point of waiver (and promissory estoppel) is that it involves a promise not to enforce the strict terms of the contract. As the clause is itself one of the terms, it follows that the party for whose benefit it is inserted may promise not to enforce this clause as well. In addition, there is little point putting in a clause stating that employees have no authority to do certain things, if practice demonstrates that this is untrue. In such cases, the court would probably interpret the contract in the light of reality and decide that the term had been varied by the seller's conduct in condoning this behaviour.

2.5.1.4 Economic duress

Even if a variation is supported by consideration, it may not be valid if it is brought about by economic duress, where one party threatens to break its side of the contract unless the other side promises to pay more than originally agreed.

An example would be where a food supplier agrees with a catering company to deliver food for a wedding. The day before the wedding, the supplier tells the caterer that it will not deliver unless the buyer pays an extra £1,000. The supplier agrees that, for the extra money, it will deliver king prawns instead of ordinary freshwater prawns (thus providing consideration at minimal cost to itself). The caterer is unable to source the food from anywhere else in time for the wedding and so agrees to pay the extra money. This would clearly amount to economic duress as there is an unlawful threat by the supplier not to perform its side of the contract, and there is no practical alternative for the caterer but to agree to pay more. It must, however, have been left with no practical alternative – mere commercial pressure will not be enough.

The variation of the contract will be voidable and the only remedy is rescission. The buyer may refuse to pay the extra money, or, if he has already paid, he may recover the money, provided that he does not delay too long or there is no other evidence that he has affirmed the contract.

2.6 Interpretation of contracts

You need to identify the terms of the contract before it can be interpreted. The court will look at the following issues:

(a) Have any statements made before the contract was concluded been included as terms of the contract, or could they be misrepresentations inducing entry into the contract, or perhaps as a 'last shot' under the 'battle of the forms' (see **2.3.3** above)?

(b) Is the contract only in writing, or is it both written and oral?

(c) Have the terms been incorporated into the contract, eg by notice or by signature?

(d) Are any terms implied into the contract by custom of that trade, or by statute, eg ss 12–15 of the SGA 1979, or by the common law?

(e) Are any terms, especially those excluding or limiting liability, rendered void by statute, eg ss 2, 3 or 6 of UCTA 1977 (see **Chapter** 7)?

(f) How are contracts to be interpreted – literally or purposively? Lord Hoffman, in *Investors Compensation Scheme Ltd v West Bromwich Building Society* [1998] 1 WLR 898, held that it was appropriate to consider the wider context and to interpret contracts with business common sense, ie purposively.

2.7 Discharge of contracts

A contract comes to an end when it has been discharged by:

(a) performance of the contract (which will be the usual situation);

(b) agreement between the parties;

(c) frustration, if the contract can no longer be performed in the manner intended by the parties;

(d) breach, if it is a repudiatory breach, ie breach of a condition not of a warranty, and that repudiation is accepted by the innocent party.

The first two are unlikely to cause any problems. The remainder of this chapter will look at the last two matters.

2.7.1 Frustration

A contract is frustrated when, after the contract is made, and without the fault of either party, the contract becomes impossible or radically different to perform, eg because the subject matter of the contract has been destroyed (*Davis Contractors v Fareham Urban DC* [1956] AC 696). The result is that the contract automatically comes to an end and both parties are relieved of their obligations under the contract. Unlike mistake (see **2.4.3**), the event must occur after the formation of the contract, and before performance.

If the contract is frustrated, the provisions of the Law Reform (Frustrated Contracts) Act 1943 will come into operation. Prima facie, the buyer can recover any payments it made before frustration (s 1(2)), and any sums which are due before the frustration date will cease to be payable. The court, however, has the discretion to allow the seller to keep all or some of any advance payment if it considers that this will be just, having regard to any expenses which the seller may have incurred in preparing to perform the contract. If one party has conferred a valuable benefit on the other, the court may allow the first party to claim a just sum in respect of that benefit (s 1(3)), although this is less likely to be relevant in a supply of goods case. It might be more relevant in a services contract, where the supplier has done some of the work but has been unable to finish it due to a frustrating event.

In sale of goods contracts, to a limited extent, the problem is dealt with by the SGA 1979. Where there is a contract for the sale of specific goods, if (again without the fault of either party) the goods perish before risk has passed to the buyer, under s 7 the contract is avoided, and the Law Reform (Frustrated Contracts) Act 1943 will not generally apply (s 2(5)). However, the common law doctrine is still of considerable significance, especially for shipping contracts.

2.7.2 Remedies for breach of contract

Not all breaches of contract will give the innocent party the right to bring the contract to an end. It is important to decide whether the term that has been breached is a condition or a warranty.

(a) Breach of a condition will give the innocent party the right to repudiate or terminate the contract. Termination means that the innocent party is discharged from all future obligations under the contract, and may recover any property transferred under the contract (including the price paid for any goods or services) and claim damages. Alternatively, the innocent party can chose to affirm the contract, in other words to hold the other party to its obligations under the contract (although this will not always be practically possible).

(b) Breach of warranty only gives the innocent party the right to claim damages (provided that it can show that it has suffered a loss). The innocent party does not have the option to terminate the contract.

2.7.3 Contractual damages

Damages are the 'usual' remedy for breach of contract and, provided that the claimant can show that it has suffered a loss, are available as of right. The purpose of contractual damages is compensatory, not punitive. Most damages in contract are assessed on an expectation basis – the aim is to put the claimant into the position that he would have been if the contract had been performed as intended. However, they are subject to certain restrictions.

2.7.3.1 Remoteness of damage

Not all loss which the claimant suffers will arise as a direct result of the breach. Damages cannot be claimed for losses that are too remote. The remoteness rule was set out in *Hadley v Baxendale* [1854] 9 Exch 341. Claims for damages are limited to:

(a) losses that flow naturally from the breach (the so-called 'first limb' of *Hadley v Baxendale* which covers all direct loss/damage). Whether or not the loss comes within this limb is an objective test, but it is important to note that ordinary loss of profit can come within this limb;

(b) losses that may reasonably be supposed to have been in the contemplation of the parties at the time they made the contract, as a result either of actual or imputed knowledge (the 'second limb'). Some loss of profit, or indirect and consequential loss will fall within this limb. For example, in *Victoria Laundry v Newman Industries* [1949] 1 All ER 997, CA, 'exceptional profit' arising as a result of a lucrative dyeing contract which had not been drawn to the attention of the defendant was too remote. Note that it is the knowledge of the parties at the time the contract is made, not at the time of the breach, which is relevant when applying this test.

In commercial contracts, most sellers will want to exclude indirect or consequential loss, although this will always be subject to UCTA 1977. However, it is not always clear whether loss of profit falls within the first or second limb. As we have seen, ordinary loss of profit can come within the first limb, but more recent cases, such as *Brown v KMR Services Ltd* [1955] 4 All ER 598 and *Transfield Shipping Inc v Mercator Shipping Inc* [2008] UKHL 48, have looked at the situation where there are exceptional losses. *Brown* involved the Lloyd's underwriting losses, and *Transfield* involved loss of profit as a result of the late delivery under a charterparty in an extremely volatile market. In *Brown,* the losses were not too remote, but in *Transfield* the House of Lords held that the loss was too remote. It is clear that the courts are drawing a distinction between different kinds of loss of profit. Most recently, the Court of Appeal in *Supershield Ltd v Siemens Building Technologies FE Ltd* [2010] EWCA Civ 7 confirmed that the *Hadley v Baxendale* test remains the 'standard rule', but held that, looking at the commercial context, the reasonable expectations and intentions of the parties may cause the court to depart from this rule. From a drafting point of view, it is important clearly to allocate responsibility for the consequences of breach in order to avoid these uncertainties (see **Chapter 8**).

2.7.3.2 Mitigation

The claimant must have made a reasonable attempt to mitigate its loss. It cannot claim for loss which it failed to mitigate. The burden of proof is on the defendant to show that the claimant did not make a reasonable attempt to mitigate.

2.7.3.3 Restitution and restitutionary damages

The aim of restitution is to prevent unjust enrichment, eg where an advance payment has been made for a service and there has been a total failure of consideration, in the sense that no benefit at all has been provided under the contract. Commercially, restitution can useful where no contractual relationship exists, and includes quasi-contractual claims for the return of money paid, or quantum meruit where work has been carried out under a contract which has never come into existence, for example as a result of mistake.

Restitutionary damages are different from other restitutionary remedies in that that they are an equitable remedy. Such damages are sometimes referred to as *Wrotham Park* damages, following the case of *Wrotham Park Estates v Parkside Homes Limited* [1974] 1 WLR 798, which established that damages might not always be based on financial loss to the claimant. Normally, as discussed at **2.7.3** above, the aim of contractual damages is to compensate the claimant for the loss suffered, not to punish the defendant for breaching the contract. There is some academic debate as to whether restitutionary damages sit outside this general purpose and so may be awarded when the defendant has made gains at the expense of the claimant, making such damages more akin to a claim for account of profit. The case law, particularly on the rationale for an award of restitutionary damages, is complex and outside the scope of this book.

Restitutionary remedies are an alternative to contractual remedies, and the claimant will not receive both. They are awarded rarely, and never where contractual remedies would produce a satisfactory result.

Chapter 3
Sale of Goods: Introduction

3.1 Introduction

The next four chapters will examine direct sales of goods from manufacturer to retailer. A brief reminder of the supply chain (see **Chapter 1**) shows the relevant contracts which will be governed by the SGA 1979.

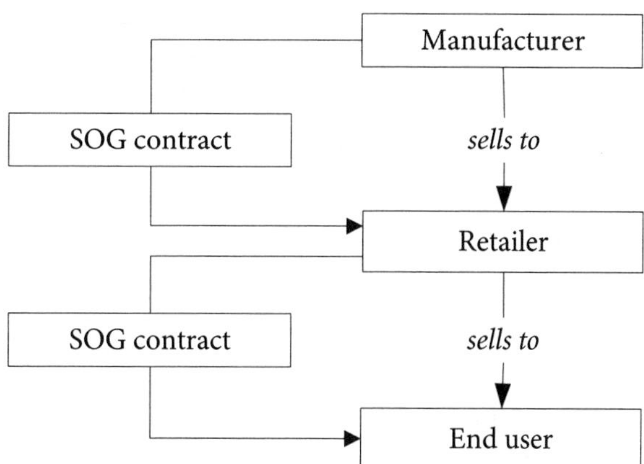

Figure 3.1 Sale of goods contracts

The sale of goods contract is probably the most commonly occurring contract type of all, with countless numbers of contracts being entered into every day. This is a vast area of law and the purpose of this chapter is to introduce you to the legal framework within which such contracts are created, and to provide a summary of the structure of the SGA 1979.

3.2 Relevant legislation

All sales of goods are governed by the SGA 1979, as amended by:

(a) the Sale and Supply of Goods Act 1994;

(b) the Sale of Goods (Amendment) Act 1994;

(c) the Sale of Goods (Amendment) Act 1995.

Where goods are supplied along with services, eg a contract to decorate a house, the Supply of Goods and Services Act 1982 (SGSA 1982) applies.

The Unfair Contract Terms Act 1977 (UCTA 1977) deals with exclusion clauses, including exclusion of the implied terms under the SGA 1979.

3.3 Sale of goods to consumers

Consumer contracts are largely beyond the scope of this book, although they are clearly important in practice. Many commercial clients will have dealings with consumers, and will need to consider the particular issues raised by dealings with this type of buyer.

There is also a large body of legislation aimed at protecting consumers, some of which will be considered in more detail in **Chapter 25**. Some examples of the most important pieces of legislation are:

(a) the Electronic Commerce (EC Directive) Regulations 2002 (SI 2002/2013);

(b) the Consumer Protection (Distance Selling) Regulations 2000 (SI 2000/2334);

(c) the Unfair Terms in Consumer Contracts Regulations 1999 (SI 1999/2083);

(d) the Sale and Supply of Goods to Consumers Regulations 2002 (SI 2002/3045);

(e) the Consumer Protection from Unfair Trading Regulations 2008 (SI 2008/1277) which implement the EU Unfair Commercial Practices Directive.

3.4 Definitions

3.4.1 What is 'sale of goods'?

The SGA 1979, s 2(1) defines a contract for the sale of goods as:

> ... a contract by which the seller transfers or agrees to transfer the property in goods to the buyer for a money consideration, called the price.

Section 2(4) defines a sale as follows:

> Where under a contract of sale the property in the goods is transferred from the seller to the buyer the contract is called a sale.

These subsections indicate how a sale of goods differs, for example, from a contract for hire of goods because the property in the goods (the title to the goods) changes hands. It differs from a gift of the goods because the buyer pays the seller money for the goods in a sale contract. It also differs from a contract of barter, in which goods are exchanged for goods or a combination of goods and money.

3.4.2 What are 'goods'?

Usually it is perfectly obvious whether the subject matter of the contract is goods (eg buying a chocolate bar in a shop). The SGA 1979, s 61 defines goods as including 'all personal chattels other than things in action and money'. An example of a thing in action is a cheque, which is in effect a promise to pay money. Land is not included, but crops and 'things attached to and forming part of the land which are agreed to be severed before sale or under the contract of sale' are within the definition of goods.

Section 5(1) differentiates between present and future goods:

> The goods which form the subject of a contract of sale may be either existing goods, owned or possessed by the seller, or goods to be manufactured or acquired by him after the making of the contract of sale, in this Act called future goods.

Existing goods can be:

(a) specific goods, which under s 62 are goods which 'can be identified and agreed upon at the time of the contract', eg 'my 2007 sky blue Mercedes SLK registration number T15 SHR';

(b) unacertained purely generic goods, eg 100 tons of potatoes;

(c) a specified quantity of goods from an identified bulk, eg 100 tons of potatoes from 200,000 tonnes currently stored in Allpress Distribution Ltd's warehouse in Chatteris.

Future goods are goods which do not yet exist, eg next year's potato crop, or goods which the seller does not yet own. Future goods can never be specific goods.

The distinction between the various types of goods is important when considering when title or property in the goods passes (see **5.2**).

Section 6 provides that where specific goods have perished, the contract is void (see **2.7.1**).

One area where there has been uncertainty is computer programs. Are they goods or services? (The point is that the implied terms in the contract would be different for goods and for services.) In *St Albans City and District Council v International Computers Ltd* [1996] 4 All ER 481, it was held *obiter* that programs were goods when they were supplied on a disk. More recently, in the case of *Horace Holman Group Ltd v Sherwood International Group Ltd* [2000] WL 491372, there was a dispute as to whether software was goods, and *St Albans* was cited as the authority. The program itself was found not to comprise a sale of goods for the purposes of UCTA 1977, although s 7 of UCTA 1977 was held to be applicable to the contract under which the program was supplied.

3.5 Structure of the SGA 1979

The SGA 1979 imposes duties on the buyer and the seller, with corresponding rights and remedies for each party, relating to transfer of ownership and performance of the contract. Under s 27, for example, the buyer's duty to pay for the goods is concurrent with the seller's duty to deliver them, and failure to perform these duties gives rise to statutory remedies over and above the ordinary contractual remedies discussed in **Chapter 2**.

The effect of a sale of goods is that ownership of, and risk in, the goods passes to the buyer. This is fundamental, but, in addition, each party to a sale of goods contract will have particular commercial concerns, which have been touched on in **Chapter 1**. For example:

(a) The main concern for both parties will be that the contract works for them financially. The seller will want to ensure that the price is right and that payment is prompt in order to avoid cash-flow problems. In relation to payment, the buyer will be looking for favourable credit periods and will be more concerned to see that delivery is prompt. The terms relating to these issues of price, payment and delivery are the 'core' terms of the contract, because they define the parties' principal obligations: the seller's obligation to deliver the goods; and the buyer's obligation to accept and pay for them.

(b) Once the goods are delivered, the buyer will want to ensure that it has got what it paid for, in the sense that the goods are exactly as described and that they are in perfect condition. The seller will be concerned to minimise its liability in relation to the buyer in the event that the goods turn out to be defective or unsuitable for any reason.

The SGA 1979 deals with these issues. Surprisingly, however, the SGA 1979 imposes very little control on a commercial sale agreement. The SGA 1979 acts, in some circumstances, to fill in voids and omissions to which the parties have not turned their minds, or where they have simply relied upon the Act. In addition, in certain circumstance the parties can opt out of some of these controls.

Provisions as to ownership and the 'core' duties, rights and remedies of both parties are summarised in **Table 3.1** below.

Duties of Seller	Duties of Buyer
• To deliver the goods (s 29) • To deliver the correct quantity (s 30) • To pass good title (s 12) • To deliver goods which: – correspond with description (s 13) – are of satisfactory quality and fit for purpose (s 14) – correspond with sample (s 15)	• To accept delivery (s 27) • To pay for the goods (s 27)
Rights/Remedies of Seller	**Rights/Remedies of Buyer**
• To terminate/repudiate the contract for breach of condition • Action for the price (s 49) • Damages for non-acceptance (s 50) • Rights of the unpaid seller: – lien (s 41) – stoppage in transit (ss 44, 45) – resale (s 48) • To retain title to the goods until paid (ss 17 and 19)	• To inspect the goods (s 34) • To reject the goods and refuse payment for breach of condition • To damages for non-delivery (s 51) • To damages when the goods are accepted (s 53) • To request specific performance (s 54)

Table 3.1 Rights and remedies of parties to a contract

The main performance obligations can be divided, albeit loosely, into three categories, as set out below.

3.5.1 Default provisions

Many of the implied terms are safety-net terms, implied only if the parties have not made their own provision. They would often be unsuitable for a commercial contract, eg s 28 implies cash on delivery, which will not be appropriate for most commercial transactions, where a buyer will normally be buying on credit.

3.5.2 Implied terms which can be excluded by agreement between the parties

Section 55 provides that some of the terms implied into a contract for the sale of goods by the 1979 Act can be excluded by the agreement of the parties, subject to UCTA 1977 (see **Chapters** 7 and **8**). It may be perfectly valid and desirable to exclude them, but the problem usually is to what extent UCTA 1977 permits this.

3.5.3 Implied terms which can never be excluded

The obligation of the seller to pass good title to the buyer can never be excluded. Any attempt to do so will be void.

Figure 3.2 below shows into which categories the main performance obligations fall. Each of these obligations will be discussed in more detail in **Chapters 4, 5** and **6**.

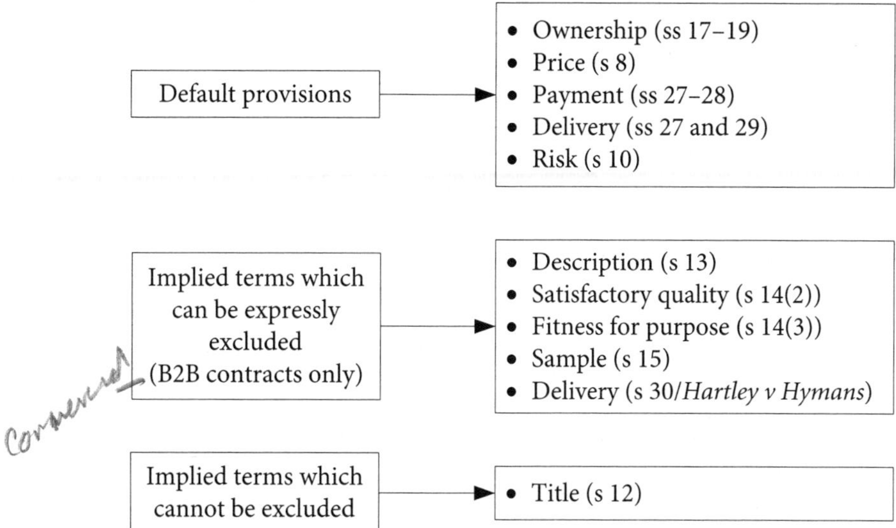

Figure 3.2 Categories of performance obligations

3.6 Effects of a sale of goods contract

The effects of a sale of goods contract are that:

(a) ownership of the goods is transferred to the buyer;

(b) the risk in the goods passes to the buyer; and

(c) the seller is paid.

3.7 Other types of contract under which goods may pass

Contracts for goods and services clearly involve the sale of goods but do not fall within the ambit of the SGA 1979. Many of the legal controls on the 'goods' part are in effect the same as for the sale of goods, but in addition there are controls on the 'services' component.

Other contracts under which goods may pass include conditional sale, hire purchase, leasing, bailment and factoring.

3.7.1 Contracts for services

Contracts for services are governed by the SGSA 1982. The main terms implied by this Act are:

(a) the service will be performed with reasonable skill and care (s 13);

(b) the work will be carried out within a reasonable time, but only if no time for performance has been fixed by the contract (s 14); and

(c) a reasonable charge will be paid, but only if no price is fixed by the contract (s 15).

3.7.2 Contracts for work and materials

A good example of a contract for work and materials (ie, goods and services) is a contract for repair, where the repairer supplies not only his own labour but also the necessary parts. These contracts are governed by the SGSA 1982. It is important to remember that it is *not* the SGA 1979 itself which applies in such cases (SGSA 1982, s 1).

It can sometimes be difficult to decide whether a contract should be categorised as a sale of goods contract, or as a contract for work and materials. Suppose, for example, that a customer engages a designer to design and build a chair. Is this a sale of goods contract (for the sale and purchase of the chair), or is it a work and materials contract? In *Samuels v Davis* [1943] KB

526, the Court of Appeal suggested that it did not matter too much how the agreement was categorised, as long as the correct terms were implied.

3.7.3 Exchange and barter

Contracts of exchange and barter are found relatively rarely in practice. In the past, they have been most frequently encountered in dealings with businesses in developing countries, where foreign currency may not be available to allow the buyer to pay in cash. There is evidence that they are now also being used in some forms of online trading.

3.7.4 Hire purchase

In a hire purchase agreement, the buyer obtains immediate possession of the goods, in return for making regular payments. However, ownership remains with the other party to the agreement. The buyer has an option to obtain ownership by paying a final instalment. The buyer 'buys' the goods not from the 'seller' but from the finance house, pursuant to the hire purchase agreement.

Hire purchase agreements are regulated under the Consumer Credit Act 1974. However, the 1974 Act does not deal with implied terms relating to title to the goods or quality. These are governed by the Supply of Goods (Implied Terms) Act 1973, which implies terms similar to those implied into sale of goods agreements by ss 12–15 of the SGA 1979.

3.7.5 Conditional sale

A conditional sale agreement achieves a very similar result to a hire purchase agreement. Again, the buyer obtains immediate possession and makes regular payments in return. Again, ownership remains with the other party, although the buyer can obtain ownership by making a final payment. However, the agreement is structured rather differently in that there is no option to purchase. Instead, it is a sale of goods agreement under which ownership does not pass until the final payment is made.

Conditional sale is often used to finance consumer purchases in exactly the same way as a hire purchase agreement. When used in this way it is regulated by the Consumer Credit Act 1974. Because they are sale of goods agreements, the SGA 1979 applies to conditional sale agreements in the normal way and so, for example, ss 12 to 15 imply terms regarding title to the goods, quality, etc.

3.7.6 Hire agreements

A hire agreement differs from a sale of goods agreement in that ownership of the goods does not pass as the hirer obtains only possession, not title to the goods. In some situations, hire agreements with consumers are regulated by the Consumer Credit Act 1974.

The SGA 1979 does not apply to hire agreements. Instead, terms relating to the right to transfer possession and quality are implied by the SGSA 1982, ss 6–11 (see **Chapter 6**). The terms are very similar to those implied in sale of goods agreements by the SGA 1979, ss 12–15. Exceptions are that s 7 of the SGSA 1982 implies a term that the owner, referred to as the 'bailor', has the right to transfer possession rather than a right to sell the goods. In a hire agreement, of course, it is only possession of the goods which is being transferred, not the title to them, so that is the important thing here.

3.7.7 Leases of goods

A lease is the contract between a lessor and a lessee for the hire of an asset. Today, this would be an expensive item of equipment, perhaps industrial machinery, a computer system, lorries or other motor vehicles. The lessor need not necessarily be the manufacturer or a seller of the equipment. It could instead be a finance company. The lessor is the owner of the equipment, and keeps the ownership. The lessee has the right to possess and use the equipment during the term of the lease. The lessee pays the lessor rental payments as specified in the lease contract. At the end of the lease, the equipment is returned to the lessor, which may lease it out again or more usually sell it. If the equipment is sold to the lessee, the danger is that the contract may instead be construed as a hire purchase contract and therefore be subject to the legislation on hire purchase.

There are two basic categories of lease:

(a) Operating leases. With an operating lease, the equipment is hired out to the user (the lessee) for a short period of time, returned to the lessor and then hired out to another user. This is, for example, how a tool hire shop would normally operate.

(b) Finance leases. With a finance lease, the equipment is supplied to one user only, which retains possession of it for substantially the whole of its working life. Most computer leases are finance leases. With a finance lease, there is no contractual relationship between the user and the supplier of the hardware. The lessor will be a finance house, which has purchased the equipment from the supplier.

3.7.8 Factoring

Factoring is where a supplier of goods sells its unpaid invoices (debts) to a third party, the factor. The supplier will not receive the full book value for the debts, as the factor will charge a fee and interest, and will also take into account the risk of the debtor defaulting. However, there are considerable advantages for the business in that it releases cash and improves cash flow. Customers will deal direct with the factor in the collection of the factored debts.

3.7.9 Bailment

Bailment is where the owner of goods (the bailor) transfers possession of the goods to another party, the bailee. The bailee will keep the goods on behalf of the bailor, subject to any express or implied conditions of the bailment contract, for example the goods may be used for a specified purpose. The bailment contract will normally provide for the eventual return of the goods to the bailor. The bailee, therefore, does not own the goods but simply has possession of them, and must take reasonable care of them, until the bailor reclaims them.

Bailment does not always depend on the existence of a bailment contract. It may arise as a result of one party assuming voluntary possession of another's goods. The bailee will still have an implied duty to take reasonable care of the goods whilst they are in his possession.

Chapter 4

Sale of Goods: Core Terms – Price, Payment and Delivery

4.1 Introduction

In a commercial context, it is unusual for the parties not to make provision about the essential terms of the contract: price, payment and delivery. Clearly, the seller and the buyer will have different agendas on these issues. Initially, each of the parties' solicitors will want to include terms which are favourable to their client in the draft contract. This will often be followed by a period of negotiation until the issues are resolved. How they are dealt with will ultimately depend on the bargaining strength of the parties.

The SGA 1979 contains default, or fallback, provisions which will be implied into the contract only where the parties have not made their own provision. In addition, in relation to delivery, there are implied duties imposed on each party, which are fundamental to the performance of the contract. These are the duty of the seller to deliver the goods and the duty of the buyer to accept delivery. Clearly, without these, the contract will not be performed at all. Finally, there are further delivery obligations imposed on the seller which will be implied into the contract as conditions, either by statute or by the common law. These are the duty to deliver the right quantity, and the duty to deliver on time where there is a specified delivery date. These implied conditions can be excluded only by agreement between the parties, and subject to UCTA 1977.

In this chapter each of the core provisions will be dealt with in turn, concentrating on the default provisions and drafting considerations relevant to each of these. The implied terms will be dealt with in more detail in **Chapter 6**.

4.2 The price

4.2.1 Definition of 'price' (SGA 1979, s 8)

Section 8 provides:

> (1) The price in a contract of sale may be fixed by the contract, or may be left to be fixed in a manner agreed by the contract, or may be determined by the course of dealing between the parties.
>
> (2) Where the price is not determined as mentioned in subsection (1) above the buyer must pay a reasonable price.
>
> (3) What is a reasonable price is a question of fact dependent on the circumstances of each particular case.

The basic position is that the parties are free to fix their own price. The fallback position is that if they fail to do so, the price will be a reasonable one. It is clearly preferable to have a specific provision as to price to avoid uncertainty. One problem with s 8 is that, if the parties have not agreed such a basic term of the contract as the price of the goods, it is debatable whether or not they have concluded a contract at all. Alternatively, the parties may conclude the contract but agree that the price will be fixed at some point in the future. This is an 'agreement to agree' which, as discussed in **Chapter 2**, will be unenforceable, unless the parties have agreed on a specific mechanism for fixing the price.

4.2.2 Agreeing the price (ss 8 and 9)

In most circumstances, the parties will agree the price. This may be done in one of several ways:

(a) The price may be fixed by use of a price list or by quotation.

(b) The price may have been agreed during negotiation. If so, it is important that such agreement should be documented.

(c) The price may also be determined by a consistent course of dealing between the parties.

(d) A further possibility is that the parties leave the price to be fixed by the valuation of a third party. If this does not happen, the contract is void (s 9).

4.2.3 Price – drafting considerations

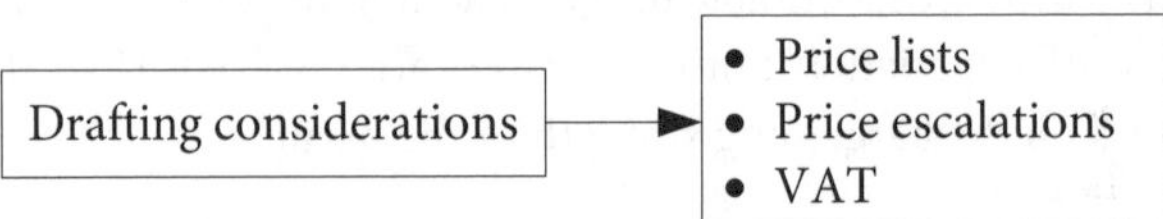

4.2.3.1 Price lists and quotations

Where the price is fixed by reference to a price list or quotation, it is important to specify the length of time for which any quoted price or price list will remain valid. Price lists and quotations should include a statement that such a price must be accepted within a specified time period, for example 28 days.

It is also important to specify clearly what is included in the price, for example whether the price includes delivery costs or insurance.

4.2.3.2 Price escalation clauses

If there is a likelihood of the cost of raw materials or labour increasing between the signing of the contract and delivery, it is advisable to put in a specific price escalation clause. In the absence of such a clause, the seller will not be able to change the price.

In a business to business contract, any provision allowing the seller to increase its price may be subject to reasonableness under s 3 of UCTA 1977, as it can render its performance under the contract substantially different from that which was reasonably expected.

4.2.4 Value added tax

A price in a contract is taken as including value added tax (VAT) unless otherwise specified (Value Added Tax Act 1994, s 19(2)). If the price is to be exclusive of VAT, that must be expressly stated. Failure to do this will result in the seller having to bear the VAT itself and not being able to pass it on to the buyer.

4.3 Payment

4.3.1 Duty to pay the price

Under s 27 of the SGA 1979, it is the buyer's duty to pay the price. Where the contract provides for cash on delivery, the buyer cannot claim possession of the goods unless it is able to pay the price in accordance with the terms of the contract. Only payment in full will discharge the buyer's liability, unless a discount has been agreed. In most commercial contracts, the buyer will want a credit period.

4.3.2 Payment – drafting considerations

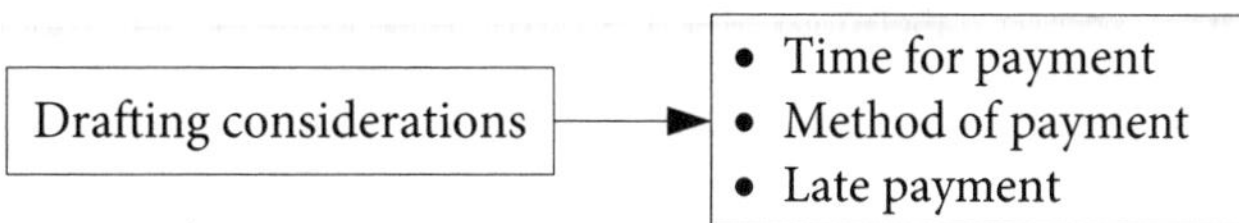

4.3.2.1 Time for payment

Unless the parties agree otherwise, s 28 of the SGA 1979 states that the time for payment is when the goods are delivered. Obviously, this is the normal position when buying goods in a shop. Delivery and payment will take place when the goods are paid for and handed over to the customer. In other commercial situations, however, this may not be the most suitable arrangement. Payment is generally linked to the issue of an invoice. The parties may wish to agree that:

(a) payment be made in advance. This is more common, for example, in international sales or where the seller is uncertain of the buyer's ability to pay;

(b) the buyer be given a credit period, say 30 days from the delivery of an invoice. It will then be important that the contract not only addresses the credit period, but also specifies when the seller has the right to issue an invoice, eg on delivery or after delivery has taken place.

Section 10(1) provides:

> Unless a different intention appears from the terms of the contract, stipulations as to time of payment are not of the essence of a contract of sale.

This has been interpreted as meaning that failure to pay is not a breach of condition entitling the seller to treat the contract as repudiated and to sell the goods elsewhere. It limits the seller's right to the price and to damages, if any, for late payment. This has been criticised, for example in Adams, JN and MacQueen, H, *Atiyah's Sale of Goods*, 12th edn (Longman, 2010), as providing a 'compulsory credit which the seller has to extend to the buyer'. The seller should therefore ensure that the contract does make time for payment of the essence.

4.3.2.2 Method of payment

Under s 28 of the SGA 1979, subject to contrary agreement between the parties, the seller is entitled to be paid in cash. Again, in ordinary retail sales, the customer gives the shopkeeper the money and takes the goods away. However, this may not always be the most practical commercial scenario:

(a) If a seller accepts a cheque or other negotiable instrument, this is treated as a conditional payment. If the cheque is not honoured, the seller may sue for the price either as breach of the sale of goods contract, or on the cheque as being a contract in itself. It is advisable to include a provision ensuring that payment takes place only when the cheque has been cleared, and that the buyer will allow for the time it will take for the cheque to clear when meeting any payment deadline.

(b) Payment by credit card will usually be treated as an absolute payment. Therefore, failure by the credit card company to pay the seller does not entitle the seller to sue the customer. The customer's only liability is to pay the credit card company, but failure to do so does not mean that it will be liable to the seller.

4.3.2.3 Late payment

In the absence of contrary agreement, damages for late payment may be awarded by the court for additional costs caused to the seller. Interest can be awarded under:

(a) the Law Reform (Miscellaneous Provisions) Act 1934;
(b) the Late Payment of Commercial Debts (Interest) Act 1998 (see **5.5.4**).

It is obviously sensible to provide in the contract for interest for late payment, as this avoids having to rely on these statutory provisions. Any contractual arrangement to recover, by way of damages or interest, for late payment must not 'amount to a penalty' but must be based upon a genuine pre-estimate of loss.

Clearly, prevention is better than cure, and an alternative to encourage the buyer to pay promptly would be to include a discount for prompt payment.

4.3.3 Right of resale

Where the buyer fails to pay, the seller has a statutory right of resale under s 48(3). However, this is limited in scope (see **4.5.1.5**) so it is advisable for the seller to reserve the right of resale in the contract in the event of undue delay in payment by the buyer. This prevents the buyer from taking advantage of the 'compulsory credit' period created by s 10(1) (see **4.3.2.1**).

4.4 Delivery

4.4.1 Duties of the seller and buyer

The SGA 1979 imposes corresponding duties on the seller and the buyer in relation to delivery. To understand the delivery provisions, the starting point is to consider three aspects of delivery, namely:

(a) definition of the word 'delivery';
(b) the duties of the seller and buyer in relation to delivery; and
(c) methods of delivery.

4.4.2 What is 'delivery'?

'Delivery' is defined in s 61(1) as the 'voluntary transfer of possession from one person to another'. It is, if you like, handing over the goods. However, it is important to distinguish between 'legal' and 'physical' delivery. 'Delivery' in the sense used in sale of goods does not mean the physical transportation of the goods from the seller's premises to another location, eg the buyer's premises. ('Physical transportation' is usually referred to as 'carriage of goods'.) Nor is delivery confined to the transfer of physical possession of the goods, as there are various ways in which goods can be 'delivered' (see **4.4.4**). It really means the point in time and space at which the parties can be seen to have agreed that the legal right to possession of the goods passes from the seller to the buyer. It is important to understand from the outset that delivery does not necessarily occur at the same point at which ownership passes – the two are separate legal issues. A clear distinction must be made between 'delivery' (ie the transfer of possession) and the passing of title (ie ownership).

4.4.3 Duties of the seller in respect of delivery

4.4.3.1 Duty of the seller to deliver the goods

Under s 27 of the SGA 1979, it is the duty of the seller to deliver, in the legal sense, the goods. There is no general duty to transport the goods to the buyer.

The seller must deliver goods which comply with the contract and which comply with the implied conditions under ss 12, 13, 14 and 15. Failure to do so will give the buyer the right to reject delivery (see **Chapter 6**).

4.4.3.2 Duty to deliver the right quantity

The seller is required to deliver goods of the right quantity:

(a) Under s 30(1), the buyer may reject the goods if the quantity is less than the contract quantity. However, if it accepts them, it must pay for them at the contract rate.

(b) If the seller delivers a quantity greater than the contracted quantity, the buyer may accept the contract quantity and reject the rest, or may reject the whole (s 30(2)). If the buyer accepts the whole quantity, it must pay for the excess quantity at the contract rate (s 30(3)). If the variation from the contract quantity is slight then the buyer may not reject the goods, unless the buyer is a consumer (s 30(2A)).

(c) Section 31(1) provides that the buyer is not obliged to accept delivery in instalments. This means that the seller cannot deliver some of the goods and promise to deliver the remainder later. In these circumstances, the buyer will be entitled to reject the goods.

4.4.4 Duties of the buyer in respect of delivery

4.4.4.1 Duty of the buyer to take delivery

Under s 27 of the SGA 1979, it is the duty of the buyer to accept and pay for the goods in accordance with the terms of the contract of sale. Failure to do so gives the seller statutory rights and remedies (see **4.4.6** and **4.5**).

4.4.4.2 Delivery and payment

As discussed at **4.3.2**, s 28 provides that delivery of the goods and payment should happen at the same time, subject to contrary agreement, but as it is commercially unlikely that the parties will want to rely on these provisions, these aspects of delivery should be provided for in the contract.

4.4.4.3 Delivery and acceptance

Although s 27 refers to the duty of the buyer to 'accept' the goods, it is important to realise that the SGA 1979 distinguishes between taking delivery of the goods and acceptance, in the legal sense, of the goods. Taking delivery of the goods does not mean that the buyer has agreed that the goods comply with the contract, ie the buyer has not yet necessarily accepted them. Acceptance is dealt with in s 35.

Under s 35(1), the buyer is deemed to have accepted the goods when:

(a) it tells the seller that it has accepted them; or

(b) it does any act in relation to them which is inconsistent with the ownership of the seller, eg uses them or sells them to a third party.

Section 35(2) provides that acceptance will not take place until the buyer has had a reasonable period to examine the goods to ensure that they conform with the contract. To give a simple example, if A agrees to sell a car to B and that the method of delivery will be the handing over of the registration documents, then B will take delivery when it collects the documents. However, the buyer will still have the opportunity to inspect the car before the buyer is deemed to have accepted the goods.

Section 35(4) is particularly important in commercial contracts. The buyer is deemed to have accepted the goods if it fails to notify the seller within a reasonable time that it wishes to reject them. Thus, if goods for some reason do not comply with the contract, eg they are faulty or do not match the description, then the buyer must notify the seller within a reasonable timescale that it wishes to reject. The problem here is that what amounts to a 'reasonable time' will be a question of fact in each case (see **Chapter 6**). The seller may therefore wish expressly to provide the number of days after which the buyer may no longer reject the goods.

4.4.5 Methods of delivery

There are various methods of delivery. The most obvious is actual delivery, ie physically handing over the goods, as would happen when a consumer is buying goods in a shop. Other methods of delivery include:

(a) transfer of a document (eg, a bill of lading: see **14.3.1**);

(b) delivery of an object giving control (eg giving the keys to premises where the goods are stored, or even the keys to a motor car);

(c) the buyer's continuance of possession (eg where the buyer already holds the goods as bailee of the seller, and then on the sale there is a notional delivery of the goods to the buyer);

(d) delivery to a carrier (see **4.4.6.1**);

(e) 'attornment', where a seller or a third party acknowledges that goods which were held by the seller, or on its behalf, are now held on behalf of the buyer.

The contract should expressly deal with how the goods are to be delivered.

4.4.6 Delivery – drafting considerations

The fallback delivery provisions raise a number of issues which should be considered when drafting the contract.

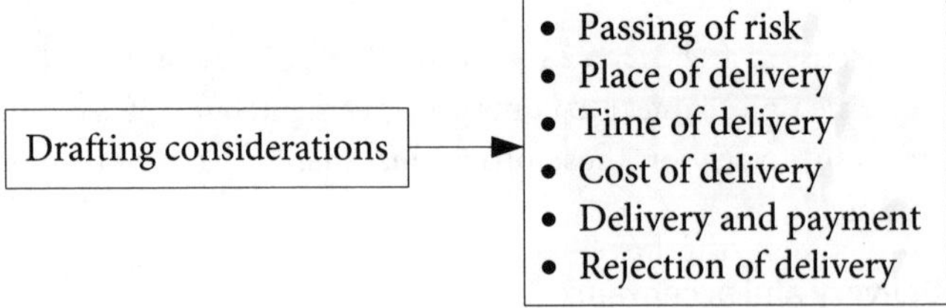

4.4.6.1 Passing of risk

Prima facie, the risk of loss or damage to the goods does not automatically pass with delivery, ie with physical possession of the goods. Under s 20(1), risk passes with the property in the goods, that is with the title to/ownership of the goods. So, it is perfectly possible for the goods to be in the buyer's (physical) possession but still be at the seller's risk, if the seller still has title to them. The seller would therefore have the trouble and expense of insuring goods that are no longer in its possession. The seller will usually want the contract to be drafted so that the risk of the goods passes to the buyer with physical possession of the goods, so that the buyer has both control of the goods and the obligation to insure them. This is particularly important in retention of title sales (see **Chapter 5**).

An example of where problems could arise is the installation of a new computer system. The buyer will not want to pay the whole price until the system is running properly, yet the goods are on the buyer's premises and under its control whilst they are being installed. In such circumstances, the contract should provide that the risk in the goods passes to the buyer when the goods arrive at the buyer's premises. It is then up to the buyer to insure the goods, for example against theft or fire.

Where goods are delivered to a carrier, the contract should deal with the passing of risk. Section 32(1) provides that where the seller is authorised or required to send the goods to the buyer, transfer of possession to the carrier constitutes delivery to the buyer. The goods are at the buyer's risk from the point at which they are in the carrier's possession. The buyer should insure them against damage or loss from that point. However, this is not invariably the case and, in any event, this arrangement is often varied by express provision in the contract.

Under s 20(2), if there is a delay in delivery then, during the period of the delay, the goods are at the risk of whichever party to the contract caused the delay. Again, this may be varied by the contract. Where the delay is beyond the control of the parties, the issue can be dealt with by the inclusion of a force majeure clause (see **Chapter 8**).

The passing of risk is also an important consideration in international sale of goods contracts (see also **Chapter 14**).

4.4.6.2 Place of delivery

In the absence of a contrary agreement, the default position under s 29(2) is that the place of delivery will be at the seller's place of business or residence. The contract between the seller and buyer should therefore specify where delivery is to occur. Alternatives include that:

(a) the seller will deliver the goods to the buyer's premises;

(b) the buyer will collect the goods from the seller's premises; or

(c) the goods will be delivered to a carrier.

4.4.6.3 Date and time of delivery

Where no provision has been made as to the date and time of delivery, the default position under s 29(3) is that delivery should take place within a reasonable time. What constitutes a 'reasonable time' depends on the facts and the circumstances at the time of delivery. To avoid commercial uncertainty, the contract should deal with the issue. The form of clause will vary, depending on what has been agreed in relation to the place of delivery:

(a) Where the seller is to deliver the goods, the time of delivery will usually be the moment when the goods are handed over to the buyer. It may be worth considering whether the seller should be given the right to deliver before any agreed delivery date, by giving reasonable notice to the buyer.

(b) Where the buyer is to collect the goods, delivery could take place when the buyer physically removes the goods from the seller's premises. An alternative is to provide that delivery takes place when the seller authorises the buyer to collect the goods.

(c) Where delivery is to a carrier, delivery will usually be when the seller hands the goods to the carrier.

Delivery must be made at a 'reasonable hour' (s 29(5)).

4.4.6.4 Express delivery dates

As discussed at **4.3.2.1**, s 10(1) states that time of payment is not of the essence in a sale of goods contract, unless the parties agree otherwise. Section 10(2) then provides that the parties can agree whether or not time is of the essence with regard to any other terms of the contract. The default position is, therefore, that time will not be of the essence, unless agreed otherwise by the parties.

With delivery, the exception to this general rule is that, in commercial contracts only, whether or not time is of the essence is governed by case law. In *Hartley v Hymans* [1920] 3 KB 475, it was held that in ordinary commercial contracts for the sale of goods, where a delivery date has been specified, time of delivery is prima facie of the essence. This has the effect of making the obligation to deliver on the specified date a condition, breach of which will give the buyer the right to repudiate the contract as well as sue for damages. This prima facie rule may be rebutted by the facts in a particular case.

In most commercial contracts, a delivery date will usually have been specifically agreed. Thus, under the common law rules, there is usually an implied condition that time will be of the essence for delivery. This clearly works in favour of the buyer, and the seller will want to ensure that the contract is drafted to avoid making time of the essence for delivery. It is important to remember that this is one of the implied conditions that may be excluded by agreement between the parties, but any attempt to do so will be subject to s 3 of UCTA 1977 (see **Chapter** 7).

Waiver

If the buyer waives the original delivery date before the goods are delivered, the buyer is entitled to give the seller reasonable notice that it will not accept the goods after a certain date. See *Charles Rickards Ltd v Oppenheim* [1950] 1 KB 616, where the buyer waived the original delivery date but then gave the seller reasonable notice of a revised date. The seller failed to meet even the revised date and the buyer was held to be entitled to refuse to accept the goods. A 'no authority clause' could be included to avoid 'accidental' waiver, eg by unauthorised employees (see **2.5.1.3**).

Force majeure

Even if there is an agreed delivery date, the duty to deliver by the agreed date could be suspended or extinguished. This is typically dealt with in a force majeure clause in the contract, which concerns events beyond the control of the parties. Again, a force majeure clause amounts to an exclusion of liability and will be subject to s 3 of UCTA 1977, and the implications will be considered in **Chapter 8**.

4.4.6.5 Cost of delivery

The parties should agree, and provision should be made in the contract, as to who will bear the costs of delivery. Usually, this will be the buyer. The only default provision is s 29(6), which relates to goods which are not yet in a deliverable state. In the absence of contrary agreement, the seller is responsible for the costs of putting the goods into a deliverable state.

4.4.6.6 Rejection of delivery

Section 36 of the SGA 1979 states that where the goods have been delivered to the buyer and the buyer rightfully rejects them, the buyer is not obliged to return them to the seller. The seller must therefore arrange for collection of the goods. This may cost the seller both time and expense, particularly where there are considerable distances involved, both in checking that rejection is justified (eg because the goods really are defective) and in arranging collection. The seller may therefore wish to include a non-rejection clause. However, this may be subject to s 6 or s 3 of UCTA 1977 (see **7.7**).

Under s 37 the buyer is liable for costs incurred by the seller due to the buyer's neglect or refusal to take delivery, ie wrongful rejection of delivery. Any attempt to make the seller pay for storage charges in this instance would be subject to s 3 of UCTA 1977, as it is an attempt to limit the buyer's liability for breach of the implied duty to accept delivery of the goods.

4.5 Rights and remedies of the seller

The seller's primary right for breach of a condition of a contract by the buyer is to terminate the contract and/or to sue for damages. In addition, the seller has the right to sue for damages for breach of warranty. Damages will always be subject to the common law rules on remoteness, in particular *Hadley v Baxendale*, and measure (see **Chapter 2**).

Where the buyer fails to accept delivery of the goods and/or to pay for them, the seller has statutory remedies under the SGA 1979 as well as the usual contract remedies. These can be divided loosely into two categories:

(a) the unpaid seller's rights against the goods ('real rights');
(b) the unpaid seller's personal rights/remedies.

4.5.1 Seller's rights against the goods

4.5.1.1 Definition of an 'unpaid seller' (s 38)

Section 38(1) of the 1979 Act defines an unpaid seller in the following manner:

> The seller of goods is an unpaid seller within the meaning of this Act—
>
> (a) when the whole of the price has not been paid or tendered;
>
> (b) when a bill of exchange or other negotiable instrument has been received as conditional payment, and the condition on which it was received has not been fulfilled by reason of the dishonour of the instrument or otherwise.

4.5.1.2 Rights of the unpaid seller under the SGA 1979, s 39

Section 39(1) gives the unpaid seller the following rights:

(a) a right of lien on the goods;

(b) a right of stopping the goods in transit;

(c) a right of re-sale.

It is important to remember that the seller is able to exercise these rights only in limited circumstances:

(a) the seller must come within the definition of an unpaid seller; and

(b) the seller has to have possession of, or at least control over, the goods.

In most circumstances, it will be unwise for the seller to rely solely on its statutory rights, and a retention of title clause should be included in the contract as a matter of course (see **Chapter 5**).

Seller's lien (ss 41, 43)

Section 41 states that an unpaid seller who is in possession of the goods is entitled to retain possession of them:

(a) until paid;

(b) where any credit period has expired; or

(c) where the buyer has become insolvent.

Under s 43, the right of lien is lost if the goods are paid for, or when the goods are consigned to a carrier without retaining title to the goods, or when the buyer has possession of the goods, or by waiver by the seller.

Stoppage in transit (ss 44–46)

Sections 44 to 46 state that the seller may stop the goods in transit where the buyer has become insolvent, and retain them until paid. Under s 46(1), the stopping could be either by:

(a) taking actual possession of the goods; or

(b) by giving notice of the seller's claim to the carrier.

Again the right is limited. It can be used only where the buyer becomes insolvent, and can be lost if the buyer manages to intercept the goods before the seller has an opportunity to exercise its right. It cannot be used if the carrier is the agent of the buyer.

Re-sale by seller (s 48)

Section 48(3) provides that an unpaid seller can re-sell the goods where:

(a) the goods are perishable; or

(b) the seller gives notice to the buyer of its intention to do so.

The limit on the right of re-sale is that the seller must give notice to the buyer of its intention to re-sell and wait to see whether the buyer tenders the price within a reasonable time. Where the goods are perishable, however, the seller does not need to serve a notice.

The unpaid seller who re-sells the goods to another buyer (ie a third party) passes good title to the goods. To do so, however, the seller must be in possession of the goods, ie must still have a lien on them or have the right to stop the goods in transit (ss 48(2), (3) and s 25).

Where the unpaid seller remains in possession of the goods and re-sells them, the original contract of sale is rescinded and the buyer is discharged from further liability to pay the price. The seller is entitled to keep the proceeds of the re-sale and to sue the original buyer for damages for non-acceptance if the seller makes any loss on the re-sale (including the expense of re-selling) as against the original price (see *RV Ward v Bignall* [1967] 2 All ER 449, CA). However, the seller is entitled to keep any profit which it makes on the re-sale.

4.5.2 Personal rights of the unpaid seller

4.5.2.1 Action for the price (s 49)

The unpaid seller can sue the buyer for the price of the goods where the buyer has the property in the goods, ie ownership of the goods, but has not paid for them, or where the price is due on 'a day certain' (s 49). This does not help if the buyer is insolvent or likely to become so, as there is no point in taking action against an 'empty vessel'.

This right is subject to statutory limitations. The result is that failure by the buyer to pay on time does not necessarily give the seller the right to bring an action for the price.

(a) Under s 49(1) the seller can bring an action for the price if, and only if, ownership in the goods has passed, and the buyer fails or refuses to pay. This subsection cannot therefore be used where, for example, the goods are subject to a retention of title clause.

(b) Section 49(2) gives the seller a limited right to bring an action for the price, irrespective of whether ownership of the goods has passed, where the price is payable on 'a day certain' and the buyer refuses to pay. The wording of this subsection is complex, but it only deals with cases where the price is payable 'irrespective of delivery'. There is no problem if payment is due on a specified date after delivery. Once the date for payment has passed, the seller can bring an action for the price.

The result is that failure by the buyer to pay on time does not necessarily give the seller the right to bring an action for the price, and the seller may have to rely on a claim for damages instead. It is therefore advisable to include a clause in the contract giving the seller a right to bring an action for the price as soon as the date for payment has passed, irrespective of whether or not ownership has passed.

4.5.2.2 Non-acceptance of the goods – assessment of damages (s 50)

Where the buyer has wrongfully refused to accept and pay for the goods, the seller can sue the buyer for damages (s 50). Section 50(2) mirrors the first limb of *Hadley v Baxendale* (see **2.7.3.1**) and provides that the measure of damages is the estimated loss directly and naturally resulting from the breach. The basis for assessment of damages is laid down in s 50(3):

> Where there is an available market for the goods in question the measure of damages is prima facie to be ascertained by the difference between the contract price and the market or current price at the time or times when the goods ought to have been accepted or (if no time was fixed for acceptance) at the time of the refusal to accept.

Presumably, where there is no available market, the measure of damages is the contract value of the goods plus any additional direct expenses caused to the seller.

A problem area is consequential loss. Such loss recovery is contemplated as 'special damages' by s 54. Beyond the prima facie measure provided by s 50(3), 'special damages' (ie damages for consequential loss recoverable under the second limb of *Hadley v Baxendale*) are recoverable.

4.5.3 The seller who is not in possession of the goods (ss 17 and 19)

As discussed, the rights of the unpaid seller against the goods apply where the seller still has possession, or at least physical control, of the goods. A more difficult situation is where the goods are in the possession or control of the buyer, but the seller has still not been paid. This is a major concern for the seller, especially where the buyer is going insolvent. The danger is that the goods will be sold by a liquidator. The seller would be only an unsecured creditor and would be unlikely to be paid much, if anything, by the liquidator, and damages would not be an appropriate remedy.

There is a right under ss 17 and 19 of the SGA 1979 to reserve title to the goods. This can be done in a contract of sale by inserting a retention of title (ROT) clause (also called a *Romalpa* clause after *Aluminium Industrie Vaassen BV v Romalpa Aluminium* [1976] 1 WLR 676). The idea behind this is to allow the seller to recover the goods if the buyer fails to pay or becomes insolvent, as the seller remains the owner of the goods which are the subject to the ROT clause. These clauses will be considered in **Chapter 5**.

4.6 Rights and remedies of the buyer

As with the seller, a breach of condition will always entitle the buyer to reject the goods, repudiate the contract and/or sue for damages. In addition, the buyer has the right to sue for damages for breach of warranty. Thus, the buyer will generally have the right to repudiate the contract for:

(a) non-delivery;

(b) late delivery, if time is of the essence;

(c) delivery of the wrong quantity, subject to s 30(2A).

4.6.1 Claim for damages (s 53)

The buyer can sue for damages for breach of a contract term, either express or implied (s 53). This is either where the term in question is classified as a warranty, or where it is a condition but the buyer has elected not to reject the goods.

Section 51 lays down the principles for calculating damages for non-delivery of the goods, and in particular s 51(3) states:

> Where there is an available market for the goods in question the measure of damages is prima facie to be ascertained by the difference between the contract price and the market or current price of the goods at the time or times when they ought to have been delivered or (if no time was fixed) at the time of the refusal to deliver.

In other words, the buyer's loss is any increase in the price of equivalent goods obtained from another source.

Where the buyer has suffered consequential loss, it too can claim for 'further damage' under s 53(4) and 'special damages' under s 54, which, as discussed above, represent damages under the second limb of *Hadley v Baxendale* (see **4.5.2.2**).

Limitation and/or exclusion clauses in sale of goods contracts are often aimed at limiting or excluding consequential loss, subject to being disallowed under UCTA 1977. The seller will not want to take on liabilities that might far exceed its profit on the sale. Such exclusions will be considered in **Chapter 6**.

4.6.2 Specific performance (s 52)

The buyer's right to apply for specific performance is regulated by s 52. The right is only for specific or ascertained goods, that is goods identified and agreed upon at the time the contract is made. It does not extend to unascertained goods, eg 5 kilos of potatoes (not yet identified) (see **Chapter 3**). The right applies whether or not the property in the goods (title to the goods) has already passed to the buyer. Whether or not specific performance is ordered is a matter within the discretion of the court. It will not be awarded in respect of goods which can be bought elsewhere by the buyer, or where damages would provide an adequate remedy.

Chapter 5
Sale of Goods: Ownership and Retention of Title

5.1 Introduction

The effect of a sale of goods contract is that ownership of the goods passes to the buyer, so the next issue to consider is the transfer of ownership in the goods. Before looking at the rules relating to ownership, it is worth briefly thinking about the terminology. The SGA 1979 refers to both 'title to goods' and 'property in goods'. Both of these terms are used to mean the same thing: 'ownership' (although this is not a term that is used in the Act itself).

The rules on ownership are complicated by the fact that the SGA 1979 provides separate rules for specific (or ascertained) goods and unascertained goods (see **Chapter 3** and **5.2.2**). Sales of specific goods are the most common in practice, but the transfer of ownership of unascertained goods gives more scope for problems to arise, particularly where the parties have not made provision for this.

It is also important to remember that the SGA 1979 itself separates ownership, possession and the passing of risk, and as discussed in **Chapter 4**, the parties can provide for each of these separately. The result is that it is perfectly possible for one party, often the buyer, to have possession but not ownership of the goods. Deciding who has ownership of the goods, and when, is important for a number of reasons.

This chapter will consider the rules relating to ownership and retention of title.

5.1.1 Insolvency

In the event of the insolvency of either of the parties, the goods come under the control of the liquidator, administrator or trustee in bankruptcy, and there is a risk that they may be sold. If the seller has delivered the goods, it would only have a claim to the proceeds as an unsecured creditor. However, if the seller has a valid retention of title over the goods (ie ownership has not passed) then it may be able to reclaim them before they are sold and thus recover the full value of the goods. Equally, where the buyer has paid for the goods but these have not been physically delivered, again its only claim will be as an unsecured creditor. If, however, the buyer has acquired ownership before the goods have been physically delivered, it can claim the goods before they are sold.

5.1.2 Risk

Under s 20, prima facie risk passes with ownership, so where the parties have not made specific provision for the passing of risk, and the goods are damaged or destroyed, it is important to know who has ownership of the goods to establish liability. If the goods are damaged or destroyed by a third party, eg a carrier, it will be necessary to establish who has the right to bring a claim against the carrier.

5.1.3 Seller's action for the price

Under s 49(1), generally, a seller can bring an action for the price only where ownership has passed (see **4.5.2.1**).

5.2 Transfer of ownership (ss 16–18)

5.2.1 Specific or ascertained goods

Ascertained goods are goods that can be identified at the time of the contract. Specific goods are goods which have been agreed on at the time of the contract. Section 17 of the SGA 1979 provides that the property in ascertained goods passes when the parties intend it to pass. This leaves the parties free to decide when ownership of the goods will pass. Their decision is often bound up with what they have agreed about delivery and payment.

5.2.2 Unascertained goods

Unascertained goods are goods which have not yet been identified. Unascertained goods can be generic goods, for example 100 kilos of potatoes or goods forming part of a bulk, or 100 kilos of potatoes out of 500 kilos. As far as unascertained goods are concerned, s 16 makes it clear that property cannot pass until the goods are ascertained. This section applies regardless of the intention of the parties, so it is not possible to make provision for the passing of ownership until the goods are ascertained. This can present serious problems for the buyer if the seller becomes insolvent.

5.2.3 Default provisions

Where the parties have failed to make provision for the passing of ownership, there are default provisions in s 18. The SGA 1979 does not really contemplate the possibility that the parties did not have any intention in relation to the transfer of ownership, and so s 18 contains complex rules for ascertaining their intention. The reason that it is important to deal with transfer of ownership as an express provision is that unintended effects can arise out of the application of the s 18 rules.

Rules 1–4 relate to specific goods. Rule 5 relates to unascertained or future goods.

(a) Rule 1 deals with unconditional contracts for the sale of specific goods in a deliverable state. Property passes when the contract is made. A simple example is when a customer buys a chocolate bar in a shop. Ownership passes when the money is handed over and the customer receives the chocolate bar.

(b) Rule 2 deals with conditional contracts where the goods exist but the buyer is bound to do something to put the goods into a deliverable state, eg the buyer agrees to buy 100 kilos of potatoes (specific goods), but the seller has to package them into 1 kilo bags before delivery. Property passes once the seller has done this and given notice to the buyer.

(c) Rule 3 deals with conditional contracts where the goods exist in a deliverable state but the seller has to weigh, measure, test the goods or 'do some other act' to ascertain the price. Property passes when the seller has done this and given notice to the buyer.

(d) Rule 4 deals with goods delivered on approval or sale and return. Property passes when the buyer approves, accepts the goods, 'otherwise adopts the transaction' or retains them beyond any fixed time for their return (or if none, beyond a reasonable time).

(e) Rule 5 provides that property in unascertained goods passes in two situations, either when:

  (i) unascertained goods are unconditionally appropriated to the contract by one party and the other party assents to this, either expressly or impliedly, for example 100 kilos of potatoes are weighed and put into a container for transportation; or

(ii) the seller delivers the goods (either to the buyer or a carrier) and the buyer assents to this, either expressly or impliedly.

The obvious danger with Rule 5 is that is that the property might pass to the buyer long before the seller wishes that to happen, ie before the seller is paid. Another serious consequence is that the risk of the goods will pass over to the buyer (under s 20(1), see **4.4.6.1**) at a time when they could easily still be in the possession of the seller. Again, this may not be the desired result at all; see *Wardars (Import & Export) Co Ltd v W Norwood & Sons Ltd* [1968] 2 QB 663, CA.

5.2.4 The basis for retention of title clauses

Section 19 provides the basis for retention of title. It provides that a seller may 'reserve the right of disposal of goods until certain conditions are fulfilled'. Therefore a seller who is allowing its buyer a credit period can stipulate that ownership will not pass to the buyer until the buyer pays for the goods. The seller retains ownership until that condition is fulfilled.

5.3 Introduction to retention of title

The effect of ss 17 and 19 (**5.2** above), therefore, is to give the seller the right to reserve title to the goods. This can be done in a contract of sale by inserting a retention of title (ROT) clause (also called a *Romalpa* clause after *Aluminium Industrie Vaassen BV v Romalpa Aluminium* [1976] 1 WLR 676). The idea of retaining title to the goods until they are paid for, or until they are sold on or used up (as with components/ingredients, etc), is that, in the last resort, the seller can recover its own goods and prevent a liquidator or trustee in bankruptcy of the buyer disposing of the goods.

The advantage for the buyer is that, up until such time as the seller might need to rely upon its retention of title clause, the buyer is free to sell or deal with the goods as it wishes. In *Fairfax Gerrard Holdings Ltd v Capital Bank plc* [2007] EWCA Civ 1226, it was held that there is no inconsistency between the inclusion of a retention of title clause and an implied or even express right to sell the goods. In practice, many retention of title clauses include a provision which states that the buyer has right to sell the goods. This does no more than restate the legal position, but provides reassurance for inexperienced buyers who are not familiar with ROT provisions.

The validity of retention of title clauses has been upheld where the goods remain identifiable (see eg *Clough Mill Ltd v Martin* [1985] 1 WLR 111 and *Armour v Thyssen Edelstahlwerke AG* [1991] 2 AC 339). In *Clough Mill*, yarn had been sold to a manufacturer of fabrics. The seller was held to have title to the unused yarn.

5.3.1 Creation of charges

A charge is a right granted over an asset or assets to secure a debt. It gives the charge holder priority to be paid ahead of unsecured creditors in the event of insolvency. Under s 870 of Companies Act 2006, charges must be registered at Companies House within 21 days of creation. If the charge is not registered, s 874 provides that it will be void against a liquidator or an administrator, and also against other unsecured creditors. However, it is important to note that it will still be valid as between the parties themselves. For a full discussion of charges, see **Chapter 12** of ***Business Law and Practice***.

Simple retention of title clauses do not generally create registrable charges over the buyer's assets. Such clauses operate by preventing the property in the goods from passing to the buyer in the first place, ie the seller still owns them until he is paid. A seller cannot (and would not) take a charge over its own property by way of security. Problems only arise where the clause attempts to go further than simply retaining title to the goods and gives the seller rights over the buyer's property. These include attempts to retain title to either the proceeds of sale of the original goods, or products which have been mixed with or manufactured into other goods.

Any such attempt would create a charge, which would be void against a liquidator, an administrator or a third party unless registered.

In practice, it is not going to be practical to register these charges. A new charge would come into existence each time the buyer resold the goods, in the case of a proceeds of sale clause, or mixed them with others, in the case of a mixed/manufactured goods clause. The seller would find it very hard to police this. It would also be onerous to complete the necessary registration forms each time, identifying the property over which the charge had been created. Registering numerous charges could also lead to adverse credit ratings for the buyer if it is a company, because the buyer's file at Companies House would show all these charges registered against it. This would discourage anyone thinking of lending money to the buyer. The effect of such actions by the seller would be to put off the buyer from contracting with the seller in the first place. In practice, therefore, the seller will not usually attempt to register any charge which a retention of title clause might create.

5.3.2 Proceeds of sale

Where the goods have been sold on to an innocent third party, under s 25 of the SGA 1979 an innocent third party will get good title to the goods. If a buyer of the goods sells them on, the sub-buyer will get good title to those goods. The proceeds of the sub-sale sale will belong to the buyer, and not to the seller. Any attempt by the seller to claim or trace the proceeds would therefore amount to an attempt to claim the buyer's property and so would amount to a charge.

Tracing has been done successfully only once, in *Aluminium Industrie Vaassen BV v Romalpa Aluminium* [1976] 1 WLR 676. The sellers there tried to claim the proceeds of sale of the goods once the goods themselves had been sold on. The Court of Appeal allowed this on the grounds that there was an express fiduciary relationship between the sellers and the buyers (with the buyers selling the goods on to a third party as agents for the sellers rather than in their own right). Subsequently, the courts have been unwilling to recognise this fiduciary relationship, which seems to have been based, in *Romalpa*, upon concessions made by one party, probably unnecessarily.

Over the years, there have been many attempts to draft retention of title clauses to permit the seller to claim sale proceeds. Very simple clauses entitling the seller to the proceeds are almost certain to be construed as charges over the proceeds. It seems from the case law that the courts will take exactly the same view of more complex attempts (eg elaborate clauses describing the existence of a fiduciary relationship between the parties).

In *Compaq Computer Ltd v Abercorn Group Ltd (t/a Osiris) and Others* [1991] BCC 484, Abercorn was appointed as an authorised dealer of Compaq's computers. The agreement contained a clause that the goods were held by Abercorn as 'bailee and agent' and proceeds of sub-sales were to be accounted for to Compaq. The court held that the relationship was a commercial buyer/seller relationship, and not a bailment, agency or fiduciary relationship. The arrangement was held to be a charge over the proceeds of the sub-sales, which was void for want of registration. It seems that even a very carefully worded clause will create only a charge.

5.3.3 Separation of proceeds

The clause may also provide that where the buyer sells the goods on, it will pay the proceeds of sale into a separate bank account, which it will hold on trust for the seller. The idea is to stop the money generated by the sale of the seller's goods from becoming mixed up with other money the buyer may have which is nothing to do with the seller. The problem here is that, whilst the clause is legally effective as between the buyer and the seller, a buyer in financial difficulties is unlikely to comply with such a provision, and may use the money to stave off creditors or to pay off its overdraft. Basic banking principles mean that once money is paid into an overdrawn account, it will be absorbed by the overdraft. Tracing will not be possible. It is therefore common to provide that the money should not be paid into an overdrawn bank account, but this is difficult to police and the seller's only remedy for breach is damages.

It is quite common to find that the clause also requires the buyer to assign the debts arising from any credit sub-sales that it makes to the seller. The problem with such a clause is that if the sub-buyer fails to comply with this or does it when it is insolvent, the seller will not usually recover the money. The rights are merely contractual and of little use in insolvency. See *Fairfax Gerrard Holdings Ltd v Capital Bank plc* [2007] EWCA Civ 1226.

5.3.4 Mixed, manufactured or altered goods

Problems also arise where the original goods have been used in a manufacturing process and have lost their original identity. Where the goods have been incorporated into other products, the original goods are considered to have been subsumed into the new products and the seller has no right to the new products. The buyer will have incurred additional costs of the manufacturing process, eg the cost of other materials and labour. The manufactured goods belong to the buyer and incorporate its profit. Again, any attempt by the seller to claim a right over the new product belonging to the buyer would create a charge.

This point was considered in *Clough Mill Ltd v Martin* [1985] 1 WLR 111, where the seller supplied yarn to a manufacturer of fabrics. Lord Goff stated:

> I find it impossible to believe that it was the intention of the parties that the plaintiff would thereby gain the windfall of the full value of the new product, deriving as it may well do not merely from the labour of the buyer but also from materials that were the buyer's without any duty to account to the buyer for any surplus of the proceeds of sale above the outstanding balance of the price due by the buyer to the plaintiff.

The seller was held not to have title to the finished fabric, only to the unused yarn.

In *Borden (UK) Ltd v Scottish Timber Products Ltd* [1981] Ch 25, the sellers sold resin to manufacturers of chipboard. It was held that they did not have title to the chipboard, or to the proceeds of its sale.

Sometimes it may not be quite so clear whether the goods have been incorporated during the manufacturing process. In *Re Peachdart Ltd* [1984] Ch 131, leather hides had been made into handbags. It was held that 'once the process of manufacture had started … work and materials provided by the company would result in the leather being converted into … other goods of a distinctive character'. A slightly more gruesome example is *Chaigley Farms Ltd v Crawford Kay and Grayshire* [1996] BCC 957, where the retention of title was over animals which were sent for slaughter. The judge held that there was 'an inescapable difference between a live animal and a dead one'. The result was the title had passed to the buyer, and the seller did not own the carcasses.

5.3.5 Detachable goods

It is important to distinguish between manufactured goods and goods which have simply been attached to other goods. Where the goods are readily detachable then it is appropriate to have a clause reserving the right of the seller to detach its goods and remove them. For example, in *Hendy Lennox (Industrial Engines) Ltd v Graham Puttick Ltd* [1984] 1 WLR 485, the seller had sold diesel engines to the buyer. The buyer had bolted the engines to electrical generators. It was therefore feasible to detach the engines without damaging the generators. A clause allowing the seller to separate and remove detachable goods will not create a charge and is likely to be upheld by the court.

5.3.6 Goods which cannot be identified

Where the goods have been mixed with other goods and are no longer identifiable, the goods will belong to the buyer. In *Re Andrabell Ltd (In Liquidation); Airborne Accessories Ltd v Goodman* [1984] 3 All ER 407, the seller sold travel bags in a number of consignments. The contracts did not have an 'all moneys' clause (see **5.4.2.1**) so any rights attached only to the consignment for which the seller had not been paid. The seller was not able to identify those bags from all the other bags, so could not recover any bags. It was also not allowed to trace the proceeds of sale through the buyer's general bank account.

5.3.7 Bulk storage

Where the seller's goods are of a type that can be stored, typically in bulk, along with the goods of the same type which belong to other suppliers or even of the buyer, eg diesel oil or grain, it may be possible to retain title to a share of the bulk. The goods must all be of the same type and specification. In such a 'commingled' mass, title does not pass to the buyer but, instead, all contributors become owners in common, generally, in proportion to their contributions to the bulk.

Glencore International AG v Metro Trading International Inc (No 2) [2001] 1 Lloyd's Rep 284 involved the storage of oil from different suppliers. The oil was all of the same type and grade, and had been stored by the buyer mixed, or co-mingled, in bulk containers. It was held that upon commingling during storage, Glencore would become an owner of the whole of the commingled bulk in common with Metro and any other persons whose oil had contributed to the bulk. Each party's share would be in proportion to the quantity of oil contributed by each of them. This illustrates the problems that such cases throw up. The big difference between this case and the earlier 'mixed goods' cases is that, in the bulk storage cases, it can be seen that the goods have not lost their identifiable nature and title does not pass to the buyer. Nevertheless, slight differences in grade or specification between the separate quantities supplied would easily cause a mixing or blending into a bulk, in which the separate sellers had lost their titles and property.

5.4 Drafting a retention of title clause: a basic checklist

It is important to appreciate at this stage that no clause can always be guaranteed to be appropriate in all situations. The solicitor drafting the clause should always check when using a precedent that it fits in with the client's needs and instructions. The following suggested provisions aim to cover the basic situation of retaining title to the goods, but also to go further and cover some of the problems mentioned above.

Any retention of title checklist should deal with:

(a) provisions which are essential to ensure that the clause is legally effective;

(b) provisions which are not legally essential, but which are desirable to make the clause work practically for the seller;

(c) clauses which may not be legally effective, but which may be included for 'bluff' value.

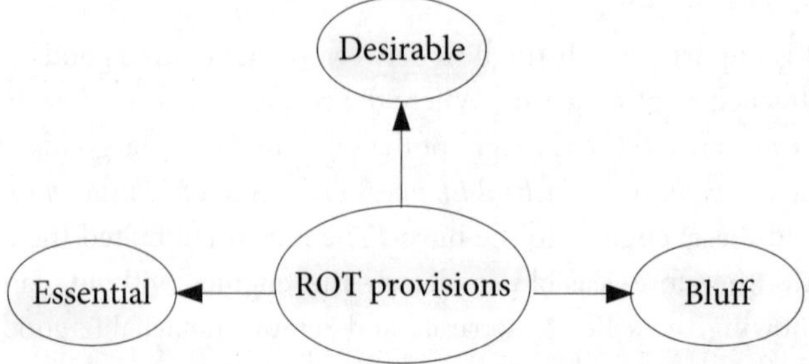

5.4.1 Essential provisions

5.4.1.1 Reserving title – simple retention of title

The seller should make it clear that it will remain the owner of the goods and that (legal) ownership will not pass to the buyer until full payment is received. This is a simple retention of title clause. To be legally effective, a retention of title clause must retain legal title to the goods, although it is not necessary to provide specifically for 'legal title' or 'legal ownership' to be retained; wording such as 'ownership', or 'title' will suffice. What is not sufficient is to retain 'equitable and beneficial ownership' as in *Re Bond Worth* [1980] Ch 228, where the seller was held to have passed title to the goods. The clause created an equitable charge which was then void for lack of registration.

It is important to remember the seller cannot recover more than it is owed. Where the seller recovers the goods and resells them under a simple retention of title clause, it must reimburse the buyer the amount of any advance or part payment which it has made. However, where the seller makes a profit on the sale, it is entitled to keep any profit which it has made, as it is selling as the owner of the goods.

5.4.1.2 Rights of entry, seizure and sale

The seller must make sure that the clause specifically provides for the right to go on to the buyer's premises (or the seller will commit trespass in doing so) to recover the goods (which would otherwise be conversion) and also to re-sell them. Clearly the seller cannot do this on a whim. The clause should contain 'triggers': events that will enable the seller to exercise these rights. The rights could be expressed as arising when the buyer is overdue in paying for the goods (ie, the consignment actually sold under *this* agreement, or any other goods which the seller has supplied to the buyer). This could be linked through to a clause in the agreement making the price become due immediately on the buyer becoming insolvent.

5.4.2 Desirable provisions

The following provisions are not essential but are desirable from the seller's point of view. All these clauses will be legally effective, although practically it may not always be possible to enforce them.

5.4.2.1 All moneys clause

Often a retention of title clause will provide that ownership will not pass to the buyer until the buyer has paid all amounts owing to the seller in respect of all goods which the seller has supplied to the buyer (ie, paid for not just this consignment of goods but any others which the buyer has bought previously). This is called an 'all moneys' (or 'all monies') clause. It aims to retain ownership of the goods until all outstanding debts owed to the seller have been paid. Many precedents are likely to include an 'all moneys' provision. It is not necessary for a retention of title clause to include this provision, but it is potentially a very useful protection where the seller is dealing with repeat orders, as it avoids the seller having to identify particular goods from particular consignments. Such clauses have been upheld as legally effective, eg in *Armour v Thyssen Edelstahlwerke AG* [1991] 2 AC 339.

5.4.2.2 Sales to sub-buyers

The clause may also provide that title will pass when the buyer sells the goods on to a sub-buyer in accordance with the agreement. This acknowledges s 25 of SGA 1979, which states that an innocent third party gets good title to the goods when the goods are sold on to it by the original buyer (see **5.3.2**).

5.4.2.3 Separate storage of the seller's goods while in the buyer's possession

A retention of title clause will be practically effective only if the seller can identify its goods once it goes to collect them. The seller needs to decide whether anything can or should be done to maximise the chances of being able to recover the goods (or at least getting some money back if something happens to them while in the buyer's possession). So, a clause could be included to provide for separate storage in order to maximise the chances that the seller can identify its own goods when trying to recover them.

A further possibility for protection of the goods is the seller marking its goods to make them easily identifiable. Where practicable, this can be a useful back-up to a separate storage clause (which the buyer may disobey). Obviously this will not always work – for example, 100 tons of gravel is impossible to mark. Note that the seller will sometimes reserve the right to inspect the buyer's premises to check if separate storage provisions are being complied with. Although this may be a useful power to have, the reality is often that separate storage provisions are impossible to police. If the buyer does disobey it will obviously be in breach of contract, the remedy for which is damages. This may be of no use to the seller (eg if the buyer is in financial difficulties or has become insolvent).

5.4.2.4 Passing of risk

It is important for sale of goods agreements to provide expressly for the passing of the risk of accidental loss of, or damage to, the goods. This may be done in a separate clause, but is often found in a retention of title clause.

Under s 20 of the SGA 1979, goods remain at the seller's risk until the property in them (ie, ownership) is transferred to the buyer, unless the parties agree otherwise (see **4.4.6.1**). This is not the desired situation in a contract with a retention of title clause, so a clause is added which displaces s 20 by contrary agreement. The seller will usually stipulate that risk passes on delivery. This will often be linked to a requirement that the buyer insures the goods and holds any proceeds of the policy on trust for the seller (see **5.4.2.5**).

5.4.2.5 Insurance

If the goods are destroyed before they can be reclaimed, the seller will want recompense. So, a clause should be included to require the buyer to insure the seller's goods and to hold the proceeds on trust for the seller. (Unlike a tracing clause (see **5.3.1**), this does not create a charge, as the ownership of the goods will not have passed when the goods are destroyed and the insurance payment becomes due.)

5.4.2.6 Detachable goods

A detachable goods clause will provide that if the goods supplied to the buyer are readily detachable without damage to the buyer's products, the seller's goods can be recovered, as in *Hendy Lennox (Industrial Engines) Ltd v Graham Puttick Ltd* [1984] 1 WLR 485 (see **5.3.5**). Such a clause should not be confused with mixed or manufactured goods clauses.

5.4.3 Bluff value clauses

Some of the tactics used by sellers are not going to be succeed because, as discussed at **5.3.1**, certain clauses create charges which are void as against liquidators, administrators or third parties if not registered. However, this does not stop such clauses being included, if only in the hope that they might serve to exert commercial pressure, even though enforcement is unlikely to succeed. These include:

(a) tracing into the proceeds of sale, separation of proceeds and assignment of debts;

(b) claiming ownership of 'mixed' or manufactured goods.

It is important to remember that each of these clauses will be valid as between the buyer and the seller, and enforceable until the buyer becomes insolvent. Thus, if the seller acts quickly it may have some chance of success, especially as against smaller companies which may not have taken legal advice. However, once the buyer is insolvent, a seller will not succeed in trying to enforce an unregistered charge against battle-hardened liquidators or administrators.

5.5 'Backing up' a retention of title clause

Even the best drafted retention of title clauses will not always be effective, and may not be appropriate commercially. There are practical and legal limitations, which need to be considered:

(a) Practically, the effectiveness of retention of title clauses depends on the nature of the goods. They will work only if the goods remain unaltered and can be identified. They will not be suitable if the goods are perishable or of low value.

(b) Legally, the clause will work only if it has been incorporated into the contract by signature, notice or previous course of dealing.

(c) A clause may be effective as between the buyer and the seller, eg a separate storage clause, but the seller's only remedy for breach will be a claim for damages, which will be useless where the buyer is in financial difficulties or insolvent.

(d) Experienced liquidators will use every opportunity to challenge a clause, and watertight drafting is not always possible. Very often, a seller will find that it is obliged to obtain a court order to enforce its retention of title clause. A further consideration, where the buyer has gone into administration, is that the Insolvency Act 1986 provides that the administrator's consent is needed to reclaim the goods. The retention of title is effectively 'frozen' during the period of the administration.

It is worth encouraging a seller to back up any retention of title clause by taking practical steps either to minimise the chances of dealing with buyers who may not pay, or to provide an incentive for the buyer to pay up, or both. The possibilities include the following.

5.5.1 Checks on the buyer/controlling the credit the buyer is given

This is likely to be a useful practical back-up to retention of title. In an ideal world, it would include the following measures:

(a) The seller should run a tight system of credit control, with frequent checks on buyers' creditworthiness. The seller should take steps to ensure that buyers always pay by the due date, send out invoices on time and chase debts before they start to become a problem. It should ensure that all relevant staff know precisely the limit of the credit that the buyer is allowed.

(b) If buyers start to fall behind in paying for the goods, the seller may want to consider reducing any credit period allowed, or even move on to demanding cash on delivery or 'up front'. Obviously, whether this is a practical solution will vary from case to case. The buyer may not agree to the new terms being imposed on it.

(c) If the contract permits, the seller should consider removing its goods from the buyer's premises at the first hint of trouble rather than waiting for a receiver or liquidator to be appointed. Once creditors become twitchy, things can happen very quickly indeed and, in practice, the goods may simply 'disappear' before they can be reclaimed.

(d) If a buyer persistently pays late, there is always the option of refusing to deal with the buyer in future.

(e) If the contract is still subsisting, the threat of termination may serve to concentrate the buyer's mind. However, such threats should be used with care, not least because the seller will not want to be sued for damages for breach of contract. Appropriate notice periods should be given. However, it may be more efficient for the seller to pay the damages and cut his losses on an uneconomic contract, rather than continue with it. (This is sometimes referred to as 'efficient' or 'economic' breach.) Again, careful thought must be given to the likely amount of any damages which the buyer may claim.

5.5.2 Debt factoring

Factoring is where the debts are sold to someone else who will then collect them (see **3.7.8**). This is an alternative to retention of title, rather than a supplement to it. Obviously, the debts cannot be sold for 100% of their value, as the factor has to make a profit. The discount can vary considerably, according to the credit period and/or the creditworthiness of the debtor.

5.5.3 Credit risk insurance

A seller may also be able to insure against the risk of the buyer not paying. Credit risk insurance may sometimes be too expensive to be worthwhile, but in the last few years it has become cheaper and more widely available. Sellers are able to obtain policies tailored to their precise needs rather than on an 'all debts' basis, which would be very expensive.

5.5.4 Providing for interest

The seller may charge interest on sums which become overdue. This may act as an incentive to the buyer to pay on time, and will give the seller some recompense if the payment is late. Normally, the best way to deal with interest is to provide for it expressly in the contract. The seller must not go over the top when providing for the amount of interest, as a provision which claimed excessive interest could be struck down as a penalty.

The Late Payment of Commercial Debts (Interest) Act 1998 provides specifically for the payment of interest in certain commercial situations. The 1998 Act works in the following way:

(a) it implies into applicable contracts a term relating to interest (basically it will apply to commercial contracts for the supply of goods or services);

(b) the term is to the effect that any 'qualifying debt' created by the contract carries simple interest in accordance with the Act, known as 'statutory interest'; and

(c) in certain circumstances, this right to interest can be ousted by contract terms if there is another 'substantial contractual remedy' for late payment, but the contract may not provide that late payment carries no remedy at all.

Many businesses which might benefit under the Act are becoming more aware of its existence, and there is some evidence that it is beginning to have an impact.

In *Banham Marshalls Services Unlimited v Lincolnshire CC* [2007] EWHC 402 (QB), the Act was even applied to payments which were being withheld because of a genuine legal dispute, where one party had delayed the commencement of proceedings.

Even if there is no express provision in the contract and the Act does not apply, there are statutory provisions for claiming interest in both the High Court and county court. This has the disadvantage that technically any award of interest is in the discretion of the court (although this is rarely a problem). Also, to be certain of its entitlement to interest, the seller must incur the cost of proceedings and wait for judgment. Debtors routinely rely on this loophole and refuse to pay interest unless proceedings are commenced.

Chapter 6

Sale of Goods: Implied Terms – Title and Quality Provisions

6.1 Introduction

The main concerns of the seller and the buyer will be the payment and delivery provisions, and, as discussed in **Chapter 4**, it is unlikely that commercial parties would not make express provision in relation to these 'core' terms. Underlying any express provisions are the implied duty of the seller to deliver (and to deliver the right quantity) and the implied duty of the buyer to accept and pay for delivery. In addition, ss 12–15 of the SGA 1979 impose further implied duties on the seller over and above its duty to deliver the goods. Commercial parties should be aware of these duties which relate to title (s 12), correspondence with description (s 13), quality and fitness for purpose (s 14) and correspondence with sample (s 15). These terms will be implied into all commercial contracts, but, with the exception of s 12, the parties may expressly agree to the contrary. Section 55 provides that various implied terms can be excluded, but any exclusion of liability will be subject to UCTA 1977. However, effective exclusion will depend on the seller knowing the extent of its liability and, in the light of that liability, anticipating what could go wrong. This chapter is intended as a reminder of the liability which arises under the implied terms. Exclusion of liability will be considered in **Chapters** 7 and **8**.

Sections 13, 14 and 15 of the SGA 1979 are all implied as strict conditions, as is the duty to pass good title under s 12(1). Any breach will, prima facie, give the buyer the right to reject the goods and terminate the contract without the need for the buyer to prove that the seller is at fault. Sections 12, 13 and 15 apply to all types of contract, whether or not the seller is acting in the course of a business or as consumer (although it is highly unlikely that a consumer seller will be making sales by sample). Section 14 only applies where the seller is acting in the course of a business. (**Table 6.1** below gives a summary of how these sections operate).

Section	Duty of seller in relation to:	Condition/warranty	Business/consumer sellers
s 12(1)	Title	Condition (s 12(5A))	Business and consumer sellers
s 12(2)	Freedom from charges and encumbrances	Warranty (s 12(5A))	Business and consumer sellers
s 12(2)	Quiet possession	Warranty (s 12(5A))	Business and consumer sellers
s 13(1)	Description	Condition (s 13(1A))	Business and consumer sellers

Section	Duty of seller in relation to:	Condition/warranty	Business/consumer sellers
s 14(2)	Satisfactory quality	Condition (s 14(6))	Business sellers only
s 14(3)	Fitness for purpose	Condition (s 14(6))	Business sellers only
s 15(1)	Sample	Condition (s 15(3))	Business and consumer sellers

Table 6.1 Operation of the SGA 1979, ss 12–15

6.2 The seller's duty to pass good title to the goods (s 12)

Section 12(1) implies into the contract a term that the seller has the right to sell the goods. In other words, it has good title to the goods. This is a condition of the contract.

In addition (and closely linked to the duty to pass good title), s 12(2) provides that there is an implied warranty:

(a) that the goods are free from any charge or encumbrance not already known to the buyer; and

(b) that the buyer will enjoy quiet possession of the goods.

For example, in *Rubicon Computer Systems Ltd v United Paints Ltd* [2000] 2 TCLR 453, it was held that the seller attaching a time lock to a computer system in order to deny access to the buyer was in breach of the 'quiet possession' term under s 12(2)(b).

6.3 Sale by description (s 13)

Section 13(1) implies a term that the goods sold should comply with their description. This could apply to goods bought from catalogues, brochures or advertisements, for example. Commercially, such sales are common, so in practice it is extremely important that commercial sellers should be aware of this duty. However, s 13 applies whether or not the seller sells in the course of a business, ie to consumer as well as commercial sellers.

In order to be a sale by description, however, the words used must be words of description rather than simply words identifying the goods. The description may go further than simply describing the goods themselves, eg any description of the packaging of the goods will be covered by s 13. In *Re Moore v Landauer & Co* [1921] 2 KB 519, the goods were not packed as had been described in the contract, which was held to be breach of description entitling the buyer to reject the entire shipment.

Section 13(1A) states that s 13(1) is a condition.

6.3.1 Reliance on the description

The buyer must know of and must have relied on the description. Where the buyer does not rely on the seller's description but on his own skill and judgement, s 13 will not apply. Whether or not the buyer has relied on the description will depend on the facts of the particular case, and will depend on factors such as the expertise of the buyer. The fact that the buyer has examined the goods will not necessarily mean that the buyer has relied on its own skill and judgment. In *Beale v Taylor* [1967] 1 WLR 1193, a car was described as a 1961 Triumph Herald. Two parts of different cars had been welded together, and only one was from the 1961 model. The sale was held to be a sale by description even though the buyer inspected the car after having seen the advertisement for it in the local paper.

6.3.2 Overlap between description and misrepresentation

A breach of s 13 may also amount to a misrepresentation. This gives the buyer the option to bring a claim for misrepresentation, although usually it will achieve a better outcome by suing for breach of contract (see **6.8.4** and **Chapter 2**).

6.4 Satisfactory quality (s 14(2))

Section 14(2) of the SGA 1979 implies a term that, in a sale in the course of a business, the goods are to be, objectively, of satisfactory quality. Under s 14(2A) the price and description of the goods will be taken into account in deciding whether or not the goods are of satisfactory quality. Section 14(2B) lists further factors which will be taken into account. These include:

(a) fitness for the common purposes of the goods;

(b) appearance and finish;

(c) freedom from minor defects;

(d) safety; and

(e) durability.

Whether or not goods are of satisfactory quality will depend on the facts of each particular case, taking into account factors such as the price of the goods, whether the goods are new or second hand and their expected durability, which can be a particular problem. If goods are fundamentally defective, for example they do not work at all or are unsafe, they will very clearly not be of satisfactory quality. However, where the defect is not fundamental or not immediately obvious (ie latent defects) then the position may not be so clear.

Britvic Soft Drinks Ltd v Messer UK Ltd [2002] EWCA Civ 548 involved the contamination of carbon dioxide gas, supplied for making soft drinks. The evidence showed that the contaminating substance, benzene, was not present in high enough quantity to be a danger to human health, but would have damaged the saleability of the drinks. This was enough for the court to hold that the gas was not of satisfactory quality for manufacturing drinks.

By contrast, in *Thain v Anniesland Trade Centre* [1997] SCLR 991, a six-year-old car, sold for £2,995, was held to be of satisfactory quality, even though the gearbox failed two weeks after purchase of the car.

Durability was an important factor in *Friarwood Ltd v Champagne Cattier SA* [2006] EWCA Civ 1105, in deciding whether or not champagne was of satisfactory quality. The champagne was alleged to have aged prematurely, resulting in 'much reduced fizz'. In this case, a retrial was ordered after the court disapproved a judge's approach in deciding that the wine was not of satisfactory quality. He had decided that the issue should be looked at from the point of view of an average, rather than a sophisticated, customer and had rejected expert evidence which should have been taken into account.

The seller will not be liable if the defect has been specifically drawn to the buyer's attention before the contract is made, or if it should have been obvious on examination of the goods (s 14(2C)).

6.5 Fitness for purpose (s 14(2) and s 14(3))

In addition to the s 14(2) requirement that the goods should be fit for their common purpose, where goods are sold in the course of a business s 14(3) implies a term that the goods are fit for any particular purpose which the buyer makes known to the seller, either expressly or by implication. In the absence of any information to the contrary, the seller is entitled to assume that the goods will be used for their normal purpose. Where a buyer requires goods for a particular (non-normal) purpose, it must inform the seller before the contract is made. For example, in *Micron Computer Systems Ltd v Wang (UK) Ltd* (HC, 9 May 1990), the buyer of a computer system failed to tell the seller of the particular purpose in question and was therefore unsuccessful in its claim.

This term does not apply where the circumstances show that the buyer does not rely upon, or it is unreasonable to rely upon, the skill or judgement of the seller.

6.5.1 Relationship between s 14(2) and s 14(3)

One problem is the overlap between s 14(2) and s 14(3). The issue is complex, but, as a rule of thumb, where goods are not of satisfactory quality, it is unlikely that they will be fit for common purpose. This would therefore be a breach of s 14(2B)(a). However, it is perfectly possible for the goods to be unfit for a particular purpose under s 14(3), but still to be fit for common purpose and therefore of satisfactory quality under s 14(2). For example, if a buyer specifies that he needs specialist trainers for running, but the seller supplies ordinary trainers, the goods may not be fit for the specified purpose, but they will still be of satisfactory quality as they are fit for their common purpose under s 14(2B)(a).

The issue was dealt with in *Jewson v Kelly* [2003] EWCA Civ 1030, where the seller was held by the Court of Appeal not to be liable for breach of the SGA 1979 in relation to the supply of electrical heating equipment. The buyers alleged that the sale was in breach of s 14(2) and (3), as the equipment had reduced the energy efficiency ratings of the flat conversions in question. The Court held:

> Although there was considerable overlap between s 14(2) and s 14(3), the function of s 14(2) was to establish a general standard, and the function of s 14(3) was to impose a particular standard tailored to the individual circumstances of the case.

The equipment did work as heating equipment, so s 14(2) was held not to be applicable. As regards s 14(3), the buyer was held not to have relied on the sellers as regards the question of the 'particular' fitness for purpose, which was the effect of the heating equipment on the flats' energy efficiency ratings. There was therefore no breach of s 14(3).

Section 14(6) provides that s 14(2) and s 14(3) are conditions.

6.5.2 Trade usage (s 14(4))

The SGA 1979, s 14(4) states that an implied condition or warranty about quality or fitness for a particular purpose may be annexed to a contract of sale by usage in the course of a particular trade. The requirements are that the usage or custom must be reasonable, universally accepted by the particular trade or profession, be certain, be lawful, and be consistent with the express or implied terms of the contract .

6.6 Sale by sample (s 15)

Section 15(2) implies a term that where the sale is by sample then the bulk of the goods will correspond with the sample in quality. The goods are also to be free of any defect, not apparent on reasonable examination, which would render the quality unsatisfactory. Section 15(1) defines a sale by sample.

In *Godley v Perry* [1960] 1 WLR 9, a retailer bought plastic catapults from a wholesaler. He tested one sample catapult and it worked satisfactorily, so he bought a consignment of them. However, a catapult sold to a customer broke, hitting the child using it, and as a result the child lost an eye. The goods were held not to comply with the sample, in breach of s 15. There had been reasonable examination of the sample which had not shown up any defects.

Section 15(3) states that s 15(2) is a condition.

6.7 Overlap between ss 13, 14 and 15

Often a sale by description may raise quality issues, eg a statement that goods are more durable than turns out to be the case (note that this could also amount to a misrepresentation).

A sale by sample will normally also amount to a sale by description. Failure to match the sample may also mean that the goods are not of satisfactory quality or fit for their purpose, as in *Godley v Perry* (**6.6** above).

6.8 Buyer's remedies for breach of the implied terms

6.8.1 Breach of condition

As discussed, all of the implied terms, with the exception of s 12(2), are conditions. Breach of any of these terms will therefore entitle the buyer to reject the goods, repudiate the contract and recover the price from the seller, as well as to claim damages if it has suffered further loss, eg loss of profit.

The buyer is not obliged to reject the goods. It can elect not to reject the goods, treat the breach as a breach of warranty and sue for damages.

6.8.2 Limits on the right to reject

In certain circumstances, the buyer will lose the right to reject the goods, although its right to claim damages will not be affected.

6.8.2.1 Slight breach (s 15A)

The Sale and Supply of Goods Act 1994 introduced s 15A into the SGA 1979. Section 15A provides that the right to reject is lost where the sale is not a consumer sale and the breach is so slight that it would be unreasonable for the buyer to reject the goods. Section 15A applies only to breach of ss 13–15 and not, for example, to breach of a stipulation concerning time of delivery.

6.8.2.2 Acceptance by the buyer (ss 34–36)

As discussed in the context of delivery, s 34 states that the buyer has a right to have a reasonable opportunity, on request, to examine the goods (see **4.4.4.3**).

Section 35 deals with the loss of the right to reject. So, for example, the buyer loses the right where it tells the seller that it has accepted the goods, or does something inconsistent with the seller's ownership after the goods have been delivered to it. The buyer also loses the right to reject if it retains the goods beyond a reasonable period of time (s 35(4)).

Whether or not the buyer has accepted the goods will be a question of fact in each case. *Clegg v Olle Andersson (t/a Nordic Marine)* [2003] EWCA Civ 320 concerned an ocean-going yacht. The buyer took three weeks to assess the situation before rejecting the goods. This was in fact many months after delivery, as the seller had been slow to respond to requests for information. The Court of Appeal held that the Sale and Supply of Goods Act 1994 (which amended the SGA 1979) allowed the buyer to have time to ascertain the actions needed to modify or repair the goods, and the buyer's rejection was upheld.

6.8.3 Breach of warranty

Section 61 states that a term which is a warranty does not give the buyer the right to reject the goods and treat the contract as repudiated, only a right to damages. This simply confirms the common law rules on breach of warranty. As for delivery, the relevant provision in relation to damages is s 54 (see **4.6.1**). The problem for the buyer is that there are situations where it may be unclear whether the term breached is a strict condition or not. Section 15A means that careful judgement is needed before rejection – a breach of, say, s 14 may be so slight as to preclude rejection.

6.8.4 Buyer's remedies for misrepresentation

This is now controlled by the Misrepresentation Act 1967 (see **2.3.2**). If a pre-contractual misrepresentation has become a term of the contract, eg as a result of s 13 of the SGA 1979, or the contract has been performed, then the buyer may still rescind the contract (Misrepresentation Act 1967, s 1). Rescission is possible for innocent misrepresentation. The buyer does not have to rely on an allegation of fraud or negligence, although rescission is also available in those circumstances. See *Shogun Finance Ltd v Hudson* [2004] 1 AC 919.

Rescission for misrepresentation is barred by affirmation, lapse of time, inability to restore the parties to their original position, or the goods being acquired by an innocent third party.

Damages for misrepresentation are also a possibility, but there can be no double recovery, ie the buyer cannot recover damages for breach of contract in respect of the same loss. See the discussion of reliance upon the misrepresentation in *Ronastone Ltd v Indigo International Holdings Ltd* [2003] All ER (D) 332 (Dec).

6.9 Additional rights under the SGA 1979 in consumer cases

Sections 48A to 48F were introduced into the SGA 1979 by Directive 1999/44/EC on Certain Aspects of the Sale of Consumer Goods and Associated Guarantees. These rights apply only to sales to consumers.

The buyer may require the seller to repair or replace goods if the goods do not comply with the implied terms under ss 13 to 15. The buyer has the right:

(a) to require the seller to replace or repair the goods (s 48B); or

(b) to reduce the purchase price or to rescind the contract (s 48A(2)).

Under s 48A(3) these rights apply if the goods do not meet the implied terms within six months of the goods being delivered to the buyer. Goods which do not conform to the contract of sale at any time within the period of six months starting with the date on which the goods were delivered to a consumer must be taken not to have so conformed at that date. So if, at any time during the six-month period following the date of delivery, a consumer discovers that the goods are faulty, it will be presumed that they were faulty on delivery. There is no need to prove that they were.

See **7.8** for a brief account of the Unfair Terms in Consumer Contracts Regulations 1999 (SI 1999/2083).

Chapter 7
Exclusion Clauses: General Principles

7.1 Introduction

Commercial clients will always be concerned about the liability which they may incur in performing their contracts, and in most cases their instinct will be to try to reduce their exposure as much as possible. Such liability may arise as the result of express terms in the contract, eg in relation to time of delivery, or terms implied by the SGA 1979 such as the implied terms in relation to quality. The solicitor is likely to be approached for advice in two respects:

(a) drafting an agreement to minimise the client's liability if things should go wrong;

(b) advising on the protection given by exclusions in an agreement once problems have arisen.

Most of this chapter deals with the first point; it looks at the various matters which the solicitor should bear in mind when drafting (or reviewing) an agreement. The use of exclusion and limitation clauses, particularly in commercial contracts, is part of the process by which the parties agree to allocate risk, liability and responsibility for performance as between themselves. Much like other clauses in the contract, the exclusions will usually reflect the nature and context of the contract, as well as the relative needs and bargaining power of the parties.

This chapter considers exclusion of liability mainly from the point of view of a solicitor drafting on behalf of a commercial seller which is entering into agreements with other commercial parties, rather than consumer buyers.

7.2 Basic rules for successful drafting of exclusion clauses

Three points are particularly important:

(a) know the commercial background;

(b) know the law;

(c) know the drafting principles.

7.2.1 Know the commercial background

Although this may seem obvious, the solicitor needs to anticipate the sort of liability that may arise in that type of business, so that he knows what to exclude. Therefore it is essential to know how a client's business operates before it is possible to draft effectively for exclusion of liability on behalf of the client. In addition, exclusion clauses in commercial contracts are in many cases subject to the reasonableness test under UCTA 1977, and many of the factors which are relevant in deciding whether or not a clause passes the reasonableness test are specific to the circumstances of each contract. Basic questions to ask would include:

(a) What sort of customers does the client normally deal with?

(b) What type of products does the client sell and what can go wrong with them?

(c) Which of the client's employees actually make the contracts (and therefore 'operate' the exclusion clauses)?

(d) How, if at all, are any exclusions introduced to the customers?

(e) Are certain exclusions/limitations or standard-form contracts common within that type of industry?

The final consideration is that, although the solicitor must try to achieve what the client has requested, the client must also be advised (as constructively as possible) that no exclusion clause can be guaranteed to work in all circumstances.

7.2.2 Tactics – drafting to litigate or to negotiate?

Once the solicitor has an idea of the commercial background, it is a good idea to consider tactics with the client. In most cases, a solicitor will be drafting to negotiate, rather than to litigate, should problems arise with the agreement in the future. It is therefore often valid to draft a clause which a court might hold unreasonable, if litigation is in fact unlikely and the clause achieves the right result for the client (eg the client deals with the type of customer which is unlikely to claim, or which will tend to settle any claim on suitable terms). Obviously, the client should be informed of what the solicitor is doing (and why) and warned that it is impossible to guarantee that the clause will achieve this result. It is also important when using this technique to distinguish between clauses which are void and clauses which are subject to the reasonableness test (see **7.7.2**).

7.2.2.1 Void clauses

The solicitor should not use any clause which is void under UCTA 1977. A clause of this nature should be easy to spot, especially if the 'victim' takes legal advice, and so is unlikely to prevent a claim being made anyway. At best, the clause will create a bad impression; at worst, it may not only be ineffective, but its use may be a criminal offence. For example, under the Consumer Transactions (Restrictions on Statements) Order 1976 (SI 1976/1813), a supplier commits a criminal offence if, in a consumer sale of goods contract, he uses a clause which is void under s 6 of UCTA 1977.

7.2.2.2 Clauses subject to the reasonableness test

Where a clause is subject to the reasonableness test, the position is quite different. It may be possible to achieve good results for the client by using a clause which might be of doubtful reasonableness if it were ever litigated, as long as the client understands and approves of the tactic.

7.2.2.3 Drafting for good public relations

In some circumstances, it is worth drafting positively rather than (as is traditional with exclusion clauses) negatively. It could be worthwhile, for example, in a contract for the performance of services, for the supplier to promise to exercise reasonable care and skill in carrying out the work under the contract, and to accept full liability for any personal injury or death caused by breach of its promise. This gives the other party no more than its legal rights, but creates the impression that the supplier is being generous. Onerous exclusions will achieve the opposite effect.

7.2.3 Know the law

Relevant areas include:

(a) the implied terms that may affect the contract, eg the implied terms in relation to delivery, title and quality;

(b) the likely remedies for breach of express or implied terms;

(c) the common law rules relating to incorporation and construction;

(d) the rules in UCTA 1977; and

(e) the factors which determine whether a clause will pass the reasonableness test or not.

7.2.4 Know the drafting principles

Although the client's instructions, or the circumstances in which the clause is to operate, may in practice limit how a clause can be put together, the way in which an exclusion clause has been drafted may have a profound influence on its effectiveness. You should bear in mind the following.

7.2.4.1 Use of precedents

Because the effectiveness of an exclusion clause will depend to a large extent on its own individual context, precedents for exclusion clauses need to be used with some caution. The solicitor should always consider how a clause might work in a particular business context, and think carefully before simply copying a precedent which appears to be suitable on paper. Having said that, precedents can be very useful in this context as a source of inspiration, or as a guide to how the layout of the exclusions within the contract might be organised.

7.2.4.2 Drafting for severance

Instead of drafting one clause to cover all the exclusions under the contract (which carries the risk that the clause may then be struck down in its entirety as unreasonable), it is usually more appropriate to draft a series of clauses or sub-clauses. If one sub-clause is found to be unreasonable, the others may still survive if the court is able to apply the normal principles of severance. To reinforce the point, the series can end with a statement that each clause or sub-clause is to be treated as separate and independent.

7.3 Preparing to draft

Before beginning to draft, there are several general considerations which the solicitor should have in mind, which will relate to the likely effectiveness of the finished clauses.

7.3.1 What is an 'exclusion clause'?

There is no really comprehensive legal definition of what constitutes an 'exclusion' or 'exemption' clause. The closest approach to a full definition is probably contained in s 13 of UCTA 1977, which defines very widely the type of clause to which that Act applies. In addition, all the relevant sections of UCTA 1977 refer to 'exclusion or restriction of liability', so the Act clearly covers limitation clauses as well as strict exclusion clauses. However, bear in mind that UCTA 1977 does not cover every case of exclusion or limitation of liability (see **7.7.1**). For the sake of simplicity, this chapter uses the expression 'exclusion clause' to cover both exclusion and limitation clauses, unless the context requires otherwise.

Practically, an exclusion clause is a clause which attempts to exclude or limit the availability of the remedies arising as the result of the happening (or more often non-happening) of a specified event, generally a breach of contract by one of the parties.

7.3.2 Ways of excluding liability

7.3.2.1 Trying to exclude everything

Sometimes, the client may want the solicitor to exclude all liability which could arise from breach of any contractual obligation. Tempting as this may be, it cannot be done:

(a) Some liability is non-excludable because of UCTA 1977 (see **7.2.1**).

(b) A contract which purports to exclude one party's liability for breach in respect of all its contractual obligations would not be a contract at all. That party would not be binding itself to do anything, and the 'contract' would be no more than a declaration of intent. Either the contract would be void for uncertainty, or a court faced with this situation would probably assume that the parties had made a mistake, and attempt to construe the contract in such a way that it does not exclude liability for everything.

(c) Commercially, this is unlikely to be practical. Customers are unlikely to want to do business where there is no prospect of recompense if things go wrong.

The solicitor will have to judge carefully how far it is possible to go if the client requests as much exclusion as possible, and advise accordingly.

7.3.2.2 Fundamental breach

A problem may arise where a client seeks to exclude liability for its own fundamental, repudiatory breach of contract. This is possible to achieve, but the scope for excluding liability in such circumstances is very narrow and will turn upon the construction of the exclusion. If the wording is clear, a clause may cover a serious repudiatory breach (see *PhotoProductions Ltd v Securicor Transport Ltd* [1980] AC 827, HL). However, following the *NetTV* case (*Internet Broadcasting Corporation (t/a NetTV) v MAR LLC (t/a MARHedge)* [2009] EWHC 844 (Ch)), there is now a rebuttable presumption that an exclusion clause does not apply to a deliberate personal repudiatory breach.

7.3.2.3 Types of exclusion clause

Table 7.1 below lists some of the main types of exclusion clause. The examples given are not intended to be watertight provisions; they are simple illustrations of the type of clause that could be encountered in practice. In a commercial contract, all of these would be subject to reasonableness under either s 3 or s 6 of UCTA 1977, and their effectiveness will be considered in **7.7.2**.

Type of clause	Effect of clause	Example
Exclusion of liability	Excludes liability altogether.	'The Seller accepts no liability for the late delivery of the Goods.'
Limitation of liability	Limits the extent of liability.	'The Seller's liability is limited to the contract price of the Goods.'
Exclusion of remedies	Limits the remedies which are available to the buyer, eg the right to terminate or the right to damages. Includes non-rejection clauses. (An alternative is to provide for substitute remedies, eg repair or replacement.)	'Where the Seller is in breach of any terms of this Agreement the Buyer may not reject the goods or terminate the contact and any claim is limited to damages.'
Exclusion of types of loss	Limits liability for a particular type of loss, eg loss of profit or consequential loss.	'The Seller accepts no liability for indirect or consequential loss or damage (whether loss of profit, loss of business or otherwise), costs, expenses or other claims for consequential compensation whatsoever (howsoever caused) which arise out of or in connection with this Agreement.'

Type of clause	Effect of clause	Example
Time bar	Excludes liability unless notice of breach is given within a specified time period.	'The Seller will not be liable for any defect in the quality of the Goods unless such defect is notified to the Seller within 7 days beginning with the date of delivery.'
Duty defining	Prevents liability arising in the first place.	'Any delivery dates specified are approximate only and whereas every attempt will be made to meet these dates the Seller cannot promise to do so.'
Force majeure	Excludes liability for failure to perform the contract as a result of events outside the seller's control.	'The Seller is not liable for any delay in performing or failure to perform any of the Seller's obligations in relation to the Goods if the delay or failure was due to circumstances outside the Seller's reasonable control.' (A non-exhaustive list of the force majeure circumstances, eg war, riot, flood, fire, abnormal weather, etc, should be included.)

Table 7.1 Exclusion clauses

7.4 Testing the clause

Although this chapter deals with the drafting of exclusion clauses, rather than the more general contractual background against which they will operate, it is often helpful at the drafting stage to consider that contractual background; this can be an extremely useful way of assessing a draft clause's potential strength. The solicitor should try to anticipate what problems may arise, and whether, if they do, a customer will be able to establish a cause of action. If it seems likely that the customer will succeed, the solicitor should then consider whether the clause will work to protect the client against such a claim. To test the clause he should consider the following.

7.4.1 Contractual background

(a) Identify the terms of the contract, both express and implied, which are likely to be relevant, ie those terms which may lead to liability if breached. (It is tempting to think that the exclusion clause is a 'relevant' term, but at this stage the solicitor is simply assessing his client's potential liability and so does not need to consider any exclusions yet.)

(b) Decide whether those terms are likely to be breached and the likely events which will lead to breach.

(c) Anticipate what remedy the injured party will be seeking and decide whether or not that remedy is legally available, eg rejection of the goods will not be available for breach of warranty.

These points will form an integral part of the process of applying the clause if problems occur, and will often provide important information at the drafting stage as to how well the clause is likely to work.

7.4.2 Three stages for effectiveness

Once the claimant has established a cause of action, the burden of proof will shift to the defendant to show that its exclusion clause is valid. A party who wishes to claim the protection of an exclusion clause must prove three things:

(a) *incorporation*: that the clause forms part of the contract;

(b) *construction*: that the wording of the clause is wide enough that, on its true construction, it covers the breach which has occurred;

(c) *UCTA 1977*: that the clause is not invalidated by UCTA 1977 (if applicable).

7.5 Incorporation

To be effective, a clause must form part of the contract. This rule applies to all contractual terms, but the courts apply it particularly strictly in relation to exclusion clauses. A clause may be incorporated in one of three ways:

(a) by signature;

(b) by notice; and

(c) by previous course of dealing.

There may be practical problems in relation to each of these methods of incorporation which the solicitor must consider.

7.5.1 Signed or unsigned documents?

If a clause is contained in a contractual document which the client's customers will sign, the chances of incorporation are very good (the normal contractual rule is that a customer will be bound by signature, whether or not he has read or understood the document). If, however, the clause is in an unsigned document, it will form part of the contract only if reasonable steps are taken to bring it to the customer's attention before the contract is made. Putting the clause into a document which is to be signed should, therefore, be less risky as far as incorporation is concerned. However, this may not be the best solution if it does not fit in with the client's normal business practices. There may also be problems over signature itself:

(a) What if the clause is in a document which should be signed but which the customer does not sign?

(b) What if a regular customer normally signs a contractual document but fails to sign on one or more occasions?

(c) Is it possible to draft and locate the clause so that it will be incorporated even if the document is not signed?

There can be no general answers to these questions; in each case, the solicitor must obtain full instructions and then draft to meet the needs of the client's particular business.

7.5.2 Timing

If the clause is contained in a document which is not intended to be signed, it will be incorporated provided that reasonable steps have been taken to bring it to the customer's attention before the contract is made. However, problems may arise if there is normally an interval between drawing the buyer's attention to the clause and the contract being made. Again, it will help to find out how the client's business operates, but the solicitor may in practice be unable to resolve this problem. There may be problems if it is intended to incorporate exclusion clauses by reference to other documents (see **8.2.5.7** below).

7.5.3 Course of dealings

If the clause is in an unsigned document, it may be incorporated into the contract by way of a regular and consistent course of dealings. Once again, the solicitor needs to know how the client's business works in order to decide whether this is likely. Questions to ask are:

(a) Does the client do a lot of business with regular customers?

(b) Is it involved mainly in 'one-off' transactions?

(c) Are there a variety of different dealings? (This is perhaps most likely.)

Incorporation by course of dealings is far more likely to happen with contracts made between commercial parties than with contracts between a commercial party and a consumer, but it may be unwise to depend too much upon a course of dealing as a reliable method of incorporation because exclusion clauses and, particularly, limitation clauses do tend to vary over time, and should in any event be regularly updated.

7.5.4 Preventing incorporation problems

If the solicitor has acquired a background knowledge of how the client actually makes contracts, it should be possible to spot potential incorporation problems and take action before they arise. This could, for example, take the form of advice to the client (eg about staff training in relation to how contracts should be entered into), or building in safeguards when drafting (eg paying particular attention to the layout of the contract and the location of the clause). Whatever method is chosen, the client should always be made aware of the dangers; in particular, that its employees' actions when making contracts on the client's behalf could actually prevent exclusions in the contract from working.

7.6 Construction

7.6.1 Does the clause cover the breach?

Even if the clause is incorporated into the contract, it will be effective only if, on its true construction by the court, it is worded to do two things:

(a) to cover the breach which actually occurs; and

(b) to exclude the seller's liability for that breach.

As with incorporation, this poses problems when drafting; the solicitor must be aware of the sort of things that can go wrong, so that the exclusion can be drafted to cover such eventualities. The problem is how far the solicitor can foresee the circumstances in which the clause will eventually operate, or what breaches might occur. Once again, knowing the client's business as thoroughly as possible and taking full instructions will help, particularly in trading contexts, such as insurance and freight contracts, where disputes and litigation arise with some frequency.

An awareness of the basic contractual principles of construction is also important. Unfortunately, this is a widely misunderstood area of the law. However, the basic principle is straightforward: when looking at the construction of a clause, the court is looking at the wording to see whether the clause does what it is intended to do, which, in the case of an exclusion clause, is to exclude liability in the event of a specified breach. So the clause must specify the breach that is likely to occur (cover the breach) and specify the liability which the client wants to exclude. The following simple examples of some poorly-drafted terms illustrate this.

Example 1

Clause: 'The Seller will not be liable for any loss suffered as a result of failure to deliver the Goods.'

Breach: The seller delivers the goods late.

Construction: The clause does not cover the breach which has occurred, as failure to deliver (non-delivery) is not the same thing as late delivery.

Example 2

Clause: 'The Seller will not be liable for loss of profit or consequential loss resulting from late delivery of the Goods.'

Breach: The seller delivers the goods late, and the buyer wants to reject the goods and recover the price.

Construction: The clause does cover the breach (late delivery), but it has not excluded the buyer's right to reject the goods and reclaim the price. It has only protected the seller from a claim for damages for indirect loss.

7.6.2 *Contra proferentem*

An exclusion clause will be construed strictly *contra proferentem* (ie any ambiguity will be construed against the person attempting to rely on it). One important aspect of this principle relates to exclusion of liability for negligence, for which clear and unambiguous words are required. From this point of view, it is therefore desirable for a clause excluding liability for negligence to refer clearly to 'negligence' (or an appropriate synonym). However, a client may be extremely reluctant to state in the contract that it is excluding liability for negligence. The solicitor may use expressions such as 'howsoever caused', but whether this (or similar wording) will be effective is uncertain; it will depend on the circumstances. Whether or not to take the risk is a matter which the solicitor must discuss fully with the client.

It should be borne in mind that the particular provision will be construed against the background of the wording within which it is set. For example, a restricted construction was given to the words 'in any circumstances' by the court in *Regus (UK) Ltd v Epcot Solutions Ltd* [2008] EWCA Civ 361. The court stated that normally one would not expect a party to exclude liability caused by fraud, recklessness or malice as it was assumed that businessmen deal with each other in good faith. Thus the phrase was construed so as to apply only to other damage. The court also took into account neighbouring sub-clauses to reach a true construction of the phrase.

7.6.3 Other principles of construction

In construing an exclusion clause, the court may apply various other principles to decide whether or not the clause covers the breach, for example:

(a) *Expressio unius est exclusio alterius*: by this principle, if a contract expressly mentions one or more matters, those not mentioned are automatically excluded. For example, if a clause lists claims which are to be barred, it will not apply to claims not mentioned.

(b) *Ejusdem generis*: this is a general aid to construction, which is sometimes seen as being more appropriate to property documents than to commercial contracts. The principle is that general words which follow two or more specific words are restricted to the same type of item or situation as the preceding specific words. (Note that this principle does not apply to a force majeure clause; see further **8.3.2**.)

7.6.4 Avoiding loose terminology

If words or phrases are used inappropriately, this may mean that a clause does not cover the breach which it was intended to cover. In particular, jargon may be misused (even by lawyers). For example, the words 'rescission', 'condition' and 'warranty' are all often used in commercial contracts in ways which pervert their strict legal meaning. A similar problem arises from the use of words which may mean different things to different readers of the contract (eg, 'consequential loss'). When drafting, therefore, the solicitor should either try to avoid expressions which may cause problems, or define clearly what a particular expression means in context (for further discussion of this point in relation to the expression 'consequential loss', see **8.3.5**). Note that even if loose terminology does not prevent the clause from covering the breach, it may make the clause less likely to pass the reasonableness test if, for example, the effect is to make it difficult to understand (see further **8.2.5** and the discussion of *Regus (UK) Ltd v Epcot Solutions* at **7.6.2** above)).

7.7 Unfair Contract Terms Act 1977

The solicitor will obviously need to be aware of statutory controls on the drafting of exclusion clauses. By far the most important of these is UCTA 1977.

7.7.1 Scope of UCTA 1977

Section 13 of UCTA 1977 gives the Act a wide scope in respect of the type of clause to which it applies, but it will by no means apply in every case. In particular, by s 1(3), the Act applies only to business liability, ie to breach of obligations arising 'in the course of a business' (or use of business premises), so it will not cover the contracts where the seller is a consumer. Business is defined in s 14 to include a profession, government department or public authority.

7.7.1.1 Contracts to which UCTA 1977 does not apply

The most important examples of this are:

(a) contracts listed in Sch 1 to UCTA 1977. By this Schedule, ss 2–4 (and to a limited extent s 7) do not apply to certain types of contract, including insurance contracts, contracts relating to land and contracts relating to intellectual property rights;

(b) international supply contracts. By s 26(2), the reasonableness test under ss 3 and 4 of UCTA 1977 does not apply to an international supply contract.

Note also that, by s 27 of UCTA 1977, if the applicable law of the contract is that of some part of the UK only because of the choice of parties (and would, apart from that choice, be the law of a country outside the UK), then ss 2–7 and 16–21 of UCTA 1977 do not operate as part of the law applicable to the contract. Thus where both parties to the contract are based outside of the UK, they will not be subject to UCTA 1977 simply because they have chosen UK law to govern their contract (see **Chapter 13**).

7.7.1.2 Clauses to which UCTA 1977 does not apply

Even if UCTA 1977 can apply generally to a particular type of contract, it may not apply to certain individual clauses within that contract. For example, in B2B contracts, s 3 of UCTA 1977 applies only if the parties are using standard terms. So if two businesses enter into a tailor-made (ie not standard-form) contract for the sale of goods and the seller inserts a clause into the contract excluding liability for late delivery of the goods, s 3 will not apply to this clause because the buyer deals neither as consumer nor on the other party's written standard terms of business: no other section of UCTA 1977 is relevant to the clause either. However, a term in the same contract excluding liability for breach of one or more of the implied terms in ss 13–15 will be subject to reasonableness by virtue of s 6 of the 1977 Act.

7.7.2 A reminder of the effect of UCTA 1977 on contractual terms

Clauses purporting to exclude or limit liability for negligence will be subject to s 2 of UCTA 1977. Clauses purporting to exclude or limit liability for losses and some clauses purporting to replace common law or statutory remedies with contractual ones will, depending on circumstances, be subject to either s 6 or s 3 of UCTA 1977.

If a clause falls within the scope of UCTA 1977, the effect of the Act is that either:

(a) the clause will be void; or

(b) the clause will be subject to the test of reasonableness.

The effect of UCTA 1977 varies depending on whether the contract is a B2B contract or a B2C contract. The expression 'deals as consumer' is defined in s 12 of UCTA 1977; perhaps surprisingly, in *R & B Customs Brokers Co Ltd v United Dominions Trust Ltd* [1988] 1 All ER 847, the Court of Appeal has held that, in certain circumstances, a company can deal as consumer. Broadly speaking, the point arises when a company does not make the contract 'in the course of a business' and the goods are of a type ordinarily supplied for private use or consumption. In this case, the company buying a car for one of its directors was held to be dealing as a consumer.

The following is a brief reminder of which of these two categories certain types of clause will fall into. (Although the word 'void' is used here to describe the effect of the relevant sections of UCTA 1977 on exclusion clauses, and is a convenient shorthand description, none of the sections of the Act actually uses this word. Instead, each section provides that the relevant liability cannot be excluded or restricted.)

7.7.2.1 Void clauses

Section 2(1)

By s 2(1) of UCTA 1977, a person cannot, by reference either to a contract term or to a notice, exclude or restrict his liability for personal injury or death resulting from negligence.

Section 6(1)

By s 6(1) of UCTA 1977, liability for breach of the implied condition of title under either s 12 of the SGA 1979 or s 8 of the Supply of Goods (Implied Terms) Act 1973 cannot be excluded or restricted by reference to any contract term.

Section 6(2)

By s 6(2) of UCTA 1977, as against a person who deals as consumer, liability for breach of the implied conditions in ss 13–15 of the SGA 1979 or ss 9–11 of the Supply of Goods (Implied Terms) Act 1973 cannot be excluded or restricted by reference to any contract term. (Note that s 7 of UCTA 1977, which applies to miscellaneous contracts under which goods pass (eg, work and materials contracts), contains provisions similar to those in s 6.)

7.7.2.2 Clauses subject to the reasonableness test

The two ways in which the contractual reasonableness test (see **8.1.1**) is most likely to apply are as follows.

Section 3

Section 3 of UCTA 1977 applies where either:

(a) one party deals as consumer; or

(b) significantly for commercial contracts, one party deals on the other party's written standard terms of business, and the clause attempts to exclude or restrict liability for breach of contract.

It imposes the reasonableness test on a wide variety of clauses.

Section 6(3)

Any attempt to exclude the liability arising under ss 13–15 of the SGA 1979 against a person who does not deal as consumer is subject to the reasonableness test.

Table 7.2 below gives a summary of these provisions.

Exclusion of liability for	Effect (B2B contract)	Effect (B2C contract)	UCTA 1977
Death or PI caused by negligence	Void	Void	s 2(1)
Damage to property caused by negligence	Subject to reasonableness	Subject to reasonableness	s 2(2)
Breach of express term	Subject to reasonableness (if dealing on STC)	Subject to reasonableness	s 3
s 12 SGA (title)	Void	Void	s 6(1)
s 13 SGA (description)	Subject to reasonableness	Void	B2C – s 6(2) B2B – s 6(3)
s 14 SGA (quality/fitness for purpose)	Subject to reasonableness	Void	B2C – s 6(2) B2B – s 6(3)
s 15 SGA (sample)	Subject to reasonableness	Void	B2C – s 6(2) B2B – s 6(3)

Table 7.2 Summary of the reasonableness test

The diagram below provides a summary of the six-stage 'exclusion clause checklist' which the solicitor should work through before starting to draft any exclusion clauses. It will also be useful for assessing their validity once problems have arisen. Provided that it is established that the clause is not void, the next stage is to think about whether the clause will pass the reasonableness test.

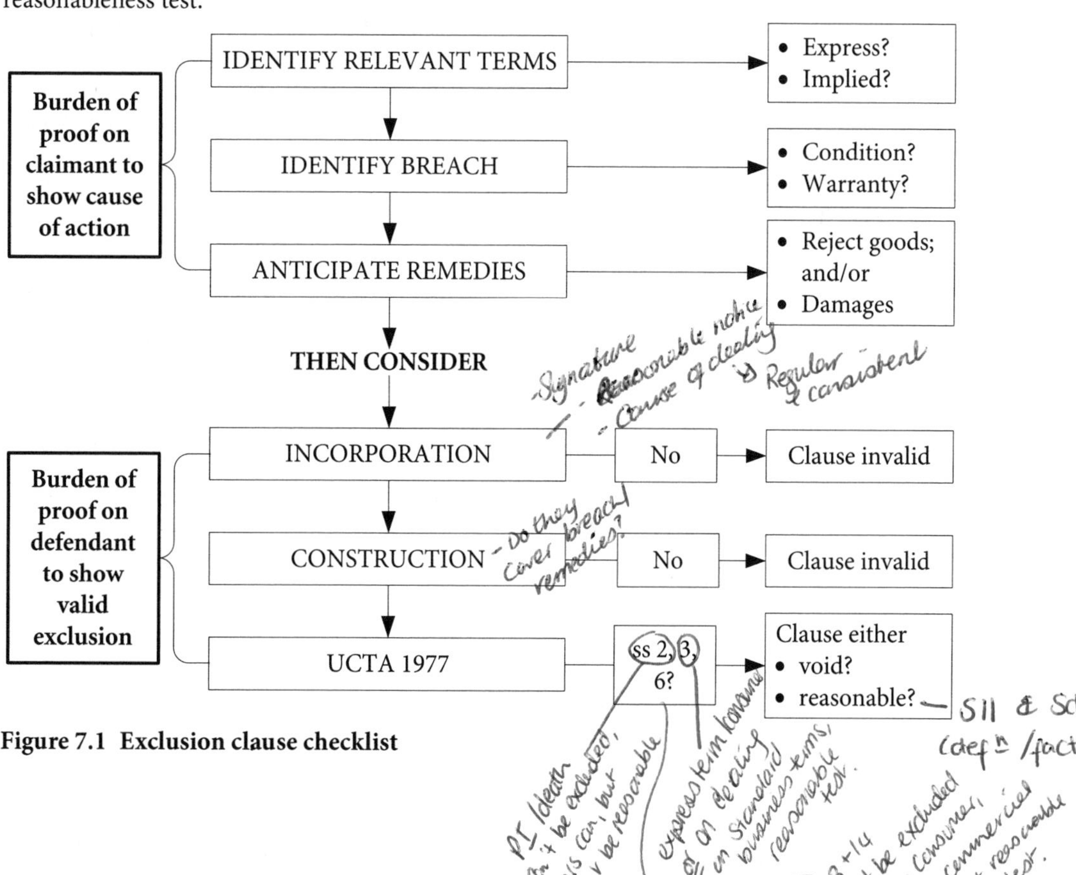

Figure 7.1 Exclusion clause checklist

7.8 Unfair Terms in Consumer Contracts Regulations 1999

These Regulations provide (in certain circumstances) a further important statutory control on drafting exclusion clauses. The Regulations do not apply to a contract between two commercial parties but where a commercial client enters into standard-form contract for the supply of goods and/or services to a consumer, their impact is likely to be significant. Like UCTA 1977, they relate only to business liability, but unlike UCTA 1977 they relate to all unfair contract terms, not just exclusion clauses.

7.8.1 The Regulations in outline

7.8.1.1 Definitions and scope of the Regulations

The definitions of 'consumer' and 'seller or supplier' require that a consumer must be a natural person who is not acting for business purposes, and that a seller or supplier must be acting for business purposes.

Regulation 4 provides that the Regulations apply 'in relation to unfair terms in contracts concluded between a seller or supplier and a consumer', and also indicates a number of terms to which the Regulations do not apply.

'Unfair term' is then defined by reg 5(1):

> a contractual term which has not been individually negotiated shall be regarded as unfair if, contrary to the requirement of good faith, it causes a significant imbalance in the parties' rights and obligations arising under the contract to the detriment of the consumer.

An 'illustrative and non-exhaustive list of terms which may be regarded as unfair' can be found in Sch 2. Regulation 6 describes how unfair terms are to be assessed. The effect of an unfair term (found in reg 8) is that it 'shall not be binding on the consumer'.

7.8.1.2 The requirement of 'plain, intelligible language'

By reg 7, a seller or supplier 'shall ensure that any written term of a contract [to which the Regulations apply] is expressed in plain, intelligible language'. This concept is not further defined in the Regulations, neither is it clear from the Regulations what will happen if a term is not expressed in plain, intelligible language. Perhaps the most appropriate conclusion is that it is one of the factors which may render a term unfair (compare the relationship of UCTA 1977 and 'plain English'; see **8.2.5**). Regulation 7 also provides that 'if there is doubt about the meaning of a written term, the interpretation most favourable to the consumer shall prevail'; compare the normal *contra proferentem* rule (see **7.6.2**).

7.8.1.3 Enforcement

Regulations 10–15 give power to the Office of Fair Trading (OFT) and 'qualifying bodies' (specified in Sch 1, including bodies such as the Consumers' Association) to consider complaints that contract terms drawn up for general use are unfair, and to take action.

7.8.2 Relationship with UCTA 1977

The Regulations apply in addition to rather than instead of UCTA 1977. Thus, a solicitor will have to advise on situations where a term is subject not only to the UCTA 1977 reasonableness test, but also to the test of fairness under the Regulations.

7.9 Proposals for reform

In December 2004, the Law Commission published a detailed review of the law on unfair contract terms, with proposals for major reform of the 1977 Act and the 1999 Regulations with the objective of replacing 'these two pieces of legislation with a single unified Act that will set out the law on unfair contract terms in a clear and accessible way' (*Report of the Law*

Commission and Scottish Law Commission into Unfair Terms in Contracts). The Commission's report contains an extensive summary of its recommendations for reform and a draft Unfair Contract Terms Bill showing how the Commission recommends that these should be put into practice. However, at the time of writing (September 2010) it remains unclear when (or whether) the Government might decide to pursue reform of this area. It is not thought to be a priority at the moment.

Chapter 8
Exclusion Clauses: Drafting for Reasonableness

8.1 General principles

8.1.1 The contractual reasonableness test

In practice, where UCTA 1977 applies to a commercial agreement, most (if not all) of the agreement's exclusion clauses will be subject to the reasonableness test, so it is usually against this test that the solicitor will need to assess a clause.

Section 11(1) of UCTA 1977 states that:

> In relation to a contract term, the requirement of reasonableness ... is that the term shall have been a fair and reasonable one to be included having regard to the circumstances which were, or ought reasonably to have been, known to or in the contemplation of the parties when the contract was made.

It is, therefore, a test of reasonableness of incorporation, not reasonableness of reliance. If (in the light of the actual and constructive knowledge of the parties at the time) it is reasonable to include a particular clause when the contract is made, it should pass the reasonableness test. The court should not look at whether it was reasonable for the 'guilty' party to rely on the clause in the light of the breach (although it has to be said that it is not uncommon in practice for courts to do this). It is for the party claiming that a term satisfies the reasonableness test to show that it does (s 11(5)).

8.1.2 The Sch 2 guidelines

The court will look at the Sch 2 guidelines to assess whether the clause is reasonable. The guidelines include:

(a) the relative bargaining power of the parties;

(b) whether any choice was available (eg could the buyer have acquired the goods elsewhere without the clause?);

(c) whether the buyer was offered any inducement to accept the clause;

(d) the extent of the parties' knowledge of the existence and effect of the terms;

(e) whether it was practicable to comply with any condition imposed on bringing a claim;

(f) whether the goods were manufactured to special order.

The list is not intended to be exhaustive and, strictly speaking, applies only when the court is assessing reasonableness under s 6(3) and s 7(3) of UCTA 1977. However, the courts often apply the guidelines by analogy when considering the reasonableness test in relation to other sections, notably s 3. This approach was confirmed as appropriate by the Court of Appeal in *Overseas Medical Supplies Ltd v Orient Transport Services Ltd* [1999] 2 Lloyd's Rep 273 and, more recently, in *Regus (UK) Ltd v Epcot Solutions Ltd* [2008] EWCA Civ 361. The former case also contains a useful discussion and summary of the factors which are generally relevant to assessing the reasonableness of a clause.

It is unusual for one factor alone to be conclusive on reasonableness; in drafting, the solicitor must take into account all the factors (often conflicting) which could apply, and try to assess on balance whether the clause is likely to be held reasonable.

The court will also look at other factors to decide whether a clause is reasonable. The clause must be a reasonable one to include in the particular circumstances in relation to that particular contract. One of the most important factors therefore is the type of contract.

8.1.3 Is it a consumer contract or a commercial contract?

In determining whether a clause will survive the application of UCTA 1977, the crucial factor is often whether the contract is a consumer contract or a commercial contract. As discussed, a clause which excludes liability for breach of ss 13–15 of SGA 1979 is subject to the reasonableness test only against a commercial buyer; it is void against a buyer who deals as consumer.

However, under s 2(2) and s 3, a clause is subject to the reasonableness test whether the 'innocent' party is a business or a consumer. The courts are often stricter in applying the test where that person is a consumer. The clause may in fact be less likely to pass the test for that reason alone. If the client deals with both commercial and consumer buyers, it is important for the solicitor to recognise this when drafting. There may be several different ways of dealing with the problem, depending on how the client does business and the other relevant circumstances. For example, the solicitor may decide to draft two different forms of contract, with the 'consumer' version either omitting certain exclusion clauses, or containing only modified versions. However, this may be risky; it would then be necessary to ensure that those operating the contract are able to distinguish between the two versions (perhaps by printing them on different coloured paper).

8.2 Drafting for reasonableness: relevant factors

8.2.1 Introduction

Looking at the cases in which the courts have applied the contractual reasonableness test, it is possible to identify a number of factors which have been held to have a bearing on reasonableness. However, even if a clause has been interpreted in a particular way or held to be reasonable on one occasion, this is no guarantee that a court will react in the same way when faced with the same clause in a different case. As a result, it is not possible to produce an exhaustive list of relevant factors on reasonableness. However, the following are factors that the court will consider in relation to each of the Sch 2 guidelines.

It is important to bear in mind that in practice there is considerable overlap between the Sch 2 guidelines. For example, the parties' knowledge of the market in which they operate and the nature of the goods will clearly affect their understanding of a particular clause, but it will also be relevant when assessing their relationship – a well-informed buyer will be in a much stronger position than one who is new to the market.

8.2.2 Case law

It is not possible to summarise the extensive case law on the subject of reasonableness, but an awareness of some of the leading cases to which reference will be made in this section is essential before considering the reasonableness factors.

Arguably, still by far the most important case in relation to reasonableness is *Watford Electronics Ltd v Sanderson CFL Ltd* [2001] EWCA Civ 317. In this case, the seller had supplied the buyer with computer hardware and software; the supply was on the seller's standard terms, which contained the following provisions:

(a) a clause limiting the seller's liability to the contract price and excluding liability for consequential or indirect losses;

(b) a clause providing that neither party relied on any representation by the other party in entering the contract; and

(c) an addendum to the contract (the 'side letter') in which the seller agreed to use its best endeavours to allocate appropriate resources to the contract to minimise any losses which might arise from its performance of the contract.

The software did not perform to the buyer's satisfaction, and the buyer sued for damages for breach of contract. The Court of Appeal held that the limitation clause passed the reasonableness test, noting generally that the parties were both experienced commercial parties and of roughly equal bargaining power; this clearly influenced the court's decision. In addition, the parties would (or should) have taken into account the risk of the software failing to perform when settling the contract price. The buyer also appeared to have taken a conscious decision to live with the exclusion clauses in return for various concessions from the seller (in particular the addendum referred to at (c) above, the side letter obliging the seller to use its best endeavours to allocate resources so as to minimise the effect of any failure). As a matter of construction, the limitation clause did not deprive the buyer of the chance to recover damages for breach of contract in all situations, and the seller's ability to rely on it was further qualified by the addendum to the contract. In the circumstances, and having regard to the Sch 2 guidelines, the clause satisfied the reasonableness test.

Other cases which are illustrative of the attitude of the courts in deciding reasonableness are the 'soft drinks' cases: *Britvic Soft Drinks Ltd v Messer UK Ltd* [2002] EWCA Civ 548 and *Bacardi-Martini v Thomas Hardy Packaging [2002]* EWCA Civ 549. Both cases involved the contamination of carbon dioxide supplied to drinks manufacturers. In both, the exclusion of liability for breach of the implied terms relating to quality and fitness for purpose was found to be unreasonable.

More recently, the Court has considered the issue again in *Regus (UK) Ltd v Epcot Solutions Ltd* [2008] EWCA Civ 361. Regus supplied serviced offices to Epcot, a small company supplying IT training services. The air conditioning in the offices failed to function properly, and Epcot stopped paying its service charges. When Regus claimed for arrears, Epcot counterclaimed for loss of profit and loss of opportunity to develop its business, as well as for distress and loss of amenity. The contract contained a wide-reaching exclusion clause which attempted to exclude liability for 'loss of business, loss of profits, loss of anticipated savings, loss of or damage to data, third party claims or any consequential loss'. At first instance this was held to be unreasonable, as the clause effectively precluded any remedy for Epcot. This decision was reversed on appeal, as the trial judge had not taken into account the damages which Epcot could claim for 'diminution in value of the services provided'. The exclusion clause did not preclude recovery for the diminution in the value of the services; it only excluded consequential loss. The Court of Appeal considered the clause in the light of the Sch 2 factors, and held that in the circumstances it met the requirement of reasonableness.

8.2.3 Bargaining strength and the relationship between the parties

The first of the Sch 2 guidelines is the relationship between the parties and the strength of their bargaining positions. For example, in a consumer case, the fact that bargaining power is normally on the side of the supplier may be a vital factor in the court's decision. Where the parties are both businesses, size alone will not always be the determining factor. The court will look at the relationship between the parties and consider some of the factors set out below.

8.2.3.1 Negotiated or standard-form contract?

If the contract was individually negotiated, so that both sides were able to influence its contents, the courts may be more likely to decide that exclusions are reasonable than they would if one party had simply imposed terms on the other (as in a standard-form contract). Note, however, that a contract may not necessarily fall neatly into one particular category. An example of this is where the original 'framework' of the contract is negotiated between the trade associations of the parties, but, by the time it goes into operation, the contract is in effect standard-form.

8.2.3.2 Market in which the parties operate

This raises a number of issues on reasonableness and bargaining power. The courts tend to hold that commercial parties which are operating in the same market may be taken to know exactly how that market works; if they have provided for this accordingly in their contracts, the courts are likely to assume that those provisions are reasonable and neither is at an unfair advantage. This conclusion may be reinforced where both parties are known to have used the same or similar clauses in their own standard-form contracts. See, for example, *Watford v Sanderson* and *Regus v Epcot* (**8.2.2** above). However, the use of an industry standard clause will not necessarily point to reasonableness. In some cases, the courts have suggested that a distinction can be drawn between types of standard-form contract which have been settled over the years to reflect the realities of a particular business operation, such as bills of lading and charterparties, and standard-form contracts which are simply imposed by the strong on the weak. If there is a very considerable imbalance of bargaining power, the courts may still be prepared to hold that a clause imposed by the stronger party is unreasonable, even if both parties operate in the same market. The court will also consider this factor when assessing the knowledge and understanding of the parties under Sch 2(c) (see **8.2.5**).

8.2.3.3 Financial pressure

One party may have been forced to accept an exclusion because its financial situation at the time of the contract means that it cannot afford to turn down the deal which the other side is offering, despite the presence of an exclusion. This may make the exclusion unreasonable.

8.2.3.4 Age and experience of the buyer

The courts may hold that an experienced buyer (whether individual or commercial) should know what it is doing when it enters into contracts, and therefore be more likely to decide that an exclusion clause against such a buyer is reasonable. Compare, for example, two cases on property surveys. In *Stevenson v Nationwide Building Society* (1984) 272 EG 663, the buyer was an estate agent, and an exclusion in the contract relating to the negligent performance of a survey was held to be reasonable. In *Smith v Bush (Eric S) (a firm); Harris v Wyre Forest District Council* [1989] 2 All ER 514, however, the buyer was inexperienced in buying property, and a similar exclusion was held to be unreasonable against him.

8.2.3.5 Effect of legal advice

If the 'victim' of the clause received legal advice, any exclusion stands a better chance of being held reasonable. However, in *Walker v Boyle* [1982] 1 All ER 634, the 'victim', the buyer in a conveyancing transaction, was legally advised (as was the seller) and the clause was a standard term in the then edition of the National Conditions of Sale. Nevertheless, it was still held to be unreasonable.

8.2.3.6 Drafting techniques

In a tailor-made (ie fully-negotiated) contract, it may be useful to include a preamble to the exclusion, referring to as many of the above factors as are relevant, and stating whether and, if so, how those factors have been taken into account in drafting the exclusion. If the court appreciates the background, it may be more likely to hold that the exclusion is reasonable.

8.2.3.7 Attitude of the courts

To sum up, as a general proposition, it seems that if the buyer is a consumer, any exclusion clause is more likely to fail the reasonableness test; if the contract is between commercial parties, it is more likely to pass.

In a commercial contract where there is no great inequality of bargaining power, and particularly where the parties have had the opportunity to identify the risks under the contract and cover them by insurance, the courts have often taken the view that they should not interfere with what the parties have done. In *Watford v Sanderson* (see **8.2.2**), Chadwick LJ stated:

> Where experienced businessmen representing substantial companies of equal bargaining power negotiate an agreement, they may be taken to have had regard to the matters known to them. They should, in my view, be taken to be the best judge of the commercial fairness of the agreement which they have made; including the fairness of each of the terms in that agreement. They should be taken to be the best judge on the question of whether the terms of the agreement are reasonable ... Unless satisfied that one party has, in effect, taken unfair advantage of the other – or a term is so unreasonable that it cannot properly have been understood or considered – the court should not interfere.

However, it must be stressed that there is no guarantee that a court will always take this view; each case must turn on its own facts. There may be particular or additional factors that will mitigate either for or against reasonableness. For example, the factor that clearly influenced the Court of Appeal in both *Watford Electronics Ltd v Sanderson CFL Ltd* and *Regus (UK) Ltd v Epcot Solutions Ltd* was that both parties in each case had used the same terms before in their respective standard-form contracts (**8.2.2** above).

8.2.4 Choice

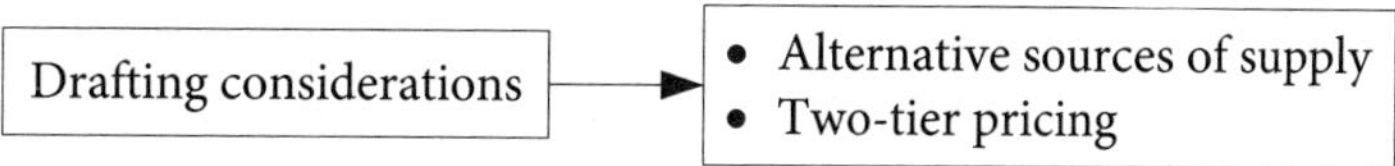
Drafting considerations
• Alternative sources of supply
• Two-tier pricing

8.2.4.1 Do other suppliers use the clause?

Could the buyer have obtained the goods or services from another supplier which does not impose the exclusion clause in question? This factor may point in either direction. If the buyer could have gone elsewhere without having the clause imposed, and yet chose to make this particular contract, this may mean that the clause is more likely to be reasonable. However, if all suppliers use a similar exclusion, lack of choice may make the exclusion unreasonable. If the supplier is the only one in a particular line of business using a particular exclusion clause, and is, therefore, out of step with its competitors, this again may be evidence that it is unreasonable to use the clause at all. The buyer's knowledge of the existence and extent of the clause (see **8.2.5**) is also likely to be relevant in these circumstances.

8.2.4.2 Two-tier pricing

In a clause of this type, the supplier of the goods or services charges a lower price if the buyer accepts the exclusion clause, and a higher price if the contract contains either a modified version of the clause or no clause at all. Using two-tier pricing can help the clause to pass the reasonableness test. For example, in *Woodman v Photo Trade Processing* (CC, 3 April 1981) it was held that a clause limiting the liability of a film processor to the cost of the film was unreasonable because (amongst other things) the processor had failed to use a two-tier pricing system recommended by its own trade association. However, the use of two-tier pricing is not an automatic guarantee of success. In *Warren v Truprint* [1986] BTLC 344, it was held that an exclusion clause based on two-tier pricing was unreasonable because its wording was too vague.

Note that two-tier pricing can work in both consumer and commercial cases. For example, in *RW Green Ltd v Cade Brothers Farm* [1987] Lloyd's Rep 602, the seller in a commercial sale of goods contract used an exclusion with two-tier pricing, and the clause passed the reasonableness test.

8.2.5 Buyer's knowledge and understanding of the clause

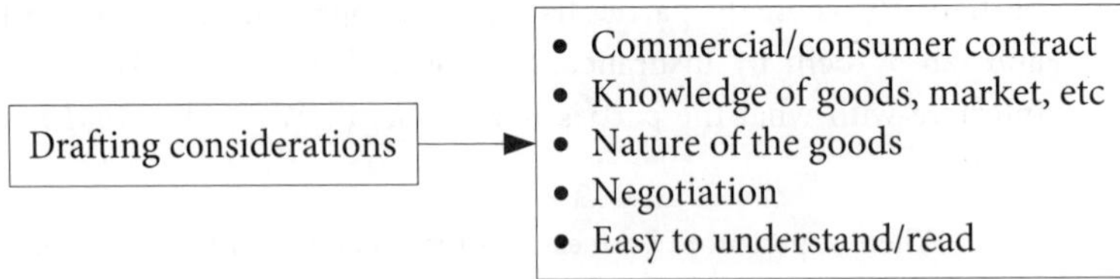

It is important to remember that it is the knowledge and understanding of the parties at the time that the contract was made that will be relevant here.

In a contract between commercial parties, to assess the knowledge and understanding of the parties the courts will look at factors such as the nature of the goods, their awareness of market conditions, and whether or not the parties have used the same standard terms and conditions themselves.

Where the buyer is a consumer, knowledge and understanding is particularly important, as the buyer is unlikely to have inside knowledge of the market. In this context, it is essential to ensure that the clauses are both readable and comprehensible, although this requirement is by no means confined to consumer contracts. Consider, for example, the following comments of Staughton J in the commercial case of *Stag Line v Tyne Ship Repair Group (The Zinnia)* [1984] 2 Lloyd's Rep 211:

> I would have been tempted to hold that all of the conditions are unfair and unreasonable for two reasons; first, they are in such small print that one can barely read them; secondly, the draftsmanship is so convoluted and prolix that one almost needs an LLB to understand them.

8.2.5.1 Nature of the goods

In *Watford v Sanderson* (see **8.2.2**) the Court of Appeal, in finding the exclusion clauses in issue to be reasonable, was clearly influenced by the nature of the product (computer software) as being likely to give rise to predictable problems (and, potentially, to extreme liability). Both parties were aware of this. In *Britvic Soft Drinks Ltd v Messer UK Ltd* (see **8.2.2**), the Court found the exclusions unreasonable and noted that the goods in question (carbon dioxide for use in manufacturing soft drinks) were not ones where the end-user of the goods would reasonably anticipate difficulties or expect to have to test them for compliance with the contract. Again, the court will also consider the nature of the goods when assessing the bargaining strength of the parties.

8.2.5.2 Negotiation

Clearly, if the parties have negotiated on the nature and extent of the term, they can be taken to know and understand its implications. This was an important factor in *Watford v Sanderson*. In *Regus v Epcot* (see **8.2.2**), the attempt by the 'buyer' (an experienced commercial tenant) to renegotiate other terms of the contract, but not the exclusion clause, was seen by the Court as a significant indication of the reasonableness of the clause.

8.2.5.3 Short and simple drafting

This can be difficult to achieve, but is worth aiming for. The solicitor should, in particular, consider the likely reading abilities of those involved with the contract, both customers and employees of the client.

8.2.5.4 Size of print, layout and appearance

Wherever possible, the solicitor should advise the client to use easily readable print, and to set documents out in a way which assists reading (if this can be done without wasting space). Devices such as different typefaces, bold type, underlining and boxes are all useful for drawing attention to significant parts of a contract.

8.2.5.5 Position of the clause

The solicitor will also need to consider where and how the exclusion should appear in the contract. There is no single correct way of doing this; it is often helpful to look at several sets of precedents to get a feel for the different methods. For example, some contracts will place each exclusion immediately after the clause to which it relates; some will have a separate section for the exclusions, cross-referring to other relevant clauses where necessary. The way in which the exclusions are presented may have a bearing on the victim's knowledge and understanding of them, and therefore affect their reasonableness.

8.2.5.6 Practical problems

Following these guidelines should increase the chances of a clause being held reasonable, but it may also create practical difficulties. For example, a clause which is well laid out and clearly expressed may not fit onto the back of an order form. Sometimes 'wall-to-wall' layout (where the print covers virtually the entire surface of the paper, without margins or adequate space between lines) is essential because space is limited. In this case it will be worth considering whether space can be increased by getting rid of redundant clauses, or deleting clauses which cover contingencies so remote that they are not worth providing for (or which would cause few problems if they did occur). It is also possible that a document written in 'plain' English may turn out to be shorter than the same thing expressed in traditional 'legal' English.

8.2.5.7 Incorporation by reference

Incorporation by reference is a common practice in both consumer and business contracts. For example, the supplier under a sale of goods agreement may wish to use standard terms laid down by its trade association as the basis of any contracts it makes. To save space, the agreement can state that the goods are sold subject to the relevant trade association's standard terms, and that the supplier will provide the buyer with a copy of the terms. This may be a useful space-saving device, but there can be problems with both incorporation and reasonableness.

8.2.5.8 Tactics

The solicitor must also be aware of tactical considerations. The client may not want the finished document to be too clear. It may be valid to obscure the meaning of a clause for tactical reasons (and some clients may be uncomfortable with a document which is not written in what they perceive to be 'legal' English). There are no clear-cut solutions to the problems which this raises: solicitor and client must discuss the pros and cons of each approach in each individual case.

8.2.5.9 Conclusion

Because of the numerous considerations, this factor will often be difficult to weigh up; solicitor and client will have to decide what the priority is in each particular case. On the one hand, if a contract is drafted and set out clearly, clauses which are subject to the reasonableness test are more likely to pass the test. On the other hand, fitting a contract into a set amount of space (eg the back of the client's order form) may be seen as more important, even though this may require a compression of drafting and layout which could render a clause unreasonable. However, there may be some room for compromise; just because a contract must fit onto an order form, it does not necessarily also have to be drafted 'wall-to-wall', difficult to read and full of jargon.

8.2.6 Compliance with conditions

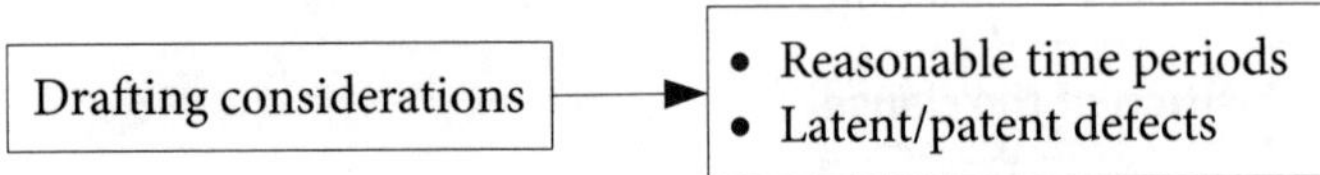

The court will consider whether it was reasonable to expect compliance with any condition for bringing action imposed by the contract, for example a time bar clause stating that the right to reject is lost if defects are not notified to the seller within a specified period. It may be reasonable to state that obvious defects should be notified within a relatively short period, but such a requirement will not be reasonable in respect of latent defects which are not likely to become apparent immediately. Again, the condition must have been reasonable at the time of the contract. Before drafting such a clause, it is therefore important that the solicitor has as much information as possible about the product to establish the type of defect likely to occur, and how quickly the buyer might be expected to notice it.

8.2.7 Goods manufactured to special order

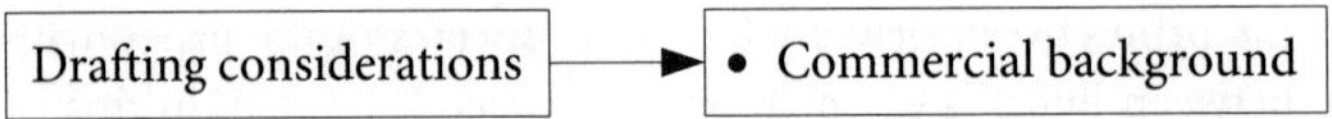

Whether it is reasonable to exclude liability in these circumstances will depend on the facts of the case. Where a seller has expended considerable time and money in manufacturing a 'one-off' product to the order of a particular customer, eg heavy industrial plant, it may find that if it is rejected by the buyer for any reason, it will be difficult to sell on to anyone else. The seller will therefore wish to exclude the buyer's right to reject. A buyer, on the other hand, may have incurred considerable expenditure in order to ensure that a product is unique or free from defects, eg where a consumer buyer commissions an item of furniture from a cabinet maker. If the product turns out to be defective, he will want to be able to return it, and it may be unreasonable to exclude the right to do so.

Tactics

Where there is a particular commercial reason to exclude liability, again, it is advisable to include a preamble explaining why the clause has been included.

8.2.8 Other factors

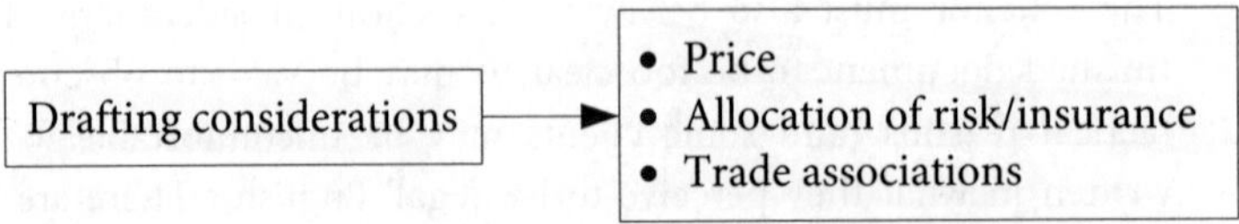

The Sch 2 guidelines can be seen as a starting point for assessing the reasonableness of the clause. However, there are further factors which the court will consider, and it is important not to overlook these.

8.2.8.1 Price

If the loss which may result from breach of contract is wholly disproportionate to the contract price, it may be reasonable for the contract to contain an exclusion (or limitation) clause. If both parties are aware of this from the outset, the chances of the clause being reasonable may be enhanced. In a tailor-made contract, a preamble can be used to set out the basis on which the parties are contracting.

8.2.8.2 Allocation of risk and insurance

The parties to a commercial contract will usually be in the best position to decide what the risks under the contract are, and how to deal with them. The court may attach considerable significance to how the parties have identified and dealt with the risks under the contract. If an exclusion or limitation clause has the effect of passing the risk of loss or damage from one party to the other, it has more chance of surviving the reasonableness test if it is clear that the contract has provided for this. Examples include:

(a) reflecting the degree of risk in the contract price, then backing this up with a limitation clause;

(b) imposing an obligation on the party with the risk to take out appropriate insurance;

(c) prefacing any insurance clause with a preamble explaining how the insurance arrangements and the exclusions have been arrived at.

Even if there is no obligation to insure, the courts place considerable emphasis on the availability of insurance to the parties respectively. For example, in *George Mitchell (Chesterhall) Ltd v Finney Lock Seeds Ltd* [1983] 2 AC 803, where defective cabbage seed was sold to a farmer, the House of Lords was obviously impressed by evidence that it would have been easy and inexpensive for the supplier to cover itself against the risk of supplying defective seed. This was one of several reasons for finding that a clause limiting liability to the price of the seed was unreasonable.

It may be worthwhile obtaining expert evidence on insurance before drafting the contract and its exclusions. The courts will not always be in the best position to assess what the risks and the most suitable insurance arrangements are, and may, therefore, in the absence of suitable evidence, make an inappropriate decision on the reasonableness of any exclusion.

Note that where a limitation clause is concerned, UCTA 1977, s 11(4)(b) specifically mentions the availability of insurance as a factor in assessing reasonableness (see further **8.3.1.2**).

8.2.8.3 Trade associations

Approval by a trade association (or similar body) may help an exclusion clause to pass the reasonableness test. For example, in *RW Green Ltd v Cade Brothers Farm* [1987] Lloyd's Rep 602, a case involving the sale of defective potato seed, the parties used a standard-form contract which had originally been negotiated between the National Farmers' Union and the National Association of Seed Potato Merchants. The limitation clause was found to be reasonable.

8.3 Effectiveness of different types of exclusion clause

In deciding whether the clause is reasonable, the court will also look at the clause itself. The extent of the exclusion and the type of clause will be relevant factors. This chapter ends with a closer look at the effectiveness of some of the different types of exclusion clause commonly found in commercial contracts:

(a) limitation clauses;

(b) force majeure clauses;

(c) time bar clauses;

(d) non-rejection clauses;

(e) exclusions and limitations of consequential loss.

8.3.1 Exclusion or limitation?

8.3.1.1 General principle

The House of Lords has held on a number of occasions that a clause which limits liability is more likely to pass the reasonableness test than one which excludes it altogether (see eg *Ailsa Craig Fishing Co Ltd v Malvern Fishing Co Ltd* [1983] 1 WLR 964). However, this principle should be treated with caution; arguably, what is important is the difference in the degree of exclusion, not simply in the type of clause. A clause which limits the supplier's liability to the contract price, where the damage likely to be caused is far in excess of this, may be as unreasonable as a total exclusion, especially if the contract price in the latter case is low.

8.3.1.2 UCTA 1977 guidelines

Note that UCTA 1977, s 11(4) contains two guidelines which apply only where a term is designed to limit liability to a specified sum of money rather than to exclude it altogether:

(a) by s 11(4)(a), the court should take account of the resources available to the person relying on the limitation to meet liability, should it arise; and

(b) by s 11(4)(b), the court should have regard to how far it was open to that person to cover himself by insurance.

In *St Albans City and District Council v ICL* [1996] 4 All ER 481, the Court of Appeal looked at the bargaining strength of the parties, and held that a limitation clause in a contract between a multinational company with substantial resources and a local authority was unreasonable. Other factors which the Court took into account were the fact that ICL was covered by product liability insurance of £50 million yet had limited its liability to £100,000, and the limited choice of similar products available to the local authority. Had the limitation clause been upheld, the cost of the loss would have been borne by the local taxpayers, so it was fairer to allocate the risk to ICL. As discussed at **8.2.2**, the Court of Appeal considered the reasonableness of a limitation clause in *Watford v Sanderson CFL Ltd* and concluded that the clause did not deprive the buyer of the right to damages in all circumstances.

8.3.2 Force majeure clauses

A force majeure clause is designed to apply where contractual performance has become impossible because of circumstances unforeseen by the parties and outside their control. In a sale of goods contract, it will normally seek to excuse the seller for failure to deliver the goods on time (or even at all) in these circumstances. A force majeure clause is normally classified as part of the boiler-plate of an agreement (see **1.5.2.8**).

8.3.2.1 Meaning of 'force majeure'

The expression 'force majeure' has been interpreted by the courts to cover a range of events, including act of God, war, strikes, embargoes, government refusal to grant licences and abnormal weather conditions. The common factor in each case is that the event is outside the contracting parties' control. However, it is usual for a force majeure clause to do more than simply state that the supplier will not be liable for non-performance caused by 'force majeure'. Instead, it will normally set out a (non-exhaustive) list of specific events which the clause is intended to cover and the consequences of any of those events arising, so that both parties know exactly where they stand. (As noted at **7.6.3**, the *ejusdem generis* rule does not apply to force majeure clauses; specifying events does not cut down the meaning of any general words which follow.)

8.3.2.2 Frustration of the contract

As discussed in **Chapter 2** (see **2.7.1**), where performance has become impossible due to events beyond the parties' control, in the absence of express provision the contract may be frustrated. Thus, for example, a contract for supply of goods will be frustrated if it becomes clear that any delivery of the goods will be so late that performance of the contract will be radically different from that envisaged by the parties.

8.3.2.3 Advantages of a specific provision in the contract

The problem with frustration is that it is rather uncertain (how long must the buyer wait before the performance of the contract will become radically different from that which the parties envisaged?), and its effects under the Law Reform (Frustrated Contracts) Act 1943 are rather arbitrary. Thus, although it will act as a kind of 'safety net' if the parties do not turn their attention to what will happen if unforeseen events occur, it is generally preferable to have a specific provision (ie, a force majeure clause) in the contract dealing with this situation. The parties can then agree that when the disrupting circumstances have been in existence for a specific time, either party may cancel the agreement by giving the other a certain period of written notice. The contract can also make specific provision for the financial consequences of such a cancellation.

8.3.2.4 Application of UCTA 1977

As long as one party deals as consumer or on the other party's written standard terms of business, a force majeure clause will be subject to the reasonableness test under s 3 of UCTA 1977, as an attempt by the party relying on the clause to render no contractual performance at all (s 3(2)(b)(ii)). Although this may appear to be a rather drastic type of exclusion at first sight, courts often are prepared to treat force majeure clauses favourably (ie hold that they are reasonable) if care is taken over drafting.

8.3.2.5 Drafting points to consider

(a) The force majeure events should be clearly defined. Knowledge of the client's business is therefore essential to anticipate the type of events to be included.

(b) If a force majeure event occurs, should the contract to be suspended or cancelled (or suspended for a certain period followed by cancellation)? Which is appropriate will depend on the client's instructions and the circumstances.

(c) If cancellation is chosen, is it more appropriate to have automatic cancellation of the contract if a force majeure event occurs, or should the party relying on the force majeure give notice of cancellation to the other? The latter will usually be preferable. (Note that the party relying on force majeure will have to prove that the event in question has arisen.)

(d) Should the party relying on force majeure refund any payments which the other party has already made to it? Providing for a refund should help to ensure that the clause is reasonable. It need not always be a full refund; a partial refund may be appropriate, especially if the supplier has already incurred expense.

8.3.3 Time bar clauses

A client who is involved in the supply of goods or services may wish to reduce the limitation period which would normally apply to claims arising from breach of the contract (the basic contractual limitation period is six years). This may be justifiable: long before the statutory limitation period expires, evidence of a breach of contract may become hard to pin down, and perishable goods will have lost any market value they may have had. In addition, a supplier will probably want to close its books on a particular contract reasonably soon after performance. In a commercial contract, therefore, it may be appropriate to include a 'time bar' clause (eg, in a sale of goods contract, stating that the buyer cannot claim in respect of defects in the goods unless it notifies those defects to the supplier within a certain period of time).

Time bar clauses will usually be effective (and reasonable) if they are included for good commercial reasons, particularly if they result from insurance consequences or requirements (see *Super Chem Products Ltd v American Life and General Insurance Co Ltd* [2004] UKPC 2).

8.3.3.1 Application of UCTA 1977

If (as will usually be the case) the effect of the time bar clause is to exclude liability for breach of the implied conditions under the SGA 1979 then s 6 of UCTA 1977 will apply, and the clause will either be void or subject to the reasonableness test, depending on whether the buyer deals as consumer or not. Otherwise, s 3 of UCTA 1977 will apply (as long as one party deals as consumer, or on the other party's written standard terms of business); the clause is an attempt by one party to exclude or restrict its liability when in breach of contract (s 3(2)(a)).

8.3.3.2 Drafting points to consider

(a) Does the party relying on the clause want to be notified of defects (ie, of the possible existence of a claim) or of the claim itself within a specified period, or to impose a time-limit for bringing proceedings, or all of these? A clause which raises too many barriers or is too complex may fail the reasonableness test.

(b) It is often sensible to distinguish between patent and latent defects, giving a longer time period for notification in respect of defects which are not immediately apparent on delivery. This is more likely to be reasonable than having the same time period for notification of both types of defect.

(c) The clause should state whether it is a particular remedy (eg rejection, damages) or the claim itself which is to be barred. If only the remedy is barred, the buyer might be able to use the claim as a defence to an action for the price by the seller.

If the contract is between members of the same trade association, a time bar clause probably has a better chance of passing the reasonableness test. Parties operating in the same market should know and accept the problems likely to arise in that market, and it may then be possible to make the clause stricter (eg, cut down the notification period) than if the other contracting party is unfamiliar with the problems of the trade.

8.3.4 Non-rejection clauses

There are two main reasons why a seller may consider a non-rejection clause:

As discussed in **Chapter 4**, for his own convenience, a seller may want to prevent SGA 1979, s 36 from applying to the contract (see **4.4.6.6**).

The seller may want to stop its buyer from taking advantage of a fall in the price of the contract goods by finding a technical breach of contract, rejecting the goods (with a view to getting its money back from the seller, or not having to pay at all) and then buying replacement goods more cheaply at the new, lower market price.

8.3.4.1 Application of UCTA 1977

A non-rejection clause may, depending on the circumstances, be subject to either s 6 or s 3 of UCTA 1977.

8.3.4.2 Drafting points to consider

(a) As there may be different reasons for including a non-rejection clause (see above), different types of clause will be necessary according to the client's needs. Again, it is important to be aware of the commercial background before drafting the clause.

(b) It may be worth using a preamble to explain why the clause has been included.

(c) Sometimes a simple reversal of s 36 of SGA 1979 will meet the seller's needs (eg allowing the buyer to reject but making it clear that, following rejection, the buyer must return the goods to the seller).

(d) Alternatively, the seller may wish to go further and state that the buyer cannot reject at all. This will also prevent the buyer claiming restitution of the purchase price, but not from suing for damages for breach of contract.

8.3.5 Loss of profits, indirect and consequential loss clauses

A common drafting technique with exclusion or limitation clauses is to try to limit liability to 'direct loss' and exclude liability for all or any of the following: 'loss of profits' or 'indirect loss' or 'consequential loss'. However, there may be problems with construction, and the terms are frequently misunderstood by clients and consequently misused. The starting point is therefore to take a brief look at terminology, as this will have a bearing on construction of the clause:

(a) *'Loss of profits'*. Clients tend to assume that all 'loss of profits' is indirect or consequential loss. However, contracts are designed to achieve profits, so loss of ordinary profits can be direct loss. In legal terms, these profits would fall within the first limb of *Hadley v Baxendale* (see **2.7.3.1**) as arising naturally from the breach. Thus, a clause excluding consequential loss or indirect loss will not exclude normal loss of profit. Clearly, ordinarily contemplated re-sale profits (as in distribution or wholesale contracts) would naturally fall within normal loss of profits; it may be more problematic where the goods are likely to be used by the seller in a way not directly linked to profit making, rather than being simply sold on.

(b) *'Indirect' or 'consequential' loss*. Consequential or indirect loss is all loss other than direct loss. In legal terms, it is loss which falls under the second limb of *Hadley v Baxendale*, so these terms will not cover ordinary loss of profits. The term does not, as clients tend to assume, cover all financial loss. Thus, a clause excluding indirect or consequential loss will not preclude a claim for direct loss.

It is perfectly acceptable to exclude liability both for loss of profits and for indirect or consequential loss. For example, in *Watford v Sanderson* (see **8.2.2**), the Court of Appeal held that where the parties were of equal bargaining power and were aware of the potential risks, 'it is reasonable to expect that the contract will make provision for the risk of indirect or consequential loss to fall on one party or the other'. The problem is just how wide the exclusion is. Clearly it is not acceptable to exclude all liability, so as to leave the buyer with no remedy at all (see, eg, *Regus v Epcot* (at **8.2.2**) and the *NetTV* case (at **7.3.2.2**)). In *Regus*, the court held that, on true construction of the clause, the exclusion of consequential loss, although wide-reaching, did not prevent recovery of direct loss.

8.3.5.1 Application of UCTA 1977

Exclusion or limitation of liability for loss of profits and indirect or consequential loss may be subject to s 3 or s 6 of UCTA 1977.

8.3.5.2 Drafting points to consider

(a) When excluding liability for loss of profits, list what types of profit are contemplated and separate loss of profits from indirect or consequential loss; otherwise 'ordinary' profits, eg anticipated re-sale profits, might well not be covered by the clause.

(b) With clauses dealing with indirect or consequential losses, the scale and type of matters within reasonable contemplation of the parties should be considered. Again, it is important to have a good grasp of the commercial background and, if necessary, investigate with the client the types of loss which could arise. The clause should specify the types of loss excluded, eg loss of contracts, loss of goodwill, loss of anticipated earnings, etc. However, the list should not be a veiled disguise for effectively excluding all types of financial loss.

(c) Consider the nature of the goods. The clause should not exclude the type of consequential loss that is always likely to result from defects in the particular type of goods, eg computer programs, leaving the buyer without any remedy.

(d) Consider including a cap on liability rather than a total exclusion, and take out insurance to cover this. The cap could be related to the extent of the seller's product liability insurance, and a preamble included explaining that this is the reason for the limit. The cap should not be set too low (see *St Albans v ICL* discussed at **8.3.1.2**). A further possibility is to link the cap to the price of the goods.

Chapter 9

Marketing Agreements: Introduction to Agency and Distribution

9.1 Introduction

The previous chapters have concentrated on the contractual arrangements into which commercial manufacturers may enter to make direct sales to retailers or the end users of the goods. However, commercial suppliers may decide, for a variety of reasons, not to market the goods themselves but to appoint an intermediary. They may lack the resources to market the goods effectively, or they may wish to break into a new and unfamiliar market where they require the expertise of a third party.

The topic of agreements for the marketing of goods and services is introduced in **Chapters 34** and **35** of ***Business Law and Practice***. This chapter gives a brief reminder of two of the most commonly encountered marketing agreements: agency and distribution. **Chapter 10** will then goes on to consider how each type of agreement might be put together.

9.2 Agency

The term 'agency' is often used very loosely in relation to commercial activities to cover a number of different types of business relationship, and it is extremely important not to take at face value the label which the parties have put on their arrangement; always check carefully the actual nature of the relationship.

A true sales agency agreement is one where the agent makes contracts with customers on behalf of its principal; in other words, the agent binds the principal, so there is a contract between the principal and the customer (but none between the agent and the customer). At this stage the agent 'drops out' of the process. However, the principal is liable for the acts of his agent.

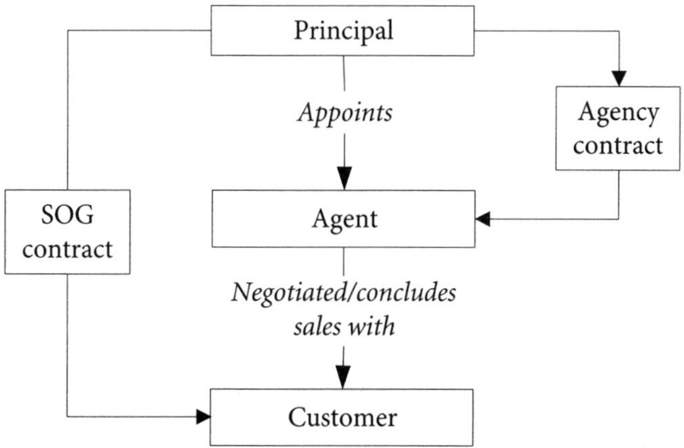

Figure 9.1 Sales agency agreement

The agent does not hold stocks of the goods, although it may have samples to show to prospective customers. When the goods are sold, title to the goods passes direct from the principal to the customer. The agent never owns the goods – it is simply an intermediary, and so will not generally incur liability, for example, if the goods are defective.

Other types of agency agreement are possible; for example marketing or 'introducing' agency. This term normally covers the situation where the agent simply finds customers and introduces them to the principal, which then negotiates and makes the contract for itself; however, it is also used where the agent finds customers and negotiates terms on the principal's behalf but without having the authority to make the contract on the principal's behalf.

In any dispute, the court is likely to attach little weight to the labelling of an agreement but will look at the relationship between the parties. In *Mercantile International Group plc v Chuan Soon Huant Industrial Group Ltd* [2002] EWCA Civ 288 the arrangement between the parties was described as an 'agency agreement'. However, the claimant was not paid by commission but (like a distributor) was remunerated by mark-up. The court looked at the substance of the agreement itself. The claimant clearly had authority to negotiate in the principal's name, the principal delivered direct to customers and the claimant never held any stock. The Court of Appeal decided that, despite the way that the claimant was paid, the agreement was in fact an agency agreement.

9.3 Distribution

In a distribution agreement, the supplier sells goods to the distributor, which buys them in order to re-sell on its own behalf. A common example of a distribution agreement is where a manufacturer sells its products to a wholesaler, which buys them to sell to its own customers to retail onwards; the relationship between manufacturer and wholesaler is a distribution agreement.

The distributor owns the goods which it sells, and title to the goods passes from the distributor to its customers. The supplier has no contractual relationship with the distributor's customers, and so will have no contractual liability, for example under ss 13–15 of the SGA 1979 (see **Chapter 6**). If the goods are defective, the supplier may, however, be liable to end users in tort or for product liability, eg under the Consumer Protection Act 1987.

Note that a distribution agreement is sometimes referred to as a 'distributorship agreement' (or simply 'distributorship'). Some commentators prefer this term, on the ground that, in practice, 'distribution agreement' is sometimes used loosely to refer to an agreement for the carriage of goods.

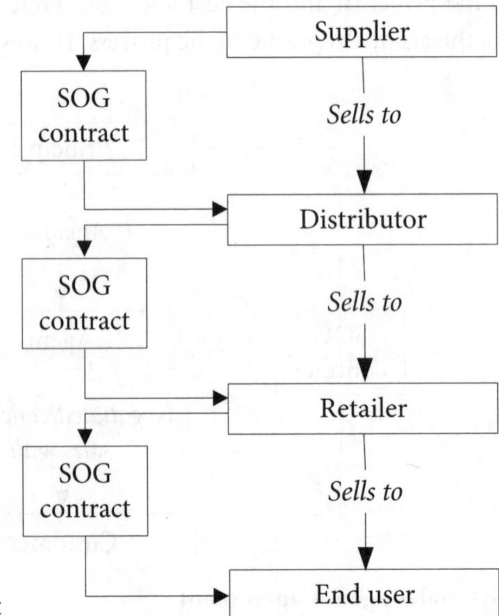

Figure 9.2
Distribution agreement

9.4 Advantages and disadvantages of each type of agreement

Table 9.1 below contains a reminder of the commercial factors to consider when deciding whether an agency or a distribution agreement would be more suitable. For a more detailed discussion, see **Chapter 35** of ***Business Law and Practice***.

Agency	**Distribution**
Agent (A) appointed by principal (P) under agency agreement. A receives commission (usually agreed percentage of sales or introductions). Can be used for marketing services as well as goods.	Supplier (S) enters distribution agreement with distributor (D). D buys the goods from S for resale, and retains all profits from resale. Generally only suitable for marketing goods.
Requires close supervision by P. Less suitable if A and P are based in different countries or P has limited time for this. More suitable for bespoke products, products requiring close contact or after-sales service. Useful to protect brand/goodwill.	Requires limited supervision. D decides how and where to market goods. More suitable for mass-produced products or where S is likely to encounter unfamiliar markets/ language problems. More difficult to protect brand/goodwill.
P remains contractually liable to his customers. A has limited financial risk, and has no initial outlay on stock, although A will probably earn less through payment of commission than profit from re-sale.	No contractual liability between S and D's customers, although S may be liable in tort or under product liability legislation. D bears the risk of non-payment, claims from customers and unsold stock.
Often more expensive for P to set up and operate.	More expensive for D to set up and operate, but can be more lucrative for D. D may have more incentive to exploit market to generate profit.
Agency agreements are unlikely to infringe UK or EU competition law (see **10.1.3.2** and **Chapter 27**).	Can give rise to competition law problems. The grant of territorial protection may infringe Article 101 of the TFEU or the Chapter 1 Prohibition (see **Chapter 27**).
Agency agreements are subject to the Commercial Agents (Council Directive) Regulations 1993, which govern areas such as payment of duties of A and P, commission, and payment on termination of the agreement (see **10.3**).	No equivalent legislation for distribution.
Where P and A are based in separate jurisdictions, they may be regarded as one undertaking for corporation tax purposes, which may have adverse tax consequences for P. P will be liable for VAT on products supplied in its name.	D will generally pay all tax on profits and VAT.

Table 9.1 Advantages of agency and distribution agrements

9.5 Exclusivity

Whether the manufacturer decides to appoint an agent or a distributor, it will be important to decide the extent to which the agent/distributor will be protected from competition within the territory where it is operating. There are three options:

(a) Exclusive agency/distributorship. The manufacturer agrees not to appoint any other agents/distributors within the territory and will not sell the products within the territory itself.

(b) Sole agency/distributorship. The manufacturer agrees not to appoint any other agents/distributors within the territory, but remains free to sell the products within the territory itself.

(c) Non-exclusive agency/distributorship. The manufacturer can appoint other agents/distributors within the territory, and can sell the products within the territory itself.

Again, in practice, clients tend to use the terminology loosely. In particular, the legal and commercial meanings of the terms 'sole' and 'exclusive' have become confused, and may even mean different things in different product markets, so it is important to establish the exact nature of the relationship between the parties.

The choice will depend on various factors, including the bargaining power of the parties. Clearly, exclusivity is preferable for the agent or distributor, and may be important to allow a new appointee to establish itself within a territory. Businesses often regard territorial exclusivity as a fundamental term, particularly in a distribution agreement, in order to benefit as much as possible from their initial investment. Without the grant of exclusivity, a potential distributor might not agree to take on the distributorship at all.

Where exclusivity is granted, the manufacturer should put in place measures to ensure that the territory is fully exploited, such as minimum target obligations.

9.6 Basic rules for successful drafting of marketing agreements

The three basic rules in relation to drafting mentioned in **Chapter 7** (know the commercial background, know the law, and know the drafting principles) are equally important in this context:

(a) Commercial background is essential to advise the client on the most appropriate type of marketing agreement.

(b) Agency agreements are regulated by the Commercial Agents Regulations 1993, and distribution agreements can be subject to both EU and UK competition law, so it is vital for the solicitor drafting the agreement to have an awareness of both of these areas of law. A cautionary tale in relation to agency is *Berry v Laytons* [2009] ECC 34, where an agent was awarded £192,189 plus interest in damages as a result of his solicitor's negligent failure to advise on his entitlement under the Regulations on termination of the agency agreement. The consequences could be a great deal worse where parties can be fined up to 10% of worldwide turnover for breach of relevant EU or UK competition provisions.

(c) Lastly, the usual health warning applies to the use of precedents, but it is important that the agreement does not fall foul of the Commercial Agents Regulations or competition law respectively, so a precedent may be helpful in deciding whether or not a clause complies.

Chapter 10

Marketing Agreements: Drafting Agency and Distribution Agreements

10.1 Drafting an agency agreement

10.1.1 Introduction

To help in considering how to approach an agency agreement, this section will refer to an expanded version of the agency example described in ***Business Law and Practice*** at **35.6**.

> **Example**
>
> Wood Magic Ltd is a medium-sized company in Chester. It has been established for about 20 years, and has built up a thriving business making custom-designed furniture in luxury woods such as yew and cherry. Its sales have been largely confined to the North of England, where it has built up an excellent reputation. However, following a recent change of management and an injection of new capital, the directors plan to expand the business. In particular, they want to target London and the South-East, but have not yet decided how best to do this. Up to now, Wood Magic has carried out its own marketing, and there are no plans to change the set-up for the existing Northern operations.
>
> The directors now feel that Wood Magic needs to find a 'trading partner' with a presence in the target market to help the furniture become established in that market. They are prepared to commit at least one director to be permanently engaged in developing this side of the business and establishing good relations with the trading partner. This commitment will be a long-term one and, despite having the trading partner to find customers for it, Wood Magic needs to maintain customer contact itself to ensure that customers get the products they need.
>
> The directors would like to know how the involvement of a trading partner might affect Wood Magic's liability to customers, but see no problem in being liable to customers if things go wrong, as they are proud of the company's reputation.

10.1.2 Initial advice

At this stage of the proposed transaction, the solicitor is likely to be asked to advise on two related areas:

(a) What sort of marketing arrangement is most suitable for Wood Magic?

(b) What factors should it take into account when looking for a trading partner?

The facts indicate that some form of agency agreement would be most appropriate:

(a) Wood Magic needs to be able to supervise its trading partner quite closely, and is prepared to commit resources to this supervision.

(b) Wood Magic needs to have some sort of contact with the buyers of its furniture to give them the products they need.

(c) Wood Magic is not concerned about being liable to its ultimate customers.

(d) The target market is in the UK, so supervision of the trading partner should be easier.

Either marketing or sales agency may be suitable, depending on whether the directors simply want the agent to find customers, or whether they want to give the agent authority to make contracts on Wood Magic's behalf. In both cases (but particularly the second), Wood Magic should be looking for a reliable, well-organised and creditworthy business, preferably with an established reputation.

10.1.3 Preliminary considerations

Assume now that Wood Magic's directors have found a suitable trading partner, a company called Lynwood Ltd, which is based in Kingston-upon-Thames. They have checked Lynwood's business credentials and are satisfied that it will make a suitable trading partner. In particular, Wood Magic is satisfied that using Lynwood will give Wood Magic an appropriate level of customer contact. The prospective parties are now negotiating the agency agreement, and have provisionally agreed certain terms, including the following:

(a) Lynwood will have authority to find customers and make contracts on Wood Magic's behalf.

(b) Wood Magic will deliver the finished furniture direct to customers.

(c) Wood Magic will pay Lynwood a monthly commission.

(d) Wood Magic will set the prices for the furniture (as it is custom-made, Wood Magic will supply Lynwood with a detailed 'pricing menu' which will allow Lynwood to work out the price for each order).

(e) Lynwood will keep certain display items of Wood Magic's furniture at its premises to show potential customers what can be achieved. Wood Magic will supply Lynwood with these items free of charge and will remain the owner of the items.

(f) The law of the contract is to be English law (for choice of law, see **Chapter 13**).

On the basis of these instructions, the solicitor is ready to begin drafting the agreement. However, there are several preliminary considerations which should be taken into account.

10.1.3.1 Statutory restrictions on drafting

Many agency agreements are now subject to the Commercial Agents Regulations 1993. The impact of these Regulations will be considered in detail at **10.3** below.

10.1.3.2 How far will the agreement be affected by competition law?

As the law of the contract is to be English law, English competition law is potentially applicable. The Competition Act 1998 contains a basic prohibition (the Chapter I Prohibition) on anti-competitive agreements which is almost identical to Article 101(1) TFEU (formerly Article 81(1) EC, prior to the renumbering of the EC Treaty by the Treaty of Lisbon).

In practice, agency agreements will fall outside the scope of Article 101 as a result of paras 12–21 of the Commission Notice of May 2010 which sets out guidelines on vertical restraints, and which replaced the previous Notice of May 2000. (The European Commission often publishes guidelines to accompany legislation. These guidelines give the background and reasoning behind the relevant legislation. They are not legally binding, but give fairly substantial assistance in interpreting the meaning of the legislation.) Part II of the Notice lists the types of agreement which generally fall outside the scope of Article 101(1), including agency agreements. (Note that, unlike the 2000 Notice, the 2010 Notice no longer refers to 'genuine agency agreements'.)

(a) Paragraph 13 of the Notice states that the determining factor in assessing whether Article 101(1) is applicable to an agency agreement is the 'financial or commercial risk borne by the agent'.

(b) Paragraphs 14–17 then indicate the types of financial or commercial risk that are relevant in deciding whether an agency agreement falls within the scope of Article 101 TFEU. The rules are complex, and a detailed discussion of these is beyond the scope of this chapter. However, the main requirement, under para 16, is that ownership of the goods must not pass to the agent. There is also a non-exhaustive list of indications that an agent is not accepting significant financial or commercial risks, including that:
   (i) the agent does not contribute to the supply of goods or services;
   (ii) the agent is not required to invest in sales promotion;
   (iii) the agent does not maintain at its own cost or risk stocks of the contract goods; and
   (iv) the agent does not create and/or operate after-sales, repair or warranty services (unless it is fully reimbursed by the principal).

On the basis of the terms agreed in principle, there seems a good chance that Wood Magic's proposed agreement will fall outside the scope of Article 101(1), and therefore the Chapter 1 prohibition, as Lynwood does not appear to be accepting financial or commercial risks. In particular:

(a) There is no evidence that Lynwood will ever be the owner of the contract goods, and although Lynwood keeps display items of furniture at its premises, these are not 'stocks' in the normal sense (Lynwood has not paid for them and does not own them).

(b) There is no evidence of Lynwood providing promotional or after-sales services.

10.1.3.3 How far should the agreement expressly refer to the basic principles of agency law?

This will depend upon the relationship of the parties and how familiar they are with the principles of agency law generally. If they are new to one another and have little experience of agency agreements (this would seem to apply to Wood Magic and Lynwood), setting out the principles could be beneficial; both parties will know exactly where they stand. If, however, the parties are both experienced and already have a long-standing relationship, express inclusion of basic agency principles may only offend both sides. If the agency falls within the ambit of the Commercial Agents Regulations 1993, wide fiduciary duties are imposed upon the parties (see **10.3.2**).

10.2 Planning, form and content of an agency agreement

The next step is to plan the structure of the agreement. Whilst doing so, it is essential to consider how the Commercial Agents Regulations 1993 affect each part of the agreement. An agency agreement is likely to follow the structure set out in **Table 10.1** below. The Regulations relevant to each part of this structure are shown in the right-hand column.

Structure of agency agreement	Relevant regulations
(a) Date, parties, recitals	(a) None
(b) Interpretation clause	(b) reg 2
(c) Appointment of agent	(c) regs 1 and 2, 14
(d) Agent's rights and duties	(d) reg 3
(e) Principal's rights and duties	(e) reg 4
(f) Financial provisions	(f) regs 6–12
(g) Termination (if not dealt with elsewhere)	(g) regs 5, 16–20
(h) Boiler-plate clauses	(h) regs 21 and 22
(i) Signatures	(i) reg 13
(j) Schedules	(j) None

Table 10.1 Structure of an agency agreement

Note that there is no requirement under the Commercial Agents Regulations 1993 that the agreement should be in writing or signed, but under reg 13 either party has the right to request a signed written document from the other. Clearly it would be unusual for a commercial agency agreement not be in writing.

This section will look at the content of a simple agency agreement, and then the effect of the Commercial Agents Regulations 1993 will be discussed in **10.3**.

10.2.1 Introduction to the agreement

This section of the agreement is likely to cover the following areas:

(a) a preliminary clause setting out the date of the agreement, the parties and any recitals which are felt to be necessary;

(b) a definitions and interpretation clause; and

(c) a clause dealing with the appointment of the agent.

10.2.1.1 Date, parties, recitals

The date of the agreement should cause few problems, but the description of the parties may need some thought. The principal will often be a manufacturer (as with Wood Magic), but, as agency can be created at any stage of the marketing chain, it could be, for example, a wholesaler.

Recitals may be useful for setting out the basis on which the parties are making their agreement. For example, Wood Magic and Lynwood might use a recital to show that their relationship is such that the agent (Lynwood) is not accepting significant financial or commercial risk, and to indicate therefore that the parties believe that the agreement will not be affected by competition law.

10.2.1.2 Definitions and interpretation

Two definitions which are likely to require some thought are 'Products' and 'Territory'.

'Products'

It is useful for the agreement to contain a comprehensive definition of the products which the agent is marketing on the principal's behalf. In the case of the agreement under consideration, this is clearly Wood Magic's furniture, but a more precise definition is likely to be needed. For example, will the agent handle the principal's whole product range, or only some of the principal's products? Will it handle all products of a particular type which the principal manufactures? This is often best dealt with by listing the relevant products in a schedule to the agreement.

Often the main problem in a continuing relationship is how to handle changes which may occur (eg what will happen if the principal ceases to manufacture a particular product or begins to manufacture a new one?). To cover this, the parties should decide matters such as:

(a) whether the agreement should include provision for a mutually agreed variation;

(b) whether the principal will force the agent to take up a new product (either with or without notice);

(c) whether any changes to the product range should be made only with the agent's consent.

The answers will obviously depend upon the relationship between the parties, their relative needs and their bargaining strengths.

'Territory'

Where will the agent market the goods? In Lynwood's case, the relevant area is to be London and the South-East of England. In many cases, defining 'territory' will be straightforward, but it should be expressed as precisely as possible. If this is not made clear, it may lead to disputes over territorial rights between different agents and between agent and principal. This may also involve disputes over exclusivity of the agency (see **10.2.1.3**, 'Agent's authority', below).

10.2.1.3 Appointment of the agent

The appointment clause defines the agent's role in the agreement, and is perhaps the single most important clause in an agency agreement. In particular, it defines the extent of the agent's authority to bind the principal, which in turn will determine a number of other matters. It is likely to cover the following areas.

Agent's authority

In a sales agency agreement, the agent is given authority to enter contracts on the principal's behalf for the sale of the products. As the agent binds the principal, the principal must honour any contracts which the agent has made on its behalf. As noted previously, a marketing agent's authority will be more restricted; it will either be limited to finding customers and introducing them to the principal, or to finding customers and conducting some negotiation on the principal's behalf without, however, binding the principal. Whatever the parties decide is best for them, the appointment clause should always make clear the extent of the agent's authority.

Agent's operations

In attempting to define the geographical limits of the agent's operations and the extent to which the agent will be protected from competition by others within this territory, the clause should be as clear as possible. As discussed in **Chapter 9,** a particular problem arises with the use of the expressions 'sole' agency and 'exclusive' agency. It is, therefore, unsafe to define the scope of the agent's protection from competition in the territory simply by using the words 'sole' or 'exclusive' in the agreement.

It is better to state clearly whether the principal can appoint other agents or market the products in the territory itself (and in what circumstances). It is also sensible to make clear how far (if at all) the agent can extend its operations beyond the territory. On this last point, note that forbidding the agent to accept unsolicited orders from outside the territory can cause real problems if Article 101 TFEU does apply to the agreement (see **10.1.3.2**).

Duration and termination

The appointment clause often also deals with duration and termination of the agreement. The parties may consider entering into a fixed-term agreement. It may be desirable to grant the agent a reasonably long initial fixed term, in order to give it an incentive to build up the business. However, there are, of course, other possibilities. If the parties want an indefinite term, or a fixed term followed by an indefinite term, a suitable notice provision should be included. (Note that under reg 15 of the Commercial Agents Regulations 1993, the agent is entitled to certain minimum periods of notice – see **10.3.5.1**.)

Del credere agency

If the agency is to be a del credere agency (ie, where the agent agrees to guarantee the customer's performance of the contract in return for an additional commission), this is likely to be an appropriate part of the agreement in which to include the del credere provision.

In the proposed agreement between Wood Magic and Lynwood, the solicitor will need to take instructions on most of the preceding matters, as there is no evidence that the parties have yet considered any of them (except the matter of Lynwood's authority).

10.2.2 The agent's rights and duties

10.2.2.1 Introduction

The principal needs to have an appropriate amount of control over its sales agent's activities, so the section on agent's duties is likely to be the longest of the agreement. Broadly speaking, the principal will want to ensure (as far as possible) that the agent observes certain limitations (eg, in a sales agency, that the agent does not make unsuitable contracts on the principal's behalf), while still encouraging the agent to exploit the agency to its full potential. It may be appropriate when drafting the agreement to have a clause relating to general duties, followed by individual clauses covering particular duties (such as advertising and promotion).

10.2.2.2 General duties

The principal may want to provide that the agent uses its 'best endeavours' in promoting and marketing the products. 'Best endeavours' does, however, put a considerable burden upon the agent (it means that the agent must make every effort possible to find customers and make contracts), and the agent may consider this duty too strict.

10.2.2.3 Specific duties

Licences and permits

It may sometimes be necessary to obtain a licence for the sale of the products in the territory, or to comply with local regulations. Clearly, this is unlikely to be a problem for Wood Magic and Lynwood. However, if this is the case, the agreement should allocate responsibility for doing so. The solicitor should consider which party is best placed to obtain any licence or comply with any regulations, and draft accordingly. It is often sensible to make the agent responsible for getting permits and licences for the sale of the products and in respect of its own performance. It is also customary to provide that the agent must comply with laws and regulations concerning the sale of the products, but not those concerning the nature of the products or their packaging; this will normally be for the principal to do.

Promotion and marketing

The principal will want the agent to promote the principal's business and to keep up good relations with customers. It is clear, for example, in the agreement under consideration, that Wood Magic and its products already enjoy an excellent reputation, and Wood Magic will obviously want this to continue. The principal may want to make this duty more specific, for example by requiring the agent's staff to be available when needed for meetings with the principal or potential customers, or for attending trade fairs and other relevant marketing events. The principal may also require the agent to provide premises which the principal considers suitable (it may also want the right to inspect these premises from time to time), and to set up proper office facilities and a suitable organisation for the efficient operation of the agency.

The parties need to agree which of them will have the responsibility and expense of advertising. It is common to find a clause which requires the agent to pay for the advertising, but to use only material which has either been supplied or approved by the principal, thus allowing the principal to keep considerable control of the agent's activities. For example, Wood Magic may want Lynwood to use advertising and promotional tactics which Wood Magic knows to be effective from its own marketing experience.

Note that under the Notice of May 2010 (see **10.1.3.2**) if the agent is 'directly or indirectly obliged to invest in sales promotion' (eg, by contributing to the principal's advertising budget), this may amount to incurring a 'risk' which would bring the agreement within the ambit of Article 101 TFEU. Caution may therefore be required.

Stock

Principal and agent may agree that the agent will itself keep stocks of the principal's products in order to fulfil the contracts it makes on the principal's behalf. If the parties have agreed, however, that the principal will supply customers direct, the stock clause could be much simpler, or perhaps omitted altogether. If the agent is to keep stocks of the products, the agreement should deal with the level of stock which the agent is to carry and what is to happen to stock while it is on the agent's premises.

The principal will not want the stock to be counted as part of the agent's assets, and therefore claimable by the agent's creditors if the agent becomes insolvent, so it is desirable to provide, for example, that the stock is clearly marked as being the principal's and is stored separately from other goods while on the agent's premises. The principal may want to add the right to inspect the agent's premises from time to time to ensure that the agent is complying with this.

Note that if it is clear that the agent bears the risk of loss while the stock is on its premises, the Notice of May 2010 would probably cease to apply, and Article 101 TFEU problems might arise (see **10.1.3.2**). Similarly, if there is any requirement for the agency to provide specialised premises or handling facilities, etc, these could be treated as 'market-specific investments' which could comprise 'risk' for these purposes. However, Wood Magic and Lynwood will not have problems in this respect: Wood Magic will deliver direct to customers.

Duty to supply information

It may be useful (eg, in order to plan future products, or to improve existing ones) for the principal to receive feedback from the agent on how customers are reacting to the products. How much information the principal wants from the agent, and on what matters, will obviously vary from case to case; for example, some principals may be satisfied with a clause which requires the agent to report 'from time to time', others may want the agent to report on a regular basis and at definite times. The principal may also wish to restrict the agent's right to get involved in disputes or proceedings concerning the products without the principal's written consent.

Confidentiality

An agency agreement will not always require highly sophisticated confidentiality provisions; if the agent is simply finding customers and making contracts, it may not be privy to any information or process which could be described as confidential. If, however, the agent will be handling confidential material, the principal will need to consider how best to protect its interests. This is usually done by making clear what information is confidential, and what the agent is and is not entitled to do in relation to confidential information. In the agreement under consideration, Wood Magic will need to decide if Lynwood needs any confidential information (eg about how the furniture is made) to be able to fulfil its role as sales agent. For more on the law of confidence (and, in particular, the implied duty of confidentiality), see **Chapter 23**.

Intellectual property

This section of the agreement is likely to vary considerably and will not be necessary at all if the agent does not 'handle' any intellectual property (IP) rights under the agreement. If such a clause is necessary, its specific nature and extent will vary according to the circumstances and the type of intellectual property involved. Generally speaking, however, the clause will be designed to protect the principal's rights in the intellectual property and prevent the agent from getting any interest in it. It may be necessary to include clauses which:

(a) require the agent to inform the principal of any infringement of the principal's rights in the territory, or any claim by a third party that the principal has infringed its rights;

(b) require the agent to act on the principal's instructions and at the principal's request to institute or defend proceedings, or to do whatever else is necessary to maintain the validity and enforceability of the principal's rights;

(c) state that the agent is not to have, or seek to gain, any interest in the principal's rights (eg, trade marks on products, goodwill);

(d) require the agent not to damage the principal's goodwill by using confusingly similar trade names or trade marks, or behaving in any way that would invalidate the principal's rights or be inconsistent with them. A clause of this type would in most agreements need to be made subject to the rights of the agent and any third party to challenge the validity of the principal's intellectual property, or Article 101 TFEU problems could arise (see **Chapter 28** for a fuller discussion of the relationship of intellectual property and competition law, and how this may affect the drafting of commercial agreements).

The solicitor will need to take full instructions from Wood Magic about IP rights which may be involved in the marketing (eg, any trade mark which Wood Magic uses, and any registered or unregistered design rights relevant to the furniture).

Miscellaneous clauses relating to the agent's duties

It is quite common to find a clause in the 'Agent's Duties' section which gathers together clauses which do not fall under any other heading. Obviously, the solicitor will need to decide whether this is appropriate or necessary in the light of Wood Magic's instructions, but a 'Miscellaneous Provisions' clause could include the following terms:

(a) that the agent will meet targets set by the principal. Depending on the nature of the agency, these might be for numbers of customers found and introduced, or numbers of contracts made on the principal's behalf;

(b) that the agent will not pledge the principal's credit;

(c) that the agent will not become involved in or try to settle any dispute about the products without first obtaining the principal's permission to do so;

(d) that the agent will not do anything which might prejudice the principal's business or the marketing of its products;

(e) that where the agent makes contracts on the principal's behalf, the contracts will be made on the principal's standard terms;

(f) that the agent will not become involved in any way with goods which compete with the products which are the subject of the agency agreement.

Note that the Commercial Agents Regulations 1993 impose mandatory duties on the agent (see **10.3.2**).

10.2.3 The principal's rights and duties

These are often less onerous than the agent's duties to the principal. Again, the solicitor will need to take instructions from Wood Magic as to what it intends its rights and duties as principal to be. However, the following provisions are commonly encountered (note how many of them complement duties which have already been imposed on the agent):

(a) the right for the principal to amend the listed products which are the subject of the agreement;

(b) the duty for the principal to pay commission to the agent. It is customary for an agent to be remunerated by commission; the duty to pay it may be stated as part of the principal's rights and duties, or it may be included as part of a complete financial provisions clause (see **10.3.4**);

(c) the duty of the principal to comply with all relevant laws relating to the composition, packaging and labelling of the goods; this is likely to make sense, as these matters will be under the principal's control;

(d) the duty for the principal to supply advertising and promotional material;

(e) the duty for the principal to pass on to the agent any information which might assist the agent in marketing the goods;

(f) if the agreement requires the agent to hold stock, the duty for the principal to supply stock (this should also encompass how and when stock is to be supplied, ordering procedure, returns and so on);

(g) the duty for the principal to provide an after-sales service for the products;

(h) the duty for the principal to indemnify the agent against any liability which the agent incurs as a result of being held out as the principal's agent (eg, costs and expenses which the agent may incur in relation to claims arising out of the agency).

Again, the Commercial Agents Regulations 1993 impose mandatory duties on the principal (see **10.3.3**).

10.2.4 Financial provisions

This section of the agreement is likely to vary considerably in content and layout. The parties are obviously free to choose the form of agreement which suits them best, and could combine the financial provisions with the principal's and the agent's duties respectively, if appropriate. However (especially where the financial provisions in the agreement are elaborate), it will often make sense to deal with them in a separate section relating to both parties.

10.2.4.1 Commission

Most genuine agency agreements deal expressly with matters such as how the commission is to be calculated, and when it is to be paid. All Wood Magic and Lynwood have agreed so far is that Wood Magic will pay Lynwood a monthly commission, so the solicitor will clearly need to take full instructions on the precise requirements. In practice, there may be considerable variation in the way commission can be dealt with, but it is important to note that under the Commercial Agents Regulations 1993 there are mandatory provisions in relation to commission, and the parties may not always be completely free to make their own arrangements (see **10.3.4**).

10.2.4.2 Accounting arrangements for commission

The agreement should also deal with how the agent is to receive the commission. A number of possibilities arise. For example, the agent may collect payment for the goods from customers, and then account to the principal after deducting its commission. If the agent collects money, the parties may prefer the agent to pay the gross sum to the principal, which then pays commission over to the agent. Alternatively, the principal may collect payment from customers and then pay the agent a regular amount of commission. If the parties are based in different countries, it is also particularly important that the agreement should state the currency in which the commission is to be paid.

10.2.4.3 Deductions

If the agent does collect money from customers on behalf of the principal, it may sometimes be obliged to deduct certain sums (eg in respect of local taxes) before handing over the balance. If this is the case, the parties should deal with the deductions expressly in the agreement.

10.2.4.4 General accounting arrangements

The parties may wish to provide, where appropriate, for the payment of interest on any sums outstanding if either side fails to account to the other (the agent in respect of money collected from customers, the principal in respect of commission). The agreement should also provide for the keeping of accounts and other financial records. This should cover not only which records each party is to keep, but also whether either party has the right to inspect or ask for copies of the other side's records.

10.2.5 Termination

10.2.5.1 What circumstances will allow either party to terminate?

Circumstances in which either side may want the right to terminate the agreement will normally include:

(a) either side getting into financial difficulties, such as receivership, winding up or making a voluntary arrangement;

(b) breach of the agreement (consider drafting a notice procedure under which the party in breach can be required to remedy the breach where possible); and

(c) change in control of the agent if the agent is a company.

It is normally desirable to set out the circumstances expressly in the agreement. See also **10.3.5.1** on notice requirements in cases within the Commercial Agents Regulations 1993.

10.2.5.2 What will the effects of termination be?

The agreement should state how termination will affect the following:

(a) any stocks of the product, samples and advertising material held by the agent;

(b) sales which the agent has already negotiated, but in respect of which no moneys have been paid over;

(c) the agent's authority to negotiate on behalf of the principal;

(d) the agent's duty of confidentiality;

(e) the agent's right to compensation on termination.

10.2.5.3 Does the principal need to pay anything to the agent on termination?

This will normally be a matter for agreement between the parties. However, there are mandatory provisions under the Commercial Agents Regulations 1993 in relation to termination which require the principal to give the agent a 'pay off' on termination of the agreement in the form of either indemnity or compensation (see **10.3.5.2**). If the Regulations apply to the agreement, it is important that the client should be advised of the options. There is still considerable debate in practice as to whether an agreement should go for indemnity or compensation, how far the agreement should deal expressly with the point (in most cases, the agent will be entitled to a pay-off regardless of what the agreement says) and how any termination payment clause should be worded.

10.2.6 Miscellaneous

An agency agreement will usually have a 'boiler-plate', containing a number of miscellaneous clauses (eg arbitration, notices, choice of law and jurisdiction). Boiler-plate clauses in general are considered in **Chapter 1**.

10.2.7 Particular points to consider when drafting a marketing agency agreement

A standard marketing agency agreement will be substantially similar in content and layout to a sales agency agreement; the main differences will result from the fact that a marketing agent has no authority to conclude contracts on the principal's behalf.

10.2.7.1 Appointment

The agreement should define the nature of the agent's operations, with a clear statement that the agent is not authorised to enter into contracts on the principal's behalf. Normally, the agent also agrees not to describe itself as a sales agent.

Care needs to be taken about defining the exact limits of the agent's authority: is it to have authority only to find potential customers and pass them on to the principal; or is it to have authority to do at least some negotiating on the principal's behalf (without actually making any contract)? Although the terms 'marketing' and 'introducing' agency are widely used, they have no legally exact meaning, and so should not be used without additional explanation to make the extent of the agent's authority clear.

Note that an agent which does not have 'continuing authority' to negotiate on the principal's behalf is not a 'commercial agent' within the meaning of the Commercial Agents Regulations 1993 (see **10.3.1.1**).

10.2.7.2 Introducing potential customers

The agreement should provide that the agent is to pass on all orders and enquiries promptly to the principal.

10.2.7.3 Principal's response to potential customers

Is it desirable or possible to provide that the principal should comply with all orders generated by the agent's efforts? A marketing agent does not bind its principal. If the principal refuses to accept an order from a particular customer introduced by the agent, however, this could damage the agent's reputation, and possibly make it more difficult for the agent to earn commission in future. The parties may be able to agree some sort of compromise, for example that the principal will comply with orders from all customers, as long as it is satisfied that they are good credit risks.

10.2.7.4 Agent's duties

A marketing agent is very unlikely to carry stock or collect payments on the principal's behalf.

10.3 Commercial Agents Regulations 1993

The Commercial Agents Regulations 1993 came into force on 1 January 1994 and enacted into English law the requirements of the EC Directive on the Co-ordination of Laws of Member States relating to Self-Employed Commercial Agents (Directive 86/653/EEC).

The Commercial Agents Regulations 1993 lay down rules in relation to a number of important areas of an agency agreement, in particular:

(a) the rights and obligations of both parties;

(b) the agent's remuneration; and

(c) the conclusion and termination of the agency contract.

Many, but not all, agency agreements will be subject to these Regulations. Where they do apply, it is essential when drafting or analysing an agency agreement to ensure that it complies with the Regulations. Provisions which do not comply will be unenforceable.

10.3.1 Scope of the Commercial Agents Regulations 1993

Before starting to draft the agreement, the solicitor should consider whether the Regulations do, in fact, apply to the agreement. The Regulations 'govern the relations between commercial agents and their principals ... in relation to the activities of commercial agents in Great Britain' (reg 1(1)). Provision is made in reg 1(3) (as amended) for agreements which are to be governed by the law of another Member State. Thus the agent must conduct his activities within Great Britain. Note that the Regulations do not extend to Northern Ireland (reg 2(5)).

10.3.1.1 Meaning of 'commercial agent'

'Commercial agent' is defined in reg 2(1) as:

> a self-employed intermediary who has continuing authority to negotiate the sale or purchase of goods on behalf of another person (the 'principal') or to negotiate and conclude the sale or purchase of goods on behalf of and in the name of that principal ...

This definition means that the type of 'marketing' agent which only has authority to find customers and is not authorised to 'negotiate' on the principal's behalf will not be a 'commercial agent'. Whether an agent falls within this definition is not always straightforward. Note that a company can be a self-employed intermediary.

In *Mercantile International Group plc v Chuan Soon Huant Industrial Group Ltd* [2002] EWCA Civ 288, because the claimant clearly had authority to negotiate in the principal's name, the Court of Appeal held the agreement was consistent with the agent being a 'commercial agent', and the Regulations therefore applied.

By contrast, see *Sagal (t/a Bunz UK) v Atelier Bunz GmbH* [2008] EWHC 789 (Comm), where, in a complex contractual relationship, the claimant was held not be a commercial agent. Despite all other appearances, the claimant did not negotiate the sale of jewellery as an intermediary; he negotiated the sale on his own behalf.

10.3.1.2 Meaning of 'negotiate'

In *PJ Pipe & Valve Co Ltd v Audco India Ltd* [2005] EWHC 1904 (QB), the claimant's role consisted of identifying opportunities for the defendant, advising it of those opportunities and promoting it to potential customers, rather than negotiating specific terms on the defendant's behalf. The High Court gave the words 'to negotiate' a broad meaning, ruling that if the agent spent time and resources on developing the principal's goodwill, and it was in the principal's commercial interest for the agent to do this, this could amount to 'negotiation', just as much as negotiating specific terms of the contract between principal and customer.

10.3.1.3 Situations in which the Regulations will *not* apply

The Regulations will not apply:

(a) where the agent's activities are not within Great Britain, (although equivalent regulations apply throughout the EEA);

(b) where the agent does not come within the definition of 'commercial agent' (reg 2(1));

(c) where the agent is an agent of a type listed in reg 2(2);

(d) where the agent's activities as a commercial agent are to be considered secondary under reg 2(3), (4) and the Schedule. The drafting of the Schedule is extremely complex, and it is not always clear when an agent is involved in secondary activities. Examples include part-time agents or agents who sell through mail order catalogues or brochures. From *Light v Ty Europe Ltd* [2004] 1 CLC 71, it seems that sub-agents who do not have a contractual relationship with the principal to a sales agency agreement would fall within this category;

(e) where the contract covers the supply of services rather than goods.

Assuming that Lynwood falls within the definition of 'commercial agent' (which it will, as long as it has in practice 'continuing authority to negotiate and conclude the sale ... of goods on behalf of another person'), the Regulations will apply to its agreement with Wood Magic.

The checklist below summarises the steps to consider to help decide whether the Commercial Agents Regulations 1993 apply.

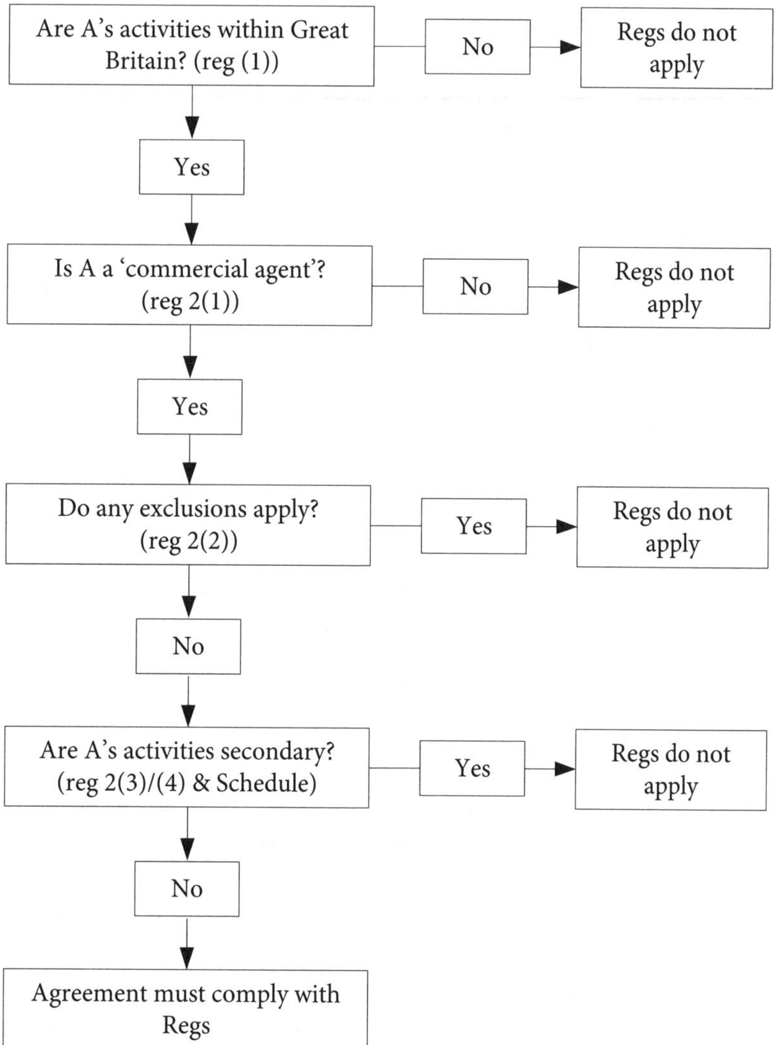

10.3.2 Agent's duties

Regulation 3 of the Commercial Agents Regulations 1993 governs the agent's duties:

(a) By reg 3(1), a commercial agent must look after the interests of his principal and act dutifully and in good faith.

(b) Regulation 3(2) deals with a number of specific developments of these general duties; for example reg 3(2)(c) requires the agent to comply with reasonable instructions.

10.3.3 Principal's duties

Regulation 4 governs the principal's duties:

(a) By reg 4(1), a principal must act dutifully and in good faith in its relations with its commercial agent.

(b) Regulation 4(2) and (3) deal with specific aspects of these general duties, for example there is a mandatory duty to notify the agent within a reasonable period once the principal anticipates that the value of commercial transactions will be significantly lower than normal expectations (see reg 4(2)(b)).

(c) Under reg 15 there is a duty to give minimum periods of notice to terminate the agreement, except where immediate termination would be justified by conduct or other exceptional circumstances (eg repudiatory breach or frustration, etc). Note that this provision applies to either party (see **10.3.5.1**).

10.3.4 Financial provisions

The principal must ensure that the remuneration provisions in the agreements are consistent with the Regulations:

(a) Regulation 7 provides for the agent's right to commission on transactions which are concluded during the agency agreement.

(b) Regulation 8 gives the agent certain rights to commission even after the agency agreement has ended. Regulation 8(a) provides that the agent will be entitled to post-termination commission if the transaction is 'mainly attributable' to its efforts whilst the agency agreement was still subsisting and the contract is concluded within 'a reasonable time' after termination. The problem here is that both phrases are somewhat vague. In *Tigana Ltd v Decoro Ltd* [2003] EWHC 23 (QB) the agent was awarded the equivalent of nine months' commission in relation to such transactions, and the court considered the circumstances where the transaction could be said to be 'mainly attributable' to the agent's efforts.

(c) Regulation 9 deals with the situation where a new agent is appointed and under reg 7 the new agent would be entitled to commission on the same transaction as the previous agent. The claim of the 'old' agent will prevail over the new agent, unless it can be shown that it is 'equitable' for them to share. Again, the terminology is vague, and it is not always clear what the new agent would have to do to meet this requirement.

(d) Regulation 10 controls when commission becomes due and when it must be paid. The agreement should deal with this.

  (i) *Payment due.* There are three options available to the parties, but they should bear in mind that payment will become due at the latest when the customer 'executes' (or performs) its part of the transaction.

  (ii) *Payment made.* Payment must then be made at the latest at the end of the month following the quarter on which it became due.

(e) The agent's right to commission can be extinguished only in the circumstances described in reg 11, ie broadly, that the contract arranged by the agent will not be carried out but that this is not the principal's fault.

(f) Regulation 12 obliges the principal to supply the agent with a statement of commission, and entitles the agent to demand the information it needs (including 'an extract from the books' to check the amount of commission due to it).

10.3.5 Termination

10.3.5.1 Notice provisions

Regulation 15(2) provides for minimum notice periods to be given by the parties:

(a) one month's notice for the first year;

(b) two month's notice for the second year;

(c) three month's notice for the third and subsequent years.

Under reg 15(3), the parties can agree to longer notice periods, but the agreement can never provide a shorter notice period for the principal than the agent. Unless there is contrary provision in the contract, the notice period must expire at the end of a calendar month.

10.3.5.2 Termination payments

The provisions of the Commercial Agents Regulations 1993 in relation to termination payments are complex, but are of crucial importance when drafting the agreement. In most cases, reg 17 obliges the principal to give the agent a 'pay-off' on termination of the agreement. This right arises automatically on termination of the agreement, not simply when the principal is in breach of contract. The pay-off may take the form of indemnity or compensation, depending on the circumstances, but the principal cannot contract out of its obligation to pay.

The position under reg 17 may be briefly summarised as follows:

(a) Regulation 17(1) provides that, on termination of the agency contract, the agent is entitled either to be 'indemnified' in accordance with reg 17(3)–(5), or to be 'compensated for damage' in accordance with reg 17(6)–(7).

(b) Regulation 17(2) states that except where the agreement provides otherwise, the agent is entitled to be compensated rather than indemnified.

(c) Regulation 18 gives the grounds for excluding the payment of either indemnity or compensation, broadly speaking, where the termination is due to the agent's conduct (which would justify termination under reg 16, eg repudiatory breach) or the agent has itself terminated the agreement or assigned its rights and duties under the agreement. The grounds for excluding payment are extremely limited. The agent will still be entitled to compensation if, for example, the agreement comes to an end as a result of:

    (i) effluxion of time; see, eg, *Cooper v Pure Fishing (UK) Ltd* [2004] 2 Lloyd's Rep 518; or

    (ii) age, illness or infirmity of the agent (reg 18(b)(ii)).

(d) Regulation 19 states that the parties cannot derogate from regs 17 or 18, which are consequently mandatory provisions. Any provision in the agreement which removes or cuts down the agent's right to a pay-off will be of no effect. See *Crane v Sky In-Home Service Ltd* [2007] EWHC 66 (Ch).

(e) Under reg 17(9) the agent must inform the principal of its intention to claim (either for indemnity or compensation) within one year from termination of the agreement, or the agent will lose its right to claim.

The indemnity option is based on German law (it is sometimes referred to as the 'German model') and may seem attractive to principals because it provides a limit on the payment the agent can get, ie no more than one year's commission, based on the agent's actual annual remuneration over the past five years (see reg 17(4)). There is also some evidence in practice that the actual payment will often be less than this.

The 1993 Regulations are considerably less clear about what 'compensation for damage' is. As far as the Directive is concerned, 'compensation' in this context is based on French agency law (sometimes referred to as the 'French model'), and often, in practice, French law allows the agent on termination a sum equivalent to two years' commission.

Authority on the meaning of 'compensation for damage' was somewhat scarce and contradictory, and it remained unclear for over a decade whether the French model would be followed in the UK. However, since July 2007 there has been House of Lords' authority on the calculation of compensation for damage: *Lonsdale v Howard & Hallam Ltd* [2007] UKHL 32. The House of Lords confirmed the approach previously taken by the Court of Appeal:

(a) It was inappropriate in the UK to apply the French law which exists in this area; in particular, there was no reason why courts in the UK should use two years' commission as a basis for calculating compensation for damage. French and English practices on damages differed, not because their respective courts were applying different rules of law but because they were operating in different markets.

(b) The House of Lords noted that, in *Honyvem Informazioni Commerciali Srl v Mariella de Zotti* (Case C-465/04) [2006] OJ C131/19, the ECJ had made it clear that the method of calculation of the damage which the agent suffers as a result of termination is a matter for the law of each Member State, as long as calculation is done consistently with the

Directive. The purpose of reg 17 was to compensate for damage to the agent's business as a result of the termination.

(c) Compensation should be calculated on the value of the agency business to the agent (including goodwill) at the date of termination of the agency. In giving the leading opinion in the House of Lords' judgment, Lord Hoffmann noted that this should be assessed on the basis of what a buyer would be prepared to pay to 'stand in the shoes' of the agent.

Even now, commentators are still somewhat divided on the likely impact of the ruling in the long term. Most agree that it brings clarity to a complex area of law, but there is some concern that the decision favours principals at the expense of agents, especially where (as in *Lonsdale* itself) the agency business is declining.

Note that reg 17(5) expressly provides that the grant of an indemnity 'shall not prevent the commercial agent from seeking damages'. It is generally assumed here that 'damages' refers to normal contractual damages, and that this provision would be relevant where, for example, the agreement has been unjustifiably terminated with no or insufficient notice. There is no express equivalent of this provision in relation to compensation for damage. In *Tigana Ltd v Decoro Ltd* (see **10.3.4**), it was held that damages for breach of contract which would otherwise be payable on termination of an agency are subsumed into compensation under reg 17; the agent would not get both. *PJ Pipe & Valve Co Ltd v Audco India Ltd* [2005] EWHC 1904 (QB) illustrates that there may be circumstances where the agent can claim damages as well as compensation, but the court will always attempt to avoid double counting, thereby limiting these claims.

10.3.6 Derogation

A final consideration is how far it is possible to derogate from the Commercial Agents Regulations 1993. Some of the Regulations contain non-derogation provisions, others do not. The literal approach would be to consider that where no derogation provision is included, it may be possible to derogate. However, in *Graham Page v Combined Shipping and Trading Co Ltd* [1997] 3 All ER 656 the Court of Appeal did emphasise that because the Regulations are implementing legislation, courts must adopt a purposive approach to their interpretation. Lord Justice Staughton was in no doubt that the main purpose of the Commercial Agents Directive was to protect the agent: 'commercial agents are a downtrodden race, and need and should be afforded protection against their principals'. Thus, if the Regulations are interpreted purposively, then derogation would not be possible. In *Ingmar v Eaton Leonard* [2002] ECC, the court was of the opinion that derogation from reg 8 would be possible only in so far as it does not thwart the purpose of the Directive. The solicitor should always advise the client of the risks of any attempt at derogation.

Derogation	
Regulations with non-derogation provisions	**Derogation not mentioned**
Regs 3 and 4 (reg 5)	Reg 6
Reg 10 (reg 10(4))	Reg 7
Reg 11 (reg 11(3))	Reg 8
Reg 12 (reg 12(3))	Reg 9
Reg 13 (reg 13(2))	Reg 14
Reg 15 (reg 15(2))	Reg 20
Regs 17 and 18 (reg 19)	

Table 10.2 Derogation

10.4 Drafting a distribution agreement

10.4.1 Introduction

This section continues with the Wood Magic example (see **10.1.1**), but in relation to a different aspect of Wood Magic's business.

> **Example**
>
> Assume that Wood Magic has, for the past five years, carried on a small sideline business of manufacturing ready-made furniture (such as coffee tables, dining tables and chairs). The directors feel that this side of the business is now ready to be developed much further. Wood Magic recently rented a stand at a trade fair in Paris to show this furniture. The response was such that the directors believe that there is an important market in France, consisting of wealthy French customers with second homes and English 'ex-pats' who have settled in France.
>
> In the short term, the directors believe that Wood Magic can spare the time and commitment needed to establish relations with a 'trading partner' in France; the directors who attended the trade fair made some promising contacts and believe that one company in particular, Bois Massif SA, could be the partner Wood Magic is looking for. However, assuming that they do establish relations with a partner they can trust, the directors would, in the long term, seek to market Wood Magic's goods in France in a way which does not require close day-to-day supervision. They believe that if they give the right training to the French partner at the outset, it will be easy for the partner to sell the ready-made furniture, without major involvement from Wood Magic.
>
> The difficulty for Wood Magic in its expansion is that it has little experience in the export trade, and it admits that its collective knowledge of the French language and of French business practices is negligible.

10.4.2 Initial advice

At this stage (as with an agency agreement) the solicitor is likely to be asked to advise on two related areas:

(a) What sort of marketing arrangement is most suitable for Wood Magic?

(b) What factors should it take into account when looking for a trading partner?

This time, the facts indicate that a distribution agreement would be appropriate:

(a) The goods can be marketed in France in the same form in which Wood Magic sells them (eg, no customising is necessary).

(b) Wood Magic needs the help of a trading partner based in the target territory, because it is not familiar with that territory's language or business practices.

(c) The marketing of the goods does not require much supervision by Wood Magic (after initial training has been given).

(d) Wood Magic will not be liable in contract to the ultimate customers.

Note that whereas some of these factors would not necessarily make an agency agreement unsuitable, they indicate that the main advantages of that type of agreement (ie supervision of agent, contact with customers: see **9.4**) are not really needed here. A distribution agreement is likely to be the cheapest and most efficient way to market these goods.

Wood Magic will need to be aware, however, that, depending on the terms which are included in the agreement with Bois Massif and the circumstances in which the agreement operates, competition law problems may arise (see **10.6** and **Chapter 27**).

As with the agency agreement, Wood Magic should check out any potential trading partner very carefully; for example, creditworthiness is even more important here than in the agency agreement, as the distributor will actually be buying the goods from Wood Magic, and therefore Wood Magic is directly at risk of non-payment by its trading partner.

10.4.3 Preliminary considerations

Assume now that Wood Magic's directors are satisfied that Bois Massif is the right trading partner for them in France, and have begun detailed negotiations over the terms of the distribution agreement which the parties will enter. They have still to decide how to deal with many areas of the agreement, but have agreed the following in principle:

(a) In order to give Bois Massif the best possible chance of getting the distributorship established, Wood Magic has agreed that it will not appoint any other distributors (or agents) for the sale of its goods in France, and that it will not sell any of its own goods in France.

(b) In return, Bois Massif has agreed to concentrate on the French market only: it will not actively seek customers from outside France (although it will be free to fulfil unsolicited orders).

What considerations arise for the solicitor in drafting the agreement?

10.4.3.1 Agency and distribution agreements: similarities and differences

It is important to note that the relationship of distributor and supplier is created and defined by the distribution agreement. Many of the clauses already discussed in relation to agency agreements are equally relevant to distribution agreements: these include interpretation, appointment, duration and many of the 'duties' clauses (allowing for some necessary modifications: see below). However, a distribution agreement is essentially an agreement for the sale of goods from the supplier to the distributor, and so matters relevant to drafting a sale of goods agreement must be considered (see **Chapter 2**).

10.4.3.2 Distribution agreements and competition law

This topic is discussed in more detail in **Chapter 27**. Briefly, however, a distribution agreement is more likely than an agency agreement to infringe Article 101(1) TFEU as, depending on the terms which the parties include and the circumstances in which the agreement operates, its potential for affecting trade and competition is greater. However, there are several ways of avoiding the impact of Article 101(1) TFEU. For example, the agreement may be ignored by the Commission if it falls within the Notice on Agreements of Minor Importance (to advise on this, it would be necessary to know the parties' market shares; see **27.5**). Even if this does not apply, it may be possible to draft the agreement to comply with a relevant block exemption.

In the agreement under consideration, Wood Magic is offering Bois Massif 'exclusive territory' and Bois Massif will agree not to sell actively outside that territory. Both parties are therefore limiting their commercial freedom, and (in theory at least) doing so in a way which may affect trade and competition (eg French buyers will have only one authorised source of supply within France) and infringe Article 101(1) TFEU. However, if in practice the agreement contained only these two restrictions, the block exemption contained in Regulation 330/2010 would apply to the agreement, and therefore Article 101(1) TFEU would not. This block exemption is discussed in more detail at **27.5.2.1**.

10.5 Planning, form and content of a distribution agreement

Again, the solicitor will need to plan the structure of the agreement and look at the competition elements, and consider how they affect each part of the agreement. A distribution agreement is likely to follow the structure set out in **Table 10.3** below. Likely anti-competitive terms relevant to each part of this structure are shown in the right-hand column:

Structure of Distribution Agreement	Anti-competitive terms
(a) Date, parties, recitals	(a) not relevant (n/r)
(b) Interpretation clause	(b) n/r
(c) Appointment of distributor	(c) Exclusivity, especially if in conjunction with territorial restrictions
(d) Standard terms of sale (may be in Schedule)	(d) n/r
(e) Distributor's rights and duties	(e) Price-fixing, export bans, non-compete obligations, no-challenge clauses (IP)
(f) Supplier's rights and duties	(f) n/r
(g) Termination (if not dealt with elsewhere)	(g) Post-termination non-compete obligations
(h) Boiler-plate clauses	(h) n/r
(i) Signatures	(i) n/r
(j) Schedules	(j) n/r

Table 10.3 Structure of a distribution agreement

10.5.1 Date, parties, recitals, interpretation

This part of the agreement is likely to be very similar to the corresponding section of a sales agency agreement (see **10.2.1.1**). In particular, similar points are likely to arise in relation to 'Products'.

10.5.2 Appointment

The appointment clause will be vitally important, in particular the question of exclusivity. How much protection will the distributor get against competition from others in its territory? The distributor may want such protection (eg against the supplier appointing other distributors or agents, or against the supplier selling within the territory) in order to benefit as much as possible from its investment in the distributorship.

It is always desirable to define the extent of the distributor's protection from competition as clearly as possible, rather than relying on the words 'sole' or 'exclusive' territory or distribution, which raise problems in the same way as they do in an agency agreement (see **10.2.1.3**). The agreement should also define the limits of the distributor's freedom to operate outside the defined territory.

The appointment clause may also deal with the duration of the agreement, although this can be done elsewhere in the agreement. Whichever method is chosen, note that an initial fixed term may be even more appropriate here than in an agency agreement, as it will give the distributor (which may have taken risks by making a large investment in the distributorship) both security and an incentive to build up the business. If this is what the parties require, the agreement must state when the fixed term is to commence. If the parties require an indefinite term, the agreement must include suitably drafted notice provisions.

10.5.3 The distributor's duties

Some of the distributor's duties will be similar to those in an agency agreement (eg in relation to confidentiality, transmission of information, training and availability of the distributor's representatives). However, other duties are likely to be significantly different because of the different nature of the agreement.

10.5.3.1 Minimum target obligations

The supplier will normally want to impose some form of minimum target obligation on the distributor to ensure that the distributor exploits the relevant market to the full, especially where the distributor has been granted exclusivity. The supplier will often see this as justifiable in return for giving the distributor an initial fixed term. A minimum target obligation can be either for:

(b) a minimum level of sales by the distributor to its customers; or

(a) a minimum level of purchases by the distributor from the supplier.

It is sometimes suggested that the latter may be more commercially flexible. For example, with a minimum purchase target, the distributor can buy extra goods from the supplier to meet the targets, and so perhaps cover a temporary bad patch more easily; purchase targets are also easier for the supplier to monitor.

If targets of either sort are imposed, the supplier must decide what is to happen if the distributor does not comply with them. The supplier may want either to end the distributor's freedom from competition in the territory, or to terminate the agreement itself. The former may appear to be less drastic from the distributor's point of view, but could be as devastating as termination of the entire agreement in the long run.

In practice, ending territorial protection for failure to meet targets is not always seen as being commercially sensible; if the distributor is finding it hard to succeed with the help of sole or exclusive territory, presumably its task will be even more difficult without it, and the supplier may not benefit in any way. The supplier should therefore consider doing this only if it is certain that matters will improve if the distributor's protection from competition is ended (eg it will encourage the distributor to make greater efforts, or the supplier will benefit by being able to appoint another distributor or market the goods itself).

10.5.3.2 Advertising and promotion

The distributor is normally made responsible for advertising and promotion. It will often be better placed than the supplier to know what sort of advertising and promotional campaigns will succeed in the territory. Wood Magic may see this as a valuable contribution which Bois Massif can make to the success of Wood Magic's furniture in France. However, the supplier may wish to reserve the right to vet the distributor's activities, especially if it wants to keep a reasonably uniform brand image over several different territories. The supplier may also wish to provide that the distributor spends a minimum sum each year (or quarter, or month as the case may be) on advertising and promotion.

10.5.3.3 Stock

The distributor will inevitably hold stock – it has actually bought the products from the supplier. The agreement will therefore need to provide for numerous matters relating to stock, including the following:

(a) How much stock should the distributor carry?

(b) What procedure should the distributor follow when it orders and pays for the goods?

(c) What procedure should the distributor follow for returning unsatisfactory goods?

(d) When are title and risk in the goods to pass to the distributor?

(e) Is it necessary to insure the products (eg, while they are in transit from supplier to distributor)? If so, who should do this?

(f) What is to happen to stock if the agreement is terminated. The supplier often faces a dilemma here, especially when Article 101 TFEU could apply to the agreement. If the distributor is still holding stock after termination, it may deal with it in ways which could damage the brand's reputation (eg, sell it cut-price in markets or through discount shops). However, because the stock is the distributor's own property, to deal with as it sees fit, any clause in the agreement which obliges the distributor to sell the stock back to the supplier on termination potentially restricts competition, and could infringe Article 101 TFEU. In most cases, the supplier will have to decide whether the risk of competition law problems is greater than that of harm to the supplier's reputation. However, note that a clause which gives the distributor the option of selling the stock back to the supplier (rather than forcing the distributor to do this) should not cause competition law problems, as the distributor is not then obliged to deal with its own property in a particular way. Subject to these points, any clause dealing with the fate of stock on termination is more likely to be an aid to negotiation than anything else.

(g) What is to happen to any advertising or promotional material on termination?

(h) What is to happen to obsolete stock? If the agreement requires the distributor to sell it back to the supplier, competition law problems may arise (in the same way as in (f) above). The parties should try to come to a workable compromise which will prevent obsolete stock affecting the market for new stock.

10.5.3.4 Confidentiality and intellectual property

The areas of confidentiality and intellectual property may be more relevant in a distribution agreement than in an agency agreement. As the distributor is actually buying the products and then selling them on, it may be necessary to supply the distributor with confidential information relating to the products, or to allow the distributor to use the supplier's intellectual property.

10.5.3.5 Competing products

The supplier may want the distributor to agree not to handle products which could compete with the products being supplied under the agreement.

10.5.4 The supplier's duties

If dealt with separately, the list of supplier's duties is likely to be comparatively small. It may be appropriate to deal with the following:

(a) Will the supplier need to supply any promotional literature, models or samples of the goods to allow the distributor to market them properly?

(b) Should the supplier be obliged to supply the distributor with information which may help the distributor to market the goods?

(c) Is the supplier prepared to offer the distributor an indemnity against defects in the products? If so, what liabilities will it cover? In addition, does the supplier wish to give limited warranties to the distributor (eg, to cut down the protection given by s 14 of the SGA 1979 if English law applies – see **6.4** and **6.5**)?

10.5.5 Sale of goods terms

Because the supplier will be selling goods to the distributor, it will be necessary to include in the agreement suitable terms to cover this sale of goods. For discussion of the basic terms in a sale of goods agreement, see **Chapters 3–7**. Consider, particularly in relation to a distribution agreement, the following:

(a) Are the supplier's sales to the distributor to be on the supplier's standard terms? If so, the agreement should make clear what these are. Perhaps the best way of doing this is to set them out in a schedule to the agreement, so that both parties are certain which terms apply.

(b) Which basic sale of goods terms (such as price, payment, delivery, description and quality) need to be included in the distribution agreement? Note that the term relating to price will be of particular importance to the distributor; it will make its money from the difference between the price at which it buys the goods from the supplier and the price at which it can sell them to its customers.

10.5.6 Termination

The termination of the agreement and the consequences of termination may be handled in a number of ways. One matter which will require particular care (for the reasons outlined in **10.5.3.3**) is disposal of stock on termination, which the solicitor may feel is better dealt with here than in the 'stock' clause.

Note that it is relatively rare for distributors to be entitled by law to compensation on termination (compare the position of agents under the Commercial Agents Regulations 1993; see **10.3.5**), but this may be relevant in certain jurisdictions (not the UK). The supplier may, however, be prepared to agree to include a term in the agreement providing for compensation.

10.5.7 Miscellaneous

Like an agency agreement, a distribution agreement usually has a 'boiler-plate'. Many of the miscellaneous clauses will be the same as those in an agency agreement (eg force majeure, arbitration, choice of law and notices).

10.6 Competition issues in distribution agreements

The impact of competition law on distribution agreements is dealt with in detail in **Chapter 27**. The following is a brief summary of some of the issues that arise in relation to the provisions discussed above.

10.6.1 Exclusivity

European case law indicates that exclusivity on its own will not necessarily cause competition problems, unless accompanied by territorial restrictions (see *Établissements Consten SA and Grundig GmbH v Commission* (Cases 56 and 58/64) [1966] ECR 299). The agreement must not forbid the distributor from exporting the goods from the territory, as this is likely to infringe Article 101(1) TFEU (and will not get the benefit of Regulation 330/2010). It is, however, possible in certain circumstances to provide that the distributor must not actively solicit orders from outside the territory, a provision that Wood Magic and Bois Massif have in mind. They could still benefit from Regulation 330/2010: see **27.5**).

10.6.2 Minimum target obligations

Although target obligations are often acceptable from a competition law point of view, care may be needed if the target is so exacting that it effectively limits the distributor's commercial freedom. The result may be that the distributor has to concentrate on promoting the supplier's products to the exclusion of others, and some purchase targets (over 80% of the distributor's total purchases of the contract goods) automatically amount to non-compete obligations. (For more on the potential competition law implications, see **Chapter 27**.)

10.6.3 Confidentiality and intellectual property

Provided that the provisions allowing the distributor to use the IP rights are not the 'primary object' of the agreement, these will not cause competition problems. However, a clause imposing a restriction on the right of the distributor to challenge the validity of the supplier's IP rights (a no-challenge clause) may be restrictive of competition.

10.6.4 Non-compete obligations

Both restrictions on handling competing products and post-termination restraint of trade clauses may amount to non-compete obligations, which may cause problems as being potentially restrictive of competition. For more detail on how these might be handled to avoid the impact of competition law, see **27.5.**

10.6.5 Severance

It is advisable to include a severance clause which will ensure that any anti-competitive (or other illegal) clause can be severed from the agreement. Clauses should be drafted for severance, using a series of clauses and sub-clauses, so that if one is found to be anti-competitive, the remainder of the agreement can survive (but see **27.5.2.1**).

10.7 Other forms of marketing arrangement

Given the nature of Wood Magic's business operations, it is unlikely that the directors will need to consider anything other than agency and distribution. A further alternative would a joint venture scheme. The nature of joint ventures and their likely advantages and disadvantages are dealt with in **Appendix 1** of ***Business Law and Practice***. A joint venture may become relevant if Wood Magic's directors come up with a project which requires input from another business with different but complementary skills. For example, assume that the directors decide to develop a range of upholstered furniture: they may seek to set up a joint venture with a company specialising in furnishing fabrics. If they did so, the two businesses could pool their resources to set up a separate joint venture company to carry out the project.

Marketing agreements involving IP rights will be discussed in **Chapter 11.**

Chapter 11

Marketing Agreements: Drafting Licensing, Merchandising and Franchising Agreements

11.1 Introduction

Chapter 10 considered the most common marketing arrangements, agency and distribution. Many businesses will not need to consider other arrangements. However, if a business continues to be successful and develops, other marketing opportunities may arise. It may, for example, be in a position to exploit its intellectual property (IP) rights. Intellectual property rights (as the name suggests) are intangible property rights which can, like any other form of property, be sold, assigned, licensed or used as security. This chapter deals with licences of intellectual property, looking at the basic structure of a licence agreement. It then goes on to give a brief introduction to other types of marketing arrangement which involve the exploitation of IP rights.

11.2 Licensing

Intellectual property rights generally are dealt with in **Chapters 16** to **23**. As discussed in these chapters, an owner of intellectual property will have certain exclusive rights over that property, eg the owner of a literary copyright has the exclusive right to copy that work; and the owner of a registered trade mark has the exclusive right to use the mark on the goods and services covered by the registration. If anyone else copies the work or uses the mark, they will infringe these rights. However, the owner may wish to license, or grant permission to, a third party to exploit these rights. The licence may cover all of the rights of the licensor, or it may be limited in its scope, so that the licensee only has the right to exploit some of these rights. For example, if a trade mark is licensed to a third party, it may only have the right to manufacture products to which the mark has been applied, but not to sell them. The scope of the licence will depend on the bargaining position of the parties.

Continuing with the example used in **Chapter 10**, assume that Wood Magic comes up with a potentially very popular design for a range of furniture, but that it does not have the resources to manufacture and distribute enough of the new product to satisfy customer demand. It is therefore considering granting a licence to a much larger furniture manufacturing business, 'Ottoman' Empire Ltd, allowing that business to use Wood Magic's designs to make and sell the furniture, initially within the UK. Very broadly, the licence agreement will permit the licensee to do this in return for payment to Wood Magic (possibly a one-off licence fee, but more likely continuing payments of royalties on chairs manufactured and sold).

Wood Magic may own design rights (see **Chapter 21**) in relation to the furniture, which it will license to the furniture manufacturer. The most suitable form of licence will be a licence of its industrial designs. However, Wood Magic may also want the furniture to be marketed using any trade mark which it may own (the Wood Magic name may not qualify for trade mark protection, but it may have registered a logo or brand name). Wood Magic may also own the copyright in any drawings of the furniture or logo. In addition, there may be trade secrets or know-how attached to the manufacturing process for Wood Magic's furniture. All these should be considered.

11.2.1 Basic rules for successful drafting of licence agreements

Again, it is extremely important to consider the three basic drafting rules, as discussed in **Chapters** 7 and **10**.

11.2.1.1 Commercial background

Researching the commercial background is important to establish what IP rights will be relevant. The solicitor may be told, for example, that the client uses a logo as a trade mark. The first thing to check is whether the mark has in fact been registered at the Intellectual Property Office. Protection is not automatic and, if not registered, the mark will only be protected by the law of passing off (see **Chapter 17**). The client may not be aware of all the relevant rights that attach to a particular item, eg is it aware that there may be copyright attached to any drawing of the logo, or the possibility of registering a design right?

11.2.1.2 Legal background

Care must be taken to check the following legal issues, which can cause difficulties in the context of IP licensing:

(a) *Ownership*. There may be problems if the right has been created by employees or commissioned from an independent contractor. Each IP right has its own rules in relation to ownership. Not only should the solicitor be aware of these, but he should also check all relevant employment contracts or commissions to satisfy himself that the rights have not been assigned to third parties.

(b) *Infringement*. The statutory rights arising in relation to each item of intellectual property are different. For example, the Trade Mark Act 1994 and the Patents Act 1977 both grant a monopoly right to the owner to use the mark or exploit the invention, but under the Copyright, Designs and Patents Act 1988, a copyright owner has more limited rights, ie only to prevent copying. In order to license the rights effectively, the licence will need to mirror the infringement provisions of the relevant statute, granting corresponding rights to the licensee.

11.2.1.3 Precedents

Extreme care is needed when using precedents, which must be carefully adapted to the requirements of the particular client. In a recent case, *Oxonica Energy Ltd v Neuftec Ltd* [2009] EWCA Civ 668, the Court of Appeal remarked on an 'appallingly drafted' patent licence and stressed the importance of giving careful thought to all the terms, rather than blindly copying from precedents.

11.2.2 Planning, form and content of the agreement

All of the rights may be included in one licence, or there may be separate licences for each right. There are advantages and disadvantages to each approach. A simple licensing agreement is likely to follow the structure below.

Structure of licence agreement
(a) Date, parties, recitals
(b) Interpretation clause
(c) Grant of licence
(d) Quality control
(e) Marketing
(f) Financial provisions
(g) Protection of IP rights
(h) Termination (if not dealt with elsewhere)
(i) Post-termination provisions
(j) [Warranties and indemnities]
(k) Boiler-plate clauses
(l) Signatures
(m) Schedules

The terms of the licence will depend to a certain extent on the bargaining position of the parties. In our example, it appears that Wood Magic is dealing with a large manufacturing company, and so may not be able to call all the shots.

11.2.2.1 Recitals

The recitals in IP licences are of particular importance. Although it may seem an obvious point, it is important that the licensor is, in fact, the owner of the particular right, and therefore has the right to license it. Problems can arise, for example, where the intellectual property is created by an employee or had been commissioned from a third party (see **11.2.1.2**). Recitals provide the background to the agreement, and can be used to set out the licensor's title to the right and that he has the right to license it. They can also be used to explain the intention of the parties, which may help to clarify the operative provisions, eg the scope of the licence.

11.2.2.2 Definitions

A clear definition of the IP rights to be licensed should be given. For example, if Wood Magic decides to license its design rights (both registered and unregistered) in the furniture, it could include these in a general definition of 'Intellectual Property Rights' or give separate definitions of each. If the licence is to include any trade marks or copyright, these should be clearly defined. The definition should also include the registration number of any registered right. The trade marks may, alternatively, be the subject of a separate licence. The rights are often defined by reference to a schedule.

The definitions should also identify the products to which the IP rights can be applied. A consideration is how broad the definition should be. Should it include the entire furniture range, or just some of it? Initially, it is probably in Wood Magic's interest to keep the definition narrow, eg chairs, as it will then be able to negotiate separate terms for other items if this product proves successful. The same is true in relation to the territory into which, for example, the licensee can sell, which should also be clearly defined. If potential markets open up outside the UK, further licences can be granted to exploit these markets.

11.2.2.3 Scope of the licence

The scope of the licence should be clearly set out. It should make clear what the licensee has the right to do, in relation to what product, where and for how long:

(a) The licence could be exclusive, sole or non-exclusive. The same considerations apply to the use of these terms as discussed in relation to agency and distribution. So far, Wood Magic appears not to have considered this point.

(b) Is the licensee to be given the right both to manufacture and to sell, or simply to manufacture the product? Here Wood Magic appears to want to give Ottoman Empire the right to both manufacture and sell the product, but the solicitor will need to check that this is what they have agreed.

(c) If the right to sell the product is included, can Ottoman Empire sell the products throughout the UK or simply in a particular region of the UK?

(d) The duration of the licence could be dealt with here, although this may be dealt with in a separate clause. The licence could be for a fixed or indefinite term.

The clause may also deal with registration. Requirements for registration (at the Intellectual Property Office) of IP licences vary depending on the right involved and whether the licence is exclusive or non-exclusive. These are set out in the table at **11.5**.

11.2.2.4 Quality control

The licence should place controls on the quality of the product and contain provisions for Wood Magic to police these. These may include a right to inspect samples and/or visit the licensee's premises to inspect the quality control systems in place.

Where trade marks are to licensed, these will often be the subject of a separate licence. Quality control provisions will be very important for the mark owner to be able to defend the integrity of any mark which is being licensed out; this is to protect the goodwill of the mark and prevent its reputation from being diluted or damaged by, say, inappropriate use by the licensee. Clearly this would affect the value of the mark.

The quality control provisions should reflect the risk of the mark being revoked, so the licence will usually provide that the licensee must not use the mark in a misleading or deceptive way, or do anything leading to loss of the mark's distinctiveness. The licensee should be required to describe the mark as a registered mark belonging to the licensor, and to specify that it is used under licence. This will ensure that the benefit of the mark's goodwill continues to accrue to the licensor.

11.2.2.5 Marketing

The licence will contain marketing requirements, for example in relation to advertising and promotion, and may require the licensor to provide marketing support to the licensee.

Furthermore, the licensee may be obliged to clear all advertising, promotional and marketing material featuring trade-marked goods/services with the licensor before use.

11.2.2.6 Financial matters

Wood Magic may want to charge a one-off flat fee for use of the rights, but more commonly will wish to charge a royalty based on a particular formula (eg based on number of items manufactured/sold by the licensee). If royalties are charged then the agreement should establish a system for record-keeping and allow for verification of the licensee's accounts by the licensor at regular intervals. Alternatives would be to provide for the licensor to take a share of the profits, an annual fee or 'milestone payments', ie the payment of fixed amounts paid on fixed dates throughout the agreement.

It is a good idea to include a minimum royalty provision, particularly if the licence is exclusive, as this will give the licensee the incentive to market the product effectively. Where a trade mark is used, this will also ensure that the mark does not become vulnerable to revocation for non-use. The consequences of failing to meet the target should be dealt with. For example, will failure to meet the target give the licensor the right to terminate the agreement?

The agreement should also provide for interest charges for late payment.

11.2.2.7 Protection of the IP rights

Provision should be made for the protection of the IP rights from infringement by third parties. In particular, the parties should decide who will have the right to bring any proceedings. In the event that the parties do not provide for this in the contract, licensees have differing statutory rights in relation to their right to bring proceedings, depending on the type of licence. These are set out in the table at **11.5**. Usually the licensor will want to retain control of infringement proceedings, but, again, whether it will be able to do so will depend on its bargaining strength.

11.2.2.8 Warranties and indemnities

The licensee will want to be sure that the use of the intellectual property does not infringe the rights of any third party, and that the rights granted are valid. Ottoman Empire is probably in a strong enough bargaining position to be able to require the Wood Magic to give express warranties (or assurances) on validity, and that the use is lawful and does not infringe any third parties' rights. Wood Magic may also be required to indemnify the licensee against liability in the event of any successful claim for infringement. A licensor will usually try to avoid giving such warranties and indemnities, but where it does, care should be taken that they are accurate.

11.2.2.9 Termination and post-termination provisions

The licence should set out the circumstances in which the agreement can be terminated, for example in the event of breach of the agreement, insolvency, or change of control of one or both of the parties. This is crucial. Surprisingly, termination provisions are often overlooked by licensors of IP rights, who fail to consider what will happen if things go wrong. Change of control provisions are particularly important to consider. A licensor should be aware that there is the possibility of its IP rights ending up in the hands of a competitor which has gained control of a licensee company. Whether the termination provisions are reciprocal will depend on the bargaining strengths of the parties.

Provision should also be made for what is to happen to the licensed products if the licence is terminated. For example, will the licensee have to deliver up any unsold stock or be given a limited period to dispose of the products, which would prevent them having to be destroyed.

Intellectual property licences may also involve competition law considerations (see **Chapter 28**).

11.2.2.10 Execution

Different statutory rules apply to execution of a licence agreement, depending again on the type of agreement and whether or not it is an exclusive licence. Again, these are set out in the table at **11.5**.

11.3 Merchandising agreements

A merchandising agreement is a form of licence agreement. They are used by media organisations to exploit their IP rights (in particular copyright and trade marks) by licensing rights for the merchandising of toys and other products based on films, television programmes, etc. The licensee is granted the right to produce products and market products based on the licensor's IP rights in return for payment, usually in the form of royalties. Merchandising agreements are of increasing importance given the huge earning potential for both the licensor and licensee. For example, Reuters reported that the Toy Story 3 film had generated more merchandise in the US than any other recent film. Tracking of shipments (using official bills of lading – see **14.3.1**) into the US showed that 724 cargo size containers of

Toy Story merchandise had been imported, mostly from China. Over and above this, there would be sales of home-produced merchandise, and this figure relates only to the merchandising of these products within the US.

A merchandising agreement will follow the same basic structure as the IP licence considered at **11.2**. It is likely to be a non-exclusive licence, and so the licensor has the right to grant licences to other licensees.

11.4 Franchising

A franchise is where a business allows a third party to use its name, concept, business format and experience. There is ongoing and close control by the franchisor over its franchisees, but they remain legally and financially separate undertakings. Well-known examples include McDonalds, KFC and the Body Shop. The most usual arrangement is between a manufacturer and retailers, but a franchise can operate at other levels of the supply chain. A franchise agreement involves the franchisor giving the franchisee the right to use the franchisor's IP rights. There may also be competition law considerations (see **Chapter 28**).

In the example given in **Chapter 10**, Wood Magic decided to extend its custom-made furniture business by opting for an agency agreement. Another way of extending this business format would be to franchise the Wood Magic 'concept' of furniture making. This would mean that Wood Magic (the franchisor) would establish a 'Wood Magic' uniform business format, which it would then authorise other businesses (the franchisees) to use in return for payment, usually an initial fee and royalties based on a percentage of turnover or profit on the product. In the franchise agreement, Wood Magic would lay down operating conditions and specifications for the franchisees to meet (eg what their premises should look like, how they should offer the furniture-making service to customers). This would allow Wood Magic to extend this part of its business without having to raise capital to do so, while still retaining considerable control over what the franchisee does with the business.

There are no legal requirements as such governing franchising, and the agreement will simply be based on normal contractual principles. However, although not legally binding, it is advisable that the agreement should comply with the European Code of Ethics for Franchising which has been adopted by the British Franchise Association.

The franchise agreement will contain many of the same terms which have been considered when looking at other marketing and licence agreements. The exact content will depend on the type of franchise, but will generally include the following: a grant of the rights, including any IP rights, obligations of the parties, payment provisions, duration, termination provisions, provisions for the protection of and warranties in relation to the IP, plus usual boiler-plate clauses. As the franchisee will be relying on the franchisor's business expertise and concept, the franchisor's obligations may include training provisions and the obligation to provide all the necessary stock and materials to set up the franchise. In addition, the agreement will impose operating obligations on the franchisee and obligations in respect of the premises, from which it will be operating, eg that it will not alter the premises or its layout or fixtures and fittings in any way.

11.5 Licences and assignments of IP rights – formalities and consequences

Right	Assignment	Exclusive licence	Non-exclusive licence
Registered trade mark	In writing and signed by or on behalf of assignor: TMA 1994, s 24(3). Prudent to register: TMA 1994, s 25.	In writing and signed by or on behalf of licensor: TMA 1994, s 28(2). Prudent to register: TMA 1994, s 25. Licensee can sue for infringement if licence agreement allows: TMA 1994, s 31(1), but must join proprietor of trade mark in action: TMA 1994, s 31(4). Licensee can call on proprietor of trade mark to sue for infringement: TMA 1994, s 30(2).	In writing and signed by or on behalf of licensor: TMA 1994, s 28(2). Prudent to register: TMA 1994, s 25. Licensee can call on proprietor of trade mark to sue for infringement: TMA 1994, s 30(2).
Copyright	In writing and signed by or on behalf of assignor: CDPA 1988, s 90(3).	In writing and signed by or on behalf of licensor: CDPA 1988, s 92(1). Licensee can sue for infringement: CDPA 1988, s 101(1), but must join the copyright owner in the action or obtain leave of the court: CDPA 1988, s 102(1).	No formalities. In certain circumstances , if the licence is in writing, the licensee can sue: CDPA 1988, s 101A.
Patent	In writing and signed by or on behalf of all parties: PA 1977, s 30(6). Prudent to register: PA 1977, s 33(3).	Prudent to register: PA 1977, s 33(3). Licensee can sue for infringement: PA 1977, s 67.	Prudent to register: PA 1977, s 33(3).
Unregistered design right	In writing and signed by or on behalf of assignor: CDPA 1988, s 222(3).	In writing and signed by or on behalf of licensor: CDPA 1988, s 225. Licensee can sue for infringement.	No formalities.

Right	Assignment	Exclusive licence	Non-exclusive licence
Registered design right	In writing and signed by or on behalf of assignor: RDA 1949, s 15B(3).	In writing and signed by or on behalf of proprietor of design (otherwise will not bind successors in title): RDA 1949, s 15C.	In writing: *Jewitt v Eckhardt* (1878) 8 Ch D 404.
	Must be registered: RDA 1949, s 19(1).	Must be registered: RDA 1949, s 19(1).	Must be registered: RDA 1949, s 19(1).
		Licensee can sue for infringement: RDA 1949, s 24F(1), but must join proprietor of design in the action: RDA 1949, s 24F(4).	

Part I Summary
Commercial Agreements

Topic	*Summary*
Definition	There is no single definition of what constitutes a 'commercial agreement' or 'commercial contract', although a basic starting point would normally be 'a deal made between two (or more) parties, both or all of whom are in business'.
Scope	A variety of elements might be relevant in a commercial agreement: the principles of commercial drafting, contracts for the sale of goods, exclusion and restriction of liability, other types of contract under which goods pass, agency and distribution agreements and the principles of consumer credit.
Contracts for the sale of goods	These are, broadly speaking, contracts between a buyer and seller, under which the ownership of goods changes hands in return for the payment of a money consideration known as the price, and where the buyer is not intending to resell the goods (cf 'Distribution agreements' below).
Sale of Goods Act 1979 (as amended)	Although normal principles of freedom of contract apply to commercial agreements, the Sale of Goods Act 1979 provides a type of regulatory framework for sale of goods agreements.
Implied terms	The Sale of Goods Act 1979 implies a variety of terms into contracts for the sale of goods; which terms will be implied depend on the circumstances of the contract (for example, some implied terms, such as those relating to price, are implied only where the parties have not expressly or impliedly decided the matter for themselves).
Duties of the parties	The Sale of Goods Act 1979 outlines the duties of the buyer and seller under a sale of goods agreement; however, virtually all these duties can be modified or excluded by agreement between the parties.
Rights of the parties	The Act also sets out the rights of the parties (eg, the buyer's right to reject the goods; the seller's rights if the buyer fails to pay for the goods).
Remedies	The Act also outlines the remedies which are available if either party breaches the contract.
Retention of title	This is a particularly important device in a commercial agreement for the sale of goods: the right of the seller to retain ownership of the goods until the buyer has paid for them.
Exclusion and restriction of liability	This is another important device: the ability of either party to exclude or restrict liability for breach of contract. Normal contractual principles of incorporation and construction apply to exemption clauses in commercial contracts; so does the Unfair Contract Terms Act 1977.

Topic	*Summary*
UCTA 1977	UCTA 1977 generally allows parties to commercial contracts more freedom to use exemption clauses than it allows for consumer contracts. With a very few exceptions (eg, purported exclusion of the implied condition relating to title, which is always void) liability can generally be excluded in a commercial agreement in so far as it is reasonable.
Other contracts under which goods pass	These include contracts of exchange, barter, hire purchase, conditional sale, work and materials and contracts of hire. They are governed by a variety of statutory provisions, all of which are closely modelled on the Sale of Goods Act 1979, so the points made above concerning implied terms are also relevant here.
Contracts for services	These are governed by the Supply of Goods (Implied Terms) Act 1982; the Act implies a small number of terms into contracts for the supply of services, including a term that the services will be provided with reasonable skill and care.
Marketing agreements	Some agreements involving goods concentrate on getting the goods to a wider market. Examples include agency agreements and distribution agreements.
Agency agreements	Although agency agreements come in a number of different types, the classic sales agency agreement involves one party (the principal) giving authority to the other party (the agent) to take actions on the principal's behalf to find customers for the principal's goods or services.
Commercial Agents Regulations 1993	Agency agreements are to a large extent governed by the normal law of contract and law of agency. However, a substantial number of agency agreements are also subject to the Commercial Agents Regulations 1993, which lay down a framework of rules concerning the rights and duties of each party (notably the agent's right to a payment on termination of the agency agreement).
Distribution agreements	A distribution agreement is fundamentally based on a sale of goods agreement. However, in a distribution agreement the parties specifically agree that the buyer of the goods (the distributor) is buying them for the purpose of re-selling them, rather than for end-use in its own business. Distribution agreements are chiefly subject to the ordinary law of contract (and sale of goods), but may have competition law implications.

Part II

INTERNATIONAL SALE AGREEMENTS

Chapter 12
Introduction to International Sale Agreements

An international sale of goods contract will need to cover the same type of issues as a domestic agreement (eg transfer of ownership, price, payment, and delivery). Generally, if the contract is subject to English law, the SGA 1979 will apply to an international contract. However, there are added complications, both legal and practical. For example, UCTA 1977 does not generally apply to international sales contracts (see s 26), and the use of exclusion clauses is prohibited in some international contracts of carriage.

The most obvious practical problem is that arrangements have to be made for transportation of the goods, often over long distances. The result, clearly, will be increased delivery periods and the associated cost of long-distance freight carriage. The parties need to decide who will arrange, and more importantly, pay for this. Language problems may cause complications and misunderstandings. Some problems can be solved by the parties using a standard contract drawn up by a trade association, or by an international body. The ones which we shall look at in Part II of this book are the Incoterms, produced by the International Chamber of Commerce. These are a set of standard form rules, produced in a variety of languages, relating to the transport arrangements. These will be considered in **Chapter 14**.

The seller will be particularly concerned with the payment arrangements. The method of payment will need to be considered. In an international sale, cash payment will usually be impractical. It may be possible to arrange for payment in advance, but more usually the buyer will demand a credit period, so payment may not take place until some time after the goods have been shipped, resulting in obvious cash flow problems. In addition, the seller will want to put in place arrangements for facilitating and guaranteeing payment. This will require complex contractual arrangements, to be put in place through a bank or banks, to which the seller can look for payment if the buyer defaults. The finance arrangements will be considered in **Chapter 15**.

Then there are various additional, or increased, risks, for example:

(a) physical risk of damage to the goods associated with sea or air transport and the associated extra handling;

(b) financial risks, for example due to changes in currency exchange rates;

(c) increased risks of not being paid, or being paid late, possibly by reason of buyer insolvency;

(d) political risks, possibly even of war, terrorist attack or blockades (a recent example is the problems for shippers with Somali pirates);

(e) legal risks if the contract is subject to foreign law (are you qualified to advise on foreign law?); and

(f) the difficulties associated with litigation, or enforcing contractual remedies outside of the seller's jurisdiction (eg how practical is it to attempt to enforce a retention of title clause?).

Some of these risks can be covered by insurance, although this can be expensive and it may not be economically viable for the seller to purchase it.

The starting point for any international sale of goods transaction will be the sale of goods contract itself but, because of these additional risks and complications, international sale of goods contracts commonly include terms dealing with international transport arrangements, insurance provision, complex financing and credit provision, and closely related payment provisions. As a result, there will be a series of additional contracts with third parties, which are essential to ensure that the parties fulfil their obligations under the principal sale of goods contract. Each contract will be governed by legislation and international conventions relevant to each area of law (international conventions are beyond the scope of this book, but an awareness of their existence is important):

(a) The freight contract between the shipper and the carrier. The party arranging (and paying for) the contract is the 'shipper'. Whether this is the buyer or seller will depend on the bargaining strength of the parties, and will be provided for in the sale contract, usually by incorporation of the relevant Incoterm. Under English law, these contracts are governed by the Carriage of Goods by Sea Acts 1971 and 1992. These Acts implement various international conventions into English law, such as the Hague and Hague-Visby rules, and regulate the rights and duties of carriers.

(b) The contract of marine insurance. Whether the buyer or seller arranges for insurance will again depend on what has been agreed between the parties and will be normally provided for in the sale contract. Where the seller is obliged to insure, the obligation will often be created by incorporation of the relevant Incoterm. Not all Incoterms oblige the seller to insure, so the buyer may need to make its own arrangements. The insurance contract will be governed by the Marine Insurance Act 1906.

(c) Again, the finance arrangements will be provided for in the sale of goods contract, and the method and the degree of security for payment will again depend on the relationship between the parties. The implementation of these arrangements will involve the buyer making the appropriate contractual arrangements with his bank, to which the seller and the seller's bank may be party. If the method of payment is to be a bill of exchange, then this will be governed by the Bills of Exchange Act 1882. The contract may require that the buyer sets up a documentary credit to guarantee payment. This is governed by the Uniform Customs and Practice for Documentary Credits (UCP) published by the ICC. (The current version is UCP 600 (2007 revision), which came into effect on 1 July 2007; a supplement, 'eUCP', deals with electronic documents.)

These additional contracts are illustrated by **Figure 12.1** below, which assumes that the goods are to be shipped by sea and that the governing law of the contract is English law.

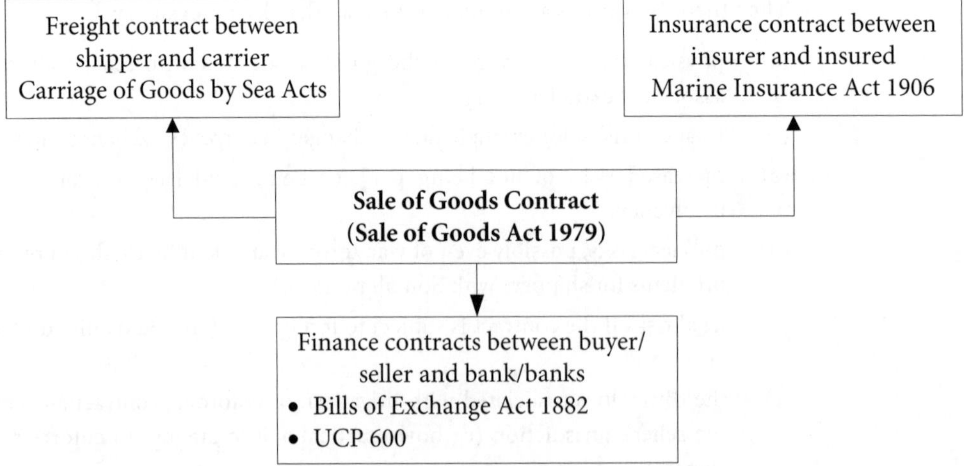

Figure 12.1 Additional contracts with third parties

Chapter 13
Choice of Jurisdiction and Law

13.1 Introduction

The whole area of jurisdiction, and of law, has been given a boost in the minds of commercial lawyers by the advent of e-commerce. Today, international contracts can be concluded at the click of a mouse. The collision of opposing jurisdictions is therefore an increasingly important issue (see further **Chapter 25**).

Chapter 13 looks at what happens when a contract goes wrong. In which jurisdiction can a client sue and be sued, and which country's laws are applicable to the contract?

Jurisdiction means the courts which would hear the dispute. Choice of law obviously means choosing which law would apply to the contract. Normally, both law and jurisdiction would be decided by a clause in the contract. If that has not been done in respect of an EU-based contract, then the two Conventions discussed below will apply.

The basic principle is that if the parties choose the law and jurisdiction which they wish to cover the contract then that choice prevails. In practice, any competently drafted written contract should have a clause covering law and jurisdiction. However, there will be circumstances where the issues need to be resolved. EU Regulation 593/2008 (Rome I) deals with choice of law.

Choice of jurisdiction is now dealt with by EU Regulation 44/2001, also known as Brussels I. The main change from its predecessor is that it gives greater protection to the consumer, including when the consumer contracts with a business on the Internet.

However, there are circumstances where the outcome of the Conventions would be different for law and for jurisdiction, so it is feasible to have an English court hearing a dispute under German law, for example. In such circumstances, the English court will be advised by experts in the law in question, here that of Germany.

13.2 Brussels I – Regulation 44/2001

This deals with jurisdiction. It applies, generally, where defendants are domiciled in Member States.

13.2.1 The basic position under Brussels I – general jurisdiction

The basic rule is that the defendant is sued in the courts of his home country, subject to the other provisions of the Regulation (Article 2). This rule is said to give 'general jurisdiction' to those courts. There are exceptions to the rule. The major ones are contracts, torts, situations where the defendant has a local branch office, real property, companies, IP, insurance, consumer contracts, and employment matters, see **13.2.2–13.2.4**.

13.2.2 Special jurisdiction – contract, tort and local branch offices

If the dispute is a contract matter then there is the option of suing the defendant in the Member State where the contract should have been performed (Article 5(1)(a)). If more than one obligation is in question, the Brussels I Regulation gives jurisdiction to the courts of the place of performance of the principal obligation.

In the case of a sale of goods contract, it is presumed that the 'place of performance of the obligation in question' is the Member State where the goods were delivered, or should have been delivered (Article 5(1)(b)). Thus, for sale of goods contracts, there is only one 'place of performance of the obligation in question' for the whole of the contract.

In matters relating to tort, the defendant may be sued in the courts of the Member State where the harmful event occurred, or may occur (Article 5(3)).

If the defendant has a branch or office in another Member State then he may also be sued there (Article 5(5)) if the dispute arises out of the operations of that branch or office.

13.2.3 Exclusive jurisdiction

Under Article 22 of Regulation 44/2001, there are situations in which certain courts are regarded as having particular expertise and so are given exclusive jurisdiction. This overrides the normal rules on general and special jurisdiction. The main instances are:

(a) proceedings concerning rights in rem in immovable property, or tenancies of immovable property: the Regulation normally gives exclusive jurisdiction to the courts of the Member State in which the property is situated;

(b) proceedings concerning the constitution or dissolution of companies: the Regulation gives exclusive jurisdiction the courts of the Member State in which the company has its 'seat' (in the UK this will usually be the registered office); and

(c) proceedings concerning the registration or validity of registered intellectual property rights: the Regulation gives exclusive jurisdiction to the courts of the Member State in which the right is registered, or in which registration has been applied for.

13.2.4 Special rules for insurance, consumer contracts and employment contracts

These are situations in which one party is considered to have greater economic power than the other. In order to redress the balance, the rules on jurisdiction are shifted in favour of the 'weaker' party. Generally he can be sued only in his own courts, but is given the choice as to whether he sues the other party in his own courts or in the other party's courts. There are limits to the extent to which the parties can contract out of these rules.

The rules on consumer contracts are contained in Articles 15–17. They apply in various situations set out in Article 15. The most usual of these is where the consumer concludes a contract with a person 'who pursues commercial or professional activities in the Member State of the consumer's domicile'. This provision should be fairly self-explanatory. However, Article 15 also applies where the other party 'by any means, directs [his commercial or professional] activities' to the Member State in which the consumer is domiciled. This is taken to include Internet selling (ie, e-commerce). So, Articles 15–18 will protect the Internet consumer by requiring that he be sued only in his own courts, whilst giving him a choice as to where he sues the seller.

This can mean that an Internet business could be sued in any jurisdiction in which its website happens to be accessible to potential customers. It might be worthwhile considering which jurisdictions the business is prepared to deal with. Most businesses that sell goods can control this by refusing orders from countries to which they are not prepared to sell, and by not sending the goods. It would be harder to exercise such control in a business involving the sale of on-line products such as plane tickets, or the downloading of software.

13.2.5 Contracting out

Article 23 allows the parties to override the rules on general and special jurisdiction by agreeing that the courts of a specified Member State are to have jurisdiction. The Article lays down the formal requirements for such an agreement. Generally, it must be in writing.

However, it is not possible to contract out of the rules on exclusive jurisdiction (in Article 22 – see **13.2.3**). There are also limits to the extent to which the parties can contract out of the rules on insurance, consumer and employment contracts.

13.2.6 First to file

The court which is first involved in the proceedings will generally have jurisdiction (Article 21). Any other court may decline jurisdiction, or stay proceedings if the actions are related (Article 22).

In England, the principle of *forum non conveniens* means that the court could stay proceedings in the English court that have also been brought in another jurisdiction.

Judgments obtained in contracting States must be recognised and enforced, but with some exceptions (Articles 27 and 28).

For another decision involving Brussels I, see *Bonnier Media Ltd v Greg Lloyd Smith* [2002] ETMR 86 (**18.9.3**).

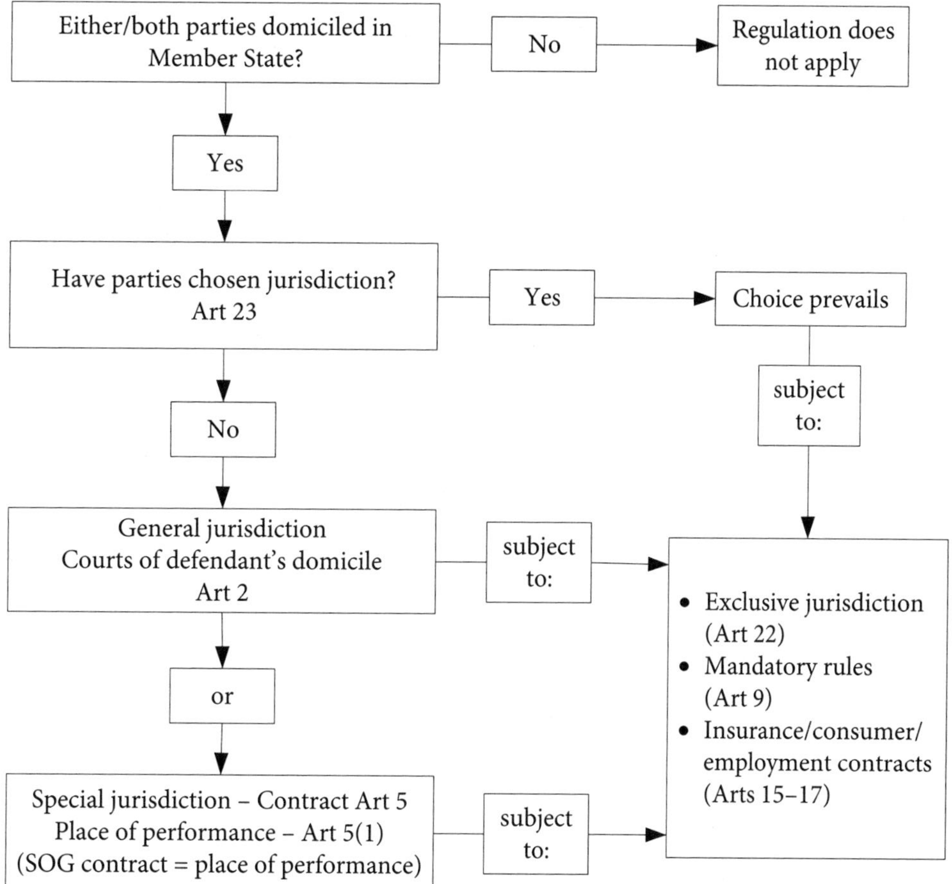

Figure 13.1 Regulation 44/2001 (Brussels I)

13.3 Rome I – Regulation 593/2008

This applies to Member States of the EU. It deals with the choice of laws, that is, the question of which law applies to the contract.

13.3.1 The basic position under Regulation 593/2008

Article 1(2) specifies the matters to which the Regulation does not apply, for example wills and probate, and matters governed by company law.

Article 3(1) allows the parties to choose the law of the contract, either expressly or impliedly. If they have done so, then that is the applicable law that governs the contract.

If no such choice has been made then the rules in Article 4 apply. Typically, in a sale of goods contract, this means that the law of the country where the seller has his habitual residence will apply, unless the buyer is a consumer, who cannot be denied the use of laws which cannot be derogated from in his own jurisdiction.

13.3.2 Other exceptions to the seller's law applying

Article 4(1)(c) deals with a right in 'immovable property'. The presumption here is that the contract is governed by the law of the country where the immovable property is situated. This does not apply to contracts for repair or construction of immovable property.

Article 5(1) provides that, in a contract for the carriage of goods (not *sale* of goods), it is the country where the carrier has its place of business if that is also the country of loading or discharging the goods, or if it is also the country where the consignor has its principal place of business.

Article 4(4) provides that the court may decide that the contract is more closely connected with another country and apply that country's laws.

13.3.3 Local 'mandatory rules'

There are limitations on the use of the applicable law. If any provisions of the applicable law conflict with local laws of the jurisdiction where the dispute is heard, relating to the contract, those conflicting provisions of the applicable law cannot validly be used. These local law provisions are the 'mandatory rules' which are referred to in Article 9 of the Regulation. These are 'rules' which cannot be derogated from (eg, in the case of the UK, the Financial Services and Markets Act 2000, the Unfair Terms in Consumer Contracts Regulations 1999, etc). Article 9 provides that the choice of foreign law by the parties will not prejudice the application of the mandatory rules of the home country to the contract. So, even if the applicable law was held to be, say, Austrian law, the Financial Services and Markets Act 2000 could also apply to a relevant dispute heard by a court in England and Wales, and would override any inconsistent provisions in Austrian law.

13.3.4 Exceptions for consumer and employment contracts

Articles 6 and 8 are intended to give protection to the weaker party to a contract.

Article 6 deals with certain types of consumer contract. Where no choice has been made, such contracts are governed by the law of the consumer's habitual residence. Where a choice has been made, the chosen law operates subject to any rules for the protection of the consumer applicable in the consumer's country of habitual residence.

Article 8 deals with individual contracts of employment. Where there is no choice of law in the contract then the presumption is that contained in Article 8(2). This is basically that the law is that of the country where the work takes place, or where the business is situated if the work takes place in a different country. However, a contractual choice of law cannot operate so as to deprive the employee of the protection of the mandatory rules which would apply under Article 8(2).

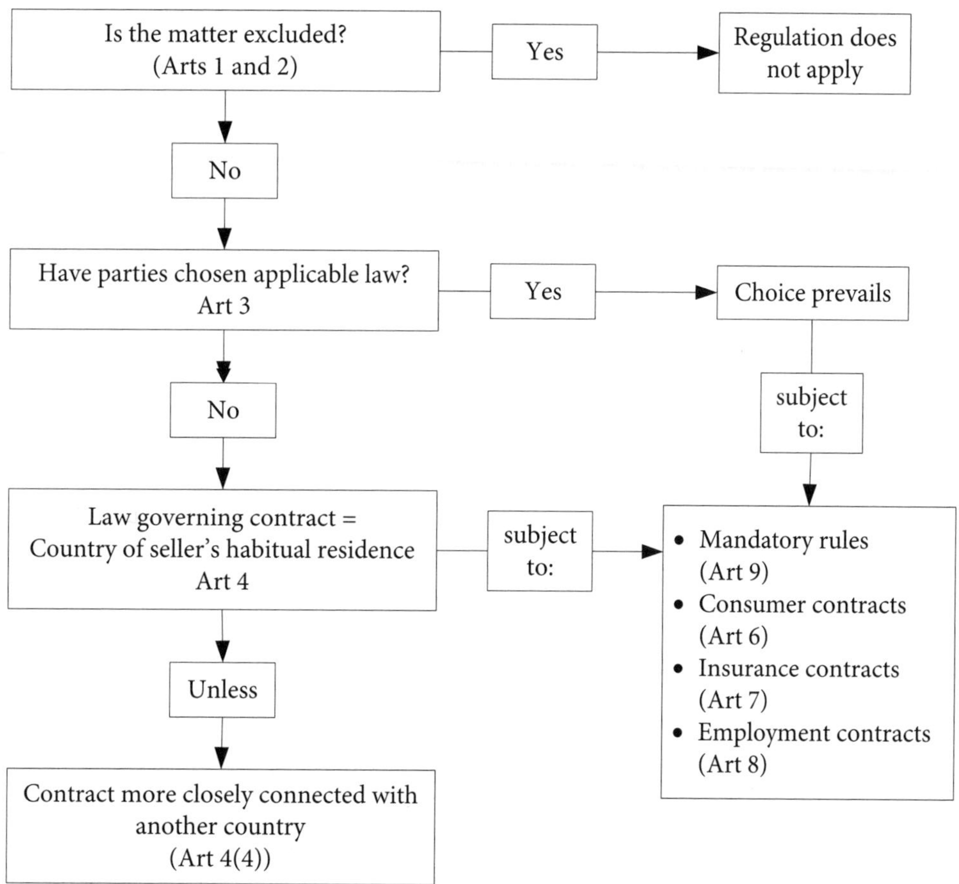

Figure 13.2 Regulation 593/2008 (Rome I)

Chapter 14
International Sale of Goods

14.1 Introduction

The typical international sale of goods transaction is one where the goods are shipped by sea over a long distance. This means there could be a considerable time delay between the goods being supplied and the seller being paid for them. The seller would ideally like to be paid when the goods are dispatched. The buyer would ideally want to pay only when he has received the goods and had a chance to inspect them.

The seller's desire to be paid is not just wishful thinking. The seller will have to pay his own suppliers, his employees and other business expenses. This is a cash flow problem that happens in all business, but the situation is exacerbated in international sale contracts because of the distances over which the goods are shipped.

In addition to the possible delay in payment, there are increased costs of insurance, to cover the sea voyage and possibly other risks.

To solve the problems of slow payment, the documents involved in an international sale have been elevated to a special status. In effect, they come to represent the goods themselves for the purposes of contract law. So, for example, delivery of the goods, in the legal sense, is performed by handing over documents.

14.2 The documents

The key documents are:

(a) the bill of lading (or alternatives – see **14.2.2** and **14.2.3**);

(b) the commercial invoice; and

(c) the policy of marine, or air, insurance.

Other documents may also be relevant (eg, export/import licences and a certificate of origin).

14.2.1 The bill of lading

The bill of lading is given by the carrier of the goods to the consignor of the goods, at the time of the goods being loaded.

The bill of lading serves three purposes:

(a) it is a receipt for the goods and evidences that they are in good condition at loading;

(b) it contains the terms of contract of carriage; and

(c) it is evidence of title to the goods, and a right to possess them.

Thus, at the destination the goods will be handed over to the person holding the bill of lading. The bill is given to the carrier in exchange for the goods. It will arrive before the goods, as the goods travel by sea but the bill is sent by airmail. A key property of a bill of lading is that its holder has title to the goods.

The disadvantage of the bill of lading is that it is intended for the sale of bulk commodities which are shipped a considerable distance by sea. Today, air transport is used more, and ships have become faster. The cargo can reach the destination before the bill of lading does. Today, sea waybills and freight forwarders receipts are often preferred to a bill of lading, as they can be sent by fax or e-mail. Although they give less legal protection, the buyer can collect the goods from the carrier by giving proof of his identity without having to produce a bill of lading, as such.

Only an original bill of lading will suffice. A photocopy or faxed copy is no good. For short (international) journeys, it is conceivable that the goods may arrive before the bill of lading, as noted above. It has been estimated that up to 50% of shipping documents are either late, or have discrepancies. In such cases, the carrier will usually deliver the goods to the buyer in return for a buyer's indemnity. Obviously, this is a bit risky for the carrier. An additional complication is that it is common practice to issue in bills of lading in sets of three. Only one copy needs to be presented to claim the goods from the carrier. The practice was originally devised to enable the resale of goods whilst at sea in days gone by, even though criticised then (see *Glyn Mills Currie & Co v East and West India Dock Co* (1882) 7 App Cas 591). Today, this practice can lead to fraud. The use of bills of lading has decreased dramatically as alternatives that are more amenable to electronic communication have gained acceptance (see **14.2.2**).

Bills of lading are still favoured in the transport of bulk cargoes, eg grain, coal, metal ores. There are attempts to produce an e-commerce equivalent by creating a network of contracts that has the same end effect as a paper bill of lading, eg the system known as BOLERO (Bills of Lading Electronic Registry Organisation). This would seem to be where the future lies for bills of lading. For further information on BOLERO, see www.bolero.net.

Bills of lading are governed in the UK by the Carriage of Goods by Sea Act 1992.

There are three types of bills of lading: inland, ocean and through bill

(a) Inland bill of lading – this is a contract between a shipper and transportation company used when transporting goods overland to an exporter's international carrier.

(b) Ocean bill of lading – this is a contract between an exporter and an international carrier for transport of merchandise to a specified foreign market overseas.

(c) Through bill of lading – this is a document that establishes the terms between a shipper and transportation company covering both the domestic and international transport of export goods between specified points for a specified charge. For example, an air shipment can be covered with a through bill of lading; however, ocean shipments require both an inland bill of lading (for domestic transport) and an ocean bill of lading (for international transport).

14.2.2 An alternative to bills of lading – waybills

A waybill is an alternative to a bill of lading. A waybill is a receipt for the goods and evidence of the carriage contract, but it does not constitute a document of title to the goods. It also specifies the person to whom delivery should be made. The original does not have to be sent to the buyer for him to be able to collect the goods from the carrier. Its disadvantage is that it does not enable the buyer to sell the goods on before he has possession of them, as he can with a bill of lading.

An advantage of waybills is that they can be sent electronically (or by fax). The transaction can thus by undertaken as e-commerce, with the payment being sent from the buyer to the seller by electronic means.

Waybills have traditionally been used for air freight. They have been used for sea freight with increasing frequency.

14.2.3 Road, rail or air transport

There is no equivalent to the bill of lading in air transport. An 'air waybill' is normally used. This would be made out to the buyer as consignee. Often, the basis is an 'FOB airport' contract (see **14.4.4**). The seller's duties end when the goods are delivered at the destination airport to the carrier or buyer's agent.

For road and rail transport, the contract would usually be made with a firm that undertakes the whole transport chain, normally using containerised transport for the goods. The contract document is a 'combined transport document'. There are various standard-form contracts from the International Chamber of Commerce (ICC) that deal with these arrangements (see **14.4**).

For a discussion of the problems of multi-modal transport, see Faber [1996] LMCLQ 503.

14.2.4 The commercial invoice

This lists and describes the contract goods (eg, '20 cases of Adams Baked Beans, each comprising 30 tins of 100g size'). It will also usually constitute a demand for payment by the buyer.

14.2.5 The policy of marine (or air) insurance

This should be worded so as to cover the goods specified in the commercial invoice for the journey described in the bill of lading. The policy would be transferred from one party to another along with the bill of lading (and would obviously need to be a transferable policy).

14.3 Effect of transfer of the documents

The Carriage of Goods by Sea Act 1992 provides a solution to any problems of privity of contract which would occur when the bill of lading is transferred from one holder to another. The Act provides that anyone who holds the bill of lading is entitled to sue the carrier on the contract of carriage. A holder also assumes the contractual burdens. (The Act also applies to other documents such as waybills, which are mentioned at **14.2.2** and **14.2.3**.) The holder also has rights in tort in relation to the goods (eg, for negligent damage).

The buyer who is in possession of the shipping documents can enforce his:

(a) contractual rights against the person who sold to him, under the contract of sale;

(b) contractual rights against the carrier under the contract of carriage; and

(c) rights against the insurer under the terms of the policy of which he is the assignee.

Motis Exports Ltd v Dampskibsselskabet AF 1912 (No 1), A/S and Another [2000] 1 All ER (Comm) 91 is an example of the problems of bills of lading. In that case, the defendant carrier delivered goods against a forged bill of lading. The owner of the goods successfully sued the carrier, as the Court of Appeal affirmed that a forged bill of lading was simply a worthless piece of paper. Delivery of the goods against a forged bill of lading was held to be misdelivery of the goods, and the carrier's general exclusion of liability for loss in transit did not cover the situation.

14.4 Arranging transportation of the goods – Incoterms

In an international sale of goods, there will be various stages in the transport chain. For example, if the goods are being exported to Korea from a factory in Manchester, they will first of all have to be taken by road or rail from Manchester in the UK to a British port, possibly Liverpool or Hull. They will then need to be loaded on to a ship and be taken by the ship from the British port to a port in Korea. Once they reach there, they will then be taken by road or rail from the Korean port to the premises of the buyer.

14.4.1 Multi-modal transport and container transport

Nowadays, it is usual for the parties to arrange so-called multi-modal transport, where the goods are transported under a single contract of carriage, using a combination of two or more modes of transport, eg road, rail, air or sea. Where, as in the example above, the parties are based in the UK and Korea, the goods will be transported by road in the UK, by sea and then by road in Korea. Although not all multi-modal transport involves the use of containers, this will most often be the case. The goods will be loaded into a container, usually at the carrier's depot in the seller's country (in the UK), and transported to a depot in the buyer's country (in Korea). Rather than a series of contracts of carriage covering the carriage by road in the UK, loading onto the ship, the sea voyage, the unloading and the carriage by road in Korea, one contract with the carrier covers all these aspects. The carrier who arranges the transport is the 'contractual carrier', which will normally arrange a series of sub-contracts to cover different aspects of the entire journey, eg the shipping arrangements. The sub-contractors are known as the 'actual carriers'.

The method of transportation will be agreed between the parties and provided for in the sale contract.

14.4.2 Legal and practical considerations

As between the seller and the buyer, there are legal and practical issues to be considered. The major ones are:

(a) who pays for each stage of the journey; and

(b) which party is responsible for the goods at each stage?

So, how do you draft the contract to take care of this?

One way is to use a standard contract. The ICC publishes Incoterms, which are sets of standard terms. The obligations of each party are laid out in simple terms in a standard book, known as Incoterms 2010 (which come into force on 1 January 2011). In addition, many contracts will continue to be in place which are based on Incoterms 2000.

Incoterms are published in more than 30 languages. This means that each party to a carriage contract can look up the relevant Incoterm in their own language, and see the buyers' and sellers' obligations laid out in simple steps. This helps to avoid misunderstandings, especially when the parties are separated by distance and by language. It thus helps to avoid disputes and litigation, with the consequent cost and time involved.

It should be realised that the Incoterms are not statutory provisions. An Incoterm will only form part of a sale of goods contract if it is expressly incorporated by reference into it, eg 'This contract is to be FOB Hull and is governed by Incoterms 2010'. Once incorporated, they do not deal with the terms of the carriage contract but merely provide which party is to arrange and pay for each of the stages of carriage. In particular, they do provide for the delivery, in the legal sense, of the goods and the passing of the risk in the goods (ie the obligation to insure the goods:). They also cover the obligation to obtain export or import clearance (not relevant for deals entirely within the EU), the buyer's obligation to take delivery, and the obligation to provide proof that the various obligations have been complied with. However, Incoterms do not attempt to cover all the terms of the sale of goods contract. They do not deal with the passing of ownership which the parties should address in the sale of goods contract.

It is also worth adding that the Incoterms use the word 'delivery' both in the legal sense of voluntary transfer of possession of the goods and in the commercial sense of transporting the goods to the buyer.

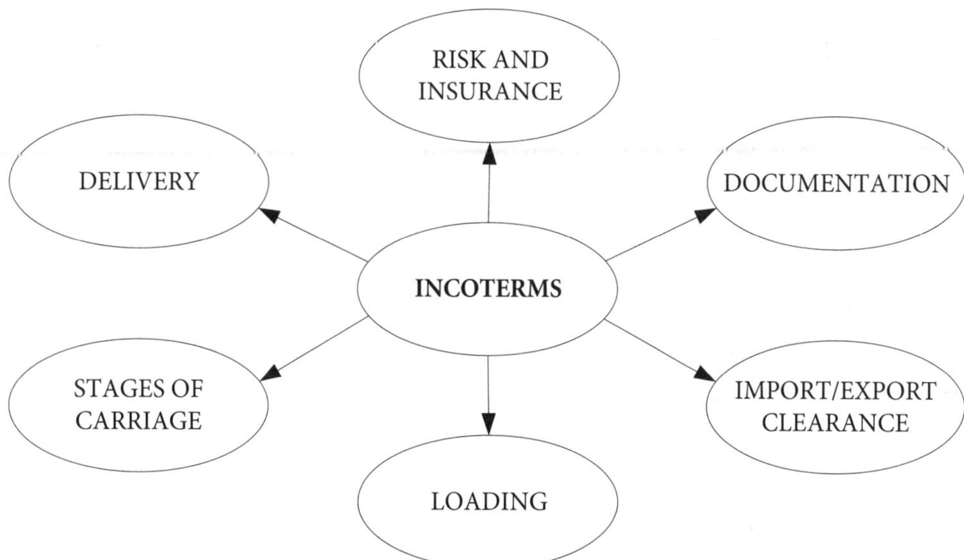

The choice of Incoterm will depend partly on the bargaining strength of the parties and partly on commercial convenience. The use of a particular Incoterm does have implications for the other contracts between the parties. For example, if the parties choose a CIF or CFR contract (see below) the mode of transport must be sea transport for these terms to work.

There is information on the ICC site at www.iccwbo.org.

Some typical Incoterms are as follows (and see **Table 14.1** on p 145):

Rules for Any Mode of Transport

EXW Ex Works
CIP Carriage and Insurance Paid
CPT Carriage Paid To
DAP Delivered at Place*
DAT Delivered at Terminal*
DDP Delivered Duty Paid
FCA Free Carrier

Rules for Sea and Inland Waterway Transport Only

CFR Cost and Freight
CIF Cost, Insurance and Freight
FAS Free Alongside Ship
FOB Free On Board

*DAP and DAT are new Incoterms to be introduced in Incoterms 2010. The new terms replace four Incoterms currently used in Incoterms 2000: DAF (delivered at frontier), DES (delivered ex-ship), DEQ (delivered ex-quay) and DDU (delivered duty unpaid).

The lightest burden on the seller is when the goods are delivered to the buyer 'ex works', that is at the seller's premises. The heaviest is when they have to be delivered to the buyer's premises with the relevant duty paid. These burdens on the seller are reflected in the price agreed for the deal. The less the burden, the less the price. However, it does mean that the buyer has to arrange and pay for the other parts of the chain of transport.

The Incoterms beginning with 'F' or 'C' are contracts where the seller fulfils its obligations in the country of shipment, ie the country of departure of the goods. Those beginning with 'D' are different in nature from those beginning with 'F' and 'C', in that the seller is responsible for the arrival of the goods in the country of destination and must bear all the risks and costs of achieving it.

The traditional sets of terms cannot always be adapted for modern shipping practice. For example, as discussed at **8.4.1**, the typical situation today is not of the ship lying at the dockside waiting for cargo to be loaded. Rather, the aim is to minimise the time spent in port. The goods are therefore in shipping containers which are stored in the docks pending arrival of the appropriate ship. It would also be typical today for goods to be put into shipping containers at the sellers' premises, or at a depot run by the carrier. They would stay in the container until they reached either the buyer, or a carrier's depot in the country of destination.

Some terms which are used for the container trade are as follows:

(a) full container load (FCL);

(b) less than full container load (LCL);

(c) free carrier (equivalent to FOB);

(d) freight, carriage paid (equivalent to CFR); and

(e) freight carriage and insurance paid (equivalent to CIF).

14.4.3 Examples of Incoterms – ex works (EXW)

The burden is lightest on the seller and heaviest on the buyer, in that the buyer has to arrange and pay for collection at the seller's premises.

The seller delivers the goods when he places the goods at the disposal of the buyer at the seller's premises (or other named location, eg a warehouse).

The first point is that the place where the 'works' are has to be specified. So, it could be 'ex works Adams Waste Recycling, Pepper Street, London', for example.

The obligations on the two parties are as follows:

(a) Seller is required to:
   (i) supply goods conforming to the contract, measured and packed;
   (ii) supply the invoice and any other documents;
   (iii) deliver the goods (in the legal sense of transfer of possession) by placing them at the buyer's disposal;
   (iv) pay for any costs incidental to placing the goods at the buyer's disposal; and
   (v) provide further assistance to the buyer for the buyer to obtain necessary licences or insurance.

(b) Buyer is required to:
   (i) accept delivery of the goods and pay for them;
   (ii) obtain appropriate licences and customs clearances; and
   (iii) pay any costs incidental to the export of the goods.

Under EXW, the seller does not arrange for export clearance (which is, of course, only relevant to sales to a buyer located outside the EU). If the buyer were unable to arrange export clearance, then the FCA set of terms should be used instead (see **14.4.4**), providing that the seller is also willing to take on the burden and risk of loading the goods.

The purchase price would always become due on delivery of the goods unless the parties agreed otherwise.

14.4.4 Examples of Incoterms – 'F' terms: main carriage unpaid

These impose more responsibility on the seller than under the ex works terms (see **14.4.3**). Incoterms beginning with 'F' require the seller to deliver the goods for the main carriage (usually sea or air transportation) as required by the buyer. The buyer will usually arrange and pay for the main carriage and the insurance for that journey. With 'F' terms, risk in the goods passes with delivery. There is a variety of 'F' terms. The difference between the 'F' terms is the hand-over point for the goods (ie, the point of legal delivery of the goods).

14.4.4.1 Free carrier (FCA) (named place)

The seller fulfils his obligations when he delivers the goods to the carrier chosen by the buyer at the named point. The risk of loss or damage is transferred at that point. The hand-over point could be the seller's premises, or it could be the carrier's depot, especially if the goods are to be sent by container. The term is frequently used when goods are shipped by container. It can also be used for air freight.

14.4.4.2 Free alongside ship (FAS) (named port of shipment)

Here, the seller fulfils his obligations when he delivers the goods alongside the ship (ie, on the dockside) at the named port of shipment (ie, the port of departure). The buyer will have arranged for the ship, and be paying for the sea carriage and insurance. The costs of loading the goods on to the ship will also be the buyer's expense.

14.4.4.3 Free on board (FOB) (named port of shipment)

These terms impose higher obligations on the seller than FAS. Here, the seller undertakes to place the goods on board a specified ship in a specified port of shipment. All charges up to and including loading the goods on to the ship are the seller's expense. The buyer has to pay the subsequent charges, including sea freight, marine insurance, unloading charges and import duties.

Under Incoterms 2000, 'free on board' means the seller delivers the goods when the goods 'pass over the ship's rail' at the port of shipment. (If this is not suitable then FCA or FAS should be used.) The buyer has the task of making the shipping arrangements and the insurance arrangements. This delivery point in FOB is the same as for CFR and CIF (see **14.4.5**). The 'over the ship's rail' provision does not always accord with modern shipping practice, that is containerised transport and roll-on, roll-off ferries. Incoterms 2010 therefore revised the point of delivery for FOB, CFR and CIF to when the goods are 'on board' the vessel.

The risk in the goods passes with delivery, that is the goods are at the seller's risk until they cross the ship's rail in Incoterms 2000, or are 'on board' in Incoterms 2010.

FOB has been declining in popularity, and losing out to alternatives, especially the CIF terms.

Under FOB, the following are the obligations on the seller and buyer:

(a) Seller is required to:
   (i) supply goods conforming to the sale of goods contract;
   (ii) deliver the goods to the buyer by placing them on board the ship;
   (iii) place them on board in the position required;
   (iv) pay any costs incidental to delivery of the goods;
   (v) obtain an export licence; and
   (vi) provide to the buyer proof of delivery to the ship.
(b) Buyer is required to:
   (i) give sufficient notice to the seller of the time and location of the delivery point (the buyer having contracted with a carrier for the sea journey, and insured the goods from the port of shipment);
   (ii) obtain any appropriate licences;
   (iii) pay costs incidental to the importation of the goods; and
   (iv) pay for the goods.

You should be aware that there are many varieties of FOB contract used in international trade. You have to be sure which one you are using (eg, Incoterms 2010 FOB Hull).

14.4.5 Examples of Incoterms – the 'C' terms: main carriage paid

These sets of terms have more onerous obligations on the seller than the 'F' terms. In the 'C' terms, the seller arranges and pays for the main carriage, usually the sea freight. Therefore, the point up to which the seller is responsible for transport costs needs to be stated after the relevant 'C' term (eg, CIF Sydney). In the CIF and CIP terms, the seller is also responsible for arranging and paying for the insurance. However, the 'C' terms are still contracts where the goods are at the seller's risk only until completion of the first leg of the journey, before the main carriage (like in 'F' terms). So, under the 'C' terms the passing of risk differs from the place to which the seller arranges transport (it is one stage earlier in the journey).

Under the 'D' terms, the risk will not pass until the goods reach their destination (see **14.4.6**).

Documentary credits are commonly used with 'C' terms. This is in line with the nature of the 'C' terms, in that the seller is not at risk once the goods have been handed over to the carrier, so can be paid against the documents received.

The most commonly used set is CIF.

14.4.5.1 Cost, insurance, freight (CIF) (named port of destination)

This is the typical contract where payment against documents would be used, usually on presentation of a bill of lading. In a CIF contract, the seller is in effect undertaking to arrange for the goods to be supplied and transported to the buyer's country.

The seller is required to:

(a) ship goods conforming to the description in the contract;
(b) clear the goods for export;
(c) arrange a contract for sea carriage to the port of destination;
(d) obtain a bill of lading or waybill when the goods are loaded;
(e) arrange and pay for insurance under which the buyer can claim, and provide insurance documents to the buyer;
(f) provide an invoice for the cost of the goods and carriage and insurance; and
(g) transmit to the buyer the bill of lading, insurance documents and invoice, and any other documents needed.

The buyer is required to:

(a) accept the documents tendered by the seller if they are in order;
(b) pay the contract price;
(c) receive the goods at the port of destination;
(d) pay any ancillary costs of the sea voyage, and costs of unloading and land transport to the buyer's premises;
(e) bear all risks of the goods after their passing over the ship's rail at the port of shipment;
(f) pay all customs dues and taxes; and
(g) obtain any import licences.

Under CIF, the price quoted to the buyer for the goods includes insurance and freight to the buyer's home port. This increases the certainty of the price for the buyer. Under an FOB contract, the buyer bears the risk of fluctuations in freight and insurance rates. The use of payment against documents means the seller will be paid quickly, and that the goods can be sold on by the buyer whilst they are still on the high seas.

The property in the goods passes when the buyer pays for them and accepts the documents. However, the risk in the goods has already passed to the buyer when the goods were loaded on to the ship in the port of shipment (ie, in the seller's country). Thus, CIF is an exception to SGA 1979, s 20, where prima facie risk passes with the property in the goods.

A CIF contract is always an export contract, and can be used only for sea or inland waterway transport.

As with FOB, there are many variations of CIF used in the commercial world. CIF and FOB are the two commonest sets of Incoterms in commercial use.

14.4.5.2 Cost and freight (CFR) (named port of destination)

The seller has to arrange and pay for the carriage of the goods to the foreign port. He is not obliged to take out insurance for the sea voyage, which is the buyer's responsibility both to arrange and to pay for, unlike CIF. If the seller fails to give the buyer enough notice for the buyer to be able to insure the goods, the goods could be regarded as travelling at the seller's risk, under SGA 1979, s 32(3).

The CFR terms lead to a rather artificial division between the arrangements for carriage and those for insurance. As such, they are not frequently used. They may be of use where the buyer's country requires its importers to insure at home, possibly for foreign exchange reasons.

14.4.5.3 Carriage and insurance paid to (CIP) (named place of destination)

This is on the borderline between being a CIF contract and one of the 'D' Incoterms (see **14.4.6**).

These terms are suitable for any mode of transport, including multimodal transport. The seller pays the freight to the place of destination (which could be a port, as with CIF), but in addition the seller arranges and pays for insurance to that place of destination for the buyer's benefit. As with CIF, the risk in the goods passes when the goods are handed over to the carrier.

14.4.5.4 Carriage paid to (CPT) (named place of destination)

This differs from CIP in that the seller is not obliged to obtain insurance cover for the transport.

14.4.6 Examples of Incoterms – the 'D' Incoterms: arrival

'D' terms impose the highest burden on the seller.

In the 'D' Incoterms, the passing of risk and delivery of the goods occur at the same time. The goods are delivered, in the legal sense, to the buyer at the place of arrival in the buyer's country, at which point risk passes as well. This is in contrast to the 'C' terms, where (legal) delivery takes place in the port of shipment (see **14.4.5**). In the case of 'D' contracts, payment by the buyer is made against the goods arriving, not against documents. However, the seller would hand over a bill of lading or a waybill to the buyer to enable the buyer to obtain delivery of the goods from the carrier.

14.4.6.1 Delivered at place (DAP) (named place of delivery)

This is a new Incoterm included in Incoterms 2010. Typically under this term, delivery is at the buyer's premises but the goods are not cleared for import. Importation formalities must be therefore arranged by the buyer, including payment of any import charges.

14.4.6.2 Delivered at terminal (DAT) (named terminal point of delivery)

This is also a new Incoterm included in Incoterms 2010. Under this term, delivery is at a container port or terminal (in other words, the goods are not delivered all the way to the buyer's premises). Other than that, it operates in the same way as DAP.

14.4.6.3 Delivered duty paid (DDP) (named place of destination in the buyer's country)

These terms place the highest burden of all the Incoterms on the seller. They would normally be used only for the supply of a small quantity of goods by air.

The goods are at the seller's risk and expense until the buyer takes delivery at the place of destination. Under DDP, the seller pays all charges, including import duties and carriage in the buyer's country.

There is no obligation on the seller to insure the goods under DDP.

Table 14.1 Incoterms 2010

TERM / SERVICE	EXW Ex-Works	FCA Free Carrier	FAS Free Alongside Ship	FOB Free On-Board Vessel	CFR Cost & Freight	CIF Cost Insurance & Freight	CPT Carriage Paid to	CIP Carriage & Insurance Paid To	DAT Delivered at Terminal	DAP Delivered at Place	DDP Delivered Duty Paid
Applicable to (eg air, sea):	All modes	All modes	Shipping only	Shipping only	Shipping only	Shipping only	All modes	All modes	All modes	All modes	All modes
Basic description	B collects from S	S gives goods to B's carrier in S's country	S delivers alongside ship	S delivers on ship	S pays for shipping	As CFR but S provides insurance	As FCA but S pays for carrier	As CPT but S pays for insurance	S delivers to named terminal (usually in B's country)	S delivers to any agreed place (usually B's premises)	As DAP or DAT but S deals with import formalities
Point of delivery (and passing of risk)	S's premises	When given to carrier	When goods alongside	When on board	When on board	When on board	When given to carrier	When given to carrier	When at terminal	At agreed place	At agreed terminal or place
	Who Pays	**Who Pays**	**Who Pays**	**Who Pays**	**Who Pays**	**Who Pays**	**Who Pays**	**Who Pays**	**Who Pays**	**Who Pays**	**Who Pays**
Loading at point of origin	Buyer	Seller	Seller	Seller	Seller	Seller	Seller	Seller	Seller	Seller	Seller
Inland freight in country of origin	Buyer	Buyer	Seller	Seller	Seller	Seller	Seller	Seller	Seller	Seller	Seller
Port receiving charges	Buyer	Buyer	Seller	Seller	Seller	Seller	Seller	Seller	Seller	Seller	Seller
Loading at port/airport	Buyer	Buyer	Buyer	Seller	Seller	Seller	Seller	Seller	Seller	Seller	Seller
Ocean/air freight charges	Buyer	Buyer	Buyer	Buyer	Seller	Seller	Seller	Seller	Seller	Seller	Seller
Customs, duties and taxes abroad	Buyer	Buyer	Buyer	Buyer	Buyer	Buyer	Buyer	Buyer	Buyer	Buyer	Seller
Inland freight to final destination	Buyer	Buyer	Buyer	Buyer	Buyer	Buyer	Buyer	Buyer	Buyer	Seller*	Seller

* The 'agreed place' is likely to be the final destination

Chapter 15

Financing and Security Arrangements in International Sale of Goods

15.1 Introduction

An international sale of goods contract, like a domestic sale contract, will set out the payment provisions agreed between the parties. However, as discussed in **Chapter 12**, there are two main problems for the seller because of the longer payment periods involved:

(a) it needs money as soon as possible to meet its own outgoings incurred in performance of the contract, eg the costs of raw materials, labour, transport, etc; and

(b) it needs some sort of security that it will actually get paid, because the commercial risks in international sale agreements are far higher. In the event of non-payment by the buyer, the chances of recovering the goods are extremely remote once they are offshore.

If the seller is in a strong enough bargaining position, it may be able to demand payment in advance or, at the latest, before the time of shipment of the goods, but this is very much an exceptional situation. In most cases, the buyer will want to arrange for a credit period, especially as it may be some time before the goods arrive at their ultimate destination. In practice, the seller may take the length of the credit period into account in setting the price of the goods, but the economic reality for the seller is that it may still encounter cash-flow problems while waiting for payment.

These problems can be resolved by the use of negotiable instruments, eg bills of exchange, or drafts, and by the use of documentary credits. These are used in conjunction with the delivery of the shipping documents by the seller as described in **Chapter 14**. The documents are used to trigger the obligation to pay on the part of the buyer. The importance of the delivery of documents in order to facilitate payment was illustrated last year when the Icelandic volcano erupted, grounding flights throughout northern Europe. The ICC reported that payments under the documentary collection system were being delayed as courier companies were prevented from delivering documents.

The law relating to bills of exchange and documentary credits has developed over centuries and involves complex networks of contractual relationships between the seller, buyer and the parties' respective banks. This chapter gives an introduction to bills of exchange and documentary credits, and some of the contractual relationships involved are discussed in more detail below. However, given the complexity of this area of law, only a broad outline is possible.

15.1.1 Methods of payment

There are three main methods of payment available in an international transaction:

(a) Cash in advance. The seller may insist on payment in advance, particularly where he has not dealt with the buyer before or lacks confidence in the buyer's creditworthiness. In practice, this is unusual, and insistence on cash in advance may cause the buyer to seek the goods from other suppliers.

(b) Payment on 'open account'. Where the parties have dealt with each other on a regular basis and the seller has complete faith in the creditworthiness of the buyer, the seller may agree to 'open account' terms. This is more favourable to the buyer than insistence on cash in advance. There are advantages for both parties, as it is cheaper than the use of a bill of exchange since bank charges will be lower. Once the seller has delivered the goods to the buyer, he will invoice the buyer. The invoice may provide for a credit period, depending on what has been agreed between the parties. There is a variety of actual payment methods, eg cheque, banker's draft, inter-bank transfer or international direct debit. Payment on 'open account' is more usual where the sale is within Europe.

(c) Bill of exchange. Where the seller is unsure of the buyer's creditworthiness, the parties may agree for payment to be made under a bill of exchange, which is a form of negotiable instrument. This method of payment is more likely to be used if the sale is outside of the EU, as it will be more difficult to enforce payment or reclaim the goods. Payment is arranged through the international banking system. The mechanics of payment under a bill of exchange will be considered at **15.2.4**. As payment is arranged through the banking system, it is a more expensive method than using 'open account' methods.

The method of payment will be agreed between the parties and will depend on a variety of factors, including the bargaining strength of the parties. It will be provided for in the sale contract.

15.1.2 Guarantee of payment

Whichever method of payment is chosen, it does not guarantee payment. Even a bill of exchange, like a cheque, may be dishonoured, eg if the buyer becomes insolvent. To secure the seller's position, it is possible for the buyer to arrange for a third party, generally a bank, to provide documentary credits. These are contractual undertakings by which the bank itself will guarantee payment, provided that the seller complies with the terms of the credit (usually by providing specified documents). The advantage of a documentary credit is that the seller can be guaranteed payment before it ships the goods. Clearly, the promise of payment by the bank to the seller is dependent on the buyer's agreement to reimburse the bank. In addition, such guarantees come at a price, and the buyer will incur considerable expense in putting in place the necessary arrangements for a documentary credit.

15.1.3 Relationship between bills of exchange and documentary credits

Documentary credits and bills of exchange have very different uses and functions; they are very different entities in law, aimed at solving very different problems.

(a) The primary function of the bill of exchange is as a means of providing payment to the seller, by way of an easily transferable document rather than the straightforward payment of cash.

(b) The function of a documentary credit is to give a security guarantee to the seller, provided by a third party bank, against the risk of the buyer's default. The provision of a documentary credit will be required where the seller is unwilling to contract with the buyer without one, eg because it has no knowledge of the credit history of the buyer, and where it is powerful enough to get its own way. Where a documentary credit has been agreed, the sale contract will oblige the buyer to open the credit within a specified time from the date of the contract. A documentary credit creates separate contractual obligations on the part of the bank additional to and independent of the sale contract and the buyer's obligation to pay for the goods.

15.2 Bills of exchange

Bills of exchange (or 'drafts') are defined in s 3(1) of the Bills of Exchange Act 1882 (BEA 1882) as follows:

> A bill of exchange is an unconditional order in writing, addressed by one person to another, signed by the person giving it, requiring the person to whom it is addressed to pay on demand or at a fixed or determinable future time, a sum certain in money to or to the order of a specified person, or to a bearer.

In other words, a bill of exchange is a document under which one party (the 'drawer') orders another party, usually a bank or financier (the 'drawee') to pay a specified sum of money to a third party (the 'payee') or to bearer. A bill of exchange will specify the place of payment (eg, 'payable in Rio de Janeiro at XY bank').

A cheque is defined as a 'bill of exchange drawn on a banker, payable on demand' (BEA 1882, s 73). A cheque is therefore a sub-species of a bill of exchange.

Typical characteristics of a bill of exchange are:

(a) every obligation in the bill must be expressed in writing;

(b) the order to pay must be unconditional;

(c) it is addressed by one person to another;

(d) it is payable on demand or at a fixed time in the future (see **15.2.1**);

(e) it is for a specific sum of money;

(f) the drawer, or his agent, must have signed it;

(g) the obligations, typically payment, can be transferred by 'negotiation', usually at a discount (see **15.2.2.1**); and

(h) performance of the obligations (eg payment) can be demanded only by the person holding the bill.

Before considering the mechanics of how payment will be made under a bill of exchange, it is useful to look at some of the terminology involved.

15.2.1 Types of bill

15.2.1.1 Sight bills and term bills

The type of bill determines when it will be paid.

(a) 'Sight' bills are payable on demand, ie on presentation to the drawee, usually a bank, so payment is immediate. They are less important commercially than term bills. A cheque is an example of a sight bill. It is payable when it is presented to the drawer's bank.

(b) 'Term' bills provide for payment at some specified date in the future. This is usually 90 or 180 days from the date of presentation, eg '90 days after sight'. The advantage of a term bill is that it can be used to provide the buyer with a credit period. The rest of this chapter will deal with term, rather than sight, bills.

15.2.1.2 Bearer bills and order bills

A bill may either be payable to 'bearer', or may direct payment to, or to the order of, a specified person.

(a) Bearer bills may be transferred merely by delivery, like a bank note. The drawee (see **15.2.3**) is simply obliged to pay out to whoever happens to possess the bill at the relevant time. There is no obligation on the drawee to check how the holder has obtained the bill. Bearer bills are clearly very insecure and are not used much in practice.

(b) Order bills specify payment to a particular person or to his order, like a cheque. In order to make a bill non-transferable, it is essential to state this specifically, eg 'pay X only'.

An order bill may be 'opened up' into a bearer bill by the present holder indorsing it in blank (ie signing his name only on the back), and then 'closed down' again by indorsing it to a particular person (ie the holder signing his name with the words 'pay X or order'). A bearer bill, however, cannot be 'closed down'. (Cheques used to be widely negotiable but, as a fraud prevention measure, most cheques are now printed with crossing lines and 'a/c payee', which prevents them being transferable by endorsement).

15.2.1.3 Documentary, clean and claused bills

Where payment of the bill is stated to be against documents, ie the seller must provide stipulated shipping documents, it is known as a 'documentary bill'. If payment is not against documents, ie the bank will pay simply on presentation of the bill, it is described as a 'clean' bill.

A bill of exchange is not normally set out as simply as a personal cheque – it has 'clauses'. There could be provisions, for example, dealing with exchange rates for currencies, or stating that the bill is payable with bankers' charges. If a bill does not stipulate that incidental charges are borne by the drawee (the bank) then they are borne by the drawer (buyer of the goods). An example of a simple draft bill of exchange (without clauses) is set out on p 154.

15.2.2 Negotiable instruments

A bill of exchange is a type of negotiable instrument. Negotiable instruments include:

(a) cheques;

(b) bills of exchange;

(c) bank notes;

(d) banker's drafts; and

(e) promissory notes (in some circumstances).

An 'instrument' is a document which evidences the holder's right to enforce a legal right, such as a promise to pay a sum of money (a 'promissory note') or an order to someone else to pay out a sum of money (a bill of exchange).

In this context, 'negotiation' means the giving and receiving of documents which evidence promises to pay and to receive money, as a 'substitute' for handing over the money itself. Where the documents are freely transferable, the documents are said to be 'negotiable'.

One significant advantage of a bill of exchange is that the document itself, the bill, is transferable, so that payment can be demanded not only by the original payee, but also by anyone who has possession of it at the relevant time for payment. Thus a bill of exchange can be bought and sold like any other commodity. The way in which a bill is transferred is by the holder 'indorsing' it (ie signing his name on the back of the bill).

15.2.2.1 Discounting

This ability to transfer a bill of exchange means that term bills can be used by the seller to raise money before payment becomes due, by selling the bill on to a third party. Whoever buys the bill will be able to present the bill for payment (unless he sells it on to someone else). The buyer will pay less than the face value of the bill to take into account the delay in receiving payment. This is known as 'discounting'. This use of a bill gives considerable flexibility to the seller in its need to raise interim finance.

For discounting to work, it is important that the buyer knows that the drawee of the bill (usually a bank) will pay up when the payment date is due. Term bills are therefore presented to the drawee which will indorse its 'acceptance' on the face of the bill, thus guaranteeing payment of the bill in the future (see **15.2.4**). When payment is due, the bill is re-presented to the drawee for payment. Thus, a term bill must be presented twice to the bank, and payment is due on the second occasion.

15.2.2.2 The 'holder in due course'

The problem for the ultimate holder is that the bill might have been stolen, or one of the previous holders of the bill might have had some other defect in his title to the bill. However, rules have developed to protect the 'holder in due course'. Under s 29(1) of the BEA 1882, a holder in due course is anyone who gives value for a bill which is still current and which appears to be perfectly regular on the face of it. Provided a holder in due course has taken the bill in good faith, and without knowledge of any defects in the title to the bill, he will take the bill 'free from equities'. This means that he can ignore any defects in the title of anyone who had held the bill before him. There is a presumption in favour of a holder that he is a holder in due course.

There are two other types of holder under the 1882 Act: 'holders for value', and mere 'holders'. They have fewer rights than a holder in due course, and are beyond the scope of this chapter.

15.2.3 Parties to the bill of exchange

There are three original parties to a bill of exchange:

(a) drawer;

(b) drawee; and

(c) payee.

Perhaps the analogy of a personal cheque is the easiest one to visualise. Here, you would be the drawer of the cheque, your bank would be the drawee (eg, Barclays Bank) and the payee would be the person you are paying (eg, your landlord). The biggest difference from a personal cheque is that with a term bill, the drawee must 'accept' the bill by signing it in order to become liable to pay out on it (see **15.2.4**). Once it has done so, it becomes known as the 'acceptor'.

15.2.4 Collection arrangements

The term 'collection arrangements' or 'documentary collection' describes the mechanics by which the seller collects payment under a documentary bill. A bill of exchange is normally drawn either against (or guaranteed by) a documentary credit, or alternatively against the documents themselves, when it will be known as a 'documentary bill'. A documentary bill is used where the seller wishes to guard against the possibility of not getting paid, but is not in a strong enough bargaining position to be able to demand a documentary credit (see **15.3**). The problem about delivering documents of title, such as a bill of lading (see **14.3.1**), direct to the buyer is that there is a serious risk of non-payment for the seller. Often the buyer sells the goods on (and transfers the bill of lading) to a third party whilst the goods are still at sea, and the seller loses control of the goods. The advantage of a documentary bill is that it uses the banking system to safeguard the seller's position so it can be reduce the risk of non-payment.

Given the analogy of a cheque (see **15.2.3**), it would be logical to assume that the basic position would be that the drawer is the buyer, the drawee is the buyer's bank, and the payee is the seller of the goods. However, with a bill of exchange, the position is as follows:

(a) the seller is the drawer;

(b) the buyer or his bank is the drawee; and

(c) the seller is the payee, ie the drawer and the payee are the same.

To see how the collection arrangements work, assume that a UK seller, Wood Magic, has entered into a CIF contract with an Australian buyer, Franklin Furnishings Ltd. The parties have agreed a 90-day credit period. The sale contract will provide for a term bill of exchange, and that the documents will be tendered against acceptance. (This is usually abbreviated in the contact to 'D/A' ('documents against acceptance').) The buyer has made the necessary arrangements through its bank in Australia.

(a) Wood Magic ships the goods as agreed in the sale contract, and forwards the bill of exchange with the shipping documents (commercial invoice, bill of lading and the insurance policy) to its own bank in the UK (known as the 'remitting bank').

(b) Wood Magic's bank will then pass the shipping documents together with the bill of exchange to Franklin's bank in Australia (known as the 'collecting bank'). The safeguard for Wood Magic is that the documents do not go directly to the buyer.

(c) The collecting bank will either forward the bill of exchange to Franklin for acceptance, or, more usually, accept the bill on behalf of the buyer. A bill is accepted by signing the front of the bill. If the bank does this, it will become the 'acceptor'. At this stage, Wood Magic can discount the bill. If the bill is not accepted it is 'dishonoured', and Wood Magic can immediately sue Franklin.

(d) The documents will be released to Franklin only on acceptance of the bill of exchange. Once Franklin has the documents, it will be able to use them to obtain possession of the goods from the carrier (or to sell them on whilst still in transit), as it now has the documents of title. A further safeguard for Wood Magic is that the collecting bank should not release the documents to Franklin until acceptance has taken place or it will be liable, even if it is not the acceptor.

(e) The collecting bank will either advise the seller of acceptance and hold the bill until the end of the credit period, or return it to Wood Magic. If Wood Magic has discounted the bill, it will transfer it to any subsequent holder of the bill.

(f) When the bill matures, the Australian bank will pay out on the bill and recover the money from Franklin.

Nevertheless, the bill can still become dishonoured by non-payment when it becomes due for payment. This is the main reason why a seller will try to get a documentary credit put in place, whenever possible (see **15.3** below).

These arrangements may be varied by the agreement of the parties, usually to suit commercial convenience. A commonly agreed practice is for the seller to draw up the bill and to present it to its own bank for acceptance. The seller's bank acts as both remitting and collecting bank. This will be the case, for example, where the parties have agreed that payment will be guaranteed by a confirmed documentary credit. (see **15.3.4.2**). This has the advantage of keeping the bill of exchange in the seller's country, which makes it easier to enforce payment. Clearly, the seller's bank will be prepared to accept the bill only if it has already agreed with the buyer's bank that the buyer's bank will reimburse it in return for the documents required to perform the sale of goods contract.

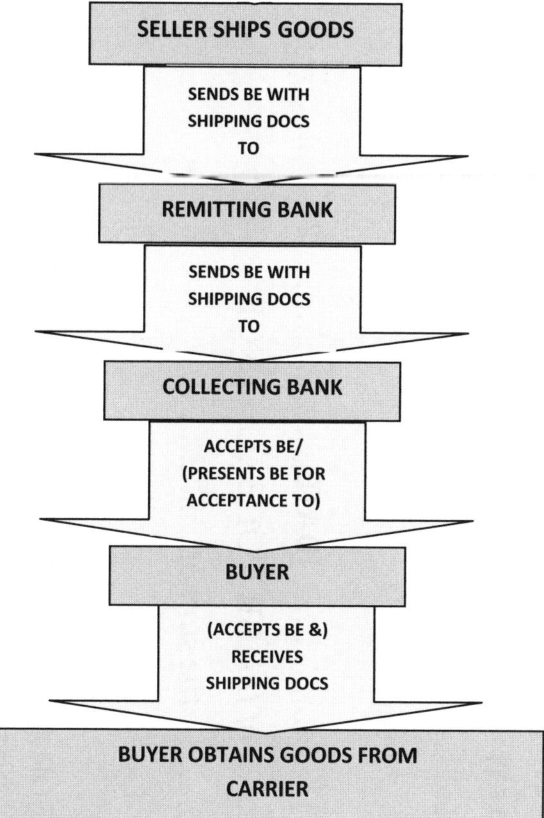

Figure 15.1 Collection arrangements

15.2.5 The relationship of the bill of exchange and underlying sales contracts

The obligation to pay on a bill of exchange is unconditional, and will not be affected by any defect or breach of the underlying sales contract on the part of the seller. Thus the obligation to pay under the bill of exchange is the result of a separate contract and remains unaffected, even if the goods are defective. In other words, a bill of exchange has an autonomy of its own.

The only real exception to this is if there is complete or partial failure of consideration by the seller. If the seller sues for payment, the buyer can raise the breach as a defence to a claim for refusal to pay the bill. The claim is a claim on the bill of exchange, on a promise that the paper could be turned into cash. It is not a claim for breach of the payment obligations under the underlying sales contract.

15.2.6 Liability on a bill of exchange

With our example (at **15.2.4**), the primary liability is clearly intended to be on the Australian bank as acceptor of the bill. If the bank refuses to accept, ie 'dishonours', the bill then Franklin will be secondarily liable. As discussed above, Wood Magic can immediately sue Franklin.

On maturity, at the end of the credit period, the bill in the Wood Magic example above will be expressed to be payable at the Australian bank. The bill will be exchanged for payment. If payment is 'in due course', the bill will be discharged and no longer be legally operative. Under s 59(1) payment 'in due course' means payment to the holder on the date the bill matures or some time afterwards, in good faith and without notice of any defect in the holder's title. If the Australian bank does not pay, the holder of the bill may sue the bank.

This is a very general statement of the liability situation, and reference should be made to other texts for dealing with detailed questions, such as liability and indemnity between different parties.

BILL OF EXCHANGE
(DRAFT)

No ....

Exchange for .... [AMOUNT] [6]................... [DATE] .... *20* ....

.... [AT SIGHT/90 DAYS AFTER DATE] [5]............... *of this* BILL OF EXCHANGE

pay to the order of [4]................. *[OURSELVES]* .... *the sum of* ....

[AMOUNT IN WORDS] ....

To NORTH EAST BANK plc[2]
COMMERCIAL ROAD, DALEBY,
EAST YORKSHIRE, DN1 72Y

FOR AND ON BEHALF OF
<u>NORTHERN SPINNERS LTD</u>[1, 3]

____
DIRECTOR

1. addressed by one person (the drawer)
2. to another (the drawee), here the seller's bank
3. signed by the person giving it (the drawer)
4. requiring the person to whom it is addressed to pay to the order of a specified person or to bearer (the payee)
5. on demand, or at a fixed or determinable future time
6. a certain sum in money.

[Note: acceptance by signature will be required with a 'term bill' (see point 5 in this example and **15.4.1**); it is quite normal to insert words of acceptance on the face of the bill, but this is not essential as signature will suffice without more. With a sight or demand bill, no signature is required.]

15.3 Documentary credits

We have just looked at the use of bills of exchange and other ways to facilitate the payment to the seller, but payment may never be made at all if the buyer refuses to, or cannot, pay for the goods, for example because of insolvency. In international (and sometimes in domestic) sales of goods, it is quite common for the seller to require a documentary credit ('letter of credit') to be opened, as a guarantee that the seller will be paid once it presents the documents specified in the credit to the bank.

Where the parties have agreed that a documentary credit will be opened, the contract of sale will provide that the buyer will arrange (and pay for) the credit. The buyer will enter into an agreement with a bank (often its own bank), under which the bank provides a written assurance (the documentary credit) that, if the seller properly performs its side of the contract, the bank will pay the seller. The bank acts directly as principal towards the seller, and not simply as a guarantor if the buyer does not pay. Therefore the bank, rather than the buyer, pays the seller, and the seller's rights are directly enforceable against it.

15.3.1 What is a documentary credit?

Almost all documentary credits are regulated by the Uniform Customs and Practice for Documentary Credits (UCP) published by the ICC. The current version is UCP 600 (2007 revision, which came into effect on 1 July 2007), which consists of 39 articles which regulate documentary credits. (Note that the UCP rules are not statutory rules. Like Incoterms (see **14.4**), they must be incorporated into the contract to be effective. Usually, the credit itself will state that it is subject to the UCP 600.)

The definition of a 'documentary credit' in Art 2 of UCP 600 is:

> Any arrangement, however named or described, ... that is irrevocable and thereby constitutes a definite undertaking of the issuing bank to honour a complying presentation.

To 'honour' means to fulfil the credit arrangement by one or another of the payment methods discussed in **15.1.1**. A 'complying presentation' of documents is one that is in accordance with the terms and conditions of the credit, the applicable provisions of the UCP and with international standard banking practice.

A specimen documentary credit is reproduced below. This will be used to illustrate how a documentary credit works.

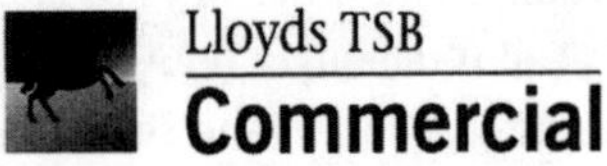

an irrevocable letter of credit

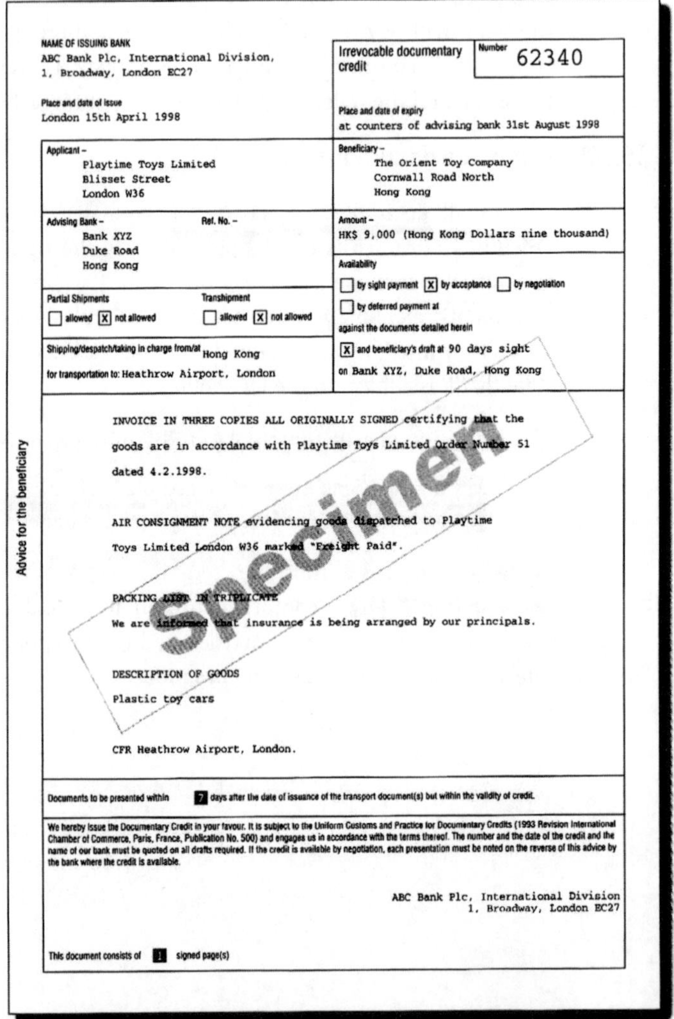

NAME OF ISSUING BANK
ABC Bank Plc, International Division,
1, Broadway, London EC27

Irrevocable documentary credit — Number 62340

Place and date of issue
London 15th April 1998

Place and date of expiry
at counters of advising bank 31st August 1998

Applicant –
Playtime Toys Limited
Blisset Street
London W36

Beneficiary –
The Orient Toy Company
Cornwall Road North
Hong Kong

Advising Bank – Ref. No. –
Bank XYZ
Duke Road
Hong Kong

Amount –
HK$ 9,000 (Hong Kong Dollars nine thousand)

Availability
☐ by sight payment ☒ by acceptance ☐ by negotiation
☐ by deferred payment at
against the documents detailed herein
☒ and beneficiary's draft at 90 days sight
on Bank XYZ, Duke Road, Hong Kong

Partial Shipments: ☐ allowed ☒ not allowed
Transhipment: ☐ allowed ☒ not allowed

Shipping/despatch/taking in charge from/at Hong Kong
for transportation to: Heathrow Airport, London

Advice for the beneficiary

INVOICE IN THREE COPIES ALL ORIGINALLY SIGNED certifying that the goods are in accordance with Playtime Toys Limited Order Number 51 dated 4.2.1998.

AIR CONSIGNMENT NOTE evidencing goods dispatched to Playtime Toys Limited London W36 marked "Freight Paid".

PACKING LIST IN TRIPLICATE

We are informed that insurance is being arranged by our principals.

DESCRIPTION OF GOODS

Plastic toy cars

CFR Heathrow Airport, London.

Specimen

Documents to be presented within 7 days after the date of issuance of the transport document(s) but within the validity of credit.

We hereby issue the Documentary Credit in your favour. It is subject to the Uniform Customs and Practice for Documentary Credits (1993 Revision International Chamber of Commerce, Paris, France, Publication No. 500) and engages us in accordance with the terms thereof. The number and the date of the credit and the name of our bank must be quoted on all drafts required. If the credit is available by negotiation, each presentation must be noted on the reverse of this advice by the bank where the credit is available.

ABC Bank Plc, International Division
1, Broadway, London EC27

This document consists of 1 signed page(s)

15.3.2 Advantages and disadvantages of documentary credits

The use of a documentary credit has advantages for all the parties, as set out in **Table 15.1** below. The main disadvantage is the cost to the buyer of using letters of credit. These are very expensive to arrange, and the less creditworthy the buyer, the more expensive the credit, because of the risk to the credit supplier. Clearly, a seller is able to obtain a documentary credit only if it has enough bargaining power. However, the buyer may be compensated by a reduction in the price of the goods.

Advantages for the seller	Advantages for the buyer	Advantages for the bank
Insolvency of B is less of a risk	Added security for the seller is likely to be reflected in price of goods.	Possession of documents protects its position if B fails to refund
Guarantees payment from an early stage in transaction	Documents examined by professional staff at bank(s) so more likely to be in order.	
Can deal with a bank in its own country		
Further protection can be offered by 'confirmed' credit		

Table 15.1 Advantages and disadvantages of a documentary credit

15.3.3 How a documentary credit works

To illustrate how a documentary credit works, assume that as well as agreeing to payment by means of a 90-day bill of exchange, Wood Magic and Franklin (see **5.2.4**) have agreed to a confirmed irrevocable letter of credit.

15.3.3.1 Arranging the credit

The buyer, Franklin, will go to a bank in its own country and ask the bank to set up a documentary credit in favour of the seller, Wood Magic. In practice, the bank to be used will have been agreed between the parties. The buyer is the 'Applicant' and the seller is the 'Beneficiary'. Clearly, the buyer will have to pay for this service, and the provision of a documentary credit, particularly a confirmed credit, is expensive. This is why it has to be a term of the sale contract between the buyer and the seller, and, as discussed, the buyer is unlikely to agree unless it is in a weak bargaining position.

15.3.3.2 Notification of the credit

Once the Australian bank has agreed to the credit being opened, it will issue the letter of credit (the bank will clearly be unwilling to do so unless it is assured that the buyer has the funds to reimburse it, so generally the buyer will either deposit funds to cover this, or have sufficient credit with the bank). It will ask another bank in the UK to advise Wood Magic that the credit has been opened. The Australian bank is the 'Issuing Bank' and the UK bank is the 'Advising Bank'. The Advising Bank is usually a bank with which the Issuing Bank has a special arrangement. (If the seller banks at one of the major international banks, it will usually be able to arrange for its own bank to be the Advising Bank.) As this is a confirmed credit, the Advising Bank will add its confirmation to the credit, thus becoming the 'Confirming Bank' (see **15.3.3.3**).

15.3.3.3 Role of the banks in relation to the documents

Once Wood Magic has been notified of the credit, it will ship the goods and send the bank the documents stipulated in the credit. The documents are examined for 'strict compliance' to ensure that they comply with the terms of the credit (see **15.3.6.2**). This will often involve two detailed examinations, one by the Advising/Confirming Bank and another by the Issuing Bank upon transfer to it of the documents. This is because either bank may be liable for wrongfully accepting or rejecting documents. If the documents comply with the credit, the Advising/Confirming Bank will pay out the seller in accordance with the chosen payment method shown on the credit itself.

Figure 15.2 below illustrates how the transaction works.

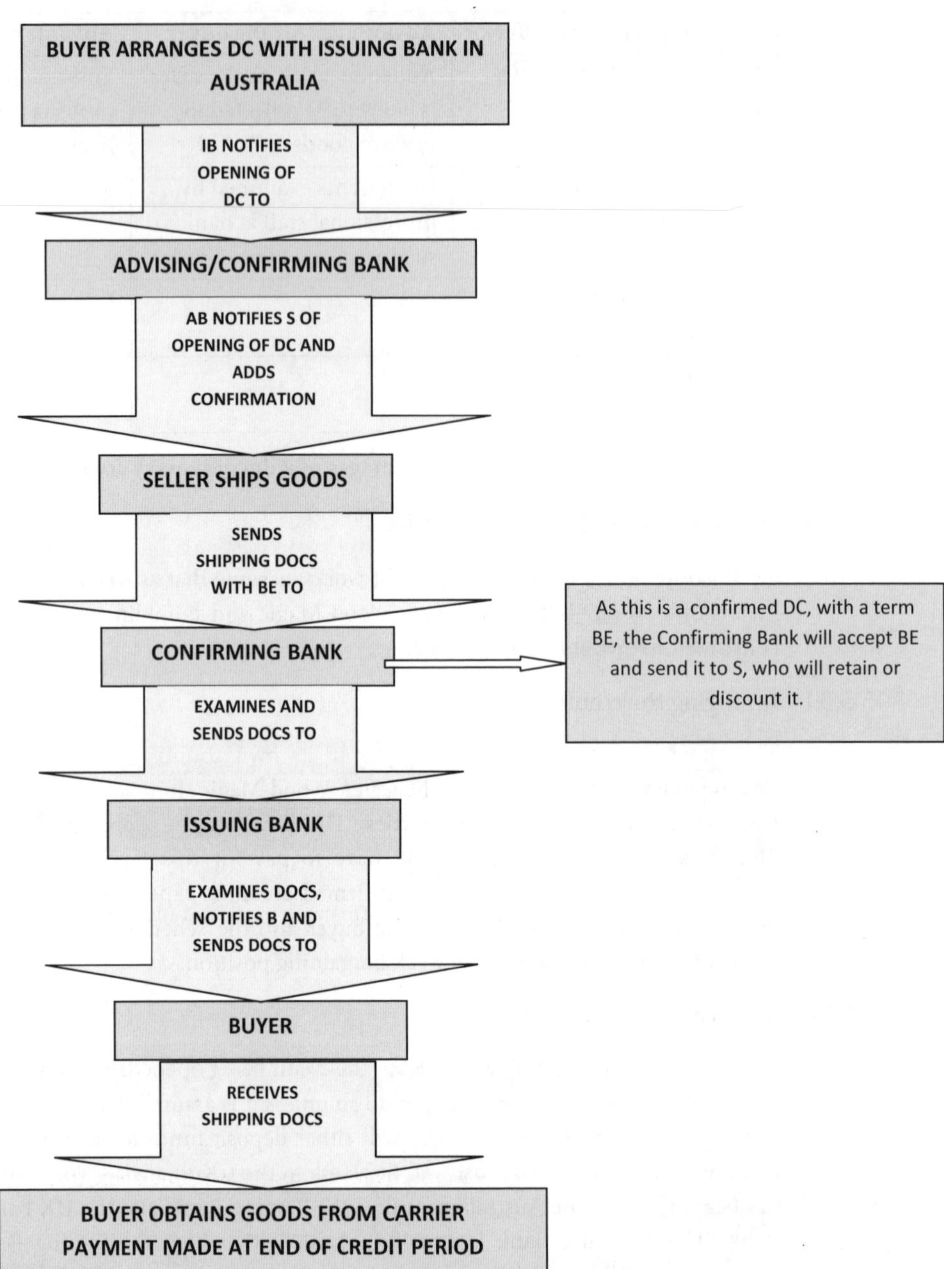

Figure 15.2 Documentary credit transaction

15.3.4 Types of documentary credit

Documentary credits can be of different types. The type of credit will be agreed between the parties and provided for in contract of sale.

15.3.4.1 Revocable and irrevocable credits

A revocable credit may be cancelled or 'revoked' by the buyer at any time. Thus it is, to all intents and purposes, useless in guaranteeing payment. Once an irrevocable letter of credit has been notified to the seller, the buyer is powerless to countermand it. Under the UCP 600, all credits are now irrevocable, unless the parties state otherwise. (The previous version, UCP 500, did extend to revocable credits, and the parties can agree to make the agreement subject to the UCP 500 rather than the UCP 600.)

The use of revocable credits is rare, and so the rest of this chapter will concentrate on irrevocable credits.

15.3.4.2 Confirmed and unconfirmed letters of credit

Even an irrevocable credit is not the ideal arrangement for the seller. If the buyer's bank does not pay for any reason, the seller will have to take action against a foreign bank in a different country. The best arrangement for the seller is to insist that the credit is 'confirmed'. Here the Advising Bank (in the seller's country) will add its own undertaking to that of the Issuing Bank that it will pay under the terms of the credit, ie it confirms the credit (and becomes the 'Confirming Bank').

15.3.5 Contractual relationships

The relationships of the parties with the banks involved depends on which type of credit is used:

(a) With an unconfirmed letter of credit, the Advising Bank is simply an agent of the Issuing Bank, and its only function is to notify the seller and receive the documents.

(b) With a confirmed letter of credit, the Confirming Bank is adding its own guarantee of payment. It is, in effect, entering into a separate banking contract (as principal, not as an agent) with the seller to pay, provided that the seller provides the documents stipulated in the letter of credit. If the Confirming Bank fails to pay, the seller can sue it direct without needing to claim against the Issuing Bank.

Thus the setting up of a documentary credit gives rise to a complex network of contractual relationships. In relation to a confirmed documentary credit, these were summarised by Lord Diplock in *United City Merchants (Investments) Ltd v Royal Bank of Canada* [1938] 1 AC 168: 'It is trite law that there are four autonomous though interconnected contractual relationships involved.' In fact, as Malek and Quest point out in *Jack: Documentary Credits* (4th edn, Bloomsbury Professional, 2009), there are in fact five separate contracts, as Lord Diplock overlooked the contract between the confirming bank and the beneficiary. These are between:

(a) Buyer and Seller (ie the sale contract);
(b) Buyer and Issuing Bank;
(c) Issuing Bank and Confirming Bank;
(d) Issuing Bank and Beneficiary;
(e) Confirming Bank and Beneficiary.

The exact nature of these contracts is beyond the scope of this book, but the case illustrates the complexity of the relationships involved.

15.3.6 Practical considerations

Where the documentary credit does not comply with the provisions of the sale contract, the buyer will be in breach of contract. In addition, the obligations of the buyer and the seller in relation to the documentary credit are regulated by the UCP 600.

15.3.6.1 What documents must be presented under a documentary credit?

As well as specifying what type of credit the buyer must arrange (eg irrevocable and unconfirmed), the sale contract will also have to specify what documents have to be presented in order to receive payment under the credit. The documents required will also be set out in the credit itself (see the specimen credit on p 156 for an example of this). This will depend on the Incoterm agreed between the parties (see **14.4**). For example, in a CIF contract, the documents will be a clean bill of lading, the insurance policy and a commercial invoice. Further documentation, eg a packing list or certificate of inspection, may be agreed between the parties. The seller must present documents that comply exactly with the terms of the credit in order to be paid (see **15.3.7.2**).

15.3.6.2 When is the credit to be provided?

The sale contract will normally specify when the credit is to be provided. If nothing is mentioned in the contract, generally the credit should be opened no later than the earliest shipping date under the contract. (If no opening date is specified in the sale contract, there will be an implied term that the credit will open and be advised to the seller within a reasonable period before the shipment date.) The seller will not be under an obligation to ship the goods unless the buyer has opened a credit in accordance with the terms of the contract. Failure to do so within the specified time period gives the seller the right to terminate the contract, or waive the breach and sue for damages.

15.3.6.3 How long must the credit last?

The sale contract will specify for how long the credit is to be opened, and this will also appear in the credit itself. Under Art 6 of UCP 600, all credits must stipulate an expiry date and a place for presentation of documents. The specimen documentary credit above has a clear issue and expiry date. The seller thus knows exactly for how long he is covered by the credit.

15.3.6.4 Presentation of the documents

The documents must be presented before the expiry date of the credit. The credit should also state a period of time after shipment within which the documents should be tendered by the seller. Under Art 14 of UCP 600, if no such period is stated, 21 days only is allowed. So, the longstop date for presenting documents is either the expiry date of the credit, or 21 days after shipment, whichever occurs first.

15.3.6.5 Methods of payment under a documentary credit

In the Wood Magic example above, the method payment chosen by the parties is a term bill of exchange. The documentary credit could provide for any one of four methods of payment:

(a) Cash on presentation of the documents by the seller – 'payment at sight'. Here the Advising/Confirming Bank will make immediate payment on receipt (or 'sight') of the documents.

(b) Cash at some future time, eg after 90 days – 'deferred payment'. The bank will examine the specified documents, but it will not make payment until the date specified in the credit.

(c) A bill of exchange drawn by the seller, probably a term bill payable at a future date – 'acceptance credit'. Here the seller presents the bill of exchange with the stipulated documents, and the bank accepts the bill of exchange. If the credit is unconfirmed, the Issuing Bank will accept the bill. If the credit is confirmed, the Confirming Bank will accept the bill.

(d) Negotiating a bill of exchange drawn by the seller – 'negotiation credit'. Once the seller has produced the correct documentation, and the bill has been accepted, the seller can negotiate the bill.

The sale contract will specify which method of payment is to be used. In addition, the method of payment will be specified in the credit itself. The specimen credit sets out four options shown on it: payment in cash on sight of the documents; by acceptance of a bill of exchange; by negotiating a bill of exchange; and by a deferred cash payment. The acceptance option has been chosen on the specimen.

15.3.6.6 Reimbursement

Clearly, where a bank has undertaken to pay out on the documentary credit, it will want to be reimbursed. Where the Confirming Bank has made the payment, the UCP 600 provides that it is entitled to be reimbursed by the Issuing Bank. The Issuing Bank is then entitled to be reimbursed by the buyer. The Issuing Bank can protect its position by retaining the documents until it is certain of payment from the buyer. As between the banks themselves, further protection is given by the Uniform Rules for Bank-to-Bank Reimbursement under Documentary Credits (URR 725).

15.3.7 Duties of the banks in relation to the documents

There are two fundamental principles of documentary credits, which affect the position of the banks involved. These are:

(a) the autonomy of the documentary credit; and

(b) the doctrine of strict compliance.

15.3.7.1 The autonomy of the documentary credit

Once in place, the credit contract is autonomous and has a separate life of its own. Although the sale contract is the contract which imposes the obligation for the documentary credit to be opened, the documentary credit itself is completely independent from the underlying sale of goods contract. It is also generally independent of any contracts arising out of the associated use of bills of exchange. The banks involved are not concerned with issues relating to either of these. For example, once an irrevocable documentary credit has been opened, the buyer cannot instruct the Issuing Bank to withdraw the credit, even if the seller has shipped goods which do not comply with the contract. Under Art 4 of UCP 600, 'banks are in no way concerned' with the underlying contracts for sale. Banks only need to ensure that the documents provided by the seller are in accordance with the instructions of the buyer. Article 5 specifically states: 'Banks deal with documents and not with goods, services or performance to which the documents may relate.'

15.3.7.2 The doctrine of strict compliance

As discussed above (**15.3.6.1**), in order to be paid the seller must present the documents to the relevant bank for examination. (In the Wood Magic example it would be the Advising/Confirming Bank which would then forward the documents to the Issuing Bank.) Under Art 14 of UCP 600, the purpose of the examination is to see whether the documents comply with the terms of the credit. The bank must only pay over the money if the seller provides exactly the right documents which strictly comply with the terms of the credit. If, for example, the documentary credit stipulates that a clean bill of lading must be provided, a claused bill will not suffice.

In *Equitable Trust Company of New York v Dawson Partners Ltd* (1927) 27 Lloyds Rep 49, which concerned a fraudulent seller and a contract to buy vanilla beans from Indonesia, Sumner LJ summed up the position: 'There is no room for documents which are almost the same or which will do just as well.'

The bank is under a duty to take 'reasonable care' in the examination of the documents. As long as the documents appear, on their face, to comply with the terms of the credit, the bank will be protected. It does not need to go 'digging' for defects. An example of this is *Gian Singh & Co Ltd v Banque de l'Indochine* [1974] 1 WLR 1234. The Privy Council allowed the defence of a bank that used reasonable care in complying with the prima facie requirements of a documentary credit, notwithstanding that one of the specified documents was in fact a forgery. Thus the visual appearance of compliance is all that needs to be determined on presentation of the documents.

If the bank wrongly accepts or rejects documents, it will be liable for the loss.

15.3.7.3 The fraud exception to acceptance of complying documents

An exception to the rule that payment must be made where the documents are in strict compliance is where the seller is guilty of fraud. This exception may be available where either the documents presented by the seller or some aspects of their presentation are tainted by fraud. Fraud affecting the underlying sale transaction is not a good reason for payment not to be made under the documentary credit. Neither is mere suspicion of fraud.

In *Mahonia Ltd v JP Morgan Chase Bank (No 1)* [2003] EWHC 1927 (Comm), the court refused to order payment against a documentary credit which had been entered into for the purpose of share swap transactions which were illegal in the US. The illegality had 'tainted' the credit arrangement.

Part II Summary
International Sale Agreements

Topic	*Summary*
Jursidiction	This term means that a court has the constitutional power to hear and decide a legal matter between parties. These powers extend to geographical limits as well as to the range of persons and issues which fall within the legal competence of any particular court or system of courts. Any attempt by a court to give a legal ruling outside of its jurisdiction will result in a nullity, both in the place for which the court has jurisdiction, as well as elsewhere in the world. Many nations and States recognise the jurisdictions and judgments of other countries as a matter of international convention.
Choice of applicable law	When any court has to decide a civil legal dispute, it also has to decide what national system of law should be applied to decide the issues. In the areas with which this text deals, these are mainly contractual issues and the question is of which national law is applicable to the contract or, if more than one system is applied to different parts of the contract, which systems should be applied. Generally, if the parties have made an express choice in a contract, that choice will be respected and applied by the court.
'Brussels I'	This started as an international agreement between the Member States of the EU and is now Regulation (EC) 44/2001, which provides the rules of jurisdiction under which the courts of those States work. It prevents disputes arising over which courts, within that system, should hear a particular matter: typically, disputes where the parties have their residence or domicile in different Member States, or indeed, if one party is not within the EU at all. An express choice of jurisdiction by the parties to a contract will usually be respected, except in matters in which any particular court has exclusive jurisdiction.
Exclusive jurisdiction	This means that there are issues in the case that extend to legal considerations, which the courts of particular Member States only can hear, to the exclusion of all others. Matters such as land, trusts, company matters and validity of intellectual property rights fall under this heading, where those matters are closely connected to a particular Member State, eg the location of land or the place of incorporation of a company etc.

Topic	*Summary*
General jurisdiction	This is the right of a Member State-domiciled defendant to expect that the courts of his own place of domicile will exercise jurisdiction and hear the case against him. There are other provisions (Special Jurisdiction) in Brussels I which, additionally, give jurisdiction to other Member States to hear the dispute, in addition to the courts having general jurisdiction. The court first applied to by the claimant will usually accept jurisdiction although there are special rules, relating to insurance, consumer and employment claims, that prevent some defendants in those matters being sued elsewhere than in their own national courts. Once the courts of one Member State accept jurisdiction, the courts of other Member States should not accept jurisdiction over the same matter.
Rome Convention	This is an international treaty between the EU Member States which provides a system of prima facie rules to help a court decide which system of law is the applicable law for any particular contract. It only applies to contractual disputes. Primacy is usually given to express contractual choice. In the absence of choice, the court looks for the law of the place with which the contract is most closely connected.
Mandatory rules	These are rules of national law that cannot be displaced by the courts of that Member State, where the court is applying an applicable law to a contract, other than the court's own national law. The mandatory rules displace the applicable law, to the extent that the two systems are incompatible.
Bill of lading	This is a document provided by a carrier of goods over water to the person who is shipping the goods, ie sending them off to somewhere else. Its function is to show that the goods have been received by the carrier, to show their quantity and condition, to show the terms under which the goods are being carried and, if necessary, to act as a document of title to show the right to sell the goods or to take possession of them from the carrier, at the end of the journey.
Multimodal transport	This term refers to the method of transporting goods from one place to another where the goods, typically packed into steel containers, can easily be carried by a succession of different vehicles and vessels. Such a trip might initially involve road transport, then cargo air transport, then further road or inland waterway transport, to its ultimate destination.

Topic	*Summary*
Incoterms	These are a comprehensive set of standard form contracts, drawn up by the International Chamber of Commerce, to allow for international transport of goods. They are based on long-settled mercantile practices and provide contracts, under which the rights and responsibilities of the parties are very clearly laid out and recognised. The terms deal particularly with demarcation of responsibility for timing and place of delivery, responsibility for cost allocation and arrangement of the different stages of the transport process, insurance obligations, etc. They are designed to be incorporated by simple reference within sale of goods contracts, with or without express modification.
Negotiable instrument	This refers to a variety of written documents, which are intended to form the subject matter of contractual promises to exchange money for the written document itself. The paper is treated as being equivalent to a certain amount of money, and the right to the money represented by the paper can be transferred by the transfer of the paper document, from one person to another, by whatever method the particular type of instrument requires, in law. Bills of exchange, cheques, banker's drafts and promissory notes are all negotiable instruments.
Bill of exchange	This is a type of negotiable instrument in which one person instructs someone else to pay money to, or to the order of, a specified person. Although these can be drawn against and addressed to private persons, they are much more commonly drawn against and payable by a person's bank ('the drawee'). Typically, they are used by a buyer of goods, who has arranged to pay the seller by the use of a bill of exchange. They are much used in international commerce. Primary liability to pay out on the bill arises upon 'acceptance', by the signature of the drawee (eg the buyer's bank).
Term bill	This is a bill of exchange which is designed to be paid out, not on the day of acceptance, but at some period later. This is often used to provide a credit period to a buyer, who can get his bill accepted and with it the acceptor's promise to pay up. In the alternative, he could take the accepted bill and attempt to negotiate it on (at a small discount) to someone else who is prepared to wait for the term to expire, in order to cash it at full face value.
Sight bill	This is a bill of exchange which is designed to be paid immediately upon acceptance ('on sight'), at full face value.

Topic	*Summary*
Documentary credit	This is a written contractual promise that the person to whom it is intended to give a benefit will be guaranteed to be paid out, provided that that beneficiary performs his part of a contractual arrangement properly. The idea is to provide a solvent and reliable assurance, independent of the buyer of goods, that the seller will be paid. Usually, the credit will be raised by a bank ('the issuing bank'), instructed and paid by the buyer, at the buyer's expense. Most documentary credits are issued under the Uniform Customs and Practice for Documentary Credits. The contract of credit itself is a separate contract from the sale of goods, so failure or insolvency of the buyer would not affect the seller, once the contract is under way. The credit may, quite independently, be confirmed by another bank, eg an offshore issuing bank and an onshore 'confirming bank'.

Part III

INTELLECTUAL PROPERTY

Chapter 16
Introduction to Intellectual Property

16.1 What is intellectual property?

The basic concept of intellectual property (IP) is that of protecting the products, results and rewards of the exercise of human intellectual and commercial endeavour. The property rights in these matters are a form of intangible property, comprising the legal right to stop others using the owner's property without permission and, in some cases, to give a monopoly right to exploit that property commercially.

A problem with protecting things that originate in a person's mind is that much of the subject matter comprised in IP gets dangerously close to claiming, as private property, some things which, at least in theory, should belong to humanity in common. Matters such as use of words of the language, shapes and forms, colours, ideas, ways of thinking and doing things, methods of manufacture, even geographical locations can form the subject matter of such rights. It follows from this that the legal framework for identifying the existence and scope of a private IP right must be very precise and technically ascertainable, if private rights are not to interfere in the free and normal conduct of a civilised society. This has become an ever-increasing problem as we have moved away from an object-based world towards a much more information-based existence, where by making a few electronic connections, a person may use and engage the IP of many different owners, possibly in many different places.

Only a limited treatment of these extensive areas of law is possible in this work and the matters are approached as follows.

The question of protection of business reputation is dealt with in **Chapters 17** and **18**, which deal with passing off and trade marks. Business exists to make profits and the surest way to make a profit is to become known and identified as a reliable and reputable supplier of whatever a market requires. It is this protection of the identity of the mark of an organisation with its own particular reputation and output, particularly through the eyes of customers, that is the binding connection between trademark law and passing off.

The second area of protection is that given to creative expression and the right of a creative person to develop property rights in the tangible results of creative talents, so as to be able to stop other persons from making free use of that property without the permission of the creator, by way of copying or otherwise, whether for gain or not. This is dealt with in **Chapters 19** and **20**, on copyright and database right protection.

A third area of protection, similar to protection of creativity, is that given to designs for shapes (both internal and external shapes) and appearances of objects, which are intended to be created to that design, typically by way of manufacture. This is a vital area for protection and one calling for some very fine distinctions, if freedom of design and manufacture is to be generally available to anyone who wishes to make use of it. **Chapter 21** deals with this area. The general idea, here, is to prevent unauthorised commercial exploitation of the designs, rather than simple copying for non-commercial purposes.

The fourth area of protection is that which allows persons of an inventive nature (in terms of being able to do or make things) to be able to take advantage of a limited time period in which they are able to exploit the commercial possibilities of their invention, in a monopolistic way, by the use of registered patents. Even during this limited time period, the underlying inventive thinking must be available to the public at large, so as to enter the collective body of human knowledge, in exchange for the monopoly right of exploitation. This area is dealt with in **Chapter 22**.

These areas of law, along with other concepts such as the protection of confidential information and 'know-how' protection (dealt with in **Chapter 23**), provide the framework within which individuals, businesses and the general public are able to benefit from a principled, reasonably predictable and equitable sharing of human intellectual output. This framework gives protection to those who create and think; it allows the public to benefit and develop from steps taken by innovators and designers; it encourages and stimulates business growth and entrepreneurial spirit; lastly, it prevents an unseemly and ultimately destructive free-for-all in the unlimited and unscrupulous use and misuse of other people's property.

A consequence of the ownership of IP is that it can come to represent much, if not all, of the real asset value of many businesses. Like most other property it can be dealt in, sold, bought, licensed or charged by way of security. Modern giants, such as the Microsoft organisation, could not have come into existence so quickly, on such a titanic, financial scale, unless they consisted primarily of IP assets.

16.2 Types of intellectual property

Intellectual property rights are now primarily statutory, supported by considerable case law. Some common law rights still exist, however, mainly passing off and breach of confidence. The main IP rights are as follows.

16.2.1 Trade marks

A trade mark is a brand name or other mark of trade origin, for example Coca-Cola for soft drinks, BMW for cars and motorcycles, or Levi's for jeans. It is a highly commercial right. Trade marks are best protected by registration (and all well-known trade marks are registered). This gives the owner of the trade mark statutory rights, under the Trade Marks Act 1994 (TMA 1994), to defend its trade mark against infringers who are using the same mark or a similar one.

The registration of a trade mark can be renewed indefinitely, provided the trade mark does not run foul of some restrictions under the TMA 1994. The oldest trade mark in the UK is the Bass red triangle for beer. It was registered in the 1870s and is still valid today.

If a trade mark is not registered then it can be protected only by the law of passing off.

16.2.2 Passing off

This is a common law tort which enables a business to defend itself from someone who is trying to take unfair advantage of the trading reputation of that business, for example by using its name or selling goods in packaging that looks similar. Passing off is less important than trade mark law, and also less certain as regards the outcome. It has also been diminished by the increased scope of registered designs (see **16.2.4**). Nevertheless, there are many situations in which the scope of passing off can reach further than trade mark protection, so the two rights can complement each other as they are not mutually exclusive, often being pleaded in the same action.

In some jurisdictions, passing off has a statutory equivalent, such as 'palming off' in the US or 'unfair commercial practices' directives in the EU.

16.2.3 Copyright

Copyright is a right to prevent copying of creative expression, such as writing, art, music, architecture, film and even computer software.

It is an unregistered system, and for an infringement to occur it has to involve 'copying'. Copyright does not stop you writing an exciting book about wizards just because JK Rowling has produced many such books. However, it does stop you copying the works and detailed plots of JK Rowling.

Copyright extends to pictorial and photographic creation, industrial plans, sculpture, recorded music and films. These media are 'artistic' but also highly commercial, if you think about the money involved in a major film, such as the James Bond films. It is the principal IP right in computer programmes and therefore of great importance today. Nevertheless, the right is not registrable and comes into existence when the work is first created.

16.2.4 Designs

Designs that relate to the appearance of an object can be registered, but ones that relate solely to its technical function (ie to how it works) cannot. Registration gives statutory protection for up to 25 years.

There is also statutory unregistered design right protecting features of shape or configuration of articles which are intended to be made available commercially. This protection can extend for between 10 and 15 years, according to circumstances.

16.2.5 Patents

Patents are a commercial IP right. A patent is protection for an invention. The invention could be a better mousetrap, or a wonder drug to treat cancer, or anything in between. A patent is a registered right, administered by the Patents Office.

A patent gives the holder the right to a monopoly for 20 years over the technology revealed in the patent. 'Revealed' is an important concept. The description of the invention is made public in return for the grant by the Crown of the period of protection. Thus, after the 20-year period expires, the invention is then public property. Anybody can use it because the technology is revealed in the patent document, known as a patent specification.

The philosophy is that inventors, and those who employ or sponsor them, should have this 20-year period in which to exploit their monopoly. Were it otherwise, it would never be worth the financial risk of the huge research and testing regimes needed for many modern inventions or patented ideas undertaken by, say, drug manufacturers.

Another possible means of exploiting a patent is by commercial exploitation of any confidential information concerning the most efficient way to make the patented invention or process work. The registered patent specification will show the world the inventive concept itself and how it broadly works, but that is very different from showing the best and most cost-effective way to make it work. Such additional information is termed 'know-how' and is, itself, highly valuable and exploitable material, as long as it remains confidential. Typically, it is not independently protected as a patent but is often ancillary to the patent, so that a patent licence will be accompanied by a know-how licence, to give the licensee the best chance of using the patent efficiently.

16.2.6 Confidential information

The law of confidence is not an IP right in a pure sense, but is often classified with the mainstream rights as it is sometimes associated with them. For example, maintaining confidentiality before submitting a patent application is vital to avoid destruction of the invention's novelty.

Case law rather than statute governs the law of confidence and, as you would expect, the vast majority of cases relate to circumstances where express obligations of confidence are lacking and implied duties of confidentiality have to be considered. It is, however, important to remember that express obligations can (and often should) be imposed (eg, on key employees or independent contractors). Where confidentiality cannot be protected by contractual means, eg once it gets to third parties, the courts may use trust principles to restrict its use.

16.2.7 What else is there?

There are various other IP rights. For example:

The IP right	What does it protect against?
Database right	Copying of information
Semiconductor topography	Copying of computer 'chips'
Plant varieties	Anyone else selling the registered new variety of plant
Moral rights	Inappropriate treatment of an artist's work
Performers rights	Copying of live performances

16.3 Public registration and administration

It can be seen that much IP is protected by the use of registration of rights in public registers. This is the work of what is now entitled the Intellectual Property Office ('the IPO') (www.ipo.gov.uk), which covers the formerly more separated functions of registration of trade marks, designs and patents and various other matters connected with different types of IP within the UK. Additionally, IP issues which have an EC component are likely to come into contact with the Office for the Harmonisation of the Internal Market ('OHIM'), based in Alicante, Spain. There is an almost seamless joint between the registration process and the way in which courts, both national and EC, deal with IP actions and proceedings, in that harmonisation and approximation of national IP legal frameworks, within the EC, has gone much further than in many other areas of business and property law. This has followed upon a long-established international tradition of according reciprocal rights to some IP, in the interests of fostering world trade and development; see **18.13** and **19.10**.

16.4 Summary of IP rights

16.4.1 Trade marks

What is protected?	a brand name and/or a logo for goods or services (also, in limited circumstances, shapes)
What benefit is there?	exclusive right to the use of the trade mark with statutory protection
How is it obtained?	registration
How long does it last?	indefinitely

16.4.2 Passing off

What is protected?	goodwill (eg, a logo or a name or associated 'get up')
What benefit is there?	gives protection against unfair imitation
How is it obtained?	arises automatically (no registration)
How long does it last?	indefinitely

16.4.3 Copyright

What is protected?	'artistic output'; creative expression
What benefit is there?	preventing copying
How is it obtained?	arises automatically (no registration)
How long does it last?	70 years from death (usually)

16.4.4 Database right

What is protected?	collections of information
What benefit is there?	protects against unauthorised copying
How is it obtained?	arises automatically (no registration)
How long does it last?	15 years from creation or revision of the database

16.4.5 Registered design right

What is protected?	new designs for products
What benefit is there?	monopoly right to use and benefit from the design commercially
How is it obtained?	registration
How long does it last?	25 years from registration (maximum)

16.4.6 Unregistered design right

What is protected?	three-dimensional shapes of articles
What benefit is there?	prevents commercial copying of articles
How is it obtained?	arises automatically (no registration)
How long does it last?	10 years in most cases (maximum of 15)

16.4.7 Patents

What is protected?	new invention or process
What benefit is there?	monopoly right to apply the technology
How is it obtained?	registration
How long does it last?	20 years from application

16.4.8 Confidential information

What is protected?	secret information
What benefit is there?	protects against unauthorised disclosure
How is it obtained?	arises automatically (no registration)
How long does it last?	indefinitely

Chapter 17
Passing Off

17.1 Introduction

Passing off is about stopping the infringer from selling his goods or services by making unfair use of the claimant's reputation. Passing off can happen in a number of different ways. Typically, passing-off cases concern the 'get-up' of goods (ie, their packaging and presentation as seen by the consumer). Passing off is often used as an additional remedy to trade mark infringement claims, and will sometimes succeed where the trade mark claim does not as it is more flexible in approach than the registered trade mark system.

The classic quote, which sums up passing off, is from Lord Halsbury in *Reddaway and Frank Reddaway & Co Ltd v Banham and George Banham & Co Ltd* [1896] AC 199: '. . . nobody has any right to represent his goods as the goods of somebody else'. If you make a potential buyer or recipient of your services think you are another party, that person has a right to claim compensation for losses suffered by the deception.

Passing off has to be in relation to a commercial activity. In *Kean v McGivan* [1982] FSR 119, an action concerning the name of a political party (the Social Democratic Party) did not succeed. Usually, something must be happening that is capable of causing people to spend money.

In the classic case of passing off, the defendant adopts some mark, or sign or other distinguishing feature (eg, the appearance of the packaging of the goods) which customers associate with the claimant. He uses this, or something confusingly similar to it, for his own goods/services, with the result that customers are fooled into thinking they are buying the claimant's product. In one of the most famous passing-off cases, *Reckitt & Colman Products Ltd v Borden Inc and Others* [1990] 1 WLR 491, the distinguishing feature of the claimants' goods was that their juice was sold in a plastic lemon. The defendant also started selling lemon juice in a plastic lemon. Reckitt & Colman succeeded in stopping the defendant using this shape of container. Today, the claimants could also use trade mark infringement as, under the TMA 1994, they have been able to register the shape of their lemon as a registered trade mark (see **Chapter 18**).

Modern marketing methods have created many hugely ingenious ways of free-riding on the business reputations and goodwill created by others. In *British Sky Broadcasting Group plc v Sky Home Services Ltd* [2006] EWHC 3165, various defendants had made use of the SKY word in corporate names, as well as in marketing material and telephone sales methods used for selling extended warranties for maintenance of satellite TV reception equipment. Passing off was established fairly easily in the circumstances of such a widely-known organisation as the claimant.

What is protected?	goodwill, eg logo or name, 'get-up'
What benefit is there?	protects against unfair use of, or damage to, business reputation
How is it obtained?	arises automatically (no registration)
How long does it last?	indefinitely

17.2 The three elements of passing off

In *Consorzio del Prosciutto di Parma v Marks & Spencer plc* [1991] RPC 351, the House of Lords judgment of Lord Oliver in *Reckitt & Colman* is quoted as a good exposition of the elements of passing off:

> More specifically, it may be expressed in terms of the elements which the plaintiff in such an action has to prove in order to succeed. These are three in number. First, he must establish a *goodwill* or reputation attached to the goods or services which he supplies in the mind of the purchasing public by association with the identifying get-up (whether it consists simply of a brand name or a trade description, or the individual features of labelling or packaging) under which his particular goods or services are offered to the public, such that the get-up is recognised by the public as distinctive specifically of the plaintiff's goods or services. Secondly, he must demonstrate a *misrepresentation* by the defendant to the public (whether or not intentional) leading or likely to lead the public to believe that goods or services offered by him are the goods or services of the plaintiff . . . Thirdly, he must demonstrate that he suffers or . . . that he is likely to suffer *damage* by reason of the erroneous belief engendered by the defendant's misrepresentation that the source of the defendant's goods or services is the same as the source of those offered by the plaintiff. (emphasis added)

17.2.1 First element: goodwill

Goodwill means business reputation. The reputation must be among customers, or prospective customers (ie, buyers, or prospective buyers of lemon juice, for example).

The reputation also needs to be in relation to some distinguishing feature, eg, in the plastic lemon. What the claimant needs to show is not only that customers associate the plastic lemon with the claimant, but also that they understand the plastic lemon as an indication or sign that the lemon juice comes from the claimant. The claimant generally demonstrates his reputation to the court by showing sales figures and expenditure on advertising (using the distinguishing feature in question), by witness evidence and survey evidence.

The distinguishing feature could be:

(a) logos, shape or style of packaging, get up, colour (eg, Heinz beans tin (colour, shape of label, name); the classic Coca-Cola bottle (shape, name); Body Shop bottle (the rounded shape and lettering); Penguin (six-pack wrapper)); or

(b) a name (eg, 'Neutrogena', where the defendant was restrained from using the similar name 'Neutralia' (*Neutrogena Corporation and Another v Golden Ltd and Another* [1996] RPC 473), or 'Harrods' (*Harrods Ltd v Harrodian School Ltd* [1996] RPC 697), although Harrods were unsuccessful in stopping the school using the same name because they could not show that this would result in damage).

In *Riddle v United Service Organisation Ltd* [2004] LTL AC9100218, the claimant was the son of the late Nelson Riddle, a composer and orchestra leader. Riddle senior and his orchestra had last toured the UK in the 1960s. It was held that there was no goodwill remaining after 40 years, so the son could not maintain a passing-off claim against defendants who ran an orchestra called the Nelson Riddle Orchestra UK. This can also be a problem for new businesses or ventures, where the goodwill has yet to become established.

The category of things in which the claimant can have reputation is not closed and cannot be conclusively defined or limited. Being common law based, the limits of the tort are potentially very wide. Reputation as a diary writer was able to be protected in *Clark (Alan Kenneth McKenzie) v Associated Newspapers* [1998] RPC 261, where parodied versions of Alan Clark's diaries were held to be passing off. Scents of products can be another tricky area, as seen in *L'Oreal SA v Bellure NV* [2006] EWHC 2355, where the scent of a fine perfume, although important to the customer, was held to be not protected, on the facts of that case, although there were trade mark infringements of other features.

17.2.2 Second element: misrepresentation, leading to confusion

There must be a misrepresentation made by the defendant in the course of trade. In the Jif lemon case (see **17.1**) the misrepresentation was the use of the plastic lemon. In most passing-off cases the misrepresentation is deliberate. In other words, there is a deliberate attempt by the defendant to 'ride on the back' of the claimant's success. For example, consider the 'Penguin and Puffin' case, *United Biscuits (UK) Ltd v Asda Stores Ltd* [1997] RPC 513, which concerned the similarity in packaging for the two brands of chocolate biscuit. Asda produced the Puffin biscuit. They had designed packaging that was very similar to that of the Penguin biscuit. They even ran an advertising campaign with the slogan 'pick up a Puffin'. This rather suggested deliberate reference to Penguin, and did not help Asda's case in court, as passing off was easily established.

However, a misrepresentation could be innocent but still actionable. The defendant need not even be aware of the claimant's products, as intention to misrepresent is not an essential element.

The misrepresentation must lead to confusion of customers or potential customers, and generally it must be confusion as to trade source. The customers must be fooled into thinking that the defendant's products come from the claimant, or that they are associated with the claimant (eg, that they are made/supplied by a company within the same group, or by a licensee). A classic example of such misrepresentation may be seen in *First Conference Services Ltd v Bracchi* [2009] EWHC 2176 (Ch), [2009] All ER (D) 56 (Oct), where a former employee of the claimant attempted to pass off conferences organised by him as those of his old employer. He did this by stating that the speakers would be 'previous speakers', ie those at conferences organised by the claimant the year before. He also misled the speakers themselves as to the identity of the true organiser of the conference.

The confusion must be at the point of sale, or before it. In *Bostik Ltd v Sellotape GB Ltd* [1994] RPC 556, the makers of Blu-tack failed to obtain an injunction in passing off against a rival manufacturer of a similar looking product. The similarity in the product could be realised only when the packaging was removed. There was no possibility of confusion by the customer at the point of sale. So far, English courts have refused to follow other jurisdictions where post-sale confusion is enough.

It is not enough that there is confusion between the claimant's and the defendant's product. Customers must believe that the defendant's products are associated with the claimant. This was illustrated in the case of *HFC Bank plc v Midland Bank plc* [2000] FSR 176. When Midland was taken over by HSBC and changed its name to HSBC, HFC Bank objected. They argued that customers would confuse HSBC with HFC. However, among other things, HFC were not able to show they had achieved sufficient brand name recognition in relation to the letters HFC. Even if customers did confuse the two acronyms, they would not necessarily think HSBC was a reference to HFC.

The removal of a distinguishing feature can result in unintentional misrepresentation. In *Sir Robert McAlpine Ltd v Alfred McAlpine plc* [2004] EWHC 630, [2004] RPC 36, it was held that the defendant's dropping of the first name 'Alfred', so that it used the name McAlpine alone, did amount to a misrepresentation. In other words, it caused confusion with the claimant's name.

There needs to be overlap between the alleged infringer and the proprietor in that there is a 'common field of activity', in the following respects:

(a) type of goods or services: would someone confuse a bicycle maker with a law firm?

(b) geographical area: a restaurant in Aberdeen is unlikely to take away trade from one in Plymouth; and

(c) time: the overlap must be more or less contemporaneous.

Unless there is a common field of activity, it will be difficult (but not impossible) to show confusion or, indeed, damage to goodwill in many cases. Nevertheless, as large national or multinational organisations, such as Tesco or BP etc, are commonly known to be involved in a hugely diverse range of goods and services, it would be very easy for passing off to take place without a common activity taking place at all, but it would still be open to the claimant to have a good chance of stopping the activity, as can be seen from the case law.

17.2.2.1 Evidence of confusion

A passing-off case will not succeed without evidence of confusion. Customer confusion is a question of fact, and it is always very difficult to predict the outcome of a passing-off claim. It is difficult to generalise about the type of thing that will lead to confusion, but the confusion must be as to trade source.

The usual evidence might be survey evidence (ie a survey of a sample of members of the public is taken, often by marketing analysts) or witness evidence, preferably from people employed in the relevant trade. In effect, they become expert witnesses on the question of likely confusion. The burden on the claimant is heavy and is often difficult to discharge. In *Julius Sämaan v Tetrosyl Ltd* (see **18.8.2**), a passing-off claim failed for lack of evidence of confusion, even though there was a clear trade mark infringement.

The courts are sceptical about survey evidence, but nevertheless it is frequently presented. Often what will be conclusive is placing the two products before the judge. Does he think customers are likely to be confused? If he agrees, he is more likely to accept the survey evidence. If he does not, he is likely to reject it.

Although the defendant may use the claimant's distinctive feature in some way, there might not be confusion if either the claimant or the defendant has clearly distinguished their products in some way. In *Arsenal Football Club plc v Reed* [2001] RPC 922, a long-standing trader in unofficial Arsenal club memorabilia was not found to have created any confusion in the minds of customers, merely by using the club's logo and name (not least, because of a clear disclaimer). The passing-off action failed (but see the trade mark case at **18.9**).

If people merely recognise the look-alike as being a cheaper copy of the branded product then this is not going to be enough for passing off. There is then no confusion as to the trade source of the goods or services. Some allowance is made for the circumstances under which the customer will look at and decide about buying the material. A quick selection from a shelf is very different from a considered examination of the matter, perhaps over days. For there to be a likelihood of confusion, it would need to confuse a more alert customer than 'a moron in a hurry' (*Morning Star v Express Newspapers* [1979] FSR 113). Next time you are in a supermarket, see if you can spot examples of where the 'own brand' supermarket version of a product is made to look similar to the well-known household name. Consider whether you are actually confused as to origin (but only glance at the shelf – the point here is that the court recognises that customers do not stare at the products, trying to spot the differences).

17.2.3 Third element: damage

The claimant must show damage, or the likelihood of damage. Often, because of the likelihood of damage, the claimant will generally be seeking an interim injunction. In the ordinary case, where the claimant and defendant are trading in the same line of business, once goodwill and misrepresentation have been established the court is usually willing to infer damage.

The main types of damage are:

(a) loss of profits – people buy the infringing product instead of the claimant's product; and

(b) loss of reputation – usually because the infringing product is of inferior quality, and customers think the infringing product is made by the claimant.

If the infringer is in a different field of activity, the claimant might not succeed because he cannot show damage. For example, in *Stringfellow and Another v McCain Foods GB Ltd and Another* [1984] RPC 501, the nightclub was not able to stop oven chips being sold under the name 'Stringfellows'. In *Wombles Ltd v Wombles Skips Ltd* [1977] RPC 99, the copyright owners of the Wombles books and television series could not stop rubbish skips being hired out under the name 'Wombles'.

However, in other cases, claimants have been able to establish damage as a result of not being able to expand into a new market. The manufacturer of 'Marigold' rubber gloves was able to stop a toilet tissue being called 'Marigold' (*LRC International Ltd and Another v Lilla Edets Sales Co Ltd* [1973] RPC 560). Also, if the infringer's product is in a field that brings disrepute on the claimant then this can be a ground of damage. In the case of *Annabel's (Berkeley Square) Ltd v Schock (t/a Annabel's Escort Agency)* [1972] RPC 838, the use in question could have created an assumption that a well-known nightclub had started an escort agency. See **12.2.2** on the significance of large organisations and common field of activity problems.

In *Global Projects Management Ltd v Citigroup Inc* [2005] EWHC 2663, the judge, in giving summary judgment for Citigroup, was prepared to accept that a domain owner, in using 'citigroup.co.uk', had created such a risk of e-mails going to unintended recipients that damage was self-evident, even if unquantifiable.

In *Irvine and Others v Talksport Ltd* [2003] EWCA Civ 423, [2003] 2 All ER 881, the matter concerned Eddie Irvine, a well-known racing driver. A photograph of him holding a mobile phone was altered so as to replace the mobile phone with a radio with the words 'Talk Radio' on it, and was then used by the defendants on a promotional leaflet for their activities. In short, they used him to advertise their product without paying him to endorse it. The Court of Appeal held that this was passing off, and that the measure of damages for a false product endorsement was the typical fee which the claimant would usually have sought.

17.3 Defences to passing off

There are a number of defences to passing off which have developed through the case law, in a random and somewhat overlapping manner. The principal ones are as follows:

(a) careful and honest use of defendant's own name, mark or get-up;

(b) defendant's or claimant's use otherwise than in trade;

(c) claimant has no goodwill or the goodwill is owned by someone else;

(d) claimant's acquiescence, encouragement or consent to use;

(e) no provable damage or loss to claimant.

17.4 Remedies for passing off

Remedies for passing off can include:

(a) an injunction;

(b) damages (nominal, if innocent passing off);

(c) an account of profits;

(d) an order to cover up marks or repackage;

(e) an order for delivery up or destruction of the offending items;

(f) declarations as to rights.

Note: remedies (b) and (c) are normally mutually exclusive.

17.5 International aspects

Other common law countries, such as Australia and New Zealand, also have laws of passing off, but their case law has developed differently on some points. Civil law countries, for example most European ones, have the law of unfair competition, which sometimes overlaps with passing off, but it is not the same in all respects. The US has the statutory claim of 'palming off', which is similar to passing off.

Chapter 18
Trade Marks

18.1 Functions and purposes of trade marks

A trade mark is simply a badge or indication of the trade origin of goods or services from a particular supplier. The legislative framework for registered marks in the United Kingdom is primarily the Trade Marks Act 1994 (TMA 1994), which implements Council Directive 89/104/EEC ([1989] OJ L40/1) so as to harmonise to a large degree the national trade mark laws of Member States with each other. As part of this purpose, the TMA 1994 deals with matters such as the implementation of the Community trade mark (CTM) scheme and other international matters affecting trade marks. Detailed discussion of the CTM is beyond the scope of this work, but the system is dealt with briefly at **18.13.1**.

Harmonisation has occurred not just at an EU level: international conventions, such as the Singapore Trade Mark Law Treaty and the Agreement on Trade Related Aspects of International Property Rights (TRIPs), have ensured that trade mark law does not vary widely around the world.

It can be said that the main functions of a registered trade mark are as follows:

(a) to indicate the trade origin of the goods or services with a particular supplier; see the definition in s 1(1) of the TMA 1994:

> In this Act 'a trade mark' means any sign capable of being represented graphically which is capable of distinguishing goods or services of one undertaking from those of other undertakings;

(b) as a likely indication of the quality of product associated with that supplier;

(c) as a measure of the ongoing and changing value of the particular brand image of particular products, or of the image of the supplier as a whole;

(d) as a useful and commercially exploitable piece of property, in itself.

18.2 Advantages and consequences of registration

The two greatest advantages of registration of trade marks are that the period of protection given by registration is, potentially, unlimited and that the scope of protection is equivalent to an exclusive right to use the mark in trade for most commercial purposes permitted by the particular registration. Almost all other advantages and consequences stem from these two incidents of registration as can be seen from the brief following analysis.

18.2.1 Duration

The period of registration is an initial 10 years, with the option to renew the mark for subsequent 10-year periods, without limit in time. Provided that the mark does not lose its ability to distinguish the particular goods or services in question and is kept in (at least limited) use, it can remain in registration. The Bass red triangle trade mark for beer has been in use for more than 130 years and still retains its validity. An incidental gain from such long use is the possibility to develop wide and immediate recognition for a good brand, possibly at international level, and, additionally, a very strong presumption that the mark was validly registered in the first place. It is possible for registered trade marks to lose their validity by various means, in due course, but this is discussed at **18.8**.

18.2.2 Exclusive rights

The starting point, here, is s 9(1) of the TMA 1994:

> The proprietor of a registered trade mark has exclusive rights in the trade mark which are infringed by use of the trade mark in the United Kingdom without his consent.

The infringing acts are then set out exhaustively in ss 10 and 11. All the various infringing acts involve use of the trade mark, 'in trade', without consent, in some way or another. This very clear statutory framework has the consequence that the public register of trade marks provides an easily accessible check on any particular trade mark, as regards ownership and current registration status. It is not necessary to develop any particular goodwill in a mark to register it initially (cf passing-off actions), and so it is quite easy to gain the maximum novelty effect and commercial impact from new, well-conceived trade marks, provided that the product bearing the mark becomes fairly quickly available itself after registration. Infringement actions are far easier to bring than typical passing-off claims; provided the elements of the statutory infringement can be evidenced and that the mark is still being used and validly in registration at the time of the infringement, the claimant will succeed.

18.3 The registration system, its problems and recent changes

Very widespread and far-reaching changes have been made to the system of registration and dealing with trade marks in the United Kingdom. For a very long time, the UK Trade Mark Registry ('the Registry') applied three quite different tests in considering whether any trade mark should be registered or not; if the mark failed to comply with any of them, registration was refused. It considered:

(a) whether the mark was capable of being a trade mark within the s 1(1) definition at all;

(b) whether, if it was, it should be refused registration under any of the absolute grounds under s 3 of the TMA 1994 (including the law on passing off); and

(c) whether it should be refused registration for any of the relative grounds in s 5 of the TMA 1994.

These steps are discussed in more detail below and at **18.4–18.6**. This system long had the advantage that trade marks registered here were seen as having a very strong presumption of validity because of the care with which the Registry formerly investigated prior registrations and, indeed, unregistered marks before allowing a mark to be registered.

The difficulty was that this was not the general practice in most of Europe, and what brought the matter into sharp focus was the very large expansion in the Community trade mark (CTM) system (see **18.13.1**). The broad rule for CTMs and trade marks throughout much of the EU (other than in the UK until recently) is that it is for objectors to registration to raise the objection themselves, rather than for the registrars to search. The registrar does, however, retain the discretion to search for prior registrations under the Trade Mark Rules 2000 (SI 2000/136), r 11A.

This created such a problem that the UK Registry has now adopted the technique of relying upon objections being raised by persons adversely affected by an application for a UK trade mark. This may well create great expense and difficulty, especially for the smaller undertaking, in protecting registered trade marks (as well as unregistered matters which might be passed off). The following description deals with the practice followed in registration. The new approach to dealing with relative grounds objections is dealt with at **18.7.3**.

Anyone can apply to register a trade mark in the UK, whether they own the trade mark or not, provided that they are using the mark for goods or services, or intend to do so. It does not matter where the applicant comes from. There is a fairly large number of formalities, which are not extensively reviewed here, but which can fairly easily be ascertained by a visit to the website at www.ipo.gov.uk. The main legal source of these requirements is the TMA 1994 and the Trade Mark Rules 2000 made under the Act. The formal and procedural stages of the registration process are not dealt with further, but they may be seen on the website mentioned above and in the Trade Mark Rules 2000.

A trade mark has to be registered in relation to named goods or services, in that a class or classes of goods or services must be chosen. Trade marks are registered in one or more of 45 classes (see **18.14**). The main purpose of the classes is to facilitate searching for trade mark registrations. A trade mark will often be registered in more than one class. For example, the trade mark for a beer would be registered in class 32, but the same trade mark could also be registered in class 25 for clothing, as the name might be used on clothing to promote the beer.

18.4 Can the trade mark meet the definition within s 1(1) of the TMA 1994?

There are two distinct questions posed by this. Can the sign be graphically represented? Can it distinguish the goods or services of the applicant from those of other undertakings?

18.4.1 Graphic representation

This is an absolutely crucial requirement, if the limits of the protection given are to be ascertainable and clear. The starting point is the Trade Mark Rules' requirement that the sign be capable of being clearly reproduced in an 8 cm by 8 cm square in the *Trade Mark Journal*, which is the official means by which applications for registration are first published to the world, in order to allow persons to object and, if it becomes registered, to illustrate how the sign will be shown on the register. It follows from this that unless the sign can be be drawn, written in words, numbers or other symbols, or described in very clear words, it is unregistrable. This raises some degree of problem for certain types of distinctive features such as sounds or scents, but even these areas are capable of being utilised for trade mark purposes, in some cases. Clearly separated colours might be able to be specified by their wavelength or by reference to agreed classification systems and there are a (very) few of these (eg BP green, Heinz turquoise etc); mostly, colour registrations involve a combination of colours and other signs such as a word or other logos, etc (known as 'device' marks).

Sounds, other than words, are problematical; about the only reliable means of ascertaining these graphically being by use of wavelength, musical notation and/or duration. Music, jingles, etc are fairly easy to deal with in this way, but other sounds are very difficult to deal with in terms of clear graphical description; see *Shield Mark BV v Kist* (Case 283/01) [2003] ETMR 822. Scent/olfactory mark registrations are almost impossible to achieve, in terms of clear graphic representation, because descriptions or chemical formulae do not evoke the scent itself but, at best, the reader's imagined perception; to achieve certainty and clarity would require a sample of the substance: see *L'Oreal SA v Bellure NV* [2006] EWHC 2355, discussed at **17.2.1**. The use of the chemical formula symbols for a substance is probably not capable of satisfying the graphic representation requirement.

18.4.2 Capable of distinguishing

Many signs and words are so commonplace in everyday use as to be incapable of having a distinctive quality in isolation. There is a strong overlap between the general limitations of the s 1(1) definition and the absolute bars to registration in s 3, so most of the discussion on the distinctiveness requirement follows in **18.5**, but it should be borne in mind that what needs to be distinctive is the mark, as a whole, rather than particular features within it. It is, therefore, quite normal to find imaginative combinations of rather commonplace symbols, words or colours achieving registration as trade marks; all that matters is to find something distinctive about the overall arrangement. A well-known example is the 'Finish' title, combined with the red 'powerball' device mark for dishwasher products. None of the component parts of the mark is particularly distinctive, but in aggregate they become highly distinctive and recognisable.

The word mark 'Deliberately Innovative' was found to lack any distinctive character in *Interactive Intelligence Inc's Registration No 873858* [2007] WL 1180.

18.5 Absolute grounds for refusal: s 3

In s 3 of the TMA 1994, the absolute grounds for refusal to register are laid down. The most common ones are in s 3(1):

> The following shall not be registered—
>
> (a) signs which do not satisfy the requirements of section 1(1),
>
> (b) trade marks that are devoid of distinctive character,
>
> (c) trade marks which consist exclusively of signs or indications which may serve, in trade, to designate the kind, quality, quantity, intended purpose, value, geographical origin, the time of production of goods or of rendering of services, or other characteristics of goods or services,
>
> (d) trade marks that consist exclusively of signs or indications which have become customary in the current language or in the bona fide and established practices of the trade:
>
> Provided that, a trade mark shall not be refused registration by virtue of paragraph (b), (c) or (d) above if, before the date of application for registration, it has in fact acquired a distinctive character as a result of the use made of it.

Distinctiveness, in the eyes of the customer, is the idea that lies behind all the paragraphs of s 3(1). A mark will undoubtedly be distinctive if it is a made-up name. The ones usually quoted are 'Kodak' or 'Exxon'. Beware of words that are merely phonetic spellings of ordinary words so that they look distinctive until pronounced (eg, 'Orlwoola' for all wool (see **18.5.5**), or 'Writs' for a sandwich bar (ie, potential problems with the Ritz restaurant)).

Clearly, the bars to registration in s 3(1)(b) to (d) can largely be bypassed by the proviso that distinctiveness has been acquired by extensive use of the trade mark. That will not, however, cure any objections under paragraph (a), such as that the sign fails the s 1(1) requirement that the mark can be graphically represented; no amount of use can get over that hurdle and that sign will remain unregistrable. Distinctiveness acquired through use is discussed in more depth at **18.6**.

The main s 3(1) problem areas in registration tend to be associated with:

(a) the use of names of individuals or businesses;

(b) aspects of the goods or services on offer; and

(c) geographical origins of the goods or services.

These matters are dealt with at **18.5.1**, **18.5.2** and **18.5.3**. The difficult question of shape marks (s 3(2)) is dealt with at **18.5.4** and public policy objections (s 3(3)) at **18.5.5**.

Intellectual property lawyers will tell you that it is very common for a client to come up with a name for a product or business which falls foul of (b) above: it sums up the product or business *too* accurately. For example, 'Shine' may be a great name for a cleaning product, but it stands little chance of registration, at least not until a reputation is built up in the name. Note that this does not mean that it cannot be used to sell the product: the client simply has no protection in the name. Often clients like their idea so much that they press ahead with the name, accepting that, at least initially, there is a risk that others will also choose to use it.

18.5.1 Use of names as trade marks

It is long established that any person is entitled to use his own personal or business name and address, fairly and honestly, without it comprising an infringement; see s 11(2) of the TMA 1994. It does not follow from this that everyone can register their own name, in that way. Many names are so common as to be unable to distinguish goods or services for the purposes of s 3(1)(b), so that the name, standing alone, is unregistrable; combine it with an address or some other distinctive feature, however, and that may solve the problem. Nevertheless, people like short, catchy trade marks. An unusual name is unlikely to create such distinctiveness problems, but common names, even if presented in an eye-catching way, can be difficult to register, although sometimes personal signatures are trade marked (consider the 'Ford' signature mark). Often, the problem is that there are already prior registered marks, using the same name.

The former Registry practice was to use a simple rule of thumb, based on the statistical incidence of the name in the London telephone directory, as a guide. This was held, with reason, to be so arbitrary as to be useless in deciding the question of distinctiveness, in the ECJ decision in *Nichols plc v The Registrar of Trade Marks* (Case C-404/02) [2004] All ER (D) 114. The approach of the ECJ was that an individual assessment needs to be made on the facts of each application, taking into account the likely scope of use of the mark, as to area of use, range of products marked and likely customer group, allowing for a certain level of reasonably informed and aware customers; see *Koninklijke Philips Electronics v Remington Consumer Products Ltd* (Case C-299/99) [2002] 2 CMLR 52, [2003] Ch 159. This approach seems now to have been adopted by the IPO, but it should still be borne in mind that even common names can acquire distinctiveness through use; see *El Du Pont de Nemours & Co v ST Dupont* [2004] FSR 15.

The trade mark use of names, other than that of the provider of the goods or services, raises different considerations such as arise in character merchandising, franchising and IP licensing. Those matters are beyond the scope of this part of the text.

18.5.2 Aspects of the goods or services themselves within s 3(1)(c)

This is a vital protection against unfair monopolisation of descriptive signs or indications by any particular person. The paragraph only strikes at trade marks consisting exclusively of such indications (which are usually terms common in the trade). In *Timken Co's Application No 2418442* (Trade Mark Registry 18/09/07) [2007] WL 2817814, the Registry refused 'friction management solutions' as far too descriptive of the services offered to be registered, as other people offering friction management solutions would not have been able to advertise what they do. If the descriptive aspect is used in combination with more distinctive features, there is usually no problem.

Signs only serving to describe the type of good cannot be registered by themselves: orange juice, cornflakes or crisps are obviously unregistrable, but even more imaginative signs may still fail for descriptiveness. 'Tastee-Freez' for ice cream and 'Weldmesh' for reinforcing mesh were too descriptive to register, whereas 'Twiglets' has long been registered for snack-type biscuits for both humans and animals. The obvious difference is that although the snacks look like twigs, they are, in fact, completely different things; the mark is not descriptive of the kind of good, only suggestive of its appearance. This imaginative mark is highly distinctive among biscuits. Put simply, coming up with the name 'Twiglets' took some ingenuity, whereas coming up with the name 'Snacks' or even 'Snax' does not.

Words of quality or value are, likewise, unregistrable, by themselves, particularly 'laudatory' words such as 'magic', 'supreme', etc. Some imagination, though, can change the situation considerably; there are very large numbers of registrations, in all sorts of classes, for variations on 'exel', 'excell', 'XL' etc. Some of the most imaginative trade mark concepts have come from the confectionery world, with imagery such as 'Mars', 'Galaxy', 'Smarties', 'Quality Street', etc. The list is endless but all have the same aspect: they do not directly, or in many cases indirectly, suggest the nature of the good itself, but may, indirectly, suggest qualities and connotations beyond the mundane and mediocre. A case that is very close to the line is *Bostik Ltd v Henkel KGAA* (Trade Mark Registry 3/09/07) [2007] WL 2573891, where the applications to register 'Hyper Glue' and 'Hypaglue' were upheld, because 'hyper' was not found to be synonymous with 'super' (which would not have been registrable). Similarly, with words or signs showing the intended purpose of the good, one needs to go beyond mere descriptiveness to achieve registration: the 'Walkman' personal stereo and 'Workmate' portable work bench illustrate the successful registration and use of such marks.

The case of *Procter & Gamble Co v Office for Harmonisation in the Internal Market (Trade Marks and Designs)* [2002] RPC 17 has widened the scope for businesses that want to use trade marks which could be descriptive. This was a case before the ECJ. The applicant appealed from a decision of the OHIM. The application was for registration as a European trade mark of 'Baby-Dry' for 'disposable diapers made out of paper or cellulose and diapers made out of textile'. The application had been rejected by OHIM as being the combination of two descriptive words, that is 'baby' and 'dry'. However, the ECJ held that while each word on its own was not distinctive, the use of the two words together produced an unusual combination which was not in common English usage.

In contrast, in *DKV Deutsche Krankenversicherung AG v Office for Harmonisation in the Internal Market* [2002] ECR I-7561, the appeal against the refusal of OHIM to allow 'Companyline' to be registered as a Community trade mark for insurance and financial advice was rejected by the ECJ. The judgment of the Court of First Instance, and therefore the refusal to register, was upheld. The ECJ held that coupling together two such general words as 'company' and 'line' created nothing distinctive in the factual circumstance. In *Easynet Group plc v Easygroup IP Licensing Ltd* [2006] EWHC 1872, Mann J confirmed that the correct approach was an overall assessment of the composite expression as to whether it is descriptive or not. If it is not, it is likely to be distinctive and registrable. The registration of 'easy.com' for a range of goods and services was upheld.

In the case of the 'Doublemint' trade mark for chewing gum, the ECJ held that the trade mark was descriptive, ambiguous and therefore deceptive, and could not be registered. Part of the reason for distinguishing this application from Baby-Dry was that Baby-Dry was an unusual combination of two ordinary words, in the reverse order from any common usage of the terms. This was not the case with 'Doublemint' (*OHIM (Doublemint) v Wrigley* (Case C-191/01) (ECJ, 23 October 2003)). The judgment followed the *Chiemsee* case, in that the ECJ held that this was a trade expression that should be kept free for other businesses to use if they so wish (see **18.5**).

18.5.3 Marks suggesting geographical origin

In the majority of cases, geographical names will not be acceptable as trade marks.

In the leading case of *Windsurfing Chiemsee Produktions und Vertriebs GmbH v Boots und Segelzubehör Walter Huber and Another* [2000] Ch 523, the ECJ refused to allow the geographical name to be registered. It held that a geographical name had to be left available for other traders to use in the future, particularly those actually located at Chiemsee (a holiday lake in Bavaria). A geographical name which did not indicate the origin of the goods would be unregistrable for being deceptive. For example, 'Swiss Miss' was refused as the chocolate was not produced in Switzerland. However, if it is totally fanciful it could succeed, for example 'Sahara' for ice cream. An objection on grounds of deceptiveness could not be overcome by any amount of use of the mark.

There are some indications that a more relaxed attitude is being taken towards geographical marks in Community trade mark applications (see **18.13.1**), particularly so with small geographical locations (see *Peek & Cloppenburg v OHIM* [2006] ETMR 35).

The problem of geographical indications can be cured, for trade marks purposes, by making certain that the mark is not exclusively geographical, eg, 'Grants of St James's', although high-class areas are not easy to use in this way because of the possibility of deceptiveness.

Another possible protection, one that often overlaps with geographical indications, is the use of 'collective marks'. These can be registered under s 49 and Sch 1 of the TMA 1994 and comprise marks which show that the goods or services are provided by a member of a particular trade association, so as to distinguish them from those of other organisations or persons. These can be registered and frequently contain indications of geographical origins (subject to most relevant traders in that product and location being willing to join the association, as with the Melton Mowbray Pork Pie Association, which has 'AUTHENTIC . MELTON MOWBRAY' as its mark); this is permitted by the Schedule, but the collective trade mark cannot be used to prevent other persons (typically, those local traders who do not wish to join up), who would be following normal, honest business practice, from using that geographical indication in their business. In a similar way, 'certification marks' can be registered under s 50 and Sch 2 of the TMA 1994 to show other highly descriptive characteristics of goods or services that would normally be caught by s 3(1)(c); things like the 'Woolmark' for textiles and 'Stilton' for cheese are registered.

There are further levels of protection available to geographical indications at the EU level by way of 'protected designations of origin' ('PDO') and 'protected geographical indications' ('PGI'), as well as at international level, where there are World Intellectual Property Organisation 'appellations of origin'. The general idea of most of this protection is to allow persons to use and register official logos and titles to show that certain products (and only those products) are designated by and linked to particular geographical origins and locations. In *Consorzio del Prosciutto di Parma v Asda Stores Ltd* (Case C-108/01) [2001] UKHL 7, the Parma Ham Association attempted to prevent Asda from further processing Parma ham, protected by a PDO, by way of slicing, labelling and packaging it in the UK. The ECJ, on a reference from the House of Lords, found that this further protection for the ham was justified by its protection under the PDO and was a valid Community right, directly enforceable in Member States (subject to its being properly publicised to the Community). The Melton Mowbray Pork Pie Association has now achieved PGI status for a range of its products. Further discussion of geographical indications is, however, beyond the scope of this book.

18.5.4 Shape marks (s 3(2))

It is now possible to register trade marks for the shape of goods or their packaging, subject to their not consisting exclusively of:

(a) the shape which result from the goods themselves;

(b) the shape of goods which is necessary to achieve a technical result; or

(c) the shape which gives substantial value to the goods.

Again, the key to these exclusions is that what needs to be shown is that the mark is distinctive, eye-catching and memorable in some way and, additionally, raises the association with a particular trade source. The main problem with allowing registration of shape marks is that the potentially unlimited duration of the mark contrasts so vividly with the limited protection period (25 years maximum) of other industrial and commercial designs (see **Chapter 21**). It is very dangerous to allow anyone a monopoly on shapes – that is why they were not capable of trade mark protection until 1994 – and it is still not easy to achieve shape mark registration.

The case law is often quite speculative in its interpretation of s 3(2) and Council Directive 89/104 EEC, to which it gives effect. It is quite clear that there is a substantial overlap between the three excluded cases in s 3(2); it is also clear that the s 3(1) provision for distinctiveness, acquired by use, does not apply to shape marks which are excluded by s 3(2), although it could apply to marks comprising, in part, matters restricted by s 3(2). That explains how the Coca-Cola bottle achieved its registration.

The key to understanding much of the case law on s 3(2) lies in the fact that to exclude a shape mark from registration, that mark must consist 'exclusively' of the proscribed shape. Many marks will consist of other things beyond mere shape. Some indication of the judicial approach is seen as follows.

18.5.4.1 The shape of the goods themselves

The Court of Appeal upheld the Registrar's refusal to register the shape of the shaver heads of the Philishave razor (*Philips Electronics NV v Remington Consumer Products Ltd (No 2)* [1999] RPC 809). On a reference to the ECJ on construction of the Directive on the Approximation of the Laws of Member States about Trade Marks (Directive 89/104/EC) from which TMA 1994 derives, the ECJ held that a shape determined by technical function of the product was not registrable as a trade mark (Case C-299/99).

In effect, the logic behind the s 3(2) exclusion is that the shape of products should be given a lesser protection as a registered design if the shape is new and has individual character (see **21.2.1**). A registered trade mark is not the appropriate right.

In *Dyson Ltd v Registrar of Trade Marks* (Case C-321/03) [2003] EWHC 1062 (Ch) Dyson attempted to achieve a very wide-ranging protection for all conceivable shapes and configurations of the external face of part of its vacuum cleaner. This was treated by the High Court, as well as the ECJ on reference, as not being a shape mark application at all, but simply a feature, which had a function and a potentially variable appearance. The ECJ was also asked whether public association of such features with Dyson was enough for it to be registrable. The ECJ found that such an infinitely variable shape could not be graphically represented so as to constitute a distinctive trade mark, because it was simply not a 'sign' in the first place. The question of distinctiveness by use did not arise on those facts.

In *Société des Produits Nestlé SA v Unilever plc* [2002] EWHC 2709 (Ch), [2003] RPC 35, it was held that it was arguable that the shape of Vienetta ice cream resulted from the nature of the product itself, which of course would render it unregistrable as a trade mark. It was also held that there was insufficient evidence that the public recognised the shape of Vienetta as a badge of origin of the goods (ie, as emanating from Unilever), which also renders it unregistrable. In *Société des Produits Nestlé SA v Mars UK Ltd* [2004] EWCA Civ 1008, the Court of Appeal confirmed the refusal of an application to register as a trade mark the three-dimensional shape of a 'Polo' mint, which did not have the word 'Polo' embossed on it. The Registrar would have allowed registration if the application had been for mint-flavoured confectionery only, and had been for the colour white and only for the size of a standard 'Polo' mint. The Court upheld his opinion.

18.5.4.2 The shape of the goods which is necessary to achieve a technical result

This was the real basis of the result in the *Philips* case (see **18.5.4.1**); the 3-rotor configuration gave the technical superiority to the shaver in the first place, and the ECJ made it clear that the exclusion was not limited to situations where the shape in question was the only available shape to achieve that particular technical result. As long as the shape is important to the technical outcome, that is likely to prevent its registration. One solid advantage of this is that interesting shapes might be registrable in other applications, where they are not technically necessary, technically, eg, a small pistol as a trade mark for '*femme fatale*' scent.

18.5.4.3 The shape which gives substantial value to the goods

This seems to be a rather difficult exclusion to apply, and it gave difficulties to the High Court and the Court of Appeal in attempting to rationalise its meaning in the *Philips* case (see **18.5.4.1**). It may well be that a shape which makes goods substantially more valuable to the user, but which is protected by way neither of patent nor design, is what is really being aimed at here. In that case, it would be a retrograde step to allow anyone to have a permanent monopoly by way of trade mark over it. Possibly, things like pistol-grip shapes, spout shapes etc, which do not fit easily into the other exclusions but are intensely used and valued by buyers, might be caught here.

In *Benetton Group SpA v G-Star International BV* (Case C-371/06) [2008] ETMR 5, ECJ, the Court held that a jeans manufacturer should not have been given registration of two shape marks for jeans where the public recognition was based upon extensive advertising of the interesting shapes. The rule in the *Philips* case was applicable, and distinctiveness acquired by use could not cure the statutory bar to registration. The marks were annulled.

18.5.5 Public interest objections (s 3(3)) and bad faith applications (s 3(6))

An application will not succeed if the trade mark in question is contrary to public policy or morality (s 3(3)(a)), is likely to deceive (s 3(3)(b)) or is made in bad faith (s 3(6)).

18.5.5.1 Likely to deceive

For example, 'Orlwoola' for clothes would be deceptive if the clothes were not made entirely of wool (and if they were, it would be descriptive). 'Instant dip' for cleaning materials was refused on the basis that some of the materials were not in fact dips (*In the matter of Application No 713,406 by Otto Seligmann for the Registration of a Trade Mark* (1954) 71 RPC 52).

Often, a significant limitation to such objections can arise if a mark has been registered for use in only particular colours. The use of a similar mark in quite different colours may not necessarily be deceptive (see *Phones 4u Ltd and Another v Phone4u.co.uk Internet Ltd* [2006] EWCA Civ 244).

18.5.5.2 Bad faith applications

An example of an existing trade mark registration being struck off as being in bad faith occurred in *Byford v Oliver and Another* [2003] EWHC 295 (Ch), [2003] All ER (D) 345 (Feb). This concerned a number of registrations obtained in 1999 by the defendants for the name 'Saxon', which was a 1980s heavy metal band that is still performing – very loudly. The membership of the band had changed over the years but the claimant had always been a member. The defendants had been members for only part of the period. The defendants were held not to own the name and goodwill of the band 'Saxon' in its various guises. There appear to be other disputes concerning the reformation of earlier successful bands and the use of associated names and marks, so more legislation is likely, shortly.

In *Jules Rimet Cup Ltd v Football Association Ltd* [2007] EWHC 2376 (Ch), the court held that the claimant had acted, both subjectively and objectively, in bad faith, in seeking to register the 'World Cup Willie' logo and words as trade marks. The claimant must have known that there was still valuable residual goodwill in the UK for such a familiar mark.

An application to strike off a mark as being deceptive was made in *Zakritoe Aktsionernoe Obchtechestvo Torgovy Dom Potomkov Postavechtchika Dvora Ego Imperatorskago Velitschestva PA Smirnova v Diageo North America Inc* [2003] All ER (D) 99 (Apr). The (Russian) appellant's argument was that the (American) respondent's 14 registrations of the word 'Smirnoff' implied an unjustified connection with the Russian Federation. Smirnoff vodka has been sold since 1952 and is described as the world's leading brand. The appeal failed, as there was held to be no deception as to the origin of the goods. The registrations for 'Smirnoff' were upheld.

18.5.5.3 Public policy or morality

In *Ghazilian's Trade Mark Application* [2002] RPC 23, the applicant appealed the refusal of the Registrar of Trade Marks to register as a trade mark for clothing the words 'Tiny Penis'. Not surprisingly, the judge agreed with the Registrar and refused registration. The judge held that the hearing officer had to consider objectively how a right-thinking, but open-minded, member of the public would view the mark in question, as in *Re Masterman's Design* [1991] RPC 89. (This concerned a Scottish doll wearing a kilt but nothing under it. Registration of the design was allowed.)

An attempt to have the FCUK registration declared invalid on public policy grounds failed; the mark had been properly registered and any objectionable use of the mark by third parties could not affect its continued validity (see *French Connection Ltd's Trade Mark Application (No 81862)* [2005] WL 3734085). This reasoning can be seen in the successful registration of many highly suggestive marks.

18.6 Evidence of use to overcome absolute grounds (the proviso to s 3(1))

In **18.5** we saw how the criteria for absolute grounds work. However, there are lots of registered trade marks which would offend these criteria. The registration system would therefore unfairly deprive the proprietors of the protection of registration, when in fact the trade marks are already well known in the trade or to the public. Examples of trade marks which prima facie offend the criteria for absolute grounds but yet have been registered include the 'York' trailer trade mark (geographical objections) and 'Premier' luggage (laudatory description). The reason is that lack of distinctiveness can often be overcome by publicly recognised use, that is, by building up goodwill in the mark. If an applicant can show that it has built up a reputation in, say, a descriptive mark by using it, then it may have acquired distinctiveness in fact through use and it can be registered. The Coca-Cola bottle shape was universally associated, by use, with the company, although the bottle shape had some distinctive features anyway. The applicant will establish reputation in the mark by sending a statutory declaration to the Trade Mark Registry giving evidence of advertising spend, turnover in the goods and length of use. (Also it needs to be use as an indicator of origin of the goods or services, sometimes referred to as 'trade mark use'.) An informal minimum number of years' use is five. If you do not have five years of use, it is not generally worth trying. Usually the client does better to choose a mark that is registrable from the outset without use but valuable marks do often arise over time.

Very few colours are registered, but the colour of Heinz tins of baked beans has now been registered on the basis of use. Usually, for colour to be considered it has to be a combination of colours, not just a single shade. See *Smith Kline & French Laboratories Ltd v Sterling-Winthrop Group Ltd* [1975] 2 All ER 578, where a complex of colours for a pharmaceutical capsule was accepted on evidence of wide recognition of the complex as distinguishing the goods. (Be aware that this case was under the old Trade Marks Act 1938.) Nevertheless, in *BP Amoco plc v John Kelly Ltd* [2002] FSR 5, it was held that BP's trade mark registration of a single colour was valid. The trade mark consisted of the shade of green defined in colour charts as Pantone 348C, which BP used as the livery for their petrol filling stations. In *Libertel Group BV v Benelux-Merkenbureau* Case (C-104/01) [2004] 2 WLR 1081, the ECJ held that in order to be capable of being registered as a trade mark, a colour had to be defined by reference to an international identification system. It was not sufficient to lodge a sample with the trade mark office in question. The colour also had to have distinctive character (ie, to have been used in relation to the goods or services in question).

A type of mark that often arises over time is in the recognised use of slogans; these can become very well known indicators of trade origin. But they have their own problems. The long-running attempt to register 'HAVE A BREAK', quite independently of the well-known 'have a break ... have a Kit Kat', has produced an ECJ reference by the Court of Appeal that appears to give support for the proposition that long use and recognition of the mark, in association with a registered trade mark, even as part of a more extensive slogan, can give the necessary distinctiveness of trade origin for registration; see *Société des Produits Nestlé SA v Mars UK Ltd* (Case C-353/03) [2005] 3 CMLR 12, [2006] All ER (EC) 348, ECJ. The problem, up to the stage of the reference, was the High Court view, supporting the refusal to register, that 'have a break', standing alone, was a common phrase that had no distinctive quality in itself.

Generally, with slogans, the more curious the expression and the less related to the particular goods or services, the greater the likelihood of registration, the downside being that the promotional value must, necessarily, be very indirect. Established use is very helpful in trying to register slogans as trade marks, in part because it allows a trial period to see whether the slogan is effective, in a commercial sense, before trying to register.

18.7 Relative grounds for refusing an application (s 5)

18.7.1 What does 'relative grounds' mean?

'Relative grounds' means a conflict with an existing registered trade mark, belonging to someone else, which is identical or similar to the one being applied for. In TMA 1994, s 5, the relative grounds for refusal are laid down. The most common ones are as follows:

> (1) A trade mark shall not be registered if it is identical with an earlier trade mark and the goods or services for which the trade mark is applied for are identical with the goods or services for which the earlier trade mark is protected.
>
> (2) A trade mark shall not be registered if because—
>
> (a) it is identical with an earlier trade mark and is to be registered for goods or services similar to those for which the earlier trade mark is protected, or
>
> (b) it is similar to an earlier trade mark and is to be registered for goods or services identical with or similar to those for which the earlier trade mark is protected,
>
> there exists a likelihood of confusion on the part of the public, which includes the likelihood of association with the earlier trade mark.
>
> (3) A trade mark which—
>
> (a) is identical with or similar to an earlier trade mark, ...
>
> (b) ...
>
> shall not be registered if, or to the extent that, the earlier trade mark has a reputation in the United Kingdom (or, in the case of a Community trade mark, in the European Community) and the use of the later mark without due cause would take unfair advantage of, or be detrimental to, the distinctive character or the repute of the earlier trade mark.

How do you find out whether your client's proposed trade mark is going to run foul of an existing registration? The answer is to do a trade mark search. Most firms have facilities for doing this online; alternatively, you can get one through an agency like Compumark. If you are inexperienced in this kind of work then it is best to go to an agency because they will analyse it for you to some extent. If you really don't know what you are doing, you instruct a trade mark agent. Beware that the results of a trade mark search are never completely up to date. The search facilities available on www.ipo.gov.uk are admirably easy to use.

Because trade marks are registered in relation to specified goods or services, the starting point is to look for trade marks registered for the same types of goods and services, that is, in the relevant classes (see **18.3** and **18.15**).

A trade mark application can also be refused on the grounds that it is likely to be the subject of a passing-off action (TMA 1994, s 5(4) and see **17.1**). To check for earlier rights in passing off, you can do a common law search by looking in telephone directories and journals (eg, in magazines on mountain bikes for marks used in connection with push bikes), etc. This common law search cannot, of course, be comprehensive. Some earlier rights may well be obvious, even without a search. See *Jules Rimet Cup Ltd v Football Association Ltd* (at **18.5.5.2**), concerning an application to register the 'World Cup Willie' logo and words.

The starting point, then, with relative ground objections, is to show an identical or similar pre-existing registration; dissimilar marks usually create few problems. The same concepts and case law come into play when considering infringements under s 10, which are discussed at **18.9**, and the same matters need to be considered. It is very important, therefore, to consider how identity and similarity are assessed in this circumstance and it is not at all easy to summarise the approaches taken. Generally, the test is one for the registration authorities and the courts, according to legal principles, a brief summary of which now follows.

18.7.1.1 Identical marks

The broad approach is for the court to put itself in the position of a reasonable, well-informed and alert customer, seeing the mark and having all the usual imperfections of recall of earlier marks that would be normal in such a person. It follows that tactile, visual and aural perceptions are important and it is probably only going to be clearly an identical mark if, without much modification, the essential elements of the earlier mark, as registered, are reproduced in the later one. Usually, the difficulties come where someone has used only part of an earlier mark, or has used all of an earlier mark and added more to it to create a larger, more complex mark, eg, if someone used the famous 'Smartie' mark in a larger composition. Generally, anyone doing the latter would infringe the earlier mark, because they have reproduced it in its entirety, albeit as part of a mark; that could be done by extending a trade marked word into a longer word or phrase; see *Decon Laboratories Ltd v Fred Baker Scientific Ltd* [2001] RPC 293 and *System 3R International AB v Erowa AG and Erowa Nordic AB* [2003] ETMR 916. Stylising the word in a different way may still amount to using an identical mark. The advantage of finding an identical mark, as compared with a similar one, is that, if used on identical goods, nothing more needs to be established to prevent registration (compare s 5(1) with s 5(2)).

18.7.1.2 Identical goods or services

This can be a problem area in some respects. It is certainly not enough that the goods or services are within the same registration class; the goods or services need to have a considerable identity in terms of what they are, in themselves, as well as with respect to what the customer is expecting to obtain. There is no requirement for direct identity between the particular appearance or other aspects of the compared matters; a square, red ceramic floor tile is identical, for these purposes, to a round, blue one.

18.7.1.3 Similarity of marks

Here, somewhat different considerations apply, because the point has been visited on many occasions and there is now a fairly well-established approach, as shown by the ECJ in *Sabel BV v Puma AG, Rudolf Dassler Sport* (Case C-251/95) [1998] ETMR 1. A court should take an overall impression of the visual, aural and conceptual similarities of the marks, looking in particular at distinctive and dominant features. To this list, scents and smells must now be added. The whole point about this test is that it concentrates upon similarities, rather than distinctions. One might well add all sorts of fancy differences on top of someone else's registered mark, but if the 'distinctive and dominant' features of the prior registered mark are still discernible enough to lead to the necessary confusion in the mind of the customer, causing him to associate the mark before him with a completely different trade source that he already associates with of those features, it will be a similar mark; see *Sir Terence Orby Conran v Mean Fiddler Holdings Ltd* [1997] FSR 856, where the 'Zinc' mark was successfully protected in opposition proceedings. The question of similarity cannot really be divorced from the question of confusion as to trade source, and similarity, in the absence of confusion or, at least, association with the registered mark, is not a relevant consideration.

In *Alticor Inc v Nutrigreen Health Products Ltd* (Trade Mark Registry 09/11/07) [2007] WL 4368242, an application was upheld to register 'NUTRILIFE' as a trade mark over opposition from the owner of the registration of 'NUTRILITE'. The mark applied for comprised 'NUTRI' and 'LIFE' on different lines, and the words were linked by other graphic imagery. Taking the totality of each mark into consideration, the differences far outweighed the similarities.

18.7.1.4 Similarity of goods and services

Here, much more emphasis is placed upon the fact that, to deny registration, there must be demonstrable confusion and wrong association of the trade source of the goods or services to be marketed under the sign for which registration is sought. Everything, here, is likely to turn upon what, exactly, the likely users of goods or services might expect to find on offer under a particular registered trade mark (bearing in mind the uses for which the trade mark is registered) and where or when those goods or services might be expected to be offered. Clearly, the closer the range and type of goods and/or services to be marketed under the new application, where they are to be marketed, and the closer the marketing techniques used are to those under the existing registration, the more likely it is that there will be found to be similarity. The conclusion to be drawn from the many cases in this area seems to be that the greater the reputation and public goodwill in the prior registered trade mark, the more the emphasis of the comparison by the court tends to shift, noticeably, from the question of similarity of the goods or services offered towards the question of confusion or wrong association of the trade source. It is a subtle point, but it is necessary in order to understand the judicial and registration approach.

18.7.2 Relative grounds, registration and specific examples

Someone trying to register 'Coca-Cola' for fizzy drinks would find it impossible on relative grounds because of the existing registrations for the real 'Coca-Cola' (ie 'identical' goods (s 5(1))). However, this could also be the case for someone trying to register 'Coca-Cola' for cars, lavatory brushes or other 'dissimilar' goods. In the case of the use in relation to cars, it would be held as obtaining an unfair advantage from the reputation of the existing trade mark. In the case of goods such as lavatory brushes, it could be held to be detrimental to the existing mark, as well as taking unfair advantage (s 5(3)).

In *Enterprise Rent-a-car Co v Eurodrive Car Rental Ltd* [2005] Lawtel 2/3/2005, the case concerned an application for a trade mark stylised letter 'E' for car rental services. The appellant objected, as it was the proprietor of various trade marks beginning with the letter 'E'. It was held that there was no likelihood of confusion under s 5(2)(b).

In *Intel Corporation v Sihra* [2003] EWHC 17 (Ch), [2003] All ER (D) 212 (Jan), registration of 'Intel-Play' was refused as it was held that it would take unfair advantage of, or be detrimental to the character and repute of the existing registered trade mark 'Intel', under s 5(3). The application was for use on constructional toys, whereas the Intel registration was for computer components.

The situation with relative grounds is very close to that under s 10 for infringement (see **18.9**), and for most purposes ss 5 and 10 can be treated as equivalent provisions. In other words, the rules on whether you can register a mark are virtually the same as the rules on whether you will infringe an existing mark if you use your mark. I cannot register 'Coca-Cola', and I will infringe it if I try to use it.

18.7.3 When might relative grounds show themselves?

The relative grounds are likely in some cases to show themselves at the first stage of application to register, where there is an initial examination and search of the Register to ensure the application complies with the substantive requirements of a trade mark and that there are no absolute or relative grounds of objection, as discussed above at **18.7.1**. The Trade Mark Manual of the IPO shows that, since October 2007, the Registrar has only been able to refuse registration on relative grounds if there is a successful objection by a proprietor of an existing trade mark or sign. If the examiner's preliminary search shows up a potential relevant ground opposition, the result of this is notified to the applicant for the new registration, so that the applicant can withdraw or amend, at this early stage. This initial check is relevant only to objections under s 5(1) and (2). Grounds of objection based upon the other parts of s 5 – s 5(3) and (4) – would not be apparent to the examiner on his initial examination.

If the relative ground difficulty has not been spotted by the examiner, or if the applicant decides to press ahead, notwithstanding potential opposition, the application is then published in the *Trade Marks Journal*, as discussed earlier at **18.4.1**. At the same time as the new application is published, the owners of the prior-registered trade mark(s) that have been identified by the initial examination will be notified of the new application. That triggers a three-month period in which any person objecting on relative grounds, in respect of prior registered marks, can bring opposition proceedings. These commence with a hearing between the parties by a hearing officer at the Registry, with available appeals either to an 'Appointed Person', appointed by the Lord Chancellor (usually a very senior practitioner), or to the Chancery Division of the High Court.

Under this more modern practice, whereby the Registrar cannot simply, on his own initiative, refuse registration on relative grounds, opposition proceedings are bound to become more frequent.

A useful case to examine the proper approach to opposition proceedings on relative grounds is seen in *Esure Insurance Ltd v Direct Line Insurance plc* [2008] EWCA Civ 842. Here, the owners of the well known 'red telephone on wheels' device trade mark for insurance objected to the application to register a computer mouse on wheels as a device mark for insurance and financial services. The Hearing Officer upheld the objection, on grounds of similarity and likelihood of confusion. On appeal to a judge, the judge disallowed the objection, mainly because of the approach to similarity taken by the Officer. The Court of Appeal, allowing the appeal from the judge below and upholding the objection, gave some useful pointers on s 5(1) and (2). First, confusion was ascertained from the point of view of the average consumer in the light of all factors, and there was no need to apply a strict threshold of similarity, completely independently of confusion. Provided that the Hearing Officer had seen evidence of the marks themselves and the class of registration, that was enough for him to come to his view. It was said that little would be gained by the use of expert evidence in such cases, except where the particular market in question might be one with which the general consumer was unfamiliar.

These changes have necessitated some amendments to the TMA 1994, and these may be seen in the Trade Marks (Earlier Trade Marks) Regulations 2008 (SI 2008/1067). The changes also include giving better protection to 'well-known' trade marks (see **18.10**) as against later registered national trade marks.

18.7.4 Summary

It can be seen, by examining the extract from s 5 shown at **18.7.1**, that all different combinations of identity/similarity of both the marks and the relevant goods/services can now be objected to on relative grounds. This is extended by s 5(3), to deal with the circumstance of identical/similar marks being used even on dissimilar goods. The position is summarised in the table below.

Goods or services	Trade mark identical	Trade mark similar
Identical	no proof of confusion needed (s 5(1))	likelihood of confusion needed (s 5(2)(b))
Similar	likelihood of confusion needed (s 5(2)(a))	likelihood of confusion needed (s 5(2)(b))
Identical, similar, dissimilar	unfair advantage or detriment needed (s 5(3))	unfair advantage or detriment needed (s 5(3))

18.8 Protecting the mark, once registered

Once the client has the registration, he needs advice on protecting the mark. If it is not protected it can become subject to misuse, including infringement, and ultimately to revocation. The most important grounds of revocation to be aware of are as follows.

18.8.1 Non-use

If the mark has not been used for five years following registration, or any subsequent five-year period, it can be struck off for non-use in that category of goods or services. It is a matter of 'use it or lose it' (ss 46(1)(a) and 6A). This happened in the *United Biscuits* case, discussed at **17.2.2**, where the successful claimants nevertheless had four trade mark registrations revoked for non-use.

18.8.2 Has become generic

A trade mark becomes generic if, as a result of action or inaction by the proprietor, it has become a common mark in the trade for a product or service for which it is registered. So, under s 1(1) of the TMA 1994, the trade mark no longer distinguishes the goods or services of one business from those of another business and would not be registrable because of s 3(1)(d). This may lead to a revocation application under s 46 of the TMA 1994; see **18.8.3**.

In *Julius Sämaan v Tetrosyl Ltd* [2006] EWHC 529, owners of fir tree marks for cardboard strip air fresheners were able to show infringement by Tetrosyl, which made similar items for use in cars. A defence that 'tree' marks were now generic was rejected as the only other relevant 'tree' mark in the market showed an oak tree.

Biro, Linoleum, Refrigerator and Launderette have become generic terms. These were once registered trade marks, but they have lost their ability to identify the goods of one business and are now simply part of the language.

How do you avoid your trade mark becoming generic? You should:

(a) use it as an adjective and not as a noun, eg, 'Gordons gin and tonic', not 'Gordons and tonic';

(b) distinguish it from the surrounding writing, eg, by putting it in bold, or in capitals or quotation marks; or

(c) acknowledge it as a trade mark (use ® if registered; but do not use ® if it is not registered because this is a criminal offence – TMA 1994, s 95).

18.8.3 Has become misleading

A trade mark can be revoked if it has become misleading because of the way the proprietor has used it, or allowed it to be used (s 46(1)(d)). One concern here is that if the mark is licensed to others then they may not produce goods of the same quality as the trade mark proprietor, or as each other. For this reason, it is essential to include quality control provisions in any licence to manufacture goods under a trade mark and to make certain that they are applied by the licensee.

18.9 Infringement of a registered trade mark

Under s 14, infringement of a registered trade mark is actionable by the proprietor of the trade mark. This is because s 9(1) says the proprietor has exclusive rights in the mark which are infringed by the use of it in the UK without his consent. It is important to realise that not every use of someone else's mark will be an infringement for these purposes. There must be a use of the mark in the course of trade, as distinct from use for non-trading purposes, eg, painting the Mercedes badge onto your wall at home out of enthusiasm. There must also be use of the mark as a trade mark, as a badge of trade origin, as distinct from serving some other purpose. These matters are discussed in more detail below.

There can only be infringement of the trade mark as actually registered. Any limits on the registration are strictly observed, as in *Phones 4u Ltd and Another v Phone4u.co.uk Internet Ltd* [2006] EWCA Civ 244. There, the registered colours of the mark limited the scope of infringement.

To constitute infringement, use of the offending mark (or 'sign', as it is referred to in s 10, to distinguish it from the mark being infringed) must be 'in the course of trade'. Thus, a painting by Andy Warhol of a can of soup did not infringe Campbells' trade mark as Andy Warhol was not in the business of making soup. The s 9 territorial limit on trade mark use within the UK may sometimes create problems involving importing and exporting trade-marked goods.

The issue of use of the mark as a badge of trade origin came up in the case of *Arsenal Football Club plc v Reed* [2003] EWCA Civ 696. Mr Reed sold football merchandise outside the ground of Arsenal Football Club on match days. He had a notice on his stall to the effect that the goods were not official Arsenal regalia. However, the goods did bear the Arsenal logo. At first instance, there was some doubt as to whether this use was use as a trade mark at all. Was the Arsenal badge being used as a trade mark, or was it just an indication of loyalty to a football team? The ECJ held that the badge was a trade mark (*Arsenal Football Club plc v Reed* (Case C-206/01) [2002] All ER (EC) 1). Professional football clubs such as Arsenal are multi-million pound businesses. They register trade marks to protect their commercial rights. The ECJ held that this was use of an identical mark on identical goods. The Court of Appeal followed the reasoning in the ECJ judgment. Aldous LJ explained that the unauthorised goods sold by Mr Reed affected the ability of the trade marks to guarantee the origin of the goods.

A different problem occurred in *R v Johnstone* [2003] UKHL 28, [2003] 3 All ER 884. In this case, the defendant dealt in bootleg copies of music CDs. Various of the artists concerned had registered their names as trade marks. Was the existence of such an artist's name on a CD merely an indication of the identity of the performer, or was it use of the name in a trade mark sense? The House of Lords held that to come within the criminal offence under s 92 of the TMA 1994, the use of the artist's name had to be use of a trade mark as an indication of trade origin of the CDs. Whilst the use of a trade mark such as 'Sony' or 'EMI' would be such a use, this was not the case with the name of an artist. Consequently, the defendant's actions did not fall within s 92.

18.9.1 The methods of infringement

The TMA 1994 now specifies four types of infringement; here you should consider the points on identical similar signs, goods/services etc at **18.7**:

(a) Use of an identical sign for identical goods or services (as determined by the statement of goods or services with which the mark was registered) (s 10(1)). The question of being 'identical' or not was examined by the Court of Appeal in *Reed Executive and Reed Solutions v Reed Business Information and Elsevier* [2004] EWCA Civ 159, [2004] RPC 40. There, the claimant argued that 'Reed Business Information' was identical under s 10(1) to its registered trade mark 'Reed'. In other words, if the registered trade mark cropped up in only part of another business name, that was use of an identical sign. The

Court rejected this argument and held that the words 'Business Information' were part of the defendant's business name. Consequently, 'Reed Business Information' was not identical to 'Reed', so the issue was not use of an identical sign in s 10(1), but rather of a 'similar' sign under s 10(2). In other words, you have to look at the whole of the allegedly infringing sign or mark.

(b) Use of an identical or similar sign for similar goods or services, or a similar sign for identical goods or services, if there is a likelihood of confusion (s 10(2)). This is a higher hurdle for the trademark proprietor to overcome, hence the argument at (a) above in the *Reed* case. Confusion must be as to the trade origin of the goods and services.

(c) Use of an identical or similar sign for goods or services, whether identical, similar or dissimilar, if the use is detrimental to, or takes unfair advantage of, the distinctive character or repute of the mark (s 10(3)). In *Conroy v SmithKline Beecham plc* (Trade Marks Registry 0-085-03, 3 April 2003), the applicant had applied to register 'Nit Nurse' in class 3 for oils and shampoos for the control of head lice. The opponents objected, successfully. They held registrations in class 5 for respiratory decongestants under the trade marks 'Night Nurse'. There were arguments that a consumer could confuse the two products, with unfortunate results. In contrast, see also *Premier Brands UK Ltd v Typhoon Europe Ltd* [2000] FSR 767, where the proprietors of 'Typhoo' for tea, objected unsuccessfully to a registration of 'Typhoon' for kitchen utensils. It should be noted that the tests in ss 5(3) and 10(3) were amended by the Trade Marks (Proof of Use) Etc Regulations 2004 (SI 2004/946). This was to fill a gap in these subsections; originally they did not extend to unfair use of a mark on similar or identical goods, only dissimilar ones. See *Adidas-Salomon AG v Fitnessworld Trading Ltd* (Case C-408/01) [2004] 1 CMLR 14, [2004] Ch 120.

It is not sufficient to show that the alleged infringer has gained an advantage; what must be shown is that the advantage was gained because the registered mark was highly distinctive, and that the reminder of it given to the public by the infringer's use of the sign is strong. The claimant was unable to show this in *Whirlpool Corporation Ltd v Kenwood Ltd* [2009] EWCA Civ 753 (application alleging infringement of a CTM shape mark, in form of a kitchen mixer, causing detriment and taking unfair advantage, was dismissed). See also the important development concerning unfair advantage claims discussed at **18.9.2** below.

(d) Any use of a trade mark which is not in accordance with honest practices in industrial and commercial matters. Honest use is not infringement, so comparative advertising is not infringement (s 10(6) (which it was under the 1938 Act)), provided it does not overstep the boundaries. A case where it did go too far is *Emaco Ltd and Another v Dyson Appliances Ltd* [1999] ETMR 903, where both parties were held to have made unfair comparisons of the goods and thereby infringed each other's trade mark registrations for Electrolux and Dyson. Note that mere advertising puffery does not count as being dishonest, but use of a mark in a manner disparaging to the mark or its owner may take the use outside of honest practice.

An extensive analysis of comparative advertising can be seen in *O2 Holdings Ltd v Hutchinson 3G Ltd* [2006] ETMR 55, where Lewison J upheld the robust, but fair, comparison of products and the validity of different 'bubble' marks used by the parties. Further questions from this case were referred to the ECJ by the Court of Appeal: see [2006] EWCA Civ 1656. The initial opinion given by Advocate-General Mengozzi in Case C-533/06 showed that permissible use of a trade mark in comparative advertising can go some way beyond merely identifying particular goods or services as originating from a competitor, and that such use need not be indispensable to the purposes of the advertiser. The opinion of the ECJ was that, taking the defendant's use of the bubble marks as a whole, it did not give rise to likelihood of confusion, was not misleading and did not suggest any commercial link between the parties. It seems likely, now, that a far more widely applicable source of guidance on the boundary between permissible comparative advertising (which will not infringe trade mark rights) and impermissible comparative advertising (which will do so) is to be seen in the *L'Oréal SA v Bellure NV case*, discussed at **18.9.2** below.

These grounds are much the same as the relative grounds for invalidity (see **18.7**).

The proprietor of a registered trade mark would usually have to produce evidence of confusion, or unfair advantage or detriment, as the case may be. This could be in the form of survey evidence, or expert witnesses from the trade in question, but the nature of the required evidence must be considered now in the light of the ECJ ruling in *L'Oréal SA v Bellure NV*, discussed in **18.9.2** below.

18.9.2 Detrimental or unfairly advantageous use

Very significant guidance has recently been given by the ECJ in *L'Oréal SA v Bellure NV* (Case C-487/07) [2009] All ER (D) 225 (Jun), on the evidential and legal requirements of an infringement claim under s 10(3) (see (c) at **18.9.1** above) and of Article 5(2) of Directive 89/104. Here, the claimant manufacturer of high-quality beauty products sought remedies, inter alia, for trade mark infringements against 'smell-alike' importers using packaging and comparison lists from which the alleged infringements arose. There were issues concerning the scope of taking unfair advantage of the reputation of a trade mark, both for the purposes of trade mark infringement and for the closely connected question of permissible comparative advertising under EC law on misleading advertisements. The matter went to the Court of Appeal, from which the following questions were referred to the ECJ (summarised here, for simplicity, as the ECJ dealt with them in a slightly different way from that in which the Court of Appeal referred them) for preliminary rulings:

(a) *Whether a third party using a sign, identical to a trade mark with a reputation, in comparative advertising in relation to identical goods, could be held to take unfair advantage where the third party gained a marketing advantage, but without causing confusion to the public as to trade origin, or causing detriment to the mark or its proprietor.* The ECJ ruled that unfair advantage could be taken of the distinctive character or the repute of the mark, without requiring a likelihood of confusion or detriment. The unfairness of the advantage lay in the third party riding 'on the coat-tails' of the trade mark, to exploit the marketing effort and expense needed to maintain the registered mark's image, without paying any compensation for it.

(b) *Whether the proprietor of a well-known registered mark could prevent such a use in comparative advertising as is described in (a) above, by a third party, where such use is not capable of jeopardising the essential function of the trade mark as an indicator of trade origin.* The ECJ ruled that the proprietor of the mark could prevent such use, even in those circumstances, provided that such use was liable to affect some other function of the mark (examples were given, in particular, of the functions of guaranteeing quality, of communication, investment or advertising). It would be for the referring court (in this case, the Court of Appeal) to determine whether the use made of the infringing sign was liable to affect one or more of the functions of the trade mark. The case law showed that the proprietor cannot oppose the use of an identical sign, if that use is not liable to cause detriment to any of the functions of the trade mark. Nevertheless, the ECJ made very clear that an advertiser, in a comparative advertisement that satisfied all the requirements of Article 3a(1) of Directive 84/450 (the Directive covering misleading advertising, which extends to comparative advertising: see further **18.9.4** below) could not be prevented from honest use of the mark by the proprietor of it. (See **18.9.4** on the point of regulation of misleading advertisements.)

(c) *Whether Article 3a(1) of Directive 84/450 means that where an advertiser indicates through a comparison list, without in any way causing confusion or deception, that his product has a major characteristic similar to that of a product marketed under a well-known trade mark, of which the advertiser's product constitutes an imitation, that advertiser takes unfair advantage of the trade mark (for the purposes of Article 3a(1) of Directive 84/50), or presents 'goods or services as imitations or replicas' for the purposes of Article 3a(1)(h).* The ECJ ruled that such an advertiser would be both taking unfair advantage of the reputation of the mark and presenting the goods or services as imitations or replicas within the meaning of Directive 84/450. It appears to follow from this ruling, and the view of the Court of Appeal in the case, that because such a use was impermissible and would be inconsistent with fair competition or honest practice, it was unlawful, and must be regarded as taking unfair advantage of the reputation of the mark, for trade mark infringement purposes, too (this point was not referred to the ECJ as being self-evident).

It seems very likely that this guidance will figure prominently in future cases on comparative advertising, both with respect to trade mark infringements per se and with respect to questions of permissible use of signs and marks in comparative advertising within Directive 84/450, as amended (see **18.9.4**).

18.9.3 Trade marks and the Internet

Trade marks are national rights (but see **18.13** below for the international dimension), so the use has to be within the UK. Thus, on the Internet, pre-emptive registration of a domain name that is similar to a registered trade mark might not necessarily be use in the course of trade within the UK. However, the Court of Appeal held it was so likely to lead to infringement that an injunction was granted (*British Telecommunications plc and Others v One in a Million Ltd and Others* [1999] 1 WLR 903). In that case, someone had registered as Internet domain names the names of various well-known businesses, including BT and Virgin. The aim presumably was to sell the domain name to the rightful owner for large sums of money. See also *Tesco Stores Ltd v Elogicom Ltd* [2006] EWHC 403 (Ch), where use of the 'Tesco' mark, as part of several domain names, constituted serious infringement of the trade mark.

A website can be accessed from anywhere in the world; this does not always mean that for trade mark purposes the trade marks are being used in the course of trade in a particular jurisdiction (see *800 Flowers, Trade Mark Application; 1-800 Flowers Incorporated v Phonenames Ltd* [2001] EWCA Civ 721, [2002] FSR 288 and *Euromarket Designs Inc v Peters and Trade & Barrel Ltd* [2001] FSR 288, where the mere possibility of accessing a site from the UK did not necessarily mean that there was infringement of a UK trade mark). In the *Euromarket* case, Jonathan Parker LJ said:

> So I think that the mere fact that websites can be accessed anywhere in the world does not mean, for trade mark purposes, that the law should regard them as being used everywhere in the world. It all depends upon the circumstances, particularly the intention of the website owner and what the reader will understand if he accesses the site. In other fields of law, publication on a website may well amount to a universal publication, but I am not concerned with that.

In *Wilson v Yahoo! UK Ltd* [2008] EWHC 361 (Ch), the defendant was granted summary judgment to strike out a claim that it had infringed the claimant's trade mark via two sponsored links on its Internet search engine. It was held that the trade mark had not been used by the defendant but only by the browser. This happened when the browser put the word mark in as a search term.

Thus, in *Bonnier Media Ltd v Greg Lloyd Smith* [2002] ETMR 86, the Scottish Court of Session held that the defendants could be sued in Scotland in regard to material accessed on the Internet, even though the originating site was outside the UK. The defendants intended to set up a website with a domain name similar to Bonnier's trade mark. It was held that the defendants' activities were aimed at damaging Bonnier's business, which was based in

Scotland. In other words, the defendants' intentions are a key part in deciding whether or not there is trade mark infringement (or passing off).

Another aspect of the international dimension of trade marks is the interface with competition law. A trade mark proprietor could not use national trade mark rights to prevent parallel importation of his goods from another EU Member State. However, he can use trade mark rights to prevent importation of goods he has produced and has sold for resale on to a non-EU market. This was the case in *Zino Davidoff SA v A & G Imports Ltd; Levi Strauss & Co and Another v Tesco Stores Ltd and Another; Levi Strauss & Co and Another v Costco Wholesale UK* (Joined Cases C-414/99, C-415/99 and C-416/99) [2002] All ER (EC) 55. Here, the claimants succeeded in preventing Tesco from continuing to import supplies of the Levi Strauss goods from North America and Mexico. The goods were for resale in the Tesco stores in the UK at lower prices than the goods officially released on to the UK market by Levi Strauss (see also the *Silhouette* case at **18.11**). In the case of *Glaxo Group v Dowelhurst Ltd* [2004] EWCA Civ 290, [2004] WL 412961, CA, pharmaceutical products were sold to the defendant company for sale in Africa but were in fact sold within the UK. An injunction was granted to prevent this activity.

Further discussion of trade mark use in Internet trading can be found at **25.5.3** below.

18.9.4 Honest and fair use of a trade mark

All the infringing acts within s 10 are subject to the proviso within s 10(6) (see (d) at **18.9.1** above), namely that any honest and fair use of another person's registered trade mark for the purpose of identifying any goods or services as being those of the proprietor or a licensee of the mark is to be allowed. This is essential, of course, to the widespread modern practice of comparative advertising, ie comparing a range of competing products on price, performance etc. This is very important, because the infringing acts set out in s 10(4) include use of the mark on business papers or in advertising.

You will have realised from your reading of the *L'Oréal SA v Bellure NV* guidance at **18.9.2** above, that where the use of a trade mark in permissible comparative advertising is concerned, the proprietor of the mark cannot prevent fair and honest use of his mark by a competitor or other advertiser. The overall framework governing what is permissible is found in Directive 84/450 EEC, as amended by Directive 97/55 EC. The object of this Directive is to provide a system of Member State regulation, under which misleading and unfair anti-competitive advertising practices (including comparative advertising) can be controlled by public enforcement authorities. It is only when the unauthorised use of a trade mark fails to comply with the regulatory requirements that the proprietor can take his own private law steps to seek remedies against the persons responsible for any misuse in comparative advertising.

United Kingdom protection for trade marks against comparative advertising has been provided by the Business Protection from Misleading Marketing Regulations 2008 (SI 2008/1276), which are intended to address confusion between, or damage to, trade marks, names or products, although these Regulations have a far wider reach than trade mark use.

18.10 'Well-known' foreign trade marks (s 56)

Section 56 was introduced as part of the UK implementation of the Paris Convention. If a foreign trade mark is well known in the UK, the foreign proprietor will be able to get an injunction to restrain the use of that mark in the UK where the use would cause confusion. This measure is to protect foreign trade marks that are not registered in the UK. The most likely instance is that of a famous shop, or restaurant or hotel which has no branches in the UK. The section limits the remedy available to injuction but, no doubt, a passing-off claim would be available if further remedies are sought.

These marks are now given better protection under the Trade Marks (Earlier Trade Marks) Regulations 2008 (see **18.7.3**).

18.11 Defences to infringement (ss 11, 12, 48)

The first line of defence to a trade mark infringement action is that the trade mark is not validly registered and should be removed from the register under s 47 of the TMA 1994. The basis of the invalidity must be that one or more of the absolute grounds for refusing registration (s 3) can be shown.

The next line of defence to consider is s 11, which limits the scope of a registered trade mark and therefore provides some defences. For example, s 11(2)(a) allows the honest use of a person's own name or address. In *Reed Executive and Reed Solutions v Reed Business Information and Elsevier* [2004] EWCA Civ 159, [2004] RPC 40, the case concerned two businesses with similar names but operating in different fields of activity. It was held that a company could avail itself of the 'own name defence', and that the existence of the word 'Limited' was not relevant. Section 11(2)(b) allows use for the purposes of indicating the nature of the goods or services, so, for example, allowing an independent business to indicate that it supplied parts for BMW cars (*Bayerische Motorenwerke AG (BMW) and Another v Deenik* (Case 63/97) [1999] All ER (EC) 235).

However, in *Aktiebolaget Volvo v Heritage (Leicester) Ltd* [2000] FSR 253, the defendant motor trader had not made it sufficiently clear that it was no longer an authorised Volvo dealer. Consequently, its use of the Volvo trade mark was held not to fall within s 11, and it had infringed the trade mark registration by using an identical mark on identical goods.

Section 12 deals with the exhaustion of rights. Goods put on to the market elsewhere in the EU by the trade mark proprietor can be legitimately sold under that trade mark in the UK. Note that this does not cover goods put on to the market elsewhere in the world (*Silhouette International Schmied GmbH and Co KG v Hartlauer Handelsgesellschaft mbH* (Case C-355/96) [1999] Ch 77 and see the *Zino Davidoff* case at **18.9**). To exhaust the rights, the owner must have actually consented to the product being placed on the market within the EEA, or there must be a strong implication of such consent. The mere fact that packaging was printed in three European languages was not enough to raise that implication in *Roche Products Ltd v Kent Pharmaceuticals Ltd* [2006] EWHC 335.

An interesting case that shows how the implication of consent can arise is *Honda Motor Co Ltd v Neesam* [2008] EWHC 338 (Ch). Here, sales by Honda to its Australian subsidiary, which sold the motor bikes to a dealer who was known to deal in the UK market, were held to show an implied consent, sufficient to exhaust the right.

Section 48 deals with the question of acquiescence. If a proprietor of an earlier mark acquiesces in someone else's use of the registered mark for a continuous period of five years, the right is lost to apply for invalidity of the later mark or to oppose its use. See *Budejovicki Budvar Narodni Podnik v Anheuser-Busch Inc* [2008] EWHC 263 (Ch). In this recent round in the lengthy litigation over the 'Budweiser' and 'Bud' marks (in which both parties have legitimate interests), an acquiescence defence was upheld, in part.

18.12 Remedies for infringement (ss 14–19)

Section 14(2) provides that the usual remedies of 'damages, injunction, accounts or otherwise' are as available as 'in respect of the infringement of any other property right'. To this are added:

(a) orders against an infringer to erase or remove the offending sign or, if that is not possible, to destroy the goods or materials (s 15);

(b) the availability of an order to deliver up infringing goods or materials held in the course of business (s 16);

(c) orders concerning the disposal of matter delivered up under (b) (s 19);

(d) relief, including damages, declaration and injunction, against groundless threats of infringement proceedings (s 21).

There are also criminal law sanctions under ss 92–98, creating offences involving unauthorised use of trade marks, subject to defences of reasonable belief that no infringement was involved. There is also the possibility of forfeiture of counterfeit goods, in connection with such offences, under s 97. Further, there is the possibility of injunction and criminal prosecution at the instance of enforcement authorities under the Business Protection from Misleading Marketing Regulations 2008.

18.13 International trade marks

We have been looking at the law of UK trade marks. If you apply for a UK trade mark, this will give you the right to stop infringements only in the UK. If you want protection in other countries (eg, US, Japan, Hong Kong) then you have to make a separate application there. So if you want to protect your mark world-wide, this will be a very expensive process.

Within Europe, two processes allow the applicant to get wider protection on the basis of a single application.

18.13.1 Community trade mark

The CTM is a single trade mark, effective throughout the European Community. You apply to the OHIM at Alicante. The CTM system is still quite new, but it is proving very popular. Between the start of the system in 1996 and the end of May 2004, there were 378,000 applications made to OHIM. If you can get a CTM then this will give you protection throughout the Community on the basis of one registration. The difficulty is that the registration can be defeated by similar prior marks anywhere in the European Community. Many well-known UK marks would not be able to achieve a Community registration for this reason. However, the CTM system does not carry out extensive investigation of existing marks but rather leaves the proprietors of existing marks to object to published applications. This happened in *Mülhens GmbH & Co KG v OHIM and Zirh International Corp* (Case C-206/04P) [2006] ETMR 57, where the owners of the earlier CTM 'Sir' were able to block the registration of 'ZIRH' for the same class of goods, on grounds of similarity.

If an applicant is unsuccessful, it is then left with the possibility of applying in each of those countries where there is no problem in order to get a bundle of national registered trade marks.

18.13.2 Madrid Protocol

This is a system that allows you to make one application in one country initially. Then an application can be made for registrations in all the other countries listed on the application form, and which are Member States of the Madrid Protocol. The system is run by the World Intellectual Property Organisation (WIPO). The European Community itself has become a member, as opposed to the individual countries. The CTM can thus now be used as a basis for an international application to obtain trade mark protection outside the EC, as well as giving protection inside it.

18.13.3 Other international aspects

International treaties such as the Paris Convention for the Protection of Intellectual Property and TRIPS (part of GATT) ensure that there are certain similarities between the intellectual property laws of many countries in the world (eg, TMA 1994, s 56 arises out of an obligation under the Paris Convention).

In addition, the TMA 1994 implements the European Trade Marks Directive, which had as its aim the partial harmonisation of European trade mark laws. However, despite this, there are many important differences between the trade mark laws of different countries, both inside and outside Europe. There are also many technical differences. One should never assume, therefore, that the position is the same in another country. Foreign legal advice is often necessary, and most intellectual property practices have foreign lawyers with whom they deal on a regular basis.

18.14 Classes used in the Register of Trade Marks (Trade Mark Rules 2000, Sch 4)

CLASSIFICATION OF GOODS AND SERVICES

When you apply to register a trade mark you must include a list of all goods and services which you want to use the mark for. You must list the goods or services in the class or classes they fall in.

The following headings give general information about the types of goods and services which belong to each class. The list is not complete. It is there to guide you to the classes that you need. If you click on the class number you will see a full list of goods or services in that class, as provided by WIPO, the international organisation which decides trade mark classification.

Goods are in classes 1–34. Services are in classes 35–45.

If you do not know which class(es) your goods or services are in, please use our Classification search.

Goods

CLASS 1

Chemicals used in industry, science and photography, as well as in agriculture, horticulture and forestry; unprocessed artificial resins, unprocessed plastics; manures; fire extinguishing compositions; tempering and soldering preparations; chemical substances for preserving foodstuffs; tanning substances; adhesives used in industry.

Includes chemicals for the making of products belonging to other classes.

Does not include fungicides, herbicides, insecticides or preparations for destroying vermin which are in Class 5.

CLASS 2

Paints, varnishes, lacquers; preservatives against rust and against deterioration of wood; colorants; mordants; raw natural resins; metals in foil and powder form for painters, decorators, printers and artists.

Does not include paint boxes for children which are in Class 16 or insulating paints and varnishes which are in Class 17.

CLASS 3

Bleaching preparations and other substances for laundry use; cleaning, polishing, scouring and abrasive preparations; soaps; perfumery, essential oils, cosmetics, hair lotions; dentifrices.

Includes deodorants for personal use.

Does not include air deodorising preparations which are in Class 5 or scented candles which are in Class 4.

CLASS 4

Industrial oils and greases; lubricants; dust absorbing, wetting and binding compositions; fuels (including motor spirit) and illuminants; candles and wicks for lighting.

Includes combustible fuels and scented candles.

Does not include fuel for nuclear reactors or electricity which are both in Class 1. CLASS 5

Pharmaceutical and veterinary preparations; sanitary preparations for medical purposes; dietetic substances adapted for medical use, food for babies; plasters, materials for dressings; material for stopping teeth, dental wax; disinfectants; preparations for destroying vermin; fungicides, herbicides.

Includes foods and beverages which are adapted for medical purposes. *Does not include* supportive bandages which are in Class 10.

CLASS 6

Common metals and their alloys; metal building materials; transportable buildings of metal; materials of metal for railway tracks; non-electric cables and wires of common metal; ironmongery, small items of metal hardware; pipes and tubes of metal; safes; goods of common metal not included in other classes; ores.

Includes unwrought and partly wrought common metals as well as simple products made of them; metallic windows and doors and also metallic framed conservatories.

CLASS 7

Machines and machine tools; motors and engines (except for land vehicles); machine coupling and transmission components (except for land vehicles); agricultural implements other than hand-operated; incubators for eggs.

Includes parts of engines and motors; some parts for vehicles (eg exhausts for vehicles); vacuum cleaners.

Does not include engines or motors for land vehicles which are in Class 12 or specialist machines (eg weighing machines are in Class 9).

CLASS 8

Hand tools and implements (hand operated); cutlery; side arms; razors.

Includes electric razors and hair cutters; cutlery made of precious metal.

Does not include surgical cutlery which is in Class 10 or hand held and electrically powered tools (eg electric drills are in Class 7).

CLASS 9

Scientific, nautical, surveying, photographic, cinematographic, optical, weighing, measuring, signalling, checking (supervision), life-saving and teaching apparatus and instruments; apparatus and instruments for conducting, switching, transforming, accumulating, regulating or controlling electricity; apparatus for recording, transmission or reproduction of sound or images; magnetic data carriers, recording discs; automatic vending machines and mechanisms for coin operated apparatus; cash registers; calculating machines, data processing equipment and computers; fire-extinguishing apparatus.

Includes computer hardware and firmware; computer software (including software downloadable from the Internet); compact discs; digital music (downloadable from the Internet); telecommunications apparatus; computer games equipment adapted for use with TV receivers; mouse mats; mobile phone accessories; contact lenses, spectacles and sunglasses; clothing for protection against accident, irradiation or fire.

Does not include printed computer manuals which are in Class 16, self contained computer games equipment which is in Class 28, various electrical items (eg electric screwdrivers are in Class 7 and electric toothbrushes are in Class 21).

CLASS 10

Surgical, medical, dental and veterinary apparatus and instruments, artificial limbs, eyes and teeth; orthopaedic articles; suture materials.

Includes electro-medical or surgical apparatus; massage apparatus.

Does not include contact lenses, spectacles or sunglasses which are in Class 9 or wheelchairs which are in Class 12.

CLASS 11

Apparatus for lighting, heating, steam generating, cooking, refrigerating, drying, ventilating, water supply and sanitary purposes.

Includes air conditioning apparatus; electric kettles; gas and electric cookers; vehicle lights.

CLASS 12

Vehicles; apparatus for locomotion by land, air or water.

Includes motors and engines for land vehicles and certain other parts and fittings (eg vehicle body parts and transmissions).

Does not include certain parts or fittings for vehicles (eg exhausts and starters are in Class 7, lights and air conditioning units are in Class 11) or children's toy bicycles which are in Class 28.

CLASS 13

Firearms; ammunition and projectiles, explosives; fireworks.

Does not include apparatus for use in playing paint ball combat games which are in Class 28.

CLASS 14

Precious metals and their alloys and goods in precious metals or coated therewith, not included in other classes; jewellery, precious stones; horological and chronometric instruments.

Includes clocks and watches; costume jewellery.

Does not include certain precious metal items (eg cutlery is in Class 8, pens are in Class 16).

CLASS 15

Musical instruments.

Includes stands and cases adapted for musical instruments.

CLASS 16

Paper, cardboard and goods made from these materials, not included in other classes; printed matter; book binding material; photographs; stationery; adhesives for stationery or household purposes; artists' materials; paint brushes; typewriters and office requisites (except furniture); instructional and teaching material (except apparatus); plastic materials for packaging (not included in other classes); printers' type; printing blocks.

Includes disposable nappies of paper for babies; printed publications.

Does not include adhesives for industrial purposes which are in Class 1, electronic publications (downloadable) which are in Class 9, providing electronic publications (not downloadable) which are in Class 41 or wallpaper which is in Class 27.

CLASS 17

Rubber, gutta-percha, gum, asbestos, mica and goods made from these materials and not included in other classes; plastics in extruded form for use in manufacture; packing, stopping and insulating materials; flexible pipes, not of metal.

Includes semi-finished plastics materials for use in further manufacture.

Does not include unprocessed plastics in the form of liquids, chips, granules etc which are in Class 1.

CLASS 18

Leather and imitations of leather, and goods made of these materials and not included in other classes; animal skins, hides; trunks and travelling bags; umbrellas, parasols and walking sticks; whips, harness and saddlery.

Includes handbags, rucksacks, purses; clothing for animals.

Does not include leather clothing which is in Class 9 (for protection against injury) or in Class 25 (ordinary apparel); certain specialist leather articles (eg cheque book holders are in Class 16).

CLASS 19

Building materials (non-metallic); non-metallic rigid pipes for building; asphalt, pitch and bitumen; non-metallic transportable buildings; monuments, not of metal.

Includes non-metallic framed conservatories, doors and windows.

CLASS 20

Furniture, mirrors, picture frames; goods (not included in other classes) of wood, cork, reed, cane, wicker, horn, bone, ivory, whalebone, shell, amber, mother-of-pearl, meerschaum and substitutes for all these materials, or of plastics.

Includes both metallic and non-metallic furniture including garden furniture; pillows and cushions.

Does not include duvets or covers for pillows, cushions or duvets which are in Class 24, furniture adapted for medical use which is in Class 10 or furniture adapted for laboratory use which is in Class 9.

CLASS 21

Household or kitchen utensils and containers (not of precious metal or coated therewith); combs and sponges; brushes (except paint brushes); brush-making materials; articles for cleaning purposes; steel wool; un-worked or semi-worked glass (except glass used in building); glassware, porcelain and earthenware not included in other classes.

Includes both electric and non-electric toothbrushes.

Does not include electric kitchen appliances (eg electric food processors are in Class 7, electric kettles are in Class 11) or kitchen and table cutlery which is in Class 8.

CLASS 22

Ropes, string, nets, tents, awnings, tarpaulins, sails, sacks and bags (not included in other classes); padding and stuffing materials (except of rubber or plastics); raw fibrous textile materials.

Includes bags and sacks for transporting bulk materials.

CLASS 23

Yarns and threads, for textile use.

CLASS 24

Textiles and textile goods, not included in other classes; bed and table covers.

Includes textile piece goods; textiles for making articles of clothing.

Does not include table linen of paper which is in Class 16 or electric blankets (not for medical use) which are in Class 11.

CLASS 25

Clothing, footwear, headgear.

Does not include clothing for the prevention of accident and injury which is in Class 9, surgeons' clothing which is in Class 10 or clothing for animals which is in Class 18.

CLASS 26

Lace and embroidery, ribbons and braid; buttons, hooks and eyes, pins and needles; artificial flowers.

Includes dressmakers' articles; badges for wear (other than precious metal badges). CLASS 27

Carpets, rugs, mats and matting, linoleum and other materials for covering existing floors; wall hangings (non-textile).

Includes wallpaper.

Does not include mouse mats which are in Class 9, mats specifically shaped/adapted for vehicles which are in Class 12 or travellers' rugs which are in Class 24.

CLASS 28

Games and playthings; gymnastic and sporting articles not included in other classes; decorations for Christmas trees.

Includes hand-held computer games equipment which is self contained (not adapted for use with TV receivers).

Does not include computer games equipment adapted for use with TV receivers or software for all types of electronic games which are in Class 9.

CLASS 29

Meat, fish, poultry and game; meat extracts; preserved, dried and cooked fruits and vegetables; jellies, jams, fruit sauces; eggs, milk and milk products; edible oils and fats.

Includes prepared meals and snacks whose main ingredients are proper to this class (eg soups and potato crisps).

Does not include sandwiches which are in Class 30 or foodstuffs for animals which are in Class 31.

CLASS 30

Coffee, tea, cocoa, sugar, rice, tapioca, sago, artificial coffee; flour and preparations made from cereals, bread, pastry and confectionery, ices; honey, treacle; yeast, baking-powder; salt, mustard; vinegar, sauces (condiments); spices; ice.

Includes prepared meals and snacks whose main ingredients are proper to this class (eg pizzas, pies and pasta dishes).

Does not include foodstuffs for animals which are in Class 31.

CLASS 31

Agricultural, horticultural and forestry products and grains not included in other classes; live animals; fresh fruits and vegetables, seeds, natural plants and flowers; foodstuffs for animals; malt.

Includes all food and beverages for animals.

CLASS 32

Beers; mineral and aerated waters and other non-alcoholic drinks; fruit drinks and fruit juices; syrups and other preparations for making beverages.

Includes shandy, de-alcoholised drinks, non-alcoholic beers and wines.

Does not include tea, coffee or chocolate-based beverages which are in Class 30.

CLASS 33

Alcoholic beverages (except beers).

Includes wines, spirits and liqueurs; alcopops.

Does not include beers which are in Class 32.

CLASS 34

Tobacco; smokers' articles; matches.

Includes lighters for smokers.

Services

CLASS 35

Advertising; business management; business administration; office functions.

Includes the organisation, operation and supervision of loyalty and incentive schemes; advertising services provided via the Internet; production of television and radio advertisements; accountancy; auctioneering; trade fairs; opinion polling; data processing; provision of business information; certain specific services provided by retailers.

Does not include computer programming which is in Class 42 or raising finance for business which is in Class 36.

CLASS 36

Insurance; financial affairs; monetary affairs; real estate affairs.

Includes building society services; banking (including home banking); stockbroking; financial services provided via the Internet; issuing of tokens of value in relation to bonus and loyalty schemes; provision of financial information.

Does not include accountancy which is in Class 35, lottery services which are in Class 41 or surveying and conveyancing services which are in Class 42.

CLASS 37

Building construction; repair; installation services.

Includes installation, maintenance and repair of computer hardware; painting and decorating.

Does not include installation, maintenance and repair of computer software which is in Class 42.

CLASS 38 Telecommunications.

Includes all telecommunications services, (eg e-mail services and those provided for the Internet); providing user access to the Internet (service providers); operating of search engines.

Does not include creating, maintaining or hosting web sites which are in Class 42. CLASS 39

Transport; packaging and storage of goods; travel arrangement.

Includes distribution of electricity; travel information.

Does not include travel insurance which is in Class 36 or booking holiday accommodation which is in Class 43.

CLASS 40

Treatment of materials.

Includes the development, duplicating and printing of photographs; generation of electricity.

CLASS 41

Education; providing of training; entertainment; sporting and cultural activities.

Includes electronic games services provided by means of the Internet; the provision of on-line electronic publications and digital music (not downloadable) from the Internet.

Does not include downloadable on-line electronic publications or digital music which are in Class 9 or educational materials in printed form which are in Class 16.

CLASS 42

Scientific and technological services and research and design relating thereto; industrial analysis and research services; design and development of computer hardware and software; legal services.

Includes installation, maintenance and repair of computer software; computer consultancy services; the following Internet related services are also proper to this class: design, drawing and commissioned writing for the compilation of web sites; creating, maintaining and hosting the web sites of others; compilation, creation and maintenance of a register of domain names; leasing of access time to a computer database (the last item reflects the leasing of access time to a computer database on a dedicated line and not access provided by Internet Service Providers to databases in general which is in Class 38).

Does not include providing access to the Internet or portal services which are in Class 38.

CLASS 43

Services for providing food and drink; temporary accommodation.

Includes restaurant, bar and catering services; provision of holiday accommodation; booking/reservation services for restaurants and holiday accommodation.

Does not include provision of permanent accommodation which is in Class 36 or the arranging of travel by tourist agencies which is in Class 39.

CLASS 44

Medical services; veterinary services; hygienic and beauty care for human beings or animals; agriculture, horticulture and forestry services.

Includes dentistry services; medical analysis for the diagnosis and treatment of persons (such as x-ray examinations and taking of blood samples); pharmacy advice; garden design services.

Does not include scientific research for medical purposes (such as research into cures for terminal diseases which is in Class 42), ambulance transportation which is in Class 39, health clubs for physical exercise which are in Class 41 or retirement homes which are in Class 43.

CLASS 45

Personal and social services rendered by others to meet the needs of individuals; security services for the protection of property and individuals.

Includes dating services; funeral services and undertaking services; fire-fighting services; detective agency services.

Does not include beauty care services for human beings or animals which are in Class 44 or educational services which are in Class 41.

Chapter 19
Copyright

19.1 What is copyright? An introduction

The law of copyright protects the results and expressions of creative ability. No formality is involved; the right comes into existence as the tangible results of that creativity appear. Copyright is said to arise 'before the ink is dry upon the paper'. It is this simple arising of property rights, concurrent with the creation of the protected copyright material, that makes copyright such a valuable protection for the creative person against intentional or unintentional, unauthorised copying. The downside of such informal creation of copyright in a piece of creative work is that it is very easy to use, without realising it, elements of other people's copyright material in creating your own new work. There is no UK 'registry' of copyright material to guide you on this and, in an age of unlimited electronic access to information and imagery of all sorts (including the computer programs that permit you to access other material), the danger of infringement is ever present. The law has, therefore, to achieve a balance between the protection of creative persons and the freedom of others to create new works.

What is protected?	creative output
What benefit is there?	prevents copying
How is it obtained?	arises automatically (no registration)
How long does it last?	70 years from death of creator (in most cases)

The first statutory copyright in England was the Statute of Anne 1709, although the history of copyright goes back much further. The Statute was passed at the request of book publishers, because they were unable to protect their rights effectively against copyists under the common law. The first items protected were therefore books. Over the years, other artistic items have been added, including music and paintings. In the 20th century, new technology allowed the development of new aspects of artistic works, such as film versions of books and plays, and protection became available to the sort of works that lie behind such creations: music, sounds, visual effects etc. This led, via technological progression, to copyright protection of the computer programs that lie behind most modern inventions.

The main legislation on copyright is the Copyright, Designs and Patents Act 1988 (CDPA 1988). In the period before the CDPA 1988, there were attempts to use copyright for industrial items (eg, *British Leyland Motor Corp Ltd v Armstrong Patents Co Ltd* [1986] 1 AC 577 on spare parts for cars) – see **21.1.1**. The philosophy behind the relevant parts of the CDPA 1988 was to push industrial items in the direction of registered and unregistered design right (which the

CDPA 1988 respectively strengthened and created), and to restrict copyright to more artistic three-dimensional items. The reason was that copyright would otherwise have given a period of protection of at least 70 years for an industrial item, whereas the duration of a registered design right is 25 years. The copyright period for artistic items which are mass-produced is now restricted to 25 years, to be in parallel with the registered design right period (see **19.2.4**).

The 'classic' copyrights are original literary, dramatic, musical, and artistic (LDMA) works.

The 'entrepreneurial' copyrights are films, sound recordings, published editions, broadcasts and cablecasts.

These copyrights protect the type of creative expression that is necessary if a work is to be made available to the wider public, recognising the effort and investment usually involved in such ventures.

It is important to be able to distinguish between the different categories of copyright, for the following reasons:

(a) If you cannot find a category for the item, copyright will not subsist in it. A good example of this is the position of computer programs, which are now in s 1 of the CDPA 1988. Until the Berne Convention (see **19.10**) clarified the position by defining software as a literary work, there was some uncertainty about whether copyright subsisted in it at all, although there had been some cases suggesting it did.

(b) The rules relating to the subsistence, duration, ownership and infringement of the copyright can vary considerably for the different types of work.

(c) If there is more than one type of work in relation to an item, the different copyright works will often be owned by different people. A film or TV production might need to take account of large numbers of copyright owners, usually by licensing or purchase of the various rights.

Let us look at the classic copyrights.

19.2 Literary, dramatic, musical and artistic (LDMA) works

These are the 'classic' copyrights, that is, the authors' and artists' rights that most people associate with copyright. These rights have many things in common, so we are going to deal with them together.

The CDPA 1988 provides as follows:

> **1 Copyright and copyright works**
>
> (1) Copyright is a property right which subsists in accordance with this Part in the following descriptions of work—
>
> (a) original literary, dramatic, musical or artistic works,
>
> (b) sound recordings, films, broadcasts or cable programmes, and
>
> (c) the typographical arrangement of published editions.
>
> ...
>
> **3 Literary, dramatic and musical works**
>
> (1) In this Part—
>
> 'literary work' means any work, other than a dramatic or musical work, which is written, spoken or sung, and accordingly includes—
>
> (a) a table or compilation other than a database,
>
> (b) a computer program,
>
> (c) preparatory design material for a computer program, and (d) a database;
>
> 'dramatic work' includes a work of dance or mime; and
>
> 'musical work' means a work consisting of music, exclusive of any words or action intended to be sung, spoken or performed with the music.

4 **Artistic works**

(1) In this Part "artistic work" means—

(a) a graphic work, photograph, sculpture or collage, irrespective of artistic quality,

(b) a work of architecture being a building or a model for a building, or

(c) a work of artistic craftsmanship.

(2) In this Part—

'building' includes any fixed structure, and a part of a building or fixed structure;

'graphic work' includes—

(a) any painting, drawing, diagram, map, chart or plan, and

(b) any engraving, etching, lithograph, woodcut or similar work;

'photograph' means a recording of light or other radiation on any medium on which an image is produced or from which an image may by any means be produced, and which is not part of a film;

'sculpture' includes a cast or model made for purposes of sculpture.

The definition of 'literary work' in s 3(1) excludes dramatic or musical works. Thus, a play or script for a film will have dramatic copyright, not literary copyright. Also, words of a song will have literary copyright, but the music will have musical copyright. This means that usually the copyright in the words and music will be separately owned and have separate duration. For example, with many of the songs of Sir Elton John, John wrote the music and Bernie Taupin wrote the words. So, the musical copyright in the music will expire 70 years after the death of Sir Elton John, and the literary copyright will expire 70 years after the death of Bernie Taupin.

A 'dramatic' work could be a play, but it also could be dance or mime. So a ballet is a dramatic work, but the music is a musical work. Again, the usual situation would be that the dramatic and musical copyrights are separately owned.

19.2.1 Originality

For LDMA works, copyright will not subsist unless the work is 'original' (see s 1(1)(a)). 'Originality' here means that the work must be the author's own work, not copied from anything else. It is very difficult to come up with completely novel expressions of creativity without borrowing something from elsewhere. Copyright in an organ solo from 'A Whiter Shade of Pale' was considered in *Fisher v Brooker* [2006] EWHC 3239 (Ch). The claimant's contribution to the musical arrangement arose out of an earlier arrangement by the first defendant (which itself was based on an original theme dating back at least three centuries!). The claimant was held, nevertheless, to have created an original arrangement because of its highly distinctive quality. The finding that the claimant was a co-author of the work was upheld by the Court of Appeal (but see the reference to this case at **19.2.5** on the question of ownership of the copyright) ([2008] EWCA Civ 287). Further declarations by the judge concerning the claimant's right to assert his copyright (after 38 years) were struck down by the Court of Appeal but subsequently restored on an appeal to the House of Lords (see **19.4.5** below).

It is originality of expression and form, not of idea or content, that is required. For example, someone could not legally copy a book by John Grisham without his consent, but he has no monopoly over thrillers based on the exciting lives of lawyers, so you could write your own. The distinction between idea and expression has received much attention in recent times in the context of the 'Da Vinci Code' case, *Baigent v Random House Group Ltd* [2006] EWHC 719 (Ch) (discussed at **19.4**), and, to a lesser degree, in musical arrangements (see *Hyperion Records Ltd v Sawkins* [2005] EWCA Civ 565).

19.2.2 Minimum effort

A work may be an original work, but it may be completely trivial. Does it still enjoy copyright protection? There will be no copyright unless a certain minimum amount of effort has gone into the work. The amount of effort required is generally low. But the exact amount depends on the category of work.

To be a joint author, a significant creative contribution as an author has to be made to the production of the work. A joint author has to do more than merely contribute ideas and has to participate actively in the writing or creation of the work (see *Ray v Classic FM plc* [1998] FSR 622).

19.2.2.1 Literary works

Generally, the level of effort required is very low. Any level of writing might attract copyright. For example, there is literary copyright in a junior school pupil's essay, or in an ordinary business letter. In *University of London Press v University Tutorial Press* [1916] 2 Ch 601, 608 it was suggested by Peterson J that almost any 'work which is expressed in print or writing, irrespective of the question whether the quality or style is high', might have the necessary minimum effort. This is slightly circular but it shows that the threshold of minimum effort and quality is quite low. The subject matter is irrelevant; the work could be highly-polished literature or a mundane memorandum or timetable.

However, the writing has to be substantial enough to constitute a 'work'. Consequently, an advertising jingle or a title will not usually be protected by copyright. The courts have been reluctant to grant copyright in single words. For example, EXXON was refused copyright protection (though it would of course get trade mark protection if validly registered) (*Exxon Corpn and Others v Exxon Insurance Consultants International Ltd* [1981] 3 All ER 241).

'Compilations', ie collections of information, are one aspect of literary copyright. Generally the English courts have been willing in the past to grant copyright in almost any compilation, eg, television listings, a directory of solicitors' names and addresses, and football pool coupons. It is likely, for example, that an ordinary, alphabetical telephone directory would have been protected by copyright under English law. However, following the adoption of the Copyrights and Rights in Database Regulations 1997 (SI 1997/3032), there is now a question mark over whether courts will in the future allow copyright in such commonplace compilations where there is nothing special about the selection or arrangement of the contents (see **20.2**). Commentators seem to think it is likely that the alphabetical telephone directory would now no longer be protected by copyright. This is because it would fall within the definition of a 'database' in the Regulations (databases do not have to be electronic) for which the Regulations impose a slightly higher standard of originality for copyright to apply. It may well be, for example, that the *Yellow Pages* would still be protected by copyright, because of the extra effort involved in dividing and classifying its contents. However, the key point is that the database right will apply and protect such collections of mundane information, and copyright will probably be largely irrelevant (see **19.5**, **20.1**).

19.2.2.2 Artistic

Artistic works divide into:

(a) those that fall under s 4, which are protected 'irrespective of artistic quality', that is, graphic works, photographs, sculptures and collages (s 4(1)(a)); and

(b) those for which a degree of artistic quality is required, that is, architecture and works of artistic craftsmanship (s 4(1)(b) and (c)).

For the first category, the standard of effort required is low. For example, copyright has been found to subsist in a very simple picture of a hand pointing, as used at a polling station to guide people round the corner. A straight line or circle would not normally be protected. In any event, it would not be substantial enough to constitute a 'work', and would be unlikely to be original. The English law approach is quite different to that applied to artistic works in some other legal systems; see *Blau v BBC* [2002] ECDR 34, where the Swiss law provided a result somewhat different to what might have followed in an English court.

Some artistic merit is required for architecture, as the words 'irrespective of artistic quality' do not appear in s 4(1)(b). Cornish and Llewelyn, in *Intellectual Property* (5th edn, Sweet & Maxwell, 2003), suggest that the artistic merit must be 'something more than the common stock'. Perhaps a mass-produced estate of similar mundane houses might not qualify, but a small development of individual 'executive' homes might. Architectural works are limited to buildings themselves, and models for buildings. Architectural drawings would be protected as graphic works, so a different standard would apply to determine copyright in the drawing to that in the building itself.

19.2.2.3 Works of artistic craftsmanship

This is a topic much beloved by academic writers but of negligible practical relevance. A work of artistic craftsmanship is a three-dimensional item which is not a sculpture, but which results from a combination of artistic and craft skills. Examples could be seen in hand-made musical instruments, furniture or wooden boats etc, provided there is evidence of both artistry and craftsmanship. For works of artistic craftsmanship, it seems that a significant degree of artistic merit is required before copyright protection will be given. The policy reason behind this is that most three-dimensional items that are not sculptures tend to be made to industrial designs, and should normally be protected by the law on designs rather than by copyright.

Unfortunately, the cases on works of artistic craftsmanship do not tell us how much artistic merit is needed for something to qualify as a work of artistic craftsmanship. In *Hensher (George) Ltd v Restawile Upholstery (Lancs)* [1976] AC 64, it was held that a mass-produced suite of furniture did not have enough artistic merit. In *Merlet and Another v Mothercare plc* [1986] RPC 115, it was held that a rain cape made by Mrs Merlet to protect her baby from the weather in Scotland did not have enough artistic merit. Most industrially manufactured articles will also lack any craft skills.

A key factor in deciding whether an item is a work of artistic craftmanship is to ask: did the author consciously intend to create a work of art? In *Guild v Eskandar Ltd* [2001] FSR 38, the claimant alleged breach of copyright in garments which she had designed for mass-production. These were held not to be works of artistic craftsmanship, because of lack of evidence of craft skills used in the manufacture, but were protected by unregistered design right as they were original and not commonplace (see **21.3.1**).

In practice, one should never rely on there being copyright in three-dimensional objects other than sculptures, but instead advise the client to register a design.

19.2.3 Recorded

For literary, dramatic and musical works, copyright will subsist only if the work is recorded (s 3(2)). This can be in writing or otherwise. Recording can be in any medium, so recording on tape, or typing into a word processor is fine.

There is no express requirement as such in the CDPA 1988 that an artistic work must be recorded, but of course it is difficult to conceive of an artistic work that is not recorded. How else could you create a drawing or a sculpture, for example, and not record it?

19.2.4 Duration of copyright

19.2.4.1 Literary, dramatic and musical works (CDPA 1988, s 12)

The normal duration is life of the author plus 70 years. The 70 years runs from the end of the year of the author's death. If copyright vests in the employer because the author was an employee, the duration of the employer's copyright is the employee's life plus 70 years. The same situation applies if the rights have been assigned. For example, in the copyright in the songs of Buddy Holly (now owned by Sir Paul McCartney), the period is 70 years from the death of Buddy Holly (ie, it expires in 1959 + 70 = 2029).

The basic term for copyright used to be life plus 50 years. The Directive on Copyright Duration (93/98/EC) increased it to 70 years. This not only extended the life of existing copyright works, but also even revived lapsed copyright if the work was still in copyright anywhere within the EU on 1 July 1995. This would have been so at that date in Germany, where the copyright term then was life plus 70 years.

If the work is of unknown authorship, the period of 70 years runs from the year of creation, or the year of first publication, whichever is the later.

For a computer-generated work, the period is 50 years from creation.

19.2.4.2 Exploited copyright works (CDPA 1988, s 52)

If a copyright work is exploited by making articles industrially then the term of copyright it enjoys is for most purposes cut down to 25 years. The 25 years are measured from the end of the calendar year in which the articles are first marketed. Examples would be a design that is put on wallpaper, or a work of artistic craftsmanship that is exploited by making it industrially (eg, a chair by Charles Rennie Mackintosh). 'Industrial' exploitation means making more than 50 articles, or making things in lengths by an industrial process (eg, wallpaper).

The term is not cut down for all purposes, but only in relation to reproducing articles. So after the 25 years are up, it will not be copyright infringement to use the wallpaper design on wallpaper or on a bread bin, but it would still be copyright infringement to make a copy of, for example, a painting that had first shown the wallpaper design.

There are exceptions to this rule limiting copyright to 25 years, and these are defined by statutory instrument. Exceptions include most sculpture, wall plaques and medals, and printed matter which is primarily of a literary or artistic character (a long list is given in the Copyright (Industrial Process and Excluded Articles) (No 2) Order 1989, SI 1989/1070). So, for example, putting a painting on a postcard will not result in the 25-year term applying. This is an important protection against premature loss of copyright protection by art galleries, artists and owners of valuable artistic copyright.

The policy reason for cutting down the term for industrially exploited copyright is that governments do not consider it appropriate that industrial designs should have long copyright protection. The period of 25 years is the same as the term of protection given to registered designs (see **21.2.7**). See also **21.3.7** for discussion of the overlap between copyright protection and design rights.

19.2.5 Ownership of copyright in LDMA works

As copyright arises 'before the ink is dry on the page', the initial copyright is owned by the author or co-authors (CDPA 1988, s 11(1)). The main exception is if the author is an employee, in which case the copyright is owned by the employer (s 11(2)). The provisos are that the work was done in the course of the employee's employment, and that there was no contrary agreement. In *Noah v Shuba and Another* [1991] FSR 14, it was held that an employed government epidemiologist had not written a document entitled 'A Guide to Hygienic Skin Piercing' in the course of his employment. He therefore owned the copyright, not his employer.

Be aware that if the work has been commissioned then the copyright rests with the author (s 11(1)), not with the person commissioning the work. A properly drafted agreement would include a clause providing for an assignment, or licence, of the copyright to the commissioner. In the absence of such a clause, a licence would usually be implied (*Blair v Alan S Tomkins and*

Frank Osborne (t/a Osborne & Tomkins (A Firm)) and Another [1971] 1 All ER 468), as otherwise the commissioner would be prevented from using the work he had paid for. Thus, the copyright in a photograph of Elvis Costello, taken at a photo shoot where the photographer had not been commissioned, was owned by the photographer (*Gabrin v Universal Music Operations Ltd* [2003] EWHC 1335 (Ch)). Some years before, a similar dispute was settled during litigation about the artwork and photographs for the famous 'Sergeant Pepper' album cover. Where a photograph or a film has been commissioned for private and domestic purposes (eg, a wedding), the person commissioning the material will have the right to prevent publication of the material (s 85).

In *R Griggs Group Ltd v Evans* [2005] EWCA Civ 11, the defendant designer was a freelance engaged by an advertising agency. The agency had been commissioned by the claimants to produce drawings for a new combined logo for their 'Dr Martens' range of footwear. The designer fulfilled the commission, but subsequently also sold the designs to an Australian rival of the claimants. It was held that the claimants were entitled in equity to the beneficial title, as a mere licence would not give them enough rights to stop the work being used by a rival. On the basis of this, it looks as if the courts are prepared to rectify the situation, save where a bona fide third party acquires title in the interim.

19.2.6 Moral rights

These are a Continental concept brought into English law by the CDPA 1988. It is the idea that the creative author or artist should retain certain rights in relation to his creation, even after he has sold the copyright to somebody else. In fact, moral rights have slightly wider implications.

The moral rights are as follows:

(a) The right to be identified ('right of paternity') (s 77). This applies only if the right has been asserted by the author. This is usually done in the copyright assignment or licence.

(b) The right to object to derogatory treatment (s 80). For example, a novelist might object if his novel were abridged in a way that compromised its artistic integrity. In *Morrison Leahy Music Ltd v Lightbond Ltd* [1993] EMLR 144, the claimants obtained an injunction to restrain the release of a recording consisting of the claimants' music interspersed with other music, as they felt this altered the character of their music. In the unusual German case of *Re Lenin's Monument* [1992] ECC 202, the son of the sculptor of a statue of Lenin failed in his attempt to assert the moral right akin to s 80. The City of Berlin was held not to be planning to destroy the statue, which could have been derogatory treatment, but merely 'to preserve it by burying it', following the demise of the former communist State of East Germany. An interesting claim to derogatory treatment of a sound recording by adding a rap line failed in *Confetti Records and Others v Warner Music UK Ltd* [2003] EWHC 1274 (Ch) because there was nothing prejudicial to the honour and reputation of the author of the original work.

(c) The right against false attribution of a work (s 84). A novel use of this right was in *Clark v Associated Newspapers* [1998] RPC 261. This concerned the *London Evening Standard*, which was then running a spoof political column called 'Alan Clark's Secret Election Diary'. Mr Clark succeeded on the basis that some people might believe that the views expressed in the column were his.

(d) The right to privacy in private photographs and films (s 85).

If the author still owns the copyright then he should not normally need to rely on these moral rights as he can control all copying of the work; for example, he can insist on being credited as a condition of allowing the work to be used. The importance of moral rights is in a situation where the author has assigned the copyright to somebody else.

Moral rights are inalienable rights, in that they cannot be assigned (s 94). However, they can be waived. Anyone acting for the assignee of copyright should always consider whether it is appropriate to insist on a waiver. You probably would not expect somebody who has produced a real work of art to waive their moral rights. However, in many commercial situations it will be appropriate (eg, for advertising copy, or designs for use on fabrics or products).

Moral rights apply only to literary, dramatic, musical and artistic works, and also to films (where the director enjoys moral rights). The most important exceptions to be aware of are computer programs and employees. In most situations employees do not enjoy moral rights.

In terms of duration, most of the moral rights will last as long as the copyright itself (s 86(1)). The exception is the paternity right, which lasts for only 20 years after the death of the author (s 86(2)).

19.3 Entrepreneurial copyrights

The descriptions 'classic' and 'entrepreneurial' copyright are not terms of art. However, the distinction is often made between:

(a) the classic LDMA copyrights, that is, the traditional authors' rights which protect creativity (see **19.2**); and

(b) the entrepreneurial copyrights which, broadly, protect people who invest in creativity, that is, production companies, broadcasters, publishers, etc.

The entrepreneurial copyrights serve the same purpose as the classic rights. That is, they give a right to stop copying of the relevant 'work'.

19.3.1 Differences between classic and entrepreneurial copyrights

The rules are slightly different for the entrepreneurial copyrights, in particular:

(a) There is no general requirement of originality and minimum effort (see **19.2.1** and **19.2.2**). Instead there are various detailed rules for each right, which have the broad aim of ensuring that there is no copyright in a mere copy. For example, if I copy somebody else's tape, with or without their permission, I have no copyright in the copy I make. These rules are beyond the scope of this book, but their broad effect can be seen in ss 5A(2), 5B(4), 6(6) and 8(2). (Note that in the case of *Norowzian v Arks Ltd and Others (No 2)* [2000] FSR 363, the claimant failed in his assertion that copyright existed in an editing process for films. The case concerned an advert for Guinness produced by the defendant by a technique devised by the claimant, termed 'jump cutting'.)

(b) Of the entrepreneurial copyrights, only films have moral rights. These vest in the director. The thinking behind this is, of course, that it is the director who has given the artistic input. He is the person who might want to defend his artistic integrity. (The director is the one who sits in the canvas chair behind the camera operator and tells the actors what to do.)

(c) The rules about ownership of the entrepreneurial rights vary (see **19.3.3**).

(d) The duration of the entrepreneurial rights varies (see **19.3.4**).

The rules are designed to give effect to the commercial, artistic and financial realities of creativity in the modern world.

19.3.2 Definitions of some entrepreneurial rights

The following definitions are taken from the CDPA 1988:

> **5A Sound recordings**
>
> (1) In this Part 'sound recording' means—
>
> (a) a recording of sounds, from which the sounds may be reproduced, or
>
> (b) a recording of the whole or any part of a literary, dramatic or musical work, from which sounds reproducing the work or part may be produced,

regardless of the medium on which the recording is made or the method by which the sounds are reproduced or produced.

(2) Copyright does not subsist in a sound recording which is, or to the extent that it is, a copy taken from a previous sound recording.

5B Films

(1) In this Part 'film' means a recording on any medium from which a moving image may by any means be produced.

(2) The sound track accompanying a film shall be treated as part of the film for the purposes of this Part.

. . .

(4) Copyright does not exist in a film which is, or to the extent that it is, a copy taken from a previous film.

. . .

6 Broadcasts

(1) In this Part a 'broadcast' means an electronic transmission of visual images, sounds or other information which—

(a) is transmitted for simultaneous reception by members of the public and is capable of being lawfully received by them, or

(b) is transmitted at a time determined solely by the person making the transmission for presentation to members of the public,

and which is not excepted by subsection (1A); and references to broadcasting shall be construed accordingly.

(1A) Excepted from the definition of 'broadcast' is any internet transmission unless it is—

(a) a transmission taking place simultaneously on the internet and by other means,

(b) a concurrent transmission of a live event, or

(c) a transmission of recorded moving images or sounds forming part of a programme service offered by the person responsible for making the transmission, being a service in which programmes are transmitted at scheduled times determined by that person.

(2) An encrypted transmission shall be regarded as capable of being lawfully received by members of the public only if decoding equipment has been made available to members of the public by or with the authority of the person making the transmission or the person providing the contents of the transmission.

(3) References in this Part to the person making a broadcast or a transmission which is a broadcast are—

(a) to the person transmitting the programme, if he has responsibility to any extent for its contents, and

(b) to any person providing the programme who makes with the person transmitting it the arrangements necessary for its transmission;

and references in this Part to a programme, in the context of broadcasting, are to any item included in a broadcast.

(4) For the purposes of this Part, the place from which a wireless broadcast is made is the place where, under the control and responsibility of the person making the broadcast, the programme-carrying signals are introduced into an uninterrupted chain of communication (including, in the case of a satellite transmission, the chain leading to the satellite and down towards the earth).

(4A) Subsections (3) and (4) have effect subject to section 6A (safeguards in case of certain satellite broadcasts).

(5) References in this Part to the reception of a broadcast include reception of a broadcast relayed by means of a telecommunications system.

(5A) The relaying of a broadcast by reception and immediate re-transmission shall be regarded for the purposes of this Part as a separate act of broadcasting from the making of the broadcast which is so re-transmitted.

(6) Copyright does not subsist in a broadcast which infringes, or to the extent that it infringes, the copyright in another broadcast.

8 Published editions

(1) In this Part 'published edition', in the context of copyright in the typographical arrangement of a published edition, means a published edition of the whole or any part of one or more literary, dramatic or musical works.

(2) Copyright does not subsist in the typographical arrangement of a published edition if, or to the extent that, it reproduces the typographical arrangement of a previous edition.

You should be aware of the following points from the above definitions of the entrepreneurial copyrights:

(a) An attempt has been made to make the definitions of 'film', 'sound recording', etc technology neutral so that they will cover future technological developments. So, for example, 'film' includes any recordings on any medium from which a moving image can be produced. It will include, for example, videos, DVDs and many 'multi-media' recordings (like computer games and websites) where you have moving images. These can be 'films' even though they may be interactive.

(b) A 'broadcast' has been redefined to make the definition generic, so as to include not only terrestrial broadcasts (BBC and ITV, etc), but also satellite (Sky) and cable broadcasts (NTL) and some Internet transmissions.

(c) The soundtrack of a film is protected by film copyright unless it is issued as a stand-alone entity, when it would be protected as a sound recording.

19.3.3 Ownership of the entrepreneurial copyrights (s 9)

The first ownership goes to the 'creator' of the copyright work (see the table, 'Ownership of entrepreneurial rights', below). So, for example, the owner of the copyright in a broadcast would be:

(a) the person providing the programme; and

(b) the person transmitting who has responsibility for its content.

This could mean that the independent television company and the broadcasting authority could jointly own the copyright.

Entrepreneurial Right	Ownership
Sound recording	Producer
Film	Producer and principal director
Broadcast	Person making the broadcast
Typographical arrangement	Publisher

Establishing the identity of the 'creator' of the work can become a problem, especially for commissioned works (see also **19.2.5**). Thus, the management company of the skaters Torville and Dean commissioned a recording of music for one of their skating routines. The company was held to be the 'maker' of the sound recording, as it had thought of the idea and taken the financial risk, not the person with whom it had contracted to organise the musicians and the studio (see *A & M Records v Video Collection* [1995] EMLR 25).

19.3.4 Duration of the entrepreneurial copyrights (ss 13A, 13B, 14)

The duration of the entrepreneurial copyrights is a bit more complex than the standard period of life of the creator plus 70 years that applies to the classic copyrights. The duration depends on the type of entrepreneurial right concerned. Thus:

(a) Sound recording – 50 years from making or being released, if later.

(b) Film – 70 years from end of life of last to die of principal director, author of screenplay, author of dialogue, or composer of specially written music.

(c) Broadcast – 50 years from first broadcast.

(d) Typographical arrangement – 25 years from end of year of publication.

19.4 Infringement of copyright

The starting point is s 16, which gives the copyright owner the exclusive right to copy, publish, perform or show in public and/or to adapt the work. If anyone else does any of those things within the UK without permission, it will be likely to infringe.

There are two types of infringement: primary infringement and secondary infringement. The primary infringer is liable regardless of his state of mind, whereas the secondary infringer is liable only if he knew, or had reason to believe, that he was dealing with an infringing copy. It is certainly not the case that the part that is copied would, standing by itself, have necessarily qualified for copyright protection, so a person might be quite unaware of any infringement. The reason for this is explained below.

Copying need not be of the whole work. The copyright is infringed if a 'substantial part' is taken. The question of what is a substantial part is considered qualitatively. So, even if you take only one line of a poem, the copyright will be infringed if it is a significant line. Similarly, a parody of a work will infringe the copyright if it amounts to a substantial copy of it. The dangers for the infringer are thus twofold: first, he may not realise that he is using a copyright work; secondly, he may not realise that he is using a legally 'substantial' part of the work.

Section 17 shows that copying of literary, dramatic, musical or artistic works means reproducing the work in any material form. That would include storing the work in any medium by electronic means. Artistic copyright can be infringed, for example, by turning a two-dimensional image into a three-dimensional solid object, and vice versa (s 17(3)).

Copyright in a literary or dramatic work will be infringed by translating it into another language, by making it into a play (or vice versa), or by making it into a cartoon. Copyright in a musical work will be infringed by making a different arrangement. These are 'adaptations' of works within s 21.

Some guidance on the judicial approach may be seen in the following cases:

(a) *Designer's Guild Ltd v Russell Williams (Textiles) Ltd* [2001] FSR 803

Here, the dispute was about alleged infringement of fabric designs, combining stripes and flowers. The House of Lords, allowing the claimants' appeal, said that the first instance finding, after comparing similarities and differences, that copying had taken place should not have been rejected by the Court of Appeal. That is the first stage of the process. Only after that should the inquiry turn to the question whether what was copied represented a qualitatively substantial part of the claimants' created output. The Court of Appeal's approach had been wrong.

(b) *Baigent v Random House Group Ltd* [2006] EWHC 719 (Ch)

In this case the writers of *The Holy Blood and the Holy Grail* ('HBHG') sued Dan Brown for breach of copyright in *The Da Vinci Code* ('DVC'). The claim was that DVC had used the central theme from HBHG and so breached copyright. The defence was that, although HBHG had been used along with many other sources, only information and general ideas had been used, not detailed copyright expression. The court held that there could be such a concept as a non-literal copying (a concept well known in software copyright claims), but where the purported copyright material largely comprised factual statements and hypotheses, this could only be protected by copyright if there was a discernible 'architecture' in the way it had been used and arranged. In this case, the supposed central theme of HBHG was at too general a level of abstraction to be protected; the claim failed. The Court of Appeal ([2007] EWCA Civ 247) confirmed the broad conclusions of Smith J, but found some faults with his approach. The judgments are very helpful in explaining the judicial approach to qualitatively substantial copying.

(c) *Newspaper Licensing Agency Ltd v Marks & Spencer plc* [2003] 1 AC 551

The House of Lords had to decide whether selective copying of cuttings from parts of newspaper editions breached, substantially, the copyright in the typographical arrangements of the editions. Although the CDPA 1988, s 8 definition extended to 'any part' of a work, what comprised a substantial part had to be decided qualitatively, not simply by reference to quantity and proportion to the whole. As none of the copied cutting sections reproduced anything like the layout of entire pages, it was not a substantial copying and the claim failed.

(d) *Nova Productions Ltd v Mazooma Games Ltd* [2007] EWCA Civ 219

In another case which turns on the distinction between idea and expression, the Court of Appeal dismissed claims that the defendant's computer game about pool infringed the claimant's copyright in its game. There were three substantial issues, all of which are helpful to an understanding of infringement. The first point was the claimant's assertion that a sequence of graphic images showed some similarity in both games. The Court said that the starting point was that each frame comprised a separate graphic; the fact of a sequence of them added nothing to that (ie, the sequence is not a graphic work in itself). There was no substantial copying of the individual graphics. The second issue was that although there was some evidence of the copying and taking of ideas, that did not mean that a substantial part of the defendant's creative form and expression had been copied (similarly with the '*Da Vinci Code*' case, above). The third issue related to the alleged copying of the computer program. The mere creation of a computer code that gave a similar effect to another one, without copying the computer code of that other, was more to do with protecting ideas than expression. The claimant's ideas had inspired the defendant, but at too general a level to constitute substantial copying.

From these cases, it can be seen that it may be possible to imitate a certain style or way of expressing things, without necessarily infringing the original. Much of today's surreal imagery can be seen to be influenced by the works of Salvador Dali, without close copying. Dali's works, in their time, were heavily influenced by the much earlier work of Hieronymus Bosch. The distinction between copying and reflecting an influence is a hard one to draw.

Copyright is not normally infringed simply by using the work. For example, you do not infringe the copyright in a book by reading it. You do not infringe a recording by playing it. This is because using it does not normally involve making copies of it. However, if you read or play it in public you do infringe. The CDPA 1988 specifically provides that performing or showing a work in public will infringe the copyright, and this is primary infringement (s 19). Similarly, including a work in a broadcast or cablecast will normally be primary infringement (s 20). So the permission (ie, the licence) of the copyright owner is necessary in these circumstances.

19.4.1 Special position of computer programs (software) (s 17(6))

Although the normal position is that you do not infringe by using a work, such as by reading it, a computer program is different in this respect. When a program is run in a computer, the computer has to make at least a transient copy of it in order to run it. This transient copying will infringe the copyright without the copyright owner's permission (s 17(6)). It is not possible, therefore, to use a program without a licence. Often this licence is express. For example, you get a licence with any program you buy off the shelf. Sometimes, this licence may be implied by the circumstances. If someone is a lawful licensee then he is also entitled to make one back-up copy of the software (s 50A). There is a special provision to permit transient copying as part of a larger technological process: see **19.9** below.

19.4.2 Primary infringement (ss 16–21)

The most usual act of primary infringement is copying. Copyright is not a monopoly right. As its name implies, it is the right not to be copied. Independently produced items cannot be objected to. It follows that you cannot infringe copyright if you have never had any access to the original. So in a copyright infringement action, if the defendant had no opportunity to copy, he will not be liable. On the other hand, if the defendant did have the opportunity to copy and the defendant's work is so similar to the claimant's that the most likely explanation is that he has copied, then there will be an inference of copying. The defendant will have to prove that he did not copy.

Having said that, copying can be indirect. Copying can occur as a result of seeing not the original work itself but a copy of it, or something derived from it. For example, if a novel has been adapted to make a play, you infringe the copyright in the novel by copying the play. (In that case the separate copyright in the play is also infringed.)

The late George Harrison was sued in the US, as it was alleged that his song 'My Sweet Lord' was a subconscious copy of an earlier work. The song which was the subject of the alleged copying was 'He's So Fine', composed by Ronald Mack and sung by The Chiffons. It was a minor hit in the UK in 1963 and a major one in the US. The Harrison song was held to have infringed the earlier song. Ultimately, George Harrison is reputed to have bought the copyright to the earlier song, so solving the problem.

In *Sony Music Entertainment (UK) Ltd and Others v Easyinternetcafé Ltd* [2003] EWHC 62 (Ch), [2003] FSR 48, the claimants obtained an injunction against the operators of some Internet cafés. They recorded music from the Internet on to CDs for their customers for a fee. This was held to be breach of ss 17 and 18. In *Independiente Ltd and Others v Music Trading On-line (HK) Ltd and Others* [2003] EWHC 470 (Ch), the claimants were seeking to stop the defendants from supplying sound recordings via the Internet to the UK, when those recordings had been licensed for use only outside the EU. (They failed because they did not have the consent of the copyright holders; although the matter was ultimately settled, there has been further litigation about the terms upon which the matter was settled.)

19.4.3 Secondary infringement (ss 22–26)

This is all about dealing with or facilitating the manufacture of 'infringing copies'. These are copies made without the copyright owner's permission. So, the trader who imports copies into the UK may be liable for secondary infringement, as will the trader who sells, distributes or stores such copies. It will extend to persons who provide the means to make the copy, or who provide premises or equipment for infringing public performances. Section 27 defines the wide range of meaning given to 'infringing copy'.

In the typical infringement situation, there will be more than one infringer. However, the main culprit will be the person who manufactures the goods. He will be the primary infringer, because he is actually copying the work in order to make the goods.

Then there will be the dealers who buy or import the goods. Maybe this is a wholesaler who buys from the manufacturer and the retailers who buy from the wholesaler. The wholesaler and retailers will be secondary infringers, but only if they knew or had reason to believe that they were dealing with infringing copies. Usually, the copyright owner is mainly concerned with stopping the manufacture. He will normally write to the retailers and the wholesalers (if known) enclosing evidence of his copyright title and asking them to stop selling the goods. If they then carry on, they will be liable for secondary infringement, because from this point on at least they will not be able to argue that they were innocent.

In *Bloomsbury Publishing Group Ltd and Another v News Group Newspapers Ltd and Others* [2003] EWHC 1205 (Ch), [2003] 3 All ER 736, the publisher and author of the 'Harry Potter' books obtained an injunction to restrain unauthorised publication of the fifth book in the series. A copy had been stolen from the printers and was being offered to some national newspapers, in advance of its official release date. The CDPA 1988, s 23 concerns 'possessing or dealing with an infringing copy'. In *Nouveau Fabrics Ltd v Voyage Decoration Ltd* [2004] EWHC 895 (Ch), the claimant's lawyers had written a letter before action informing the defendant of the claimant's copyright. The defendant was thus held to have had reason to believe that the fabrics it was importing were copies which infringed the claimant's copyright.

19.4.4 Defences – 'fair dealing'

In certain circumstances some use of a copyright work is allowed without the permission of the copyright owner. The approach usually followed by the courts is, first, to ascertain whether the defendant's act falls within the particular statutory purpose, and then, even if it is within that purpose, to see that the copying has not gone any further than necessary to comprise 'fair dealing' (*Hyde Park Residence Ltd v Yelland and Others* [2000] RPC 604). The important ones to be aware of are as follows.

19.4.4.1 Fair dealing for the purposes of research or private study (s 29)

This applies to LDMA works and to published editions. It basically allows the taking of copies of pages of books in the course of non-commercial studying or researching. It does not allow the librarian to take lots of copies, one for each student. In practice it must be read together with the provisions about librarians and archives and about schools, which are very complicated.

In *HM Stationery Office v Green Amps Ltd* [2007] EWHC 2755 (Ch), a private company, which had obtained unlicensed access to a mapping database which HMSO made available for licensed research, made use of the data for commercial purposes. The unlicensed infringement was not protected by s 29.

Implementation of Directive 2001/29/EC on copyright and related rights in the information society has inserted the words 'non-commercial' into this defence in relation to research, thus restricting it severely.

19.4.4.2 Fair dealing for the purpose of criticism and review (s 30(1))

If one wished to comment in an article on, say, the quality of a textbook on intellectual property, this fair dealing provision will permit copied extracts from the book to be used without the author's permission. The question whether this use is within the exception depends mainly on:

(a) the purpose of the use of the quote – if I copy what the textbook says in order to tell people about the law rather than in order to comment on the textbook then I am just letting the textbook do my work for me and this would not be within the exception; and

(b) how much I quote.

The Publishers' Association publishes guidelines on how much you can quote.

19.4.4.3 Fair dealing for the purpose of reporting current events (s 30(2))

This allows all works, other than photographs, to be used for reporting current events. If the report is in a newspaper or magazine there must be acknowledgement. If the report is on television, radio, etc then no acknowledgement is required (though in practice an acknowledgement is often given). Again, the question whether the dealing is fair depends on:

(a) the purpose; and

(b) how much is taken.

The purpose must truly be for reporting current events and not simply using something that has become of interest because of a particular current event. For example, the death of the Duchess of Windsor did not justify the publication of an exchange of letters between her and the Duke of Windsor without the permission of the copyright holder (*Associated Newspapers Group plc v News Group Newspapers Ltd* [1986] RPC 515). It also did not come under fair dealing for criticism and review (see **19.4.4.2**).

19.4.4.4 Artistic works on public display (s 62)

Section 62 provides an important general provision that making graphic or photographic images, broadcasts or films of buildings, sculptures, models for buildings and works of artistic craftsmanship is not an infringement of any copyright in those things. This applies to things which can be seen, permanently sited, in public places or premises open to the public. This provision also protects any further publication or copying of images or representations of those things.

19.4.5 Other defences and licensing

In proceedings for infringement of an IP right, the defendant will often argue that the right in question is not valid and/or the claimant does not have the right to sue for infringement. Another defence is that the copying has been done with the consent of the copyright holder (ie, there is a licence). Such a licence could be express or implied from the circumstances of the case. A licence might be implied, if it were necessary to give business efficacy to or to reflect the true intentions of parties to an agreement, but only to the minimum extent necessary.

19.5 Remedies

By s 96(2) of the CDPA 1988, 'in an action for infringement of copyright all such relief by way of damages, injunctions, accounts or otherwise is available to the plaintiff as is available in respect of any other property right'. This range of remedies is open to the copyright owner and, to the extent that licensed material is infringed, it is also open to an exclusive licensee against third parties, concurrently with the copyright owner. A non-exclusive licensee of copyright may have that range of remedies if the licence is in writing and expressly grants the non-exclusive licensee a right of action (ss 101, 101A). Where the rights of action are held concurrently between the owner and the exclusive licensee, usually whichever one initiates the action will need to join the other as second claimant or as defendant, according to the circumstances (s 102).

Damages are available, usually based upon the tortious, compensatory measure, often (but not always) based upon what the infringer would have had to pay for a notional licence to achieve what he has attempted to do without permission. Damages are not available against an innocent infringer, or someone has no knowledge of or reason to believe in the existence of copyright in the material (s 97(1)), although that does not prejudice the availability of other remedies. Under s 97(2), there is a provision for 'additional damages' to be awarded according to the circumstances, particularly the flagrancy of the infringement and the likely benefit accruing to the defendant. This usually depends upon some seriously questionable behaviour by the defendant, over and beyond the simple question of copying (see *Cantor Fitzgerald International v Tradition (UK) Ltd* [2000] RPC 95).

Injunctions, particularly interim ones, are fairly widely used in copyright disputes, the courts deciding the matter upon the weight of the issues and consequences for each party. The test for the court, in interim matters, is usually one of whether there is a serious triable issue. If damages could fairly easily restore the position, without more, an injunction application is unlikely to succeed.

Account of profit is a broad alternative to damages in an appropriate case against any infringer, knowing or innocent. The usual problem applies, in that if the court orders an account to be taken and it turns out that little or no profit has accrued, it will not be possible to fall back upon a substantial damages claim; only nominal damages would be available. The claimant will need to think long and hard about his election.

Orders are available for delivery up of infringing copies or articles held in the reasonable knowledge or belief that they are used, or have been used, for infringement purposes, both in civil and in criminal proceedings (ss 99, 108). This is supported by forfeiture of such similar copies and articles as are found during criminal investigations or proceedings under s114A. There can also be orders to forfeit such articles to the copyright owner, for destruction or whatever the court may think fit as to disposal (s 114).

The CDPA 1988, s 100 allows a copyright owner to seize offending articles. However, the right is in fact very weak. It can be used only against market or street traders as the right excludes business premises. The police also have to be informed beforehand. Section 107 provides for criminal liability for making or dealing with infringing articles. Sections 108 and 114 allow for the delivery up or destruction of infringing copies. Section 111 allows for an order to prevent the importation of infringing copies.

19.6 Databases

The Copyright and Rights in Database Regulations 1997 implemented the Directive on the Legal Protection of Databases (Directive 96/9/EC) ('Database Directive') and introduced a new 'database right' which is not the same as copyright but which gives some safeguards which are similar to copyright (see **Chapter 20**).

The new right was introduced to protect the interests of database owners (eg, news agencies), though it applies both to electronic and paper databases. Under English law, many such databases would generally have qualified for copyright as compilations in the past, but in many European countries they might not have been protected by copyright (because they would not be regarded as sufficiently original – see **19.2.2.1**). Even where there was copyright protection, if somebody extracted just one or two pieces of information then this might not amount to substantial copying, so might not be an infringement. See how the database right deals with this at **20.6**.

The individual items from which the database was composed could each also get copyright as a literary work, if substantial enough to constitute a 'work'.

19.7 Copyright and information technology

An enormous practical problem in respect of information technology (IT) and the law is that technological advances constantly outstrip the law. For example, it was suggested at the time that the CDPA 1988 was going through Parliament that parts of it were already out of date.

Arguably, copyright is the most important of the 'general' IP rights in relation to IT matters. It is of more direct significance than either trade marks or patents (see also **Chapter 24**).

19.7.1 Computer programs

Perhaps the most important aspect of the application of copyright to IT is that computer programs are protected by literary copyright (see **19.4.1**). Unauthorised copying (including simple down-loading) of a program therefore amounts to breach of copyright (that is, basically, normal rules and remedies apply). So, the resulting anomaly is that something functional is protected by a literary right. It is also more likely that non-literal copying can be shown to infringe software copyright than other forms of literary copyright. This problem has been much considered under US copyright law.

The CDPA 1988, s 3(1), and the Copyright (Computer Programs) Regulations 1992 (SI 1992/3233) provide that software is protected as a literary work. (Note that there are also proposals to give patent protection to at least some computer programs; see **22.3.4**.)

19.7.2 The Internet

There seems to be a strongly held view in some quarters that the law cannot apply to or control the Internet at all. Nevertheless, the law undoubtedly does apply to the Internet. The fact is that copyright infringement is no less of an infringement simply because it involves the Internet. The only real issues concern the most effective method of dealing with jurisdictional and evidential problems that arise in pursuing large numbers of people in different countries.

Most Internet use, where the material is available to the public in the UK, will fall within s 20 of the CDPA 1988 as a 'communication to the public'; any unauthorised use of copyright material can, therefore, infringe. The section is expressed to apply to making works available by 'electronic transmission'. This sweeps up the former s 7 of the CDPA 1988, which dealt with 'cablecasts'. It does not matter where the host website is located.

There have already been cases which have decided that unauthorised use of material from the Internet can amount to breach of copyright (see, eg, *Shetland Times Ltd v Wills and Another* [1997] FSR 604, discussed at **24.6.2**). There is also the opposite situation where copyright material is used on the Internet without permission. For example, in January 1999, a considerable number of musicians and pop singers took out advertisements in newspapers to protest against the unauthorised Internet use of their material, and to demand tighter legal controls. You may be familiar with the litigation in the USA on the 'Napster' site, which various record companies sued for breach of copyright in their recordings. Napster has returned as a licensed site, where you have to pay money to download the recordings. However, other sites have sprung up, such as Gnutella, Blubster, Newtella, MusicCity and KaZaA. These do not use a centralised server so it is harder to take action against them. They use P2P, software which enables one computer to communicate with another computer without going through a centralised server (P2P stands for 'peer to peer').

See the case of *Sony Music Entertainment (UK) Ltd and Others v Easyinternetcafé Ltd* at **19.4.2** for an instance of copyright infringement on the Internet. In the *Daily Telegraph*, 24 April 2003, it was reported that EMI is making 140,000 of its tracks available to customers via the Internet. It will charge customers, but less than they would have to pay to buy a CD version.

More recently, the Recording Industry Association of America (RIAA) has instituted proceedings against many people in the United States for allegedly using P2P copying, and this policy is now being actively pursued in the United Kingdom.

Despite these steps in defence of their rights, it does seem as if the emphasis is beginning to shift away from attempts to enforce IP rights against mass users of the Internet, towards a recognition by producers of mass media/entertainment that they will have to live with widespread publication of their products. The way forward is more likely to be by way of agreements between the entertainment providers and ISPs/advertisers.

19.8 Public performances – the collecting societies

It would be very difficult for the creators of music and songs, in particular, to enforce their rights acting individually, not least as their copyright could be infringed by a public performance anywhere in the country. To overcome this problem, the collecting societies have existed for many years. They operate either as licensees of the relevant copyrights, or as agents acting on behalf of the copyright holders. They employ staff to travel round the country to find places where public performances are taking place without a licence from one of the collecting societies. The typical problem locations are pubs and restaurants.

The Performing Rights Society (PRS) and the Mechanical Copyright Protection Society (MCPS) act for writers of music and lyrics and their publishers. The MCPS acts on behalf of its composer and publisher members. It negotiates agreements with those who wish to record the music of its members. It collects and distributes the 'mechanical' royalties which are generated from recording of the music on to many different formats. The PRS collects licence fees on behalf of composers, lyricists and music publishers for public performance or broadcast of their works. They co-operate closely under the name 'The Music Alliance'. Phonographic Performance Limited (PPL) acts for over 3,000 record companies, both large and small, and deals primarily with the copyright in sound recordings. Video Performance Limited (VPL) is responsible for music videos.

As well as their policing role, the collecting societies license performance of their works, including to broadcasters such as the BBC, ITV and Sky. All the societies cooperate closely to ensure that the copyright holders in each aspect of a work receive their fair share of a licence fee from a user. Disputes about the terms and other aspects of this system are heard by the Copyright Tribunal, formerly the Performing Right Tribunal. See *Phonographic Performance Ltd v Candy Rock Recording Ltd* [2000] EMLR 618, CA.

In the publishing world, the Copyright Licensing Agency Ltd (CLA) seeks to enforce its members' copyright in their works. It licenses businesses to copy protected works. The CLA is owned by the Authors Licensing and Collecting Society (ALCS) and the Publishers Licensing Society (PLS). The Newspaper Licensing Agency Ltd (NLA) was set up in 1996 to enforce newspaper proprietors' rights in their copyright. It licenses businesses to copy newspapers, and was involved in a high-profile case with Marks & Spencer (see **19.4** and **19.4.4.3**).

19.9 Developments in the law of copyright

Directive 2001/29/EC on Copyright and Related Rights in the Information Society ('Copyright Directive') deals with harmonisation of copyright through the EU. In particular, it addresses the issue of copyright protection on the Internet and satellite and cable broadcasts. It provides for an exemption from liability for an intermediary which carries out transient or incidental copying as part of a technological process. Articles 6 and 7 of the Directive are intended to outlaw the making and selling of devices which circumvent anti-copying technology. The Directive has now been implemented by the Copyright and Related Rights Regulations 2003 (SI 2003/2498), as of October 2003, and has amended the CDPA 1988 in this respect by the insertion of s 28A.

This important provision has been examined in detail by Kitchin J in *Football Association Premier League Ltd v QC Leisure* [2008] EWHC 1411 (Ch). The case concerns the use of foreign origin decoder cards for the purpose of allowing UK screening of Premier League matches in bars and similar places. The cards were necessary to allow UK access to broadcasts intended to be seen only in Greece, the Middle East and North Africa. The Premier League claimant controls the filming and the licensing of its matches; the use by the defendants of the cards was claimed to be an infringement of the copyrights involved, and as undermining the value of the licensing rights to licensor and licensees alike. In a very extensive preliminary examination of the law, the judge decided that the matter is so closely connected to European Community law, and that the issues are of such considerable significance to commercial and legal policies of the Community, that the only safe course was an adjournment to allow references on certain points to be made to the ECJ for a ruling.

This is a matter of very great importance to the whole question of cross-border satellite broadcasting and its reception; beyond this, it is likely to shed light on the larger question of the copyright implications of transient or incidental passage of copyright material within any computer operation which, as an operational part of a technological process, has no independent economic significance. It appears, from the preliminary analysis of the matter by Kitchin J, that he sees the question of independent economic significance as being of central importance to the need for the ECJ's view, both as to transient copies made within the cards themselves and also as to the transient copies produced on the TV screens. The ECJ ruling is expected shortly (late 2010).

Directive 2001/84/EC on the Resale Right for the Benefit of the Author of an Original Work of Art should have been implemented in Member States by 1 January 2006. This gives the creator of a copyright work a percentage of the sale price (the 'resale right' – reg 3) when the work is re-sold on the open market during the period of copyright protection (ie, up to 70 years after the author's death). There was some delay, following extensive consultation, but the Artist's Resale Rights Regulations 2006 (SI 2006/346) came into effect on 14 February 2006.

The resale right can be 'transmitted', under regs 9 and 16, to persons who become beneficially entitled, on the death of the author, either to the work itself or to the copyright in the work. The resale right will be exercisable on such 'transmitted rights' only for resale contracts after 1 January 2010. The resale right is capped at €12,500 per sale (max), and has already collected £5 million or so for living artists, which is unlikely to make much impact on a market worth several billion pounds each year.

19.10 International copyright protection

Internationally, there are two distinct levels of recognition and protection of copyright material. The first lies in the various measures taken by the European Community; the second is seen in international treaty obligations of the UK. It is only possible to give a brief outline of these matters here, but they can be summarised as follows.

Within the EU, the matter has been dealt with by directives, leading to national legislation, showing some degree of harmonisation. Examples are discussed at **19.9** above. Other examples are seen in computer programs (Directive 91/250/EEC), rental and lending rights in copyright (Directive 92/100/EEC), and database protection (Directive 96/9/EC). The general effect of all this legislation is that most national legislation within the EC is fairly consistent in its effect and application, but there are still anomalous situations, particularly with respect to performance and moral rights.

On the broader international stage, the UK is a signatory to two major treaties, the Berne Copyright Convention and the Universal Copyright Convention. Both treaties have a similar effect: they provide assurance, as between the signatory nations, that mutual recognition, availability of jurisdiction and national legal remedies will be given to the owners of copyright within the different signatory states. It is a sort of copyright club arrangement.

The Berne Convention was ratified by the UK in 1887 and has a wide international membership, including all EC members, the USA and China. It is administered by the World Intellectual Property Organisation. The broad effect of the Convention is that the qualification for protection part of the CDPA 1988, Chapter IX, extends the protection of the Act to citizens and bodies incorporated within the signatory nations of the Convention. The degree of protection may be limited in some cases where the courts of another signatory state would not give as much protection to a UK citizen as is available in the UK. Much depends upon the amount of protection available under national copyright law, which is not overridden by the Convention. Some rights suggested by the Convention are not generally available under English law; in some matters (notably, duration of protection), English law gives longer periods than the Convention and many other national laws. Very significantly, the Berne Convention is based upon the complete lack of formality that English law gives to the creation and recognition of copyright.

The Universal Copyright Convention ('UCC') is run by UNESCO and has a quite different membership to the Berne Convention, although the UK and the larger nations are signatories. The biggest difference from the Berne Convention lies in the UCC's requirement for quite a high degree of formality being required of the contracting states as well as the mandatory, prominent display upon the material of the copyright symbol, the owner's name and the date of first publication (even though that is not strictly required under English law).

There are other international agreements and organisations that can affect copyright matters, but these fall outside the remit of this work.

Chapter 20
The Database Right

20.1 Background and introduction

There has been a difference of approach between English law and the Continental civil law systems on the protection of utilitarian information such as lists of customers' names and addresses, or entries in a phone directory. The English approach has been to grant copyright protection, but the Continental view was that such functional documents were not literary works and therefore could not be protected by copyright. This difference of approach was resolved by Directive 96/9/EC on the Legal Protection of Databases ('the Database Directive'). This was implemented by the Copyright and Rights in Databases Regulations 1997 ('the 1997 Regulations') (SI 1997/3032). These amended the CDPA 1988. The protection given by the 1997 Regulations is known as the 'database right'.

What is protected?	collections of information
What benefit is there?	protects against unauthorised copying
How is it obtained?	arises automatically (no registration)
How long does it last?	15 years from creation or substantial revision of the database

There remains a class of databases that is protected by copyright (see **19.2** and **20.2**). This class will, in almost all cases, be protected by both copyright and the database right under the 1997 Regulations. The problem that commonly arose for copyright database owners, prior to the 1997 Regulations, was that copying often took the form of repeated, low level use of the material, which usually failed to be a 'substantial' copying for infringement purposes. This gap has now been filled by reg 16(2) (see **20.6**).

20.2 Definition of a database

A database is defined in the CDPA 1988, s 3A, as follows:

> **3A Databases**
>
> (1) In this Part 'database' means a collection of independent works, data or other materials which—
>
> (a) are arranged in a systematic or methodical way, and
>
> (b) are individually accessible by electronic or other means.
>
> (2) For the purposes of this Part a literary work consisting of a database is original if, and only if, by reason of the selection or arrangement of the contents of the database the database constitutes the author's own intellectual creation.

The definition of a 'database' covers information held in electronic form and also that held only as paper documents. This definition is also applied by the 1997 Regulations.

In practice, a database could, for example, be information on the daily price of stocks and shares, a telephone directory, Lexis or the CD-ROM law reports. Copyright protection may also be afforded to a database specifically as a literary work, although the standard is not only that of originality, but also that it is the 'author's own intellectual creation'. This seems to be a higher standard than for copyright in literary works in general, and so a database is unlikely to have copyright protection.

Whether or not it is protected by copyright, a database attracts the database right, which arises automatically. The database right runs for 15 years from the end of the year of completion. It prevents unauthorised use of the database or a substantial part of it.

Under reg 13 of the 1997 Regulations, the database right exists where there is 'substantial investment in obtaining, verifying or presenting the contents of the database.' Thus, data arrangements have the protection of the database right if there is a substantial investment (including any investment, whether of financial, human or technical resources):

(a) in quality or quantity; or
(b) in obtaining, verifying or presenting the data.

Further points to consider in relation to database right are discussed below.

20.3 Qualifications for the database right

There are copyright-style qualification requirements (1997 Regulations, reg 18) based on nationality, or corporate seat.

20.4 Ownership of the database right

The maker of a database protected by the database right is the person who takes the initiative in obtaining, verifying or presenting the contents of the database and who assumes the risk of investing in that obtaining (see 1997 Regulations, reg 14).

The maker is the first owner of the database right (reg 15).

Care is needed in asserting ownership of database rights. In *Google Inc v Copiepresse SCRL* [2007] ECDR 5, a database right infringement claim by a management company failed, simply because the company did not hold the database right but only managed copyright on behalf of various newspapers which were subjected to automatic searches by Google. Copyright infringements were upheld by the Belgian court.

20.5 Duration of database protection

The database right lasts for the longer of 15 years from the end of the calendar year:

(a) of completion of the database; or
(b) during which the database was first made available to the public (reg 17).

A 'substantial new investment', under s 17(3) will 'top up' the right so the period starts again. So, a telephone directory would in effect have a rolling 15-year protection, as a new edition is produced every year.

20.6 Infringement of the database right

Infringement is the extraction or re-utilisation of all or a substantial part of the contents of a database without the consent of the owner (reg 16).

'Extraction' means the permanent or temporary transfer of the contents of a database to another medium by any means, or in any form.

'Re-utilisation' means making those contents available to the public by any means.

'Substantial' is in terms of quality, or quantity or both.

'Substantial part' can include repeated extraction and/or re-utilisation of insubstantial parts (reg 16(2)). This is the most useful aspect of the right, in that it can prevent repeated, low-level use of the database by unauthorised persons.

20.7 Exceptions from the database right

Database rights are not infringed (regs 19 and 20):

(a) by fair dealing with a substantial part of a database made available to the public if:
   (i) such dealing is for illustration in teaching or research; and
   (ii) sufficient acknowledgement is given; or

(b) generally, by copying or use with the authority of the keeper of a database available for public inspection as a statutory record.

The database right can be licensed or assigned (as can the copyright in the database).

20.8 Application of the database right

The database right was introduced to give the database owner an action against people who extract information from the database without its permission, whether or not this would constitute copyright infringement.

In *British Horseracing Board v William Hill*, the British Horseracing Board operated a computerised database containing the details of horse owners, trainers and jockeys, racing colours, horses and other information relating to races to be run in Great Britain. Information on the database was updated after each race. William Hill, a bookmaker with 1,500 licensed betting shops in the UK, legitimately used information from the British Horseracing Board service. In 2000, William Hill started an Internet betting service which used information from the British Horseracing Board service. This was outside the terms of William Hill's licence agreement. The British Horseracing Board therefore sued for breach of the database right, and the case was referred to the ECJ.

In essence, the ECJ held that there needed to be economic investment in resources used to create a database in order for the database right to arise. This was distinct from re-presenting existing materials, which was held to be the case here. The British Horseracing Board would have had to collect the information on runners and riders in any event for its own purposes as the supervisor of horseracing in the UK. The view of the ECJ was therefore that the database in question did not benefit from the database right, and so William Hill could not have infringed it.

An interesting point was considered in *Cantor Gaming Ltd v Gameaccount Global Ltd* [2007] EWHC 1914 (Ch). The claimant had inserted a clause in its online game licence that if any use of its intellectual property were made by third party bookmakers, via the defendant, that would be a material breach of the licence. It was decided that the claimant's database, even though not used in a conventional way, had been stored, backed up, reproduced and accessed. That was sufficient to constitute an unlawful use of the database.

In *Cureton v Mark Insulations Ltd* [2006] EWHC 2279, an agent who had been given the task of selling insulation to his principal's customers began to collate more information about them for his own private purposes, unrelated to the agency function. In a termination dispute, the principal claimed ownership of the database. The court held that although the principal was justified in summarily dismissing the agent, the work in creating the database had been done by the agent and he was, therefore, the owner under reg 14 (see **20.4**).

Chapter 21
Design Rights

21.1 Introduction to design protection

So far, in looking at IP rights, we have examined the protection of business reputation and creative expression through trade marks, passing off and copyright, all areas which provide clear and obvious examples of matters that require legal protection. The creator or owner of a business or a copyright work really does look like an owner of property in some form. In dealing with designs, however, somewhat different considerations come into play. Here, we are dealing with the way things look and with the shape and appearance of manufactured articles – often, the quite mundane objects that surround us in our everyday world. It is not so easy or practicable to accept that shapes and appearances of things should remain the monopoly of any particular person for any extensive length of time. Nevertheless, successful shapes and appearances cost money to design and are worth a great deal to their owner, commercially. In consequence, the law has had to develop to give a range of more limited rights to owners of designs, in terms both of period of protection and the scope of the protection offered, than those you have seen in the IP rights studied so far. There is a delicate balancing act here, between over-protection of design owners and the maintenance of general design freedom for other competing designers and manufacturers, who wish to use similar design features on the same, or even on different, types of article.

A simple example illustrates the point: a person buys an article, perhaps a motor cycle, and then decides it is so good that he wishes to keep it for a long time. If the manufacturer changes models after a short while and ceases to make spare parts for the earlier bike, can the enthusiastic owner go to someone else who is willing to make and sell a spare part to that design? It would be a great problem if the original manufacturer could exercise design rights to prevent such a thing permanently, or even stop other manufacturers, as competitors, from making the millions of genuine spare parts used in the everyday world. Design protection has to be able to deal with this practicality; the law has to recognise that where there is plenty of design freedom, an interesting design will merit protection for a period. Where there is little or no room to vary the design (such as with many spare parts, or in interfaces between component parts, or between scart, 3-pin or other cable connections, etc), the law will usually not provide protection for those design features.

The protections we look at below fall into two categories: the most protected category is achieved by initial registration of a design and maintenance of that registration up to a maximum of 25 years, this protection being limited to external shapes and appearances ('registered design right' or 'RDR'); a lesser, unregistered design right will give a shorter period of protection to shapes and forms, but is capable of dealing with the often invisible internal shapes and forms of articles which cannot be protected by registration ('unregistered design right' or 'UDR'). It should be understood though, that it is not always the whole of an article that will be protected; the protection will apply only to those features which are capable of meeting the requirements of the relevant legislation, which tends to exclude many features as being unprotectable.

It is important to realise that RDR and UDR are not mutually exclusive; it is often the case that both rights may co-exist in the same design features or, alternatively, that the separate rights exist in separate features of the same article – eg, RDR protecting the surface decoration of it (to which UDR cannot apply, see **21.1.1** below), while UDR protects inner, unseen shapes and configurations (to which RDR cannot apply, see **21.1.2** below).

The law explained in the following paragraphs is discussed mainly by reference to the current English statutes and cases. Note, though, that this area has had to respond directly to the European Community (now European Union) interventions of the last 20 years or so. There have been, and continue to exist, some differences between the approaches to designs (and other IP rights) seen in national legal systems within the Community, but the current English design statutes are fairly closely aligned now with the law applicable throughout the Community, by virtue of the 'Design Directive' mentioned at **21.1.1** below. This alignment of Community and national laws has proceeded in parallel with the development of the 'Community Registered Design' ('CRD'), as well as the 'Community Unregistered Design' ('CUD'), administered by OHIM in Alicante (these are dealt with in outline at **21.2.11** and **21.3.9** respectively below). The strong similarities between domestic and Community law on these matters, particularly in registered designs, will become clear as the chapter proceeds. Consequently, little direct reference is made to the Community legislation, as much of our domestic legislation closely follows the EC form and drafting. It will be seen that several cases referred to, if examined in detail, have used Community Design terms and provisions, but detailed examination of the differences between domestic and Community law in this area is not necessary, or desirable, for the present purposes of this chapter. The English High Court, Court of Appeal and Patents County Court have jurisdiction to hear Community Design matters.

21.1.1 Registered design right (RDR) – overview

Registered designs have existed in England since at least the 1830s. They were bolstered at that time to protect the designs of fabrics from being copied by cheap imports. Registered design right was strengthened in the CDPA 1988, with the aim of promoting its use for a wider range of articles. At the same time, copyright was pushed in the direction of artistic output, not least to resist the trend that had developed of trying to use copyright for industrial items such as, say, spare parts for cars, etc, to gain longer periods of protection. The interface between copyright and design protection is discussed at **21.3.7** below. Directive 98/71/EC on the Legal Protection of Design (the Design Directive), implemented by the Registered Design Regulations 2001 (SI 2001/3949), made further amendments to the legislation governing registered designs, the Registered Designs Act 1949 (RDA) 1949, effective from 9 December 2001. Regulation 6/2002 EC sets up the framework of the Community Design Scheme (see **21.2.11** and **21.3.9**).

Registered design right protects the visible, external appearance, during ordinary use, of all or part of a product, 'product' being very widely defined so as to include consumer or industrial products.

A visit to the IPO website (www.ipo.gov.uk) and its registered designs search area, under 'products', will reveal designs for just about anything that can be manufactured, from the most artistically designed consumer articles to the most functional industrial items. The range is very wide, from tools, to clothes, to transport, so the protection has come a long way from fabric designs and purely consumer articles. The form of protection given is similar to other registered IP rights: the fact of registration gives notice to the world at large of the existence of the right, so that any commercial use or exploitation of the design, or of articles made to that design, with or without knowledge or intention, is within the scope of the protection (see infringements and remedies at **21.3.5** and **21.3.6**). In effect, RDR gives the owner of the design a monopoly period of up to 25 years (an initial five-year period, renewable in subsequent five-year periods) in which to use and exploit the design.

What is protected?	new designs for manufactured items
What benefit is there?	monopoly right
How is it obtained?	registration
How long does it last?	25 years from registration

21.1.2 Unregistered design right (UDR) – origins and overview

Unregistered design right is a relatively modern form of protection for designs. One of the essential components of most replicable designs is some sort of design document. Such a document is almost sure to be protected by the law of copyright, potentially for a long period, and prior to the CDPA 1988, most industrial and manufacturer's design documents had artistic/graphic protection, capable of preventing unauthorised replication of the designs for the long periods associated with artistic copyright. More significantly, unauthorised reproduction of articles from those design documents also infringed the copyright, under the 2D to 3D transformation, as the law then stood. This was even more dangerous as, because of the informal nature of copyright creation and protection, no registration was required and a person could easily infringe copyright without knowing it.

What the 1988 Act did was to eradicate this long-term copyright protection of designs by the creation of UDR, the effect being that to reproduce the design document, without permission, will certainly infringe any copyright in it (but the period of protection will typically be only for a maximum of 25 years); if the document is reproduced for the purpose of the unauthorised creation of articles to that design, that reproduction will also be an infringement of any UDR in the design (but protection is only for the maximum period of up to 15 years, more typically 10). The most significant change, though, is that any unauthorised making of articles from that infringing copy of the design document will not be an infringement of copyright but will be an infringement of any UDR in the design. The whole idea of this change was effectively to suppress the extensive copyright protection in favour of the much more limited UDR protection (the relationship between copyright and UDR, in a manufacturing, design or production context, is quite complex and more detail is given below, see **21.3.7**). So if I photocopy your design document, I have infringed your copyright, but if I look at your design document and make the object represented in it, I have not infringed your copyright but I have infringed your UDR.

The scope of the protection given by UDR is quite wide, as it protects designs of any aspect of the shape or configuration, internal or external, of all or part of an article. It can be seen, at once, that this goes further than RDR in protecting internal shapes; but, as will be seen, it is more limited than RDR in that it cannot protect surface decoration. Both RDR and UDR therefore have their individual characteristics. To maximise protection, use of both may be necessary.

What is protected?	3-dimensional shapes and configurations
What benefit is there?	prevents copying
How is it obtained?	arises automatically (no registration)
How long does it last?	10 years in most cases (15 years maximum)

21.2 Registered design right

21.2.1 Definitions – 'new' and 'individual character'

'Registered design' is defined in RDA 1949, s 1(2) as:

> ... the appearance of the whole or part of a product resulting from the features of, in particular, the lines, contours, shape, texture and/or materials of the product itself and/or its ornamentation.

'Product' is defined in s 1(3) as:

> any industrial or handicraft item other than a computer program; and in particular, includes packaging, get-up, graphic symbols, typographic type-faces and parts intended to be assembled into a complex product.

This definition now includes things that were not covered before (the amendments referred to at **21.1**), perhaps most notably the packaging and get-up (presentation) of goods. Thus, it would now be possible to register the appearance of packaging as a registered design. This would give such items the increased protection of a registered right.

A design must be '*new*' and have '*individual character*', which terms are defined as follows:

> **1B Requirement of novelty and individual character**
>
> (1) A design shall be protected by a right in a registered design to the extent that the design is new and has individual character.
>
> (2) For the purposes of subsection (1) above, a design is new if no identical design or no design whose features differ only in immaterial details has been made available to the public before the relevant date.
>
> (3) For the purposes of subsection (1) above, a design has individual character if the overall impression it produces on the informed user differs from the overall impression produced on such a user by any design which has been made available to the public before the relevant date.

As to the requirement for novelty, the test in s 1B(2) is clearly one of whether that design is available to the public, which raises further subordinate questions as to what is meant by 'available to the public' in terms of time, geographical scope and purpose of exposure of the design. The answers to these questions can be found in further examination of the rest of s 1B, particularly s 1B(5), (6) and (7). In broad terms, the time at which the novelty test must be met is when the application to register is first filed. The 'public' in question is probably now somewhat wider than the previous statutory test of the public within the UK. Section 1B(6)(a) indicates that the likely scope may well be as large as the purchasing public and the business community throughout the European Economic Area (EEA).

The question whether the design is new, at that date, is one of whether any largely identical design already exists in 'the prior art in the sector concerned'; that is the sort of designs which are already known of or in use at that date, both by buyers and by 'persons carrying on business . . . and specialising in the sector concerned' (s 1B(6)(a)). So, much depends upon what 'the sector' means. According to Lewison J, in *Green Lane Products Ltd v PMS International Group Ltd* [2007] EWHC 1712 (Pat), 'the sector concerned' is the sector in which the 'prior art' is located rather than the particular product sector for which the new registration was applied. That is an important finding, if it is right, in that it means that a design cannot be pirated simply by trying to use that design in a different product sector, as was being attempted in that case. This view has now been upheld by the Court of Appeal ([2008] EWCA Civ 358). This decision suggests that registration of a design for, say, a car, could prevent use of that design on a cake or a toy. The extent of 'the prior art' probably extends to almost any design, wherever located in the world, that is 'available' within the EEA. Registrations will not usually be invalidated by earlier designs in remote places, of which European industry would be unlikely to be aware. The Design Registry will not search prior art but will rely on third parties to object to the application when it is published.

The question of 'individual character' in s 1B(3) is also determined as at the date of first filing and really boils down to a question of evidence as to the overall impression made upon an 'informed user', presumably a person familiar with the designs used in the sector in question. In *J Choo (Jersey) Ltd v Towerstone Ltd* [2008] EWHC 346 (Ch), in a pirated handbag claim, the 'informed user' was said to be neither the woman in the street nor a handbag designer, but rather someone with knowledge of handbag design. The real question is usually whether the creator of the new design has taken advantage of any freedom of design that is available to him to make his new design different from what is already available; if he has not, it is likely that the new design will not have individual character. This is given statutory force in s 1B(4). It should be borne in mind that the different overall impression test might be passed by combining features from several different products to give a completely new amalgam of those features – see *In the Matter of Registered Design No 2044802 in the Name of Household Articles Ltd*, Ch D (Patents Ct) 22/1/98, [1998] FSR 676, a case under the old law, but one which would probably be decided the same way now. There are suggestions in the cases that evidence of both novelty and individual character should be limited to that of purchasers of or traders in the product in question. There is little room for any expert evidence and the court will not usually require it.

It appears, in many cases, that 'individual character' might not add much to the basic requirement that the design be new.

Some helpful guidance on the 'overall different impression' test for individual character has now been given by the Court of Appeal in *Procter & Gamble Co v Reckitt Benckiser (UK) Ltd* [2007] EWCA Civ 936. In the context of a CRD infringement claim, concerning air freshener spray containers, the Court gave some general guidance as follows:

(a) The first point is that a different overall impression is sufficient and it does not need to be 'clearly' different.

(b) The notional informed user would be taken as being fairly familiar with design issues.

(c) Protection would be correspondingly greater for products which were novel, as compared to those only incrementally different from the prior art.

(d) The test for validity of the registered design remained 'Is the overall impression different?'.

(e) The court needed to identify the 'overall impression' with some care.

(f) The level of generality was very important and should be that of the notional informed user, rather than the casual customer.

(g) The court should than repeat this exercise with the alleged infringing design.

(h) The court should ask finally whether the overall impression of each design was different.

In the instant case, the judge had taken the similarities at too general a level and had come to a finding that there had been infringement. The Court of Appeal held that the informed user would have formed different overall impressions of the products and that therefore there was no infringement. Also, on the appeal, the claimant's original registration was upheld.

21.2.2 'Grace period' of 12 months

The amended RDA 1949 now provides a grace period of 12 months during which a designer may disclose the design to others without affecting the design's novelty, or the assessment of its individual character in an application for registration by the end of the 12-month period (s 1B(5), (6)). There is no right to claim for infringement before the design has been granted registration (s 7A(6)). The very point was in issue in *Oakley Inc v Animal Ltd*, because the disclosure date created problems as to which law and tests applied. There are other provisions in s 1B(6) to protect against unauthorised or abusive disclosures of the design during the grace period.

It would still be important to keep evidence of the date of creation of the design (eg, by storing original drawings which should be dated and signed). Thus, if someone else claimed during the 12-month grace period that he had created the design in question, there would be evidence available to refute that claim. Once the design has been registered, any such disputes would be resolved by the registration, if it is valid.

21.2.3 Design features that cannot be protected

21.2.3.1 Technical function (s 1C)

There is an exclusion from registrability for features dictated 'solely by the product's technical function'. The requirement of 'solely' dictated raises the question of how much design freedom is available (see **21.2.3.2**); if there is some freedom to give a different appearance to the design, it is probably registrable, provided it is new and has individual character.

Section 1C(1) states: 'A right in a registered design shall not subsist in features of appearance of a product which are solely dictated by the product's technical function.' An example of such a feature would be the serrated blades of a dressmaker's crimping shears, which create a sawtooth edge on what is cut.

21.2.3.2 Interface features (s 1C(2))

Section 1C(2) excludes registration for any features of the design of a product which are *compelled* to be of a certain exact shape in order to be able to fit into, around or up against some other product so that either or both of the products can perform their proper function. The remaining features of either product may well be registrable, but the interface features are not. If it had to be that design then no design flair has been shown, so why should it gain protection?

One of the more pervasive features of modern designs has been the increasing use of modular ranges (ie things designed to lock together) of products of all types – tools, furniture, utensils, household and vehicle fittings. By itself, s 1C(2) would create a problem for protecting the many ingenious designs for the interfaces between modular items. Section 1C(3) removes this problem by stating that s 1C(2) does not apply to features that allow for assembly or connection of mutually interchangeable products within a modular system; such features can now be registered and protected (although they would still need to be new and of individual character). That tends to cut back the rigour of both s 1C(2) and the earlier case law rule (seen in *Amp Inc v Utilux Pty Ltd* [1971] RPC 397) that such interface connections could never be registered. So, for example, stacking chairs are not automatically excluded from registration (but may fail on other grounds).

21.2.4 Designs that can now be protected

Under the law pre-December 2001, it was not possible to have a design registration for a spare part (see *R v Registered Designs Appeal Tribunal, ex p Ford Motor Co* [1995] 1 WLR 18). However, it is now possible to have such a registration, provided the part is visible during the normal use of the whole product. For example, a new design of radio aerial for a car would be registrable as it would be visible, but a new design for an oil filter for a car would not, as it would be hidden during normal use. Thus, s 1B(8), (9) provide:

> (8) For the purposes of this section, a design applied to or incorporated in a product which constitutes a component part of a complex product shall only be considered to be new and to have individual character—
>
> (a) if the component part, once it has been incorporated into the complex product, remains visible during normal use of the complex product; and
>
> (b) to the extent that those visible features of the component part are in themselves new and have individual character.
>
> (9) In subsection (8) above "normal use" means use by the end user; but does not include any maintenance, servicing or repair work in relation to the product.

'Normal use' means that the visible parts of a wing mirror, in the *Ford* case, could now be registered as they are visible in the ordinary use of a car.

A design registration cannot be used against someone supplying a spare part for the repair of a complex product, 'so as to restore its original appearance' (eg, the car radio aerial mentioned above (s 7A(5)). So, while the registration can be used to stop another manufacturer from using that design for a car radio aerial on its make of car, it cannot be used to stop someone supplying spare aerials so as to restore the appearance of a car, made by the owner of the registered design. Care would be needed, of course, to avoid reproducing any logos or marks that had any separate rights, such as trade marks or passing off protection; licences would be needed to reproduce those.

21.2.5 The scope of the right

The proprietor has the exclusive right (subject to any compulsory licensing by the Crown under the RDA 1949, Sch 1) to use the design and 'any design which does not produce on the informed user a different overall impression' (s 7(1)). This in effect includes use of the design on any product. It will extend to manufacture, dealing in, importing, exporting, stocking and use of a product incorporating the design (see **21.2.9**).

Unlike the situation under the old law, designs no longer have to be registered in regard to certain types of product. So, use of a design intended for crockery on, say, tee shirts would be infringement of the design registration. That can be seen from an examination of the *Green Lane Products Ltd* case discussed at **21.2.1** above.

21.2.6 Duration of protection

The duration of protection is a maximum of 25 years (s 8). This is achieved by an initial registration of five years, renewable in five-year periods.

21.2.7 Ownership of registered designs (s 2)

The prima facie rule is that first ownership of the design rests in the 'author', ie the actual designer (s 2(1)). That is subject to the following points:

(a) If the design is created in the course of someone's employment, the ownership of the design belongs to the employer (s 2(1B)). This in effect is the same as copyright (see **19.2.5**).

(b) If the design is created as a result of a commission (eg freelance work), then the ownership belongs to the commissioner, not to the designer (s 2(1A)). This is in contrast to the situation with copyright (see **19.2.5**).

21.2.8 Exhaustion of rights

Registered design right cannot be used to hinder parallel importing (s 7A(4)), where the product has been put on the market within the EEA by the registered proprietor, or with his consent. So if you sell your product in France, you cannot use RDR to stop it being imported and sold in the UK.

21.2.9 Infringement of registered designs

Knowledge or intention is not required for infringement. The fact of registration gives notice to all, regardless of knowledge. Knowledge becomes relevant only in considering what remedies are available (see **21.2.10**).

The registration of a design gives the registered proprietor the exclusive right to use the design and 'any design which does not produce on the informed user a different overall impression' (s 7(1)). Care is needed, here, to distinguish between an overall design concept and the particular features of the design that are protected by registration. These are quite different things, as can be seen in *Rowlawn Ltd v Turfmech Machinery Ltd* [2008] EWHC 989 (Pat). The defendant had clearly followed much of the broad concept of the claimant's registered design, but that was not what was protected by the registration. In the finer detail of the machinery (a type of mowing machine) the defendant's design differed and had been developed without copying.

'Using' the design is defined in s 7(2), including a reference to '… the making, offering, putting on the market, importing, exporting or using of a product in which the design is incorporated or to which it is applied'.

'Infringement' is defined in s 7A as doing anything that is the exclusive right of the proprietor without its consent. Exceptions in s 7A(2) include:

(a) an act which is done privately and for purposes which are not commercial;
(b) an act which is done for experimental purposes;
(c) an act of reproduction for teaching purposes …;
(d) …
(e) [these concern foreign ships and aircraft but which are temporarily in the UK]
(f) …

There are qualifications to the exceptions, in s 7A(3); if these are complied with, there is no infringement:

(a) the act of reproduction is compatible with fair trade practice and does not unduly prejudice the normal exploitation of the design, and
(b) mention is made of the source.

There can be no infringement before the date of the certificate of registration (s 7A(6)).

21.2.10 Remedies

Damages may not be awarded against an infringer who had no knowledge that the design was registered (despite the existence of the public register) (s 24B). It is not enough to mark a design with the word 'registered' to overcome this; rather, the registration number of the design must also be marked on the product in question. Apart from this concession to a lack of awareness, the rest of the remedies are available without regard to knowledge of infringement. The position seems to be different where infringement of a Community design is concerned. In *J Choo (Jersey) Ltd v Towerstone Ltd* [2008] EWHC 346 (Ch), Floyd J held that s 24B, although effective in a claim under the RDA 1949, had no application to a claim based on a Community right.

Remedies can include:

(a) an injunction;
(b) damages;
(c) an account of profits; and
(d) an order for delivery up or destruction of the offending items.

The RDA 1949, s 26 provides for a remedy for groundless threats of infringement proceedings. This comprises a declaration, damages and an injunction. The reason for these types of provisions in the legislation governing IP rights is that the threat of infringement proceedings is a severe danger to a business.

There are also criminal offences of falsely representing a design as registered, both against individuals and against corporate bodies.

21.2.11 EU-registered design right – the Community registered design (CRD)

Regulation 6/2002 set up an EU-registered design system, which deals with CRD registration. The system has been registering CRDs since 2003 under the Regulation. It is run by the EU Trade Marks Office (OHIM) in Alicante. For the purposes of this edition we are not dealing with this development in depth, but it will affect you when you are in practice, sooner or later. See **21.3.9** for the equivalent measure in unregistered designs.

Community registered designs are similar in many respects to RDR examined at **21.2** above. The broad tests of novelty and individual character are very much the same, and a maximum 25-year term of protection is available. The big difference is that a CRD is effective throughout the Community (now Union), and is recognised by all Member States. There is no search mechanism before registration and it is for third parties, Member States or the Commission itself to appeal against registration to the OHIM, with an ultimate appeal to the ECJ.

21.3 Unregistered design right

This is referred to in the CDPA 1988 as 'design right'. 'Design' is defined in s 213(2) as 'any aspect of the shape or configuration (whether internal or external) of the whole or part of an article'. The design must be 'original' (s 213(1)), which is further explained as being 'not commonplace in the design field in question'.

No right subsists unless the design is recorded in a document, or an article has been made to the design (s 213(6)).

A further complication of the UDR regime is the necessity for the work to 'qualify' for protection within s 217. This depends upon the design having a qualifying connection to the UK via specified qualifying persons (including designers and commissioners), qualifying countries (in which trading or legal residence is established), or qualifying first marketing within the UK or the EU.

21.3.1 Originality

The requirement of originality for UDR has two aspects:

(a) that it should be original, in the copyright sense of not itself being a copy; and
(b) that it should not be 'commonplace in the design field in question' (s 213(4)).

There have been some cases which have considered what it means to be 'commonplace'. The idea is that UDR protects a design against copying. For that concept to work, the design in question has to be distinguishable from all the other goods of that type in the marketplace. For example, see the following cases.

In *Farmers Build Ltd v Carrier Bulk Materials Handling Ltd* [1999] RPC 461, concerning a slurry separator, it was held that putting a number of different commonplace features together in a new way can result in a design that is not commonplace.

In *Jo-Y-Jo Ltd v Matalan Retail Ltd* [1999] EIPR 627, it was held that flowers embroidered on vests were commonplace.

In *Ocular Sciences Ltd and Another v Aspect Vision Care Ltd and Others; Galley v Ocular Sciences Ltd (No 2)* [1997] RPC 289, a design for contact lenses was held to be commonplace if trite, common-or-garden, or hackneyed. In that case, many features of the contact lenses were held to be commonplace, or subject to the 'must fit' exclusion (ie must fit the eye – see **21.3.2**).

In *Lambretta Clothing Company Ltd v Teddy Smith (UK) Ltd & Next Retail plc* [2003] EWHC (Ch), the subject matter was a 'retro-vintage' track top. On the existence of UDR, it was held that:

(a) the outline shape of the track top was not original as it had itself been copied from another garment;
(b) the Lambretta logos were surface decoration and therefore excluded from UDR (see **21.3.2.4**);

(c) mere juxtaposition of patches of colour on the garment did not fall within the meaning of 'configuration' in s 213(2), so did not attract UDR; and

(d) two-dimensional colour applied to the garment did not generate an original three-dimensional design.

Overall, there was no UDR existing in the garment.

In *A Fulton Co Ltd v Grant Barnett & Co Ltd* [2001] RPC 16, there was held to be UDR in the handle of an umbrella, which had been designed by a director of the claimant company. The designs were held to be original and not to be commonplace. They were also held to have been infringed by the defendant.

In *Guild v Eskandar Ltd* [2001] FSR 38, UDR was held to exist in garments based on Iranian ethnic clothing, that is, there was sufficient originality in the designs in question (see **19.2.2.3**).

In *Dyson Ltd v Qualtex (UK) Ltd* [2006] EWCA Civ 166, the Court of Appeal upheld a judge's approach of looking at originality by taking a short cut, considering, first, whether the whole of an article was original and, secondly, unless there was a special point about a particular aspect, taking the view that each and every aspect of the design of that article was original. That is very helpful to a designer, in that it is less likely that someone will be able to challenge his design by attempting to 'pick off' features, in a piecemeal way, as being commonplace, so as to challenge the originality of the whole. The Court also added the helpful observation that a very good design (the Dyson handle) did not lose its protection simply by becoming well known and recognised as a good design.

21.3.2 Exclusions

The CDPA 1988, s 213(3) sets out the exclusions from UDR.

21.3.2.1 Methods or principles of construction (s 213(3)(a))

These are excluded on the basis that methods of construction are the subject of patent law rather than design law. 'Method of construction' has been defined as a process or operation by which a shape is produced, as opposed to the design of the shape itself. In *Landor & Hawa International Ltd v Azure Designs Ltd* [2006] EWCA Civ 1285, this principle was applied to 'piping' arrangements, which cloaked the expanding joint in luggage when unexpanded. It was held not to be part of a method of construction and copying it was an infringement.

In *Christopher Tasker's Design Right References; Re Patent Office* [2001] RPC 3, various aspects of sliding doors for wardrobes were held to be subject to UDR, and therefore to come within s 213(2). However, the hiding from view of aluminium runners by the use of wooden mouldings was a method of construction, and excluded from UDR by s 213(3).

21.3.2.2 Must fit (s 213(3)(b)(i))

This is similar to the interface exclusion for RDR (see **21.2.3.2**). Functional designs are not excluded from UDR; indeed, one of the main purposes of this right is to protect more functional designs. There is, however, an exclusion for those aspects of the design which 'must fit' with other articles in order that either article may perform its function. It is only the 'interface' that is excluded from protection, ie the bits that have to fit into, up to or around the other object. Again, attention will focus on whether the designer truly has any freedom of design open to him. If the shape had to be like that to fit something else, then no design flair has been used and protection should not be granted. The exclusion applies only to the interface connections between objects which are designed to be connected at some stage.

This exclusion would also apply to human spare parts (prostheses), or contact lenses (*Ocular Sciences Ltd and Another v Aspect Vision Care Ltd and Others; Galley v Ocular Sciences Ltd (No*

2) [1997] RPC 289). Another instance concerned a holder for a mobile phone, many features of which did not get UDR as its shape was dictated by the phone (*Parker v Tidball* [1997] FSR 680).

21.3.2.3 Must match (s 213(3)(b)(ii))

Unregistered design right cannot apply to design features of an article if the appearance of those features is dependent on that of a larger article of which it is intended to form an integral part. There could, for example, be no UDR in spare parts (for cars or prostheses for people, eg artificial limbs) where shapes are dependent on the larger object.

The scope of the exclusion was considered in *Dyson Ltd v Qualtex (UK) Ltd* [2004] EWHC 2981 (Ch). Here, Dyson was seeking to prevent the sale of spare parts made by Qualtex to fit and match Dyson vacuum cleaners. The Qualtex spares in question were intended to resemble closely the Dyson spares, not least as they were visible in the normal use of the vacuum cleaners. It was held that the 'must match' exclusion will not apply if the design of the spare part could be itself be changed without radically changing the overall appearance of the whole article, ie a vacuum cleaner in this case. In other words, it was not necessary for the Qualtex spares to be identical in appearance to the Dyson ones, so the must match exclusion did not save Qualtex from infringement of Dyson's unregistered design right.

In *Dyson Ltd v Qualtex (UK) Ltd* [2006] EWCA Civ 166, the Court of Appeal broadly upheld the judge's approach and confirmed that it was for the spare parts dealer or manufacturer to show that, as a practical matter, there was a real need to copy some feature of shape or configuration (because the appearance of the entire article was dependent upon the relevant design feature of the spare part). If there was no such dependence, the consequence would be that any UDR subsisting in that feature of the original design and article could properly be protected; it would not be excluded by 'must match' and the spare part would constitute an infringing article.

21.3.2.4 Surface decoration (s 213(3)(c))

Surface decoration is excluded from UDR. This is really part of the definition, as UDR protects only the shape of a product (see the *Lambretta* case at **21.3.1**). There can be some difficulty in distinguishing surface decoration from 3-dimensional features of an article.

An interesting case on this problem is *Helmet Integrated Systems Ltd v Mitchell Tunnard*, PCC 10/2/2006, LTL 15/12/2006, [2006] FSR 41. The dispute was about design features of a modular, state-of-the-art fire helmet and, in particular, scalloping features along the sides of the helmet. The evidence showed that scalloping had resulted in some advantages of strength, but the features had not been designed for anything other than appearance's sake. The feature was held to be surface decoration and fell within the exclusion.

21.3.3 Ownership of unregistered designs

If the design is created in the course of someone's employment, the ownership of the design belongs to the employer (s 215). This in effect is the same as copyright (see **19.2.5**).

In *Ultraframe (UK) Ltd v Clayton and Others; Ultraframe (UK) Ltd v Fielding and Others* [2002] EWHC 1964 (Ch), the claimant company was held to be the owner of unregistered designs created by the person who had been managing director and major shareholder. In *A Fulton Co Ltd v Grant Barnett & Co Ltd* [2001] RPC 16, the claimant company was also held to own an unregistered design created by a director, despite the lack of a service contract between company and director.

As with RDR, if the design is created as a result of a commission then the ownership belongs to the commissioner, not to the designer. This is in contrast to the situation with copyright (see **19.2.5** and **21.2.7**).

If the UDR arises by 'first marketing' qualifications (see **21.3**), the person who first markets the design will be the first owner of the UDR (s 215(4)).

Ownership is the same for both registered and unregistered designs. Why the difference from copyright? Primarily because design rights are thought of as commercial rights, so it makes sense that 'he who pays the piper calls the tune'. With copyright the position is more subtle. Although it covers other things as well, copyright is often considered to be the realm of the creative artist, so there the starting point is that the author should own his own creation.

21.3.4 Duration of protection

Unregistered design right lasts for 15 years from the end of the calendar year in which the design was first created, or 10 years from being made available for sale or hire (s 216).

21.3.5 Infringement of unregistered designs

Unregistered design right follows copyright in that there is primary and secondary infringement. Secondary infringement requires knowledge.

The owner of UDR has the exclusive right to reproduce the design for commercial purposes by making articles to that design, or by reproducing his design document for the purpose of making articles to that design (s 226(1)). The latter is seen in *Societa Esplosivi Industriali Spa v Ordnance Technologies (UK) Ltd* [2007] EWHC 2875 (Ch). Here, the defendant had used the designs for multiple warhead systems, which it had obtained in a collaborative enterprise with the claimant, for purposes different from those originally contemplated by the parties. The end result would have been that weapons would have been made to those designs by third parties. That did not protect the defendant. It did not need to make the weapons itself, to infringe the UDR.

Primary infringement is, therefore, for commercial purposes, directly or indirectly making articles to the design, or making a design document for the purpose of enabling such articles to be made, without the UDR owner's permission, or authorising anyone else to do so (s 226(3)).

Secondary infringement includes importation, possessing for commercial purposes, selling and hiring, but is relevant only if the person had knowledge or reason to believe that the items were infringing items (s 227).

21.3.6 Remedies

Remedies are damages, injunctions, accounts of profits (s 229(1)), order for delivery up of infringing articles (s 230), and an order for disposal of infringing articles (s 231). Damages are not available against an innocent primary infringer (s 233), although other remedies are available. Innocence requires an absence of knowledge of the existence of the UDR and no reason to believe in its existence.

There is a provision providing remedies against groundless threats of infringement proceedings (s 253). The remedies are a declaration, injunction and damages.

By contrast with RDR, exclusive licensees have the same remedies available, concurrently with the owner of UDR.

21.3.7 Overlap with copyright

As we have seen in **Chapter 19**, a three-dimensional article cannot be protected by copyright unless it is itself an artistic object, typically either a sculpture or a 'work of artistic craftsmanship', or an engraving. The intention of the CDPA 1988 is to exclude from copyright protection any industrial or manufactured object that would itself not be protected by copyright. Thus, s 51 also excludes, from copyright protection, the use of any design *document* where an article has been made from that design. In other words, it is not possible to use copyright by the back door to protect the article in question by asserting the copyright in the design drawings (see **21.1.2**). It is simply not an infringement of any copyright that might exist in the design document (s 51(1)).

Instead, the creation of a three-dimensional article can only be protected by UDR, or by registered design right. It would, of course, have to meet the criteria for the design right in question. (Do not forget that if copyright does still apply to the article in question, the period of protection is shortened to 25 years from first production of the article if it is produced industrially – see s 52 and **19.2.4.2**.) The overall effect is that copyright protection is suppressed in favour of UDR protection.

Section 236 provides that any UDR that subsists in the article will be ignored if the article is protected by copyright. This would be the case if the article were, say, a sculpture. So, in this situation, copyright prevails (if in fact copyright does apply to the article – see s 51). The combined effect of s 51 and s 236 is to prevent overlap between copyright and design right protection.

By contrast, any registered design right can co-exist with the copyright in a three-dimensional article.

An interesting case that shows the working of s 51 is *Flashing Badge Co Ltd v Groves* [2007] EWHC 1372 (Ch). Here, the defendant had imported flat, flashing badges which were virtually identical to badges made by the claimant. The claimant owned copyright in the surface decoration on the badges. When this was asserted in infringement proceedings, the defendant raised s 51 as a defence, saying that the drawings on the face of the badges were designs for the creation of an article, the badge, and therefore protected by s 51(1). Rimer J held that the designs were surface decoration caught by s 51(3), which removed the disputed material outside the reach of being a 'design document' for the purposes of s 51(1). It was a straightforward copyright infringement.

21.3.8 Licences of right

In the last five years of the term of an unregistered design, anyone can apply for a licence to use the unregistered design (s 237). If terms cannot be agreed between the parties, then the terms are settled by the Designs Registry, which is part of the UK Intellectual Property Office (IPO).

21.3.9 Community unregistered design right – the CUD

Regulation 6/2002 introduced a Community unregistered design right. This right lasts for three years. However, it seems that the Community right is merely intended to protect registrable designs in the period before registration is applied for. In *Landor & Hawa International v Azure Designs* (see **21.3.2.1**), there was infringement of both design right and the Community unregistered design right.

In many respects, the CUD can be seen to be a short-term, interim form of protection with a dual purpose. It gives a short period of informal protection to many short-lived designs with commercial lives of not much more than three years. It also gives initial protection to many designs of longer commercial life, while consideration is given to obtaining more long-term protection by registration.

21.4 Semiconductor topography design right

It is no exaggeration to claim that the modern developed world is largely built around the computer. You will already realise that computer programs get literary copyright protection (see **19.2**). At the heart of computer operation is the integrated circuit or micro-chip, which is a tiny, complex pattern of hairsbreadth electrical circuits, formed by etching within a sandwich of insulating ('semiconducting') material. Under impetus from the USA, the European

Community turned its attention to the necessity to offer some protection to the designs of the circuits within these vital components, resulting in a European Council Directive on the matter in 1987.

The designs of the chips and their functioning manner had largely been patent-protected, but once that stage was achieved, the precise patterns of etched circuits would not be suitable for patent protection, as there is no inventive step involved in simply using chips to make the computers carry out different operations. Copyright protection is also largely removed by the effect of s 51 of the CDPA 1988. Design protection was the obvious solution, and the result is that a specialised application of informal protection by UDR is given to these circuits, by protecting the topography (the 'map') of the circuits.

The solution eventually arrived at is found in the Design Right (Semiconductor Topographies) Regulations 1989 (SI 1989/1100). The way protection is achieved is to use the framework of the UDR provisions in the CDPA 1988 and to make such amendments as are necessary for precise application to microchips. The basis for protection is, as with UDR, originality, not being commonplace and a qualifying situation for protection. The infringing and permitted acts are, however, rather different from those applicable to UDR and resemble, in many ways, the 'fair dealing' provisions that apply to copyright material. This is clearly in contemplation of the need for a general freedom to use the technology to its limits by encouraging analysis and further development. Ownership and duration are very similar to UDR, and the doctrine of exhaustion applies to any articles using the protected material once they are sold, hired or imported into the EC by, or with the licence of, the topography right owner. Further discussion of this area is beyond the scope of this work.

21.5 Registered and unregistered designs

A summary of registered and unregistered designs is provided in the table below.

	RDR	**UDR**
Statute	RDA 1949 as amended by Registered Designs Regulations 2001	CDPA 1988
Definition	Appearance of whole or part of a product resulting from features of, in particular: (a) lines (b) contours (c) colours (d) shape (e) texture or materials (f) ornamentation 'Product' includes packaging, get up, graphic symbols, typographic type-faces and visible parts	Any aspect of: (a) shape, or (b) configuration of the whole or part of an article NB no right subsists unless the design is recorded in a document or an article has been made to the design

	RDR	UDR
Originality	**New**: no identical design/design differing in only immaterial details has previously been made available to public, *and* **Individual character**: overall impression to informed user differs from that of any other design that has been made available to public, and **The design has not been made available to public:** ie not published, exhibited or used in the trade NB 12 months grace period	Must be **original**, ie must be: (a) **the result of independent effort** ie not copied, and (b) **not commonplace** in design field in question
Exclusions	(a) features solely dictated by technical function (b) interface (mechanical fittings only) (but modular designs are registrable)	(a) methods of construction (b) must fit (c) must match (d) surface decoration
Ownership	Commissioner; the employer; the designer, in that order	Commissioner; the employer; the designer, in that order
Duration	25 years in total (maximum)	The shorter of: (a) 15 years from the end of the year of creation/recording; or (b) 10 years from the end of the year of first sale/hire
Infringement	Making, offering, putting on market, importing or exporting any product incorporating the design or any design which does not produce a different overall impression. No need to prove copying NB private non-commercial acts are excluded	Primary: making articles to the design/making document for purposes of making articles. Need to prove copying: substantial similarity is enough. Secondary: import, sell, hire, offer, possess with knowledge/reason to believe is an infringing article.

Chapter 22
Patents

22.1 Introduction

Patents are monopoly rights granted by the Government to protect inventions under the Patents Act 1977 (PA 1977). If a patent is granted, the inventor gets a monopoly over use of his invention for (generally) 20 years (ie, he can stop anybody else using it for this time). The quid pro quo of getting a patent so far as the inventor is concerned is that before the patent is granted, details of the invention go on a public register at the Patent Office which everyone may study. So, a patented invention cannot be kept secret. The idea is that others should be able to learn from the patent. It contributes to the general body of technological understanding. After the 20 years are up, the invention is available for anyone to use, but the general thinking behind the new invention will have been available to the rest of the world for those 20 years, during which time the knowledge of how the invention works may have sparked ideas in the minds of other inventors.

The main justification for patents is that if there were no patents, commercial organisations would not invest in the research needed to produce new inventions or would keep the invention a secret. They need to have a chance to recoup their expenditure on the invention that is a success, as well as the time spent on abortive projects. The estimated cost of putting a new pharmaceutical product on the market is £200 million, and it takes about 12 years. A business will need to recover this cost from its product, hence patent protection is very important in the business world.

What is protected?	new invention
What benefit is there?	monopoly right
How is it obtained?	registration
How long does it last?	20 years from application

22.2 Obtaining a patent

The patent system is a 'first to file' system, not a 'first to invent'. In other words, the crucial step is the bureaucratic step of filing the application at the Patent Office. You may recall the tale of Elisha Gray, who filed his application for the telephone four hours later than Alexander Graham Bell. Bell therefore was awarded the patent by the US Supreme Court and became famous. Gray has been largely forgotten by history (but he in fact patented a telegraph system and founded the Western Electric Company, so do not feel too sorry for him).

A patent for the UK can be obtained:

(a) by applying to the UK Patent Office;

(b) by applying to the European Patent Office under the European Patent Convention ('EPC'); or

(c) via an international application under the Patent Co-operation Treaty 1970 ('PCT').

The PCT would be used, for example, if the proprietor of a US or Japanese patent was also seeking to apply for a patent in the UK. It would then be assigned the priority date of the non-UK patent (see **22.4.1**), which is one big advantage of an application through either the PCT or EPC. There are more than 100 countries which are members of the PCT, including most major centres of technology.

The EPC does not provide a true European Patent (but see below for developments on this aspect). It awards a bundle of national patents for countries which are parties to the EPC. Not all EPC patent applications will specify all the countries of the EPC. It is a European system, not an EU one, and encompasses countries that are not EU Member States (eg, Switzerland), though all the EU Member States are individual members of the EPC.

The cost of a European patent (EPC) is high, being about £31,000, as opposed to perhaps £2,000 plus VAT for drafting and filing a UK patent. The headquarters of the European Patent Office (EPO) are in Munich and its search branch is in The Hague.

The PCT 1970 is administered by the WIPO in Geneva. It provides for a single application and preliminary search. The WIPO then sends the application on to national offices for them to decide whether to award a patent for their territory.

There have been discussions at EU level for several years aimed at setting up a Community patent system. The discussions have been dogged by disputes over which languages can be used, and the role of the national patent offices. On 3 March 2003, the Member States finally agreed on the approach to be taken. The key areas are:

(a) the existing framework of the EPC should be utilised;

(b) the EPO would run the Community patent system;

(c) it would grant a patent 'for the territory of the Community';

(d) the EU as such will need to ratify the EPC, though all current members of the EU are individual members of the EPC;

(e) the full patent specification could be filed in any one of English, French or German at the European Patent Office with the claims, only, translated into the other two languages; and

(f) a court to be called 'the Community Intellectual Property Court' will be established by Council Regulation (this proposal has now been overtaken by events and will be some years yet in becoming a reality).

Patents can be categorised as 'product' patents, which claim the end product of a manufacturing process (eg, a new drug, or a better vacuum cleaner), or as 'process' patents, which claim the manufacturing process itself (eg, the method for making 'Gore-Tex' waterproofing for outdoor clothing). It would of course be sensible to try to patent both the product and the method of making it. This would have to be done in separate patents. At present, the Community patent framework is still moving through an extensive consultation stage and there is no immediate sign of a clear timescale for implementation. There are some indications that some major decisions could be taken by 2011, but it is thought that implementation could take six to eight years. The process has now evolved into a plan to create a 'Unified Patent Litigation System'. This may achieve some tangible form by 2013, but at present many stages of consultation and negotiation remain to be dealt with.

22.3 Patentability

An invention will be patentable if it satisfies four conditions. It must:

(a) be *new* (PA 1977, s (1)(a));

(b) constitute an *inventive step* (s 1(1)(b));

(c) be capable of *industrial application* (s 1(1)(c)); and

(d) not be within any of the *exclusions* in s 1(2).

22.3.1 New

Novelty is judged by reference to the 'state of the art' at the 'priority date' (see **22.4.1**). In essence, the question is: 'Is this new information, or can we find the information in an existing source?' Under Article 54(2) of the EPC:

> The state of the art shall be held to compromise everything made available to the public by means of a written or oral description, by use, or in any way, before the date of filing of the European patent application.

The information sources utilised would be:

(a) other granted patents or published applications, both UK and relevant foreign jurisdictions;

(b) published descriptions of relevant technology, eg in scientific journals or PhD theses; and

(c) existing products or processes that are in the public domain.

As a matter of practicality, these are matters known about within, or are accessible from, the jurisdiction. Third parties can bring material to the attention of the Patent Office when the application is published (see below).

So this involves a factual investigation (ie, has the invention been thought of before and has it been made public?). The investigation will be carried out by the Patent Office in its initial examination of the patent application. Third parties can also object after publication of the application by the Patent Office. The whole topic of novelty is also highly relevant in patent infringement actions, when the usual defence of the alleged infringer is to challenge the validity of the patent. This means that the topic of the prior art is examined again, but this time in retrospect, perhaps 20 years or more after the original patent application (see **22.8**). A common-form defence to infringement claims is that the patent should never have been granted in the first place and is invalid.

A problem that has arisen more significantly, since the EPC and the European patent system, is the uneasy relationship between the test for novelty and the exclusion, within s 1(2)(a) of the PA 1977, of the patentability of 'discoveries' (see **22.3.4**). Perhaps the greatest gain arising from (particularly) medical or pharmaceutical patents is that surprising and unexpected results can arise from their actual use; great progress can be achieved this way. Sometimes it is achieved by discoveries that radically different dosages bring about different effects. Is such a new development patentable? Is it an excluded 'discovery'? The EPC and the national courts have really taken the bull by the horns on this, and it is clear that many such developments are patentable, despite the prior disclosure of the drugs, etc in earlier patents. In *Actavis Ltd v Merck & Co Inc* [2008] EWCA Civ 444, the Court of Appeal held that novelty could be conferred by new dosage regimes or other forms of administration of a substance (known as 'Swiss-type' claims). This was in line with Article 52(4) of the EPC, and such claims were not simply excluded as discoveries or methods of treatment. Although this was a European patent matter, it is probably in line with the established English court approach, that a claim directed to the practical application of the technical effect of a discovery may well be patentable, as distinct from trying to patent the discovery itself.

The question is one of whether the invention has been 'disclosed' to the public before the date of filing of the application (or the priority date). It will only be treated as having been previously disclosed if there has been an 'enabling disclosure'. If there has been an enabling disclosure, the applicant will fail. As the term suggests, an enabling disclosure means a disclosure that would enable somebody to make the product, or work the process, as the case may be. The question the Patent Office asks is whether, at the priority date, a skilled worker could by observation or analysis reproduce the applicant's invention from the disclosure in question. So, if a newspaper reports that Professor X has created a new process for cloning sheep, this would not be an enabling disclosure. For it to be an enabling disclosure the report would have to describe the process in a way that would allow others to reproduce the invention. (A detailed scientific paper would undoubtedly give such information.)

In what circumstances might an enabling disclosure arise? In the case of product patents, disclosure of the product will usually be an enabling disclosure, especially where the invention is a mechanical device. An obvious example is where there is already a product on the market which discloses the invention. For example, if the patent application is for a bagless vacuum cleaner and there is already a bagless vacuum cleaner on the market. This is clearly an enabling disclosure, because anyone taking the vacuum cleaner apart can see how the invention works. Similarly, if a vacuum cleaner embodying the invention had been exhibited at a trade fair then this would be an enabling disclosure (but some trade fairs are specifically excluded under PA 1977). The enabling disclosure could arise from a third-party product where the third party had thought of the idea first. Alternatively, it could be the applicant for the patent marketing/ exhibiting his invention before the filing date. This is called 'self-publication'. So you can defeat your own application by showing the invention to the public prior to making your patent application.

In *Synthon BV v Smithklein Beecham plc* [2006] 1 All ER 685, HL, an interesting enabling disclosure was seen where the claimant had disclosed the nature of a chemical compound in an earlier initial patent application, which was not proceeded with. It was enough to have the defendant's later patent declared invalid.

In one case, the invention was a hay-raking machine in which the rake wheels were turned by contact with the ground rather than by an engine (*C Van der Lely NV v Bamfords Ltd* [1963] RPC 61). A photograph of the machine was printed in a newspaper. The question was whether the photograph was clear enough to show how the invention worked. If so, it was an enabling disclosure, and in this case it was held to be so.

In some cases the product may not disclose the invention. This would often be the case in relation to process patents. The end product of the patented process will not necessarily reveal the process itself. A consequence is that it may be possible to disclose the existence of a new product without showing how the process works. An example is *Quantel Ltd v Spaceward Microsystems Ltd* [1990] RPC 83, where the demonstration at an exhibition of a complex computer for creating visual effects on television would not have enabled someone to work out how it operated. Falconer J said in relation to this aspect:

> Demonstration of a prototype of the claimed invention at an exhibition where no-one was allowed near the actual machine and no engineering description was given, although individuals were allowed to use the stylus to draw a picture, could not possibly have been an enabling disclosure so as to anticipate any claim.

22.3.2 Inventive step

An invention might be new but it also needs to be a quantum leap over the existing technology. This second criterion for patentability is that the invention should involve an 'inventive step' (ie, it shows thinking which has not been seen before). The question asked here is whether the invention would be obvious to a somewhat unimaginative person skilled in the art, taking into account the state of the art at the priority date (see the *Vericore* case at **22.3.1**). The person skilled in the art here refers to the 'uninventive technician'. This is someone who is knowledgeable, but lacking that inventive spark. In the *Rockwater* case (see

22.6.3), Jacobs LJ described the uninventive skilled man thus: 'It is settled that this man, if real, would be very boring – a nerd.'

In using the 'uninventive technician', the following limitation was referred to by Aldous LJ in *Amersham Pharmacia Biotech AB v Amicon Ltd and Others* [2001] EWCA Civ 1042:

> A fiction in patent law is that the notional uninventive skilled man in the art is deemed to have read and assimilated any piece of prior art pleaded by the party attacking the patent claim ...
>
> The more distant a prior art document is from the field of technology covered by the patent, the greater the chance that an intelligent but uninventive person skilled in the art will fail to make the jump to the solution found by the patentee.

In other words, the prior art being used in an attempt to strike out a patent has to be highly relevant to the patent in question, rather than just anything, anywhere that just happens to cover the same matter but in a different application or use.

A widely-cited test is in *Windsurfing International Inc v Tabur Marine* [1985] RPC 59. Here, Oliver LJ described the test as having four stages:

(a) the court must identify the inventive concept embodied in the patent;

(b) it must assume the mantle of the normally skilled but unimaginative addressee in the art at the priority date and impute to him what was, at that date, common general knowledge in the art in question;

(c) it must identify what, if any, differences exist between the matters cited as being 'known or used' and the alleged invention; and

(d) it must ask itself whether, viewed without any knowledge of the alleged invention, those differences constituted steps which would have been obvious to the skilled man, or whether they required any degree of invention.

Put simply, what you have to do is, first, identify what the invention adds to the state of the art. If this new bit is not obvious to the uninventive technician then you have an inventive step.

Some useful guidance on this area is to be seen in *Generics (UK) Ltd v Lundbeck A/S* [2008] EWCA Civ 311, where a patentee brought infringement proceedings and the respondent generic drug manufacturer had raised defences of lack of novelty and inventive step. The Court of Appeal held that in ordinary product patents (as distinct from process patents), where the application satisfied the requirements of s 1, the product itself was the invention and the technical contribution to the world art is the product itself, rather than the process by which it was made. This was so, even if that process provided the only inventive step. In other words, the inventive step taken was in being able to make, for the first time, that new product. It did not matter if that manufacturing process had been used to make a thousand different earlier products; the first-instance judge had taken his eyes off the real invention, which was the new drug itself. The patentee's appeal succeeded.

The classic case was the 'sausage machine case' (*Williams v Nye* (1890) 7 RPC 62, CA). A patent was struck out for lack of inventive step because it was simply the combination of two known machines, a mincing machine and a sausage-filling machine. There were also arguments along these lines in the case of *Hickman v Andrews and Others* [1983] RPC 174, concerning infringement of the patent for the Black and Decker 'Workmate', invented by Ron Hickman. Clamping arrangements of this type were known before Ron Hickman invented the Workmate. However, the Court of Appeal upheld the patent.

In *IDA Ltd v Southampton University* [2006] EWCA Civ 145, the question of inventive step also decided the identity of the 'sole deviser' (and ownership) of a type of insect trap. Two fairly similar designs were only distinguishable because one inventor had used a new and different material. That was the inventive step.

Commercial success of the product is taken as being a good indicator of the patent having an inventive step. So is fulfilling a 'long felt want', that is, plugging a gap in the market. In other words, if it was such an obvious step from the existing technology, why had no one done it before the patentee had come up with his invention?

In *Biogen v Medeva* [1997] RPC 1, the House of Lords held:

> Anything inventive done for the first time was the result of adding a new idea to the existing stock of knowledge. If it was the idea of using established techniques to do something which no one had previously thought of doing, the inventive idea would be doing the new thing.

The question of inventive step is, of course, a question of fact in each case, and if there is no inventive step, the application will fail for 'obviousness' (see *Pozzoli SpA v BDMO SA* [2007] EWCA Civ 588 – an application for a storage device for CDs which failed for obviousness).

22.3.3 Industrial application

It must be possible to make the product/carry out the process. Patents are not about abstract ideas. The invention must be able to be put into practice. In effect, this requirement is taken care of by the exclusions in the PA 1977, s 1(2) and (3) (see **22.3.4**). There is a temptation to avoid disclosing too much detail about the invention, which may cause objections based upon insufficiency, as in *Rex v Arkwright* (1785) 1 WPC 64. There may also be objections that the device cannot be built or made to work at all. In *Duckett v Patent Office* [2005] EWHC 3140 (Pat), a perpetual motion device was rejected because its energy principle was contrary to all accepted views of physics. Its mechanical arrangement, linking a generator with a battery, failed for obviousness.

The desire to avoid too much information being disclosed at the early stage of a patent application often can cause problems of revocation applications, both on insufficiency (s 72(1)(c)), and on grounds of 'added material', (s 72(1)(d)). The latter happens where the matter disclosed in the specification extends beyond that disclosed in the filed application for the patent, ie 'drip-feeding' the information to the registry.

22.3.4 Exclusions

The exclusions are listed in s 1(2) and (3) of the 1977 Act:

> (2) It is hereby declared that the following (among other things) are not inventions for the purposes of this Act, that is to say, anything which consists of—
>
> (a) a discovery, scientific theory or mathematical method;
>
> (b) a literary, dramatic, musical or artistic work or any other aesthetic creation whatsoever;
>
> (c) a scheme, rule or method for performing a mental act, playing a game or doing business, or a program for a computer;
>
> (d) the presentation of information;
>
> but the foregoing provision shall prevent anything from being treated as an invention for the purposes of this Act only to the extent that a patent or application for a patent relates to that thing as such.
>
> (3) A patent shall not be granted for an invention the commercial exploitation of which would be contrary to public policy or morality.

Section 1(2)(a) deals with discoveries of natural phenomena. These have not been invented by any human, so are not patentable. The paragraph also excludes methods of doing things. In *Citibank NA v Comptroller-General of Patents* (ChD, 9 June 2006), a computerised method for checking, statistically, the accuracy of data inputted into systems was not excluded as a 'business method' within s 1(2)(c). It was, however, excluded as a 'mathematical method' by s 1(2)(a). The rationale for excluding methodology is to prevent attempts at monopolising the thinking process itself.

Section 1(2)(b) deals with aesthetic creations which are protected by another IP right, that is copyright (see **Chapter 19**).

Section 1(2)(c) deals with mental acts, as explained above. How would you know if someone else was performing the mental act in question? Obviously, you could not, so making such matters patentable would be impractical as well as undesirable.

The borderline between a non-patentable method and a patentable technical contribution to the known art is hard to discern. In *Aerotel Ltd v Telco Holdings Ltd; Macrossan's Patent Application (No 0314464.9)* [2006] EWCA Civ 1371, in a conjoined appeal, the Court held that an automated method of assembling documents required to incorporate a company was excluded methodology. By contrast, the other appeal was successful because it involved a new physical combination of hardware items. That comprised a technical contribution and was patentable. It brought about the effect of making a computer run at a higher speed.

Computer programs are also in theory excluded (s 1(2)(c). However, this does not actually mean that computer programs can never be patented. The tendency in recent years has been to grant patents to more and more computer programs. Very broadly, the test is whether the program has a 'technical effect', that is, has it a practical application? One example is *Vicom's Application* [1987] OJ EPO 14, where a program for doing computer-aided design (CAD) of engineering products was held to be patentable. This case has greatly influenced the approach to computer program patents in both European and UK applications. This is a very complex area, but it might be summarised by saying that, for a computer program to form part of a patent, it must bring about some effect or consequence that, itself, as distinct from the computer program, is new and shows an inventive step. This was applied to exclude *Macrossan's Patent Application*, referred to above.

The approach of the EPO has been more inclined toward granting computer patents since its decisions in two cases – *IBM/Computer Programs* (Case T-935/97) [1999] EPOR 301 and *IBM/Computer Programs* (Case T-1173/97) [1999] EPOR 219. The EPO technical board of appeal held that the 'technical effect' requirement simply meant that to be patentable, the application had to go beyond the mere routine operation of a computer.

As matters presently stand, the UK Patent Office considers that the correct and definitive approach has been expressed by the Court of Appeal in the *Aerotel Ltd/Macrossan* appeals case discussed above, because the Court considered and evaluated all relevant UK and EPO authorities. The Court took the view that the EPO practice to exclusions had not stabilised sufficiently to be a firm guide in itself. Jacob LJ, after considering the decisions of the EPO boards of appeal, had suggested a four-step approach to dealing with the exclusions within s 1(2). The steps are:

(a) properly construe the claim;

(b) identify the actual contribution to the known art;

(c) ask whether it falls solely within the excluded subject matter (if it does, that would exclude the application);

(d) check whether the actual or alleged contribution is actually technical in nature (if it is not, that would exclude it).

The Patent Office considers this to replace all previous tests applied to exclusion issues under s 1(2); it has been used in many applications since and seems to work well.

Section 1(2)(d) deals with presentation of information. This could not constitute an 'invention' in itself, but a new mechanism or process of presentation could be patented.

Genetic engineering inventions are patentable, and indeed are a major area of activity for patent agents and lawyers (see **22.3.2**). Also, producing new varieties of plants is protectable under the Plant Varieties Act 1997, which is outside the scope of this book. In the US case on gene engineering (*Diamond v Chakrabarty* 65 Law Ed (2d) 144 (1980)), the Supreme Court held that 'anything under the sun', apart from a human being, should be regarded as patentable. Directive 98/44/EC on legal protection of biotechnological inventions led to changes to the PA 1977, by way of the Patent Regulations 2000 (SI 2000/2037), to take account of technical progress in this field.

22.4 The patent specification

The documents required for filing an application are a request for grant and the patent specification. A request for grant is what it says it is: a document asking for a patent to be granted. The specification contains three sections: an abstract, the description and the claims.

The abstract is a summary which is used for reference purposes (essentially this allows the Patent Office to decide who has the specialism to deal with the application). The description must disclose the invention sufficiently for it to be performed by a skilled person. Obviously, this may be a very lengthy section where the invention is complex.

The claims indicate the extent of the patent applied for. It is this section which will be used in the event of the patent (assuming it is granted) being enforced in court: the patent owner has protection only over the matters listed in the claims.

The description and the claims must be a consistent match for each other. A case needs to be shown for the grant of a patent, in particular that there has been an inventive step above and beyond the existing technology.

A patent specification is a complex technical and legal document. A patent agent normally drafts it. This is someone with a scientific or engineering qualification, depending on the particular field they are working in. The costs of drafting a specification and dealing with the initial filing of the application are about £2,000 plus VAT. If there are queries from the patent examiner in the Patent Office then this will increase that cost.

If the patent is granted then it is the claims that define the scope of the monopoly granted to the inventor. The analogy of a fence is sometimes used. The idea is that the claims form a fence that surrounds the area which the inventor claims as his own. For someone to be liable for patent infringement, it is enough to infringe one claim in the patent specification (ie, to have crossed the fence in only one place).

In drafting the claims, the aim is to include all possible alternatives, whilst excluding those that already exist or are obvious. If an alternative is omitted, a competitor could claim that to be their own invention, or could use the gap to exploit the technology themselves. On the other hand, if too much is said in the claims, one danger is that improvements in the technology may not be patentable when they arise in the future. The reason is that a patent specification itself becomes part of the state of the art once it is published, so a new application would have to show that it has achieved an inventive step over the previous patent.

The first claim will be the widest. It will state the invention claimed in fairly general terms. Subsequent claims refine the first claim. Each claim usually narrows the invention down a bit. The final claims usually describe the commercial product that is going to be on the market.

The idea is that the wider the area of technology which is claimed, the further away the patent owner can keep rival inventors. In patent litigation, an inevitable area of dispute is that some of the patent claims are too wide and need to be narrowed, or struck out, as being unjustifiable.

The invention must be described in enough detail to allow a person with the requisite skills to carry out the invention. So, if the patent is for interleaving chocolate and ice-cream, the specification must describe the process in sufficient detail to allow a skilled ice cream maker to set up the process. See the cases on 'sufficiency' at **22.3.3** and also *Schering-Plough Ltd v Norbrook Laboratories Ltd* [2005] EWHC 2532 (Pat), where a patent was revoked because much more research was needed to make the invention work. A patent specification which is refused on this ground is said to lack 'sufficiency'. In *European Central Bank v Document Security Systems Inc* [2008] EWCA Civ 192, a European patent for producing security documents, such as shares or banknotes, that were copy-proof, was held to be invalid. It was only possible to work the invention by adding material not disclosed by the original application.

You should be aware of the difference between this and manufacturing 'know-how'. Manufacturing know-how is the extra tricks of the trade that help you make the process run with greatest efficiency. For example, it might be the speed of the production line to get the most cost-effective results, how much air to blow into the ice-cream, or the temperature at which the room should be maintained. So, even though the patent specification describes the basic invention, the know-how is often also needed for a licensee because it makes it economically feasible to set up and run the process.

22.4.1 The priority date

The 'first to file' basis of the patent system increases the pressure to be the first person to reach the Patent Office with an application.

Normally, the application or 'filing' date is the patent's priority date. The priority date is the date on which we judge whether the invention is new. The usual reason for the priority date being earlier than the date the papers were filed is that the proprietor is claiming priority from an earlier overseas patent under one of the international conventions (see **22.2**). (An alternative reason, which is much less common, is that the PA 1977, s 15 allows the inventor to file an 'outline application' at an early stage in order to secure an early priority date. The outline application will be less detailed than a full application. A full application must be filed within 12 months.)

22.4.2 Timescale

The Patent Office takes about 18 months to do the initial examination. It is then published as an application and is on the public register (ie, the invention can no longer be kept secret). Third parties then have the opportunity to object to the grant of the patent. If there are no major problems then the patent will be granted six months or so after publication, that is two years after filing the papers. This period counts as part of the 20-year period for the life of the patent. If there is a major problem that delays grant of the patent, the useful life of the patent once granted could be severely reduced. However, the maximum period between publication and grant of the patent is now 36 months. In addition, there can be other regulatory problems which reduce the useful life of the patent, such as obtaining permission to market a new pharmaceutical product, or plant protection product. There are EU provisions which allow for an extension of up to five years to the life of a pharmaceutical patent (Regulation 1768/92), or to the life of a patent for a plant protection product (Regulation 1610/96). These are intended to compensate for the regulatory delays.

22.5 Who is entitled to grant of a patent?

The general rule is that the inventor is the first person entitled (s 7(2)). The inventor is the person who devised the invention. This can be more complicated than it seems, for example if there are multiple parties involved (eg, *Henry Bros (Magherafelt) Ltd v Ministry of Defence* [1999] RPC 442, where the Court of Appeal held that the test was to determine who had contributed to the main concept of the invention). This was applied in *IDA Ltd v Southampton University* [2006] EWCA Civ 145 (see **22.3.2**).

22.5.1 Employees

Under the PA 1977, s 39(1), if the inventor is an employee, the patent will belong to the employer if the invention is made in the course of the employee's normal duties, provided an invention might reasonably be expected to result from his duties. This is also the outcome if he owes the employer a special duty (eg, a director's duty to his company). In *Greater Glasgow Health Board's Application* [1996] RPC 207, it was held that a hospital doctor who had invented a new device for examining eyes owned the invention himself. He was employed to treat patients, not to invent, so the invention did not belong to his employer.

The rule is slightly different from the rule for ownership of copyright (see **19.2.5**) but the result is similar. Copyright also does not have any equivalent of the provision relating to employees with a special duty (PA 1977, s 39(1)(b)).

Another important difference is that PA 1977, s 42 does not allow contracting out of these provisions. With copyright there is nothing to stop the employer from putting a provision in the contract of employment that all copyright relevant to the employer's business will belong to the employer. With patents, any such provision would be void. However, there is nothing to stop the employer drafting the job description to emphasise that the employee is employed to make inventions. Also, the employer is still entitled to enforce contractual or common law confidentiality requirements (s 42(3)).

22.5.2 Compensation for employee inventors

Under the PA 1977, s 40, an employee who invents something may be entitled to compensation where the patent belongs to the employer. This is the case if:

(a) having regard among other things to the size and nature of the employer's undertaking, the invention or the patent for it (or the combination of both) is of outstanding benefit to the employer; and

(b) it is just that compensation is awarded.

The statutory test is awkward to apply in practice because the criterion is the benefit of the patent or the invention, not the benefit the product which was sold in the marketplace. In the case of *Garrison's Patent* [1997] CIPA 297, an invention which provided 2%–3% of the turnover of a small company was held not to be of outstanding benefit, and therefore no compensation was awarded.

In determining the amount of compensation, s 41 gives guidance, including factors listed in s 41(3) (eg, the nature of the employee's duties and the amount of his remuneration).

Disputes of this type are often settled, and recorded cases are rare (but see **22.10**).

22.6 Infringement

22.6.1 Definition of infringment

Infringement arises where a third party engages in the acts prohibited under the PA 1977, s 60. As patents are national rights, to infringe a UK patent the prohibited acts have to occur within the UK:

> **60 Meaning of infringement**
>
> (1) Subject to the provisions of this section, a person infringes a patent for an invention if, but only if, while the patent is in force, he does any of the following things in the United Kingdom in relation to the invention without the consent of the proprietor of the patent, that is to say—
>
> (a) where the invention is a product, he makes, disposes of, offers to dispose of, uses or imports the product or keeps it whether for disposal or otherwise;

(b) where the invention is a process, he uses the process or he offers it for use in the United Kingdom when he knows, or it is obvious to a reasonable person in the circumstances, that its use there without the consent of the proprietor would be an infringement of the patent;

(c) where the invention is a process, he disposes of, offers to dispose of, uses or imports any product obtained directly by means of that process or keeps any such product whether for disposal or otherwise.

You should note the distinction between infringing acts for a product patent and for a process patent; s 60(1)(b) requires actual or imputed knowledge of infringement, whereas s 60(1)(a) and (c) do not. However, even with a process patent, dealing with the products of that process will be infringement even though the products themselves are not patented.

Section 60(2) makes it an offence to supply or offer to supply 'any means ... for putting the invention into effect'. So, in *Lacroix Duarib SA v Kwikform (UK) Ltd* [1998] FSR 493, the supply of a kit of parts would have infringed the claims in a patent for the completed article.

22.6.2 How do you judge if infringement has occurred?

The first thing to establish is whether the allegedly infringing product or process comes within one of the claims in the patent specification. That is, has the third party crossed the 'fence line' which is constituted by the claims and stepped on to the patentee's monopoly? It is enough for patent infringement if one of the patent claims is infringed.

Sometimes a supposed infringement is not what it seems to be. In *Novartis AG v Ivax Pharmaceuticals UK Ltd* [2007] EWCA Civ 971, the patentee had a patent for making a 'microemulsion' of a drug which was very resistant to solution in water. The defendant was not an infringer when it managed to achieve the same effect by dispersing tiny particles of the drug in a liquid which was not a microemulsion (ie there was no 'oil in water' carrier).

The first claim is often the most important as it will be the broadest. So a patent for a Dyson vacuum cleaner might have as its first claim that it sucks up dust and other particles using a cyclone of air. Later claims would then be more specific about how it achieves this. So why bother with the other claims that narrow this first claim down? The reason is that when you sue somebody for patent infringement, they will invariably counterclaim by saying that the patent is invalid. The patentee then has to defend his claims, particularly in relation to novelty and inventive step (see **22.3**). (The 'infringer' will go digging round in the prior art to try to find reasons why the patent should never have been granted in the first place.) The broader the claim, the more difficult it is to defend. So that is why you have the narrower claims too. If claim 1 falls by the wayside, you may still be able to defend one of the later claims. It is only necessary to show infringement of one claim to succeed against the infringer.

22.6.3 Interpreting the claims in the patent specification

How does the court approach the interpretation of the claims? The court takes a 'middle road' between interpreting the claims strictly, ie literally, and taking into account what the patentee must have intended. Although the courts are said to be taking the 'purposive' approach from *Catnic Components Ltd and Another v Hill & Smith Ltd* [1982] RPC 183, they tend to be a lot less generous to patentees than this might suggest. In effect, the courts tend to hold the view that if the patentee meant to cover a particular variation then he should have claimed it expressly. (It should be remembered that *Catnic* was decided under the PA 1949. It concerned a patent for steel lintels for use above doors and windows. The patent claimed a right angle in the cross-sectional shape of the lintel. The defendant's lintel was 4–5 degrees away from a right angle, but was still held to infringe.)

Improver Corporation and Others v Remington Consumer Products Ltd and Others [1990] FSR 181 was a case which reformulated the test. This was the case about the 'Epilady' device for removing hair. Here, the patented device featured a rotating spring mechanism. The defendant's device performed the same task, but a rubber tube mechanism with slits removed the hairs.

Hoffmann J restated the issues as two of fact and one of construction:

(a) Does the variant have a material effect upon the way the invention works? If so, the variant is outside the claim. If not . . .

(b) Would this (ie, that the variant had no material effect) have been obvious at the date of publication of the patent to a reader skilled in the art? If not, the variant is outside the claim. If so . . .

(c) Would the reader skilled in the art nevertheless have understood from the language of the claim that the patentee intended that strict compliance with the primary meaning was an essential requirement of the invention? If so, the variant is outside the claim.

There was held to be no infringement. It is regarded as an example of poor drafting by the patent agent, who apparently did not draft the first claim widely enough to catch the rubber tube variation but restricted it to a helical spring. This is a good illustration of how patent infringement litigation hinges on the precise wording of the claims in the patent specification (see also *Vericore* at **22.3.1**).

The distinctions made can be very fine indeed. In *Archibald Kenrick & Sons Ltd v Laird Security Hardware Ltd* [2006] EWHC 1675 (Ch), an amended claim showing the range and direction of movement of an internal bolt for sliding window panels was upheld. It had a material effect on how the system worked.

It is in the extension of the *Improver* questions away from the area of mechanical devices to chemical compounds that greatest difficulties have arisen. The Court of Appeal has re-affirmed the *Improver* approach in *Wheatley v Drillsafe Ltd* [2001] RPC 133, though the tests are now referred to as the 'Protocol questions', after the Protocol on the interpretation of Article 69 of the European Patent Convention (see **22.2**). This corresponds to the PA 1977, s 125(1), on how to interpret the word 'invention'. In *Kirin-Amgen Inc v Hoechst Marion Roussel Ltd* [2004] UKHL 46, a case concerning genetic engineering, Lord Hoffmann said that it was important to distinguish between two matters. On the one hand, there were the guidelines set out in *Improver Corp* for deciding whether or not equivalent technology fell within the scope of the relevant patent claims. On the other hand, there was the principle of purposive construction established by *Catnic*. *Catnic* was expressed to be the bedrock of patent construction. It was important that the patentee be given the full extent, but no more than that, of the monopoly which the person skilled in the art would think he was intending to claim in the patent specification.

This question, of the precise range of monopoly claimed by the patentee, came up in the *Novartis AG* case mentioned in **22.6.2**. In *M-Systems Flash Disk Pioneers Ltd v Trek 2000 International Ltd* [2008] EWHC 102 (Pat), Kitchin J confirmed that the correct approach to interpretation of a patent specification is that it is to be read, as a whole, through the eyes of a skilled person, giving the words a purposive construction. See this case at **22.6.4** on revocation.

On the construction of the claims generally, in *Dyson Appliances Ltd v Hoover* [2001] EWCA Civ 1440, [2002] RPC 42, the Court of Appeal said that this was a matter for the judge. Evidence as to the factual situation was helpful, especially to explain the technology, but it was not acceptable to have expert witnesses who gave their own interpretation of the meaning of the claims.

It is also worth noting the words of the Court of Appeal in *Scanvaegt International AS v Pelcombe Ltd* [1998] FSR 786:

> lack of clarity ... can result in the patentee being unable to establish infringement. If you cannot define the invention claimed, you cannot conclude that it is being used.

As an illustration of the detail into which patent litigation goes, in the case of *Rockwater v Technip France SA* [2004] EWCA 381 the dispute hinged on the meaning of the words 'last means for guiding the flexible conduit' in claim 3 of the patent in question. It was held that the defendant's ship did infringe the words in claim 3, and therefore the patent. (The patent concerned technology for laying pipes at sea.)

22.6.4 Amendments to the specification, invalidity and revocation

There is a very close connection between a patentee claiming infringement and the possibility of counterclaims that the patent is invalid for some reason and should be revoked. If the patent is invalid, it should not have been granted, and consequently there cannot have been an infringement. It does not follow that revocation proceedings cannot take place without infringement claims, but the two claims often go together; also, the Comptroller of Patents can revoke a patent on his own initiative, under s 73.

The only grounds for revocation are found s 72(1) and are:

(a) the invention is not a patentable invention (failure to comply with ss 1–4);

(b) the patent was granted to a person who was not entitled to that patent (failure to comply with s 7);

(c) the specification of the patent did not disclose the invention clearly enough and completely enough for it to be performed by a person skilled in the art (insufficiency);

(d) the matter disclosed in the specification extends beyond that disclosed in the patent application as filed ('added matter', forbidden by s 76);

(e) the protection conferred by the patent has been extended by an amendment which should not have been allowed (also forbidden by s 76).

These are the only grounds on which the validity of a patent may be 'put in issue' (s 74(3)), and the only proceedings in which validity can be raised are limited by s 74(1). It is not possible, for example, simply to seek only a declaration as to the validity or invalidity of a patent (s 74(2)). Validity can be put in issue in infringement cases (by way of defence), in proceedings for groundless threats of infringement or declarations of non-infringement, in revocation proceedings or in disputes as to Crown use under s 58. This greatly reduces the possibilities for unjustified claims or proceedings.

In infringement or revocation proceedings where validity is in issue, there is a limited power, under s 75, to allow the proprietor of the patent to amend the specification to try to bring the patent to a state of validity. In no circumstances can an amendment be permitted that results in the specification disclosing added matter, or which extends the protection conferred by the patent (s 76(3)). Many recent cases have involved disputes about material added on amendments (usually to try to overcome 'inventive step' or 'sufficency' problems).

22.7 Infringers

The acts listed in s 60 (see **22.6.1**) would cover those making a product, using a process or disposing of the product of a process. Section 60 covers disposing and keeping, so would cover all the parties in a supply chain, even including the ultimate customer. Do not forget that the acts have to take place in the UK for there to be infringement of a UK patent. In the case of *Stena Rederi Aktiebolag and Another v Irish Ferries Ltd* [2002] EWHC 737 (Ch), [2002] RPC 990; [2003] EWCA Civ 66, [2003] RPC 36, the infringing article, a high-speed passenger ship, came into UK waters for periods of only three hours at a time. The defendants were able to use the provisions in the PA 1977, s 60(5)(d), which give exemptions for temporary entry into the UK of ships and aircraft.

If protection outside of the UK is required, applications in other countries should be made for foreign patents (there are of course the options of applying for a European Patent or patents under the PCT).

22.8 Defences

The first possible defence is that the patentee has consented to the use by granting a licence.

The chief line of defence is an attack on the validity of the patent, in part or in total, as described at **22.6.4**. If the patent can be proved to be invalid, or at least some claims can be struck out, then the defendant could not be liable for having infringed an invalid claim.

Patent litigation can, however, become extremely complex and costly, and a very good example of this can be seen in *Edwards Lifesciences AG v Cook Biotech Incorporated* [2009] EWHC 1304 (Pat), and the subsequent costs hearing at [2009] EWHC 1443. This case illustrates how revocation proceedings and infringement claims interact, often at great expense to the parties, and also shows how easy it is for litigation to get somewhat out of control. Edwards ('E') initially sought revocation of a patent registered to Cook ('C'). C counterclaimed that E had infringed its patent by manufacturing a bio-prosthetic, implantable heart valve (C did not manufacture such things). A preliminary issue was ordered to be tried as to whether a product description, which accompanied the sold valves, could properly be described as confidential. The reason for this was that E was being asked to disclose this material for the purposes of the litigation to independent experts acting for C. The court gave its directions on this matter at [2008] All ER (D) 368 (Jul), broadly protecting the material. During the trial of the claim and counterclaim, C originally maintained that all 34 of its claims made in respect of the invention had independent validity; on being required to serve the details of these by the court, the number was reduced to 25. Eventually, just nine claims were considered by the court. The consequence of this was to greatly increase the costs incurred by E.

During the trial, C persisted in seeking disclosure of many documents, which the court subsequently held were irrelevant to the issues, further increasing the legal costs incurred by E. Subsequently, it was held that much of this disclosure was neither necessary nor proportionate. E won on its main points, that C's patent was not valid and that therefore E could not have infringed it, so C's counterclaim failed. Nevertheless, E was held to have failed on a number of the points that it had made, or had withdrawn them. The judge in the costs hearing ordered a reduction of 20% in the costs awarded to E, to reflect those points argued unsuccessfully by E.

A major use for trainees in an IP department is to have them spend weeks in the bowels of the libraries looking for documents on the topic in question which have been date stamped with a date earlier than the priority date. The patentee is fixed with such knowledge in any language, provided the document is within the jurisdiction. The documents may help to strike out some or all of the claims of the patent.

Another defence is that the alleged infringer is in fact a co-owner of the patent, and therefore is entitled to work the patent himself (PA 1977, s 36).

The use in question could be the subject of an implied licence under the patent. Likewise, repair of a patented product is not infringement of the patent. However, reconditioning the patented article may be regarded as going too far and be an infringing act.

Defences may be raised, relying on EU rules for free movement of goods. Goods sold on other markets by the patentee or its licensees may be parallel imported into the UK from other EU Member States, under Articles 34 and 36 of the Treaty on the Functioning of the European Union. The cases that arise usually concern pharmaceuticals, which are high-value items and often have their price regulated by national governments (eg, *Centrafarm BV and Adrian de Peijper v Sterling Drug Inc* (Case 15/74) [1974] ECR 1147). The exercise of patent rights was held to be incompatible with the free movement of goods in that case. (Centrafarm bought a

Sterling product in the UK and re-sold it in The Netherlands for twice the UK price.) In such circumstances, the patentee's rights are said to be exhausted. See generally **27.5** and **27.6**.

The PA 1977 provides for two general defences in s 60(5):

> An act which, apart from this subsection, would constitute an infringement of a patent for an invention shall not do so if—
>
> (a) it is done privately and for purposes which are not commercial;
>
> (b) it is done for experimental purposes relating to the subject matter of the invention.

The activities in s 60(5) are regarded as being for the public good, and therefore the patent system should not be a restraint. The type of activities covered include research by scientists in universities and research institutes.

Section 64 allows a defence of prior use where the defendant was using the relevant technology before the priority date. In practice, this is a very limited defence, as you cannot expand your use, only go on using the process or product exactly as you did before the priority date.

22.9 Remedies

Under s 61, the claimant may seek:

(a) an injunction restraining the defendant;

(b) an order for delivery up or destruction of the offending goods;

(c) damages;

(d) an account of profits (but not as well as damages); or

(e) a declaration that the patent is valid and has been infringed by the defendant.

Section 62 states that damages may not be awarded against an innocent infringer. See s 62(1) for the rules on notice to persons who claim innocent infringement.

Section 72 allows the court or the Patent Office to revoke a patent on the grounds of failing to meet the criteria for patentability in s 1(1). Section 75 allows for the amendment of patents under the control of the court or the Patent Office (see **22.6.4**).

You need to beware of a threats action under the PA 1977, s 70. This is where the patentee can be held liable for a threat to sue someone for patent infringement if the threat turns out to be unjustified. The person threatened can sue for a declaration (that the threats are not justifiable), injunction and damages. An example of such an action is *Cintec International v Parkes* [2003] EWHC 2328. There, the patent proprietor alleged, without justification, that C's process infringed P's patents for water-filled bags for suppressing the effects of explosions. C was granted an order restraining P. Consequently, initial letters in patent disputes are very restrained! There is also a similar provision in relation to various IP rights (see **18.12**, **21.2.10** and **21.3.6**).

Chapter 23
Basics of the Law of Confidential Information

23.1 Introduction to the law of confidential information

Basically, the law will uphold a person's obligation to keep a secret, in certain circumstances. The law of confidence is not an IP right in a pure sense but is often classified with some of the mainstream rights. For example, maintaining confidentiality before submitting a patent application is vital to avoid destruction of the invention's novelty.

On the other hand, the law here can give protection in its own right. For example, the owner of confidential information relating to a product or process may decide to keep this 'know-how' secret, rather than formalise matters by seeking patent protection. The benefit of this is that a well-guarded secret may be protected indefinitely, rather than simply for the limited period afforded to IP rights (eg, 20 years for patents).

Case law rather than statute has governed and shaped the law of confidence and, as you would expect, the vast majority of cases relate to circumstances where express obligations of confidence are lacking and implied duties of confidentiality have to be considered. It is, however, important to remember that express obligations can (and often should) be imposed (eg, on key employees or independent contractors). See, for example, *Attorney-General v Observer Ltd and Others; Attorney-General v Times Newspapers Ltd and Another* [1990] AC 109, which concerned the book *Spycatcher* written by Peter Wright, an ex-employee of the security services. However, even an express confidentiality agreement may not be upheld by the court. For example, in *London Regional Transport v Mayor of London* [2003] EMLR 4, the Court of Appeal upheld the decision not to prevent publication of the report in question, as publication was held to be in the public interest.

So, what is the legal basis for giving such valuable protection? The principle arises from the equitable jurisdiction of the court to restrain unconscionable behaviour, where such behaviour may result in damage to a person. An early example is seen in the well-known case of *Prince Albert v Strange* (1849) 1 Mac & G 25, where an attempt was made by unscrupulous persons to show to the public some etchings, which were committed to a printer for the private purposes of Queen Victoria and the Prince Consort. This case set an early precedent by showing a readiness to injunct third-party recipients of confidential information or matter, within the court's discretion. The courts have been ready, ever since, to entertain such proceedings and to give a remedy, in appropriate cases.

Another factor that has supervened upon this area has been the way in which the European Convention on Human Rights has required English courts, via the Human Rights Act 1998, to deal with the Convention rights of respect for private life and freedom of expression (Articles 8 and 10). These matters have certainly made a subtle alteration to the way in which such applications to the court are dealt with, and pleaded, in the first place, but this chapter will attempt to give an overview of the way in which the courts deal with purely commercial-type disputes about confidentiality, rather than extending to a broad survey of the more rights-based claims (see **23.4** for these matters). The fairly consistent approach of the English courts in commercial/business confidence matters is somewhat easier to grasp and to explain than the more contentious interplay between individual rights and freedoms shown in the HRA 1998 claims.

The whole area has been given considerable publicity, in recent times, by the Michael Douglas and Catherine Zeta-Jones wedding photographs litigation, which raised the interesting point of whether there could be an analogous type of confidential material in photographs, intended for mass publication, but through only one intended publicity outlet (see **23.4** and *Douglas and Others v Hello! Ltd and Others (No 3)* [2007] 2 WLR 920). A person obtained surreptitiously taken photographs, knowing that this was in breach of all rules concerning the occasion. Aspects of this case will be mentioned at points where some of the basic elements of confidentiality are discussed below.

What is protected?	secret information
What benefit is there?	protects against unauthorised disclosure
How is it obtained?	arises automatically (no registration)
How long does it last?	indefinitely

23.2 The elements of confidentiality

The case of *De Maudsley v Palumbo and Others* [1996] FSR 447 demonstrates the difficulties faced by a claimant where no express obligation of confidentiality has been imposed. The facts related to the Ministry of Sound, the celebrated nightclub in Southeast London. The case report states:

> At a supper party held on November 1, 1989 between the plaintiff, the first defendant and the latter's girlfriend, the plaintiff communicated to the first defendant his idea for a night club which he claimed had five novel features:
>
> (1) it would be legally open all night long;
>
> (2) of large size with decor of a 'high tech industrial' warehouse style;
>
> (3) it would have separate areas for dancing, resting and socialising, and a VIP lounge;
>
> (4) an enclosed dance area of acoustic design ensuring excellent sound quality, light and atmosphere, with no leakage of those elements beyond its environment; and
>
> (5) it would employ top disc jockeys from the United Kingdom and around the world.

In the autumn of 1991 the defendants opened a nightclub called the Ministry of Sound, featuring some but not all of the plaintiff's ideas. The plaintiff was excluded from the project and subsequently sued for (inter alia) breach of confidence.

The judge (Knox J) relied on the three-point test from *Coco v AN Clark (Engineers) Ltd* [1969] RPC 41:

(a) Did the information have the necessary quality of confidence about it?

(b) Was the information imparted in circumstances importing an obligation of confidence?

(c) Was there any unauthorised use of the information?

23.2.1 Did the information have the necessary quality of confidence about it?

In the *De Maudsley* case, Knox J stated:

> Before the status of confidential information can be achieved by a concept or an idea, it is necessary to have gone far beyond identifying a desirable goal. A considerable degree of preliminary development of a definite product needs to be shown.

He found that the plaintiff's ideas were too vague to constitute confidential information.

He also found that, in order to merit protection, the idea must contain some element of originality. He took each element of the plaintiff's proposal, and criticised them for lack of novelty and/or vagueness.

Knox J accepted Hirst J's analysis in *Fraser and Others v Thames Television Ltd and Others* [1984] 1 QB 44 of the requirements for a literary, creative or entertainment idea to be protected as confidential information. This case concerned use of the law of confidential information to protect an idea for a television series about a female pop group. (Copyright will not protect a mere idea in these circumstances, see *Green v Broadcasting Corporation of New Zealand* [1989] 2 All ER 1086, which concerned the format for a game show.)

Hirst J said that the idea must:

(a) contain some element of originality;

(b) be clearly identifiable (as an idea of the confider);

(c) be of potential commercial attractiveness; and

(d) be sufficiently well developed to be capable of actual realisation.

In the *Douglas* case (see **23.1**), the highly valuable photographic rights to the wedding, and the resulting photographs, were held to be proper matters in which a quality of confidence would arise. This would extend to the wedding occasion itself having an obligation of confidence, so far as photography was concerned. All guests were under strict obligation in this respect, and this was enforced by security staff.

23.2.2 Was the information imparted in circumstances importing an obligation of confidence?

The problem here for the plaintiff in *De Maudsley* was that the relevant occasion on which he had imparted the information was a social one, not a business context. The plaintiff acknowledged in his evidence that he had deliberately refrained from explaining that the information was confidential, 'because [he] did not want to blow the deal there and then'. Lastly, there was no accepted trade practice in this area to substantiate the plaintiff's claim.

Failure to make confidentiality clear also caused the claimant's case to fail in *Shaw v API Group plc* (QBD District Registry (Manchester)), 10 April 2008, WL.

See *Vitof Ltd v Altoft* [2006] EWHC 1678, where computer source code, created in contemplation of the incorporation of a company which would exploit the code commercially, was held to have been imparted under an obligation of confidence.

This requirement can also extend to persons who obtain information in circumstances where they know or have reason to believe that they should not have it. This can be seen in cases such as the *Douglas* case and *Prince Albert v Strange* (see **23.1**). In the case of the photographer at the Douglas wedding, he knew at all times that what he was doing was a serious breach of trust.

In *Northern Rock plc v Financial Times Ltd* [2007] EWHC 2677 (QB), a highly confidential memorandum came into the hands of various publishing organisations. Financial Times Ltd published the whole memorandum, but others published only extracts. Northern Rock contended that the memorandum had been leaked by an employee in breach of his or her contract. An injunction was granted to prevent further publication of the full memorandum but not of the small, extracted parts that had already been widely circulated. There was detailed commercial information in the full document, and the public interest lay in enforcing the duties of confidence in the report.

23.2.3 Was there any unauthorised use of the information?

Here, the judge in *De Maudsley* held that the plaintiff's ideas and the defendants' club did not overlap to a sufficient degree to constitute unauthorised use.

The plaintiff's action therefore failed on all three counts. However, the judge summarised the situation as follows:

> Mr de Maudsley was in my view rather shabbily treated in that he was encouraged to think that he would be part of the enterprise but was only told that this would not be so, long after Mr Palumbo and Mr Waterhouse had decided, almost certainly justifiably because of Mr de Maudsley's rather difficult character and limited abilities, that he would not be included in their project.

The moral of the story is not to rely upon an implied duty of confidence. It is far better to inject certainty into the situation with the use of a written confidentiality agreement.

In *Cray Valley Ltd v Deltech Europe Ltd and Others* [2003] EWHC 728 (Ch), an action for breach of confidence in relation to the manufacture of industrial resins failed. There were no express undertakings of confidence by the former employees in question. It was held that the information did not have the necessary quality of confidence, not least as much of it had been published already and was easy to reverse engineer. It was not imparted in circumstances importing an obligation of confidence, but merely in the normal running of a factory, without any express instructions to employees to treat it as confidential. A claim for breach of copyright did succeed. See also *HRH Prince of Wales v Associated Newspapers Ltd* [2006] EWCA Civ 1776, [2008] Ch 57.

23.3 Remedies and their availability

The most important measure will often be an injunction to prevent disclosure of the information, that is, a restraining order in advance. Once the information has been released it is usually too late to seek an injunction (but see *Northern Rock plc v Financial Times Ltd* at **23.2.2**). However, an injunction may be granted in regard to confidential information that is of commercial value where:

(a) there are two rival businesses and not to grant an injunction would give the wrong-doer an advantage (eg, *Speed Seal Products Ltd v Paddington and Another* [1986] 1 All ER 91); or

(b) the 'springboard' doctrine applies, ie where one business would gain an unfair advantage over its rivals because of unauthorised disclosure to it of commercial information (eg, *Terrapin Ltd v Builders' Supply Co (Hayes) Ltd* [1967] RPC 375; *Roger Bullivant v Ellis* [1987] FSR 172). The court will try to prevent such advantage, by injunction, where appropriate (see **23.3.1**).

Compensatory damages are available for breach of confidence (see *Seager v Copydex Ltd* [1967] 2 All ER 415).

An account of the defendant's profits is also possible (see *Peter Pan Manufacturing Corporation v Corsets Silhouette Ltd* [1964] 1 WLR 96).

An order for delivery up, or destruction under oath, of the offending document or articles made by use of the information is also possible (see *Industrial Furnaces Ltd v Reaves and Another* [1970] RPC 605).

23.3.1 Whether remedy is available

It will be clear, by now, that the law of confidential information rests upon the equitable jurisdiction to prevent unconscionable use of confidential information; any remedies or reliefs are available only as a matter of the court's discretion, not as of right. Nevertheless, the courts try to exercise their jurisdiction consistently, and a very helpful exposition of the principles involved is given by Arnold J in *Vestergaard Frandsen A/S v Bestnet Europe Ltd* [2009] EWHC 1456 (Ch), [2009] All ER (D) 57 (Oct).

The case arose out of the defendants' (former employees of the claimant) misuse of the claimant's trade secrets to develop a polytex mosquito net, which incorporated an insecticide in the material. The information came to them from their knowledge of the claimant's process for making a protective cattle net, also incorporating an insecticide. The court (at [2009] EWHC 657 (Ch)) held that the defendants had breached the confidentiality of the information, having applied the *Coco v AN Clark* three-point test discussed in **23.2**. The question then became one of how the court should exercise its discretion in granting the remedies sought. The following list is a summary of the valuable guidance given:

(a) *The general principles involved.* Where the claimant establishes that the defendant had acted in breach of confidence and that there was a sufficient risk of repetition, if there were no specific discretionary reasons to refuse an injunction, one would normally be granted, save in exceptional circumstances.

(b) *Where the 'springboard' doctrine was involved* (see **23.3** above). There was no sound authority that an injunction could be granted once the information had ceased to be confidential; publication of the confidential information, whether by confider, by confidant, or by stranger, ended the possibility of obtaining an injunction.

(c) *Where information had only a limited degree of confidence.* Here, as, for example, in circumstances where the information might be obtained by research in the public domain, an injunction could be ordered only for a limited period.

(d) *Whether an injunction could be granted to prevent a defendant from benefiting from a past misuse of confidential information.* In general, it was not clear that such an injunction could be granted, as the primary remedy should be financial. Great care should be exercised, in granting such an injunction, to ensure that the claimant was not thereby put in a position better than if there had been no misuse at all. The duration of such an injunction should not go beyond the period for which the defendant's illegitimate advantage could be expected to last.

(e) *Where a product derived from, or was manufactured using, confidential information.* An injunction could be granted to restrain the manufacture or sale of such product, where the manufacture represented a continued use of the information, always having regard to the extent and importance of the use of it. Otherwise, the appropriate remedy in respect of manufacture and sale of products derived from a past misuse of information was a financial one.

The resulting orders for the claimant were that the defendants should be restrained from using or disclosing the claimant's trade secrets (except any information which was now in the public domain). An injunction restrained any further production or sale of the first derived product, but did not extend to later developed products, where the derivation from the original information was not so clearly illustrated.

See also *First Conference Services Ltd v Bracchi* [2009] EWHC 2176 (Ch), where an employee, having decided that he would leave his job, e-mailed confidential information to a company that he himself had set up. He was held to have misappropriated the information; he had also involved himself in passing off. The court ordered injunctive relief.

23.3.2 The position of former employees

The majority of breach of confidence claims involve former employees as defendants, and it is important to realise that certain considerations should be added to those already examined where an employment situation is involved. The first point is that it is open to an employer to secure some protection for his secrets or other confidential information by requiring the employee to enter into a covenant in restraint of trade and confidentiality agreements. If the employer fails to do this, the court may take the view that some information, of an otherwise confidential nature, might not be viewed by either party as so significant as to be protected; it might blend in with information that the employee should feel free to use or to pass on, and the court may be unwilling to step in (see *AT Poeton (Gloucester Plating) Ltd v Horton* [2001] FSR 169, CA).

The second point is that there is considerable judicial guidance as to the different types of information that might come to an employee during his employment. The widely-cited analysis by Goulding J, at first instance, in *Faccenda Chicken v Fowler* [1985] 1 All ER 724, is instructive and helpful here. The judge categorised the types of information and consequent confidentiality status as falling into three groups:

(a) *Class 1* – mundane, easily obtained information (for all that it might be very technical) that is already in the public domain; such information is not confidential and cannot be protected.

(b) *Class 2* – confidential information that the employee knows, or ought to know, is confidential (perhaps something equivalent to a trade secret), but which enters the employee's mind as part of his own 'stock in trade' of skill and experience, to be used in his own future employment; this will normally remain confidential during the term of employment, but will not usually be protected after termination in the absence of an express covenant.

(c) *Class 3* – highly confidential information in the nature of trade secrets, customer information, etc; this type of information would be protected under an implied term of good faith between the parties, both during the employment and after termination, regardless of the absence of a restrictive covenant.

The Court of Appeal has repeatedly used this analysis in appeals and, despite some elaborations, the classification remains good guidance; judges have been criticised, on appeals, for not following this approach.

The main issue in such cases is often about whether the confidential information is easily isolated from other information that the employee is free to use; that will always depend upon the facts of the case (in the *AT Poeton* case, the claim was dismissed on appeal on this point). You should be clear, however, that the above guidance deals only with the nature of the confidential information and its consequent protectable status; it does not attempt to go further than that.

23.4 A right of privacy and the Human Rights Act 1998?

In the somewhat unusual case of *Douglas and Others v Hello! Ltd and Others* [2003] EWHC 786 (Ch), [2003] All ER (D) 209 (Apr); [2005] EWCA Civ 595, breach of confidence was used to prevent publication by a rival magazine of wedding coverage granted by two film stars to a magazine. It was held that the photographs of the event had the necessary quality of confidence about them, and deserved protection as a trade secret. The illicit photographer from the rival magazine (the defendant) had been under a duty of confidentiality when attending the wedding. The defendant knew of the arrangement between the couple and the other magazine, but had deliberately ignored it and took covert photographs. The law of confidence was held to have protected the claimants' right to respect for private life under the Human Rights Act 1998, Sch 1, Pt I, Art 8. It was therefore held that it was unnecessary to consider whether the Act had created a new right of privacy. The wedding and the party were private events held on private property. These were key factors in the Douglases succeeding. The Lords appeal concerned the nature and protectability of the obligation of confidence, rather than the privacy issue. In another case, the privacy of Princess Caroline of Monaco was protected by the European Convention on Human Rights under Article 8, even though the invasion of her privacy occurred in a public place (*von Hanover v Germany*, Application No 59320/00).

In *A v B (A Company) and Another* [2002] EWCA Civ 337, [2002] 2 All ER 545, the Court of Appeal refused to uphold an injunction under the 'respect for private life' provisions of the Act restraining two newspapers from publishing details of the extra-marital affairs of the claimant, a professional footballer.

In *Campbell v MGN Ltd* [2002] EWCA Civ 1373, [2003] QB 633, the Court of Appeal refused to uphold an injunction against a newspaper restraining publication of sensitive information about a well-known media personality, Naomi Campbell. She had been having treatment for drug addiction, having previously denied drug abuse. The Court held that the public interest in publishing the story overrode her privacy rights under the Human Rights Act 1998. However, the House of Lords overruled the Court of Appeal ([2004] 2 All ER 995). It held that the information about Ms Campbell seeking treatment for drug addiction and photographs of Ms Campbell attending treatment were unnecessary intrusions into her private life. Ms Campbell's right to respect for her private life under the Human Rights Act 1998, Sch 1, Pt I, Art 8, was held to outweigh M's freedom of expression under Article 10. A similar result followed in *HRH Prince of Wales v Associated Newspapers Ltd* [2007] EWHC 1685 (Ch), where the Prince of Wales was able to obtain summary judgment in his claims for breach of confidence and privacy, and infrigement of the copyright in his private journals.

Chapter 24
Information Technology

24.1 Introduction

The computer is a universal presence in offices, homes and schools throughout the developed world. The increase in computer use in the last 20 years or so has come about through the amazing reduction in the price of computing power. For comparison, if a new car had decreased in price to the same degree that computers have over the 20-year period, the car would now cost something less than a tankful of petrol.

However, it should not be forgotten that a computer is basically a calculating machine with a very large memory. It needs to be told what to do. This chapter addresses some of the main legal and related issues which this raises:

(a) IP issues;

(b) semiconductor chip protection;

(c) hardware contracts;

(d) software contracts;

(e) the Internet;

(f) computer crime;

(g) data protection; and

(h) rights in databases.

Many of these issues are relevant to areas of law already covered elsewhere in this book, so, where appropriate, this chapter is cross-referenced to that material.

24.2 Information technology and intellectual property rights

All the major forms of legal protection of IP rights pre-date the electronic computer by a century or more. As they were not developed with the computer in mind, there have therefore been many problems in deciding whether a particular activity comes within the remit of the existing IP law. Indeed, there has been a considerable need to produce new forms of legal protection to deal with problems that have emerged. The following paragraphs summarise the way in which the various IP rights may be relevant to computer software and hardware.

24.2.1 Copyright

For the main points on the law of copyright itself, see **Chapter 19**. The relevance of copyright to computers is as protection for the software; in other words, the instructions required to enable the computer to perform the desired task. In order to be protected, the software would have to have been 'written down' on some medium at some stage of its existence, although of course when bought by the customer, the software will usually be on floppy disks or a CD. (For the avoidance of doubt, note that 'software' = 'computer programs'.)

A computer program is a series of written instructions telling a computer what to do. It will contain thousands of lines of instructions, each one of which relates to a simple step; but put together as a program, it enables the computer to be used, for example, for word processing. As already noted in **Chapter 19**, copyright exists in software as a literary work (CDPA 1988, s 3(1)); see further **24.5.2**.

Unauthorised use of a computer program (which includes simple down-loading) is therefore breach of copyright. The commercial arrangement for use of software is usually a licence, ie, a copyright licence.

(For the law on copyright in databases, and the relatively new 'database right', see **Chapter 19** and **24.9**.)

24.2.2 Patents

As noted in **Chapter 22**, the PA 1977, s 1(2) excludes 'computer programs' from the remit of the patent system (although, as indicated in **22.3.4**, this does not necessarily mean that a program can never be patented).

The reality is that patents for computer programs are being granted in increasing numbers. The attitude of the UK Patent Office and the European Patent Office has become more relaxed over recent years, though not to the extent of the 'open doors' policy of the US Patent Office. The patent is really being granted for the technical effect brought about by the use of the program, as distinct from the program itself.

Patents do, of course, have relevance to protection of inventions in relation to computer hardware (ie, the electronics) if the necessary conditions for patentability are satisfied.

24.2.3 Trade marks

Trade marks are covered in **Chapter 18**. This becomes particularly relevant in the context of Internet 'domain' names, where trade mark infringement and passing off are the relevant causes of action (see further, **24.6**).

(Trade marks are, of course, also relevant in the usual context of being used in relation to goods and services, for example Microsoft, Dell, Compaq and so on will have various registered and unregistered marks which they use in connection with their businesses.)

24.2.4 Design rights

Registered and unregistered design rights (see **Chapter 21**) are intended to protect the outward appearance of items. The design rights are not often directly relevant to information technology (IT) (although they may be used to protect the outward appearance of a piece of hardware). However, note that the right which protects semiconductor chips is akin to a design right (see **24.3**).

24.3 Semiconductor chip protection

The chip is the brain of the computer. It is made up of millions of transistors and other electronic components, yet is only 2cm by 2cm or so in size. The 'Pentium' chip, made by Intel, is the commonest chip in desktop computers.

Obviously, such a marvel of miniaturisation could not be made by sitting at a work bench and soldering all the bits together. Rather, chips are made by a special type of photographic process, whereby the design of the circuit is etched on to the blank chip. As it is made by such a process, it can be copied in a similar manner.

The design of chips is protected in the EU by Directive 87/54/EEC. This has now been implemented in the UK by the Design Right (Semiconductor Topographies) Regulations 1989 (SI 1989/1100). Regulation 2(1) defines a semiconductor topography as a design within s 213 of the CDPA 1988 and which relates to a semiconductor product or component thereof. The design has to be recorded in a design document (see **21.4**).

Under the 1989 Regulations, there is prohibition on:

(a) unauthorised copying of a chip; and

(b) importation into, or sale in, the UK of unauthorised copy chips (but note that exhaustion of rights applies to sales within the EU; see further on this, **Chapter 28**).

Note that reverse engineering is not prohibited, so it is permissible for a third party to work out from the chip topography how it works, and then to produce a chip that performs the same function, without copying the topography or 'map' of the original.

The right lasts for 15 years from creation of the design, or 10 years from first sale of objects made to that design, whichever is the shorter (cf the period for UDR; see further **Chapter 21**).

24.4 Hardware contracts

The 'hardware' is the computer equipment. If you buy a computer, you are simply buying electrical equipment; therefore the contract for the purchase of computer hardware is a contract for sale of goods, and is in principle the same as, for example, buying a fridge from Comet. However, there is one important practical difference: it is fairly obvious when a fridge is not working properly, but it is more debatable whether or not a particular computer is doing all the things it is supposed to. Part of this problem is that it is the software which tells the hardware what to do (for more detail on software, see **24.5**).

Consequently, it is suggested that in producing a specification for a new computer system, it is better to specify the software first and then that the hardware to be supplied has to be able to run it (ie, make the buyer's particular purpose expressly known). Many of the contractual disputes in this area arise from a lack of clarity in specifying the performance requirements of the equipment.

Note that, in practice, it is possible either to buy or to lease hardware. With the decrease in the cost of hardware, buying has become more common in recent years. However, if the system is a major installation, leasing would still be encountered. In this case, the contract would be of a different type (see **24.4.2**).

The remainder of this section considers some of the legal issues which may arise in relation to computer hardware.

24.4.1 Pre-contract issues: negotiation

In *Mackenzie Patten & Co v British Olivetti Ltd* (1984) 1 CL&P 92, a firm of solicitors bought a computer system to run their accounts. The sales representative made various claims for the system. However, there was an exclusion clause in the contract in relation to his statements. The firm signed the contract. The system proved to be slow and hard to use. It was held that Olivetti were bound by the representative's claims, on the basis of a collateral contract. See *Watford Electronics Ltd v Sanderson* at **8.2.2**.

24.4.2 Leasing

With a lease of computer hardware, the lessee has the right to use the equipment but the lessor remains the owner of it. The SGSA 1982 is relevant here (the 1982 Act characterises a contract of this type as a contract of hire, but the term 'lease' is more commercially usual in practice).

Most computer leases will be 'finance leases'. This is a commercial term used to distinguish such a lease from an 'operating lease'. With an operating lease, the equipment is hired out to the user (the lessee) for a short period of time, returned to the lessor and then hired out to another user (this is, eg, how a tool-hire shop would normally operate). With a finance lease, the equipment is supplied to one user only, who retains possession of it for substantially the whole of its working life.

A finance lease basically works as follows. The finance company (lessor) acquires the computer hardware by buying it from a supplier. The finance company pays the supplier for the hardware. It then leases the hardware to the user, and the user pays the finance company a leasing payment, probably monthly. At the end of the lease, the hardware will have little residual value and will be sold off by the lessor. The lessor may credit the user with the sale proceeds (depending on the terms of the lease), but the user must not have the right to acquire title to the hardware, otherwise it will be a hire purchase contract, not a lease.

24.4.3 Sale

As noted at **24.4**, a contract for the sale of hardware is in principle the same as for the sale of any other electrical item. However, the following points will require particular care.

24.4.3.1 Delivery

Depending on the terms of a sale of goods contract, non-delivery or late delivery may entitle the buyer of goods to reject them (see **4.4.6.6**). Remember, however, that this is possible only if the time for delivery is of the essence (ie a condition of the contract: see **4.6**). Problems with hardware contracts can arise if the equipment is being specially produced or modified, or because the supplier is itself waiting for supplies of parts. In such cases, it may not be feasible for the parties to nominate a specific delivery date. It then has to be decided whether the goods have been delivered within a reasonable time. If the delay means that the intended use is no longer practicable then a reasonable time has elapsed. It is advisable for the buyer to inform the supplier at the outset of the intended uses of the equipment. However, it would be best also for the buyer to specify an end-stop date after which the equipment will not be accepted.

24.4.3.2 Payment and changes of specification

Terms on price and payment will need careful consideration.

In major hardware contracts, some changes of specification are likely (eg, it emerges in discussions between the supplier and the buyer that the buyer's future business plans make it advisable to increase the number of file servers, or the specification of the desktop computers). Changes should be categorised as those which are at the buyer's expense and those which are at the seller's expense.

24.4.3.3 Passing of risk and property

The SGA 1979, s 20(1) provides that risk (of accidental loss or damage to the goods) passes at the same time as property (ie, ownership). Sections 16–19 dictate when the property in the goods passes. The issue is important in deciding which party should bear the risk, and therefore the cost of insurance, so remember that ss 16–20 can be ousted by contrary agreement. The parties should consider what is important to them, and provide accordingly.

24.4.3.4 Retention of title

A properly drafted retention of title clause provides added protection for the seller, particularly where standard, non-bespoke equipment is being supplied (see **Chapter 5**).

24.4.3.5 Seller's obligations

Remember that in a sale of goods agreement, various conditions will be implied into the agreement by the SGA 1979:

(a) s 12 – that the seller will give good title and quiet possession (eg, the hardware will be free of third-party IP rights);

(b) s 13 – sale by description (the Misrepresentation Act 1967 could also be relevant);

(c) s 14(2) – satisfactory quality (it is, however, normally better to define 'quality' in the contract than to rely on the statutory implied condition); and

(d) s 14(3) – reasonable fitness for buyer's purpose (remember that the buyer has to make his purpose known to the seller).

Note that because the functioning of hardware is controlled by the software (ie, the program), it is often difficult to assess the hardware independently in relation to quality issues.

The implied terms in ss 13 and 14 can be excluded from the contract subject to UCTA 1977. This would often be done in computer supply contracts. In their place, the supplier would offer a warranty that the system complies with the specification agreed with the customer.

24.4.3.6 Buyer's remedies

Under the SGA 1979, s 11(3), the buyer can reject the goods for breach of condition (see **4.6**).

Rejection of the goods is the buyer's primary remedy if the seller commits breach of condition. However, this may not be feasible commercially (eg, if the hardware is specially adapted, or made so that it would be difficult for the buyer to find an alternative supplier at short notice, or possibly at all).

In any event, the right to reject is lost if the goods have been accepted (see SGA 1979, s 35). Acceptance may arise in the following ways:

(a) Hardware contracts will contain acceptance-testing clauses, which would require that the hardware is able to perform certain defined tasks which demonstrate its capabilities. Passing the tests constitutes acceptance. Ordering more hardware from the same seller would normally also constitute acceptance.

(b) Using the goods beyond mere testing may also constitute acceptance.

(c) Retaining the goods beyond a reasonable time could also be acceptance. This could happen if the hardware is delivered in instalments.

Note that a buyer can elect not to reject the goods and can claim damages instead (SGA 1979, s 11(2)). A buyer could waive his right to reject, for example, where the hardware is not delivered on time and the buyer presses the seller to make delivery as soon as possible.

24.4.3.7 Seller's remedies

If the buyer refuses to accept the goods, the seller can sue for the price, but will have to mitigate by trying to re-sell the hardware. The question will then arise: is there a market for this particular hardware, and will the seller be able to get the same price? The seller could be awarded his lost profit under SGA 1979, s 50(2), if he can show that there are few alternative buyers.

24.4.3.8 Exclusion clauses

In many cases, UCTA 1977 will apply to a hardware contract. The most likely application is in relation to attempted exclusions of the SGA 1979, ss 13–14 (ie, the implied conditions of description, satisfactory quality and reasonable fitness for purpose). In a commercial sale, the test will be one of 'reasonableness' (UCTA 1977, s 6).

The leading computer case on exclusion clauses is *St Albans City and District Council v ICL* [1996] 4 All ER 481. The loss suffered by St Albans District Council as a result of the computer system supplied by ICL failing to work properly was £1.3m, but the contract contained an exclusion of loss clause for losses over £100,000 (ie, compensation for loss caused was limited to this sum). This was held to be unreasonable because:

(a) ICL had more resources than the council did;
(b) ICL had product liability insurance of £50m worldwide;
(c) ICL could not justify the £100,000 limit;
(d) the contract was signed on superseded standard terms;
(e) local authorities are limited in what they can insure against;
(f) St Albans received no inducement to agree; and
(g) ICL had said that negotiation over terms would delay implementation of the deal.

The tide has gone the other way to an extent with the case of *Watford Electronics Ltd v Sanderson CFL Ltd* [2001] EWCA Civ 317, [2001] 1 All ER (Comm) 696. An interesting point that went against the claimants is that they themselves used a similar limitation of liability clause in their own terms. They were therefore held to be aware of the commercial considerations and the effect on the price agreed for the job.

24.4.4 Maintenance agreements

Computer hardware will normally come with a guarantee (usually called a warranty) – an express promise from the supplier that it will do or provide certain things if the hardware goes wrong.

After the warranty expires, it makes sense for a buyer to set up a maintenance agreement for commercial hardware.

The key points for the owner of the hardware and the provider of the maintenance to consider when setting up such an agreement are:

(a) should it provide for repair on site, or return to base?
(b) the desired response time from the provider (the faster it is, the more expensive it is);
(c) is replacement equipment to be provided in the interim whilst repair is carried out?
(d) duration of the contract – the older the equipment, the more repairs it will need and the more it will cost to maintain; and
(e) is transfer of the agreement to a new owner of the hardware permitted, as this will increase the second-hand value of the hardware?

24.4.5 System supply contracts

A system supply contract is where the buyer receives some or all of the following:

(a) hardware;
(b) software;
(c) cabling, power supply;
(d) services (eg, installation, maintenance, support, systems integration).

Note that in a 'turnkey' contract (where the system is supplied ready to run, usually with all software and peripherals such as printers), the supplier may buy in various aspects of the goods or services, almost certainly including the software. This would be licensed direct to the user, rather than by licence to the supplier and sub-licence from him to the user. It is important that the user evaluates the terms of the licences to see if they are suitable for his purposes.

24.5 Software

Software can be 'off the peg' (ie, a standard package), or 'made to order'. Standard package software will be cheaper than made to order, but may not fulfil the user's requirements adequately. A middle way for the buyer of software to choose is to adapt standard software, in effect customising it. The trend is toward increased sales of standard software.

There is also a distinction between system software, which organises the way the hardware operates, and applications software, which performs the function required by the user (eg, 'Word' or 'Powerpoint' are applications software). System software is normally supplied by the maker of the hardware (eg, the BIOS – the Basic Input/Output System).

24.5.1 Software licensing

Software supply contracts are basically copyright licences (see **Chapter 19**), but also contain terms dealing with the supply of the physical manifestations of the software (eg, sometimes retaining title to the disks, or forbidding the possession of more than one set of back-up disks, or forbidding use other than on specified hardware).

As noted at **24.2.1,** there is specific legal provision on the IP position for software. Under s 17(2) of the CDPA 1988, unauthorised storage of a program in a computer is copyright infringement. Directive 91/250/EEC specifies further legal protection for software. It is implemented in the UK by the Copyright (Computer Programs) Regulations 1992 (SI 1992/3233).

Even where software is sold over the counter, licensing is still relevant. In this case, the software house tries to impose a licence on the user by specifying that opening the cellophane in which the software is wrapped constitutes acceptance of the terms of the standard-form licence visible through the wrapper (this is known as a 'shrink-wrap' licence, and is considered further at **24.5.2**).

(What will in practice happen in this sort of 'consumer' sale of software and shrink-wrap licence is that the software creator (eg, Microsoft) will sell the software to a retailer (eg, computer shop). The shop sells the software on to the customer; it is, however, Microsoft which imposes the shrink-wrap licence on the customer.)

24.5.2 Shrink-wrap or click-wrap licensing

Most software today is bought off the shelf; that is, the software is a standard product, such as the 'Word' program used to create this document. As noted at **24.5.1** above, in order to create a licence between the software creator and the user, the device known as a 'shrink-wrap licence' is used (there would otherwise be a contractual link only between the user and the retailer). This means that terms of use can therefore be imposed by the software creator on the user.

The terms of the licence are set out on the outside of the packaging and are visible through the clear wrapping. The licence purportedly comes into being when the user opens the packaging, supposedly having read the terms and agreed to them.

A licensing method which has become more common in recent years, both with software downloaded through the Internet and being downloaded from a CD-ROM, is that of the 'click-wrap' licence. This is where customers are faced with the text of a licence agreement on screen. The customers have to click on the 'I agree' button before they are allowed access to the software.

24.5.2.1 Terms

Typical terms in a consumer licence include that:

(a) the licence is for use on one computer only;

(b) the software must not be copied (save for one back-up copy);

(c) the software must not be altered; and

(d) the licensor will replace defective disks and supply updates.

All other warranties or conditions are excluded (subject, of course, to the impact of UCTA 1977, or other provisions controlling exclusion or restriction of liability). As the licence will be a pure licence of the software creator's IP rights, the only heads of liability for the software creator are likely to be negligence or product liability. (Remember that exclusion of negligence will be subject to UCTA 1977, s 2; product liability cannot be excluded under s 7 of the Consumer Protection Act 1987.)

If the sale of software is a consumer sale, the Consumer Transactions (Restrictions on Statements) Order 1976 (SI 1976/1813) will apply. This requires there to be a statement that any warranty given does not affect the consumer's statutory rights. The Unfair Terms in Consumer Contracts Regulations 1999 (SI 1999/2083) may also be relevant in this situation (as noted in **Chapter** 7, these Regulations can only apply to consumer agreements).

24.5.3 Bespoke software

Bespoke software (ie, software 'tailored' to the precise needs of a particular user) is expensive, and will be the subject of a specific contract negotiated between the software house and the user, who in legal terms is the commissioner of the software (this is relevant to the ownership of the IP rights in the software; see below).

In this case, software is written to fulfil the functional specification put forward by the user. The software house will depend on the user supplying information on its business and how it is run in order to create a satisfactory program.

The specification may change during the design of the program, and the costs of such alterations need to be allocated between the parties.

Acceptance tests will need to be devised. The user will not accept the software until these have been passed.

A key problem will be that of ownership of the copyright in the program. As noted in **Chapter 19**, the copyright will (subject, of course, to any contrary agreement) vest in the creator (ie author) of the work, not in the person who commissions it. However, this may not fulfil the desires of the parties to the agreement here; the user might ideally want to have exclusive rights to the program which it paid the creator to devise, even if only to prevent third parties from benefiting from the program. The creator, on the other hand, would want to have the right to use at least some aspects of the program in future programs which it may write, not least because it regards it as part of its evolving expertise. In practice, this is another matter which will be determined by bargaining power; basically, users are unlikely to get exclusivity unless they are prepared to pay a substantial amount for it.

24.6 The Internet

It goes without saying that IP laws have been tested quite heavily by the advance of the Internet and, as with the growth of computing generally since their introduction, have had to adapt quickly to react to the new challenges it brings.

24.6.1 Using a name

In order to send a message over the Internet, it has to have an address to go to. An Internet Protocol address has the form '130.132.59.234'. As the Internet Protocol addresses are essentially forgettable, the Domain Name System (DNS) was devised. 'Domain names' are names rather than numbers, and are translated into Internet Protocol addresses by some of the computers in the Internet. An example of a domain name is 'lawcol.co.uk'. So, for example, a message could be sent to Trevor.Adams@lawcol.co.uk.

Domain names have different 'levels'; for example, the top-level domain name in the above example is 'uk'. Obviously, this is the country where the relevant party is located. Other examples of top-level domain names are '.com', '.gov' or '.org'. There is little dispute about these. Rather, the problems which arise in relation to domain names usually concern the second-level names, especially where that name is the trade mark, registered or not, of a commercial product or organisation (eg, 'McDonalds.com'). Clearly, unauthorised use of that domain name would upset a certain chain of burger restaurants.

In the UK, the organisation known as Nominet allocates domain names and does so on the basis of first come, first served. It is located at www.nominet.org.uk.

In the United States, and in effect internationally as well, the body known as the Internet Corporation for Assigned Names and Numbers (ICANN) deals with many domain name issues also, and is located at www.icann.org. It has set up some new top-level domain names, for example '.pro' for lawyers and accountants. WIPO also has an input into domain name issues, especially from the trade mark perspective, and runs a dispute resolution procedure.

In England, in the case of *British Telecommunications plc and Others v One in a Million Ltd and Others* [1999] 1 WLR 903, the Court of Appeal held that the use of various business names as domain names without consent was passing off and infringement of the registered trade marks under the TMA 1994. The claimants were BT, Sainsbury's, Virgin, Ladbrokes and Marks & Spencer. Following this case, it seems clear that unauthorised use of a business name as a domain name will be taken by the English courts as constituting passing off and trade mark infringement (assuming that there is a valid trade mark registration). In *Bonnier Media Ltd v Greg Lloyd Smith* [2002] ETMR 86 (see **18.9**), it was held by the Scottish Court of Session that the intent of the infringer was a critical factor, ie were they intending to defraud the legitimate user of the trade mark?

If a domain name is a registered trade mark, the criteria used to decide if there is infringement are those under the TMA 1994. In particular, the criteria identified in the case of *British Sugar plc v James Robertson & Sons Ltd* [1996] RPC 281, concerning the use of the word 'Treat' in relation to sweet sauces and syrups, where it was held that it was not necessary for the infringing use to be use as a trade mark as such, provided it was use in the course of trade. See, at **18.9**, *Wilson v Yahoo! UK Ltd* [2008] EWHC 361 (Ch), on the non-infringing use of trade-marks in sponsored links in Internet search engines.

Even if the trade mark is not in use in the UK, it may be protected in the UK as a 'well known mark' under s 56 of the 1994 Act (see **18.10**).

24.6.2 Copyright issues

In the case of *Shetland Times Ltd v Wills and Another* [1997] FSR 604, the Shetland News Internet site had a link which enabled the reader to access pages from the *Shetland Times*, but without seeing the front page of the *Times*. Such unauthorised use of the *Times* pages was held to be breach of copyright. Unauthorised use of copyright material on the Internet now falls within s 20 of the CDPA 1988, which covers infringement by communication to the pubic within the UK, by electronic means.

The BBC has undertaken similar action with regard to infringement via the Internet of its copyright in the Teletubbies.

24.6.3 Intercepting communications

The Regulation of Investigatory Powers Act 2000 makes it illegal for a business to intercept communications without the consent of both the sender and recipient. Permitted interceptions may be allowed under the Telecommunications (Lawful Business Practice) (Interception of Communications) Regulations 2000 (SI 2000/2699). However, even permitted interceptions may fall foul of the Human Rights Act 1998, or the Data Protection Act 1998. See *Copland v United Kingdom*, Application No 62617/00, (2007) 45 EHRR 37.

See also the offences under the Computer Misuse Act 1990 at **24.7**.

24.7 Computer crime

There have been attempts in the past to use the law of theft and criminal damage in relation to problems related to computers (eg, problems caused by hackers, people who attempt to gain unauthorised access to computer systems). The problems in using the conventional law proved to be immense; what has been stolen, or what has been damaged? The Computer Misuse Act 1990 seeks to avoid such esoteric questions by creating offences that are specific to computers.

24.7.1 Section 1 – unauthorised access, hacking and like activities

Section 1 of the Computer Misuse Act 1990 makes it an offence to obtain unauthorised access to a computer system, as follows:

> (1) A person is guilty of an offence if—
>
> (a) he causes a computer to perform any function with intent to secure access to any program or data held in any computer;
>
> (b) the access he intends to secure is unauthorised; and
>
> (c) he knows at the time when he causes the computer to perform the function that that is the case.

The punishment is a maximum of six months' imprisonment and/or a fine.

24.7.2 Section 2 – the ulterior intent offence

This is committed by a person who secures unauthorised access to a computer system with the intent of using that access to facilitate the commission of a further serious criminal offence. Such offences are those where the sentence is fixed by law (eg, murder), or where a first offender aged over 18 years could be sentenced to five years in jail. For example, a case has been reported in France where access was sought to medical records in order to blackmail sufferers of AIDS. If such facts arose within the UK, they would be capable of giving rise to the s 2 offence.

The offence in s 2 is triable either way. The maximum sentence is five years' imprisonment.

24.7.3 Section 3 – modification of computer material

The act must be intended to impair the operation of a computer, or to prevent or hinder access to any programs or data, or to impair the operation of any program or reliability of the data. Sending out a computer virus would come within s 3, as would deleting or altering data, or indeed adding jocular comments to the Duke of Edinburgh's e-mail (*R v Gold* [1988] 2 WLR 984, where the prosecution failed under the then law).

The offence in s 3 is triable either way. The maximum sentence is five years' imprisonment.

24.7.4 Jurisdiction

The Computer Misuse Act 1990 introduced the concept of a 'significant link' with one of the UK jurisdictions. In the case of the s 1 or s 3 offences, it is enough that either the offender or the victim was located within the jurisdiction. For the s 2 offence, the court has jurisdiction only if the further act would be an offence in the country where it was intended that it should occur.

24.8 Data protection

The Data Protection Act 1998 has revised the law in this area. See **Chapter 26** for more detailed discussion.

The Act, which is complex, extends the principles of the Data Protection Act 1984. Broadly, it consists of provisions for:

(a) notification by those who use data;

(b) general data protection principles; and

(c) a supervisory body headed by the Information Commissioner.

The 1998 Act includes manual records, not just computer ones, as was the case under the 1984 Act.

Key definitions include:

(a) 'processing', which includes altering, retrieving, or disposing of data;

(b) 'data controller', who is the person who determines the purposes for which data are to be processed; and

(c) 'data processor', who is the person who processes data on behalf of the data controller. (Note that the data controller is responsible for the actions of the data processor.)

Common conditions that have to be met are:

(a) that the data subject (ie, the person to whom the data relate) has given his consent to processing; or

(b) that processing is necessary for the performance of a contract to which he is a party.

Data subjects have the right to:

(a) be informed that data are being processed;

(b) be informed of the nature of the data;

(c) require that data are not processed if it causes them damage or distress; and

(d) object to direct marketing.

For transfers of data outside the EEA, the countries of destination have to have an equivalent level of data protection. For example, Japan and the USA do *not* meet this requirement, though an agreement with the USA looks as if it will take shape around the European Commission's gradual acceptance of the US voluntary 'Safe Harbor' principle. See European Commission Decision of 27 July 2000.

24.9 The database right

As noted in **Chapter 20**, this is a relatively new right relating to the keeping of information. The Copyright and Rights in Databases Regulations 1997 (SI 1997/3032) implement Directive 96/9/EC on the Legal Protection of Databases by amending the Copyright Designs and Patents Act 1988 (CDPA 1988).

A 'database' is defined in the CDPA 1988, s 3A(1) (see **20.2**). In practice, a database could, for example, be information on the daily price of stocks and shares, a telephone directory, 'Lexis', or the CD-ROM law reports. Copyright protection is also afforded to a database specifically as a literary work, although the standard is not only that of originality, but also that it is the 'author's intellectual creation'. To obtain 'database right' protection, only s 3A(1) needs to be met. For copyright protection, both s 3A(1) and (2) must be met.

Whether or not it is protected by copyright, a database also attracts a new database right, which arises automatically. The database right runs for 15 years from the end of the year of completion. It prevents unauthorised use of the database, or a substantial part of it.

As noted in **20.2,** data arrangements have the protection of database right if there is a substantial investment (including any investment, whether of financial, human or technical resources):

(a) in quality or quantity;
(b) in obtaining, verifying or presenting the data.

Further points to consider in relation to the database right are as follows.

24.9.1 Qualifications for the database right

There are copyright-style qualification requirements (Copyright and Rights in Databases Regulations 1997, reg 18) based on nationality or corporate seat.

24.9.2 Ownership of the database right

The maker of a database protected by the database right is the person who takes the initiative in obtaining, verifying or presenting the contents of the database and who assumes the risk of investing in that obtaining. (See Copyright and Rights in Databases Regulations 1997, reg 14.)

The maker is the first owner of the database right (reg 15).

24.9.3 Duration of lesser protection

The database right lasts for the longer of 15 years from the end of the calendar year:

(a) of completion of the database; or
(b) during which the database was first made available to the public (reg 17).

A 'substantial new investment' (see **24.9**) will 'top up' the right so the period starts again.

24.9.4 Infringement of the database right

Infringement is the extraction or re-utilisation of all or a substantial part of the contents of a database without the consent of the owner (reg 16).

'Extraction' means the permanent or temporary transfer of the contents of a database to another medium by any means, or in any form.

'Re-utilisation' means making those contents available to the public by any means.

'Substantial' is in terms of quality, or quantity or both.

'Substantial part' can include repeated extraction and/or re-utilisation of insubstantial parts (reg 16(2)). This is very important, as it means that copying of small extracts, which would not comprise a qualitatively sufficient copying for copyright infringement purposes, may still comprise a database right infringement, if done often enough.

24.9.5 Exceptions from the database right

Database rights are not infringed (regs 19 and 20):

(a) by fair dealing with a substantial part of a database made available to the public if:
    (i) such dealing is for illustration in teaching or research; and
    (ii) sufficient acknowledgement is given;
(b) generally, by copying or use with the authority of the keeper of a database available for public inspection as a statutory record.

The database right can be licensed or assigned (as can the copyright in the database).

Chapter 25
E-commerce

25.1 Introduction

The exponential growth in the commercial use of the Internet in the last decade and a half, the developments in Internet shopping, and the general adaptation to online contracting by commercial parties and the consumer alike, arguably may be the most fundamental change to commercial activity in centuries. But is it such a change? At first sight one might think so, but the reality is that much of this, from the point of view of the lawyer, is a case of adapting existing, well-known principles to suit new fact situations. A good example of this is the way in which encryption and digital signatures have been introduced to give the legal certainty that would otherwise reside in a confidential agreement, signed by the parties, with a pen. That is not to say that this area of law is easy to understand and to apply; it is not, for the simple reason that the pace of technological and commercial developments has caused the courts and legislators to struggle to keep up. What follows is a summary of the main areas of legal issues and recent developments.

The term 'e-commerce' is used here to describe both contracts between business parties (B2B) and those between businesses and consumers (B2C). To arrive at a satisfactory definition of e-commerce, it is probably not necessary to go much further than to say that it covers business transactions in goods and services between remote parties, who communicate with each other by electronic means. Often, there will also be questions about the use of the Internet for advertising, and these are dealt with at **25.5** below. The aim of this chapter is to provide a preliminary understanding of some of the legal aspects of e-commerce for the budding commercial lawyer, and to highlight problem areas.

25.2 The legal framework

The very real difficulty with e-commerce is that parties can come to agreements without regard to national frontiers or distance; so can the parties simply forget about law and have a fine old time dealing together? Clearly that would never work, because there would be no legal way in which the parties could either enforce the contract or settle disputes. Consequently, all the major trading countries of the world have had to wrestle with the problem of applying legal systems to e-commerce, but there are still very wide differences in the approaches taken under different national legal systems. For the purposes of this chapter, the main focus will be on the harmonised laws of the EU and English domestic law; much of the law derives from the so-called E-commerce Directive, ie Council Directive 2000/31 EC. This is given effect in the UK by the Electronic Commerce (EC Directive) Regulations 2002 (SI 2002/2013) ('the 2002 Regulations') and is discussed in more depth at **25.7**.

While the Directive is generally about the provision of electronic services by Internet Service Providers (ISPs), it can extend out towards most types of commercial provision of electronic information. It can cover, in particular, website selling of goods and services, but the type of e-commerce that is concluded by parties using an exchange of e-mails is generally not affected by it. Nevertheless, by Article 9(1), Member States are required to ensure that national legal systems effectively facilitate the making of valid contracts by electronic means. The particular position of the consumer in a B2C contract is dealt with at **25.7**.

A distinction that should be raised at the outset is between the use of websites and the use of simple communication between parties by electronic means, such as e-mails. Most of the controlling legislation in this area is aimed at the former, by reference to 'information society services' (ISSs), which covers most of the business activity carried out by the use of websites. The general approach followed below is to deal with this distinction as and when required by the particular point being examined.

25.3 Formation and proof of contract

25.3.1 Offer and acceptance

Although the Internet is supra-national, every contract requires an applicable law before it can be legally analysed. The issues of law and jurisdiction of e-commerce contracts are dealt with at **25.4** below but, for the purposes of this chapter, it is assumed that the contract will be governed by English law. In essence, the law of offer and acceptance in contract, with which you are already familiar, works in exactly the same way in e-commerce; the point to remember is that the familiar steps and distinctions have to be looked at in the light of the particular way in which online transactional communications work. Thus:

(a) *Offer or invitation to treat*? This vital distinction applies just as much in e-commerce as when contracting elsewhere; the point of departure comes when one considers that e-commerce might be entered into either by a simple exchange of e-mails, or by using a website. If the matter is transacted by e-mail, the question will be dealt with exactly as with a traditional exchange of letters, ie whether the communication is an expression of willingness to contract on specified terms, made with the intention that it becomes binding as soon as it is accepted by the person to whom it is addressed. If it is anything less than this, it may be an invitation to treat but is not an offer.

With a website, however, the details displayed by the supplier are much more likely to have been designed so as to constitute an invitation to treat. The reason for that is that the customer is required to make the offer, usually establishing his identity and payment assurance, before the seller will enter the contract by acceptance. The statutory assumption in the 2002 Regulations, reg 12, is that the customer's order will usually comprise the contractual offer, the supplier's acknowledgement being the acceptance.

(b) *Acceptance*. In e-commerce by exchanges of e-mail, the well-established rule of convenience and certainty analogous to the 'postal rule' is probably applicable. Under this, acceptance occurs when the offeree does the last act that is seen as contemplated by the parties: if that is acceptance by letter, the last act is posting the letter; if it is during an exchange of e-mails, the last act is the sending of the acceptance message. It remains possible, of course, for a 'battle of the forms' situation to arise even in this circumstance.

Where the acceptance taking place is by the use of a website in a transaction to which the 2002 Regulations apply, the recipient of a service must have had explained to him by the provider, prior to placing an order, 'the different technical steps to follow to conclude the contract' (reg 9(1)(a)); additionally, 'the order and acknowledgement of receipt will be deemed to be received when the parties to whom they are addressed are able to access them' (reg 11(2)(a)), but note that parties who are non-consumers are free to agree other arrangements. That suggests that acceptance may take place at the earliest time at which the customer can access the supplier's acknowledgement of the order/

offer, regardless of whether the customer actually does so. There seems to be no particular reason why the special telex rule in *Entores Ltd v Miles Far East Corporation* [1955] 2 QB 327 should apply to e-commerce transactions.

(c) *Incorporation of terms.* In general, the same rules are likely to be applied to the incorporation of terms as in other contractual circumstances, including the court's jurisdiction to decide about the 'battle of forms' where standard-form contract terms are involved.

25.3.2 Electronic execution of documents, encryption and security

Most commercial transactions do not require formal execution by signature as a matter of law, but there are circumstances in which a signature may be required, either by the terms of the contract, or by the common law or by statute. The Electronic Signatures Regulations 2002 (SI 2002/318), made in response to Directive 1999/93 EC, constitute the United Kingdom's framework for providing for the supervision and liability of signature-certification service providers, related data protection measures and admissibility into evidence of electronic signatures (see also Pt II of the Electronic Communications Act 2000). Some statutory requirements for a 'signature' and 'writing' can, it seems, be met by e-mail exchanges (see *Mehta v J Pereira Fernandes SA* [2006] EWHC 813 (Ch), although on the facts of the case an e-mail address not contained in the body of the message did not comprise a 'signature' for the purpose of the Statute of Frauds 1677, s 4).

The security aspects of many online contractual arrangements and negotiations can be of extreme importance, and the problem may become even greater where bank details or the availability of a person's electronic signature are concerned. The ingenuity of fraudsters and computer hackers has no limit, and e-commerce would not be possible without the ability of encryption techniques to help safeguard the confidentiality of much of the material that is transmitted electronically. Such technical questions raise no particular legal problems, but you should be aware of the part that encryption plays in the role of certification providers, and in the use of card and bank details in commercial and consumer transactions.

25.4 Law and jurisdiction, choices and application

In many respects, the question of the system of law properly applicable to an e-commerce contract is very similar to what you have already looked at in **Chapter 13**, **13.3**, on the Rome Convention and its replacement, Regulation (EC) No 593/2008. Primacy is given to the choice of law of the parties, subject only to the interposition of mandatory rules of law. Special provision is made to protect the positions of consumers and employees, and a most important provision is in place to deal with Internet selling to consumers; under Regulation (EC) 593/2008, Article 6.1(b), where any person exercising his trade or profession directs his activities by any means (including the Internet) at a Member State where the consumer has his habitual residence, the governing law of the contract will be that of the particular Member State.

As regards choice or determination of jurisdiction, this again is dealt with in **Chapter 13**; and the special rules for determining the jurisdiction in consumer cases, particularly the rule on Internet selling to consumers in Member States under Regulation 44/2001 ('Brussels II'), Article 15, is explained at **13.2**.

In situations where, for whatever reason, none of the above provisions applies, the questions of jurisdiction and applicable law will be determined by the rules on jurisdiction and conflict of laws of the forum where the dispute is heard.

25.5 The application of intellectual property law to e-commerce

This is a highly complex and technical matter, some of which has already been been discussed, briefly, when looking at the separate types of IP rights in earlier chapters. A summary of the main areas relating to IP disputes is given below.

25.5.1 Domain name disputes

There have probably been more squabbles about the right to use domain names as such, or about IP-related claims that have a domain name angle to them, than about most other areas of e-commerce, so that a brief examination of the problem is called for. In respect of the right to the 'ownership' and use of any particular domain name, without any additional claim that someone's IP rights are infringed, this will sometimes involve a claimant who claims the right to use a domain name or stop others from using it; the defendants will often be the bodies concerned with the allocation or registration of such names, such as ICANN (US-based allocation system) and Nominet (the UK allocation body). These disputes are essentially contractual. Such a matter may be resolved by litigation, as in *Pitman Training Ltd v Nominet UK* [1997] FSR 797, but nowadays the issue will more usually be dealt with by recourse to the dispute resolution mechanism used by the particular allocation body.

Such disputes, often with an international aspect, can involve difficult constitutional law problems at times, as in *Pocket Kings Ltd v Safenames Ltd* [2009] EWHC 2529, [2009] All ER (D) 205 (Oct), where the High Court refused to enforce a penal forfeiture order against a domain name, made by the State of Kentucky, USA (the order was made on the basis that the activities promoted by the site were illegal in that state).

The other main problem area with domain names lies in the potential infringement of IP rights, where the domain name is the same as, or close to, a word trade mark which is owned by someone else. These issues are examined below.

25.5.2 Passing off

There are many cases where the use of a domain name allegedly passes off the user's products or services as those of another. The law on this is very much the same as with any other form of passing off. A very clear example is seen in *Phones 4u Ltd and Another v Phone4u.co.uk Internet Ltd* [2006] EWCA Civ 244, where the defendant, having registered the domain name 'Phone4u.co.uk' at a time when a chain of shops owned by the claimant had established a thriving business using the 'Phones 4u' mark, was held to have passed off its products as those of the claimant. From the date of acquisition of the domain name, there could not be any realistic use of the name without deception; to register and use the name of a well-known company as a domain name to draw in custom was fraudulent.

Beyond the mere use of the domain name, the way in which any e-commerce transmission, or website, uses or displays material may constitute a passing off of someone else's good or services, provided that the classic indicia of the tort – reputation, misrepresentation leading to confusion and damage – can be established. Indeed, the very width of the common law tort (relating to 'get up', display and promotional technique, etc, as well as marks) makes passing off a serious possibility in e-commerce.

25.5.3 Trade marks

Again, the potential infringement of a registered trade mark, either in the domain name or in the other transmitted material, arises in the same way as with any other circumstance, by coming within the statutory acts of infringement. You will have seen already (at **13.9**) that there are very many trade mark cases involving the use of websites, so it is not necessary to repeat that material here. Nevertheless, a case of huge importance to the use of trade marks on the Internet is presently on foot: in *Interflora Inc v Marks and Spencer plc* [2009] EWHC 1095

(Ch), [2009] All ER (D) 217 (May), Arnold J has agreed to refer to the ECJ for guidance certain questions that may have extensive repercussions. The case concerns the use by the defendant of Google's 'Adword' and sponsored link systems for allowing potential advertisers to purchase the use of keywords, many of which are the same as registered trade marks, urls and domain names (here, 'Interflora' signs and variations on them). Curiously, Google's current policy seems to be to accept notification by any affected mark owners and block the purchase of 'their' keywords by other would-be users in all the Member States of the EC, except for the UK and Ireland; this may, perhaps, be because Google feels that the last-named national courts would be more acquiescent to this policy.

This case and the ECJ reference should be watched with care, as the consequent guidance should be helpful to all persons interested in e-commerce, advertising and search engine design. The eventual result of the *L'Oréal SA v Bellure NV* litigation, in consequence of the ECJ reference, discussed at **18.9.2** above, should also help to clarify the limits of permissible use of trade marks in comparative advertising, both for the purposes of the UK law and for Community law.

Another very important case, in which guidance is being sought from the ECJ, is *L'Oréal SA v eBay International AG* [2009] EWHC 1094 (Ch). Here, the question is whether eBay can be held liable for the infringements of trade marks by the users of eBay, in arranging sales; Arnold J is, at the time of writing, in the process of referring several questions on this matter to the ECJ, and this is discussed, in the context of statutory defences available to 'information society service providers', ie websites, at **25.7.1** below.

25.5.4 Copyright

This is a vast topic, and a couple of paragraphs can do no more than skim over its surface; nevertheless, you should be aware of the enormous potential for problems from this direction. Almost everything that ever gets onto a website or into an electronic transmission has some sort of copyright in it, or would have were the material not out of its copyright period. The rules for the substantive existence and infringement of copyrights of different types have been explored in **Chapter 19**; in particular, you will have realised that the simple downloading of material by a computer will constitute a copying which, if it is not licensed by the owner of the right, may comprise an infringing act. You will also know that there are many defences to copying, such as 'fair use' for various purposes, as well as transient copying as part of a technological process under s 28A of the CDPA 1988.

The most widespread defence available to the users of websites is that they use the site under the licence of the copyright owner, but that can avail them nothing where the person who put the material on the site did not own the copyright in it in the first place – he might have infringed the copyright and, theoretically, the person downloading it might become a secondary infringer (and, if he passes it on, a primary infringer). That has led to enormous problems involving 'framing' (placing material on a website so that it is displayed on a different site), 'deep linking' (linking one site to the inside pages on another site) and 'peer to peer/information/file sharing' sites.

All sorts of counter-measures have been tried to deal with unauthorised use of copyright material, but the one potent extension of legal powers in this area is probably the Copyright and Related Rights Regulations 2003 (SI 2003/2498), which aim to prevent the circumvention of technological measures which are in place to protect the copyright (and other IP rights such as the database right, etc), where copyright works are made available to the public by electronic means. This has led, inter alia, to the amendment of s 296 and the insertion of ss 296ZA–296ZG of the CDPA 1988. Nevertheless, copyright issues are likely to provide the greatest IP challenge to the future development of the information society, the Internet and e-commerce; time alone will tell whether there is any achievable and practical answer. In the meantime, the courts and enforcement authorities wrestle with the problem using the tools currently available to them, on a case-by-case basis.

25.6 Business to business e-commerce

As explained at **25.1** above, most of the legislation in this area is aimed at the use of websites by consumers to obtain goods and services, not two businesses arranging a contract by e-mail, except in one crucial respect – almost all of this legislation is based upon the European Union requirement for a level playing field in respect of the conduct of business and commerce. Vital to that end are the requirements for fair consumer practice, for freedom of movement of goods and services, for rights of establishment and for fair competition practices. It would therefore be a great mistake to assume that the use of e-commerce would somehow release the parties from any of these requirements, if the contract could potentially generate any EU Member State effects at all. When one adds in the fact that electronic communications leave an indelible trail for the skilled investigator to follow (who may have impressive powers of investigation and enforcement where these EU or domestic matters are involved), it becomes clear that the apparent freedom from legislation is a dangerous trap for the unwary. The speed with which transactions can be entered into electronically only adds to the danger. The parties to a B2B arrangement, set up without the use of a public access website, should take very great care about the content and legal effect of all of their electronic communications.

Some of the likely risks for B2B arrangements come from competition law (dangers of 'concerted practices' arising out of frequent communications, even if there are no express agreements, for Article 101 TFEU purposes); from impermissible use of confidential information, or copyright or other protected material in e-mails or attachments; and from failing to deal with important points (such as law or jurisdiction points, or incorporation of terms) given the pressure, as regards pace and time, to enter a deal. If B2B contracts are entered into using a website, consideration has to be given to whether there is any way that one party (who must be a natural person) might be seen as acting as a 'consumer' in the transaction; although it will be a rare occurrence, that is not an impossibility, and it could make a great deal of difference as to statutory rules governing the contract (see **25.7** below).

25.7 Business to consumer e-commerce

Here, the emphasis moves to the consumer (in an extended sense) protection requirements of European and domestic law. This section is premised on the assumption that the consumer purchase of goods and/or services is via a website. The three main areas of statutory regulation that should be considered are set out in **25.7.1** to **25.7.3** below.

25.7.1 The Electronic Commerce (EC Directive) Regulations 2002

The 2002 Regulations were enacted, in response to the E-commerce Directive, to regulate the provision of goods, services and information to consumers by electronic means by 'information society service providers' (ISSPs). This is mainly aimed at the Internet, although it can extend to other means of electronic communication. The definition of an ISS, given in reg 2 (see the **Appendix** to this work), is

> any service normally provided for remuneration, at a distance, by means of electronic equipment for the processing … and storage of data, and at the individual request of the recipient of the service.

'Consumer' is defined as 'any natural person who is acting for purposes other than his trade, business or profession'. 'Recipient of the service' extends, by contrast, to 'any person who, *for professional ends or otherwise*, uses an information society service, in particular for the purposes of seeking information or making it accessible'(emphasis added). You will see, from this last definition, that the reach of the 2002 Regulations goes beyond mere consumer protection.

Regulation 6 (see **Appendix**) governs the detailed information that must be provided by the ISSP. Regulation 6(1) deals with the requirement for transparency regarding the identity, location and contact details of the ISSP, and other professional and regulatory information, including the ISSP's VAT identification number (reg 6(1)(g)). Regulation 6(2) requires, vitally, that where an ISS refers to prices, they must be indicated clearly, unambiguously and indicate, in particular, whether they are inclusive of tax and delivery costs.

Regulation 7 deals with the required attributes and content of 'commercial communications'. A commercial communication is defined in reg 2 as:

> a communication, in any form, designed to promote, directly or indirectly, the goods, services or image of any person pursuing a commercial, industrial or craft activity or exercising a regulated profession ...

This is a very wide definition indeed, clearly extending to advertising. Where such a communication is made, it must be identifiable as such, it must identify the person on whose behalf it is made, it must clearly identify any promotional offer as such, and it must ensure that any conditions are made accessible and are clear and unambiguous (reg 7(a)–(d)).

Regulations 9 and 11 are concerned with the provision of information and the placing of the order where a contract is to be concluded by electronic means (see **Appendix**). Where a consumer is involved, reg 9 requires that, *prior* to the placing of an order, certain information that is vital to the interests of the consumer must be provided in a clear and unambiguous form by the ISSP. Of fundamental importance, where the ISSP provides terms and conditions applicable to the contract, it must make these available to the service recipient in a way that allows for their storage and reproduction (reg 9(3)); this last provision is mandatory, even if the contract is concluded by individual e-mail exchange, whereas the other requirements of reg 9 do not apply in such non-website contracting situations. Regulation 11 deals with the requirements where an order is placed by 'technological means' (not defined); the ISSP must acknowledge receipt to the service recipient, without undue delay and by electronic means.

Non-compliance with the requirements of the 2002 Regulations is actionable at the instance of enforcement authorities (which may involve civil or criminal law proceedings) and at the instance of ISS recipients, whether parties to a contract covered by the 2002 Regulations or not. The principal statutory remedies are:

(a) a claim for damages for breach of statutory duty (reg 13);

(b) a court order to require the supply of contract terms or conditions to comply with reg 9(3) (reg 14);

(c) the right to apply to the court for rescission, if the ISSP does not provide the means for correcting input errors required by reg 11(1)(b) (reg 15);

(d) protection of the right of any person to seek court relief to stop infringement of any rights (reg 20).

25.7.2 The Consumer Protection (Distance Selling) Regulations 2000

The Consumer Protection (Distance Selling) Regulations 2000 (SI 2000/2334) ('the Distance Selling Regulations'), in contrast to the 2002 Regulations (see **25.7.1** above), really are a consumer protection measure, enacted in response to Council Directive 97/7/EC on Distance Selling. As this work is not primarily aimed at consumer protection law, only a brief explanation of the provisions is given below, to show the demands upon the suppliers of goods and services, mainly as regards the information requirements of 'distance communications' under contracts having a distance selling component ('distance contract'). It must be said that the Distance Selling Regulations came into being before today's white-knuckle ride into website selling really developed, and it is not always easy to apply the language of the Regulations to the modern retail situation. Nevertheless, the following points may be made:

(a) Under reg 3, a 'distance contract' means a consumer contract for goods or services under an organised distance sales or service provision scheme run by the supplier who, for the purpose of the contract, makes exclusive use of one or more means of distance communication, up to and including the moment when the contract is concluded.

(b) Regulations 5 and 6 concern 'excepted contracts' and contracts in which the Regulations apply only to parts. The main exceptions are land, building, financial services and auction contracts. Regulation 6(2) provides that the requirements imposed by regs 7–18 and 19(1) are not applicable to contracts for food, beverages or other everyday consumption articles delivered to a consumer's home or workplace by regular roundsmen (reg 6(2)(a)). Bearing in mind the massive increase in home deliveries of daily necessaries by the large general store groups, this raises a considerable question of applicability of the 2000 Regulations. Neither do those particular regulations apply to specific date/period provision of accommodation, transport, catering or leisure services (reg 6(2)(b)).

(c) Regulation 7 requires the provision, in good time prior to the conclusion of the contract, of details of the supplier and his commercial purpose; details of the goods or services; prices, including taxes and delivery costs; payment, delivery and performance details and requirements; notice of cancellation rights; period of validity of price or offer; details of substitutability of goods, etc and other matters. Regulation 8 deals with other written and additional information that may be required, according to circumstances, relating to rights of cancellation (reg 8(2)), obligations to return goods, complaints, after-sales service and guarantees, etc.

(d) Regulation 10(1) provides a powerful consumer protection measure, consisting of a right of cancellation by notice (as modified or excepted by regs 11–13). The effect of such notice, if properly given, is that the contract is treated as if it had never been made (reg 10(2)). The notice must be written or in other durable medium, available and accessible to the buyer; the available modes of giving the notice are prescribed (by reg 10(4)) as hand delivery, post, fax or e-mail.

(e) Regulation 14 provides for the return, on a cancellation, of sums paid by the consumer as soon as possible, and in any case within 30 days starting with the day of notice of cancellation.

(f) Regulation 19(1) is important: unless the parties agree otherwise, the supplier shall perform the contract within a maximum of 30 days, beginning with the day after the day the consumer sent his order. A contract that has not been performed within that period (or whatever was otherwise agreed) is treated as if it had not been made, save for any rights that the consumer has under it for non-performance (reg 19(5)).

(g) Regulation 24 deals with the situation of inertia selling, ie unsolicited goods sent to a person with a view to that person acquiring them, where there has been no agreement by the recipient to acquire or return them. The recipient is entitled to treat those goods (as between himself and the sender) as an unconditional gift.

Enforcement of the Distance Selling Regulations takes two main forms. First, the enforcement authorities may apply for injunctions to secure compliance under reg 27. The secondary form (but which is probably the most effective) is that there is no contracting out of the Regulations; any contract term that is inconsistent with the consumer protection provided by the Regulations is void to that extent (reg 25(1)).

25.7.3 The Privacy and Electronic Communications (EC Directive) Regulations 2003

The Privacy and Electronic Communications (EC Directive) Regulations 2003 (SI 2003/2426) ('the 2003 Regulations') came into being as a result of Directive 2002/58/EC. They provide a specialised and focused regime of data protection in the realm of electronic communications, which are, of course, essential to the functioning of e-commerce. The 2003 Regulations have wider application than just to e-commerce, in that many of the provisions concern both

Internet use and telephone network applications. The main provisions, for present purposes are regs 4–8 and 22–23.

Regulation 4 provides that nothing in the 2003 Regulations relieves a person of obligations under the Data Protection Act 1998 in respect of personal data. Really, the only concern, for present purposes, is with personal data, which is discussed at **26.2.1**. A good deal of the Act is concerned with the security and regulation of public electronic communications, which is beyond the direct relevance of this chapter.

Regulation 5 requires the provider of a public electronic communications service and the provider of any communications network by means of which that service is provided, between them to take appropriate measures to safeguard the security of that service.

Regulation 6 deals with confidentiality of information, and prevents the accessing or storing of information from a subscriber's or user's computer terminal, except where that person is told about the purpose for the access or storage and is given the opportunity to refuse access or storage. This is the basis of the famous 'cookie' box on websites. Regulation 7 deals with the necessary limitations on 'traffic data', the normal electronic nuts and bolts that make the whole electronic communication transmission work. These data must be erased or modified so they cease to be 'personal' data, when no longer required for transmission purposes, unless the subscriber has given permission for their retention for the time necessary for specific marketing or 'value-adding' purposes. Regulation 8 further expands upon the scope of activities for which such permission may be sought, but provides the usual saving for provision of traffic data to competent authorities acting under statutory powers, or under any provision relating to the settlement of disputes (reg 8(4)).

Regulations 22 and 23 deal with transmission of unsolicited communications and for direct marketing, where the identity or address of the sender is concealed. They really are dealing with spam/junk. In both cases, the practices are forbidden by the Regulations, except that there is a provision in reg 22(3) which allows transmissions, for direct marketing purposes, of unsolicited communications where the recipient has 'opted in' to such communications.

25.8 Payment aspects of e-commerce transactions

Again, it is necessary to draw distinctions between B2B e-commerce, using e-mails etc, and the use of website selling, the latter having far more B2C use. With B2B e-commerce, the risk of fraud (which is usually in obtaining something, without any intention of paying for it) can often be minimised where the supplier is in a strong enough bargaining position to obtain independent credit guarantees or money 'up front'. Where the supplier is not in such a strong position, there are considerable risks, but some of these might be reduced, at the supplier's expense, by credit insurance.

With B2C transactions, using websites, the situation can be better for the supplier, and particularly so for the consumer. A great deal of electronic selling involves credit card payment, and the supplier is largely safeguarded against fraudulent customers by the fact that the cost of any card fraud falls back on the credit supplier, the supplier's position being enhanced, in most cases, by the requirement that the credit/payment is available before any performance is made. The risk for a consumer of a fraudulent supplier trying to obtain either money or the customer's details is, nevertheless, quite high. A fair measure of protection for loss of money is provided by the Consumer Credit Act 1974 (CCA 1974), ss 83 and 84, to limit losses to £50 prior to notification to the bank that the card is lost, stolen or being misused. Further protection is given by the Distance Selling Regulations 2000, reg 21, which provides that consumers can cancel a payment where fraudulent use is made of credit cards in contracts covered by the Distance Selling Regulations; the consumer is then entitled to be re-credited, or to have money returned to him. The burden is on the card issuer to show that any use of the card was authorised by the card holder (reg 21(3)). Regulation 21 does not apply to any contract falling within s 83 of CCA 1974; these two mutually-exclusive provisions, between them, provide quite comprehensive protection to the consumer.

25.9 Liabilities of ISSPs and others

You will have already come across many instances of liability during your reading of this chapter, and it will perhaps help if a short summary of the position is offered. This is a rapidly developing field, and the courts will be likely to have to react to new techniques and novel legal questions with some rapidity over the coming years.

25.9.1 The position with contracts arranged by exchange of electronic mail

Normally, the situation here is as with any paper or oral contract: provided the parties have restricted their communications to what was necessary for the contract, the only liabilities to arise will usually be as between the parties. It would still be possible for liability to third parties to arise, under normal legal principles, if the arrangement created any tort (such as publishing defamatory statements, procuring breaches of contract or other economic torts, or breaches of trust, etc). Nevertheless, potential third-party liability is probably much less than where widely accessible websites are concerned.

25.9.2 The position with website e-commerce

Here, the situation is very different: the whole idea of a person being provided with virtually free access to a site from which links and connections may lead to an almost unlimited amount of data, belonging to and referring to all sorts of legal entities, is truly a modern Pandora's box. The potential for legal liability to arise is, frankly, immense, particularly if one considers the further possibilities of defamation, IP infringements etc, associated with many sites.

The position of the ISSP's liability has been discussed already in various contexts; it might be summed up by saying that whatever it provides or facilitates is designed to be part of the information society, and there is no particular reason why it should not be responsible for whatever harms ensue to others, within the limits permissible under whatever laws are in place at the particular time. The material discussed at **25.7.1**, concerning the E-commerce Directive and the 2002 Regulations, shows that the liability of the ISSP can be very wide, but that we should be in a better position to understand the matter, and the position with regard to statutory hosting defences, once the ECJ has delivered rulings and guidance on the cases before it at the moment (late 2010). Probably the greatest immediate problems arise from the use of link/keyword practices (although the ECJ has decided that Google cannot be held liable for trade mark infringements of advertisers on its webpages that select trade mark keywords without permission of the trade mark owner), and from the questions concerning accessory liability for torts and other wrongs committed by service users using interactive sites.

The position between the ISSP and its own users is normally contractual, so that is probably easier to analyse than third-party liability; it will simply depend upon the terms of the contract between the parties, subject to the power of the governing legislation to affect or to invalidate those terms, including the effects of UCTA 1977.

25.10 Conclusion

As you will have seen, a body of law and practice has had to be created and applied with completely unprecedented rapidity, to deal with the growth of the information society and e-commerce. There are probably many more questions still to be asked and answered than have already been considered by the legislators and the courts, but the general framework of workable legal systems for e-commerce is discernible on both sides of the Atlantic. The real challenge will come as the giant nations of Asia begin to make their influence and impact felt – upon commerce generally, upon e-commerce in particular, and upon the world of the commercial lawyer. The emphasis is clearly becoming one of globalisation, so that the budding commercial lawyer is well advised to keep abreast of the information available from sources relevant to the growth in world trade. Some useful source locations are given below:

- International Chamber of Commerce – www.iccwbo.org
- ICANN (Internet Corporation for Assigned Names and Numbers) – www.icann.com
- Nominet UK – www.nominet.org.uk
- World Intellectual Property organisation – www.wipo.org
- World Trade Organisation – www.wto.org

Chapter 26
Data Protection and Freedom of Information

26.1 Introduction

Data about persons or businesses have always been valuable and sensitive commodities, but in the last 30 years or so, the exponential growth and availability of computer systems to assemble, arrange and transfer data has posed a challenge for legal systems worldwide. The demand for such data is insatiable, and to allow unrestricted holding of, and access to them would rapidly lead to chaos and criminality. The only applicable English law, prior to the recent information explosion, worked on the basis of the protection of confidence (see **Chapter 23**), and there was little statutory control of data beyond that. That case law has the broad effect of treating certain confidential information as being within the reach and protection of the equitable jurisdiction. This was completely inadequate to deal with the huge proliferation of potentially accessible databases, containing mundane but highly valuable information. After major investigations and various government reports, coupled with the need to have legal protections compatible with those of the rest of the EU, the Data Protection Act 1984 was enacted. This Act was regulatory in effect and it could not cover paper-based systems; it set out certain guiding principles and its enforcement was largely in the hands of a Data Protection Registrar, with some compensation available for affected individuals. Its effect was to make the handling of personal information subject to controls which had not existed before.

26.1.1 Data Protection Act 1998

The 1984 Act proved a somewhat tentative start, but it was overtaken by a much more robust approach in the European Data Protection Directive of 1995 (95/46/EC). This was enacted as the Data Protection Act 1998 (DPA 1998), which is the current governing legislation. The main effects of the Act are to protect the right of individual privacy and to harmonise UK law with that of other Member States. At first glance, one might consider that this legislation is all about individual protection, but that would be a mistake. Directive 95/46/EC originated out of the highly protectionist attitudes, in some EU Member States, towards the national legal limitations that might be imposed upon the free flow of personal data between, and within, Member States. Data are a valuable source of commercial advantage, and it was certainly the case that, prior to the Directive, trade barriers effectively were being created by national rules on data protection and dissemination. The aim of the Directive is to give no more protection to data processing than is commensurate with a balance between the rights of natural persons and the maintenance of a free market within the EU, by harmonising national legal rules. This will be seen in some of the case law referred to below.

The scheme of the DPA 1998 is to require a 'data controller' to be registered (and to maintain registration) before he can lawfully 'process' any 'personal data' about a 'data subject' (see **26.2** for the meaning of these terms). In other words, before anyone can obtain or deal with any personal information about an identifiable individual, in a systematic way, that data controller must be on a publicly accessible register. Once on the register and in a position to deal with the data, the data controller may deal with the data only for the purposes and within the limits imposed by the Act; and even then, some 'sensitive personal data' will require further special treatment and protection.

The data subject is always in a position to require the data controller to give him basic rights of access to information about what data the controller holds and what is being done, or is likely to be done, with the data. There is a wide range of criminal sanctions available against persons who fail to comply with the requirements of the Act (see **26.7**). The enforcement of the Act is in the hands of the Information Commissioner (formerly known as the Data Protection Commissioner), who, along with his department, regulates, enforces and prosecutes on behalf of the public. The Commissioner is also involved in all aspects of data protection, including European cooperation, advice to the public and to individuals, and the encouragement of good practice, as well as the development and publication of codes of practice. There was formerly a Data Protection Tribunal, now known as the Information Tribunal ('the Tribunal'), which hears a variety of appeals against various regulatory steps taken under the DPA 1998 and the Freedom of Information Act 2000 (FOIA 2000).

26.1.2 Freedom of Information Act 2000

The emergence of data protection legislation has been mainly about protecting the individual's expectation to the privacy of personal data. Over the same period of time, another public expectation has arisen: that of open government and freedom of information about the acts of public authorities. Always a contentious matter, the 'right to know' was not particularly European in origin but has developed more in the common law nations of the world over the last half century. English public law and criminal law show many cases in which the relationship between public access to information and the privacy of the decision-making process is hard to discern with clarity. There was a clear public demand and need for more to be done. Following a period from 1994 during which the Government used a voluntary 'Code of Practice on Public Access to Government Information' (overseen by the Parliamentary Ombudsman), the FOIA 2000 was passed.

The big difference between the DPA 1998 and the FOIA 2000 is that the former deals with the private protection of personal data, whereas the latter is concerned with public access to government information. Nevertheless, there can be overlap, as public authorities, for FOIA 2000 purposes, may also be data controllers for the purpose of the DPA 1998. However, detailed discussion of that overlap is beyond the scope of this work. This chapter deals first with data protection and then with freedom of information.

26.2 Overview and scope of the DPA 1998

The DPA 1998 improved upon the DPA 1984 in a number of ways:

(a) manual files are now included as well as automated data;

(b) new conditions for legal processing of data were laid down;

(c) a new category of personal data was created – 'sensitive data';

(d) transfer of personal data to countries outside the European Economic Area was prohibited, unless certain conditions were met;

(e) minimum security requirements for data were introduced; and

(f) more rights for individuals were introduced, including the right to compensation for damage or distress caused by unlawful processing.

The effects of the DPA 1998 fall into two categories. The first is to allow individuals access to information held about them, for example the information held about people by credit reference agencies. This may be inaccurate and a person would probably want to correct such inaccuracies. The second effect is to protect information about individuals from being disclosed improperly. So, if you give your bank or gas supplier certain information, you might not want them to disclose that information to another business, for example an insurance company, without your consent. Such information is very valuable commercially, and it should not be available for sale without your consent.

Nevertheless, protection of privacy has its limits; the DPA 1998 was given an unusual level of public attention following the murder of two young girls in the town of Soham in 2002. The killer would probably not have been given a job in proximity to children if background checks by two police forces had been carried out properly. In the resulting public inquiry conducted by Sir Michael Bichard, he rejected the suggestion that the DPA 1998 had prevented one police force adequately recording information about the man in question. To quote from the findings of the report:

> It is, as a member of the judiciary said recently, an 'inelegant and cumbersome' piece of legislation, but the legislation was not the problem. I suggest, however, that better guidance is needed on the collection, retention, deletion, use and sharing of information, so that police officers, social workers and other professionals can feel more confident in using information properly.

To understand the working of the Act, it is necessary first to look at some definitions which are closely interdependent (see **26.2.1**), then at some further interpretative measures (see **26.2.2**), and then to examine the principles of good practice and the preconditions for fair processing (see **26.2.3** and **26.2.4**).

26.2.1 The definitions of 'data controller', 'personal data', 'processing' and 'data subject'

These terms are defined in s 1(1) of the DPA 1998, by reference to each other, so that each and every definition and element must be satisfied in order to apply the law to the particular fact situation:

> 'data controller' means . . . a person who (either alone or jointly or in common with other persons) determines the purposes for which and the manner in which personal data are, or are to be, processed;
>
> 'personal data' means data which relate to a living individual who can be identified—
>
> (a) from those data, or
>
> (b) from those data and other information which is in the possession of, or is likely to come into the possession of, the data controller,
>
> and includes any expression of opinion about the individual and any indication of the intentions of the data controller or any other person in respect of the individual;
>
> 'processing', in relation to information or data, means obtaining, recording or holding the information or data or carrying out any operation or set of operations on the information or data, including—
>
> (a) organisation, adaptation or alteration of the information or data,
>
> (b) retrieval, consultation or use of the information or data,
>
> (c) disclosure of the information or data by transmission, dissemination or otherwise making available, or
>
> (d) alignment, combination, blocking, erasure or destruction of the information or data;
>
> 'data subject' means an individual who is the subject of personal data.

So, it is fairly easy to see the general scheme of the Act from the connection of these interpretative definitions; the data controller becomes responsible to the data subject from the first moment of dealing with any personal information that could identify the data subject as a living individual. At first sight, the DPA 1998 seems to have almost limitless scope, but that is deceptive because the Act has only limited application to the various processing methods by which data or information can be dealt with, as well as there being a wide range of exemptions provided for reasons of public policy; also, there have been some restrictive views of the courts as to how some parts of the Act are to be interpreted (see **26.2.2**).

In *Johnson v Medical Defence Union Ltd* [2007] EWCA Civ 262, the Court of Appeal, in a majority judgment, gave a restrictive view of the meaning of 'processing', after consideration of Directive 95/46/EC. The practice, at the defendant's business, whereby a risk manager summarised and made observations about selected files concerning the appellant, was held (Arden LJ dissenting) not to be 'processing' at all, for the purposes of the DPA 1998. The majority in the Court of Appeal took the view that the only matter complained about, which was the 'unfair' selecting of material by the risk manager, had been done by her own personal selection choice, there had been no automatic process at all at work. This seems to be an indication that the English courts view the purpose behind the Directive and the DPA 1998 to be that it is aimed at highly automated processing and retrieval schemes (see *Durant v FSA* at **26.2.2**).

26.2.2 'Personal data', 'data' and 'relevant filing systems'

We have already seen how the DPA 1998 works in a broad sense, but now it is necessary to see how far the provisions can reach. The definition of 'personal data' in s 1(1) is itself defined by reference to 'data'. The problem with that is that the s 1(1) definition of 'data' includes five, alternative classes of information, of which the most significant involves a 'relevant filing system', which term is then further defined in s 1(1).

The starting point is to find out what can comprise 'data' for these purposes:

> 'data' means information which—
>
> (a) is being processed by means of equipment operating automatically in response to instructions given for that purpose;
>
> (b) is recorded with the intention that it should be processed by means of such equipment;
>
> (c) is recorded as part of a relevant filing system or with the intention that it should form part of a relevant filing system;
>
> (d) does not fall within paragraph (a), (b) or (c) but forms part of an accessible record as defined by section 68; or
>
> (e) is recorded information held by a public authority and does not fall within any of paragraphs (a) to (d) …

It is enough that the data fit within one class, although they may fit within more than one. Classes (a) and (b) are reasonably clear. Class (c) is very broad and can include paper-based systems. Class (d) can extend to health and education records that do not fit into other classes. Class (e) was added by the FOIA 2000.

Class (c) is likely to have much the most common application, and the definition of a 'relevant filing system' has caused, and will probably continue to cause, problems. That definition is as follows:

> 'relevant filing system' means any set of information relating to individuals to the extent that, although the information is not processed by means of equipment operating automatically in response to instructions given for that purpose, the set is structured, either by reference to individuals, or by reference to criteria relating to individuals, in such a way that specific information relating to a particular individual is readily accessible …

In *Durant v Financial Services Authority* [2003] EWCA Civ 1746, the Court of Appeal restricted the meaning of a 'relevant filing system', and thus restricted the meaning of 'personal data'. Auld LJ held that the structure of a manual filing system would have to be 'on a par' with a computerised system for it to fall within the definition of a 'relevant filing system'. In other words, it would have to be highly organised. A mere collection of documents would not suffice. In the case in question, the effect was that the information did not have to be disclosed under the DPA 1998.

As regards the definition of 'personal data', the Court of Appeal held that data would 'relate to' an individual only if the data concerned a person's privacy. Two tests were suggested:

(a) Is the information *biographical* in a significant sense?

(b) Does the information have the *individual* as its focus, rather than other persons or matters?

The Information Commissioner has published guidance following the decision in *Durant*; see www.ico.gov.uk (search 'Durant'). Thus, it is suggested that the individual's name will be 'personal data' only where the name appears together with other information about the named individual such as address, telephone number or information regarding his hobbies. This comes from the decision of the ECJ in *Lindquist v Kammaraklagaren* (Case C-101/01) (ECJ, 6 November 2003). The Information Commissioner suggests that the following are also examples of personal data, provided the information in question can be linked to an identifiable individual:

(a) information about the medical history of an individual;

(b) an individual's salary details;

(c) information concerning an individual's tax liabilities;

(d) information comprising an individual's bank statements; and

(e) information about an individual's spending preferences.

In contrast, the Information Commissioner suggests that the following examples of information would not normally be personal data:

(a) mere reference to a person's name where the name is not associated with any other personal information;

(b) incidental mention in the minutes of a business meeting of an individual's attendance at that meeting in an official capacity; or

(c) where an individual's name appears on a document or e-mail indicating only that it has been sent or copied to that particular individual, the content of that document or e-mail does not amount to personal data about the individual unless there is other information about the individual within it.

Further, the Information Commissioner suggests that information which has as its focus something other than the individual will not constitute 'personal data'. For example, information which focuses on a property is not 'personal data'. The reason is that such information is not taken as something that will 'relate to' the individual. In contrast to this, there are circumstances where information about a house could be 'personal data'. For example, this could be a valuation of a house which was used in the context of divorce proceedings.

If an individual cannot be identified from the data in question then the data are not 'personal data', and therefore not subject to the DPA 1998. So, for example, if the information about patients taking part in a clinical experiment has the identifying information about individuals removed from the results, the results are not 'personal data'. The results are thus not subject to the access rights under the 1998 Act.

26.2.3 The eight principles of good practice

Anyone processing personal information must comply with eight enforceable principles of good information handling practice (DPA 1998, s 4(4)). These principles, contained in Sch 1, state that data must be:

1. fairly and lawfully processed;
2. processed for limited purposes;
3. adequate, relevant and not excessive;
4. accurate and up-to-date;
5. not kept longer than necessary;
6. processed in accordance with the individual's rights;
7. secure; and
8. not transferred to countries outside the European Economic Area unless the country has adequate protection for the individual.

To assist in facilitating good practice, s 51(3) of the DPA 1998 provides for the Information Commissioner and trade associations to be proactive in providing appropriate codes of practice to achieve industry/activity specific best practice in data protection. There are some widely used codes, including The Employment Practices Data Protection Code and The British Code of Advertising, Sales Promotion and Direct Marketing. This type of self-guidance and regulation is further supported by such measures as the Privacy and Electronic Communications (EC Directive) Regulations 2003 (SI 2003/2426), which generally apply to the area of electronic communication, including online marketing.

26.2.4 The six conditions for fair data processing and the obligation to register

At least one of the following conditions, seen in Sch 2 to the DPA 1998, must be met for personal information to be considered as having been processed fairly:

(a) the individual has consented to the processing;

(b) processing is necessary for the performance of a contract with the individual or for taking steps at the request of the individual with a view to entering into a contract;

(c) processing is required under a legal obligation (other than one imposed by the contract);

(d) processing is necessary to protect the vital interests of the individual;

(e) processing is necessary to carry out public functions, eg administration of justice; and

(f) processing is necessary in order to pursue the legitimate interests of the data controller or third parties (unless it could unjustifiably prejudice the interests of the individual).

In the *Johnson* case, discussed at **26.2.1**, it was said, obiter, in the Court of Appeal, that 'fairness' required consideration of both data subject and data user. The Court took the view that the defendant Medical Defence Union was running its business, as a mutual society for health professionals, for the benefit of all its members, as a whole. There was no suggestion of bad faith and it had adopted a clearly thought-out policy that was not, at its lowest, clearly unjustified. There were no grounds to interfere with the first instance finding that the processing was not unfair in any relevant respect. The defendant Union had acted as it did for the purpose of fulfilling its obligations to all its members; that can be seen to fit easily within, at the very least, conditions (c) and (f), above.

Where 'sensitive personal data' are to be processed (see **26.2.5**), one of the above conditions (at least) as well as at least one of a further set of conditions, found in Sch 3, must be met.

The requirement for data controllers to be on a public register stems from the 1995 Data Protection Directive, Article 18, which requires all Member States to provide that controllers notify supervisory authorities before carrying out any processing of personal data. This is put into effect by s 17 of the DPA 1998, which, in combination with s 21(1), makes it a criminal offence to process such data in the absence of registration of 'registrable particulars' and certain other matters concerning the data controller and its methods of achieving compliance with the seventh principle referred to in **26.2.3**: maintaining the security of the data. Currently, the registration period is 12 months, renewable in 12-month periods, for a fee of

£35 per data controller, regardless of the amount of processing involved. It must be stressed that s 17 must be complied with before any type of processing is commenced (including obtaining the data in the first place; see **26.2.1**); any unlawfulness cannot be cured retrospectively. See **26.7** for notification offences.

26.2.5 Sensitive personal data

Sensitive personal data are a sub-set of personal data. There are tighter controls on the processing of sensitive personal data. The relevant definition of 'sensitive personal data' is in s 2:

> In this Act 'sensitive personal data' means personal data consisting of information as to—
>
> (a) the racial or ethnic origin of the data subject,
>
> (b) his political opinions,
>
> (c) his religious beliefs or other beliefs of a similar nature,
>
> (d) whether he is a member of a trade union (within the meaning of the Trade Union and Labour Relations (Consolidation) Act 1992),
>
> (e) his physical or mental health or condition,
>
> (f) his sexual life,
>
> (g) the commission or alleged commission by him of any offence, or
>
> (h) any proceedings for any offence committed or alleged to have been committed by him, the disposal of such proceedings or the sentence of any court in such proceedings.

Sensitive personal data must be processed in accordance with the requirements of Sch 3, 'Conditions relevant for purposes of the first principle: processing of sensitive personal data'. For example:

> 1. The data subject has given his *explicit* [emphasis added] consent to the processing of the personal data.
>
> 2. (1) The processing is necessary for the purposes of exercising or performing any right or obligation which is conferred or imposed by law on the data controller in connection with employment.

There is a broad range of such conditions, based on public policy grounds. The conditions are alternatives and at least one must apply in any particular case.

26.2.6 Checklist to application of the DPA 1998

At this point it is possible to see that some caution is needed in ascertaining whether the DPA 1998 applies to a situation in the first place. It is suggested that the following checklist order might be helpful:

(a) the data subject must be a living individual;

(b) data (within s 1(1)) must be in question; that may, but will not necessarily, involve consideration of whether a relevant filing system is involved;

(c) the data are personal data;

(d) some processing is involved;

(e) at least one precondition for processing within Sch 2 is met, and if sensitive personal data are involved, at least one from Sch 3 is met too;

(f) the data are processed in accordance with all the relevant data protection principles in Sch 1.

26.3 The rights of the data subject and other persons under the DPA 1998

These matters are dealt with in Pt II of the Act. This Part recognises that personal data about one individual may well, if disclosed, identify other individuals and disclose information about those persons too. The rights, therefore, may extend to more than one individual in any particular case. The seven rights are as described at **26.3.1** to **26.3.7** below.

26.3.1 The right to subject access (s 7)

A data controller is not required to notify a data subject automatically about data held in respect of him. However, s 7 entitles a data subject to be informed by a data controller, upon request in writing, whether any personal data are being processed, what they comprise, the purposes for which they are being processed, and to whom the data are or may be disclosed. This is subject to some limits where multiple individuals might be identified and confidentiality is involved, but the right is enforceable by court order in difficult cases. Any request for information from a credit reference agency is deemed to be limited to personal data about financial standing, unless the contrary is clearly indicated in the request (s 9).

26.3.2 The right to prevent processing likely to cause damage or distress (s 10)

Any data subject is entitled to require, by written notice, that a data controller cease or not commence processing, or restrict processing, of his personal data, where the processing would otherwise be likely to cause unwarranted damage or distress to anyone at all. This right does not apply where any of the conditions in paras 1–4 of Sch 2 is fulfilled. These include where the data subject has already consented to processing, or the processing is necessary for the purposes of complying with contractual arrangements of the data subject, to meet legal or regulatory requirements upon the data holder or to protect the vital interests of the data subject. The data controller must reply to the notice within 21 days, stating just what he intends to do about the notice.

26.3.3 The right to prevent processing for purposes of direct marketing (s 11)

This is a very important right for any data subject to require, in writing, a data holder to cease, or not begin, any processing carried out for the purposes of allowing any person to direct advertising or marketing material towards particular individuals.

26.3.4 Rights in relation to automated decision taking (s 12)

This is a right that is likely to grow in significance. Any individual is allowed to object to decisions being taken that significantly affect that individual and which are based solely upon the automated processing of his or her personal data. Non-exclusive examples of such decision-making areas as work performance, creditworthiness, reliability and conduct are given in the section. The section provides that a data subject can require a data controller to ensure that such a decision is not to be made based solely on the automatic processing, or, if one has already been made, the data subject is to be notified that it was made on that basis, as soon as reasonably practicable. The data subject then has 21 days to require the data controller to reconsider the decision, or to take a fresh decision on a different basis. There are some categories of 'exempt decisions' in s 12(6) and (7), and these may be added to, in due course, by the Secretary of State; the existing exemptions mainly involve contractual matters of the data subject, or are based upon safeguarding the interests of the data subject.

26.3.5 The right to compensation (s 13)

Any individual, whether data subject or otherwise, can sue one or more data controllers as primarily or vicariously liable for breaches of the Act that lead to damage and/or distress. Distress claims seem to be limited to circumstances where the distress is accompanied by quantifiable damage, or where the personal data were processed for journalistic, artistic or literary purposes (see s 3). There is a defence against compensation claims if the data controller has taken reasonable care to comply with the Act (s 13(3)).

26.3.6 The right to rectification, blocking, erasure and destruction (s 14)

This gives the court, at the instance of a data subject, the power to order the data controller to rectify, block, erase or destroy any personal data, about the data subject or anyone else, which are inaccurate and personal data which contain expressions of opinion which appear to be based upon the inaccurate data. If the inaccurate data have been accurately recorded by the data holder, wherever they came from, the court may order that the data remain but be supplemented by an approved statement of correction.

26.3.7 The right to ask the Commissioner to assess whether the Act has been contravened (s 42)

This gives a discretion to the Commissioner as to the form and manner of making such an assessment, at the instance of any person who is, or who believes himself to be, directly affected by any processing. There is no discretion as to whether to assess; that is subject to the saving that the Commissioner must receive enough information from the complainant to be able to identify the complainant and to identify the particular processing. This remedy is used very widely, and the consequence is normally that the Commissioner serves an 'information notice' on the controller, stating how the notice came to be served and seeking information. This is backed up by criminal sanctions under s 47 if there is failure in compliance with the notice. A data controller has a right of appeal to the Tribunal against service of such notices.

26.4 The obligations of the data controller and disclosure restrictions

As we saw at **21.2.3**, data controllers must abide by the data protection principles. The two principles of most concern in regard to disclosure of personal data are the first two, namely that data must be fairly and lawfully processed, and processed for limited purposes. Let us now look at these two principles in further detail.

26.4.1 First principle of good practice: fair and lawful processing

As 'processing' is defined widely, the first principle has wide application to all use of personal data. It can be divided into four obligations:

(a) to process personal data fairly;

(b) to process such data lawfully;

(c) to comply with *at least one* of the Sch 2 conditions; and

(d) to comply additionally with *at least one* of the Sch 3 conditions if sensitive personal data are processed.

You will recall that the Sch 2 conditions include consent by the data subject, as well as such matters as being necessary for performance of contracts involving the data subject. It is not necessary for all of the Sch 2 conditions to be met, but clearly, if consent is safely to be relied upon as a precondition, that data subject would need to know, in advance, that consent is being given or strongly implied, and for what purposes any consent is given. 'Pushy' data controllers need to be careful about that. Where sensitive personal data are involved, consent must be 'explicit'.

In *British Gas Trading Ltd v Data Protection Registrar* [1998] Info TLR 393 (Data Protection Tribunal), British Gas were found to be processing customers' information unfairly. If a customer did not wish to receive information about other products and services, including from third parties, he had to return a form to British Gas. The tribunal found the processing of personal data was unfair unless done with the consent of the data subject, and that silence did not equate to acceptance. (The case was in fact decided under the 1984 Act, though the facts would still have breached the DPA 1998.) See also *Johnson v Medical Defence Union Ltd* [2007] EWCA Civ 262, discussed at **26.2.1** and **26.2.4**.

There are other conditions in Sch 2 which could be used to justify processing, depending on the circumstances. For example, condition 5(a), that the processing is necessary for the administration of justice. Condition 6(1) provides wide grounds for data processing:

> The processing is necessary for the purposes of legitimate interests pursued by the data controller or by the third party or parties to whom the data are disclosed, except where the processing is unwarranted in any particular case by reason of prejudice to the rights and freedoms or legitimate interests of the data subject.

In *Totalise plc v Motley Fool Ltd* [2001] EWCA Civ 1897, the defendants ran an Internet bulletin board. A third party posted defamatory statements about the claimants. The claimants sought information from the defendants as to the true identity of the third party, who used a pseudonym on the bulletin board. The defendants refused to supply the information, stating that release might breach the DPA 1998. The Court of Appeal held that a court would need to pay attention to condition 6 of Sch 2 before granting an order to reveal the third party's identity. In particular, the rights of the third party would need to be considered and to be balanced against those of the claimant. The right of the third party to respect for his or her private life under Article 8 of the European Convention on Human Rights would also need to be taken into account.

Processing of sensitive personal data is subject to the conditions in Sch 3. The conditions here are harder to satisfy than those in Sch 2. In practice, many instances of requests for the release of sensitive personal data are made in connection with a criminal investigation, or in regard to potential civil proceedings. Thus, under condition 6 in Sch 3, release of sensitive personal data can be justified if:

> the processing . . . is necessary for the purpose of, or in connection with, any legal proceedings (including prospective legal proceedings).

Under condition 10 of Sch 3, there is a power for the Secretary of State to make an order setting out the additional conditions where processing of sensitive personal data may take place on the grounds of substantial public interest. For example, the Data Protection (Processing of Sensitive Personal Data) Order 2000 (SI 2000/417) sets out a number of conditions concerning crime prevention or detection.

In many of the conditions in Schs 2 and 3, the processing of personal data must be 'necessary'. The Information Commissioner suggests that in judging whether processing is necessary, data controllers would need to consider whether:

(a) the purposes for which the data are being processed are valid;

(b) such purposes can be achieved only by the processing of personal data; and

(c) the processing is proportionate to the end pursued.

26.4.2 Second principle of good practice: processed for limited purposes

There is a lot of overlap between the first and second principles. The concept of processing for limited purposes means that the data should be processed only for the purposes to which the data subject has consented. The legal guidance from the Information Commissioner is in fact slightly wider and refers to different purposes which are not being 'envisaged' by the data subject at the time of the collection of the information. As we will see below, there are exceptions which may apply in various circumstances to this and other principles, for example in connection with crime prevention or legal proceedings.

26.5 Exemptions

Part IV of the DPA 1998 deals with the very wide range of exemptions to the provisions of the Act. These are seen in ss 27 to 39 and Schs 7 and 8. The reasons for most of the exempt situations are based on public policy. None of the matters provides absolute blanket exemption from all the effects of the Act, but instead work on the basis that certain disclosure and processing restrictions, normally required by the data protection principles, are removed in certain circumstances. Matters such as national security, crime, taxation, social work, examination marks, legal professional privilege, etc are included, and the range extends to almost all areas where there is a strong justification, based upon public interest, that the Act should not apply to its fullest extent. Because different heads of exemption receive different statutory treatment, consideration of the full range of matters is beyond the scope of this work, but two examples are given at **26.5.1**.

26.5.1 Exemptions for crime prevention and legal proceedings

Under s 29(3), personal data are exempt from the non-disclosure provisions and the right of subject access where the disclosure is for the purposes of preventing or detecting crime, apprehending or prosecuting offenders, or assessing or collecting tax, if the application of those provisions would prejudice any of those vital matters. It will still be necessary to show that at least one of the preconditions to processing is present. This exemption is further facilitated by the effect of the Data Protection (Processing of Sensitive Personal Data) Order 2000 (SI 2000/417; see **26.4.1**), which allows sensitive personal data to be processed without breaching the first principle, if processing is necessary for various purposes based upon 'the substantial public interest'. That provision covers police work as well as the other matters contained in s 29.

Under s 35(2):

> Personal data are exempt from the non-disclosure provisions where the disclosure is necessary—
>
> (a) for the purpose of, or in connection with, any legal proceedings (including prospective legal proceedings), or
>
> (b) for the purpose of obtaining legal advice,
>
> or is otherwise necessary for the purposes of establishing, exercising or defending legal rights.

So, a data controller might be required to disclose information to a third party in connection with legal proceedings, as indicated in the two subsections above. This could cover telecommunications companies who receive requests under the Regulation of Investigatory Powers Act 2000. It would also cover orders made under the Drug Trafficking Act 1994, or obligations to disclose information under the Money Laundering Regulations 2003 (SI 2003/3075). Less dramatically, it would also cover disclosure under the Civil Procedure Rules 1998. A court order would normally be required in this last instance (see the *Totalise* case at **26.4.1**).

Thus, it is clear that a data controller may be faced with a very wide range of matters, in which he may be required to disclose information that would normally be protected by the Act. On closer examination, it can be seen that the disclosure is usually going to be made to government agencies or to parties to legal proceedings; the obvious safeguard for the data controller is that, if necessary, the aid of the court may be sought to decide the matter.

In *Sayers v Smithkline Beecham Plc* [2007] EWHC 1346, the High Court was asked to authorise the supply of some copy documents of expert reports, which had been used in the English court in the MMR/MR vaccine litigation. These were required for use by the US Government, as it was a defendant in litigation in the US concerning alleged autism links to the MMR vaccine. This application was opposed by various claimants in the UK proceedings, on grounds that release of the documents would be contrary to the DPA 1998, as the data subjects had not given permission for this use in America. Keith J granted the US application on the basis that:

(a) the US courts could be trusted to use the documents only for the proper purpose of the litigation and on condition that anonymity could be preserved properly;

(b) the claimants would probably have consented to the use of the documents by the claimants in the US, so it was not in the interests of justice to deny their use to the defendants; and

(c) provided that the documents were properly anonymised, so as to prevent any link to identifiable persons, there could be no infringement of the DPA 1998 or of Article 8 of the European Convention on Human Rights (ECHR).

In *L v L* [2007] EWHC 140 (QB), the court was asked to order delivery up of all copies of the claimant husband's laptop hard drive that had been made or taken by his former wife, her solicitors and any of their agents. This was against a backdrop of financial proceedings, concerning the now-dissolved marriage, in the Swedish courts. The husband argued that the hard drive held much material, some protected by legal professional privilege, some confidential material that was not protected by privilege, and information about the personal and business affairs of identifiable friends and colleagues. He based his application on Article 8 of the ECHR, on the DPA 1998 and on the Computer Misuse Act 1990, s 1. The Court ordered delivery up into the hands of the husband's solicitors, subject to any subsequent requirement to give relevant disclosure in accordance with the rules of litigation.

It can be seen, from the above cases, that the courts take a balanced and principled view of the matter, and there seems to be no real problem in applying the current data protection law to litigation situations.

26.6 Requests from outside the EU

The eighth data protection principle prohibits the transfer of personal data to countries outside the European Economic Area, not just the EU, unless the country in question has an equivalent level of protection for personal data. A particular problem area is the United States. There are a number of exemptions to this prohibition which are broadly similar to those under s 35(2) (in effect that release is required or allowed by law; see **26.5.1**) but not identical to them. The Information Commissioner has stated that there is no blanket exemption allowing the transfer of information in regard to the law of another country. The transfer might be necessary for reasons of substantial public interest, or necessary in connection with legal proceedings, but a judgement has to be made in each case. Section 54 deals with international cooperation. The *Sayers v Smithkline Beecham plc* case gives a good illustration of the process in operation (see **26.5.1**).

An example of these difficulties has emerged with the increased requirements for security of aircraft. The US Bureau of Customs and Border Protection required EC airlines to disclose data comprising passenger lists. However, the European Commission considered that the release of these data would not be in compliance with the Directive on Data Protection from which the DPA 1998 stems. The problem was overcome by the adoption of a bilateral arrangement between the EC (now EU) and the US in 2004. This contained assurances as to how the United States authorities would use and protect the data. Generally, the powers of the Commissioner are limited by the DPA 1998, and any further steps usually require government intervention. In summary, the prevailing ECJ view is that passenger name records, dealt with for security purposes, fall within the exemptions for public safety and crime prevention.

26.7 Enforcement, offences and civil damages

We have already seen how the Commissioner might assist the data subject by assessing what a data controller is doing, or is likely to be doing, with personal data and what steps the controller is taking to comply with the DPA 1998. Now it is necessary to see how these statutory requirements are enforced. The Act creates a wide range of criminal offences, but these fall, generally, within one of three classes: notification offences, enforcement offences, and disclosure offences. Most are 'either way' offences, punishable by fine.

Notification offences are those matters arising out of Pt III of the Act, which deals with the obligations of the data controller to notify the Commissioner of 'registrable particulars', to ask to be put on the register and to notify the Commissioner of any changes to the particulars. Processing without registration and failure to notify changes are offences under s 21.

Enforcement offences are found in Pt V of the Act and arise where there is a failure by the data controller to comply with the enforcement mechanisms employed by the Commissioner. If the Commissioner becomes involved in assessment of any particular processing by a data holder, the first step taken will be service of an information notice (see **26.3.6**). Then, if the Commissioner becomes satisfied that the data controller is, or will become, in contravention of any of the data protection principles, an 'enforcement notice' will be served, requiring the data controller to remedy the situation (subject to appeal against the notice to the Tribunal). Under s 47, failure to comply with any of these notices is a criminal offence.

Disclosure offences can arise in various ways. The definition of 'processing' is wide enough to cover improper disclosure, which can thus fall within the offences under s 21 discussed above (eg, simply handling data without being registered). Section 55 creates a wide-ranging offence where personal data (or information contained within the personal data) are obtained or disclosed without the consent of the data controller (usually catching errant employees or others in league with them). This can catch persons who procure the disclosure in such circumstances and anyone who sells, or offers to sell, personal data obtained in that way. This is very useful to prevent further dissemination or use of the data, after an initial illegal disclosure. For this purpose, advertising the sale is treated as offering to sell the data (s 55(6)). Interestingly, s 59 creates an offence of wrongful disclosure by the Commission itself (Commissioner, staff or agents).

Most claims for damages are likely to be brought, unreported, in the county court, because of the level of damages involved. Nevertheless, if injunctive relief is sought, some may get into the High Court. Two reported cases where the court awarded damages for breach of the DPA 1998 are *Campbell v MGN Ltd* [2002] EWCA Civ 1373 and *Douglas and Others v Hello! Ltd and Others* [2003] EWHC 786 (Ch) (see **23.4**). It may be that more claims might be brought for distress arising from breach of the Act, but the principles of assessment for distress are not clear yet.

26.8 Conclusion on data protection

There have been valuable and practical benefits to the general public being able to prevent, for example, utility providers – or anyone else with vast amounts of commercially valuable personal data – simply selling that data to the highest bidder. It has also been of the greatest importance that individuals have been able to find out just what personal data are held by data controllers, and to what end.

The legal framework seems to be reasonably applicable and workable, considering the exceptional difficulties in regulating the holding and processing of data in an information-based society. There are, currently, some signs that the commercial pressure to make the fullest use and exploitation of data is creating some unease for many people; the Information Commissioner and Parliament are beginning to respond to public concerns about this. Nevertheless, that should not be seen as any failure of the basic data protection legislative structure. A more difficult problem is the purely technical aspect of keeping data processing systems secure against fraudsters, theft and negligence. There have recently been some massive failures of security around data held by government departments and other large organisations; data protection law can do little to prevent such failures and the matter is not discussed further.

Overall, the practical problems have been more about organisations failing to disclose information, rather than organisations disclosing information too readily. As we have said, the tendency is for bureaucrats to treat the DPA 1998 as a charter to keep things secret. The obvious examples are the Soham murder case, resulting in the Bichard Report, mentioned at **26.2** above, and the reported failure by British Gas to disclose information to social services about vulnerable pensioners who might have problems surviving in cold weather. This is really a question of the interface problems between data protection, freedom of information and human rights law. This area must, necessarily, be left to the courts to examine as and when it becomes necessary to do so.

26.9 Freedom of information

Freedom of information appears, at first glance, to be quite the opposite of data protection, but there is no fundamental reason for the two concepts to be incompatible. All that is necessary is for public authority users and holders of information to be aware of the difference between duties owed to the general public and those duties owed to the private individual. The Information Commissioner is responsible for both data protection and freedom of information; a very wide range of further information can be found at ico.gov.uk.

The basic approach of British bureaucracy, up until the last 20 years or so, was to deal with most information on a strict 'need to know' basis, usually claiming that it was covered by the Official Secrets Act and therefore protected from disclosure. Even very mundane information was treated in a similar way. This became an ever-more pressing problem with the growth in number and powers of public agencies and local government authorities. There were many piecemeal initiatives and steps taken to widen access in various areas, such as access to medical records, housing records, meetings of local authorities, etc; but much a more general advance was demanded, so the FOIA 2000 was enacted, coming fully into force on 1 January 2005. The Act has enhanced many of the existing statutory access rights, but many of those earlier rights still remain and, where this is the case, the FOIA 2000 is not applicable (FOIA 2000, s 21). The philosophy of the Act is to allow much wider citizen participation in the development of public policy and the decision-making process. It also has the merit of increasing the public awareness and accountability of public bodies.

An important limitation on public access under the Act is that it applies only to recorded information held by a public body. So, matters which are not so recorded, but which may well be known to public servants, are beyond the reach of the Act; other methods will need to be employed to find out about those matters. Another considerable limitation is that any request by the data subject which involves any of his personal data can be made only under the DPA 1998. Such a matter is exempted under s 40(1) of the FOIA 2000. It is possible to obtain data concerning individuals other than the applicant in very restricted circumstances set out in s 40(2)–(4)

26.9.1 Application of the Freedom of Information Act 2000

The 2000 Act applies only to information held by 'public authorities', as defined in s 3(1). These include:

(a) central government departments and agencies;
(b) local government;
(c) the police;
(d) the NHS;
(e) State schools, colleges and universities; and
(f) publicly-owned companies such as the Royal Mail.

The Secretary of State is empowered under s 5 to designate an entity as a public authority. The above list can therefore be added to by that means. This could apply, for example, to a contractor providing services on behalf of a government department. The Act also provides that certain public authorities come within it only in respect of information of a specified description (s 7). See *BBC v Sugar* [2008] EWCA Civ 191.

26.9.2 Accessible information

Section 1 of the 2000 Act defines the right to information. Section 1(1) deals with the basic right:

> (1) Any person making a request for information to a public authority is entitled:
>
> (a) to be informed in writing by the public authority whether it holds information of the description specified in the request, and
>
> (b) if that is the case, to have that information communicated to him.

The provisions of para (a) are referred to as the 'duty to confirm or deny'. 'Awareness Guidance No 21' from the Information Commissioner deals with this matter. In essence, the thinking behind these provisions is quite straightforward. If information has been requested but is not held by the authority in question, it would normally be reasonable to inform the applicant of that fact. However, there may be some exceptional cases where it would not even be right to confirm or deny that information requested is held. An obvious example is the area of policing, where it would not make sense to allow criminals to discover whether they were under suspicion or not.

Basically, all information held by a public authority is available to an individual under the provisions of the Act, but there are seven absolute exemptions and 16 qualified exemptions from the general right (see **26.9.5**). The right is to 'information', not to documents or to a file. The public authority can therefore edit documents or files, where they also contain information that would be subject to an exemption. The public authority should not refuse a request for access on the basis that there is exempt information as well as accessible information in the document or file. Considerable editing may result, in practice.

The Act has given rise to a very wide range and complexity of requests, and there is some concern in public bodies about the cost of compliance. There is a discretion, where the cost of compliance would exceed a statutory limit, to require the applicant to agree to pay the actual cost, or part of it, in advance. The response time allowed is normally a maximum of 20 days, but this may be extended by notice to the applicant, where reasonable to do so.

The accessible information is that 'held' by the public authority, not that 'created' by the authority. Thus, information from or about businesses which is held by a public authority is accessible to the public, if it is not subject to an exemption. This could cover, for example, details of a bid made for government work under the Public Private Partnership. This aspect of the Act is a key concern to businesses and their lawyers.

The Act applies to information obtained by a public authority before the Act came into force (s 1(4)). In other words, information is not exempted from disclosure because it was obtained before the implementation date of the Act.

26.9.3 Publication schemes

A voluntary code of practice on access to government information was introduced in 1994. Government departments, their agencies and some other public bodies followed this code. It promoted the disclosure of information by public bodies, subject to some exemptions. It was sufficiently flexible that the departments in question could operate either a relatively open or a restrictive regime and still come within the code. The code ceased to have effect from 1 January 2005.

All public authorities which are subject to the FOIA 2000 have been obliged to operate approved publication schemes since 30 June 2004, under s 19. These schemes have to be approved by the Information Commissioner. The schemes must have regard to the public interest in, for example, the publication of reasons for decisions which have been made by a public authority. There is a wide range of schemes under the 2000 Act, including, for example, a number for the NHS. A publication scheme will usually comprise four sections:

(a) information about the public authority, its responsibilities and the scheme;
(b) classes of information published or to be published;
(c) the manner in which the information is to be published;
(d) whether the publication is to be free of charge or not.

The presence of a publication scheme does not, of itself, prevent successful applications for further, more detailed information under the Act. In *Corporate Officer of the House of Commons v Information Commissioner* [2008] EWHC 1084 (Admin), the decisions of the Information Commissioner and Information Tribunal, to order the provision of detailed breakdowns of claims for accommodation allowances by 14 Members of Parliament, were upheld by the Divisional Court. The consideration of the publication of private addresses had been properly dealt with and had been found to be outweighed by the deeply flawed allowances system; public scrutiny was justified.

26.9.4 Codes for access to information and for management of information

Under s 45 of the 2000 Act, the Secretary of State is required to issue a code of practice giving guidance to public authorities. The Information Commissioner has to be consulted, and the code must be approved by Parliament. This code gives guidance relating to the following:

(a) the provision of advice by public authorities to applicants – public authorities must provide advice and assistance;
(b) the transfer of requests by a public authority to another authority which may be the holder of the information;
(c) consultation with persons to whom the information relates, or whose interests are likely to be affected;
(d) the inclusion in contracts entered into by public authorities of terms relating to the disclosure of information;
(e) the provision by public authorities of procedures for dealing with complaints about requests for information.

This code is available at www.dca.gov.uk/foi/reference/imprep/codepafunc.htm.

Under s 46, the Lord Chancellor is obliged to issue a code for public authorities relating to the keeping, management and destruction of their records. This is available at www.dca.gov.uk/foi/reference/imprep/codemanrec.htm. Once a record has been destroyed, there is no access to the information that was contained within it. In some other jurisdictions, the recollections of civil servants are treated as accessible information, but this is not the case in the UK system under the FOIA 2000.

26.9.5 Absolute and qualified exemptions

Section 2 of the FOIA 2000 sets out the circumstances in which a public authority may refuse a request for information. These fall into two categories, namely, absolute exemptions and qualified exemptions. If an absolute exemption applies there is no legal right of access at all, for example information relating to public security matters. If a qualified exemption applies, a public authority must consider whether there is a greater public interest in, first, confirming or denying the existence of the information requested and, secondly, providing the information to the applicant or not.

The *absolute exemptions* are:

(a) information accessible by other means (s 21);

(b) information supplied by, or relating to, bodies dealing with security matters (s 23);
(c) court records (s 32);
(d) parliamentary privilege (s 34);
(e) personal information (s 40);
(f) information provided in confidence (s 41); and
(g) information the disclosure of which is prohibited by law (s 44).

An example of (d) above is seen in *Office of Government Commerce v Information Commissioner* [2008] EWHC 737 (Admin). Here, Parliamentary privilege was held to apply to review documents prepared for the use of Parliament in connection with the Government's identity card programme. The court allowed an appeal against the Information Commissioner's decision to order disclosure.

Examples of (f) are seen in *Secretary of State for the Home Office v British Union for the Abolition of Vivisection* [2008] EWHC 892 (QB) and *Bluck v Information Commissioner*, Information Tribunal (2007) 98 BMLR. In the first case, the High Court allowed an appeal against a decision of the Information Tribunal that information held by the Home Office should be disclosed. The information that had been obtained by the Home Office was commercially sensitive and had been obtained under statutory powers, with a very strong implication of confidentiality; the Tribunal's approach had been wrong in law. In the *Bluck* case, a father lost his appeal against a decision of the Information Commissioner that medical records concerning his daughter should not be disclosed without the consent of her husband. The daughter had died in hospital, the hospital had admitted liability and a settlement had been reached with the husband. The Tribunal held that the public interest, that patients retained trust in the confidentiality of their records, greatly outweighed any public interest in their disclosure. Interestingly, the Tribunal took the view that the right to enforce and protect confidentiality, relating to medical records, probably passed to personal representatives, despite earlier authorities to the contrary.

Note that much personal information is exempted from the FOIA 2000, and can only be accessed via the DPA 1998.

The *qualified exemptions* are:

(a) information intended for future publication (s 22);
(b) national security (ss 23–24);
(c) defence (s 26);
(d) international relations (s 27);
(e) relations within the UK (s 28);
(f) the economy (s 29);
(g) investigations and proceedings (s 30);
(h) law enforcement (s 31);
(i) audit functions (s 33);
(j) formulation of government policy (s 35);
(k) prejudice to effective conduct of public affairs (s 36);
(l) communications with Her Majesty (s 37);
(m) health and safety (s 38);
(n) some personal information (s 40);
(o) legal professional privilege (s 42); and
(p) commercial interests (s 43).

Qualified exemptions may be class-based, or not. Class exemptions under the Act are intended to give protection to *all* information falling within a particular category, for example legal professional privilege.

On the other hand, a qualified exemption could be prejudice-based. Such exemptions come into force only if a disclosure of particular information would cause prejudice to that category of activity, for example prejudice to international relations. If it does not then the information must be disclosed. This applies in relation to the following qualified exemptions:

(a) defence;
(b) international relations;
(c) relations within the UK;
(d) the economy;
(e) law enforcement;
(f) audit functions; and
(g) commercial interests.

In addition, two sections use alternative words for 'prejudice'. These are:

(a) prejudice to effective conduct of public affairs (s 36), where 'inhibit' is used in s 36(2)(b); and
(b) health and safety (s 38).

Both class- and prejudice-based exemptions are subject to the public interest test, unless the Act states that they are absolute exemptions.

26.9.6 Policing the Act

The Information Commissioner enforces the 2000 Act and is required to promote good practice (s 18). He was previously the Data Protection Commissioner, but now combines that role with his role under the FOIA 2000. He is also responsible for enforcement of the Environmental Information Regulations 2004, which operate separately from the FOIA 2000.

Under s 50, a dissatisfied applicant can apply to the Information Commissioner for a decision. The applicant must have exhausted any complaints procedure which is provided by the public authority. (Such a procedure is required by the access code – see **26.9.4**.)

If the Information Commissioner believes that the public authority has failed to abide by the Act, he can issue an enforcement notice. Under s 54, if the public authority fails to comply with the notice, the Information Commissioner may apply to the court. If the court agrees with the notice, failure to comply is contempt of court. There is an appeal from the decision of the Commissioner to the Information Tribunal under s 57 by either the complainant or the public authority, or both. These appeals apply to decision notices, information notices and enforcement notices. This is a complex area, and in some circumstances it can appear that the Commissioner has reached a decision whereas the reality is that what he has decided is that the matter complained of is beyond his jurisdiction under the Act. That happened in the *BBC v Sugar* case (see **26.9.1**). In this circumstance, the appropriate recourse would be to seek judicial review of the Commissioner's decision, rather than to appeal under the Act.

26.9.7 Interface with the Human Rights Act 1998

Under s 6 of the Human Rights Act 1998, it is unlawful for a public authority to act in a way which is incompatible with a Convention right. Under s 12, the right to free speech is upheld. So, suppose that a business wished to obtain an injunction to stop a public authority from releasing confidential information which had originally been obtained from that business, eg a tender for a contract. The business would have to show, in effect, that it was likely to succeed at the full trial. This is a very heavy evidential burden. The court must in any event consider whether it would be in the public interest for the information to be disclosed. (For a case on the public interest in disclosing information, see *London Regional Transport v Mayor of London* [2001] EWCA Civ 1491.)

A more recent case which involved consideration of the situation where data protection, freedom of information and human rights are engaged is *Michael Stone v South East Coast Strategic Health Authority and Others* [2006] EWHC 1668 (Admin). Here, the decision to publish a report following an independent inquiry into the care, treatment and supervision of Michael Stone prior to his committing two murders and attempting another was upheld. The public interest justified the decision, and the publication was not in breach of the claimant's human rights or his rights under the DPA 1998.

There are hints in the *Corporate Officer of the House of Commons v Information Commissioner* case, discussed at **26.9.3**, that the privacy of private addresses would need to be of a very pressing nature to defeat the public interest in freedom of information in matters which disclose serious shortfalls in the conduct of public bodies. See also *L v L* at **26.5.1**.

Part III Summary
Intellectual Property

Topic	*Summary*
Passing off	This is a common law tort, in which a person misrepresents his goods or services as being those of some other person, or one of numerous variations on that theme. For a person to succeed in proving passing off, he must show that he has some discernible goodwill in some particular aspect of his own goods or services, that the defendant is misrepresenting that aspect, in some way, so that customers are likely to be confused as to the trade origin of the goods or services that they are purchasing, and that there is some identifiable damage to the claimant's business.
Trade mark	This is a sign, capable of graphic representation, that is capable of distinguishing the goods and services of one undertaking from those of another. It must be capable of performing its feature of providing distinctiveness if it is to be registered. Without registration, the mark will not get the statutory protection and the right to a potentially permanent monopoly over that mark in the form in which it is registered.
Descriptive marks	Trade marks which only serve to describe aspects of the type, origin, quality or quantity of the goods are not usually registrable. Often, combining these aspects with other non-excluded matters, such as a logo or different wording, will get around the problem, as can distinctiveness acquired through use of the mark.
Shape marks	There is a limited possibility for registration of trade marks which comprise shapes, but, in general, it is quite difficult to obtain long-term protection by trade mark for shape marks.
Generic marks	These are trade marks which, over time, have lost their ability to distinguish the objects bearing them from similar objects emanating from different trade sources. If a registered trade mark becomes generic, the registration may be revoked. The term simply becomes part of general trade usage.
Community Trade Mark	This is trade mark registration system that applies right across the EU and which is available provided there is no ground of objection arising in any one of the Member States. The system is administered by the Office for the Harmonisation of the Internal Market (OHIM).
Registered Design Right	This is available to protect aspects of the visible external appearance of objects for a limited period of up to 25 years. The main limitation is that the design feature requiring protection must be new (not available before) and of individual character (creating a different overall impression to what had previously been available to the public).

Topic	*Summary*
Unregistered Design Right	This is a residual form of protection that applies to features of the shape or configuration of manufactured articles, internally or externally. The protection is available for up to a maximum of 15 years, more usually 10. To get protection, the feature must be original, in the sense of not being copied, and not commonplace in the design field in question.
Exhaustion of rights	This term describes the process by which the owner of intellectual property rights such as trade marks, patents or design rights loses the power to prevent the further marketing of objects within the EU, once the first dealing in or importation into the EU of the object has taken place, with the right owner's express or implied permission. His rights are said to be exhausted.
Copyright	This is a property right comprising the right to prevent a person copying, for other than a very limited group of 'fair dealing' purposes, an original work of literature, drama, music or art. The right comes into being upon the creation of the work itself and, in most cases, lasts for 70 years from the year in which the creator dies.
Moral rights	These are statutory rights which exist in parallel with the original copyright in most literary, dramatic, musical and artistic works and films. They are designed to remain to the advantage, use and protection of the creator of the work, in the event that he assigns his copyright to someone else.
Entrepreneurial copyright	This is a class of rights that arise out of the exploitation and commercialisation of original copyright works. In the main, they arise as a second generation of rights and are more limited in duration than the original copyright works from which they come. Matters such as films, broadcasts and sound recordings can fall within this category.
Database right	This is a statutory protection that can arise on the creation of databases, that is collections of data or other material that are arranged in a systematic way and which are individually accessible. It applies to both copyright-protected databases as well as non-copyright protected databases. The difference is that, to be copyright protected, the database must have had some human intellectual input in arranging and selecting the material; this is not necessary for non-copyright databases and could be computer created. The right arises automatically on creation and does not need registration. It lasts for 15 years from creation or substantial revision.

Topic	*Summary*
Patent	The grant of a patent is the giving of a monopoly right to use and exploit an invention of some sort. The right is given in exchange for the invention being made public, so that whatever inventive step is comprised within the idea can enter the 'world art' and become known to all. The effect is that the inventor has a 'lead time' of 20 years in which to exploit his invention to the full, but the rest of the world is able to see, throughout that period, what he has developed and is free to build upon the inventor's thinking, for further developments and inventions. The invention, to be patentable, must be new, comprise some inventive step, be capable of industrial application and not be caught by any statutory exclusion.
Inventive step	This means some new aspect of an invention that, at the time of applying for a patent for it, would not be obvious to a person reasonably skilled in the relevant field of invention and development, but who was not of a particularly imaginative or intuitive mind.
Patent claims	These are a part of the patent specification that must be provided by applicants for grant of patent. They comprise a series of numbered paragraphs, in which the inventor describes features of his invention which are, arguably, things or ways of doing things that no person has done or thought about before. The approach is normally to claim, as the first claim, the widest and most general feature of the invention and then, progressively, to narrow and refine the features and qualities claimed as being new to the world art. A person only needs to infringe any one of the claims to infringe a patent.
Confidential information	Some types of confidential information can be protected from disclosure, even though the information is not intellectual property in itself. Material that has been disclosed to someone else, under circumstances where that other person has reason to believe that he has received it under an obligation of confidentiality, can sometimes be the subject of restraining injunctions as well as compensatory damages for unauthorised disclosure. The legal principles involved are trust and fiduciary in nature. Often, the matter is expressly covered in contractual non-disclosure clauses, but where these are not present or applicable the court must be approached.

Topic	*Summary*
Data protection	This is a statutory form of protection which applies where persons obtain or deal with information about individuals, identifiable from the data, in a systematic way. Where this is the case, the persons who are creating, holding or dealing with the information, become liable to registration on a publicly-accessible register. They also become subject to eight statutory principles of good practice and must meet, at least, one of six preconditions before they can be seen as having processed any personal information fairly and lawfully. The individual who is the data subject has a number of statutory rights available, with respect to the processing of the data relating to him.

Part IV

COMPETITION LAW

Chapter 27
Competition Law and Commercial Agreements

27.1 Introduction

You may recall from previous study of competition law that there is a huge degree of overlap between the EU and UK systems. This is no surprise, as the substantive law under the UK system is based on that of the EU. As such, both systems are 'effects based', which means that the law is concerned with the effect that an arrangement may have upon the competitive dynamic of a market. Accordingly, a commercial lawyer must understand the basics of the law, as it can impact on commercial arrangements in numerous ways.

In this chapter we shall again visit the relevant EU and UK legislation. However, here we are going to use the relevant legislation to provide a structure by which you can analyse a commercial agreement in order to determine:

(a) whether an agreement potentially breaches the law;
(b) what sanctions can be imposed for breach; and
(c) how an agreement can be amended, or how it can take advantage of exemptions, so as to be compliant.

Given the degree of overlap between the two systems under discussion here, the approach of this chapter will be to outline the position under EU law and then highlight (where necessary) any additional points which arise under UK law. This approach has been taken to avoid, as much as possible, unnecessary repetition. In addition, not only is the substantive law very similar, there is also an express provision under the Competition Act 1998 (CA 1998), s 60, requiring UK law to be interpreted:

> ... to ensure that so far as is possible ... questions arising ... in relation to competition within the United Kingdom are dealt with in a manner which is consistent with the treatment of corresponding questions arising in Community law in relation to competition within the Community.

27.1.1 Who investigates?

Before we look at how to analyse an agreement, let us deal with a couple of issues that can cause some confusion when studying competition law:

(a) which competition authority will investigate; and
(b) what is the legal basis for its investigation and prosecution?

Looking at the first of these questions, here we are concerned with two of the major regulating bodies: in the EU context, the Competition Directorate of the European Commission (Commission); and in the UK, the Office of Fair Trading (OFT).

In regard to the second question, this was once a very straightforward issue. The Commission was the only body that could investigate and prosecute infringements of EU competition law, and the OFT was responsible for the prosecution of UK competition rules. (It should be noted that under the UK system, other public bodies responsible for the regulation of particular sectors – for example, electricity and gas markets – also have authority to apply UK and EU competition rules; however, these are beyond the scope of this book.)

The arrangement outlined above changed in May 2004, when the OFT (along with the national competition authorities – NCAs – of other Member States) was given the power to apply EU law as well as national competition rules. This delegation of powers from the Commission (or, more correctly, the sharing of power) was due to the expansion of the EU and the fact that the Commission simply did not have the resources to investigate all breaches of EU competition law in the (then) 25 Member States of the EU. The sharing of power to investigate and prosecute infringements of EU law has freed the Commission to concentrate on the most serious, pan-European infringements of the rules. An outline of the position is contained in the following table.

Institution	Which law can it apply?	Comment
Commission	EU competition law only	Will concentrate on serious pan-European infringements
OFT	EU competition law UK competition law	Where there is a potential breach of European competition rules, the Commission will consult with NCAs to assess whether the Commission or the NCA should conduct the investigation and prosecution of the infringement. As pointed out above, the Commission will normally investigate only the most serious pan-European infringements.

As you can see from the above, the OFT can apply either set of rules. We shall look at which set of rules it can use later in this chapter (see see **27.2.6.2**). The important thing for our purposes is that any analysis of an agreement under either EU or UK competition rules will be almost identical.

As a final introductory point, most commercial arrangements will fall to be considered under rules relating to anti-competitive agreements. As such this chapter will concentrate on Article 101 of the Treaty of the Functioning of the European Union (TFEU) (previously Article 81 EC Treaty) and the corresponding UK legislation contained in the Chapter I prohibition. However, it will also briefly deal with Article 102 TFEU (previously, Article 82 EC Treaty) relating to abuse of market power and the UK's Chapter II prohibition.

27.2 Article 101/Chapter I prohibition

27.2.1 EU competition law

Article 101(1) TFEU relates to anti-competitive agreements and prohibits:

> … agreements between undertakings, decisions by associations of undertakings and concerted practices which may affect trade between Member States and which have as their object or effect the prevention, restriction or distortion of competition within the internal market.

As you can see, this is a complex provision. We shall look at each element separately, and this will provide a structure by which we can analyse a commercial agreement under either EU or UK competition rules relating to anti-competitive agreements.

27.2.2 'Agreement(s)'

The term 'agreements' has been interpreted widely by the European courts and covers all types of commercial arrangements, whether they are in writing or agreed verbally. The interpretation is wide enough also to include arrangements that are not legally binding and includes so-called 'gentlemen's agreements'. Accordingly, outside a traditional understanding of the term 'agreements', it is sufficient that the undertakings concerned have expressed their joint intention to conduct themselves on the market in a specified way for the definition to be satisfied.

27.2.3 'Between undertakings'

The term 'undertakings' covers virtually all legal or natural persons carrying on economic or commercial activities. It therefore covers companies, partnerships and sole traders. It also includes non-profit making organisations (such as FIFA, the governing body of football).

27.2.3.1 Parent and subsidiary

For an agreement to come within Article 101(1), it must be between two separate undertakings (plural). Competition law looks at whether the undertakings form *separate economic entities* (this differs from most systems of company law, which consider each company to form a separate legal entity).

As such, parent and subsidiary companies will generally be considered as one and the same economic entity, and therefore agreements between such companies will not be 'between undertakings' for the purposes of Article 101(1).

27.2.3.2 Agency agreements

Applying the same principle, pure agency agreements will generally fall outside Article 101(1) (see 'Guidelines on Vertical Restraints' in the **Appendix**). A pure agency agreement is one where the financial or commercial risk associated with the agency agreement is borne by the principal. Here the agent is not a separate economic undertaking (as it is not accepting any individual economic risk) and, as such, the arrangement between agent and principal in this case will fall outside Article 101(1).

27.2.4 'Decisions by associations of undertakings'

This category would include decisions taken by, for example, a trade association. Such decisions could clearly provide the potential for anti-competitive conduct by facilitating the co-ordination of market behaviour through, for example, price fixing.

27.2.5 'Concerted practices'

By adding concerted practices to the prohibition in Article 101(1), the legislation extends to include conduct that impacts on competition but is made outside an agreement or decision. Although a concerted practice will breach Article 101(1) (if the other elements of Article 101(1) are satisfied), the problem with establishing a concerted practice is one of evidence and intent. As such this is a specialist area of competition law and will not be considered further here.

27.2.6 'Affect trade between Member States'

27.2.6.1 EU law

For Article 101(1) to apply, there must be an effect on trade *between Member States*. If there is no such effect, then Article 101(1) simply does not apply.

The concept of effect on trade became more prominent with the expansion of the EU in May 2004. As we have seen at **27.1.1**, until this time only the Commission could investigate and prosecute breaches of Articles 101 and 102. With the sharing of powers to apply these Treaty articles, it became particularly important to establish when a national competition authority could apply EU rules and where it could apply national rules. Accordingly, the requirement that an agreement should have an effect on trade between Member States defines the boundaries between conduct which is subject to EU rules under Articles 101 and 102, and conduct which is subject to the domestic competition law of the Member States. In essence this is an issue of jurisdiction.

To ensure that the concept of effect on trade was fully understood and applied consistently between the Member States, the Commission published *Guidelines on the effect on trade concept contained in Articles 81 and 82 of the Treaty*, Commission Notice [2004] OJ C101/81 ('the Effect on Trade Guidelines'). The Effect on Trade Guidelines provide guidance under the following three heads:

(a) the concept of 'trade between Member States':
(b) the notion of 'may affect'; and
(c) the concept of 'appreciability'.

Of particular interest in the Effect on Trade Guidelines is the 'not capable of appreciably affecting trade' or 'NAAT' rule, whereby agreements are regarded by the Commission, in principle, not to affect trade between Member States if the combined market shares of the parties to the agreement are less than 5% on the relevant market, provided that, in the case of horizontal agreements, the parties' aggregate turnover in the EU is below €40 million. In the case of vertical agreements, the seller's turnover must be below €40 million in the EU for the NAAT rule to apply.

27.2.6.2 UK law

Thus far, we have considered only EU law. Effect on trade is the most obvious difference between EU and UK law. Section 2(1) of the CA 1998 applies to:

> ... agreements between undertakings, decisions by associations of undertakings or concerted practices which (a) may affect trade within the *United Kingdom* ... (emphasis added)

This is referred to as the Chapter I prohibition.

As you can see, s 2(1) of the CA 1998 is almost identical to Article 101(1) (**27.2.1**), the only difference being the requirement that there must be an effect on competition within the United Kingdom.

Given the OFT's ability to enforce both EU and UK competition law (see **27.1.1**), this is an important difference. Where rules relating to anti-competitive agreements are being used to investigate an agreement the impact of which is felt within the UK and in other Member States, then the OFT can apply both Article 101 (as there will be an effect on trade between Member States) and the Chapter I prohibition (as there will be an effect on trade within the UK). Whether in fact the OFT or the Commission will be the body that investigates the potential breach of Article 101 will be the subject of liaison and agreement between the two regulatory bodies.

However, where an agreement's impact is felt solely in the UK then the OFT can apply only the CA 1998 and not Article 101. The Commission has no power to apply the CA 1998.

27.2.7 'Object or effect the prevention, restriction or distortion of competition within the internal market'

If an agreement has as its object or effect the prevention, restriction or distortion of competition, it will be caught by Article 101(1). The distinction between object and effect is an important one in relation to the prosecution of an infringement.

27.2.7.1 Object

There is a relatively limited list of anti-competitive behaviour that will be classified as 'object infringements'. These will include the most serious types of behaviour, and will be dependent on whether the relationship between the parties is horizontal or vertical.

In terms of vertical relationships, ie those between parties at different levels of the supply chain (eg, between a supplier and distributor) and considered in this chapter, the list consists of the following two infringements:

(a) to fix minimum resale prices; and

(b) to impose export bans.

The substance of these infringements is considered in more detail at **27.3** below.

It should be noted that the above list of object infringements is not an official list published by the competition authorities (and indeed what these authorities classify as 'object infringements' may change over time).

The most significant difference in the prosecution of an object infringement is that the competition authorities do not have to prove that there would have been an effect on competition; the mere existence of the infringement is enough to establish liability.

27.2.7.2 Effect

As indicated above, outside the classification of an arrangement as an object infringement, the competition authorities must show that the infringement has an appreciable effect on competition before liability can be imposed.

In the absence of an appreciable effect on competition, the agreement will fall outside Article 101(1). This is considered in more detail below at **27.5.1**.

27.2.7.3 'Prevention, restriction or distortion of competition within the internal market'

The terms 'prevention', 'restriction' and 'distortion' are generally used interchangeably, and evidence of the least anti-competitive of the terms, a distortion, is sufficient under Article 101(1). In practice, where the anti-competitive object and/or effect of an arrangement is established, it is generally assumed that this element of the test will also be satisfied.

27.3 Analysing an agreement

Now that we have outlined the elements of Article 101(1) (and, by implication, the elements of the Chapter I prohibition), we can analyse an agreement to see whether it potentially falls within the sanction. We can then consider whether we can 'save' the arrangement.

Consider the following scenario. X Ltd (X) manufactures widgets. It is very successful and enjoys a market share of 20% of the widgets market in the EU. X has traditionally focused its sales in the UK, but has sold directly to customers all over the EU. Although this has been successful, X's sales have levelled out over the past few years. X believes that it can increase sales in mainland Europe (and particularly France) by appointing a company with detailed knowledge of the French market. Consequently, X has been in negotiation with Y (an unconnected company) with the aim of appointing Y as its exclusive distributor in France.

The proposed terms of the agreement are as follows:

- Y will distribute only in France – it will not be allowed to supply any customer outside France; and
- Y can only sell at prices set by X – Y is thus prevented from discounting.

Using the legislation as a structure, we can quickly come to a preliminary conclusion as to whether the proposed arrangement could (if entered into) potentially breach Article 101(1) (and/or the Chapter I prohibition).

Agreement?	Yes	Clearly the distribution agreement satisfies this element of the test. Note that the agreement does not even need to be written down.
Between undertakings?	Yes – we are told that the two businesses are unconnected – so this is not a parent or subsidiary relationship, neither is the arrangement an agency agreement.	So no need to consider: (a) decisions by association of undertakings; or (b) concerted practices.
Effect on trade between Member States?	Yes – the agreement is between a UK supplier and a French distributor. It also appears to prevent the sale of goods outside France – so it would appear there is some effect on trade between Member States. In practice you would consult the Effect on Trade Guidelines to finalise this point – however, given the fact that X's market share is 20%, it exceeds the NAAT criteria (and so an effect on trade between Member States is likely to be established).	As a cross-border effect, Article 101 is likely to apply – however, there may also be an effect on trade within the UK. For example, what if a UK consumer wanted to purchase widgets from the French distributor because it was cheaper. The Chapter I prohibition may also apply here.
Object or effect, etc?	Yes – there are potential object infringements as the agreement contains a market share provision and resale price maintenance. The most obvious anti-competitive activity is price fixing. Clearly, if X dictates the price at which the goods can be sold by Y, Y is not capable of discounting the goods. Each of Y's buyers will have to pay the same (presumably) inflated price. It is a fundamental principle of competition that price should be set by the market and not artificially. In terms of market sharing, this again can have serious implications for competition. Let us assume that X sells the good directly to customers in the UK. It does so at very high prices. A consumer, angered by the price she has to pay for widgets in the UK, does some research and finds that she can buy widgets more cheaply from Y in France. However, as Y is prevented from selling outside France, Y cannot supply potential customers in the UK, allowing X to continue to charge very high prices. X's position in the UK is protected from potential competition.	As object infringements there is no need to consider whether the effect is 'appreciable'.

From the above analysis, there is clearly a competition law issue here. Given this fact, this is now a suitable point to look at the consequences of breaching the rules.

27.4 The sanctions

As we have seen, the substantive law is very similar in both the EU and UK systems. However, in terms of the consequences of breach, although some similarities still exist, there is more divergence when it comes to the issue of sanctions. As a general point, the OFT has a far greater range of sanctions at it disposal (many of which have derived from US competition law).

27.4.1 Fines

27.4.1.1 EU law

This is by far the most well-known sanction. The Commission can impose fines not exceeding 10% of the worldwide turnover of the undertaking for breaches of Article 101 and/or Article 102. This power, as with many of the Commission's powers of enforcement, is contained in the Modernisation Regulation 1/2003 [2004] OJ L1/1 (in this case Article 23(2)). The fact that fines can relate to turnover (rather than profit) means that the level of fines can be very high. For example, in May 2009, Intel (the computer chip manufacturer) was fined €1.06 billion (the largest individual fine to date) for a breach of Article 102.

27.4.1.2 UK law

The OFT also has the power to impose a fine of up to 10% of an undertaking's worldwide turnover. It should be noted that where an undertaking has committed an infringement under both UK and EU competition rules, the undertaking will not be fined twice for the same anti-competitive behaviour (see para 5.3 of OFT Guide 407 – Enforcement).

Under s 39 of the CA 1998, there is 'limited immunity' from the Chapter I prohibition for what it refers to as 'small agreements'. This means that the agreement is immune from penalties (ie fines) under s 36. A 'small agreement' is one where the parties' joint turnover does not exceed £20 million. It is very important to note, however, that a 'price-fixing agreement' cannot be a small agreement (s 39(1)(b)).

Note that this 'limited immunity' does not apply to breaches of Article 101(1). So where the OFT is investigating under European competition rules, the immunity will not apply.

27.4.2 Cease and desist

27.4.2.1 EU law

Article 7 of the Modernisation Regulation allows the Commission to order that the infringement is stopped immediately. In practice, most undertakings that become subject to enforcement proceedings will stop the infringement in any event.

27.4.2.2 UK law

The OFT can address directions to a party that has or parties that have breached the CA 1998. These directions may involve the requirement to cease the activity in question, and can also require a party to modify its conduct.

27.4.3 Voidness

27.4.3.1 EU law

Although not a penalty that is imposed by the Commission, agreements that are found to have infringed Article 101(1) are automatically void under Article 101(2). Although rarely an issue in a serious infringement case (as it is highly unlikely that a party would attempt to uphold an agreement that was clearly anti-competitive), voidness is more likely to be raised where there is a commercial dispute. For example, if a party to an agreement is being sued for breach, a possible defence to that claim would be to argue that the agreement (or a particular term of the agreement) was in fact void as it breached EU (or indeed UK) competition rules.

27.4.3.2 UK law

Under UK law, the corresponding sanction rendering agreements automatically void for infringements of the Chapter I prohibition is outlined in s 2(4) of the CA 1998.

27.4.4 Other consequences of breach

27.4.4.1 Third party actions

So far we have considered the sanctions that can be imposed by the competition authorities. These sanctions will form part of the public enforcement procedure. Outside public enforcement, private individuals can take action against the infringing business (note that Articles 101 and 102 are directly effective). These private actions normally concern a claim for damages – either after the public enforcement process has been completed or, more rarely, independently of public enforcement actions. It should be noted that a private action could result in an award of damages that exceeds the level of any fine imposed by the competition authorities.

27.4.4.2 Management time/publicity

Although not sanctions as such, the breach of competition law will result in a number of additional consequences for the business. First, an investigation launched by the competition authorities will take up a huge amount of management and staff time. A typical investigation could take a number of years to conclude. Secondly, although it is sometimes said that 'all publicity is good publicity', the fact that a business has been found to have breached competition rules is unlikely to endear it to the general public. This possible impact on the company's image/brand is like to be magnified in the event that the breach concerns the fact that customers have been charged higher prices due to the infringement. It should be noted that both the EU and UK systems allow the possibility of third party 'class actions' to allow consumer organisations to recover losses suffered by consumers.

27.4.5 UK law – the criminal cartel offence – the Enterprise Act 2002

The EA 2002 introduced new penalties that can be imposed *on an individual* for breaches of the Chapter I prohibition or Article 101 and/or the Chapter II prohibition or Article 102. The important thing to note here is that it is only the OFT that can impose these sanctions (when applying either EU or UK competition rules) – the Commission has no power to impose criminal sanctions on an individual.

27.4.5.1 Imprisonment/fine

An individual can be imprisoned for up to five years for the most serious anti-competitive behaviour, such as price fixing, limitation of supply or production. market sharing, or bid rigging. In addition, he may be subject to an unlimited fine. Again, this sanction is only available to the OFT.

27.4.5.2 Director disqualification

A director found to have breached the competition rules can be disqualified from acting as a director for up to 15 years by the OFT. It should be noted that disqualification orders may be made in respect of any type of anti-competitive behaviour and not just the infringements which could give rise to imprisonment or the imposition of a fine described above.

27.5 Saving the agreement

When looking at how to save an agreement that potentially falls within Article 101/the Chapter I prohibition, there are effectively three methods that may be employed:

(a) to establish that, although the agreement in hand may have an effect on competition, the effect is not appreciable (see **27.5.1**);

(b) to ensure that the agreement conforms with a relevant block exemption (see **27.5.2**); or

(c) if the two methods above are not available, to establish whether the agreement might benefit from individual exemption (either Article 101(3) under EU law, or s 9 of the CA 1998 under UK rules) (see **27.5.3**).

Before we look at these potential ways to 'save' an agreement, it is important to note as a general point that these methods are not available where there is an 'object' or 'hardcore' infringement of the rules. Therefore, as an initial step in most cases, the legal adviser will have to remove or amend hardcore restrictions within the agreement to avoid the possibility of breaching competition rules.

27.5.1 Appreciable effect on competition

A legal adviser looking to save an agreement will first aim to establish whether or not the agreement is likely to have an appreciable effect on competition.

As we have seen (**27.2.7**), outside 'objects', or hardcore restrictions, are generally always prohibited. In other cases, EU and UK competition law will impose liability only where any effect on competition is appreciable. In order to assess whether an agreement has an appreciable effect on competition (or otherwise), a legal adviser should refer to the Commission's Notice on Agreements of Minor Importance [2001] OJ C368/13 (NAOMI). Note that although NAOMI is a Commission Notice, the OFT has indicated that it will use the same principles contained within NAOMI when analysing the CA 1998.

Broadly, NAOMI can apply to any type of agreement that does not contain any hardcore restrictions, such as price fixing or export bans. In addition, the market share of the parties to the arrangement must be below the following thresholds in order to benefit from NAOMI:

(a) agreements between competitors (horizontal agreements) – the *aggregate* market share of the parties to the agreement does not exceed 10%; or

(b) agreements between non-competitors (vertical agreements) – the market share *held by each* of the parties to the agreement does not exceed 15%.

(emphasis added)

As can been seen from the above, the thresholds for vertical agreements are much more generous than those for horizontal agreements which generally give rise to greater competition concerns.

NAOMI is a very useful place to start when looking to save an agreement. However, the market share thresholds contained within NAOMI are relatively low. Accordingly, only parties with low market share will be able to take advantage of the Notice. In addition, the market share of parties to an arrangement may increase over time, so although the arrangement may be able to take advantage of NAOMI, the parties' subsequent market share may preclude its application. In any event, the legal adviser should always inform the client that market share needs to be kept under review to ensure continued reliance on NAOMI.

27.5.2 Block exemptions

The next option for the legal adviser is to assess whether the agreement might benefit from a block exemption. Block exemptions, which are produced by the Commission, provide a 'safe harbour' for agreements. In essence, if an agreement comes within certain criteria it will be exempted from Article 101(1). As such, block exemptions provide a very useful device for avoiding infringements of that provision. They also recognise the fact that certain agreements, although technically coming within Article 101(1), should be exempted as the pro-competitive effects of the arrangements outweigh their anti-competitive effects. In this section we examine how one block exemption attempts to achieve this balance.

First, a few more introductory points need to be made. Block exemptions generally have higher market share thresholds than those contained in NAOMI. It is important that the legal adviser indentifies the correct block exemption for the agreement under consideration. As with NAOMI, and as a general point, block exemptions will not apply where the agreement contains hardcore (or objects) restrictions. When assessing a block exemption, the legal adviser should also consult any accompanying guidelines published by the Commission.

The block exemption considered in this book (and which will apply to the distribution agreement we are examining) is Commission Regulation 330/2010 on the application of Article 101(3) of the Treaty on the Functioning of the European Union to categories of vertical agreements and concerted practices. This Regulation is more commonly referred to as the Vertical Restraints Block Exemption (VRBE), and it will referred to as such for the purpose of this chapter.

Lastly, we have already seen that NAOMI will apply to an analysis of an agreement under the Chapter I prohibition. In the same way, a UK analysis under Chapter I would also benefit from the VRBE under s 10 of the CA 1998, which expressly provides an exemption from Chapter I if an agreement complies with a Commission regulation.

27.5.2.1 The VRBE

The VRBE (reproduced in the **Appendix**) applies to certain vertical agreements entered into on or after 1 June 2010. Below, we consider the specific rules contained in the VRBE and how these rules balance the pro- and anti-competitive effects of the vertical agreements we considered above.

The exemption

The exemption from Article 101(1), pursuant to Article 101(3), is contained in Article 2(1) of the VRBE.

The type of agreement

As with all block exemptions, the VRBE relates to a fairly narrow sphere of commercial activity, and it will apply only to vertical agreements, which are defined in Article 1(1)(a). Clearly, a legal adviser must ensure that the agreement he is considering comes within the block exemption he intends to use. This may sound obvious, but many commercial arrangements do not neatly fit within the definition given by a block exemption.

The entry requirements

In addition to the type of agreement, the VRBE sets out (as with other block exemptions) other conditions that must be met before it will apply. These conditions are contained in Article 2(2) to (4) and Article 3. For our purposes, Article 3 is the most important; it outlines the market share thresholds of the parties, above which the parties cannot use the VRBE. Both the supplier's and buyer's market share are relevant here. The VRBE states that the exemption will apply only where:

> ... the market share held by the supplier does not exceed 30% of the relevant market on which it sells the contract goods or services and the market share held by the buyer does not exceed 30% of the relevant market on which it purchases the contract goods or services. (Article 3(1))

The substantive rules

Once the type of agreement is established and the entry requirements are satisfied then the substantive terms of the agreement may be assessed by reference to the VRBE's conditions. The main conditions contained in the VRBE are found in Articles 4 and 5 (and these will be considered in the context of distribution agreements).

(a) Article 4 – hardcore restrictions

This Article applies to hardcore (or object) restrictions contained within a vertical agreement. The Article states that the exemption contained in Article 2 of the VRBE 'shall not apply to *vertical agreements* which, directly or indirectly ... have as their object' any of the restrictions contained in Article 4 (emphasis added).

Accordingly, if a restriction prohibited in Article 4 is contained within the agreement then the *whole* agreement falls outside the VRBE. In this event, the only option left to 'save' the agreement is by individual exemption (see **27.5.3**). However, given that an agreement containing hardcore restrictions is highly unlikely to come within the rules relating to individual exemption, legal advisers will ensure that no hardcore restrictions, as outlined in Article 4, remain within the agreement. Some of the restrictions contained in Article 4 are examined in a little more detail below.

(i) Pricing restrictions

Article 4(a) prevents any restriction on the buyer's ability to set its sale price – in particular the setting of a fixed or minimum price. In the context of a distribution agreement, and as we saw in the example at **27.3** above, the supplier cannot dictate to the distributor the price at which it sells the goods to retailers. This activity will clearly restrict price competition. This type of infringement is referred to as 'resale price maintenance', which is a form of price fixing.

(ii) Territorial restrictions

Another way in which competition may be severely restricted or removed is by the imposition of territorial restrictions. This is particularly sensitive in the context of the EU, as free movement of goods and services is one of the founding principles of the Treaty of Rome.

Article 4(b) is a good example of how the VRBE attempts to balance the pro- and anti-competitive effects of vertical agreements. The general position under Article 4(b) is that no restriction can be placed on the buyer as regards the customers to which or territories in which it can sell the goods or services which are the subject of the vertical agreement. However, such a wide-ranging restriction could cause as many problems as it attempts to solve.

For example, although such a wide-ranging restriction would initially seem a good thing for competition, it would not afford any protection to the distributors (who may have invested significant sums and who are essential to the competitive dynamic). If distributors could not be protected (to some extent), they might simply not wish to make the necessary investment, and consumers within the EU would be denied access to a new product. Accordingly, Article 4(b) attempts to reach a compromise between restrictions on buyers and protection for distributors. In this regard, the VRBE makes a distinction between active and passive sales. 'Active sales' describes the process where a seller (in our case, the distributor) approaches potential buyers. 'Passive sales' describes the process where consumers approach the seller. This is outlined in **Figure 27.1** below.

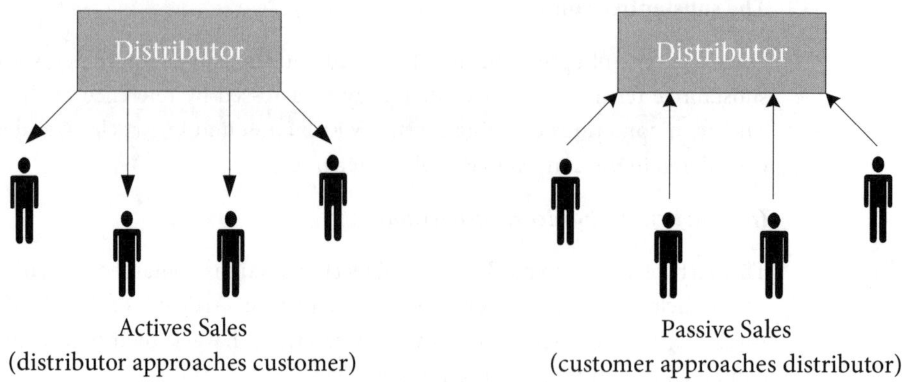

Figure 27.1 Active and passive sales

Article 4(b)(i) allows restrictions to be placed on distributors, preventing them from actively seeking customers in territories that have been awarded on an exclusive basis (or reserved to the supplier). Note that Article 4(b)(i) is an exception to the general prohibition contained in Article 4(b) (you need to read the last word of Article 4(b) to appreciate this – see **Appendix**).

Accordingly, a supplier can provide protection for an exclusive distributor by placing in *other* distribution agreements a restriction which prevents those distributors from actively seeking orders in the exclusive territory. Given this protection, the distributor will be more willing to make the necessary investment (and consumers will get access to the product).

This can be confusing, so let us look at this by way of an example. Assume that a supplier appoints distributors in four territories (A, B, C and D). Only one of these territories has been awarded on an exclusive basis, Territory C. In these circumstances, the supplier can place restrictions in the agreements of the distributors in Territories A, B and D, preventing them from actively seeking customers in Territory C (see **Figure 27.2** below).

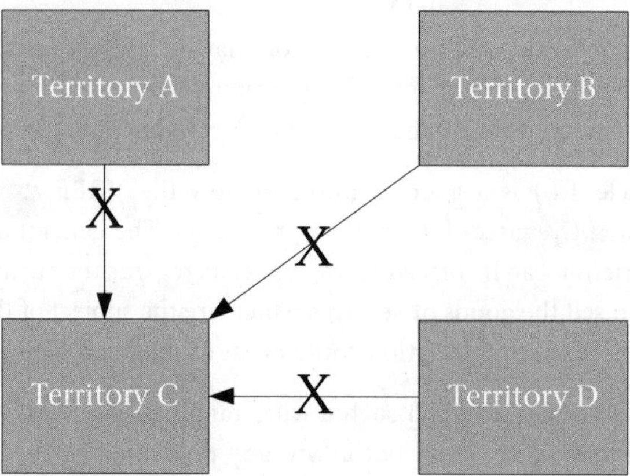

Figure 27.2 Territory C appointed on an exclusive basis – restriction of active selling

As the exclusive distributor in Territory C is protected from other distributors actively attempting to take away its customers, the distributor is more likely to make the necessary investment that an exclusive distributor would be required to make.

Note that Article 4(b)(i) only provides for a partial restriction on active selling, and as such provides no acceptable restriction on passive sales. Accordingly, a customer in Territory C cannot be prevented from approaching the distributors in Territories A, B and D to source the product (see **Figure 27.3** below). In theory, the distributor in Territory C, aware that customers are able to source the product elsewhere, will not charge excessive prices.

As there can be no restrictions in the agreements operating in Territories A, B and D preventing them from responding to passive sales requests, restrictions such as total export bans will be prohibited.

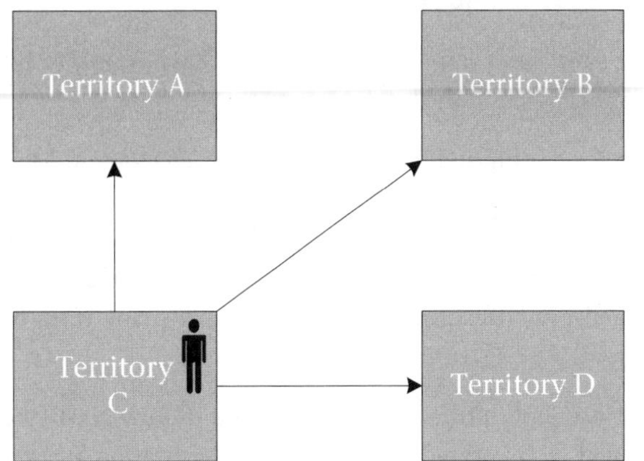

Figure 27.3 Passive sales request

The above discussion deals with the most common instance of territorial restrictions contained in the VRBE. Note that Article 4 contains other rules relating to territorial and customer groups, and which ones apply will be dependent on the type of agreement in contemplation. A detailed discussion of these rules is beyond the scope of this book.

(b) Article 5 – non-hardcore restrictions

There is an important difference between the restrictions in Article 4 and Article 5. If an agreement contains any of the restrictions contained in Article 5, the VRBE will not apply to *that obligation*, but the rest of the agreement can still benefit from the block exemption. It will, of course, be necessary to consider whether the infringing restrictions are severable from the 'legitimate' parts of the agreement as a matter of the governing law of the contract.

Article 5 is generally concerned with non-compete provisions. A non-compete obligation can take many forms and will clearly impact on the competitive dynamic. A definition of 'non-compete' can be found at Article 1(1)(d) (see **Appendix**).

Again, the VRBE attempts to balance the interests of the supplier (for example, the buyer will not manufacturer competing goods) with the wider need to ensure that the supplier is not completely immune from competition. The VRBE therefore allows non-compete clauses, but only for a limited period. During the term of any vertical agreement, a non-compete obligation cannot exceed five years (Article 5(1)(a)). However, a non-compete obligation in such an agreement can be renewed before the five-year limit (and thereby give a longer period of protection for the supplier) as long as the obligation does not simply roll over but is subject to some form of negotiation (see the last paragraph of Article 5(1)).

In terms of post-termination non-compete obligations, the general rule is that these cannot be longer than one year from the date of termination of the agreement, although additional conditions also apply (see Article 5(3)).

The VRBE contains a number of other operative provisions that are beyond the scope of this book, although in practice they would need to be considered by the legal adviser. In addition, the Commission has published a Notice, 'Guidelines on Vertical Restraints', which accompanies the VRBE and is an invaluable source of information (regularly consulted by practitioners) on the substance and interpretation of the VRBE. A copy of the Guidelines can be found on the Commission's website or in [2010] OJ C130/01. Extracts are also provided in the **Appendix** to this book.

The VRBE, along with other block exemptions, has a finite period of validity and will expire on 31 May 2022.

27.5.3 Individual exemption

If the agreement cannot benefit from either NAOMI or the VRBE, individual exemption is the last resort open to the legal adviser.

The system of individual exemption was changed in May 2004. Until that time, parties could notify their agreements to the Commission for an individual exemption. However, under this system (and given the consequences of breach of competition rules) a very large number of parties adopted this route. This imposed a huge burden on the Commission's resources and resulted in notification applications taking many years before they received an exemption (if ever).

The system of notification was dropped in May 2004 (the UK system of notification was also dropped at this time). Under the Modernisation Regulation (**27.4.1.1**) it is not possible to notify agreements, and therefore the possibility of relying on immunity from being fined is no longer available. Undertakings have to make their own assessment of the compatibility of their arrangements in the light of EU competition law and case law. It should be noted that it is for the undertaking or association of undertakings invoking Article 101(3) to prove that the exemption conditions have been satisfied.

Note that the individual exemption under UK competition rules outlined in s 9 of the CA 1998 is identical to that under EU competition law.

To obtain an exemption, an agreement must satisfy four conditions contained in Article 101(3), two positive and two negative. The two positive conditions are:

(a) the agreement must contribute to an improvement in the production or distribution of goods, or to the promotion of technical or economic progress; and

(b) consumers will get a fair share of the resulting benefit.

The two negative conditions are:

(c) the agreement does not impose on the undertakings restrictions which are not indispensable; and

(d) the agreement will not afford them the possibility of substantially eliminating competition.

It should be noted that under EU/UK individual exemption, it is theoretically possible for 'object' or hardcore restrictions to be exempted, in broad terms, where the anti-competitive effects are outweighed by pro-competitive effects. However, although the possibility exists, it is highly unlikely that a serious infringement could be justified in this way.

27.5.4 Application

Let us now look again at X's proposed agreement with Y (the facts of the scenario are at **27.3** above). As you will recall, we concluded that the agreement fell within Article 101(1). Now consider whether the agreement might take advantage of any of the ways in which an agreement that comes with Article 101(1) (and by implication the Chapter I prohibition) can be 'saved' and avoid liability being placed upon the parties.

	Application	**Comment**
NAOMI	This will not apply as X Ltd's market share is 20% (over the 15% limit under NAOMI).	In addition to the market share issue the proposed agreement contains hardcore infringements.

	Application	Comment
Block exemption	The VRBE will clearly apply to the agreement. The arrangement is a vertical agreement and the market shares of X and Y appear to be within the thresholds contained in the VRBE.	Although the VRBE will potentially apply, the two terms considered in the distribution agreement are 'hardcore' restrictions as defined in Article 4, which would result in the agreement falling outside the VRBE. Clearly, a legal adviser would need to remove or adapt the offending terms so that the agreement could take advantage of the safe harbour afforded by the VRBE.
Individual exemption	Individual exemption is not subject to a market share threshold and is potentially open to all agreements.	Even if the agreement contained hardcore restrictions, in theory it could be saved by individual exemption. However, the parties will have to show (in broad terms) that the anti-competitive effects of the arrangement outweigh the pro-competitive effects.

27.6 Article 102/Chapter II prohibition

Thus far we have concentrated on the law relating to anti-competitive agreements. Here we briefly consider how competition law deals with abuses of market power. As an initial point, you should note that the rules on abuse of market power are additional to those on anti-competitive agreements and, as such, undertakings with a high market share will need to consider both sets of rules

Article 102 TFEU states:

> Any abuse by one or more undertakings of a dominant position within the internal market or in a substantial part of it shall be prohibited as incompatible with the internal market in so far as it may affect trade between Member States

Contained within the sanction are terms that are common to both Articles 101 and 102 (and by implication the Chapter I and II prohibitions) and which will be interpreted in the same way under European rules. Accordingly, the types of business vehicles that fall within the term 'undertakings' will be the same as those outlined above at **27.2.3**. The important thing to note here, however, is that unlike under Article 101 there is no need to establish separate undertakings, and abuse by *one* undertaking (so-called unilateral behaviour) will be sufficient to impose liability on a dominant firm.

In addition to 'undertakings', Article 102 also refers to 'trade between Member States'. We have already considered this concept above at **27.2.8**.

Section 18 of the CA 1998 contains the UK sanction on abuse by dominant undertakings. The sanction is referred to as the 'Chapter II prohibition' and mirrors Article 102. As with Article 101, the only substantive difference between the two pieces of legislation is that the Chapter II prohibition relates to abusive conduct that 'may affect trade within the *United Kingdom*'.

In order for there to be a breach of Article 102/the Chapter II prohibition, two elements must be present: a dominant position (or market power); and abuse.

27.6.1 Dominance

Establishing whether an undertaking has market power (or holds a 'dominant position' as it is referred to under European rules) is crucial to identifying the types of commercial activity that undertakings can enter into.

The ECJ laid down the legal test for dominance in Case 27/76 *United Brands v Commission* [1978] ECR 207:

> The dominant position thus referred to by Article [102] relates to a position of economic strength enjoyed by an undertaking which enables it to prevent effective competition being maintained on the relevant market by affording it the power to behave to an appreciable extent independently of its competitors, customers and ultimately of its consumers.

Indicative of an undertaking's ability to act independently is the market share that the undertaking enjoys on the market (although it is important to note that market share does not, in itself, establish dominance). Clearly, in order to ascertain market share, the market (or markets) on which the undertaking operates must be established. This will be done by consideration of both the relevant product market on which the undertaking operates as well as the relevant geographic market.

Once the relevant market (or markets) has been established, the undertaking's market share can be calculated. When assessing market share figures for the purpose of establishing dominance, the European Commission (and OFT) does not apply rigid rules but considers that certain market share figures give rise to presumptions (which are capable of rebuttal). An outline of these presumptions is given below.

27.6.1.1 Market share of 50% or more – presumption of dominance

Clearly, any presumption is capable of being rebutted; however, the higher the market share, the less likely that the presumption will be rebutted. Accordingly, very high market share, of say 80%, would almost certainly result in a finding of dominance.

27.6.1.2 Market share between 40% and 50% – no presumption either way

Within roughly these market share figures, there is no presumption either way. Other factors would also need to be considered in order to establish dominance. For example, the market share of the undertaking's competitors on the market would also need to be assessed. It is less likely there will be a finding of dominance, for example, where the two main competitors to the undertaking also held a significant share of the market.

27.6.1.3 Market share below 40% – presumption of non-dominance?

There have very rarely been findings of dominance below a 40% market share. Clearly, the lower the market share, the less likely it is that dominance will be established – a market share figure significantly lower than 40% is very unlikely to give rise to dominance.

27.6.1.4 Dominance – other factors

Although market share is an important element in establishing dominance, it should be noted that other factors will also be considered, for example the length of time the dominant position is held (the longer the time, the more likely the undertaking is dominant). In addition, how easily other undertakings can enter the market (so-called 'barriers to entry') will be considered: the more easily others can enter the market, the less likely dominance will be established.

27.6.2 Abuse

Occupying a dominant position in the relevant market will not of itself breach Article 102/the Chapter II prohibition. It is the abuse of that position that will impose liability.

Some examples of abusive conduct follow.

27.6.2.1 Charging excessive prices

Clearly, the most obvious way in which a dominant undertaking may abuse its position is by charging its customers an excessive price. Although this may appear to be an obvious abuse, in practice it raises some difficult questions, not least what price amounts to an excessive price.

27.6.2.2 Predatory pricing

This type of practice aims to reduce prices to such a level that a competitor is forced to exit the market as it cannot match the very low prices being offered. In theory, once all competition is removed from the market, the dominant firm can then raise prices, in the knowledge that customers cannot turn to an alternative source of supply.

27.6.2.3 Refusal to supply

Competition may also be affected where a dominant firm refuses to supply its products. This can be particularly problematic where the dominant firm's refusal impacts on the ability of the potential buyer to compete in another market.

27.6.2.4 Tying

A typical example of a tying or 'bundling' abuse will involve placing a condition on a buyer that, in order to obtain supplies of one product (that the buyer requires), the buyer must also purchase a product that it does not want.

27.6.2.5 Price discrimination

This may arise where a dominant undertaking charges different prices to different customers for the same product, without justification on the grounds of quality, quantity or other characteristics.

27.6.3 Saving the arrangement

In regard to abuses of market power, there are no equivalent exception/exemptions similar to NAOMI, the VRBE or individual exemptions which apply to Article 101 (and the Chapter I prohibition) (see **27.5**). However, some limited ways in which the arrangement may be justified/exempted from penalty are set out below.

27.6.3.1 Objective justification

Certain types of behaviour carried out by a dominant undertaking may be commercially legitimate and not caught by Article 102. This will be the case if the conduct of the dominant firm can be justified as being objectively necessary (ie reasonably needed to protect its commercial interests) and proportionate to the objective (ie not more restrictive than necessary to achieve the objective). For example, a dominant supplier may refuse to supply (a potential abuse) on the basis that a buyer has a poor credit rating and/or history.

27.6.3.2 UK law

Section 40 of the CA 1998 provides for limited immunity for breaches of the Chapter II prohibition for conduct of minor significance. The immunity provides for the possibility that an undertaking that has a turnover of under £50m a year may be immune from fines. The exemption applies only to breaches of UK law and does not extend to breaches of Article 102 which the OFT may also investigate.

Chapter 28
EU Law and Intellectual Property Rights

28.1 Introduction

This chapter looks at the relationship between EU law and IP rights. It concentrates on the competition law problems which may arise in relation to the exploitation of IP rights (with particular reference to the licensing of patents), but also briefly considers the ways in which IP rights may come into conflict with the provisions of the Treaty on the Functioning of the European Union (TFEU) relating to the free movement of goods (Articles 34–36 TFEU, formerly Articles 28–30 EC).

28.1.1 Exploiting intellectual property rights

Assume that Frodsby Engineering Ltd, a small company, has developed a revolutionary new machine, in respect of which it has obtained patents in the UK and other Member States, including France. Frodsby's directors are now looking for ways to make money out of the 20-year monopoly right which English law has conferred on the company (not least so that it gets a return on the time and money spent on developing the machine; the directors see this as a just reward for the company's creativity and effort).

Their two main options are:

(a) make money by Frodsby manufacturing and selling the machine itself; and/or

(b) make money by licensing the right to other businesses to manufacture and sell the machine (ie, allowing other businesses to make use of the patent).

The advantages of licensing are covered briefly in **Chapter 34** of ***Business Law and Practice***. It is possible here that Frodsby may choose to license the patent because it is not geared up to manufacture the machine in sufficient quantities, or in other ways lacks the resources to exploit the patent fully, or because it finds a licensee with a better knowledge of the machine's target market.

28.1.2 How might the patent holder's actions cause competition law problems?

English law gives Frodsby as patent holder a right which arguably in itself could restrict trade and competition. Frodsby can rely on the patent to stop anyone else making or selling the machine, or even developing a similar machine which comes too close to the patent. Even if Frodsby allows other businesses to use the patent (by licensing it out), it could directly or indirectly restrict trade and competition by the terms which it includes in the licence; for example, it could grant a licensee exclusive territory, or stop a licensee exporting the machine from that territory.

28.1.3 The response of EU law

European Union law has a balancing act to perform in this situation. It must try to deal fairly with two potentially conflicting situations: on the one hand, the desire of the patent holder to be rewarded for its creativity (failure to permit this could stifle innovation and the development of new markets); and on the other hand, the need to stop IP rights granted under national law interfering with trade and competition within the common market.

The TFEU does not try to stop Member States passing laws which grant IP rights (although, increasingly, attempts are being made to harmonise national systems: see **Part III**). Article 345 TFEU (formerly Article 295 EC) provides that the Treaty 'shall in no way prejudice the rules in Member States governing the system of property ownership', which has led the EU competition authorities to take the view that EU law should not seek to control the mere existence of IP rights. What the law does seek to control, however, is the exploitation (or, as it is more commonly expressed, the 'exercise') of rights (see further **28.2**).

28.1.4 Which rights may cause problems?

Many of the points covered by this chapter are relevant to all types of IP right. However, problems arise most often in relation to three of the rights because of their particular characteristics. Patents (on which the chapter concentrates) are particularly likely to pose problems because of their monopoly aspect. Trade marks can, if regularly re-registered, last for an indefinite period of time. Copyright cannot last indefinitely but has the longest periods of guaranteed validity of any IP right (ie, 70 years from the end of the year of the author's death in the case of most LDMA works).

28.2 Attempting to resolve the conflict

The distinction mentioned in **28.1.3** between the existence of an IP right and its exercise was developed by the ECJ as an attempt to reconcile Article 345 TFEU with other, possibly conflicting, Treaty provisions. Briefly, the ECJ's interpretation is that Article 345 TFEU is concerned with safeguarding the existence of national IP rights; other Articles (such as Articles 34–36 TFEU and Articles 101–102 TFEU) with controlling their exercise. As a basic rule, if the exercise of an IP right interferes with a Treaty provision (other than Article 345 TFEU), that right will be compromised; its exercise will be forbidden or restricted.

28.3 Article 101 TFEU and the exploitation of intellectual property rights

If the holder of an IP right licenses it out, as Frodsby is contemplating doing in the example in **28.1.1**, this will involve an agreement between the holder and the licensee (a licensing agreement, sometimes simply called a 'licence'). Broadly speaking, any IP right can be licensed in this way. In Frodsby's case, the right happens to be a patent, and the agreement would be referred to as a patent licensing agreement, or patent licence. Because there is an agreement, Article 101 TFEU may apply (depending, of course, on the terms of the agreement). The existence of the IP rights which are being licensed will not, as such, infringe Article 101(1) TFEU. However, the licence agreement itself could, if it might affect trade and competition within the common market. In addition, the bringing of proceedings to stop infringement of an IP right may infringe Article 101(1) TFEU if the proceedings may affect trade within the common market, and are brought as a result of an agreement. In other words, exercise of the right may be restricted if there is evidence that the exercise infringes Article 101(1) TFEU. (Note that if Article 101 TFEU applies to an agreement and the competition authorities suspect a breach, the authorities can take action because of their duty to enforce Article 101 TFEU. However, the authorities have no similar power to intervene where Articles 34–36 TFEU are at issue: see **28.6**.) Depending on the circumstances and the terms of the agreement, the licensing of any IP right may give rise to competition law problems. However, it is convenient to concentrate on patent licensing, in the light of the Frodsby example.

Assume that Frodsby is contemplating licensing the patent for the machine to Megaco, a French company. Megaco will use the patent to manufacture the machine. The parties have agreed the following licence terms in principle:

(a) Frodsby has agreed that it will not appoint any licensees in France other than Megaco; and

(b) Megaco will sell the machines at a price which Frodsby will determine.

Would an agreement on these terms run into difficulties with Article 101(1) TFEU; and, if so, would it be possible to avoid this happening?

28.4 Licensing agreements and competition law

28.4.1 Likely competition law problems

The two terms outlined above could both give rise to some competition concerns. For example, term (a) concerns a territorial exclusion, and as such would prevent Frodsby appointing another licensee in France. Clearly, the inability to appoint an alternative, competing licensee may have an impact on competition. However, looking at this from Megaco's perspective, it may have invested heavily in the manufacture of the machine and will want some protection. In the event that Megaco (or indeed other such potential licensees) is not afforded some protection by competition rules, it may simply not be prepared to take on such a commercial risk, and therefore no new product will be produced or sold in France.

In this simple example, it can be seen that competition rules have to be sufficiently flexible to give some protection to Megaco in these circumstances, whilst ensuring that any protection is limited so as to take into account competition concerns.

Conversely, there are other types of commercial behaviour that are highly unlikely to be excused from a competition law perspective. Term (b), relating to the fact that Frodsby can dictate the price at which Megaco can sell the machines, is unlikely to be justified on any grounds (you will have considered 'object' infringement – of which this is one example – in **Chapter 27**).

As we have seen at **27.5**, in the event that an agreement contains anti-competitive terms or arrangements, it may be justified in one of three ways:

(a) the Notice on Agreements of Minor Importance (NAOMI);

(b) a relevant block exemption; or

(c) individual exemption under Article 101(3) TFEU.

As a general rule, object (or hardcore) restrictions cannot benefit from any of the three ways to justify an agreement outlined above. Consequently, a legal adviser would remove or reword any such restriction to ensure that it was capable of benefiting from one of these methods.

In terms of our approach here, although NAOMI could potentially apply, in practice it is rarely relied upon due to the fact that the market share thresholds are very low. In addition, where there is a relevant block exemption, it is far more likely that any analysis of an agreement will ensure that it conforms with the terms of a block exemption in any event. Accordingly, we shall not consider NAOMI further here (however, for more information on how to apply NAOMI, see **27.5.1**).

28.4.2 Technology Transfer Block Exemption

The relevant block exemption relating to IP licensing is Commission Regulation (EC) No 772/2004 of 27 April 2004 on the application of Article 81(3) of the Treaty [Article 101(3) TFEU] to categories of technology transfer agreements. The Technology Transfer Block Exemption

Regulation (TTBER), as it is more commonly known, is also accompanied by guidance published by the Commission.

The TTBER adopts a broadly similar approach to many other block exemptions. The Preamble to the TTBER explains that certain types of technology transfer agreement (defined in Article 1, para 1(b) as patent licensing agreements, know-how licensing agreements, software copyright licensing agreements, or a combination of any of these) can improve economic efficiency and be pro-competitive because they can (amongst other things) reduce the need for duplication of research and development, and can make it easier for new technologies to reach the market, thus increasing competition.

As with vertical agreements, the presumption under the TTBER is broadly that technology transfer agreements will qualify for exemption from the prohibition in Article 101(1) TFEU where the parties' market shares do not exceed specified thresholds, and where the agreements do not contain certain severely anti-competitive ('hardcore') terms.

The structure and content of the block exemption are set out below in outline.

28.4.2.1 Competitors and non-competitors

There is one major difference between the operation of the TTBER and many other block exemptions. The difference arises because the Commission is concerned that IP licences can be used by businesses which would normally compete with one another, as a means of dividing markets up between themselves. The classic situation arises where competitors license technologies to each other, and in return agree not to compete with each other in other fields. What looks like a licence, designed to make technology more widely available, is therefore in fact little more than a cover for an agreement not to compete. The technology covered by the licences may even be relatively unimportant to the parties; what really matters to them is the non-compete agreement.

Because of this danger, the TTBER applies different rules to agreements between competitors and agreements between non-competitors. The market share thresholds are different, as are the lists of 'hardcore' anti-competitive terms. The TTBER makes a further distinction between two types of agreement between competitors. On the one hand there is the 'reciprocal' agreement, where each licenses technology to the other. This is seen as open to the sort of abuse described above. The other type of agreement between competitors is the 'non-reciprocal' agreement, where one competitor licenses technology to another. This is more likely to be a genuine licence and less likely to be used as a cover for an agreement dividing markets between the parties, and so is subject to fewer restrictions.

28.4.2.2 The structure of the TTBER

Like many modern block exemptions, the TTBER begins in Article 1 with a list of definitions. The exemption itself is contained in Article 2. Article 3 sets the market share thresholds.

Article 4 contains the 'hardcore' restrictions. The inclusion of such a 'hardcore' term will mean that the exemption provided for in Article 2 will not apply to the *entire agreement*. Here, there are two lists. Article 4, para 1 deals with restrictions in agreements between competitors; Article 4, para 2 deals with agreements between non-competitors.

Article 5 outlines the non-hardcore or excluded restrictions. The exemption provided for in Article 2 will not apply to a particular *obligation*, but the rest of the agreement may still benefit from the TTBER.

Article 6 allows the Commission and the national competition authorities of the Member States to withdraw the block exemption from any given agreement if they find that the agreement is anti-competitive and so does not qualify for exemption under Article 101(3) TFEU. One of the situations in which they can do this is where the parties do not exploit the licensed technology; this may be a 'sham' licence agreement of the sort mentioned at **28.4.2.1**. Article 7 allows the Commission to disapply the block exemption from entire markets which are dominated by parallel networks of similar technology transfer agreements. Article 8 sets out detailed rules for the calculation of market share for the purposes of Article 3.

28.4.2.3 Does the Frodsby–Megaco agreement fall within the TTBER?

The proposed agreement appears to fall within Article 2, in that it is a 'technology transfer agreement' (a patent licensing agreement) which contemplates the production of products made with the licensed technology, and which is between two undertakings, Frodsby and Megaco (agreements between more than two undertakings are not covered). We do not know whether Frodsby and Megaco are competing or non-competing undertakings, and we do not know whether the market shares of the undertakings fall within Article 3. However, there is definitely a hardcore restriction, in that Megaco cannot determine its prices when selling the machines to third parties. This is a hardcore restriction regardless of whether the parties to the agreement are competing or non-competing (Article 4(1)(a) and 4(2(a)), and so even if the market shares do fall within Article 3, the presence of this hardcore restriction will prevent the block exemption from applying.

Accordingly, in regard to term (b), the parties would need to remove this from the agreement, or at the very least ensure that it is redrafted to conform with the TTBER. The TTBER does allow a licensor to impose a maximum or to recommend a sale price in certain circumstances (see Article 4(2)(a) – for example where the parties are non-competitors for the purposes of the TTBER). The legal adviser would need to discuss these points with his client.

In addition, term (a) (territorial protection) may also be acceptable under the TTBER. For example, a licensor can be restricted from actively seeking sales, or passively responding to sales, outside its allotted territory in certain circumstances – where the agreement is between non-competitors and for a limited period of time (see Article 4(2)(b) – for a definition of passive and active sales, see **27.5.2.1**). Here it can be seen that a restriction on all licensees from exporting the licensed products may give protection to Megaco, as other licensees situated in other Member States will be unable to export their machines to France (for a limited period), thereby protecting Megaco's market.

28.5 Article 102 TFEU and intellectual property rights

The ownership of IP rights may confer a dominant position on an undertaking within a particular geographic or product market. For example, a business may become dominant in a relevant product market by acquiring a patent; the patented item may form a market by itself if its novelty and inventiveness mean that consumers do not regard any other product as a substitute for it. However, this of itself (ie, the existence of the IP right) will not infringe Article 102 TFEU. Infringement requires abuse of a dominant position, which would mean improper exercise of the right in question. Not all exercises will be improper and, therefore, 'abusive'; it will depend on the circumstances, and in particular the effect on competition in the markets concerned. These general principles were confirmed by the ECJ in *Radio Telefis Eireann and Another v Commission of the European Communities and Another* (Cases C-241/91P and C-242/91P) [1995] ECR 1-801 (the 'Magill' case). However, some uncertainty still remains about the relationship between Article 102 TFEU and the exercise of IP rights; notably, exactly how far a right-holder's refusal to license its right to others amounts to abusive behaviour. For a more recent ECJ ruling on the matter, see *IMS Health GmbH and Co OHG v NDC Health GmbH and Co KG* (Case C-418/01) [2004] ECR I-5039.

28.6 Articles 34–36 TFEU and intellectual property rights

28.6.1 Introduction

The competition authorities of the EU cannot resolve all the problems which arise from the existence and exercise of IP rights by using Articles 101–102 TFEU). For example, in many cases, Article 101 TFEU does not apply because the situation does not involve a business arrangement of the type to which it can apply. It will then be necessary for the authorities to control the exercise of IP rights by relying on the principles of free movement of goods (Articles 34–36 TFEU).

28.6.2 How Articles 34–36 TFEU may be relevant

Assume that Frodsby Engineering Ltd puts its patented machine on the market in Germany as well as in the UK. Market conditions in Germany mean that Frodsby can afford to sell the machine more cheaply there than it can in the UK. Fred, a businessman, realises that he can make money by (lawfully) buying the machine in Germany and reselling it in the UK at a price which still undercuts Frodsby's UK price. What if Frodsby were to try to rely on its patent rights under English law to prevent Fred from importing the machines into the UK, claiming that those rights give it absolute control over what happens to the machines at all times?

Fred may try to argue that English patent law is a 'measure having equivalent effect' to a quantitative restriction on imports under Article 34 TFEU, as the patent holder is attempting to use the law to stop imports of patented goods into the UK. Article 34 TFEU prohibits such measures, so use of the UK patent rights to stop the imports may not be justified, being incompatible with the free movement of goods around the common market.

However, Article 34 TFEU must be read subject to Article 36 TFEU. This permits derogations from Article 34 TFEU in certain circumstances, such as where the measure is necessary for 'the protection of industrial or commercial property rights', an expression which will cover IP rights such as patents. Thus, under Article 36 TFEU, the national measure (ie, the law on patents) may be justified if it protects something about the patent which needs protection.

There are, in turn, however, limits on the use of Article 36 TFEU. The Article itself provides that it cannot be invoked to justify a measure which amounts to 'arbitrary discrimination' or 'a disguised restriction on trade', and the ECJ has used this to ensure that any derogations from Article 34 TFEU do not go too far (the Court has also indicated that the measure must be proportionate). In particular, the Court has developed the doctrine that Article 36 TFEU can be invoked by the holder of an IP right only if the infringement action is necessary to protect the 'specific subject-matter' of the right. In other words, although EU law recognises that national IP rights need protection in certain circumstances, it also attempts to ensure that they do not interfere too much with trade within the common market.

28.6.3 Specific subject-matter

What constitutes the specific subject-matter of an IP right will vary according to the right concerned. The ECJ has held that the specific subject-matter of a patent is 'the guarantee that the patentee, to reward the creative effort of the inventor, has the exclusive right to use an invention with a view to manufacturing industrial products and putting them into circulation for the first time, either directly or by the grant of licences to third parties, as well as the right to oppose infringement' (*Centrafarm BV and Adrian de Peijper v Sterling Drug Inc* (Case 15/74) [1974] ECR 1147). For a trade mark, however, the specific subject-matter is 'the guarantee that the owner of the trade mark has the exclusive right to use that trade mark, for the purpose of putting products protected by the mark into circulation for the first time, and is, therefore, intended to protect him against competitors wishing to take advantage of the status and reputation of the trade mark by selling products illegally bearing that trade mark' (*Centrafarm BV and Adrian de Peijper v Winthrop BV* (Case 16/74) [1974] ECR 1183). The position in relation to copyright is less clear; this is at least partly because national systems of copyright law within the EU still vary quite considerably.

The specific subject-matter of an IP right may, therefore, be seen as a limit on the use of the principles relating to free movement of goods. The Court recognises that there is something central to each IP right which needs protection, but is reluctant to allow the right to be exercised in an uncontrolled manner; the Court will always be prepared to stop the use of IP rights if they are being used to restrict trade and competition within the common market.

28.6.4 Exhaustion of rights

This is further illustrated by the concept of 'exhaustion of rights', which the ECJ has applied to most IP rights, including patents, copyright and trade marks. Its effect is that when goods which are subject to an IP right are lawfully put on the market for the first time in the EEA (either by the right holder, or with its consent), this 'exhausts' the right holder's opportunities to control what subsequently happens to the goods. In particular, the right holder cannot use the right to prevent the goods being imported into another Member State. However, note that this only applies to attempts by the right holder to control the movement of the goods around the EEA; it does not take away the holder's right to take action if the right has actually been infringed.

The case of *Silhouette International Schmied GmbH and Co KG v Hartlauer Handelsgesellschaft mbH* (Case C-355/96) [2000] All ER (EC) 769 showed the doctrine at work in relation to trade marks. The ECJ interpreted Article 7 of the Trade Marks Directive (89/140/EEC) to mean that exhaustion occurred only in the circumstances described above (lawful marketing in the EEA by the owner, or with the owner's consent). Thus, the owner of a trade mark would be entitled to stop products bearing the mark being imported into the EEA from outside that area (in this case, spectacle frames bearing Silhouette's mark being imported from Bulgaria into Austria). However, even after the *Silhouette* case, this area continued to prove problematic, particularly on the issue of the trade mark owner's consent. For example, how far could the owner's consent to imports of its goods into the EEA be implied when the owner had put its goods on the market outside the EEA without express restrictions as to where they could be re-sold?

The questions relating to consent now appear to have been answered by the ECJ's ruling in the joined cases of *Zino Davidoff SA v A & G Imports Ltd; Levi Strauss & Co and Another v Tesco Stores Ltd and Another; Levi Strauss & Co and Another v Costco Wholesale UK* (Joined Cases C-414/99, C-415/99 and C-416/99) [2002] All ER (EC) 55. The Court in effect ruled that there had to be some positive expression of consent by the trade mark owner to its goods being imported into the EEA from outside. Consent cannot be implied from silence; there would have to be some unequivocal demonstration from the circumstances that the trade mark owner had given up its right to control the import into and marketing of the goods within the EEA. This ruling appears greatly to have strengthened the hand of trade mark owners: for example, it appears that there is now no need to state expressly in an agreement for goods which are to be sold outside the EEA that they must not be imported into and sold in the EEA.

28.7 Article 34 TFEU and Articles 101–102 TFEU: relationship

It seems clear that some attempts to use IP rights to prevent the import of goods from one Member State into another may be capable of infringing both Article 34 TFEU and Article 101 or 102 TFEU (*Nungesser (LC) and Kurt Eisle v Commission for the European Communities* (Case 258/78) [1982] ECR 2015: the 'Maize Seeds' case). Application of the rules on free movement of goods to a case does not necessarily preclude the application of the competition rules, although in practice it is comparatively rare for both to be argued actively in the same case.

Appendix

Legislation

Registered Designs Act 1949
1949 c. 88

An Act to consolidate certain enactments relating to registered designs

[16th December 1949]

Registrable designs and proceedings for registration

1. Registration of designs

(1) A design may, subject to the following provisions of this Act, be registered under this Act on the making of an application for registration.

(2) In this Act "design" means the appearance of the whole or a part of a product resulting from the features of, in particular, the lines, contours, colours, shape, texture or materials of the product or its ornamentation.

(3) In this Act—

"complex product" means a product which is composed of at least two replaceable component parts permitting disassembly and reassembly of the product; and

"product" means any industrial or handicraft item other than a computer program; and, in particular, includes packaging, get-up, graphic symbols, typographic type-faces and parts intended to be assembled into a complex product.

1B. Requirement of novelty and individual character

(1) A design shall be protected by a right in a registered design to the extent that the design is new and has individual character.

(2) For the purposes of subsection (1) above, a design is new if no identical design or no design whose features differ only in immaterial details has been made available to the public before the relevant date.

(3) For the purposes of subsection (1) above, a design has individual character if the overall impression it produces on the informed user differs from the overall impression produced on such a user by any design which has been made available to the public before the relevant date.

(4) In determining the extent to which a design has individual character, the degree of freedom of the author in creating the design shall be taken into consideration.

(5) For the purposes of this section, a design has been made available to the public before the relevant date if—

- (a) it has been published (whether following registration or otherwise), exhibited, used in trade or otherwise disclosed before that date; and
- (b) the disclosure does not fall within subsection (6) below.

(6) A disclosure falls within this subsection if—

- (a) it could not reasonably have become known before the relevant date in the normal course of business to persons carrying on business in the European Economic Area and specialising in the sector concerned;
- (b) it was made to a person other than the designer, or any successor in title of his, under conditions of confidentiality (whether express or implied);

(c) it was made by the designer, or any successor in title of his, during the period of 12 months immediately preceding the relevant date;

(d) it was made by a person other than the designer, or any successor in title of his, during the period of 12 months immediately preceding the relevant date in consequence of information provided or other action taken by the designer or any successor in title of his; or

(e) it was made during the period of 12 months immediately preceding the relevant date as a consequence of an abuse in relation to the designer or any successor in title of his.

(7) In subsections (2), (3), (5) and (6) above "the relevant date" means the date on which the application for the registration of the design was made or is treated by virtue of section 3B(2), (3) or (5) or 14(2) of this Act as having been made.

(8) For the purposes of this section, a design applied to or incorporated in a product which constitutes a component part of a complex product shall only be considered to be new and to have individual character—

(a) if the component part, once it has been incorporated into the complex product, remains visible during normal use of the complex product; and

(b) to the extent that those visible features of the component part are in themselves new and have individual character.

(9) In subsection (8) above "normal use" means use by the end user; but does not include any maintenance, servicing or repair work in relation to the product.

1C. Designs dictated by their technical function

(1) A right in a registered design shall not subsist in features of appearance of a product which are solely dictated by the product's technical function.

(2) A right in a registered design shall not subsist in features of appearance of a product which must necessarily be reproduced in their exact form and dimensions so as to permit the product in which the design is incorporated or to which it is applied to be mechanically connected to, or placed in, around or against, another product so that either product may perform its function.

(3) Subsection (2) above does not prevent a right in a registered design subsisting in a design serving the purpose of allowing multiple assembly or connection of mutually interchangeable products within a modular system.

2. Proprietorship of designs

(1) The author of a design shall be treated for the purposes of this Act as the original proprietor of the design, subject to the following provisions.

(1A) Where a design is created in pursuance of a commission for money or money's worth, the person commissioning the design shall be treated as the original proprietor of the design.

(1B) Where, in a case not falling within subsection (1A), a design is created by an employee in the course of his employment, his employer shall be treated as the original proprietor of the design.

(2) Where a design becomes vested, whether by assignment, transmission or operation of law, in any person other than the original proprietor, either alone or jointly with the original proprietor, that other person, or as the case may be the original proprietor and that other person, shall be treated for the purposes of this Act as the proprietor of the design.

(3) In this Act the "author" of a design means the person who creates it.

(4) In the case of a design generated by computer in circumstances such that there is no human author, the person by whom the arrangements necessary for the creation of the design are made shall be taken to be the author.

7. Right given by registration

(1) The registration of a design under this Act gives the registered proprietor the exclusive right to use the design and any design which does not produce on the informed user a different overall impression.

(2) For the purposes of subsection (1) above and section 7A of this Act any reference to the use of a design includes a reference to—

(a) the making, offering, putting on the market, importing, exporting or using of a product in which the design is incorporated or to which it is applied; or

(b) stocking such a product for those purposes.

(3) In determining for the purposes of subsection (1) above whether a design produces a different overall impression on the informed user, the degree of freedom of the author in creating his design shall be taken into consideration.

(4) The right conferred by subsection (1) above is subject to any limitation attaching to the registration in question (including, in particular, any partial disclaimer or any declaration by the registrar or a court of partial invalidity).

7A. Infringements of rights in registered designs

(1) Subject as follows, the right in a registered design is infringed by a person who, without the consent of the registered proprietor, does anything which by virtue of section 7 of this Act is the exclusive right of the registered proprietor.

(2) The right in a registered design is not infringed by—

(a) an act which is done privately and for purposes which are not commercial;

(b) an act which is done for experimental purposes;

(c) an act of reproduction for teaching purposes or for the purpose of making citations provided that the conditions mentioned in subsection (3) below are satisfied;

(d) the use of equipment on ships or aircraft which are registered in another country but which are temporarily in the United Kingdom;

(e) the importation into the United Kingdom of spare parts or accessories for the purpose of repairing such ships or aircraft; or

(f) the carrying out of repairs on such ships or aircraft.

(3) The conditions mentioned in this subsection are—

(a) the act of reproduction is compatible with fair trade practice and does not unduly prejudice the normal exploitation of the design; and

(b) mention is made of the source.

(4) The right in a registered design is not infringed by an act which relates to a product in which any design protected by the registration is incorporated or to which it is applied if the product has been put on the market in the European Economic Area by the registered proprietor or with his consent.

(5) The right in a registered design of a component part which may be used for the purpose of the repair of a complex product so as to restore its original appearance is not infringed by the use for that purpose of any design protected by the registration.

(6) No proceedings shall be taken in respect of an infringement of the right in a registered design committed before the date on which the certificate of registration of the design under this Act is granted.

8. Duration of right in registered design

(1) The right in a registered design subsists in the first instance for a period of five years from the date of the registration of the design.

(2) The period for which the right subsists may be extended for a second, third, fourth and fifth period of five years, by applying to the registrar for an extension and paying the prescribed renewal fee.

(3) If the first, second, third or fourth period expires without such application and payment being made, the right shall cease to have effect; and the registrar shall, in accordance with rules made by the Secretary of State, notify the proprietor of that fact.

(4) If during the period of six months immediately following the end of that period an application for extension is made and the prescribed renewal fee and any prescribed additional fee is paid, the right shall be treated as if it had never expired, with the result that—

(a) anything done under or in relation to the right during that further period shall be treated as valid,

(b) an act which would have constituted an infringement of the right if it had not expired shall be treated as an infringement, and

(c) an act which would have constituted use of the design for the services of the Crown if the right had not expired shall be treated as such use.

8A. Restoration of lapsed right in design

(1) Where the right in a registered design has expired by reason of a failure to extend, in accordance with section 8(2) or (4), the period for which the right subsists, an application for the restoration of the right in the design may be made to the registrar within the prescribed period.

(2) The application may be made by the person who was the registered proprietor of the design or by any other person who would have been entitled to the right in the design if it had not expired; and where the design was held by two or more persons jointly, the application may, with the leave of the registrar, be made by one or more of them without joining the others.

(3) Notice of the application shall be published by the registrar in the prescribed manner.

(4) If the registrar is satisfied that the failure of the proprietor to see that the period for which the right subsisted was extended in accordance with section 8(2) or (4) was unintentional, he shall, on payment of any unpaid renewal fee and any prescribed additional fee, order the restoration of the right in the design.

(5) The order may be made subject to such conditions as the registrar thinks fit, and if the proprietor of the design does not comply with any condition the registrar may revoke the order and give such consequential directions as he thinks fit.

(6) Rules altering the period prescribed for the purposes of subsection (1) may contain such transitional provisions and savings as appear to the Secretary of State to be necessary or expedient.

8B. Effect of order for restoration of right

(1) The effect of an order under section 8A for the restoration of the right in a registered design is as follows.

(2) Anything done under or in relation to the right during the period between expiry and restoration shall be treated as valid.

(3) Anything done during that period which would have constituted an infringement if the right had not expired shall be treated as an infringement—

(a) if done at a time when it was possible for an application for extension to be made under section 8(4); or

(b) if it was a continuation or repetition of an earlier infringing act.

(4) If, after it was no longer possible for such an application for extension to be made and before publication of notice of the application for restoration, a person—

(a) began in good faith to do an act which would have constituted an infringement of the right in the design if it had not expired, or

(b) made in good faith effective and serious preparations to do such an act,

he has the right to continue to do the act or, as the case may be, to do the act, notwithstanding the restoration of the right in the design; but this does not extend to granting a licence to another person to do the act.

(5) If the act was done, or the preparations were made, in the course of a business, the person entitled to the right conferred by subsection (4) may—

(a) authorise the doing of that act by any partners of his for the time being in that business, and

(b) assign that right, or transmit it on death (or in the case of a body corporate on its dissolution), to any person who acquires that part of the business in the course of which the act was done or the preparations were made.

(6) Where a product is disposed of to another in exercise of the rights conferred by subsection (4) or subsection (5), that other and any person claiming through him may deal with the product in the same way as if it had been disposed of by the registered proprietor of the design.

(7) The above provisions apply in relation to the use of a registered design for the services of the Crown as they apply in relation to infringement of the right in the design.

Property in and dealing with registered designs and applications

15B. Assignment, &c of registered designs and applications for registered designs

(1) A registered design or an application for a registered design is transmissible by assignment, testamentary disposition or operation of law in the same way as other personal or moveable property, subject to the following provisions of this section.

(2) Any transmission of a registered design or an application for a registered design is subject to any rights vested in any other person of which notice is entered in the register of designs, or in the case of applications, notice is given to the registrar.

(3) An assignment of, or an assent relating to, a registered design or application for a registered design is not effective unless it is in writing signed by or on behalf of the assignor or, as the case may be, a personal representative.

(4) Except in Scotland, the requirement in subsection (3) may be satisfied in a case where the assignor or personal representative is a body corporate by the affixing of its seal.

(5) Subsections (3) and (4) apply to assignment by way of security as in relation to any other assignment.

(6) A registered design or application for a registered design may be the subject of a charge (in Scotland, security) in the same way as other personal or moveable property.

(7) The proprietor of a registered design may grant a licence to use that registered design.

(8) Any equities (in Scotland, rights) in respect of a registered design or an application for a registered design may be enforced in like manner as in respect of any other personal or moveable property.

15C. Exclusive licences

(1) In this Act an "exclusive licence" means a licence in writing signed by or on behalf of the proprietor of the registered design authorising the licensee to the exclusion of all other persons, including the person granting the licence, to exercise a right which would otherwise be exercisable exclusively by the proprietor of the registered design.

(2) The licensee under an exclusive licence has the same rights against any successor in title who is bound by the licence as he has against the person granting the licence.

Register of designs, etc.

19. Registration of assignments, etc.

(1) Where any person becomes entitled by assignment, transmission or operation of law to a registered design or to a share in a registered design, or becomes entitled as mortgagee, licensee or otherwise to any other interest in a registered design, he shall apply to the registrar in the prescribed manner for the registration of his title as proprietor or co-proprietor or, as the case may be, of notice of his interest, in the register of designs.

(2) Without prejudice to the provisions of the foregoing subsection, an application for the registration of the title of any person becoming entitled by assignment to a registered design or a share in a registered design, or becoming entitled by virtue of a mortgage, licence or other instrument to any other interest in a registered design, may be made in the prescribed manner by the assign or, mortgagor, licensor or other party to that instrument, as the case may be.

(3) Where application is made under this section for the registration of the title of any person, the registrar shall, upon proof of title to his satisfaction—

(a) where that person is entitled to a registered design or a share in a registered design, register him in the register of designs as proprietor or co-proprietor of the design, and enter in that register particulars of the instrument or event by which he derives title; or

(b) where that person is entitled to any other interest in the registered design, enter in that register notice of his interest, with particulars of the instrument (if any) creating it.

(3A) Where national unregistered design right subsists in a registered design, the registrar shall not register an interest under subsection (3) unless he is satisfied that the person entitled to that interest is also entitled to a corresponding interest in the national unregistered design right.

(3B) Where national unregistered design right subsists in a registered design and the proprietor of the registered design is also the design right owner, an assignment of the national unregistered design right shall be taken to be also an assignment of the right in the registered design, unless a contrary intention appears.

(4) ...

(5) Except for the purposes of an application to rectify the register under the following provisions of this Act, a document in respect of which no entry has been made in the register of designs under subsection (3) of this section shall not be admitted in any court as evidence of the title of any person to a registered design or share of or interest in a registered design unless the court otherwise directs.

24A. Action for infringement

(1) An infringement of the right in a registered design is actionable by the registered proprietor.

(2) In an action for infringement all such relief by way of damages, injunctions, accounts or otherwise is available to him as is available in respect of the infringement of any other property right.

(3) This section has effect subject to section 24B of this Act (exemption of innocent infringer from liability).

24B. Exemption of innocent infringer from liability

(1) In proceedings for the infringement of the right in a registered design damages shall not be awarded, and no order shall be made for an account of profits, against a defendant who proves that at the date of the infringement he was not aware, and had no reasonable ground for supposing, that the design was registered.

(2) For the purposes of subsection (1), a person shall not be deemed to have been aware or to have had reasonable grounds for supposing that the design was registered by reason only of the marking of a product with—

(a) the word 'registered' or any abbreviation thereof, or

(b) any word or words expressing or implying that the design applied to, or incorporated in, the product has been registered,

unless the number of the design accompanied the word or words or the abbreviation in question.

(3) Nothing in this section shall affect the power of the court to grant an injunction in any proceedings for infringement of the right in a registered design.

24C. Order for delivery up

(1) Where a person—

(a) has in his possession, custody or control for commercial purposes an infringing article, or

(b) has in his possession, custody or control anything specifically designed or adapted for making articles to a particular design which is a registered design, knowing or having reason to believe that it has been or is to be used to make an infringing article,

the registered proprietor in question may apply to the court for an order that the infringing article or other thing be delivered up to him or to such other person as the court may direct.

(2) An application shall not be made after the end of the period specified in the following provisions of this section; and no order shall be made unless the court also makes, or it appears to the court that there are grounds for making, an order under section 24D of this Act (order as to disposal of infringing article, &c).

(3) An application for an order under this section may not be made after the end of the period of six years from the date on which the article or thing in question was made, subject to subsection (4).

(4) If during the whole or any part of that period the registered proprietor—

(a) is under a disability, or

(b) is prevented by fraud or concealment from discovering the facts entitling him to apply for an order,

an application may be made at any time before the end of the period of six years from the date on which he ceased to be under a disability or, as the case may be, could with reasonable diligence have discovered those facts.

(5) In subsection (4) 'disability'—

(a) in England and Wales, has the same meaning as in the Limitation Act 1980;

(b) in Scotland, means legal disability within the meaning of the Prescription and Limitation (Scotland) Act 1973;

(c) in Northern Ireland, has the same meaning as in the Statute of Limitations (Northern Ireland) 1958.

(6) A person to whom an infringing article or other thing is delivered up in pursuance of an order under this section shall, if an order under section 24D of this Act is not made, retain it pending the making of an order, or the decision not to make an order, under that section.

(7) The reference in subsection (1) to an act being done in relation to an article for 'commercial purposes' are to its being done with a view to the article in question being sold or hired in the course of a business.

(8) Nothing in this section affects any other power of the court.

24D. Order as to disposal of infringing articles, &c

(1) An application may be made to the court for an order that an infringing article or other thing delivered up in pursuance of an order under section 24C of this Act shall be—

(a) forfeited to the registered proprietor, or

(b) destroyed or otherwise dealt with as the court may think fit,

or for a decision that no such order should be made.

(2) In considering what order (if any) should be made, the court shall consider whether other remedies available in an action for infringement of the right in a registered design would be adequate to compensate the registered proprietor and to protect his interests.

(3) Where there is more than one person interested in an article or other thing, the court shall make such order as it thinks just and may (in particular) direct that the thing be sold, or otherwise dealt with, and the proceeds divided.

(4) If the court decides that no order should be made under this section, the person in whose possession, custody or control the article or other thing was before being delivered up is entitled to its return.

(5) References in this section to a person having an interest in an article or other thing include any person in whose favour an order could be made in respect of it—

(a) under this section;

(b) under section 19 of Trade Marks Act 1994 (including that section as applied by regulation 4 of the Community Trade Mark Regulations 2006 (SI 2006/1027));

(c) under section 114, 204 or 231 of the Copyright, Designs and Patents Act 1988; or

(d) under regulation 1C of the Community Design Regulations 2005 (SI 2005/2339).

24E. Jurisdiction of county court and sheriff court

(1) In Northern Ireland a county court may entertain proceedings under the following provisions of this Act—

section 24C (order for delivery up of infringing article, &c),

section 24D (order as to disposal of infringing article, &c), or

section 24F(8) (application by exclusive licensee having concurrent rights),

where the value of the infringing articles and other things in question does not exceed the county court limit for actions in tort.

(2) In Scotland proceedings for an order under any of those provisions may be brought in the sheriff court.

(3) Nothing in this section shall be construed as affecting the jurisdiction of the Court of Session or the High Court in Northern Ireland.

Legal proceedings and appeals

24F. Rights and remedies of exclusive licensee

(1) In relation to a registered design, an exclusive licensee has, except against the registered proprietor, the same rights and remedies in respect of matters occurring after the grant of the licence as if the licence had been an assignment.

(2) His rights and remedies are concurrent with those of the registered proprietor; and references to the registered proprietor in the provisions of this Act relating to infringement shall be construed accordingly.

(3) In an action brought by an exclusive licensee by virtue of this section a defendant may avail himself of any defence which would have been available to him if the action had been brought by the registered proprietor.

(4) Where an action for infringement of the right in a registered design brought by the registered proprietor or an exclusive licensee relates (wholly or partly) to an infringement in respect of which they have concurrent rights of action, the proprietor

or, as the case may be, the exclusive licensee may not, without the leave of the court, proceed with the action unless the other is either joined as a claimant or added as a defendant.

(5) A registered proprietor or exclusive licensee who is added as a defendant in pursuance of subsection (4) is not liable for any costs in the action unless he takes part in the proceedings.

(6) Subsections (4) and (5) do not affect the granting of interlocutory relief on the application of the registered proprietor or an exclusive licensee.

(7) Where an action for infringement of the right in a registered design is brought which relates (wholly or partly) to an infringement in respect of which the registered proprietor and an exclusive licensee have concurrent rights of action—

(a) the court shall, in assessing damages, take into account—

(i) the terms of the licence, and

(ii) any pecuniary remedy already awarded or available to either of them in respect of the infringement;

(b) no account of profits shall be directed if an award of damages has been made, or an account of profits has been directed, in favour of the other of them in respect of the infringement; and

(c) the court shall if an account of profits is directed apportion the profits between them as the court considers just, subject to any agreement between them;

and these provisions apply whether or not the proprietor and the exclusive licensee are both parties to the action.

(8) The registered proprietor shall notify any exclusive licensee having concurrent rights before applying for an order under section 24C this Act (order for delivery up of infringing article, &c); and the court may on the application of the licensee make such order under that section as it thinks fit having regard to the terms of the licence.

24G. Meaning of 'infringing article'

(1) In this Act 'infringing article', in relation to a design, shall be construed in accordance with this section.

(2) An article is an infringing article if its making to that design was an infringement of the right in a registered design.

(3) An article is also an infringing article if—

(a) it has been or is proposed to be imported into the United Kingdom, and

(b) its making to that design in the United Kingdom would have been an infringement of the right in a registered design or a breach of an exclusive licensing agreement relating to that registered design.

(4) Where it is shown that an article is made to a design which is or has been a registered design, it shall be presumed until the contrary is proved that the article was made at a time when the right in the registered design subsisted.

(5) Nothing in subsection (3) shall be construed as applying to an article which may be lawfully imported into the United Kingdom by virtue of an enforceable Community right within the meaning of section 2(1) of the European Communities Act 1972.

26. Remedy for groundless threats of infringement proceedings

(1) Where any person (whether entitled to or interested in a registered design or an application for registration of a design or not) by circulars, advertisements or otherwise threatens any other person with proceedings for infringement of the right in a registered design, any person aggrieved thereby may bring an action against him for any such relief as is mentioned in the next following subsection.

(2) Unless in any action brought by virtue of this section the defendant proves that the acts in respect of which proceedings were threatened constitute or, if done, would constitute, an infringement of the right in a registered design the registration of which is not shown by the claimant to be invalid, the claimant shall be entitled to the following relief, that is to say:—

(a) a declaration to the effect that the threats are unjustifiable;

(b) an injunction against the continuance of the threats; and

(c) such damages, if any, as he has sustained thereby.

(2A) Proceedings may not be brought under this section in respect of a threat to bring proceedings for an infringement alleged to consist of the making or importing of anything.

(3) For the avoidance of doubt it is hereby declared that a mere notification that a design is registered does not constitute a threat of proceedings within the meaning of this section.

Patents Act 1977
1977 c. 37

An Act to establish a new law of patents applicable to future patents and applications for patents; to amend the law of patents applicable to existing patents and applications for patents; to give effect to certain international conventions on patents; and for connected purposes [29th July 1977]

Part I
New Domestic Law

Patentability

1. Patentable inventions

(1) A patent may be granted only for an invention in respect of which the following conditions are satisfied, that is to say—

(a) the invention is new;

(b) it involves an inventive step;

(c) it is capable of industrial application;

(d) the grant of a patent for it is not excluded by subsections (2) and (3) or section 4A below;

and references in this Act to a patentable invention shall be construed accordingly.

(2) It is hereby declared that the following (among other things) are not inventions for the purposes of this Act, that is to say, anything which consists of—

(a) a discovery, scientific theory or mathematical method;

(b) a literary, dramatic, musical or artistic work or any other aesthetic creation whatsoever;

(c) a scheme, rule or method for performing a mental act, playing a game or doing business, or a program for a computer;

(d) the presentation of information;

but the foregoing provision shall prevent anything from being treated as an invention for the purposes of this Act only to the extent that a patent or application for a patent relates to that thing as such.

(3) A patent shall not be granted for an invention the commercial exploitation of which would be contrary to public policy or morality.

(4) For the purposes of subsection (3) above exploitation shall not be regarded as contrary to public policy or morality only because it is prohibited by any law in force in the United Kingdom or any part of it.

(5) The Secretary of State may by order vary the provisions of subsection (2) above for the purpose of maintaining them in conformity with developments in science and technology; and no such order shall be made unless a draft of the order has been laid before, and approved by resolution of, each House of Parliament.

2. Novelty

(1) An invention shall be taken to be new if it does not form part of the state of the art.

(2) The state of the art in the case of an invention shall be taken to comprise all matter (whether a product, a process, information about either, or anything else) which has at any time before the priority date of that invention been made available to the public (whether in the United Kingdom or elsewhere) by written or oral description, by use or in any other way.

(3) The state of the art in the case of an invention to which an application for a patent or a patent relates shall be taken also to comprise matter contained in an application for

another patent which was published on or after the priority date of that invention, if the following conditions are satisfied, that is to say—

(a) that matter was contained in the application for that other patent both as filed and as published; and

(b) the priority date of that matter is earlier than that of the invention.

(4) For the purposes of this section the disclosure of matter constituting an invention shall be disregarded in the case of a patent or an application for a patent if occurring later than the beginning of the period of six months immediately preceding the date of filing the application for the patent and either—

(a) the disclosure was due to, or made in consequence of, the matter having been obtained unlawfully or in breach of confidence by any person—

(i) from the inventor or from any other person to whom the matter was made available in confidence by the inventor or who obtained it from the inventor because he or the inventor believed that he was entitled to obtain it; or

(ii) from any other person to whom the matter was made available in confidence by any person mentioned in sub-paragraph (i) above or in this sub-paragraph or who obtained it from any person so mentioned because he or the person from whom he obtained it believed that he was entitled to obtain it;

(b) the disclosure was made in breach of confidence by any person who obtained the matter in confidence from the inventor or from any other person to whom it was made available, or who obtained it, from the inventor; or

(c) the disclosure was due to, or made in consequence of the inventor displaying the invention at an international exhibition and the applicant states, on filing the application, that the invention has been so displayed and also, within the prescribed period, files written evidence in support of the statement complying with any prescribed conditions.

(5) In this section references to the inventor include references to any proprietor of the invention for the time being.

3. Inventive step

An invention shall be taken to involve an inventive step if it is not obvious to a person skilled in the art, having regard to any matter which forms part of the state of the art by virtue only of section 2(2) above (and disregarding section 2(3) above).

4. Industrial application

(1) An invention shall be taken to be capable of industrial application if it can be made or used in any kind of industry, including agriculture.

4A. Methods of treatment or diagnosis

(1) A patent shall not be granted for the invention of—

(a) a method of treatment of the human or animal body by surgery or therapy, or

(b) a method of diagnosis practised on the human or animal body.

(2) Subsection (1) above does not apply to an invention consisting of a substance or composition for use in any such method.

(3) In the case of an invention consisting of a substance or composition for use in any such method, the fact that the substance or composition forms part of the state of the art shall not prevent the invention from being taken to be new if the use of the substance or composition in any such method does not form part of the state of the art.

(4) In the case of an invention consisting of a substance or composition for a specific use in any such method, the fact that the substance or composition forms part of the state of

the art shall not prevent the invention from being taken to be new if that specific use does not form part of the state of the art.

Property in patents and applications, and registration

30. Nature of, and transactions in, patents and applications for patents

(1) Any patent or application for a patent is personal property (without being a thing in action), and any patent or any such application and rights in or under it may be transferred, created or granted in accordance with subsections (2) to (7) below.

(2) Subject to section 36(3) below, any patent or any such application, or any right in it, may be assigned or mortgaged.

(3) Any patent or any such application or right shall vest by operation of law in the same way as any other personal property and may be vested by an assent of personal representatives.

(4) Subject to section 36(3) below, a licence may be granted under any patent or any such application for working the invention which is the subject of the patent or the application; and—

(a) to the extent that the licence so provides, a sub-licence may be granted under any such licence and any such licence or sub-licence may be assigned or mortgaged; and

(b) any such licence or sub-licence shall vest by operation of law in the same way as any other personal property and may be vested by an assent of personal representatives.

(5) Subsections (2) to (4) above shall have effect subject to the following provisions of this Act.

(6) Any of the following transactions, that is to say—

(a) any assignment or mortgage of a patent or any such application, or any right in a patent or any such application;

(b) any assent relating to any patent or any such application or right;

shall be void unless it is in writing and is signed by or on behalf of the assignor or mortgagor (or, in the case of an assent or other transaction by a personal representative, by or on behalf of the personal representative).

(6A) If a transaction mentioned in subsection (6) above is by a body corporate, references in that subsection to such a transaction being signed by or on behalf of the assignor or mortgagor shall be taken to include references to its being under the seal of the body corporate.

(7) An assignment of a patent or any such application or a share in it, and an exclusive licence granted under any patent or any such application, may confer on the assignee or licensee the right of the assignor or licensor to bring proceedings by virtue of section 61 or 69 below for a previous infringement or to bring proceedings under section 58 below for a previous act.

33. Effect of registration, etc., on rights in patents

(1) Any person who claims to have acquired the property in a patent or application for a patent by virtue of any transaction, instrument or event to which this section applies shall be entitled as against any other person who claims to have acquired that property by virtue of an earlier transaction, instrument or event to which this section applies if, at the time of the later transaction, instrument or event—

(a) the earlier transaction, instrument or event was not registered, or

(b) in the case of any application which has not been published, notice of the earlier transaction, instrument or event had not been given to the comptroller, and

(c) in any case, the person claiming under the later transaction, instrument or event, did not know of the earlier transaction, instrument or event.

(2) Subsection (1) above shall apply equally to the case where any person claims to have acquired any right in or under a patent or application for a patent, by virtue of a transaction, instrument or event to which this section applies, and that right is incompatible with any such right acquired by virtue of an earlier transaction, instrument or event to which this section applies.

(3) This section applies to the following transactions, instruments and events—

(a) the assignment or assignation of a patent or application for a patent, or a right in it;

(b) the mortgage of a patent or application or the granting of security over it;

(c) the grant, assignment or assignation of a licence or sub-licence, or mortgage of a licence or sub-licence, under a patent or application;

(d) the death of the proprietor or one of the proprietors of any such patent or application or any person having a right in or under a patent or application and the vesting by an assent of personal representatives of a patent, application or any such right; and

(e) any order or directions of a court or other competent authority—

(i) transferring a patent or application or any right in or under it to any person; or

(ii) that an application should proceed in the name of any person;

and in either case the event by virtue of which the court or authority had power to make any such order or give any such directions.

(4) Where an application for the registration of a transaction, instrument or event has been made, but the transaction, instrument or event has not been registered, then, for the purposes of subsection (1)(a) above, registration of the application shall be treated as registration of the transaction, instrument or event.

Employees' inventions

39. Right to employees' inventions

(1) Notwithstanding anything in any rule of law, an invention made by an employee shall, as between him and his employer, be taken to belong to his employer for the purposes of this Act and all other purposes if—

(a) it was made in the course of the normal duties of the employee or in the course of duties falling outside his normal duties, but specifically assigned to him, and the circumstances in either case were such that an invention might reasonably be expected to result from the carrying out of his duties; or

(b) the invention was made in the course of the duties of the employee and, at the time of making the invention, because of the nature of his duties and the particular responsibilities arising from the nature of his duties he had a special obligation to further the interests of the employer's undertaking.

(2) Any other invention made by an employee shall, as between him and his employer, be taken for those purposes to belong to the employee.

(3) Where by virtue of this section an invention belongs, as between him and his employer, to an employee, nothing done—

(a) by or on behalf of the employee or any person claiming under him for the purposes of pursuing an application for a patent, or

(b) by any person for the purpose of performing or working the invention,

shall be taken to infringe any copyright or design right to which, as between him and his employer, his employer is entitled in any model or document relating to the invention.

40. Compensation of employees for certain inventions

(1) Where it appears to the court or the comptroller on an application made by an employee within the prescribed period that—

(a) the employee has made an invention belonging to the employer for which a patent has been granted,

(b) having regard among other things to the size and nature of the employer's undertaking, the invention or the patent for it (or the combination of both) is of outstanding benefit to the employer, and

(c) by reason of those facts it is just that the employee should be awarded compensation to be paid by the employer,

the court or the comptroller may award him such compensation of an amount determined under section 41 below.

(2) Where it appears to the court or the comptroller on an application made by an employee within the prescribed period that—

(a) a patent has been granted for an invention made by and belonging to the employee;

(b) his rights in the invention, or in any patent or application for a patent for the invention, have since the appointed day been assigned to the employer or an exclusive licence under the patent or application has since the appointed day been granted to the employer;

(c) the benefit derived by the employee from the contract of assignment, assignation or grant or any ancillary contract ("the relevant contract") is inadequate in relation to the benefit derived by the employer from the invention or the patent for it (or both); and

(d) by reason of those facts it is just that the employee should be awarded compensation to be paid by the employer in addition to the benefit derived from the relevant contract;

the court or the comptroller may award him such compensation of an amount determined under section 41 below.

(3) Subsections (1) and (2) above shall not apply to the invention of an employee where a relevant collective agreement provides for the payment of compensation in respect of inventions of the same description as that invention to employees of the same description as that employee.

(4) Subsection (2) above shall have effect notwithstanding anything in the relevant contract or any agreement applicable to the invention (other than any such collective agreement).

(5) If it appears to the comptroller on an application under this section that the application involves matters which would more properly be determined by the court, he may decline to deal with it.

(6) In this section—

"the prescribed period", in relation to proceedings before the court, means the period prescribed by rules of court, and

"relevant collective agreement" means a collective agreement within the meaning of the Trade Union and Labour Relations (Consolidation) Act 1992, made by or on behalf of a trade union to which the employee belongs, and by the employer or an employers' association to which the employer belongs which is in force at the time of the making of the invention.

(7) References in this section to an invention belonging to an employer or employee are references to it so belonging as between the employer and the employee.

41. Amount of compensation

(1) An award of compensation to an employee under section 40(1) or (2) above shall be such as will secure for the employee a fair share (having regard to all the circumstances) of the benefit which the employer has derived, or may reasonably be expected to derive, from any of the following—

(a) the invention in question;

(b) the patent for the invention;

(c) the assignment, assignation or grant of—

(i) the property or any right in the invention, or

(ii) the property in, or any right in or under, an application for the patent,

to a person connected with the employer.

(2) For the purposes of subsection (1) above the amount of any benefit derived or expected to be derived by an employer from the assignment, assignation or grant of—

(a) the property in, or any right in or under, a patent for the invention or an application for such a patent; or

(b) the property or any right in the invention;

to a person connected with him shall be taken to be the amount which could reasonably be expected to be so derived by the employer if that person had not been connected with him.

(3) Where the Crown or a Research Council in its capacity as employer assigns or grants the property in, or any right in or under, an invention, patent or application for a patent to a body having among its functions that of developing or exploiting inventions resulting from public research and does so for no consideration or only a nominal consideration, any benefit derived from the invention, patent or application by that body shall be treated for the purposes of the foregoing provisions of this section as so derived by the Crown or, as the case may be, Research Council.

In this subsection "Research Council" means a body which is a Research Council for the purposes of the Science and Technology Act 1965 or the Arts and Humanities Research Council (as defined by section 1 of the Higher Education Act 2004).

(4) In determining the fair share of the benefit to be secured for an employee in respect of an invention which has always belonged to an employer, the court or the comptroller shall, among other things, take the following matters into account, that is to say—

(a) the nature of the employee's duties, his remuneration and the other advantages he derives or has derived from his employment or has derived in relation to the invention under this Act;

(b) the effort and skill which the employee has devoted to making the invention;

(c) the effort and skill which any other person has devoted to making the invention jointly with the employee concerned, and the advice and other assistance contributed by any other employee who is not a joint inventor of the invention; and

(d) the contribution made by the employer to the making, developing and working of the invention by the provision of advice, facilities and other assistance, by the provision of opportunities and by his managerial and commercial skill and activities.

(5) In determining the fair share of the benefit to be secured for an employee in respect of an invention which originally belonged to him, the court or the comptroller shall, among other things, take the following matters into account, that is to say—

(a) any conditions in a licence or licences granted under this Act or otherwise in respect of the invention or the patent for it;

(b) the extent to which the invention was made jointly by the employee with any other person; and

(c) the contribution made by the employer to the making, developing and working of the invention as mentioned in subsection (4)(d) above.

(6) Any order for the payment of compensation under section 40 above may be an order for the payment of a lump sum or for periodical payment, or both.

(7) Without prejudice to section 32 of the Interpretation Act 1889 (which provides that a statutory power may in general be exercised from time to time), the refusal of the court or the comptroller to make any such order on an application made by an employee under section 40 above shall not prevent a further application being made under that section by him or any successor in title of his.

(8) Where the court or the comptroller has made any such order, the court or he may on the application of either the employer or the employee vary or discharge it or suspend any provision of the order and revive any provision so suspended, and section 40(5) above shall apply to the application as it applies to an application under that section.

(9) In England and Wales any sums awarded by the comptroller under section 40 above shall, if a county court so orders, be recoverable *by execution issued from the county court* or otherwise as if they were payable under an order of that court.

(10) In Scotland an order made under section 40 above by the comptroller for the payment of any sums may be enforced in like manner as an extract registered decree arbitral bearing a warrant for execution issued by the sheriff court of any sheriffdom in Scotland.

(11) In Northern Ireland an order made under section 40 above by the comptroller for the payment of any sums may be enforced as if it were a money judgment.

Note. The italicized words in subsection (9) are substituted by the words 'under section 85 of the County Courts Act 1984' by the Tribunals, Courts and Enforcement Act 2007, s. 62(3), Sch. 13, paras. 39, 40, as from a day to be appointed.

42. Enforceability of contracts relating to employees' inventions

(1) This section applies to any contract (whenever made) relating to inventions made by an employee, being a contract entered into by him—

(a) with the employer (alone or with another); or

(b) with some other person at the request of the employer or in pursuance of the employee's contract of employment.

(2) Any term in a contract to which this section applies which diminishes the employee's rights in inventions of any description made by him after the appointed day and the date of the contract, or in or under patents for those inventions or applications for such patents, shall be unenforceable against him to the extent that it diminishes his rights in an invention of that description so made, or in or under a patent for such an invention or an application for any such patent.

(3) Subsection (2) above shall not be construed as derogating from any duty of confidentiality owed to his employer by an employee by virtue of any rule of law of otherwise.

(4) This section applies to any arrangement made with a Crown employee by or on behalf of the Crown as his employer as it applies to any contract made between an employee and an employer other than the Crown, and for the purposes of this section "Crown employee" means a person employed under or for the purposes of a government department or any officer or body exercising on behalf of the Crown functions conferred by any enactment or a person serving in the naval, military or air forces of the Crown.

Infringement

60. Meaning of infringement

(1) Subject to the provisions of this section, a person infringes a patent for an invention if, but only if, while the patent is in force, he does any of the following things in the United Kingdom in relation to the invention without the consent of the proprietor of the patent, that is to say—

(a) where the invention is a product, he makes, disposes of, offers to dispose of, uses or imports the product or keeps it whether for disposal or otherwise;

(b) where the invention is a process, he uses the process or he offers it for use in the United Kingdom when he knows, or it is obvious to a reasonable person in the circumstances, that its use there without the consent of the proprietor would be an infringement of the patent;

(c) where the invention is a process, he disposes of, offers to dispose of, uses or imports any product obtained directly by means of that process or keeps any such product whether for disposal or otherwise.

(2) Subject to the following provisions of this section, a person (other than the proprietor of the patent) also infringes a patent for an invention if, while the patent is in force and without the consent of the proprietor, he supplies or offers to supply in the United Kingdom a person other than a licensee or other person entitled to work the invention with any of the means, relating to an essential element of the invention, for putting the invention into effect when he knows, or it is obvious to a reasonable person in the circumstances, that those means are suitable for putting, and are intended to put, the invention into effect in the United Kingdom.

(3) Subsection (2) above shall not apply to the supply or offer of a staple commercial product unless the supply or the offer is made for the purpose of inducing the person supplied or, as the case may be, the person to whom the offer is made to do an act which constitutes an infringement of the patent by virtue of subsection (1) above.

(5) An act which, apart from this subsection, would constitute an infringement of a patent for an invention shall not do so if—

(a) it is done privately and for purposes which are not commercial;

(b) it is done for experimental purposes relating to the subject-matter of the invention;

(c) it consists of the extemporaneous preparation in a pharmacy of a medicine for an individual in accordance with a prescription given by a registered medical or dental practitioner or consists of dealing with a medicine so prepared;

(d) it consists of the use, exclusively for the needs of a relevant ship, of a product or process in the body of such a ship or in its machinery, tackle, apparatus or other accessories, in a case where the ship has temporarily or accidentally entered the internal or territorial waters of the United Kingdom;

(e) it consists of the use of a product or process in the body or operation of a relevant aircraft, hovercraft or vehicle which has temporarily or accidentally entered or is crossing the United Kingdom (including the air space above it and its territorial waters) or the use of accessories for such a relevant aircraft, hovercraft or vehicle;

(f) it consists of the use of an exempted aircraft which has lawfully entered or is lawfully crossing the United Kingdom as aforesaid or of the importation into the United Kingdom, or the use or storage there, of any part or accessory for such an aircraft;

(g) it consists of the use by a farmer of the product of his harvest for propagation or multiplication by him on his own holding, where there has been a sale of plant propagating material to the farmer by the proprietor of the patent or with his consent for agricultural use;

(h) it consists of the use of an animal or animal reproductive material by a farmer for an agricultural purpose following a sale to the farmer, by the proprietor of the patent or with his consent, of breeding stock or other animal reproductive material which constitutes or contains the patented invention.

(i) it consists of—

(i) an act done in conducting a study, test or trial which is necessary for and is conducted with a view to the application of paragraphs 1 to 5 of article 13 of Directive 2001/82/EC or paragraphs 1 to 4 of article 10 of Directive 2001/83/EC, or

(ii) any other act which is required for the purpose of the application of those paragraphs.

(6) For the purposes of subsection (2) above a person who does an act in relation to an invention which is prevented only by virtue of paragraph (a), (b) or (c) of subsection (5) above from constituting an infringement of a patent for the invention shall not be treated as a person entitled to work the invention, but—

(a) the reference in that subsection to a person entitled to work an invention includes a reference to a person so entitled by virtue of section 55 above, and

(b) a person who by virtue of section 20B(4) or (5) above or section 28A(4) or (5) above or section 64 below or section 117A(4) or (5) below is entitled to do an act in relation to the invention without it constituting such an infringement shall, so far as concerns that act, be treated as a person entitled to work the invention.

(6A) Schedule A1 contains—

(a) provisions restricting the circumstances in which subsection (5)(g) applies; and

(b) provisions which apply where an act would constitute an infringement of a patent but for subsection (5)(g).

(6B) For the purposes of subsection (5)(h), use for an agricultural purpose—

(a) includes making an animal or animal reproductive material available for the purposes of pursuing the farmer's agricultural activity; but

(b) does not include sale within the framework, or for the purposes, of a commercial reproduction activity.

(6C) In paragraphs (g) and (h) of subsection (5) "sale" includes any other form of commercialisation.

(7) In this section—

"relevant ship" and "relevant aircraft, hovercraft or vehicle" mean respectively a ship and an aircraft, hovercraft or vehicle registered in, or belonging to, any country, other than the United Kingdom, which is a party to the Convention for the Protection of Industrial Property signed at Paris on 20th March 1883 or which is a member of the World Trade Organisation; and

"exempted aircraft" means an aircraft to which section 89 of the Civil Aviation Act 1982 (aircraft exempted from seizure in respect of patent claims) applies.

"Directive 2001/82/EC" means Directive 2001/82/EC of the European Parliament and of the Council on the Community code relating to veterinary medicinal products as amended by Directive 2004/28 of the European Parliament and of the Council;

"Directive 2001/83/EC" means Directive 2001/83/EC of the European Parliament and of the Council on the Community code relating to medicinal products for human use, as amended by Directive 2002/98/EC of the European Parliament and of the Council, by Commission Directive 2003/63/EC and by Directives 2004/24/EC and 2004/27/EC of the European Parliament and of the Council.

61. Proceedings for infringement of patent

(1) Subject to the following provisions of this Part of this Act, civil proceedings may be brought in the court by the proprietor of a patent in respect of any act alleged to infringe the patent and (without prejudice to any other jurisdiction of the court) in those proceedings a claim may be made—

(a) for an injunction or interdict restraining the defendant or defender from any apprehended act of infringement;

(b) for an order for him to deliver up or destroy any patented product in relation to which the patent is infringed or any article in which that product is inextricably comprised;

(c) for damages in respect of the infringement;

(d) for an account of the profits derived by him from the infringement;

(e) for a declaration or declarator that the patent is valid and has been infringed by him.

(2) The court shall not, in respect of the same infringement, both award the proprietor of a patent damages and order that he shall be given an account of the profits.

(3) The proprietor of a patent and any other person may by agreement with each other refer to the comptroller the question whether that other person has infringed the patent and on the reference the proprietor of the patent may make any claim mentioned in subsection (1)(c) or (e) above.

(4) Except so far as the context requires, in the following provisions of this Act—

(a) any reference to proceedings for infringement and the bringing of such proceedings includes a reference to a reference under subsection (3) above and the making of such a reference;

(b) any reference to a claimant or pursuer includes a reference to the proprietor of the patent; and

(c) any reference to a defendant or defender includes a reference to any other party to the reference.

(5) If it appears to the comptroller on a reference under subsection (3) above that the question referred to him would more properly be determined by the court, he may decline to deal with it and the court shall have jurisdiction to determine the question as if the reference were proceedings brought in the court.

(6) Subject to the following provisions of this Part of this Act, in determining whether or not to grant any kind of relief claimed under this section and the extent of the relief granted the court or the comptroller shall apply the principles applied by the court in relation to that kind of relief immediately before the appointed day.

(7) If the comptroller awards any sum by way of damages on a reference under subsection (3) above, then—

(a) in England and Wales, the sum shall be recoverable, if a county court so orders, *by execution issued from the county court* or otherwise as if it were payable under an order of that court;

(b) in Scotland, payment of the sum may be enforced in like manner as an extract registered decree arbitral bearing a warrant for execution issued by the sheriff court of any sheriffdom in Scotland;

(c) in Northern Ireland, payment of the sum may be enforced as if it were a money judgment.

Note. The italicized words in subsection (7)(a) are substituted by the words 'under section 85 of the County Courts Act 1984' by the Tribunals, Courts and Enforcement Act 2007, s. 62(3), Sch. 13, paras. 39, 41, as from a day to be appointed.

62. Restrictions on recovery of damages for infringement

(1) In proceedings for infringement of a patent damages shall not be awarded, and no order shall be made for an account of profits, against a defendant or defender who proves that at the date of the infringement he was not aware, and had no reasonable grounds for supposing, that the patent existed; and a person shall not be taken to have been so aware or to have had reasonable grounds for so supposing by reason only of the application to a product of the word "patent" or "patented", or any word or words expressing or implying that a patent has been obtained for the product, unless the number of the patent accompanied the word or words in question.

(2) In proceedings for infringement of a patent the court or the comptroller may, if it or he thinks fit, refuse to award any damages or make any such order in respect of an infringement committed during the further period specified in section 25(4) above, but before the payment of the renewal fee and any additional fee prescribed for the purposes of that subsection.

(3) Where an amendment of the specification of a patent has been allowed under any of the provisions of this Act, the court or the comptroller shall, when awarding damages or making an order for an account of profits in proceedings for an infringement of the patent committed before the decision to allow the amendment, take into account the following—

(a) whether at the date of infringement the defendant or defender knew, or had reasonable grounds to know, that he was infringing the patent;

(b) whether the specification of the patent as published was framed in good faith and with reasonable skill and knowledge;

(c) whether the proceedings are brought in good faith.

Infringement

67. Proceedings for infringement by exclusive licensee

(1) Subject to the provisions of this section, the holder of an exclusive licence under a patent shall have the same right as the proprietor of the patent to bring proceedings in respect of any infringement of the patent committed after the date of the licence; and references to the proprietor of the patent in the provisions of this Act relating to infringement shall be construed accordingly.

(2) In awarding damages or granting any other relief in any such proceedings the court or the comptroller shall take into consideration any loss suffered or likely to be suffered by the exclusive licensee as such as a result of the infringement, or, as the case may be, the profits derived from the infringement, so far as it constitutes an infringement of the rights of the exclusive licensee as such.

(3) In any proceedings taken by an exclusive licensee by virtue of this section the proprietor of the patent shall be made a party to the proceedings, but if made a defendant or defender shall not be liable for any costs or expenses unless he enters an appearance and takes part in the proceedings.

70. Remedy for groundless threats of infringement proceedings

(1) Where a person (whether or not the proprietor of, or entitled to any right in, a patent) by circulars, advertisements or otherwise threatens another person with proceedings for any infringement of a patent, a person aggrieved by the threats (whether or not he is the person to whom the threats are made) may, subject to subsection (4) below, bring proceedings in the court against the person making the threats, claiming any relief mentioned in subsection (3) below.

(2) In any such proceedings the claimant or pursuer shall, subject to subsection (2A) below, be entitled to the relief claimed if he proves that the threats were so made and satisfies the court that he is a person aggrieved by them.

(2A) If the defendant or defender proves that the acts in respect of which proceedings were threatened constitute or, if done, would constitute an infringement of a patent—

(a) the claimant or pursuer shall be entitled to the relief claimed only if he shows that the patent alleged to be infringed is invalid in a relevant respect;

(b) even if the claimant or pursuer does show that the patent is invalid in a relevant respect, he shall not be entitled to the relief claimed if the defendant or defender proves that at the time of making the threats he did not know, and had no reason to suspect, that the patent was invalid in that respect.

(3) The said relief is—

(a) a declaration or declarator to the effect that the threats are unjustifiable;

(b) an injunction or interdict against the continuance of the threats; and

(c) damages in respect of any loss which the claimant or pursuer has sustained by the threats.

72. Power to revoke patents on application

(1) Subject to the following provisions of this Act, the court or the comptroller may by order revoke a patent for an invention on the application of any person (including the proprietor of the patent) on (but only on) any of the following grounds, that is to say—

(a) the invention is not a patentable invention;

(b) that the patent was granted to a person who was not entitled to be granted that patent;

(c) the specification of the patent does not disclose the invention clearly enough and completely enough for it to be performed by a person skilled in the art;

(d) the matter disclosed in the specification of the patent extends beyond that disclosed in the application for the patent, as filed, or, if the patent was granted on a new application filed under section 8(3), 12 or 37(4) above or as mentioned in section 15(9) above, in the earlier application, as filed;

(e) the protection conferred by the patent has been extended by an amendment which should not have been allowed.

74. Proceedings in which validity of patent may be put in issue

(1) Subject to the following provisions of this section, the validity of a patent may be put in issue—

(a) by way of defence, in proceedings for infringement of the patent under section 61 above or proceedings under section 69 above for infringement of rights conferred by the publication of an application;

(b) in proceedings under section 70 above;

(c) in proceedings in which a declaration in relation to the patent is sought under section 71 above;

(d) in proceedings before the court or the comptroller under section 72 above for the revocation of the patent;

(e) in proceedings under section 58 above.

(2) The validity of a patent may not be put in issue in any other proceedings and, in particular, no proceedings may be instituted (whether under this Act or otherwise) seeking only a declaration as to the validity or invalidity of a patent.

(3) The only grounds on which the validity of a patent may be put in issue (whether in proceedings for revocation under section 72 above or otherwise) are the grounds on which the patent may be revoked under that section.

125. Extent of invention

(1) For the purposes of this Act an invention for a patent for which an application has been made or for which a patent has been granted shall, unless the context otherwise requires, be taken to be that specified in a claim of the specification of the application or patent, as the case may be, as interpreted by the description and any drawings contained in that specification, and the extent of the protection conferred by a patent or application for a patent shall be determined accordingly.

(2) It is hereby declared for the avoidance of doubt that where more than one invention is specified in any such claim, each invention may have a different priority date under section 5 above.

(3) The Protocol on the Interpretation of Article 69 of the European Patent Convention (which Article contains a provision corresponding to subsection (1) above) shall, as for the time being in force, apply for the purposes of subsection (1) above as it applies for the purposes of that Article.

Copyright, Designs and Patents Act 1988
1988 c. 48

An Act to restate the law of copyright, with amendments; to make fresh provision as to the rights of performers and others in performances; to confer a design right in original designs; to amend the Registered Designs Act 1949; to make provision with respect to patent agents and trade mark agents; to confer patents and designs jurisdiction on certain county courts; to amend the law of patents; to make provision with respect to devices designed to circumvent copy-protection of works in electronic form; to make fresh provision penalising the fraudulent reception of transmissions; to make the fraudulent application or use of a trade mark an offence; to make provision for the benefit of the Hospital for Sick Children, Great Ormond Street, London; to enable financial assistance to be given to certain international bodies; and for connected purposes [15th November 1988]

Part I
Copyright

Chapter I
Subsistence, ownership and duration of copyright

Introductory

1. Copyright and copyright works

(1) Copyright is a property right which subsists in accordance with this Part in the following descriptions of work—

(a) original literary, dramatic, musical or artistic works,

(b) sound recordings, films or broadcasts, and

(c) the typographical arrangement of published editions.

(2) In this Part "copyright work" means a work of any of those descriptions in which copyright subsists.

(3) Copyright does not subsist in a work unless the requirements of this Part with respect to qualification for copyright protection are met (see section 153 and the provisions referred to there).

2. Rights subsisting in copyright works

(1) The owner of the copyright in a work of any description has the exclusive right to do the acts specified in Chapter II as the acts restricted by the copyright in a work of that description.

(2) In relation to certain descriptions of copyright work the following rights conferred by Chapter IV (moral rights) subsist in favour of the author, director or commissioner of the work, whether or not he is the owner of the copyright—

(a) section 77 (right to be identified as author or director),

(b) section 80 (right to object to derogatory treatment of work), and

(c) section 85 (right to privacy of certain photographs and films).

Descriptions of work and related provisions

3. Literary, dramatic and musical works

(1) In this Part—

"literary work" means any work, other than a dramatic or musical work, which is written, spoken or sung, and accordingly includes—

(a) a table or compilation other than a database,

(b) a computer program,

(c) preparatory design material for a computer program and

(d) a database;

"dramatic work" includes a work of dance or mime; and

"musical work" means a work consisting of music, exclusive of any words or action intended to be sung, spoken or performed with the music.

(2) Copyright does not subsist in a literary, dramatic or musical work unless and until it is recorded, in writing or otherwise; and references in this Part to the time at which such a work is made are to the time at which it is so recorded.

(3) It is immaterial for the purposes of subsection (2) whether the work is recorded by or with the permission of the author; and where it is not recorded by the author, nothing in that subsection affects the question whether copyright subsists in the record as distinct from the work recorded.

3A. Databases

(1) In this Part "database" means a collection of independent works, data or other materials which—

(a) are arranged in a systematic or methodical way, and

(b) are individually accessible by electronic or other means.

(2) For the purposes of this Part a literary work consisting of a database is original if, and only if, by reason of the selection or arrangement of the contents of the database the database constitutes the author's own intellectual creation.

4. Artistic works

(1) In this Part "artistic work" means—

(a) a graphic work, photograph, sculpture or collage, irrespective of artistic quality,

(b) a work of architecture being a building or a model for a building, or

(c) a work of artistic craftsmanship.

(2) In this Part—

"building" includes any fixed structure, and a part of a building or fixed structure;

"graphic work" includes—

(a) any painting, drawing, diagram, map, chart or plan, and

(b) any engraving, etching, lithograph, woodcut or similar work;

"photograph" means a recording of light or other radiation on any medium on which an image is produced or from which an image may by any means be produced, and which is not part of a film;

"sculpture" includes a cast or model made for purposes of sculpture.

5A. Sound recordings

(1) In this Part "sound recording" means—

(a) a recording of sounds, from which the sounds may be reproduced, or

(b) a recording of the whole or any part of a literary, dramatic or musical work, from which sounds reproducing the work or part may be produced,

regardless of the medium on which the recording is made or the method by which the sounds are reproduced or produced.

(2) Copyright does not subsist in a sound recording which is, or to the extent that it is, a copy taken from a previous sound recording.

5B. Films

(1) In this Part "film" means a recording on any medium from which a moving image may by any means be produced.

(2) The sound track accompanying a film shall be treated as part of the film for the purposes of this Part.

(3) Without prejudice to the generality of subsection (2), where that subsection applies—

(a) references in this Part to showing a film include playing the film sound track to accompany the film,

(b) references in this Part to playing a sound recording, or to communicating a sound recording to the public, do not include playing or communicating the film sound track to accompany the film,

(c) references in this Part to copying a work, so far as they apply to a sound recording, do not include copying the film sound track to accompany the film, and

(d) references in this Part to the issuing, rental or lending of copies of a work, so far as they apply to a sound recording, do not include the issuing, rental or lending of copies of the sound track to accompany the film.

(4) Copyright does not subsist in a film which is, or to the extent that it is, a copy taken from a previous film.

(5) Nothing in this section affects any copyright subsisting in a film sound track as a sound recording.

6. Broadcasts

(1) In this Part a "broadcast" means an electronic transmission of visual images, sounds or other information which—

(a) is transmitted for simultaneous reception by members of the public and is capable of being lawfully received by them, or

(b) is transmitted at a time determined solely by the person making the transmission for presentation to members of the public,

and which is not excepted by subsection (1A); and references to broadcasting shall be construed accordingly.

(1A) Excepted from the definition of "broadcast" is any internet transmission unless it is—

(a) a transmission taking place simultaneously on the internet and by other means,

(b) a concurrent transmission of a live event, or

(c) a transmission of recorded moving images or sounds forming part of a programme service offered by the person responsible for making the transmission, being a service in which programmes are transmitted at scheduled times determined by that person.

(2) An encrypted transmission shall be regarded as capable of being lawfully received by members of the public only if decoding equipment has been made available to members of the public by or with the authority of the person making the transmission or the person providing the contents of the transmission.

(3) References in this Part to the person making a broadcast or a transmission which is a broadcast are—

(a) to the person transmitting the programme, if he has responsibility to any extent for its contents, and

(b) to any person providing the programme who makes with the person transmitting it the arrangements necessary for its transmission;

and references in this Part to a programme, in the context of broadcasting, are to any item included in a broadcast.

(4) For the purposes of this Part, the place from which a wireless broadcast is made is the place where, under the control and responsibility of the person making the broadcast, the programme-carrying signals are introduced into an uninterrupted chain of communication (including, in the case of a satellite transmission, the chain leading to the satellite and down towards the earth).

(4A) Subsections (3) and (4) have effect subject to section 6A (safeguards in case of certain satellite broadcasts).

(5) References in this Part to the reception of a broadcast include reception of a broadcast relayed by means of a telecommunications system.

(5A) The relaying of a broadcast by reception and immediate re-transmission shall be regarded for the purposes of this Part as a separate act of broadcasting from the making of the broadcast which is so re-transmitted.

(6) Copyright does not subsist in a broadcast which infringes, or to the extent that it infringes, the copyright in another broadcast.

8. Published editions

(1) In this Part "published edition", in the context of copyright in the typographical arrangement of a published edition, means a published edition of the whole or any part of one or more literary, dramatic or musical works.

(2) Copyright does not subsist in the typographical arrangement of a published edition if, or to the extent that, it reproduces the typographical arrangement of a previous edition.

Authorship and ownership of copyright

9. Authorship of work

(1) In this Part "author", in relation to a work, means the person who creates it.

(2) That person shall be taken to be—

(aa) in the case of a sound recording, the producer;

(ab) in the case of a film, the producer and the principal director;

(b) in the case of a broadcast, the person making the broadcast (see section 6(3)) or, in the case of a broadcast which relays another broadcast by reception and immediate re-transmission, the person making that other broadcast;

(d) in the case of the typographical arrangement of a published edition, the publisher.

(3) In the case of a literary, dramatic, musical or artistic work which is computer-generated, the author shall be taken to be the person by whom the arrangements necessary for the creation of the work are undertaken.

(4) For the purposes of this Part a work is of "unknown authorship" if the identity of the author is unknown or, in the case of a work of joint authorship, if the identity of none of the authors is known.

(5) For the purposes of this Part the identity of an author shall be regarded as unknown if it is not possible for a person to ascertain his identity by reasonable inquiry; but if his identity is once known it shall not subsequently be regarded as unknown.

11. First ownership of copyright

(1) The author of a work is the first owner of any copyright in it, subject to the following provisions.

(2) Where a literary, dramatic, musical or artistic work, or a film, is made by an employee in the course of his employment, his employer is the first owner of any copyright in the work subject to any agreement to the contrary.

(3) This section does not apply to Crown copyright or Parliamentary copyright (see sections 163 and 165) or to copyright which subsists by virtue of section 168 (copyright of certain international organisations).

Duration of copyright

12. Duration of copyright in literary, dramatic, musical or artistic works

(1) The following provisions have effect with respect to the duration of copyright in a literary, dramatic, musical or artistic work.

(2) Copyright expires at the end of the period of 70 years from the end of the calendar year in which the author dies, subject as follows.

(3) If the work is of unknown authorship, copyright expires—

(a) at the end of the period of 70 years from the end of the calendar year in which the work was made, or

(b) if during that period the work is made available to the public, at the end of the period of 70 years from the end of the calendar year in which it is first so made available,

subject as follows.

(4) Subsection (2) applies if the identity of the author becomes known before the end of the period specified in paragraph (a) or (b) of subsection (3).

(5) For the purposes of subsection (3) making available to the public includes—

(a) in the case of a literary, dramatic or musical work—

(i) performance in public, or

(ii) communication to the public;

(b) in the case of an artistic work—

(i) exhibition in public,

(ii) a film including the work being shown in public, or

(iii) communication to the public;

but in determining generally for the purposes of that subsection whether a work has been made available to the public no account shall be taken of any unauthorised act.

(6) Where the country of origin of the work is not an EEA state and the author of the work is not a national of an EEA state, the duration of copyright is that to which the work is entitled in the country of origin, provided that does not exceed the period which would apply under subsections (2) to (5).

(7) If the work is computer-generated the above provisions do not apply and copyright expires at the end of the period of 50 years from the end of the calendar year in which the work was made.

(8) The provisions of this section are adapted as follows in relation to a work of joint authorship—

(a) the reference in subsection (2) to the death of the author shall be construed—

(i) if the identity of all the authors is known, as a reference to the death of the last of them to die, and

(ii) if the identity of one or more of the authors is known and the identity of one or more others is not, as a reference to the death of the last whose identity is known;

(b) the reference in subsection (4) to the identity of the author becoming known shall be construed as a reference to the identity of any of the authors becoming known;

(c) the reference in subsection (6) to the author not being a national of an EEA state shall be construed as a reference to none of the authors being a national of an EEA state.

(9) This section does not apply to Crown copyright or Parliamentary copyright (see sections 163 to 166D) or to copyright which subsists by virtue of section 168 (copyright of certain international organisations).

Chapter II
Rights of Copyright Owner

The acts restricted by copyright

16. The acts restricted by copyright in a work

(1) The owner of the copyright in a work has, in accordance with the following provisions of this Chapter, the exclusive right to do the following acts in the United Kingdom—

(a) to copy the work (see section 17);

(b) to issue copies of the work to the public (see section 18);

(ba) to rent or lend the work to the public (see section 18A);

(c) to perform, show or play the work in public (see section 19);

(d) to communicate the work to the public (see section 20);

(e) to make an adaptation of the work or do any of the above in relation to an adaptation (see section 21);

and those acts are referred to in this Part as the "acts restricted by the copyright".

(2) Copyright in a work is infringed by a person who without the licence of the copyright owner does, or authorises another to do, any of the acts restricted by the copyright.

(3) References in this Part to the doing of an act restricted by the copyright in a work are to the doing of it—

(a) in relation to the work as a whole or any substantial part of it, and

(b) either directly or indirectly;

and it is immaterial whether any intervening acts themselves infringe copyright.

(4) This Chapter has effect subject to—

(a) the provisions of Chapter III (acts permitted in relation to copyright works), and

(b) the provisions of Chapter VII (provisions with respect to copyright licensing).

17. Infringement of copyright by copying

(1) The copying of the work is an act restricted by the copyright in every description of copyright work; and references in this Part to copying and copies shall be construed as follows.

(2) Copying in relation to a literary, dramatic, musical or artistic work means reproducing the work in any material form.

This includes storing the work in any medium by electronic means.

(3) In relation to an artistic work copying includes the making of a copy in three dimensions of a two-dimensional work and the making of a copy in two dimensions of a three-dimensional work.

(4) Copying in relation to a film or broadcast includes making a photograph of the whole or any substantial part of any image forming part of the film or broadcast.

(5) Copying in relation to the typographical arrangement of a published edition means making a facsimile copy of the arrangement.

(6) Copying in relation to any description of work includes the making of copies which are transient or are incidental to some other use of the work.

18. Infringement by issue of copies to the public

(1) The issue to the public of copies of the work is an act restricted by the copyright in every description of copyright work.

(2) References in this Part to the issue to the public of copies of a work are to—

(a) the act of putting into circulation in the EEA copies not previously put into circulation in the EEA by or with the consent of the copyright owner, or

(b) the act of putting into circulation outside the EEA copies not previously put into circulation in the EEA or elsewhere.

(3) References in this Part to the issue to the public of copies of a work do not include—

(a) any subsequent distribution, sale, hiring or loan of copies previously put into circulation (but see section 18A: infringement by rental or lending), or

(b) any subsequent importation of such copies into the United Kingdom or another EEA state,

except so far as paragraph (a) of subsection (2) applies to putting into circulation in the EEA copies previously put into circulation outside the EEA.

(4) References in this Part to the issue of copies of a work include the issue of the original.

18A. Infringement by rental or lending of work to the public

(1) The rental or lending of copies of the work to the public is an act restricted by the copyright in—

(a) a literary, dramatic or musical work,

(b) an artistic work, other than—

(i) a work of architecture in the form of a building or a model for a building, or

(ii) a work of applied art, or

(c) a film or a sound recording.

(2) In this Part, subject to the following provisions of this section—

(a) "rental" means making a copy of the work available for use, on terms that it will or may be returned, for direct or indirect economic or commercial advantage, and

(b) "lending" means making a copy of the work available for use, on terms that it will or may be returned, otherwise than for direct or indirect economic or commercial advantage, through an establishment which is accessible to the public.

(3) The expressions "rental" and "lending" do not include—

(a) making available for the purpose of public performance, playing or showing in public or communication to the public;

(b) making available for the purpose of exhibition in public; or

(c) making available for on-the-spot reference use.

(4) The expression "lending" does not include making available between establishments which are accessible to the public.

(5) Where lending by an establishment accessible to the public gives rise to a payment the amount of which does not go beyond what is necessary to cover the operating costs of the establishment, there is no direct or indirect economic or commercial advantage for the purposes of this section.

(6) References in this Part to the rental or lending of copies of a work include the rental or lending of the original.

19. Infringement by performance, showing or playing of work in public

(1) The performance of the work in public is an act restricted by the copyright in a literary, dramatic or musical work.

(2) In this Part "performance", in relation to a work—

(a) includes delivery in the case of lectures, addresses, speeches and sermons, and

(b) in general, includes any mode of visual or acoustic presentation, including presentation by means of a sound recording, film or broadcast of the work.

(3) The playing or showing of the work in public is an act restricted by the copyright in a sound recording, film or broadcast.

(4) Where copyright in a work is infringed by its being performed, played or shown in public by means of apparatus for receiving visual images or sounds conveyed by

electronic means, the person by whom the visual images or sounds are sent, and in the case of a performance the performers, shall not be regarded as responsible for the infringement.

20. Infringement by communication to the public

(1) The communication to the public of the work is an act restricted by the copyright in—

(a) a literary, dramatic, musical or artistic work,

(b) a sound recording or film, or

(c) a broadcast.

(2) References in this Part to communication to the public are to communication to the public by electronic transmission, and in relation to a work include—

(a) the broadcasting of the work;

(b) the making available to the public of the work by electronic transmission in such a way that members of the public may access it from a place and at a time individually chosen by them.

21. Infringement by making adaptation or act done in relation to adaptation

(1) The making of an adaptation of the work is an act restricted by the copyright in a literary, dramatic or musical work.

For this purpose an adaptation is made when it is recorded, in writing or otherwise.

(2) The doing of any of the acts specified in sections 17 to 20, or subsection (1) above, in relation to an adaptation of the work is also an act restricted by the copyright in a literary, dramatic or musical work.

For this purpose it is immaterial whether the adaptation has been recorded, in writing or otherwise, at the time the act is done.

(3) In this Part "adaptation"—

(a) in relation to a literary work, other than a computer program or a database, or in relation to a dramatic work, means—

(i) a translation of the work;

(ii) a version of a dramatic work in which it is converted into a non-dramatic work or, as the case may be, of a non-dramatic work in which it is converted into a dramatic work;

(iii) a version of the work in which the story or action is conveyed wholly or mainly by means of pictures in a form suitable for reproduction in a book, or in a newspaper, magazine or similar periodical;

(ab) in relation to a computer program, means an arrangement or altered version of the program or a translation of it;

(ac) in relation to a database, means an arrangement or altered version of the database or a translation of it;

(b) in relation to a musical work, means an arrangement or transcription of the work.

(4) In relation to a computer program a "translation" includes a version of the program in which it is converted into or out of a computer language or code or into a different computer language or code.

(5) No inference shall be drawn from this section as to what does or does not amount to copying a work.

Secondary infringement of copyright

22. Secondary infringement: importing infringing copy

The copyright in a work is infringed by a person who, without the licence of the copyright owner, imports into the United Kingdom, otherwise than for his private and domestic use, an article which is, and which he knows or has reason to believe is, an infringing copy of the work.

23. Secondary infringement: possessing or dealing with infringing copy

The copyright in a work is infringed by a person who, without the licence of the copyright owner—

(a) possesses in the course of a business,

(b) sells or lets for hire, or offers or exposes for sale or hire,

(c) in the course of a business exhibits in public or distributes, or

(d) distributes otherwise than in the course of a business to such an extent as to affect prejudicially the owner of the copyright,

an article which is, and which he knows or has reason to believe is, an infringing copy of the work.

24. Secondary infringement: providing means for making infringing copies

(1) Copyright in a work is infringed by a person who, without the licence of the copyright owner—

(a) makes,

(b) imports into the United Kingdom,

(c) possesses in the course of a business, or

(d) sells or lets for hire, or offers or exposes for sale or hire,

an article specifically designed or adapted for making copies of that work, knowing or having reason to believe that it is to be used to make infringing copies.

(2) Copyright in a work is infringed by a person who without the licence of the copyright owner transmits the work by means of a telecommunications system (otherwise than by communication to the public), knowing or having reason to believe that infringing copies of the work will be made by means of the reception of the transmission in the United Kingdom or elsewhere.

25. Secondary infringement: permitting use of premises for infringing performance

(1) Where the copyright in a literary, dramatic or musical work is infringed by a performance at a place of public entertainment, any person who gave permission for that place to be used for the performance is also liable for the infringement unless when he gave permission he believed on reasonable grounds that the performance would not infringe copyright.

(2) In this section "place of public entertainment" includes premises which are occupied mainly for other purposes but are from time to time made available for hire for the purposes of public entertainment.

26. Secondary infringement: provision of apparatus for infringing performance, &c.

(1) Where copyright in a work is infringed by a public performance of the work, or by the playing or showing of the work in public, by means of apparatus for—

(a) playing sound recordings,

(b) showing films, or

(c) receiving visual images or sounds conveyed by electronic means,

the following persons are also liable for the infringement.

(2) A person who supplied the apparatus, or any substantial part of it, is liable for the infringement if when he supplied the apparatus or part—

(a) he knew or had reason to believe that the apparatus was likely to be so used as to infringe copyright, or

(b) in the case of apparatus whose normal use involves a public performance, playing or showing, he did not believe on reasonable grounds that it would not be so used as to infringe copyright.

(3) An occupier of premises who gave permission for the apparatus to be brought onto the premises is liable for the infringement if when he gave permission he knew or had reason to believe that the apparatus was likely to be so used as to infringe copyright.

(4) A person who supplied a copy of a sound recording or film used to infringe copyright is liable for the infringement if when he supplied it he knew or had reason to believe that what he supplied, or a copy made directly or indirectly from it, was likely to be so used as to infringe copyright.

Designs

51. Design documents and models

(1) It is not an infringement of any copyright in a design document or model recording or embodying a design for anything other than an artistic work or a typeface to make an article to the design or to copy an article made to the design.

(2) Nor is it an infringement of the copyright to issue to the public, or include in a film or communicate to the public, anything the making of which was, by virtue of subsection (1), not an infringement of that copyright.

(3) In this section—

"design" means the design of any aspect of the shape or configuration (whether internal or external) of the whole or part of an article, other than surface decoration; and

"design document" means any record of a design, whether in the form of a drawing, a written description, a photograph, data stored in a computer or otherwise.

52. Effect of exploitation of design derived from artistic work

(1) This section applies where an artistic work has been exploited, by or with the licence of the copyright owner, by—

(a) making by an industrial process articles falling to be treated for the purposes of this Part as copies of the work, and

(b) marketing such articles, in the United Kingdom or elsewhere.

(2) After the end of the period of 25 years from the end of the calendar year in which such articles are first marketed, the work may be copied by making articles of any description, or doing anything for the purpose of making articles of any description, and anything may be done in relation to articles so made, without infringing copyright in the work.

(3) Where only part of an artistic work is exploited as mentioned in subsection (1), subsection (2) applies only in relation to that part.

(4) The Secretary of State may by order make provision—

(a) as to the circumstances in which an article, or any description of article, is to be regarded for the purposes of this section as made by an industrial process;

(b) excluding from the operation of this section such articles of a primarily literary or artistic character as he thinks fit.

(5) An order shall be made by statutory instrument which shall be subject to annulment in pursuance of a resolution of either House of Parliament.

(6) In this section—

(a) references to articles do not include films; and

(b) references to the marketing of an article are to its being sold or let for hire or offered or exposed for sale or hire.

Chapter IV
Moral Rights

Right to be identified as author or director

77. Right to be identified as author or director

(1) The author of a copyright literary, dramatic, musical or artistic work, and the director of a copyright film, has the right to be identified as the author or director of the work in the circumstances mentioned in this section; but the right is not infringed unless it has been asserted in accordance with section 78.

(2) The author of a literary work (other than words intended to be sung or spoken with music) or a dramatic work has the right to be identified whenever—

(a) the work is published commercially, performed in public or communicated to the public; or

(b) copies of a film or sound recording including the work are issued to the public;

and that right includes the right to be identified whenever any of those events occur in relation to an adaptation of the work as the author of the work from which the adaptation was made.

(3) The author of a musical work, or a literary work consisting of words intended to be sung or spoken with music, has the right to be identified whenever—

(a) the work is published commercially;

(b) copies of a sound recording of the work are issued to the public; or

(c) a film of which the sound-track includes the work is shown in public or copies of such a film are issued to the public;

and that right includes the right to be identified whenever any of those events occur in relation to an adaptation of the work as the author of the work from which the adaptation was made.

(4) The author of an artistic work has the right to be identified whenever—

(a) the work is published commercially or exhibited in public, or a visual image of it is communicated to the public;

(b) a film including a visual image of the work is shown in public or copies of such a film are issued to the public; or

(c) in the case of a work of architecture in the form of a building or a model for a building, a sculpture or a work of artistic craftsmanship, copies of a graphic work representing it, or of a photograph of it, are issued to the public.

(5) The author of a work of architecture in the form of a building also has the right to be identified on the building as constructed or, where more than one building is constructed to the design, on the first to be constructed.

(6) The director of a film has the right to be identified whenever the film is shown in public or communicated to the public or copies of the film are issued to the public.

(7) The right of the author or director under this section is—

(a) in the case of commercial publication or the issue to the public of copies of a film or sound recording, to be identified in or on each copy or, if that is not appropriate, in some other manner likely to bring his identity to the notice of a person acquiring a copy,

(b) in the case of identification on a building, to be identified by appropriate means visible to persons entering or approaching the building, and

(c) in any other case, to be identified in a manner likely to bring his identity to the attention of a person seeing or hearing the performance, exhibition, showing or communication to the public in question;

and the identification must in each case be clear and reasonably prominent.

(8) If the author or director in asserting his right to be identified specifies a pseudonym, initials or some other particular form of identification, that form shall be used; otherwise any reasonable form of identification may be used.

(9) This section has effect subject to section 79 (exceptions to right).

Right to object to derogatory treatment of work

80. Right to object to derogatory treatment of work

(1) The author of a copyright literary, dramatic, musical or artistic work, and the director of a copyright film, has the right in the circumstances mentioned in this section not to have his work subjected to derogatory treatment.

(2) For the purposes of this section—

(a) "treatment" of a work means any addition to, deletion from or alteration to or adaptation of the work, other than—

(i) a translation of a literary or dramatic work, or

(ii) an arrangement or transcription of a musical work involving no more than a change of key or register; and

(b) the treatment of a work is derogatory if it amounts to distortion or mutilation of the work or is otherwise prejudicial to the honour or reputation of the author or director;

and in the following provisions of this section references to a derogatory treatment of a work shall be construed accordingly.

(3) In the case of a literary, dramatic or musical work the right is infringed by a person who—

(a) publishes commercially, performs in public or communicates to the public a derogatory treatment of the work; or

(b) issues to the public copies of a film or sound recording of, or including, a derogatory treatment of the work.

(4) In the case of an artistic work the right is infringed by a person who—

(a) publishes commercially or exhibits in public a derogatory treatment of the work, or communicates to the public a visual image of a derogatory treatment of the work,

(b) shows in public a film including a visual image of a derogatory treatment of the work or issues to the public copies of such a film, or

(c) in the case of—

(i) a work of architecture in the form of a model for a building,

(ii) a sculpture, or

(iii) a work of artistic craftsmanship,

issues to the public copies of a graphic work representing, or of a photograph of, a derogatory treatment of the work.

(5) Subsection (4) does not apply to a work of architecture in the form of a building; but where the author of such a work is identified on the building and it is the subject of derogatory treatment he has the right to require the identification to be removed.

(6) In the case of a film, the right is infringed by a person who—

(a) shows in public or communicates to the public a derogatory treatment of the film; or

(b) issues to the public copies of a derogatory treatment of the film,

(7) The right conferred by this section extends to the treatment of parts of a work resulting from a previous treatment by a person other than the author or director, if those parts are attributed to, or are likely to be regarded as the work of, the author or director.

(8) This section has effect subject to sections 81 and 82 (exceptions to and qualifications of right).

False attribution of work

84. False attribution of work

(1) A person has the right in the circumstances mentioned in this section—

(a) not to have a literary, dramatic, musical or artistic work falsely attributed to him as author, and

(b) not to have a film falsely attributed to him as director;

and in this section an "attribution", in relation to such a work, means a statement (express or implied) as to who is the author or director.

(2) The right is infringed by a person who—

(a) issues to the public copies of a work of any of those descriptions in or on which there is a false attribution, or

(b) exhibits in public an artistic work, or a copy of an artistic work, in or on which there is a false attribution.

(3) The right is also infringed by a person who—

(a) in the case of a literary, dramatic or musical work, performs the work in public or communicates it to the public as being the work of a person, or

(b) in the case of a film, shows it in public or communicates it to the public as being directed by a person,

knowing or having reason to believe that the attribution is false.

(4) The right is also infringed by the issue to the public or public display of material containing a false attribution in connection with any of the acts mentioned in subsection (2) or (3).

(5) The right is also infringed by a person who in the course of a business—

(a) possesses or deals with a copy of a work of any of the descriptions mentioned in subsection (1) in or on which there is a false attribution, or

(b) in the case of an artistic work, possesses or deals with the work itself when there is a false attribution in or on it,

knowing or having reason to believe that there is such an attribution and that it is false.

(6) In the case of an artistic work the right is also infringed by a person who in the course of a business—

(a) deals with a work which has been altered after the author parted with possession of it as being the unaltered work of the author, or

(b) deals with a copy of such a work as being a copy of the unaltered work of the author,

knowing or having reason to believe that that is not the case.

(7) References in this section to dealing are to selling or letting for hire, offering or exposing for sale or hire, exhibiting in public, or distributing.

(8) This section applies where, contrary to the fact—

(a) a literary, dramatic or musical work is falsely represented as being an adaptation of the work of a person, or

(b) a copy of an artistic work is falsely represented as being a copy made by the author of the artistic work,

as it applies where the work is falsely attributed to a person as author.

Right to privacy of certain photographs and films

85. Right to privacy of certain photographs and films

(1) A person who for private and domestic purposes commissions the taking of a photograph or the making of a film has, where copyright subsists in the resulting work, the right not to have—

(a) copies of the work issued to the public,

(b) the work exhibited or shown in public, or

(c) the work communicated to the public;

and, except as mentioned in subsection (2), a person who does or authorises the doing of any of those acts infringes that right.

(2) The right is not infringed by an act which by virtue of any of the following provisions would not infringe copyright in the work—

(a) section 31 (incidental inclusion of work in an artistic work, film or broadcast);

(b) section 45 (parliamentary and judicial proceedings);

(c) section 46 (Royal Commissions and statutory inquiries);

(d) section 50 (acts done under statutory authority);

(e) section 57 or 66A (acts permitted on assumptions as to expiry of copyright, &c.).

Chapter V
Dealings with Rights in Copyright Works

Copyright

90. Assignment and licences

(1) Copyright is transmissible by assignment, by testamentary disposition or by operation of law, as personal or moveable property.

(2) An assignment or other transmission of copyright may be partial, that is, limited so as to apply—

(a) to one or more, but not all, of the things the copyright owner has the exclusive right to do;

(b) to part, but not the whole, of the period for which the copyright is to subsist.

(3) An assignment of copyright is not effective unless it is in writing signed by or on behalf of the assignor.

(4) A licence granted by a copyright owner is binding on every successor in title to his interest in the copyright, except a purchaser in good faith for valuable consideration and without notice (actual or constructive) of the licence or a person deriving title from such a purchaser; and references in this Part to doing anything with, or without, the licence of the copyright owner shall be construed accordingly.

92. Exclusive licences

(1) In this Part an "exclusive licence" means a licence in writing signed by or on behalf of the copyright owner authorising the licensee to the exclusion of all other persons, including the person granting the licence, to exercise a right which would otherwise be exercisable exclusively by the copyright owner.

(2) The licensee under an exclusive licence has the same rights against a successor in title who is bound by the licence as he has against the person granting the licence.

Moral rights

94. Moral rights not assignable

The rights conferred by Chapter IV (moral rights) are not assignable.

Chapter VI
Remedies for Infringement

Rights and remedies of copyright owner

96. Infringement actionable by copyright owner

(1) An infringement of copyright is actionable by the copyright owner.

(2) In an action for infringement of copyright all such relief by way of damages, injunctions, accounts or otherwise is available to the plaintiff as is available in respect of the infringement of any other property right.

(3) This section has effect subject to the following provisions of this Chapter.

97. Provisions as to damages in infringement action

(1) Where in an action for infringement of copyright it is shown that at the time of the infringement the defendant did not know, and had no reason to believe, that copyright subsisted in the work to which the action relates, the plaintiff is not entitled to damages against him, but without prejudice to any other remedy.

(2) The court may in an action for infringement of copyright having regard to all the circumstances, and in particular to—

(a) the flagrancy of the infringement, and

(b) any benefit accruing to the defendant by reason of the infringement,

award such additional damages as the justice of the case may require.

99. Order for delivery up

(1) Where a person—

(a) has an infringing copy of a work in his possession, custody or control in the course of a business, or

(b) has in his possession, custody or control an article specifically designed or adapted for making copies of a particular copyright work, knowing or having reason to believe that it has been or is to be used to make infringing copies,

the owner of the copyright in the work may apply to the court for an order that the infringing copy or article be delivered up to him or to such other person as the court may direct.

(2) An application shall not be made after the end of the period specified in section 113 (period after which remedy of delivery up not available); and no order shall be made unless the court also makes, or it appears to the court that there are grounds for making, an order under section 114 (order as to disposal of infringing copy or other article).

(3) A person to whom an infringing copy or other article is delivered up in pursuance of an order under this section shall, if an order under section 114 is not made, retain it pending the making of an order, or the decision not to make an order, under that section.

(4) Nothing in this section affects any other power of the court.

100. Right to seize infringing copies and other articles

(1) An infringing copy of a work which is found exposed or otherwise immediately available for sale or hire, and in respect of which the copyright owner would be entitled to apply for an order under section 99, may be seized and detained by him or a person authorised by him.

The right to seize and detain is exercisable subject to the following conditions and is subject to any decision of the court under section 114.

(2) Before anything is seized under this section notice of the time and place of the proposed seizure must be given to a local police station.

(3) A person may for the purpose of exercising the right conferred by this section enter premises to which the public have access but may not seize anything in the possession, custody or control of a person at a permanent or regular place of business of his, and may not use any force.

(4) At the time when anything is seized under this section there shall be left at the place where it was seized a notice in the prescribed form containing the prescribed particulars as to the person by whom or on whose authority the seizure is made and the grounds on which it is made.

(5) In this section—

"premises" includes land, buildings, moveable structures, vehicles, vessels, aircraft and hovercraft; and

"prescribed" means prescribed by order of the Secretary of State.

(6) An order of the Secretary of State under this section shall be made by statutory instrument which shall be subject to annulment in pursuance of a resolution of either House of Parliament.

Rights and remedies of exclusive licensee

101. Rights and remedies of exclusive licensee

(1) An exclusive licensee has, except against the copyright owner, the same rights and remedies in respect of matters occurring after the grant of the licence as if the licence had been an assignment.

(2) His rights and remedies are concurrent with those of the copyright owner; and references in the relevant provisions of this Part to the copyright owner shall be construed accordingly.

(3) In an action brought by an exclusive licensee by virtue of this section a defendant may avail himself of any defence which would have been available to him if the action had been brought by the copyright owner.

101A. Certain infringements actionable by a non-exclusive licensee

(1) A non-exclusive licensee may bring an action for infringement of copyright if—

(a) the infringing act was directly connected to a prior licensed act of the licensee; and

(b) the licence—

(i) is in writing and is signed by or on behalf of the copyright owner; and

(ii) expressly grants the non-exclusive licensee a right of action under this section.

(2) In an action brought under this section, the non-exclusive licensee shall have the same rights and remedies available to him as the copyright owner would have had if he had brought the action.

(3) The rights granted under this section are concurrent with those of the copyright owner and references in the relevant provisions of this Part to the copyright owner shall be construed accordingly.

(4) In an action brought by a non-exclusive licensee by virtue of this section a defendant may avail himself of any defence which would have been available to him if the action had been brought by the copyright owner.

(5) Subsections (1) to (4) of section 102 shall apply to a non-exclusive licensee who has a right of action by virtue of this section as it applies to an exclusive licensee.

(6) In this section a "non-exclusive licensee" means the holder of a licence authorising the licensee to exercise a right which remains exercisable by the copyright owner.

102. Exercise of concurrent rights

(1) Where an action for infringement of copyright brought by the copyright owner or an exclusive licensee relates (wholly or partly) to an infringement in respect of which they have concurrent rights of action, the copyright owner or, as the case may be, the exclusive licensee may not, without the leave of the court, proceed with the action unless the other is either joined as a plaintiff or added as a defendant.

(2) A copyright owner or exclusive licensee who is added as a defendant in pursuance of subsection (1) is not liable for any costs in the action unless he takes part in the proceedings.

(3) The above provisions do not affect the granting of interlocutory relief on an application by a copyright owner or exclusive licensee alone.

(4) Where an action for infringement of copyright is brought which relates (wholly or partly) to an infringement in respect of which the copyright owner and an exclusive licensee have or had concurrent rights of action—

(a) the court shall in assessing damages take into account—

(i) the terms of the licence, and

(ii) any pecuniary remedy already awarded or available to either of them in respect of the infringement;

(b) no account of profits shall be directed if an award of damages has been made, or an account of profits has been directed, in favour of the other of them in respect of the infringement; and

(c) the court shall if an account of profits is directed apportion the profits between them as the court considers just, subject to any agreement between them;

and these provisions apply whether or not the copyright owner and the exclusive licensee are both parties to the action.

(5) The copyright owner shall notify any exclusive licensee having concurrent rights before applying for an order under section 99 (order for delivery up) or exercising the right conferred by section 100 (right of seizure); and the court may on the application of the licensee make such order under section 99 or, as the case may be, prohibiting or permitting the exercise by the copyright owner of the right conferred by section 100, as it thinks fit having regard to the terms of the licence.

Offences

107. Criminal liability for making or dealing with infringing articles, &c.

(1) A person commits an offence who, without the licence of the copyright owner—

(a) makes for sale or hire, or

(b) imports into the United Kingdom otherwise than for his private and domestic use, or

(c) possesses in the course of a business with a view to committing any act infringing the copyright, or

(d) in the course of a business—

(i) sells or lets for hire, or

(ii) offers or exposes for sale or hire, or

(iii) exhibits in public, or

(iv) distributes, or

(e) distributes otherwise than in the course of a business to such an extent as to affect prejudicially the owner of the copyright,

an article which is, and which he knows or has reason to believe is, an infringing copy of a copyright work.

(2) A person commits an offence who—

(a) makes an article specifically designed or adapted for making copies of a particular copyright work, or

(b) has such an article in his possession,

knowing or having reason to believe that it is to be used to make infringing copies for sale or hire or for use in the course of a business.

(2A) A person who infringes copyright in a work by communicating the work to the public—

(a) in the course of a business, or

(b) otherwise than in the course of a business to such an extent as to affect prejudicially the owner of the copyright,

commits an offence if he knows or has reason to believe that, by doing so, he is infringing copyright in that work.

(3) Where copyright is infringed (otherwise than by reception of a communication to the public)—

(a) by the public performance of a literary, dramatic or musical work, or

(b) by the playing or showing in public of a sound recording or film,

any person who caused the work to be so performed, played or shown is guilty of an offence if he knew or had reason to believe that copyright would be infringed.

(4) A person guilty of an offence under subsection (1)(a), (b), (d)(iv) or (e) is liable—

(a) on summary conviction to imprisonment for a term not exceeding six months or a fine not exceeding £50,000, or both;

(b) on conviction on indictment to a fine or imprisonment for a term not exceeding ten years, or both.

(4A) A person guilty of an offence under subsection (2A) is liable—

(a) on summary conviction to imprisonment for a term not exceeding three months or a fine not exceeding £50,000, or both;

(b) on conviction on indictment to a fine or imprisonment for a term not exceeding two years, or both.

(5) A person guilty of any other offence under this section is liable on summary conviction to imprisonment for a term not exceeding three months or a fine not exceeding level 5 on the standard scale, or both.

(6) Sections 104 to 106 (presumptions as to various matters connected with copyright) do not apply to proceedings for an offence under this section; but without prejudice to their application in proceedings for an order under section 108 below.

107A. Enforcement by local weights and measures authority

(1) It is the duty of every local weights and measures authority to enforce within their area the provisions of section 107.

(2) The following provisions of the Trade Descriptions Act 1968 apply in relation to the enforcement of that section by such an authority as in relation to the enforcement of that Act—

section 27 (power to make test purchases),

section 28 (power to enter premises and inspect and seize goods and documents),

section 29 (obstruction of authorised officers), and

section 33 (compensation for loss, &c of goods seized).

(3) Subsection (1) above does not apply in relation to the enforcement of section 107 in Northern Ireland, but it is the duty of the Department of Economic Development to enforce that section in Northern Ireland.

For that purpose the provisions of the Trade Descriptions Act 1968 specified in subsection (2) apply as if for the references to a local weights and measures authority and any officer of such an authority there were substituted references to that Department and any of its officers.

(4) Any enactment which authorises the disclosure of information for the purpose of facilitating the enforcement of the Trade Descriptions Act 1968 shall apply as if section 107 were contained in that Act and as if the functions of any person in relation to the enforcement of that section were functions under that Act.

(5) Nothing in this section shall be construed as authorising a local weights and measures authority to bring proceedings in Scotland for an offence.

108. Order for delivery up in criminal proceedings

(1) The court before which proceedings are brought against a person for an offence under section 107 may, if satisfied that at the time of his arrest or charge—

(a) he had in his possession, custody or control in the course of a business an infringing copy of a copyright work, or

(b) he had in his possession, custody or control an article specifically designed or adapted for making copies of a particular copyright work, knowing or having reason to believe that it had been or was to be used to make infringing copies,

order that the infringing copy or article be delivered up to the copyright owner or to such other person as the court may direct.

(2) For this purpose a person shall be treated as charged with an offence—

(a) in England, Wales and Northern Ireland, when he is orally charged or is served with a summons or indictment;

(b) in Scotland, when he is cautioned, charged or served with a complaint or indictment.

(3) An order may be made by the court of its own motion or on the application of the prosecutor (or, in Scotland, the Lord Advocate or procurator-fiscal), and may be made whether or not the person is convicted of the offence, but shall not be made—

(a) after the end of the period specified in section 113 (period after which remedy of delivery up not available), or

(b) if it appears to the court unlikely that any order will be made under section 114 (order as to disposal of infringing copy or other article).

(4) An appeal lies from an order made under this section by a magistrates' court—

(a) in England and Wales, to the Crown Court, and

(b) in Northern Ireland, to the county court;

and in Scotland, where an order has been made under this section, the person from whose possession, custody or control the infringing copy or article has been removed may, without prejudice to any other form of appeal under any rule of law, appeal against that order in the same manner as against sentence.

(5) A person to whom an infringing copy or other article is delivered up in pursuance of an order under this section shall retain it pending the making of an order, or the decision not to make an order, under section 114.

(6) Nothing in this section affects the powers of the court under section 143 of the Powers of Criminal Courts (Sentencing) Act 2000, Part II of the Proceeds of Crime (Scotland) Act 1995 or Article 11 of the Criminal Justice (Northern Ireland) Order 1994 (general provisions as to forfeiture in criminal proceedings).

114. Order as to disposal of infringing copy or other article

(1) An application may be made to the court for an order that an infringing copy or other article delivered up in pursuance of an order under section 99 or 108, or seized and detained in pursuance of the right conferred by section 100, shall be—

(a) forfeited to the copyright owner, or

(b) destroyed or otherwise dealt with as the court may think fit,

or for a decision that no such order should be made.

(2) In considering what order (if any) should be made, the court shall consider whether other remedies available in an action for infringement of copyright would be adequate to compensate the copyright owner and to protect his interests.

(3) Provision shall be made by rules of court as to the service of notice on persons having an interest in the copy or other articles, and any such person is entitled—

(a) to appear in proceedings for an order under this section, whether or not he was served with notice, and

(b) to appeal against any order made, whether or not he appeared;

and an order shall not take effect until the end of the period within which notice of an appeal may be given or, if before the end of that period notice of appeal is duly given, until the final determination or abandonment of the proceedings on the appeal.

(4) Where there is more than one person interested in a copy or other article, the court shall make such order as it thinks just and may (in particular) direct that the article be sold, or otherwise dealt with, and the proceeds divided.

(5) If the court decides that no order should be made under this section, the person in whose possession, custody or control the copy or other article was before being delivered up or seized is entitled to its return.

(6) References in this section to a person having an interest in a copy or other article include any person in whose favour an order could be made in respect of it—

(a) under this section or under section 204 or 231 of this Act;

(b) under section 24D of the Registered Designs Act 1949;

(c) under section 19 of Trade Marks Act 1994 (including that section as applied by regulation 4 of the Community Trade Mark Regulations 2006 (SI 2006/1027)); or

(d) under regulation 1C of the Community Design Regulations 2005 (SI 2005/2339).

Part III
Design Right

Chapter I
Design Right in Original Designs

Introductory

213. Design right

(1) Design right is a property right which subsists in accordance with this Part in an original design.

(2) In this Part "design" means the design of any aspect of the shape or configuration (whether internal or external) of the whole or part of an article.

(3) Design right does not subsist in—

(a) a method or principle of construction,

(b) features of shape or configuration of an article which—

(i) enable the article to be connected to, or placed in, around or against, another article so that either article may perform its function, or

(ii) are dependent upon the appearance of another article of which the article is intended by the designer to form an integral part, or

(c) surface decoration.

(4) A design is not "original" for the purposes of this Part if it is commonplace in the design field in question at the time of its creation.

(5) Design right subsists in a design only if the design qualifies for design right protection by reference to—

(a) the designer or the person by whom the design was commissioned or the designer employed (see sections 218 and 219), or

(b) the person by whom and country in which articles made to the design were first marketed (see section 220),

or in accordance with any Order under section 221 (power to make further provision with respect to qualification).

(5A) Design right does not subsist in a design which consists of or contains a controlled representation within the meaning of the Olympic Symbol etc. (Protection) Act 1995.

(6) Design right does not subsist unless and until the design has been recorded in a design document or an article has been made to the design.

(7) Design right does not subsist in a design which was so recorded, or to which an article was made, before the commencement of this Part.

214. The designer

(1) In this Part the "designer", in relation to a design, means the person who creates it.

(2) In the case of a computer-generated design the person by whom the arrangements necessary for the creation of the design are undertaken shall be taken to be the designer.

215. Ownership of design right

(1) The designer is the first owner of any design right in a design which is not created in pursuance of a commission or in the course of employment.

(2) Where a design is created in pursuance of a commission, the person commissioning the design is the first owner of any design right in it.

(3) Where, in a case not falling within subsection (2) a design is created by an employee in the course of his employment, his employer is the first owner of any design right in the design.

(4) If a design qualifies for design right protection by virtue of section 220 (qualification by reference to first marketing of articles made to the design), the above rules do not apply and the person by whom the articles in question are marketed is the first owner of the design right.

216. Duration of design right

(1) Design right expires—

(a) fifteen years from the end of the calendar year in which the design was first recorded in a design document or an article was first made to the design, whichever first occurred, or

(b) if articles made to the design are made available for sale or hire within five years from the end of that calendar year, ten years from the end of the calendar year in which that first occurred.

(2) The reference in subsection (1) to articles being made available for sale or hire is to their being made so available anywhere in the world by or with the licence of the design right owner.

Chapter II
Rights of Design Right Owner and Remedies

Infringement of design right

226. Primary infringement of design right

(1) The owner of design right in a design has the exclusive right to reproduce the design for commercial purposes—

(a) by making articles to that design, or

(b) by making a design document recording the design for the purpose of enabling such articles to be made.

(2) Reproduction of a design by making articles to the design means copying the design so as to produce articles exactly or substantially to that design, and references in this Part to making articles to a design shall be construed accordingly.

(3) Design right is infringed by a person who without the licence of the design right owner does, or authorises another to do, anything which by virtue of this section is the exclusive right of the design right owner.

(4) For the purposes of this section reproduction may be direct or indirect, and it is immaterial whether any intervening acts themselves infringe the design right.

(5) This section has effect subject to the provisions of Chapter III (exceptions to rights of design right owner).

227. Secondary infringement: importing or dealing with infringing article

(1) Design right is infringed by a person who, without the licence of the design right owner—

(a) imports into the United Kingdom for commercial purposes, or

(b) has in his possession for commercial purposes, or

(c) sells, lets for hire, or offers or exposes for sale or hire, in the course of a business,

an article which is, and which he knows or has reason to believe is, an infringing article.

(2) This section has effect subject to the provisions of Chapter III (exceptions to rights of design right owner).

Remedies for infringement

229. Rights and remedies of design right owner

(1) An infringement of design right is actionable by the design right owner.

(2) In an action for infringement of design right all such relief by way of damages, injunctions, accounts or otherwise is available to the plaintiff as is available in respect of the infringement of any other property right.

(3) The court may in an action for infringement of design right, having regard to all the circumstances and in particular to—

(a) the flagrancy of the infringement, and

(b) any benefit accruing to the defendant by reason of the infringement,

award such additional damages as the justice of the case may require.

(4) This section has effect subject to section 233 (innocent infringement).

230. Order for delivery up

(1) Where a person—

(a) has in his possession, custody or control for commercial purposes an infringing article, or

(b) has in his possession, custody or control anything specifically designed or adapted for making articles to a particular design, knowing or having reason to believe that it has been or is to be used to make an infringing article,

the owner of the design right in the design in question may apply to the court for an order that the infringing article or other thing be delivered up to him or to such other person as the court may direct.

(2) An application shall not be made after the end of the period specified in the following provisions of this section; and no order shall be made unless the court also makes, or it appears to the court that there are grounds for making, an order under section 231 (order as to disposal of infringing article, &c.).

(3) An application for an order under this section may not be made after the end of the period of six years from the date on which the article or thing in question was made, subject to subsection (4).

(4) If during the whole or any part of that period the design right owner—

(a) is under a disability, or

(b) is prevented by fraud or concealment from discovering the facts entitling him to apply for an order,

an application may be made at any time before the end of the period of six years from the date on which he ceased to be under a disability or, as the case may be, could with reasonable diligence have discovered those facts.

(5) In subsection (4) "disability"—

(a) in England and Wales, has the same meaning as in the Limitation Act 1980;

(b) in Scotland, means legal disability within the meaning of the Prescription and Limitation (Scotland) Act 1973;

(c) in Northern Ireland, has the same meaning as in the Statute of Limitations (Northern Ireland) 1958.

(6) A person to whom an infringing article or other thing is delivered up in pursuance of an order under this section shall, if an order under section 231 is not made, retain it pending the making of an order, or the decision not to make an order, under that section.

(7) Nothing in this section affects any other power of the court.

231. Order as to disposal of infringing articles, &c.

(1) An application may be made to the court for an order that an infringing article or other thing delivered up in pursuance of an order under section 230 shall be—

(a) forfeited to the design right owner, or

(b) destroyed or otherwise dealt with as the court may think fit,

or for a decision that no such order should be made.

(2) In considering what order (if any) should be made, the court shall consider whether other remedies available in an action for infringement of design right would be adequate to compensate the design right owner and to protect his interests.

(3) Provision shall be made by rules of court as to the service of notice on persons having an interest in the article or other thing, and any such person is entitled—

(a) to appear in proceedings for an order under this section, whether or not he was served with notice, and

(b) to appeal against any order made, whether or not he appeared;

and an order shall not take effect until the end of the period within which notice of an appeal may be given or, if before the end of that period notice of appeal is duly given, until the final determination or abandonment of the proceedings on the appeal.

(4) Where there is more than one person interested in an article or other thing, the court shall make such order as it thinks just and may (in particular) direct that the thing be sold, or otherwise dealt with, and the proceeds divided.

(5) If the court decides that no order should be made under this section, the person in whose possession, custody or control the article or other thing was before being delivered up is entitled to its return.

(6) References in this section to a person having an interest in an article or other thing include any person in whose favour an order could be made in respect of it—

(a) under this section or under section 114 or 204 of this Act;

(b) under section 24D of the Registered Designs Act 1949;

(c) under section 19 of Trade Marks Act 1994 (including that section as applied by regulation 4 of the Community Trade Mark Regulations 2006 (SI 2006/1027)); or

(d) under regulation 1C of the Community Design Regulations 2005 (SI 2005/2339).

233. Innocent infringement

(1) Where in an action for infringement of design right brought by virtue of section 226 (primary infringement) it is shown that at the time of the infringement the defendant did not know, and had no reason to believe, that design right subsisted in the design to which the action relates, the plaintiff is not entitled to damages against him, but without prejudice to any other remedy.

(2) Where in an action for infringement of design right brought by virtue of section 227 (secondary infringement) a defendant shows that the infringing article was innocently acquired by him or a predecessor in title of his, the only remedy available against him in respect of the infringement is damages not exceeding a reasonable royalty in respect of the act complained of.

(3) In subsection (2) "innocently acquired" means that the person acquiring the article did not know and had no reason to believe that it was an infringing article.

Chapter III
Exceptions to Rights of Design Right Owners

Infringement of copyright

236. Infringement of copyright

Where copyright subsists in a work which consists of or includes a design in which design right subsists, it is not an infringement of design right in the design to do anything which is an infringement of the copyright in that work.

Trade Marks Act 1994
1994 c. 26

An Act to make new provision for registered trade marks, implementing Council Directive No. 89/104/EEC of 21st December 1988 to approximate the laws of the Member States relating to trade marks; to make provision in connection with Council Regulation (EC) No. 40/94 of 20th December 1993 on the Community trade mark; to give effect to the Madrid Protocol Relating to the International Registration of Marks of 27th June 1989, and to certain provisions of the Paris Convention for the Protection of Industrial Property of 20th March 1883, as revised and amended; and for connected purposes [21st July 1994]

Part I
Registered Trade Marks

Introductory

1. Trade Marks

(1) In this Act a "trade mark" means any sign capable of being represented graphically which is capable of distinguishing goods or services of one undertaking from those of other undertakings.

A trade mark may, in particular, consist of words (including personal names), designs, letters, numerals or the shape of goods or their packaging.

(2) References in this Act to a trade mark include, unless the context otherwise requires, references to a collective mark (see section 49) or certification mark (see section 50).

Grounds for refusal of registration

3. Absolute grounds for refusal of registration

(1) The following shall not be registered—

(a) signs which do not satisfy the requirements of section 1(1),

(b) trade marks which are devoid of any distinctive character,

(c) trade marks which consist exclusively of signs or indications which may serve, in trade, to designate the kind, quality, quantity, intended purpose, value, geographical origin, the time of production of goods or of rendering of services, or other characteristics of goods or services,

(d) trade marks which consist exclusively of signs or indications which have become customary in the current language or in the bona fide and established practices of the trade:

Provided that, a trade mark shall not be refused registration by virtue of paragraph (b), (c) or (d) above if, before the date of application for registration, it has in fact acquired a distinctive character as a result of the use made of it.

(2) A sign shall not be registered as a trade mark if it consists exclusively of—

(a) the shape which results from the nature of the goods themselves,

(b) the shape of goods which is necessary to obtain a technical result, or

(c) the shape which gives substantial value to the goods.

(3) A trade mark shall not be registered if it is—

(a) contrary to public policy or to accepted principles of morality, or

(b) of such a nature as to deceive the public (for instance as to the nature, quality or geographical origin of the goods or service).

(4) A trade mark shall not be registered if or to the extent that its use is prohibited in the United Kingdom by any enactment or rule of law or by any provision of Community law.

(5) A trade mark shall not be registered in the cases specified, or referred to, in section 4 (specially protected emblems).

(6) A trade mark shall not be registered if or to the extent that the application is made in bad faith.

5. Relative grounds for refusal of registration

(1) A trade mark shall not be registered if it is identical with an earlier trade mark and the goods or services for which the trade mark is applied for are identical with the goods or services for which the earlier trade mark is protected.

(2) A trade mark shall not be registered if because—

(a) it is identical with an earlier trade mark and is to be registered for goods or services similar to those for which the earlier trade mark is protected, or

(b) it is similar to an earlier trade mark and is to be registered for goods or services identical with or similar to those for which the earlier trade mark is protected,

there exists a likelihood of confusion on the part of the public, which includes the likelihood of association with the earlier trade mark.

(3) A trade mark which—

(a) is identical with or similar to an earlier trade mark,

shall not be registered if, or to the extent that, the earlier trade mark has a reputation in the United Kingdom (or, in the case of a Community trade mark or international trade mark (EC), in the European Community) and the use of the later mark without due cause would take unfair advantage of, or be detrimental to, the distinctive character or the repute of the earlier trade mark.

(4) A trade mark shall not be registered if, or to the extent that, its use in the United Kingdom is liable to be prevented—

(a) by virtue of any rule of law (in particular, the law of passing off) protecting an unregistered trade mark or other sign used in the course of trade, or

(b) by virtue of an earlier right other than those referred to in subsections (1) to (3) or paragraph (a) above, in particular by virtue of the law of copyright, design right or registered designs.

A person thus entitled to prevent the use of a trade mark is referred to in this Act as the proprietor of an "earlier right" in relation to the trade mark.

(5) Nothing in this section prevents the registration of a trade mark where the proprietor of the earlier trade mark or other earlier right consents to the registration.

Effects of registered trade mark

9. Rights conferred by registered trade mark

(1) The proprietor of a registered trade mark has exclusive rights in the trade mark which are infringed by use of the trade mark in the United Kingdom without his consent.

The acts amounting to infringement, if done without the consent of the proprietor, are specified in section 10.

(2) References in this Act to the infringement of a registered trade mark are to any such infringement of the rights of the proprietor.

(3) The rights of the proprietor have effect from the date of registration (which in accordance with section 40(3) is the date of filing of the application for registration):

Provided that—

(a) no infringement proceedings may be begun before the date on which the trade mark is in fact registered; and

(b) no offence under section 92 (unauthorised use of trade mark, &c in relation to goods) is committed by anything done before the date of publication of the registration.

10 Infringement of registered trade mark

(1) A person infringes a registered trade mark if he uses in the course of trade a sign which is identical with the trade mark in relation to goods or services which are identical with those for which it is registered.

(2) A person infringes a registered trade mark if he uses in the course of trade a sign where because—

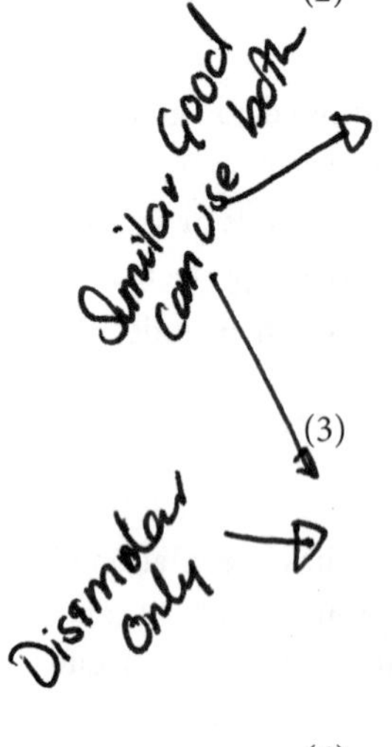

(a) the sign is identical with the trade mark and is used in relation to goods or services similar to those for which the trade mark is registered, or

(b) the sign is similar to the trade mark and is used in relation to goods or services identical with or similar to those for which the trade mark is registered,

there exists a likelihood of confusion on the part of the public, which includes the likelihood of association with the trade mark.

(3) A person infringes a registered trade mark if he uses in the course of trade, in relation to goods or services, a sign which—

(a) is identical with or similar to the trade mark,

where the trade mark has a reputation in the United Kingdom and the use of the sign, being without due cause, takes unfair advantage of, or is detrimental to, the distinctive character or the repute of the trade mark.

(4) For the purposes of this section a person uses a sign if, in particular, he—

(a) affixes it to goods or the packaging thereof;

(b) offers or exposes goods for sale, puts them on the market or stocks them for those purposes under the sign, or offers or supplies services under the sign;

(c) imports or exports goods under the sign; or

(d) uses the sign on business papers or in advertising.

(5) A person who applies a registered trade mark to material intended to be used for labelling or packaging goods, as a business paper, or for advertising goods or services, shall be treated as a party to any use of the material which infringes the registered trade mark if when he applied the mark he knew or had reason to believe that the application of the mark was not duly authorised by the proprietor or a licensee.

(6) Nothing in the preceding provisions of this section shall be construed as preventing the use of a registered trade mark by any person for the purpose of identifying goods or services as those of the proprietor or a licensee.

But any such use otherwise than in accordance with honest practices in industrial or commercial matters shall be treated as infringing the registered trade mark if the use without due cause takes unfair advantage of, or is detrimental to, the distinctive character or repute of the trade mark.

11. Limits on effect of registered trade mark

(1) A registered trade mark is not infringed by the use of another registered trade mark in relation to goods or services for which the latter is registered (but see section 47(6) (effect of declaration of invalidity of registration)).

(2) A registered trade mark is not infringed by—

(a) the use by a person of his own name or address,

(b) the use of indications concerning the kind, quality, quantity, intended purpose, value, geographical origin, the time of production of goods or of rendering of services, or other characteristics of goods or services, or

(c) the use of the trade mark where it is necessary to indicate the intended purpose of a product or service (in particular, as accessories or spare parts),

provided the use is in accordance with honest practices in industrial or commercial matters.

(3) A registered trade mark is not infringed by the use in the course of trade in a particular locality of an earlier right which applies only in that locality.

For this purpose an "earlier right" means an unregistered trade mark or other sign continuously used in relation to goods or services by a person or a predecessor in title of his from a date prior to whichever is the earlier of—

(a) the use of the first-mentioned trade mark in relation to those goods or services by the proprietor or a predecessor in title of his, or

(b) the registration of the first-mentioned trade mark in respect of those goods or services in the name of the proprietor or a predecessor in title of his;

and an earlier right shall be regarded as applying in a locality if, or to the extent that, its use in that locality is protected by virtue of any rule of law (in particular, the law of passing off).

12. Exhaustion of rights conferred by registered trade mark

(1) A registered trade mark is not infringed by the use of the trade mark in relation to goods which have been put on the market in the European Economic Area under that trade mark by the proprietor or with his consent.

(2) Subsection (1) does not apply where there exist legitimate reasons for the proprietor to oppose further dealings in the goods (in particular, where the condition of the goods has been changed or impaired after they have been put on the market).

Infringement proceedings

14. Action for infringement

(1) An infringement of a registered trade mark is actionable by the proprietor of the trade mark.

(2) In an action for infringement all such relief by way of damages, injunctions, accounts or otherwise is available to him as is available in respect of the infringement of any other property right.

15. Order for erasure, &c. of offending sign

(1) Where a person is found to have infringed a registered trade mark, the court may make an order requiring him—

(a) to cause the offending sign to be erased, removed or obliterated from any infringing goods, material or articles in his possession, custody or control, or

(b) if it is not reasonably practicable for the offending sign to be erased, removed or obliterated, to secure the destruction of the infringing goods, material or articles in question.

(2) If an order under subsection (1) is not complied with, or it appears to the court likely that such an order would not be complied with, the court may order that the infringing goods, material or articles be delivered to such person as the court may direct for erasure, removal or obliteration of the sign, or for destruction, as the case may be.

16. Order for delivery up of infringing goods, material or articles

(1) The proprietor of a registered trade mark may apply to the court for an order for the delivery up to him, or such other person as the court may direct, of any infringing goods, material or articles which a person has in his possession, custody or control in the course of a business.

(2) An application shall not be made after the end of the period specified in section 18 (period after which remedy of delivery up not available); and no order shall be made unless the court also makes, or it appears to the court that there are grounds for making, an order under section 19 (order as to disposal of infringing goods, &c.).

(3) A person to whom any infringing goods, material or articles are delivered up in pursuance of an order under this section shall, if an order under section 19 is not made, retain them pending the making of an order, or the decision not to make an order, under that section.

(4) Nothing in this section affects any other power of the court.

19. Order as to disposal of infringing goods, material or articles

(1) Where infringing goods, material or articles have been delivered up in pursuance of an order under section 16, an application may be made to the court—

(a) for an order that they be destroyed or forfeited to such person as the court may think fit, or

(b) for a decision that no such order should be made.

(2) In considering what order (if any) should be made, the court shall consider whether other remedies available in an action for infringement of the registered trade mark would be adequate to compensate the proprietor and any licensee and protect their interests.

(3) Provision shall be made by rules of court as to the service of notice on persons having an interest in the goods, material or articles, and any such person is entitled—

(a) to appear in proceedings for an order under this section, whether or not he was served with notice, and

(b) to appeal against any order made, whether or not he appeared;

and an order shall not take effect until the end of the period within which notice of an appeal may be given or, if before the end of that period notice of appeal is duly given, until the final determination or abandonment of the proceedings on the appeal.

(4) Where there is more than one person interested in the goods, material or articles, the court shall make such order as it thinks just.

(5) If the court decides that no order should be made under this section, the person in whose possession, custody or control the goods, material or articles were before being delivered up is entitled to their return.

(6) References in this section to a person having an interest in goods, material or articles include any person in whose favour an order could be made —

(a) under this section (including that section as applied by regulation 4 of the Community Trade Mark Regulations 2006 (SI 2006/1027));

(b) under section 24D of the Registered Designs Act 1949;

(c) under section 114, 204 or 231 of the Copyright, Designs and Patents Act 1988; or

(d) under regulation 1C of the Community Design Regulations 2005 (SI 2005/2339).

21. Remedy for groundless threats of infringement proceedings

(1) Where a person threatens another with proceedings for infringement of a registered trade mark other than—

(a) the application of the mark to goods or their packaging,

(b) the importation of goods to which, or to the packaging of which, the mark has been applied, or

(c) the supply of services under the mark,

any person aggrieved may bring proceedings for relief under this section.

(2) The relief which may be applied for is any of the following—

(a) a declaration that the threats are unjustifiable,

(b) an injunction against the continuance of the threats,

(c) damages in respect of any loss he has sustained by the threats;

and the plaintiff is entitled to such relief unless the defendant shows that the acts in respect of which proceedings were threatened constitute (or if done would constitute) an infringement of the registered trade mark concerned.

(3) If that is shown by the defendant, the plaintiff is nevertheless entitled to relief if he shows that the registration of the trade mark is invalid or liable to be revoked in a relevant respect.

(4) The mere notification that a trade mark is registered, or that an application for registration has been made, does not constitute a threat of proceedings for the purposes of this section.

Registered trade mark as object of property

24. Assignment, &c. of registered trade mark

(1) A registered trade mark is transmissible by assignment, testamentary disposition or operation of law in the same way as other personal or moveable property.

It is so transmissible either in connection with the goodwill of a business or independently.

(2) An assignment or other transmission of a registered trade mark may be partial, that is, limited so as to apply—

(a) in relation to some but not all of the goods or services for which the trade mark is registered, or

(b) in relation to use of the trade mark in a particular manner or a particular locality.

(3) An assignment of a registered trade mark, or an assent relating to a registered trade mark, is not effective unless it is in writing signed by or on behalf of the assignor or, as the case may be, a personal representative.

Except in Scotland, this requirement may be satisfied in a case where the assignor or personal representative is a body corporate by the affixing of its seal.

(4) The above provisions apply to assignment by way of security as in relation to any other assignment.

(5) A registered trade mark may be the subject of a charge (in Scotland, security) in the same way as other personal or moveable property.

(6) Nothing in this Act shall be construed as affecting the assignment or other transmission of an unregistered trade mark as part of the goodwill of a business.

25. Registration of transactions affecting registered trade mark

(1) On application being made to the registrar by—

(a) a person claiming to be entitled to an interest in or under a registered trade mark by virtue of a registrable transaction, or

(b) any other person claiming to be affected by such a transaction,

the prescribed particulars of the transaction shall be entered in the register.

(2) The following are registrable transactions—

(a) an assignment of a registered trade mark or any right in it;

(b) the grant of a licence under a registered trade mark;

(c) the granting of any security interest (whether fixed or floating) over a registered trade mark or any right in or under it;

(d) the making by personal representatives of an assent in relation to a registered trade mark or any right in or under it;

(e) an order of a court or other competent authority transferring a registered trade mark or any right in or under it.

(3) Until an application has been made for registration of the prescribed particulars of a registrable transaction—

(a) the transaction is ineffective as against a person acquiring a conflicting interest in or under the registered trade mark in ignorance of it, and

(b) a person claiming to be a licensee by virtue of the transaction does not have the protection of section 30 or 31 (rights and remedies of licensee in relation to infringement).

(4) Where a person becomes the proprietor or a licensee of a registered trade mark by virtue of a registrable transaction and the mark is infringed before the prescribed particulars of the transaction are registered, in proceedings for such an infringement, the court shall not award him costs unless—

(a) an application for registration of the prescribed particulars of the transaction is made before the end of the period of six months beginning with its date, or

(b) the court is satisfied that it was not practicable for such an application to be made before the end of that period and that an application was made as soon as practicable thereafter.

(5) Provision may be made by rules as to—

(a) the amendment of registered particulars relating to a licence so as to reflect any alteration of the terms of the licence, and

(b) the removal of such particulars from the register—

(i) where it appears from the registered particulars that the licence was granted for a fixed period and that period has expired, or

(ii) where no such period is indicated and, after such period as may be prescribed, the registrar has notified the parties of his intention to remove the particulars from the register.

(6) Provision may also be made by rules as to the amendment or removal from the register of particulars relating to a security interest on the application of, or with the consent of, the person entitled to the benefit of that interest.

Licensing

28. Licensing of registered trade mark

(1) A licence to use a registered trade mark may be general or limited.

A limited licence may, in particular, apply—

(a) in relation to some but not all of the goods or services for which the trade mark is registered, or

(b) in relation to use of the trade mark in a particular manner or a particular locality.

(2) A licence is not effective unless it is in writing signed by or on behalf of the grantor.

Except in Scotland, this requirement may be satisfied in a case where the grantor is a body corporate by the affixing of its seal.

(3) Unless the licence provides otherwise, it is binding on a successor in title to the grantor's interest.

References in this Act to doing anything with, or without, the consent of the proprietor of a registered trade mark shall be construed accordingly.

(4) Where the licence so provides, a sub-licence may be granted by the licensee; and references in this Act to a licence or licensee include a sub-licence or sub-licensee.

30. General provisions as to rights of licensees in case of infringement

(1) This section has effect with respect to the rights of a licensee in relation to infringement of a registered trade mark.

The provisions of this section do not apply where or to the extent that, by virtue of section 31(1) below (exclusive licensee having rights and remedies of assignee), the licensee has a right to bring proceedings in his own name.

(2) A licensee is entitled, unless his licence, or any licence through which his interest is derived, provides otherwise, to call on the proprietor of the registered trade mark to take infringement proceedings in respect of any matter which affects his interests.

(3) If the proprietor—

(a) refuses to do so, or

(b) fails to do so within two months after being called upon.

the licensee may bring the proceedings in his own name as if he were the proprietor.

(4) Where infringement proceedings are brought by a licensee by virtue of this section the licensee may not, without the leave of the court, proceed with the action unless the proprietor is either joined as a plaintiff or added as a defendant.

This does not affect the granting of interlocutory relief on an application by a licensee alone.

(5) A proprietor who is added as a defendant as mentioned in subsection (4) shall not be made liable for any costs in the action unless he takes part in the proceedings.

(6) In infringement proceedings brought by the proprietor of a registered trade mark any loss suffered or likely to be suffered by licensees shall be taken into account; and the court may give such directions as it thinks fit as to the extent to which the plaintiff is to hold the proceeds of any pecuniary remedy on behalf of licensees.

(7) The provisions of this section apply in relation to an exclusive licensee if or to the extent that he has, by virtue of section 31(1), the rights and remedies of an assignee as if he were the proprietor of the registered trade mark.

31. Exclusive licensee having rights and remedies of assignee

(1) An exclusive licence may provide that the licensee shall have, to such extent as may be provided by the licence, the same rights and remedies in respect of matters occurring after the grant of the licence as if the licence had been an assignment.

Where or to the extent that such provision is made, the licensee is entitled, subject to the provisions of the licence and to the following provisions of this section, to bring infringement proceedings, against any person other than the proprietor, in his own name.

(2) Any such rights and remedies of an exclusive licensee are concurrent with those of the proprietor of the registered trade mark, and references to the proprietor of a registered trade mark in the provisions of this Act relating to infringement shall be construed accordingly.

(3) In an action brought by an exclusive licensee by virtue of this section a defendant may avail himself of any defence which would have been available to him if the action had been brought by the proprietor of the registered trade mark.

(4) Where proceedings for infringement of a registered trade mark brought by the proprietor or an exclusive licensee relate wholly or partly to an infringement in respect of which they have concurrent rights of action, the proprietor or, as the case may be, the exclusive licensee may not, without the leave of the court, proceed with the action unless the other is either joined as a plaintiff or added as a defendant.

This does not affect the granting of interlocutory relief on an application by a proprietor or exclusive licensee alone.

(5) A person who is added as a defendant as mentioned in subsection (4) shall not be made liable for any costs in the action unless he takes part in the proceedings.

(6) Where an action for infringement of a registered trade mark is brought which relates holly or partly to an infringement in respect of which the proprietor and an exclusive licensee have or had concurrent rights of action—

(a) the court shall in assessing damages take into account—

(i) the terms of the licence, and

(ii) any pecuniary remedy already awarded or available to either of them in respect of the infringement;

(b) no account of profits shall be directed if an award of damages has been made, or an account of profits has been directed, in favour of the other of them in respect of the infringement; and

(c) the court shall if an account of profits is directed apportion the profits between them as the court considers just, subject to any agreement between them.

The provisions of this subsection apply whether or not the proprietor and the exclusive licensee are both parties to the action, and if they are not both parties the court may give such directions as it thinks fit as to the extent to which the party to the proceedings is to hold the proceeds of any pecuniary remedy on behalf of the other.

(7) The proprietor of a registered trade mark shall notify any exclusive licensee who has a concurrent right of action before applying for an order under section 16 (order for delivery up), and the court may on the application of the licensee make such order under that section as it thinks fit having regard to the terms of the licence.

(8) The provisions of subsections (4) to (7) above have effect subject to any agreement to the contrary between the exclusive licensee and the proprietor.

Duration, renewal and alteration of registered trade mark

42. Duration of registration

(1) A trade mark shall be registered for a period of ten years from the date of registration.

(2) Registration may be renewed in accordance with section 43 for further periods of ten years.

46. Revocation of registration

(1) The registration of a trade mark may be revoked on any of the following grounds—

(a) that within the period of five years following the date of completion of the registration procedure it has not been put to genuine use in the United Kingdom, by the proprietor or with his consent, in relation to the goods or services for which it is registered, and there are no proper reasons for non-use;

(b) that such use has been suspended for an uninterrupted period of five years, and there are no proper reasons for non-use;

(c) that, in consequence of acts or inactivity of the proprietor, it has become the common name in the trade for a product or service for which it is registered;

(d) that in consequence of the use made of it by the proprietor or with his consent in relation to the goods or services for which it is registered, it is liable to mislead the public, particularly as to the nature, quality or geographical origin of those goods or services.

(2) For the purposes of subsection (1) use of a trade mark includes use in a form differing in elements which do not alter the distinctive character of the mark in the form in which it was registered, and use in the United Kingdom includes affixing the trade mark to goods or to the packaging of goods in the United Kingdom solely for export purposes.

(3) The registration of a trade mark shall not be revoked on the ground mentioned in subsection (1)(a) or (b) if such use as is referred to in that paragraph is commenced or

resumed after the expiry of the five year period and before the application for revocation is made:

Provided that, any such commencement or resumption of use after the expiry of the five year period but within the period of three months before the making of the application shall be disregarded unless preparations for the commencement or resumption began before the proprietor became aware that the application might be made.

(4) An application for revocation may be made by any person, and may be made either to the registrar or to the court, except that—

(a) if proceedings concerning the trade mark in question are pending in the court, the application must be made to the court; and

(b) if in any other case the application is made to the registrar, he may at any stage of the proceedings refer the application to the court.

(5) Where grounds for revocation exist in respect of only some of the goods or services for which the trade mark is registered, revocation shall relate to those goods or services only.

(6) Where the registration of a trade mark is revoked to any extent, the rights of the proprietor shall be deemed to have ceased to that extent as from—

(a) the date of the application for revocation, or

(b) if the registrar or court is satisfied that the grounds for revocation existed at an earlier date, that date.

47. Grounds for invalidity of registration

(1) The registration of a trade mark may be declared invalid on he ground that the trade mark was registered in breach of section 3 or any of the provisions referred to in that section (absolute grounds for refusal of registration).

Where the trade mark was registered in breach of subsection (1)(b), (c) or (d) of that section, it shall not be declared invalid if, in consequence of the use which has been made of it, it has after registration acquired a distinctive character in relation to the goods or services for which it is registered.

(2) The registration of a trade mark may be declared invalid on the ground—

(a) that there is an earlier trade mark in relation to which the conditions set out in section 5(1), (2) or (3) obtain, or

(b) that there is an earlier right in relation to which the condition set out in section 5(4) is satisfied,

unless the proprietor of that earlier trade mark or other earlier right has consented to the registration.

(2A) But the registration of a trade mark may not be declared invalid on the ground that there is an earlier trade mark unless—

(a) the registration procedure for the earlier trade mark was completed within the period of five years ending with the date of the application for the declaration,

(b) the registration procedure for the earlier trade mark was not completed before that date, or

(c) the use conditions are met.

(2B) The use conditions are met if—

(a) within the period of five years ending with the date of the application for the declaration the earlier trade mark has been put to genuine use in the United Kingdom by the proprietor or with his consent in relation to the goods or services for which it is registered, or

(b) it has not been so used, but there are proper reasons for non-use.

(2C) For these purposes—

(a) use of a trade mark includes use in a form differing in elements which do not alter the distinctive character of the mark in the form in which it was registered, and

(b) use in the United Kingdom includes affixing the trade mark to goods or to the packaging of goods in the United Kingdom solely for export purposes.

(2D) In relation to a Community trade mark or international trade mark (EC), any reference in subsection (2B) or (2C) to the United Kingdom shall be construed as a reference to the European Community.

(2E) Where an earlier trade mark satisfies the use conditions in respect of some only of the goods or services for which it is registered, it shall be treated for the purposes of this section as if it were registered only in respect of those goods or services.

(2F) Subsection (2A) does not apply where the earlier trade mark is a trade mark within section 6(1)(c).

(3) An application for a declaration of invalidity may be made by any person, and may be made either to the registrar or to the court, except that—

(a) if proceedings concerning the trade mark in question are pending in the court, the application must be made to the court; and

(b) if in any other case the application is made to the registrar, he may at any stage of the proceedings refer the application to the court.

(4) In the case of bad faith in the registration of a trade mark, the registrar himself may apply to the court for a declaration of the invalidity of the registration.

(5) Where the grounds of invalidity exist in respect of only some of the goods or services for which the trade mark is registered, the trade mark shall be declared invalid as regards those goods or services only.

(6) Where the registration of a trade mark is declared invalid to any extent, the registration shall to that extent be deemed never to have been made:

Provided that this shall not affect transactions past and closed.

56. Protection of well-known trade marks: Article 6bis

(1) References in this Act to a trade mark which is entitled to protection under the Paris Convention or the WTO agreement as a well known trade mark are to a mark which is well-known in the United Kingdom as being the mark of a person who—

(a) is a national of a Convention country, or

(b) is domiciled in, or has a real and effective industrial or commercial establishment in, a Convention country,

whether or not that person carries on business, or has any goodwill, in the United Kingdom.

References to the proprietor of such a mark shall be construed accordingly.

(2) The proprietor of a trade mark which is entitled to protection under the Paris Convention or the WTO agreement as a well known trade mark is entitled to restrain by injunction the use in the United Kingdom of a trade mark which, or the essential part of which, is identical or similar to his mark, in relation to identical or similar goods or services, where the use is likely to cause confusion.

This right is subject to section 48 (effect of acquiescence by proprietor of earlier trade mark).

(3) Nothing in subsection (2) affects the continuation of any bona fide use of a trade mark begun before the commencement of this section.

Competition Act 1998
1998 c. 41

An Act to make provision about competition and the abuse of a dominant position in the market; to confer powers in relation to investigations conducted in connection with Article 85 or 86 of the treaty establishing the European Community; to amend the Fair Trading Act 1973 in relation to information which may be required in connection with investigations under that Act; to make provision with respect to the meaning of "supply of services" in the Fair Trading Act 1973; and for connected purposes.

[9th November 1998]

The prohibition

2. Agreements etc preventing, restricting or distorting competition

(1) Subject to section 3, agreements between undertakings, decisions by associations of undertakings or concerted practices which—

(a) may affect trade within the United Kingdom, and

(b) have as their object or effect the prevention, restriction or distortion of competition within the United Kingdom,

are prohibited unless they are exempt in accordance with the provisions of this Part.

(2) Subsection (1) applies, in particular, to agreements, decisions or practices which—

(a) directly or indirectly fix purchase or selling prices or any other trading conditions;

(b) limit or control production, markets, technical development or investment;

(c) share markets or sources of supply;

(d) apply dissimilar conditions to equivalent transactions with other trading parties, thereby placing them at a competitive disadvantage;

(e) make the conclusion of contracts subject to acceptance by the other parties of supplementary obligations which, by their nature or according to commercial usage, have no connection with the subject of such contracts.

(3) Subsection (1) applies only if the agreement, decision or practice is, or is intended to be, implemented in the United Kingdom.

(4) Any agreement or decision which is prohibited by subsection (1) is void.

(5) A provision of this Part which is expressed to apply to, or in relation to, an agreement is to be read as applying equally to, or in relation to, a decision by an association of undertakings or a concerted practice (but with any necessary modifications).

(6) Subsection (5) does not apply where the context otherwise requires.

(7) In this section "the United Kingdom" means, in relation to an agreement which operates or is intended to operate only in a part of the United Kingdom, that part.

(8) The prohibition imposed by subsection (1) is referred to in this Act as "the Chapter I prohibition".

9. Exempt agreements

(1) An agreement is exempt from the Chapter I prohibition if it—

(a) contributes to—

(i) improving production or distribution, or

(ii) promoting technical or economic progress,

while allowing consumers a fair share of the resulting benefit; and

(b) does not—

(i) impose on the undertakings concerned restrictions which are not indispensable to the attainment of those objectives; or

(ii) afford the undertakings concerned the possibility of eliminating competition in respect of a substantial part of the products in question.

(2) In any proceedings in which it is alleged that the Chapter I prohibition is being or has been infringed by an agreement, any undertaking or association of undertakings claiming the benefit of subsection (1) shall bear the burden of proving that the conditions of that subsection are satisfied.

10. Parallel exemptions

(1) An agreement is exempt from the Chapter I prohibition if it is exempt from the Community prohibition—

(a) by virtue of a Regulation, or

(b) because of a decision of the Commission under Article 10 of the EC Competition Regulation.

(2) An agreement is exempt from the Chapter I prohibition if it does not affect trade between Member States but otherwise falls within a category of agreement which is exempt from the Community prohibition by virtue of a Regulation.

(3) An exemption from the Chapter I prohibition under this section is referred to in this Part as a parallel exemption.

(4) A parallel exemption—

(a) takes effect on the date on which the relevant exemption from the Community prohibition takes effect or, in the case of a parallel exemption under subsection (2), would take effect if the agreement in question affected trade between Member States; and

(b) ceases to have effect—

(i) if the relevant exemption from the Community prohibition ceases to have effect; or

(ii) on being cancelled by virtue of subsection (5) or (7).

(5) In such circumstances and manner as may be specified in rules made under section 51, the OFT may—

(a) impose conditions or obligations subject to which a parallel exemption is to have effect;

(b) vary or remove any such condition or obligation;

(c) impose one or more additional conditions or obligations;

(d) cancel the exemption.

(6) In such circumstances as may be specified in rules made under section 51, the date from which cancellation of an exemption is to take effect may be earlier than the date on which notice of cancellation is given.

(7) Breach of a condition imposed by the OFT has the effect of cancelling the exemption.

(8) In exercising its powers under this section, the OFT may require any person who is a party to the agreement in question to give it such information as it may require.

(9) For the purpose of this section references to an agreement being exempt from the Community prohibition are to be read as including references to the prohibition being inapplicable to the agreement by virtue of a Regulation other than the EC Competition Regulation or a decision by the Commission.

(10) In this section—

"the Community prohibition" means the prohibition contained in—

(a) Article 81(1);

(b) any corresponding provision replacing, or otherwise derived from, that provision;

(c) such other Regulation as the Secretary of State may by order specify; and

"Regulation" means a Regulation adopted by the Commission or by the Council.

(11) This section has effect in relation to the prohibition contained in paragraph 1 of Article 53 of the EEA Agreement (and the EFTA Surveillance Authority) as it has effect in relation to the Community prohibition (and the Commission) subject to any modifications which the Secretary of State may by order prescribe.

39. Limited immunity in relation to the Chapter I prohibition

(1) In this section "small agreement" means an agreement—

(a) which falls within a category prescribed for the purposes of this section; but

(b) is not a price fixing agreement.

(2) The criteria by reference to which a category of agreement is prescribed may, in particular, include—

(a) the combined turnover of the parties to the agreement (determined in accordance with prescribed provisions);

(b) the share of the market affected by the agreement (determined in that way).

(3) A party to a small agreement is immune from the effect of section 36(1) so far as that provision relates to decisions about infringement of the Chapter I prohibition; but the OFT may withdraw that immunity under subsection (4).

(4) If the OFT has investigated a small agreement, it may make a decision withdrawing the immunity given by subsection (3) if, as a result of its investigation, it considers that the agreement is likely to infringe the Chapter I prohibition.

(5) The OFT must give each of the parties in respect of which immunity is withdrawn written notice of its decision to withdraw the immunity.

(6) A decision under subsection (4) takes effect on such date ("the withdrawal date") as may be specified in the decision.

(7) The withdrawal date must be a date after the date on which the decision is made.

(8) In determining the withdrawal date, the OFT must have regard to the amount of time which the parties are likely to require in order to secure that there is no further infringement of the Chapter I prohibition with respect to the agreement.

(9) In subsection (1) "price fixing agreement" means an agreement which has as its object or effect, or one of its objects or effects, restricting the freedom of a party to the agreement to determine the price to be charged (otherwise than as between that party and another party to the agreement) for the product, service or other matter to which the agreement relates.

Enterprise Act 2002
(2002 c. 40)

An act to . . . to create an offence for those entering into certain anti-competitive agreements . . .

[7th November 2002]

Part 6
Cartel Offence

Cartel offence

188. Cartel offence

(1) An individual is guilty of an offence if he dishonestly agrees with one or more other persons to make or implement, or to cause to be made or implemented, arrangements of the following kind relating to at least two undertakings (A and B).

(2) The arrangements must be ones which, if operating as the parties to the agreement intend, would—

(a) directly or indirectly fix a price for the supply by A in the United Kingdom (otherwise than to B) of a product or service,

(b) limit or prevent supply by A in the United Kingdom of a product or service,

(c) limit or prevent production by A in the United Kingdom of a product,

(d) divide between A and B the supply in the United Kingdom of a product or service to a customer or customers,

(e) divide between A and B customers for the supply in the United Kingdom of a product or service, or

(f) be bid-rigging arrangements.

(3) Unless subsection (2)(d), (e) or (f) applies, the arrangements must also be ones which, if operating as the parties to the agreement intend, would—

(a) directly or indirectly fix a price for the supply by B in the United Kingdom (otherwise than to A) of a product or service,

(b) limit or prevent supply by B in the United Kingdom of a product or service, or

(c) limit or prevent production by B in the United Kingdom of a product.

(4) In subsections (2)(a) to (d) and (3), references to supply or production are to supply or production in the appropriate circumstances (for which see section 189).

(5) 'Bid-rigging arrangements' are arrangements under which, in response to a request for bids for the supply of a product or service in the United Kingdom, or for the production of a product in the United Kingdom—

(a) A but not B may make a bid, or

(b) A and B may each make a bid but, in one case or both, only a bid arrived at in accordance with the arrangements.

(6) But arrangements are not bid-rigging arrangements if, under them, the person requesting bids would be informed of them at or before the time when a bid is made.

(7) 'Undertaking' has the same meaning as in Part 1 of the 1998 Act.

189. Cartel offence: supplementary

(1) For section 188(2)(a), the appropriate circumstances are that A's supply of the product or service would be at a level in the supply chain at which the product or service would at the same time be supplied by B in the United Kingdom.

(2) For section 188(2)(b), the appropriate circumstances are that A's supply of the product or service would be at a level in the supply chain—

(a) at which the product or service would at the same time be supplied by B in the United Kingdom, or

(b) at which supply by B in the United Kingdom of the product or service would be limited or prevented by the arrangements.

(3) For section 188(2)(c), the appropriate circumstances are that A's production of the product would be at a level in the production chain—

(a) at which the product would at the same time be produced by B in the United Kingdom, or

(b) at which production by B in the United Kingdom of the product would be limited or prevented by the arrangements.

(4) For section 188(2)(d), the appropriate circumstances are that A's supply of the product or service would be at the same level in the supply chain as B's.

(5) For section 188(3)(a), the appropriate circumstances are that B's supply of the product or service would be at a level in the supply chain at which the product or service would at the same time be supplied by A in the United Kingdom.

(6) For section 188(3)(b), the appropriate circumstances are that B's supply of the product or service would be at a level in the supply chain—

(a) at which the product or service would at the same time be supplied by A in the United Kingdom, or

(b) at which supply by A in the United Kingdom of the product or service would be limited or prevented by the arrangements.

(7) For section 188(3)(c), the appropriate circumstances are that B's production of the product would be at a level in the production chain—

(a) at which the product would at the same time be produced by A in the United Kingdom, or

(b) at which production by A in the United Kingdom of the product would be limited or prevented by the arrangements.

190. Cartel offence: penalty and prosecution

(1) A person guilty of an offence under section 188 is liable—

(a) on conviction on indictment, to imprisonment for a term not exceeding five years or to a fine, or to both;

(b) on summary conviction, to imprisonment for a term not exceeding six months or to a fine not exceeding the statutory maximum, or to both.

(2) In England and Wales and Northern Ireland, proceedings for an offence under section 188 may be instituted only—

(a) by the Director of the Serious Fraud Office, or

(b) by or with the consent of the OFT.

(3) No proceedings may be brought for an offence under section 188 in respect of an agreement outside the United Kingdom, unless it has been implemented in whole or in part in the United Kingdom.

(4) Where, for the purpose of the investigation or prosecution of offences under section 188, the OFT gives a person written notice under this subsection, no proceedings for an offence under section 188 that falls within a description specified in the notice may be brought against that person in England and Wales or Northern Ireland except in circumstances specified in the notice.

Commercial Agents (Council Directive) Regulations 1993 (S.I. 1993 No. 3053)

Part I
General

1. Citation, commencement and applicable law

(1) These Regulations may be cited as the Commercial Agents (Council Directive) Regulations 1993 and shall come into force on 1st January 1994.

(2) These Regulations govern the relations between commercial agents and their principals and, subject to paragraph (3), apply in relation to the activities of commercial agents in Great Britain.

(3) A court or tribunal shall:

(a) apply the law of the other member State concerned in place of regulations 3 to 22 where the parties have agreed that the agency contract is to be governed by the law of that member State;

(b) (whether or not it would otherwise be required to do so) apply these regulations where the law of another member State corresponding to these regulations enables the parties to agree that the agency contract is to be governed by the law of a different member State and the parties have agreed that it is to be governed by the law of England and Wales or Scotland.

2. Interpretation, application and extent

(1) In these Regulations—

"commercial agent" means a self-employed intermediary who has continuing authority to negotiate the sale or purchase of goods on behalf of another person (the "principal"), or to negotiate and conclude the sale or purchase of goods on behalf of and in the name of that principal; but shall be understood as not including in particular:

(i) a person who, in his capacity as an officer of a company or association, is empowered to enter into commitments binding on that company or association;

(ii) a partner who is lawfully authorised to enter into commitments binding on his partners;

(iii) a person who acts as an insolvency practitioner (as that expression is defined in section 388 of the Insolvency Act 1986) or the equivalent in any other jurisdiction;

"commission" means any part of the remuneration of a commercial agent which varies with the number or value of business transactions;

"EEA Agreement" means the Agreement on the European Economic Area signed at Oporto on 2nd May 1992 as adjusted by the Protocol signed at Brussels on 17th March 1993;

"member State" includes a State which is a contracting party to the EEA Agreement;

"restraint of trade clause" means an agreement restricting the business activities of a commercial agent following termination of the agency contract.

(2) These Regulations do not apply to—

(a) commercial agents whose activities are unpaid;

(b) commercial agents when they operate on commodity exchanges or in the commodity market;

(c) the Crown Agents for Overseas Governments and Administrations, as set up under the Crown Agents Act 1979, or its subsidiaries.

(3) The provisions of the Schedule to these Regulations have effect for the purpose of determining the persons whose activities as commercial agents are to be considered secondary.

(4) These Regulations shall not apply to the persons referred to in paragraph (3) above.

(5) These Regulations do not extend to Northern Ireland.

Part II
Rights and Obligations

3. Duties of a commercial agent to his principal

(1) In performing his activities a commercial agent must look after the interests of his principal and act dutifully and in good faith.

(2) In particular, a commercial agent must—

- (a) make proper efforts to negotiate and, where appropriate, conclude the transactions he is instructed to take care of;
- (b) communicate to his principal all the necessary information available to him;
- (c) comply with reasonable instructions given by his principal.

4. Duties of a principal to his commercial agent

(1) In his relations with his commercial agent a principal must act dutifully and in good faith.

(2) In particular, a principal must—

- (a) provide his commercial agent with the necessary documentation relating to the goods concerned;
- (b) obtain for his commercial agent the information necessary for the performance of the agency contract, and in particular notify his commercial agent within a reasonable period once he anticipates that the volume of commercial transactions will be significantly lower than that which the commercial agent could normally have expected.

(3) A principal shall, in addition, inform his commercial agent within a reasonable period of his acceptance or refusal of, and of any non-execution by him of, a commercial transaction which the commercial agent has procured for him.

5. Prohibition on derogation from regulations 3 and 4 and consequence of breach

(1) The parties may not derogate from regulations 3 and 4 above.

(2) The law applicable to the contract shall govern the consequence of breach of the rights and obligations under regulations 3 and 4 above.

Part III
Remuneration

6. Form and amount of remuneration in absence of agreement

(1) In the absence of any agreement as to remuneration between the parties, a commercial agent shall be entitled to the remuneration that commercial agents appointed for the goods forming the subject of his agency contract are customarily allowed in the place where he carries on his activities and, if there is no such customary practice, a commercial agent shall be entitled to reasonable remuneration taking into account all the aspects of the transaction.

(2) This regulation is without prejudice to the application of any enactment or rule of law concerning the level of remuneration.

(3) Where a commercial agent is not remunerated (wholly or in part) by commission, regulations 7 to 12 below shall not apply.

7. Entitlement to commission on transactions concluded during agency contract

(1) A commercial agent shall be entitled to commission on commercial transactions concluded during the period covered by the agency contract—

(a) where the transaction has been concluded as a result of his action; or

(b) where the transaction is concluded with a third party whom he has previously acquired as a customer for transactions of the same kind.

(2) A commercial agent shall also be entitled to commission on transactions concluded during the period covered by the agency contract where he has an exclusive right to a specific geographical area or to a specific group of customers and where the transaction has been entered into with a customer belonging to that area or group.

8. Entitlement to commission on transactions concluded after agency contract has terminated

Subject to regulation 9 below, a commercial agent shall be entitled to commission on commercial transactions concluded after the agency contract has terminated if—

(a) the transaction is mainly attributable to his efforts during the period covered by the agency contract and if the transaction was entered into within a reasonable period after that contract terminated; or

(b) in accordance with the conditions mentioned in regulation 7 above, the order of the third party reached the principal or the commercial agent before the agency contract terminated.

9. Apportionment of commission between new and previous commercial agents

(1) A commercial agent shall not be entitled to the commission referred to in regulation 7 above if that commission is payable, by virtue of regulation 8 above, to the previous commercial agent, unless it is equitable because of the circumstances for the commission to be shared between the commercial agents.

(2) The principal shall be liable for any sum due under paragraph (1) above to the person entitled to it in accordance with that paragraph, and any sum which the other commercial agent receives to which he is not entitled shall be refunded to the principal.

10. When commission due and date for payment

(1) Commission shall become due as soon as, and to the extent that, one of the following circumstances occurs:

(a) the principal has executed the transaction; or

(b) the principal should, according to his agreement with the third party, have executed the transaction; or

(c) the third party has executed the transaction.

(2) Commission shall become due at the latest when the third party has executed his part of the transaction or should have done so if the principal had executed his part of the transaction, as he should have.

(3) The commission shall be paid not later than on the last day of the month following the quarter in which it became due, and, for the purposes of these Regulations, unless otherwise agreed between the parties, the first quarter period shall run from the date the agency contract takes effect, and subsequent periods shall run from that date in the third month thereafter or the beginning of the fourth month, whichever is the sooner.

(4) Any agreement to derogate from paragraphs (2) and (3) above to the detriment of the commercial agent shall be void.

11. Extinction of right to commission

(1) The right to commission can be extinguished only if and to the extent that—

(a) it is established that the contract between the third party and the principal will not be executed; and

(b) that fact is due to a reason for which the principal is not to blame.

(2) Any commission which the commercial agent has already received shall be refunded if the right to it is extinguished.

(3) Any agreement to derogate from paragraph (1) above to the detriment of the commercial agent shall be void.

12. Periodic supply of information as to commission due and right of inspection of principal's books

(1) The principal shall supply his commercial agent with a statement of the commission due, not later than the last day of the month following the quarter in which the commission has become due, and such statement shall set out the main components used in calculating the amount of the commission.

(2) A commercial agent shall be entitled to demand that he be provided with all the information (and in particular an extract from the books) which is available to his principal and which he needs in order to check the amount of the commission due to him.

(3) Any agreement to derogate from paragraphs (1) and (2) above shall be void.

(4) Nothing in this regulation shall remove or restrict the effect of, or prevent reliance upon, any enactment or rule of law which recognises the right of an agent to inspect the books of a principal.

Part IV
Conclusion and Termination of the Agency Contract

13. Right to signed written statement of terms of agency contract

(1) The commercial agent and principal shall each be entitled to receive from the other, on request, a signed written document setting out the terms of the agency contract including any terms subsequently agreed.

(2) Any purported waiver of the right referred to in paragraph (1) above shall be void.

14. Conversion of agency contract after expiry of fixed period

An agency contract for a fixed period which continues to be performed by both parties after that period has expired shall be deemed to be converted into an agency contract for an indefinite period.

15. Minimum periods of notice for termination of agency contract

(1) Where an agency contract is concluded for an indefinite period either party may terminate it by notice.

(2) The period of notice shall be—

(a) 1 month for the first year of the contract;

(b) 2 months for the second year commenced;

(c) 3 months for the third year commenced and for the subsequent years;

and the parties may not agree on any shorter periods of notice.

(3) If the parties agree on longer periods than those laid down in paragraph (2) above, the period of notice to be observed by the principal must not be shorter than that to be observed by the commercial agent.

(4) Unless otherwise agreed by the parties, the end of the period of notice must coincide with the end of a calendar month.

(5) The provisions of this regulation shall also apply to an agency contract for a fixed period where it is converted under regulation 14 above into an agency contract for an indefinite period subject to the proviso that the earlier fixed period must be taken into account in the calculation of the period of notice.

16. Savings with regard to immediate termination

These Regulations shall not affect the application of any enactment or rule of law which provides for the immediate termination of the agency contract—

(a) because of the failure of one party to carry out all or part of his obligations under that contract; or

(b) where exceptional circumstances arise.

17. Entitlement of commercial agent to indemnity or compensation on termination of agency contract

(1) This regulation has effect for the purpose of ensuring that the commercial agent is, after termination of the agency contract, indemnified in accordance with paragraphs (3) to (5) below or compensated for damage in accordance with paragraphs (6) and (7) below.

(2) Except where the agency contract otherwise provides, the commercial agent shall be entitled to be compensated rather than indemnified.

(3) Subject to paragraph (9) and to regulation 18 below, the commercial agent shall be entitled to an indemnity if and to the extent that—

(a) he has brought the principal new customers or has significantly increased the volume of business with existing customers and the principal continues to derive substantial benefits from the business with such customers; and

(b) the payment of this indemnity is equitable having regard to all the circumstances and, in particular, the commission lost by the commercial agent on the business transacted with such customers.

(4) The amount of the indemnity shall not exceed a figure equivalent to an indemnity for one year calculated from the commercial agent's average annual remuneration over the preceding five years and if the contract goes back less than five years the indemnity shall be calculated on the average for the period in question.

(5) The grant of an indemnity as mentioned above shall not prevent the commercial agent from seeking damages.

(6) Subject to paragraph (9) and to regulation 18 below, the commercial agent shall be entitled to compensation for the damage he suffers as a result of the termination of his relations with his principal.

(7) For the purpose of these Regulations such damage shall be deemed to occur particularly when the termination takes place in either or both of the following circumstances, namely circumstances which—

(a) deprive the commercial agent of the commission which proper performance of the agency contract would have procured for him whilst providing his principal with substantial benefits linked to the activities of the commercial agent; or

(b) have not enabled the commercial agent to amortize the costs and expenses that he had incurred in the performance of the agency contract on the advice of his principal.

(8) Entitlement to the indemnity or compensation for damage as provided for under paragraphs (2) to (7) above shall also arise where the agency contract is terminated as a result of the death of the commercial agent.

(9) The commercial agent shall lose his entitlement to the indemnity or compensation for damage in the instances provided for in paragraphs (2) to (8) above if within one year following termination of his agency contract he has not notified his principal that he intends pursuing his entitlement.

18. Grounds for excluding payment of indemnity or compensation under regulation 17

The indemnity or compensation referred to in regulation 17 above shall not be payable to the commercial agent where—

(a) the principal has terminated the agency contract because of default attributable to the commercial agent which would justify immediate termination of the agency contract pursuant to regulation 16 above; or

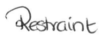

(b) the commercial agent has himself terminated the agency contract, unless such termination is justified—

  (i) by circumstances attributable to the principal, or

  (ii) on grounds of the age, infirmity or illness of the commercial agent in consequence of which he cannot reasonably be required to continue his activities; or

(c) the commercial agent, with the agreement of his principal, assigns his rights and duties under the agency contract to another person.

19. Prohibition on derogation from regulations 17 and 18

The parties may not derogate from regulations 17 and 18 to the detriment of the commercial agent before the agency contract expires.

20. Restraint of trade clauses

(1) A restraint of trade clause shall be valid only if and to the extent that—

  (a) it is concluded in writing; and

  (b) it relates to the geographical area or the group of customers and the geographical area entrusted to the commercial agent and to the kind of goods covered by his agency under the contract.

(2) A restraint of trade clause shall be valid for not more than two years after termination of the agency contract.

(3) Nothing in this regulation shall affect any enactment or rule of law which imposes other restrictions on the validity or enforceability of restraint of trade clauses or which enables a court to reduce the obligations on the parties resulting from such clauses.

Part V
Miscellaneous and Supplemental

21. Disclosure of information

Nothing in these Regulations shall require information to be given where such disclosure would be contrary to public policy.

22. Service of notice etc.

(1) Any notice, statement or other document to be given or supplied to a commercial agent or to be given or supplied to the principal under these Regulations may be so given or supplied:

  (a) by delivering it to him;

  (b) by leaving it at his proper address addressed to him by name;

  (c) by sending it by post to him addressed either to his registered address or to the address of his registered or principal office;

  or by any other means provided for in the agency contract.

(2) Any such notice, statement or document may—

  (a) in the case of a body corporate, be given or served on the secretary or clerk of that body;

(b) in the case of a partnership, be given to or served on any partner or on any person having the control or management of the partnership business.

23. Transitional provisions

(1) Notwithstanding any provision in an agency contract made before 1st January 1994, these Regulations shall apply to that contract after that date and, accordingly any provision which is inconsistent with these Regulations shall have effect subject to them.

(2) Nothing in these Regulations shall affect the rights and liabilities of a commercial agent or a principal which have accrued before 1st January 1994.

Copyright and Rights in Databases Regulations 1997 (S.I. 1997 No. 3032)

Part III
Database Right

12. Interpretation

(1) In this Part—

'database' has the meaning given by section 3A(1) of the 1988 Act (as inserted by Regulation 6);

'extraction', in relation to any contents of a database, means the permanent or temporary transfer of those contents to another medium by any means or in any form;

'insubstantial', in relation to part of the contents of a database, shall be construed subject to Regulation 16(2);

'investment' includes any investment, whether of financial, human or technical resources;

'jointly', in relation to the making of a database, shall be construed in accordance with Regulation 14(6);

'lawful user', in relation to a database, means any person who (whether under a licence to do any of the acts restricted by any database right in the database or otherwise) has a right to use the database;

'maker', in relation to a database, shall be construed in accordance with Regulation 14;

're-utilisation', in relation to any contents of a database, means making those contents available to the public by any means;

'substantial', in relation to any investment, extraction or re-utilisation, means substantial in terms of quantity or quality or a combination of both.

(2) The making of a copy of a database available for use, on terms that it will or may be returned, otherwise than for direct or indirect economic or commercial advantage, through an establishment which is accessible to the public shall not be taken for the purposes of this Part to constitute extraction or re-utilisation of the contents of the database.

(3) Where the making of a copy of a database available through an establishment which is accessible to the public gives rise to a payment the amount of which does not go beyond what is necessary to cover the costs of the establishment, there is no direct or indirect economic or commercial advantage for the purposes of paragraph (2).

(4) Paragraph (2) does not apply to the making of a copy of a database available for on-the-spot reference use.

(5) Where a copy of a database has been sold within the EEA or the Isle of Man by, or with the consent of, the owner of the database right in the database, the further sale within the EEA or the Isle of Man of that copy shall not be taken for the purposes of this Part to constitute extraction or re-utilisation of the contents of the database.

13. Database right

(1) A property right ("database right") subsists, in accordance with this Part, in a database if there has been a substantial investment in obtaining, verifying or presenting the contents of the database.

(2) For the purposes of paragraph (1) it is immaterial whether or not the database or any of its contents is a copyright work, within the meaning of Part I of the 1988 Act.

(3) This Regulation has effect subject to Regulation 18.

14. The maker of a database

(1) Subject to paragraphs (2) to (4), the person who takes the initiative in obtaining, verifying or presenting the contents of a database and assumes the risk of investing in that obtaining, verification or presentation shall be regarded as the maker of, and as having made, the database.

(2) Where a database is made by an employee in the course of his employment, his employer shall be regarded as the maker of the database, subject to any agreement to the contrary.

(3) Subject to paragraph (4), where a database is made by Her Majesty or by an officer or servant of the Crown in the course of his duties, Her Majesty shall be regarded as the maker of the database.

(4) Where a database is made by or under the direction or control of the House of Commons or the House of Lords—

(a) the House by whom, or under whose direction or control, the database is made shall be regarded as the maker of the database, and

(b) if the database is made by or under the direction or control of both Houses, the two Houses shall be regarded as the joint makers of the database.

(4A) Where a database is made by or under the direction or control of the Scottish Parliament, the Scottish Parliamentary Corporate Body shall be regarded as the maker of the database.

(5) For the purposes of this Part a database is made jointly if two or more persons acting together in collaboration take the initiative in obtaining, verifying or presenting the contents of the database and assume the risk of investing in that obtaining, verification or presentation.

(6) References in this Part to the maker of a database shall, except as otherwise provided, be construed, in relation to a database which is made jointly, as references to all the makers of the database.

15. First ownership of database right

The maker of a database is the first owner of database right in it.

16. Acts infringing database right

(1) Subject to the provisions of this Part, a person infringes database right in a database if, without the consent of the owner of the right, he extracts or re-utilises all or a substantial part of the contents of the database.

(2) For the purposes of this Part, the repeated and systematic extraction or re-utilisation of insubstantial parts of the contents of a database may amount to the extraction or re-utilisation of a substantial part of those contents.

17. Term of protection

(1) Database right in a database expires at the end of the period of fifteen years from the end of the calendar year in which the making of the database was completed.

(2) Where a database is made available to the public before the end of the period referred to in paragraph (1), database right in the database shall expire fifteen years from the end of the calendar year in which the database was first made available to the public.

(3) Any substantial change to the contents of a database, including a substantial change resulting from the accumulation of successive additions, deletions or alterations, which would result in the database being considered to be a substantial new investment shall qualify the database resulting from that investment for its own term of protection.

(4) This Regulation has effect subject to Regulation 30.

18. Qualification for database right

(1) Database right does not subsist in a database unless, at the material time, its maker, or if it was made jointly, one or more of its makers, was—

(a) an individual who was a national of an EEA state or habitually resident within the EEA,

(b) a body which was incorporated under the law of an EEA state and which, at that time, satisfied one of the conditions in paragraph (2),

(c) a partnership or other unincorporated body which was formed under the law of an EEA state and which, at that time, satisfied the condition in paragraph (2)(a),

(d) an individual who was habitually resident within the Isle of Man,

(e) a body which was incorporated under the law of the Isle of Man and which, at that time, satisfied one of the conditions in paragraph (2A), or

(f) a partnership or other unincorporated body which was formed under the law of the Isle of Man and which, at that time, satisfied the condition in paragraph (2A)(a).

(2) The conditions mentioned in paragraphs (1)(b) and (c) are—

(a) that the body has its central administration or principal place of business within the EEA, or

(b) that the body has its registered office within the EEA and the body's operations are linked on an ongoing basis with the economy of an EEA state.

(2A) The conditions mentioned in paragraphs (1)(e) and (f) are—

(a) that the body has its central administration or principal place of business within the Isle of Man, or

(b) that the body has its registered office within the Isle of Man and the body's operations are linked on an ongoing basis with the economy of the Isle of Man.

(3) Paragraph (1) does not apply in any case falling within Regulation 14(4).

(4) In this Regulation—

(a) "EEA" and "EEA state" have the meaning given by section 172A of the 1988 Act;

(b) "the material time" means the time when the database was made, or if the making extended over a period, a substantial part of that period.

19. Avoidance of certain terms affecting lawful users

(1) A lawful user of a database which has been made available to the public in any manner shall be entitled to extract or re-utilise insubstantial parts of the contents of the database for any purpose.

(2) Where under an agreement a person has a right to use a database, or part of a database, which has been made available to the public in any manner, any term or condition in the agreement shall be void in so far as it purports to prevent that person from extracting or re-utilising insubstantial parts of the contents of the database, or of that part of the database, for any purpose.

20. Exceptions to database right

(1) Database right in a database which has been made available to the public in any manner is not infringed by fair dealing with a substantial part of its contents if—

(a) that part is extracted from the database by a person who is apart from this paragraph a lawful user of the database,

(b) it is extracted for the purpose of illustration for teaching or research and not for any commercial purpose, and

(c) the source is indicated.

(2) The provisions of Schedule 1 specify other acts which may be done in relation to a database notwithstanding the existence of database right.

23. Application of copyright provisions to database right

The following provisions of the 1988 Act apply in relation to database right and databases in which that right subsists as they apply in relation to copyright and copyright works—

sections 90 to 93 (dealing with rights in copyright works)
sections 96 to 102 (rights and remedies of copyright owner and exclusive licensee)
sections 113 and 114 (supplementary provisions relating to delivery up)
section 115 (jurisdiction of county court and sheriff court).

Consumer Protection (Distance Selling) Regulations 2000 (S.I. 2000 No. 2334)

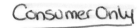

Consumer Only

3. Interpretation

(1) In these Regulations—

"the 2000 Act" means the Financial Services and Markets Act 2000;

"appointed representative" has the same meaning as in section 39(2) of the 2000 Act;

"authorised person" has the same meaning as in section 31(2) of the 2000 Act;

"breach" means contravention by a supplier of a prohibition in, or failure to comply with a requirement of, these Regulations;

"business" includes a trade or profession;

"consumer" means any natural person who, in contracts to which these Regulations apply, is acting for purposes which are outside his business;

"court" in relation to England and Wales and Northern Ireland means a county court or the High Court, and in relation to Scotland means the Sheriff Court or the Court of Session;

"credit" includes a cash loan and any other form of financial accommodation, and for this purpose "cash" includes money in any form;

"OFT" means the Office of Fair Trading;

"distance contract" means any contract concerning goods or services concluded between a supplier and a consumer under an organised distance sales or service provision scheme run by the supplier who, for the purpose of the contract, makes exclusive use of one or more means of distance communication up to and including the moment at which the contract is concluded;

"EEA Agreement" means the Agreement on the European Economic Area signed at Oporto on 2 May 1992 as adjusted by the Protocol signed at Brussels on 17 March 1993;

"enactment" includes an enactment comprised in, or in an instrument made under, an Act of the Scottish Parliament;

"enforcement authority" means the OFT, every weights and measures authority in Great Britain, and the Department of Enterprise, Trade and Investment in Northern Ireland;

"excepted contract" means a contract such as is mentioned in regulation 5(1);

"financial service" means any service of a banking, credit, insurance, personal pension, investment or payment nature;

"means of distance communication" means any means which, without the simultaneous physical presence of the supplier and the consumer, may be used for the conclusion of a contract between those parties; and an indicative list of such means is contained in Schedule 1;

"Member State" means a State which is a contracting party to the EEA Agreement;

"operator of a means of communication" means any public or private person whose business involves making one or more means of distance communication available to suppliers;

"period for performance" has the meaning given by regulation 19(2);

"personal credit agreement" has the meaning given by regulation 14(8);

"regulated activity" has the same meaning as in section 22 of the 2000 Act;

"related credit agreement" has the meaning given by regulation 15(5);

"supplier" means any person who, in contracts to which these Regulations apply, is acting in his commercial or professional capacity; and

"working days" means all days other than Saturdays, Sundays and public holidays.

(2) In the application of these Regulations to Scotland, for references to an "injunction" or an "interim injunction" there shall be substituted references to an "interdict" or an "interim interdict" respectively.

5. Excepted contracts

(1) The following are excepted contracts, namely any contract—

(a) for the sale or other disposition of an interest in land except for a rental agreement;

(b) for the construction of a building where the contract also provides for a sale or other disposition of an interest in land on which the building is constructed, except for a rental agreement;

(c) relating to financial services, a non-exhaustive list of which is contained in Schedule 2;

(d) concluded by means of an automated vending machine or automated commercial premises;

(e) concluded with a telecommunications operator through the use of a public pay-phone;

(f) concluded at an auction.

(2) References in paragraph (1) to a rental agreement—

(a) if the land is situated in England and Wales, are references to any agreement which does not have to be made in writing (whether or not in fact made in writing) because of section 2(5)(a) of the Law of Property (Miscellaneous Provisions) Act 1989;

(b) if the land is situated in Scotland, are references to any agreement for the creation, transfer, variation or extinction of an interest in land, which does not have to be made in writing (whether or not in fact made in writing) as provided for in section 1(2) and (7) of the Requirements of Writing (Scotland) Act 1995; and

(c) if the land is situated in Northern Ireland, are references to any agreement which is not one to which section II of the Statute of Frauds, (Ireland) 1695 applies.

(3) Paragraph (2) shall not be taken to mean that a rental agreement in respect of land situated outside the United Kingdom is not capable of being a distance contract to which these Regulations apply.

6. Contracts to which only part of these Regulations apply

(1) Regulations 7 to 20 shall not apply to a contract which is a "timeshare agreement" within the meaning of the Timeshare Act 1992 and to which that Act applies.

(2) Regulations 7 to 19(1) shall not apply to—

(a) contracts for the supply of food, beverages or other goods intended for everyday consumption supplied to the consumer's residence or to his workplace by regular roundsmen; or

(b) contracts for the provision of accommodation, transport, catering or leisure services, where the supplier undertakes, when the contract is concluded, to provide these services on a specific date or within a specific period.

(3) Regulations 19(2) to (8) and 20 do not apply to a contract for a "package" within the meaning of the Package Travel, Package Holidays and Package Tours Regulations 1992 which is sold or offered for sale in the territory of the Member States.

(4) Regulations 7 to 14, 17 to 20 and 25 do not apply to any contract which is made, and regulation 24 does not apply to any unsolicited services which are supplied, by an authorised person where the making or performance of that contract or the supply of those services, as the case may be, constitutes or is part of a regulated activity carried on by him.

(5) Regulations 7 to 9, 17 to 20 and 25 do not apply to any contract which is made, and regulation 24 does not apply to any unsolicited services which are supplied, by an appointed representative where the making or performance of that contract or the supply of those services, as the case may be, constitutes or is part of a regulated activity carried on by him.

7. Information required prior to the conclusion of the contract

(1) Subject to paragraph (4), in good time prior to the conclusion of the contract the supplier shall—

(a) provide to the consumer the following information—

(i) the identity of the supplier and, where the contract requires payment in advance, the supplier's address;

(ii) a description of the main characteristics of the goods or services;

(iii) the price of the goods or services including all taxes;

(iv) delivery costs where appropriate;

(v) the arrangements for payment, delivery or performance;

(vi) the existence of a right of cancellation except in the cases referred to in regulation 13;

(vii) the cost of using the means of distance communication where it is calculated other than at the basic rate;

(viii) the period for which the offer or the price remains valid; and

(ix) where appropriate, the minimum duration of the contract, in the case of contracts for the supply of goods or services to be performed permanently or recurrently;

(b) inform the consumer if he proposes, in the event of the goods or services ordered by the consumer being unavailable, to provide substitute goods or services (as the case may be) of equivalent quality and price; and

(c) inform the consumer that the cost of returning any such substitute goods to the supplier in the event of cancellation by the consumer would be met by the supplier.

(2) The supplier shall ensure that the information required by paragraph (1) is provided in a clear and comprehensible manner appropriate to the means of distance communication used, with due regard in particular to the principles of good faith in commercial transactions and the principles governing the protection of those who are unable to give their consent such as minors.

(3) Subject to paragraph (4), the supplier shall ensure that his commercial purpose is made clear when providing the information required by paragraph (1).

(4) In the case of a telephone communication, the identity of the supplier and the commercial purpose of the call shall be made clear at the beginning of the conversation with the consumer.

8. Written and additional information

(1) Subject to regulation 9, the supplier shall provide to the consumer in writing, or in another durable medium which is available and accessible to the consumer, the information referred to in paragraph (2), either—

(a) prior to the conclusion of the contract, or

(b) thereafter, in good time and in any event—

(i) during the performance of the contract, in the case of services; and

(ii) at the latest at the time of delivery where goods not for delivery to third parties are concerned.

(2) The information required to be provided by paragraph (1) is—

(a) the information set out in paragraphs (i) to (vi) of Regulation 7(1)(a);

(b) information about the conditions and procedures for exercising the right to cancel under regulation 10, including—

(i) where a term of the contract requires (or the supplier intends that it will require) that the consumer shall return the goods to the supplier in the event of cancellation, notification of that requirement; . . .

(ii) information as to whether the consumer or the supplier would be responsible under these Regulations for the cost of returning any goods to the supplier, or the cost of his recovering them, if the consumer cancels the contract under regulation 10;

(iii) in the case of a contract for the supply of services, information as to how the right to cancel may be affected by the consumer agreeing to performance of the services beginning before the end of the seven working day period referred to in regulation 12;

(c) the geographical address of the place of business of the supplier to which the consumer may address any complaints;

(d) information about any after-sales services and guarantees; and

(e) the conditions for exercising any contractual right to cancel the contract, where the contract is of an unspecified duration or a duration exceeding one year.

10. Right to cancel

(1) Subject to regulation 13, if within the cancellation period set out in regulations 11 and 12, the consumer gives a notice of cancellation to the supplier, or any other person previously notified by the supplier to the consumer as a person to whom notice of cancellation may be given, the notice of cancellation shall operate to cancel the contract.

(2) Except as otherwise provided by these Regulations, the effect of a notice of cancellation is that the contract shall be treated as if it had not been made.

(3) For the purposes of these Regulations, a notice of cancellation is a notice in writing or in another durable medium available and accessible to the supplier (or to the other person to whom it is given) which, however expressed, indicates the intention of the consumer to cancel the contract.

(4) A notice of cancellation given under this regulation by a consumer to a supplier or other person is to be treated as having been properly given if the consumer—

(a) leaves it at the address last known to the consumer and addressed to the supplier or other person by name (in which case it is to be taken to have been given on the day on which it was left);

(b) sends it by post to the address last known to the consumer and addressed to the supplier or other person by name (in which case, it is to be taken to have been given on the day on which it was posted);

(c) sends it by facsimile to the business facsimile number last known to the consumer (in which case it is to be taken to have been given on the day on which it is sent); or

(d) sends it by electronic mail, to the business electronic mail address last known to the consumer (in which case it is to be taken to have been given on the day on which it is sent).

(5) Where a consumer gives a notice in accordance with paragraph (4)(a) or (b) to a supplier who is a body corporate or a partnership, the notice is to be treated as having been properly given if—

(a) in the case of a body corporate, it is left at the address of, or sent to, the secretary or clerk of that body; or

(b) in the case of a partnership, it is left with or sent to a partner or a person having control or management of the partnership business.

11. Cancellation period in the case of contracts for the supply of goods

(1) For the purposes of regulation 10, the cancellation period in the case of contracts for the supply of goods begins with the day on which the contract is concluded and ends as provided in paragraphs (2) to (5).

(2) Where the supplier complies with regulation 8, the cancellation period ends on the expiry of the period of seven working days beginning with the day after the day on which the consumer receives the goods.

(3) Where a supplier who has not complied with regulation 8 provides to the consumer the information referred to in regulation 8(2), and does so in writing or in another durable medium available and accessible to the consumer, within the period of three months beginning with the day after the day on which the consumer receives the goods, the cancellation period ends on the expiry of the period of seven working days beginning with the day after the day on which the consumer receives the information.

(4) Where neither paragraph (2) nor (3) applies, the cancellation period ends on the expiry of the period of three months and seven working days beginning with the day after the day on which the consumer receives the goods.

(5) In the case of contracts for goods for delivery to third parties, paragraphs (2) to (4) shall apply as if the consumer had received the goods on the day on which they were received by the third party.

12. Cancellation period in the case of contracts for the supply of services

(1) For the purposes of regulation 10, the cancellation period in the case of contracts for the supply of services begins with the day on which the contract is concluded and ends as provided in paragraphs (2) to (4).

(2) Where the supplier complies with regulation 8 on or before the day on which the contract is concluded, the cancellation period ends on the expiry of the period of seven working days beginning with the day after the day on which the contract is concluded.

(3) Where a supplier who has not complied with regulation 8 on or before the day on which the contract is concluded provides to the consumer the information referred to in regulation 8(2) and (3), and does so in writing or in another durable medium available and accessible to the consumer, within the period of three months beginning with the day after the day on which the contract is concluded, the cancellation period ends on the expiry of the period of seven working days beginning with the day after the day on which the consumer receives the information.

(4) Where neither paragraph (2) nor (3) applies, the cancellation period ends on the expiry of the period of three months and seven working days beginning with the day after the day on which the contract is concluded.

13. Exceptions to the right to cancel

(1) Unless the parties have agreed otherwise, the consumer will not have the right to cancel the contract by giving notice of cancellation pursuant to regulation 10 in respect of contracts—

(a) for the supply of services if the performance of the contract has begun with the consumer's agreement—

(i) before the end of the cancellation period applicable under regulation 12(2); and

(ii) after the supplier has provided the information referred to in regulation 8(2);

(b) for the supply of goods or services the price of which is dependent on fluctuations in the financial market which cannot be controlled by the supplier;

(c) for the supply of goods made to the consumer's specifications or clearly personalised or which by reason of their nature cannot be returned or are liable to deteriorate or expire rapidly;

(d) for the supply of audio or video recordings or computer software if they are unsealed by the consumer;

(e) for the supply of newspapers, periodicals or magazines; or

(f) for gaming, betting or lottery services.

14. Recovery of sums paid by or on behalf of the consumer on cancellation, and return of security

(1) On the cancellation of a contract under regulation 10, the supplier shall reimburse any sum paid by or on behalf of the consumer under or in relation to the contract to the person by whom it was made free of any charge, less any charge made in accordance with paragraph (5).

(2) The reference in paragraph (1) to any sum paid on behalf of the consumer includes any sum paid by a creditor who is not the same person as the supplier under a personal credit agreement with the consumer.

(3) The supplier shall make the reimbursement referred to in paragraph (1) as soon as possible and in any case within a period not exceeding 30 days beginning with the day on which the notice of cancellation was given.

(4) Where any security has been provided in relation to the contract, the security (so far as it is so provided) shall, on cancellation under regulation 10, be treated as never having had effect and any property lodged with the supplier solely for the purposes of the security as so provided shall be returned by him forthwith.

(5) Subject to paragraphs (6) and (7), the supplier may make a charge, not exceeding the direct costs of recovering any goods supplied under the contract, where a term of the contract provides that the consumer must return any goods supplied if he cancels the contract under regulation 10 but the consumer does not comply with this provision or returns the goods at the expense of the supplier.

(6) Paragraph (5) shall not apply where—

(a) the consumer cancels in circumstances where he has the right to reject the goods under a term of the contract, including a term implied by virtue of any enactment, or

(b) the term requiring the consumer to return any goods supplied if he cancels the contract is an "unfair term" within the meaning of the Unfair Terms in Consumer Contracts Regulations 1999.

(7) Paragraph (5) shall not apply to the cost of recovering any goods which were supplied as substitutes for the goods ordered by the consumer.

(8) For the purposes of these Regulations, a personal credit agreement is an agreement between the consumer and any other person ("the creditor") by which the creditor provides the consumer with credit of any amount.

15. Automatic cancellation of a related credit agreement

(1) Where a notice of cancellation is given under regulation 10 which has the effect of cancelling the contract, the giving of the notice shall also have the effect of cancelling any related credit agreement.

(2) Where a related credit agreement is cancelled by virtue of paragraph (1), the supplier shall, if he is not the same person as the creditor under that agreement, forthwith on receipt of the notice of cancellation inform the creditor that the notice has been given.

(3) Where a related credit agreement is cancelled by virtue of paragraph (1)—

(a) any sum paid by or on behalf of the consumer under, or in relation to, the credit agreement which the supplier is not obliged to reimburse under regulation 14(1) shall be reimbursed, except for any sum which, if it had not already been paid, would have to be paid under subparagraph (b);

(b) the agreement shall continue in force so far as it relates to repayment of the credit and payment of interest, subject to regulation 16; and

(c) subject to subparagraph (b), the agreement shall cease to be enforceable.

(4) Where any security has been provided under a related credit agreement, the security, so far as it is so provided, shall be treated as never having had effect and any property lodged with the creditor solely for the purposes of the security as so provided shall be returned by him forthwith.

(5) For the purposes of this regulation and regulation 16, a "related credit agreement" means an agreement under which fixed sum credit which fully or partly covers the price under a contract cancelled under regulation 10 is granted—

(a) by the supplier, or

(b) by another person, under an arrangement between that person and the supplier.

(6) For the purposes of this regulation and regulation 16—

(a) "creditor" is a person who grants credit under a related credit agreement;

(b) "fixed sum credit" has the same meaning as in section 10 of the Consumer Credit Act 1974;

(c) "repayment" in relation to credit means repayment of money received by the consumer, and cognate expressions shall be construed accordingly; and

(d) "interest" means interest on money so received.

17. Restoration of goods by consumer after cancellation

(1) This regulation applies where a contract is cancelled under regulation 10 after the consumer has acquired possession of any goods under the contract other than any goods mentioned in regulation 13(1)(b) to (e).

(2) The consumer shall be treated as having been under a duty throughout the period prior to cancellation—

(a) to retain possession of the goods, and

(b) to take reasonable care of them.

(3) On cancellation, the consumer shall be under a duty to restore the goods to the supplier in accordance with this regulation, and in the meanwhile to retain possession of the goods and take reasonable care of them.

(4) The consumer shall not be under any duty to deliver the goods except at his own premises and in pursuance of a request in writing, or in another durable medium available and accessible to the consumer, from the supplier and given to the consumer either before, or at the time when, the goods are collected from those premises.

(5) If the consumer—

(a) delivers the goods (whether at his own premises or elsewhere) to any person to whom, under regulation 10(1), a notice of cancellation could have been given; or

(b) sends the goods at his own expense to such a person,

he shall be discharged from any duty to retain possession of the goods or restore them to the supplier.

(6) Where the consumer delivers the goods in accordance with paragraph (5)(a), his obligation to take care of the goods shall cease; and if he sends the goods in accordance with paragraph (5)(b), he shall be under a duty to take reasonable care to see that they are received by the supplier and not damaged in transit, but in other respects his duty to take care of the goods shall cease when he sends them.

(7) Where, at any time during the period of 21 days beginning with the day notice of cancellation was given, the consumer receives such a request as is mentioned in paragraph (4), and unreasonably refuses or unreasonably fails to comply with it, his duty to retain possession and take reasonable care of the goods shall continue until he delivers or sends the goods as mentioned in paragraph (5), but if within that period he does not receive such a request his duty to take reasonable care of the goods shall cease at the end of that period.

(8) Where—

(a) a term of the contract provides that if the consumer cancels the contract, he must return the goods to the supplier, and

(b) the consumer is not otherwise entitled to reject the goods under the terms of the contract or by virtue of any enactment,

paragraph (7) shall apply as if for the period of 21 days there were substituted the period of 6 months.

(9) Where any security has been provided in relation to the cancelled contract, the duty to restore goods imposed on the consumer by this regulation shall not be enforceable before the supplier has discharged any duty imposed on him by regulation 14(4) to return any property lodged with him as security on cancellation.

(10) Breach of a duty imposed by this regulation on a consumer is actionable as a breach of statutory duty.

19. Performance

(1) Unless the parties agree otherwise, the supplier shall perform the contract within a maximum of 30 days beginning with the day after the day the consumer sent his order to the supplier.

(2) Subject to paragraphs (7) and (8), where the supplier is unable to perform the contract because the goods or services ordered are not available, within the period for performance referred to in paragraph (1) or such other period as the parties agree ("the period for performance"), he shall—

(a) inform the consumer; and

(b) reimburse any sum paid by or on behalf of the consumer under or in relation to the contract to the person by whom it was made.

(3) The reference in paragraph (2)(b) to any sum paid on behalf of the consumer includes any sum paid by a creditor who is not the same person as the supplier under a personal credit agreement with the consumer.

(4) The supplier shall make the reimbursement referred to in paragraph (2)(b) as soon as possible and in any event within a period of 30 days beginning with the day after the day on which the period for performance expired.

(5) A contract which has not been performed within the period for performance shall be treated as if it had not been made, save for any rights or remedies which the consumer has under it as a result of the non-performance.

(6) Where any security has been provided in relation to the contract, the security (so far as it is so provided) shall, where the supplier is unable to perform the contract within the period for performance, be treated as never having had any effect and any property lodged with the supplier solely for the purposes of the security as so provided shall be returned by him forthwith.

(7) Where the supplier is unable to supply the goods or services ordered by the consumer, the supplier may perform the contract for the purposes of these Regulations by providing substitute goods or services (as the case may be) of equivalent quality and price provided that—

(a) this possibility was provided for in the contract;

(b) prior to the conclusion of the contract the supplier gave the consumer the information required by regulation 7(1)(b) and (c) in the manner required by regulation 7(2).

(8) In the case of outdoor leisure events which by their nature cannot be rescheduled, paragraph 2(b) shall not apply where the consumer and the supplier so agree.

25. No contracting-out

(1) A term contained in any contract to which these Regulations apply is void if, and to the extent that, it is inconsistent with a provision for the protection of the consumer contained in these Regulations.

(2) Where a provision of these Regulations specifies a duty or liability of the consumer in certain circumstances, a term contained in a contract to which these Regulations apply, other than a term to which paragraph (3) applies, is inconsistent with that provision if it purports to impose, directly or indirectly, an additional duty or liability on him in those circumstances.

(3) This paragraph applies to a term which requires the consumer to return any goods supplied to him under the contract if he cancels it under regulation 10.

(4) A term to which paragraph (3) applies shall, in the event of cancellation by the consumer under regulation 10, have effect only for the purposes of regulation 14(5) and 17(8).

(5) These Regulations shall apply notwithstanding any contract term which applies or purports to apply the law of a non-Member State if the contract has a close connection with the territory of a Member State.

Electronic Commerce (EC Directive) Regulations 2002
(S.I. 2002 No. 2013)

2. Interpretation

(1) In these Regulations and in the Schedule—

"commercial communication" means a communication, in any form, designed to promote, directly or indirectly, the goods, services or image of any person pursuing a commercial, industrial or craft activity or exercising a regulated profession, other than a communication—

(a) consisting only of information allowing direct access to the activity of that person including a geographic address, a domain name or an electronic mail address; or

(b) relating to the goods, services or image of that person provided that the communication has been prepared independently of the person making it (and for this purpose, a communication prepared without financial consideration is to be taken to have been prepared independently unless the contrary is shown);

"the Commission" means the Commission of the European Communities;

"consumer" means any natural person who is acting for purposes other than those of his trade, business or profession;

"coordinated field" means requirements applicable to information society service providers or information society services, regardless of whether they are of a general nature or specifically designed for them, and covers requirements with which the service provider has to comply in respect of—

(a) the taking up of the activity of an information society service, such as requirements concerning qualifications, authorisation or notification, and

(b) the pursuit of the activity of an information society service, such as requirements concerning the behaviour of the service provider, requirements regarding the quality or content of the service including those applicable to advertising and contracts, or requirements concerning the liability of the service provider, but does not cover requirements such as those applicable to goods as such, to the delivery of goods or to services not provided by electronic means;

"the Directive" means Directive 2000/31/EC of the European Parliament and of the Council of 8 June 2000 on certain legal aspects of information society services, in particular electronic commerce, in the Internal Market (Directive on electronic commerce);

"EEA Agreement" means the Agreement on the European Economic Area signed at Oporto on 2 May 1992 as adjusted by the Protocol signed at Brussels on 17 March 1993;

"enactment" includes an enactment comprised in Northern Ireland legislation and comprised in, or an instrument made under, an Act of the Scottish Parliament;

"enforcement action" means any form of enforcement action including, in particular—

(a) in relation to any legal requirement imposed by or under any enactment, any action taken with a view to or in connection with imposing any sanction (whether criminal or otherwise) for failure to observe or comply with it; and

(b) in relation to a permission or authorisation, anything done with a view to removing or restricting that permission or authorisation;

"enforcement authority" does not include courts but, subject to that, means any person who is authorised, whether by or under an enactment or otherwise, to take enforcement action;

"established service provider" means a service provider who is a national of a member State or a company or firm as mentioned in Article 48 of the Treaty and who effectively pursues an economic activity by virtue of which he is a service provider using a fixed establishment in a member State for an indefinite period, but the presence and use of the technical means and technologies required to provide the information society service do not, in themselves, constitute an establishment of the provider; in cases where it cannot be determined from which of a number of places of establishment a given service is provided, that service is to be regarded as provided from the place of establishment where the provider has the centre of his activities relating to that service; references to a service provider being established or to the establishment of a service provider shall be construed accordingly;

"information society services" (which is summarised in recital 17 of the Directive as covering "any service normally provided for remuneration, at a distance, by means of electronic equipment for the processing (including digital compression) and storage of data, and at the individual request of a recipient of a service") has the meaning set out in Article 2(a) of the Directive, (which refers to Article 1(2) of Directive 98/34/EC of the European Parliament and of the Council of 22 June 1998 laying down a procedure for the provision of information in the field of technical standards and regulations, as amended by Directive 98/48/EC of 20 July 1998);

"member State" includes a State which is a contracting party to the EEA Agreement;

"recipient of the service" means any person who, for professional ends or otherwise, uses an information society service, in particular for the purposes of seeking information or making it accessible;

"regulated profession" means any profession within the meaning of either Article 1(d) of Council Directive 89/48/EEC of 21 December 1988 on a general system for the recognition of higher-education diplomas awarded on completion of professional education and training of at least three years' duration or of Article 1(f) of Council Directive 92/51/EEC of 18 June 1992 on a second general system for the recognition of professional education and training to supplement Directive 89/48/EEC;

"service provider" means any person providing an information society service;

"the Treaty" means the treaty establishing the European Community.

(2) In regulation 4 and 5, "requirement" means any legal requirement under the law of the United Kingdom, or any part of it, imposed by or under any enactment or otherwise.

(3) Terms used in the Directive other than those in paragraph (1) above shall have the same meaning as in the Directive.

6. General information to be provided by a person providing an information society service

(1) A person providing an information society service shall make available to the recipient of the service and any relevant enforcement authority, in a form and manner which is easily, directly and permanently accessible, the following information—

- (a) the name of the service provider;
- (b) the geographic address at which the service provider is established;
- (c) the details of the service provider, including his electronic mail address, which make it possible to contact him rapidly and communicate with him in a direct and effective manner;
- (d) where the service provider is registered in a trade or similar register available to the public, details of the register in which the service provider is entered and his registration number, or equivalent means of identification in that register;
- (e) where the provision of the service is subject to an authorisation scheme, the particulars of the relevant supervisory authority;
- (f) where the service provider exercises a regulated profession—
    - (i) the details of any professional body or similar institution with which the service provider is registered;

(ii) his professional title and the member State where that title has been granted;

(iii) a reference to the professional rules applicable to the service provider in the member State of establishment and the means to access them; and

(g) where the service provider undertakes an activity that is subject to value added tax, the identification number referred to in Article 22(1) of the sixth Council Directive 77/388/EEC of 17 May 1977 on the harmonisation of the laws of the member States relating to turnover taxes—Common system of value added tax: uniform basis of assessment.

(2) Where a person providing an information society service refers to prices, these shall be indicated clearly and unambiguously and, in particular, shall indicate whether they are inclusive of tax and delivery costs.

7. Commercial communications

A service provider shall ensure that any commercial communication provided by him and which constitutes or forms part of an information society service shall—

(a) be clearly identifiable as a commercial communication;

(b) clearly identify the person on whose behalf the commercial communication is made;

(c) clearly identify as such any promotional offer (including any discount, premium or gift) and ensure that any conditions which must be met to qualify for it are easily accessible, and presented clearly and unambiguously; and

(d) clearly identify as such any promotional competition or game and ensure that any conditions for participation are easily accessible and presented clearly and unambiguously.

9. Information to be provided where contracts are concluded by electronic means

(1) Unless parties who are not consumers have agreed otherwise, where a contract is to be concluded by electronic means a service provider shall, prior to an order being placed by the recipient of a service, provide to that recipient in a clear, comprehensible and unambiguous manner the information set out in (a) to (d) below—

(a) the different technical steps to follow to conclude the contract;

(b) whether or not the concluded contract will be filed by the service provider and whether it will be accessible;

(c) the technical means for identifying and correcting input errors prior to the placing of the order; and

(d) the languages offered for the conclusion of the contract.

(2) Unless parties who are not consumers have agreed otherwise, a service provider shall indicate which relevant codes of conduct he subscribes to and give information on how those codes can be consulted electronically.

(3) Where the service provider provides terms and conditions applicable to the contract to the recipient, the service provider shall make them available to him in a way that allows him to store and reproduce them.

(4) The requirements of paragraphs (1) and (2) above shall not apply to contracts concluded exclusively by exchange of electronic mail or by equivalent individual communications.

11. Placing of the order

(1) Unless parties who are not consumers have agreed otherwise, where the recipient of the service places his order through technological means, a service provider shall—

(a) acknowledge receipt of the order to the recipient of the service without undue delay and by electronic means; and

(b) make available to the recipient of the service appropriate, effective and accessible technical means allowing him to identify and correct input errors prior to the placing of the order.

(2) For the purposes of paragraph (1)(a) above—

(a) the order and the acknowledgement of receipt will be deemed to be received when the parties to whom they are addressed are able to access them; and

(b) the acknowledgement of receipt may take the form of the provision of the service paid for where that service is an information society service.

(3) The requirements of paragraph (1) above shall not apply to contracts concluded exclusively by exchange of electronic mail or by equivalent individual communications.

Privacy and Electronic Communications (EC Directive) Regulations 2003 (S.I. 2003 No. 2426)

2. Interpretation

(1) In these Regulations—

"bill" includes an invoice, account, statement or other document of similar character and "billing" shall be construed accordingly;

"call" means a connection established by means of a telephone service available to the public allowing two-way communication in real time;

"communication" means any information exchanged or conveyed between a finite number of parties by means of a public electronic communications service, but does not include information conveyed as part of a programme service, except to the extent that such information can be related to the identifiable subscriber or user receiving the information;

"communications provider" has the meaning given by section 405 of the Communications Act 2003;

"corporate subscriber" means a subscriber who is—

(a) a company within the meaning of section 735(1) of the Companies Act 1985;

(b) a company incorporated in pursuance of a royal charter or letters patent;

(c) a partnership in Scotland;

(d) a corporation sole; or

(e) any other body corporate or entity which is a legal person distinct from its members;

"the Directive" means Directive 2002/58/EC of the European Parliament and of the Council of 12 July 2002 concerning the processing of personal data and the protection of privacy in the electronic communications sector (Directive on privacy and electronic communications);

"electronic communications network" has the meaning given by section 32 of the Communications Act 2003;

"electronic communications service" has the meaning given by section 32 of the Communications Act 2003;

"electronic mail" means any text, voice, sound or image message sent over a public electronic communications network which can be stored in the network or in the recipient's terminal equipment until it is collected by the recipient and includes messages sent using a short message service;

"enactment" includes an enactment comprised in, or in an instrument made under, an Act of the Scottish Parliament;

"individual" means a living individual and includes an unincorporated body of such individuals;

"the Information Commissioner" and "the Commissioner" both mean the Commissioner appointed under section 6 of the Data Protection Act 1998;

"information society service" has the meaning given in regulation 2(1) of the Electronic Commerce (EC Directive) Regulations 2002;

"location data" means any data processed in an electronic communications network indicating the geographical position of the terminal equipment of a user of a public electronic communications service, including data relating to—

(f) the latitude, longitude or altitude of the terminal equipment;

(g) the direction of travel of the user; or

(h) the time the location information was recorded;

"OFCOM" means the Office of Communications as established by section 1 of the Office of Communications Act 2002;

"programme service" has the meaning given in section 201 of the Broadcasting Act 1990;

"public communications provider" means a provider of a public electronic communications network or a public electronic communications service;

"public electronic communications network" has the meaning given in section 151 of the Communications Act 2003;

"public electronic communications service" has the meaning given in section 151 of the Communications Act 2003;

"subscriber" means a person who is a party to a contract with a provider of public electronic communications services for the supply of such services;

"traffic data" means any data processed for the purpose of the conveyance of a communication on an electronic communications network or for the billing in respect of that communication and includes data relating to the routing, duration or time of a communication;

"user" means any individual using a public electronic communications service; and

"value added service" means any service which requires the processing of traffic data or location data beyond that which is necessary for the transmission of a communication or the billing in respect of that communication.

(2) Expressions used in these Regulations that are not defined in paragraph (1) and are defined in the Data Protection Act 1998 shall have the same meaning as in that Act.

(3) Expressions used in these Regulations that are not defined in paragraph (1) or the Data Protection Act 1998 and are defined in the Directive shall have the same meaning as in the Directive.

(4) Any reference in these Regulations to a line shall, without prejudice to paragraph (3), be construed as including a reference to anything that performs the function of a line, and "connected", in relation to a line, is to be construed accordingly.

6. Confidentiality of communications

(1) Subject to paragraph (4), a person shall not use an electronic communications network to store information, or to gain access to information stored, in the terminal equipment of a subscriber or user unless the requirements of paragraph (2) are met.

(2) The requirements are that the subscriber or user of that terminal equipment—

(a) is provided with clear and comprehensive information about the purposes of the storage of, or access to, that information; and

(b) is given the opportunity to refuse the storage of or access to that information.

(3) Where an electronic communications network is used by the same person to store or access information in the terminal equipment of a subscriber or user on more than one occasion, it is sufficient for the purposes of this regulation that the requirements of paragraph (2) are met in respect of the initial use.

(4) Paragraph (1) shall not apply to the technical storage of, or access to, information—

(a) for the sole purpose of carrying out or facilitating the transmission of a communication over an electronic communications network; or

(b) where such storage or access is strictly necessary for the provision of an information society service requested by the subscriber or user.

22. Use of electronic mail for direct marketing purposes

(1) This regulation applies to the transmission of unsolicited communications by means of electronic mail to individual subscribers.

(2) Except in the circumstances referred to in paragraph (3), a person shall neither transmit, nor instigate the transmission of, unsolicited communications for the purposes of direct marketing by means of electronic mail unless the recipient of the electronic mail has previously notified the sender that he consents for the time being to such communications being sent by, or at the instigation of, the sender.

(3) A person may send or instigate the sending of electronic mail for the purposes of direct marketing where—

(a) that person has obtained the contact details of the recipient of that electronic mail in the course of the sale or negotiations for the sale of a product or service to that recipient;

(b) the direct marketing is in respect of that person's similar products and services only; and

(c) the recipient has been given a simple means of refusing (free of charge except for the costs of the transmission of the refusal) the use of his contact details for the purposes of such direct marketing, at the time that the details were initially collected, and, where he did not initially refuse the use of the details, at the time of each subsequent communication.

(4) A subscriber shall not permit his line to be used in contravention of paragraph (2).

23. Use of electronic mail for direct marketing purposes where the identity or address of the sender is concealed

A person shall neither transmit, nor instigate the transmission of, a communication for the purposes of direct marketing by means of electronic mail—

(a) where the identity of the person on whose behalf the communication has been sent has been disguised or concealed; or

(b) where a valid address to which the recipient of the communication may send a request that such communications cease has not been provided.

Treaty on the Functioning of the European Union

Article 101

1. The following shall be prohibited as incompatible with the internal market: all agreements between undertakings, decisions by associations of undertakings and concerted practices which may affect trade between Member States and which have as their object or effect the prevention, restriction or distortion of competition within the internal market, and in particular those which:
   (a) directly or indirectly fix purchase or selling prices or any other trading conditions;
   (b) limit or control production, markets, technical development, or investment;
   (c) share markets or sources of supply;
   (d) apply dissimilar conditions to equivalent transactions with other trading parties, thereby placing them at a competitive disadvantage;
   (e) make the conclusion of contracts subject to acceptance by the other parties of supplementary obligations which, by their nature or according to commercial usage, have no connection with the subject of such contracts.
2. Any agreements or decisions prohibited pursuant to this Article shall be automatically void.
3. The provisions of paragraph 1 may, however, be declared inapplicable in the case of:
   - any agreement or category of agreements between undertakings,
   - any decision or category of decisions by associations of undertakings,
   - any concerted practice or category of concerted practices,

   which contributes to improving the production or distribution of goods or to promoting technical or economic progress, while allowing consumers a fair share of the resulting benefit, and which does not:
   (a) impose on the undertakings concerned restrictions which are not indispensable to the attainment of these objectives;
   (b) afford such undertakings the possibility of eliminating competition in respect of a substantial part of the products in question.

Article 102

Any abuse by one or more undertakings of a dominant position within the internal market or in a substantial part of it shall be prohibited as incompatible with the internal market in so far as it may affect trade between Member States.

Such abuse may, in particular, consist in:

(a) directly or indirectly imposing unfair purchase or selling prices or other unfair trading conditions;
(b) limiting production, markets or technical development to the prejudice of consumers;
(c) applying dissimilar conditions to equivalent transactions with other trading parties, thereby placing them at a competitive disadvantage;
(d) making the conclusion of contracts subject to acceptance by the other parties of supplementary obligations which, by their nature or according to commercial usage, have no connection with the subject of such contracts.

Commission Regulation (EU) on the application of Article 101(3) of the Treaty on the Functioning of the European Union to categories of vertical agreements and concerted practices No. 330/2010

THE EUROPEAN COMMISSION,

Having regard to the Treaty on the Functioning of the European Union,

Having regard to Regulation No 19/65/EEC of the Council of 2 March 1965 on the application of Article 85(3) of the Treaty to certain categories of agreements and concerted practices, and in particular Article 1 thereof,

Having published a draft of this Regulation,

After consulting the Advisory Committee on Restrictive Practices and Dominant Positions,

Whereas:

(1) Regulation No 19/65/EEC empowers the Commission to apply Article 101(3) of the Treaty on the Functioning of the European Union by regulation to certain categories of vertical agreements and corresponding concerted practices falling within Article 101(1) of the Treaty.

(2) Commission Regulation (EC) No 2790/1999 of 22 December 1999 on the application of Article 81(3) of the Treaty to categories of vertical agreements and concerted practices defines a category of vertical agreements which the Commission regarded as normally satisfying the conditions laid down in Article 101(3) of the Treaty. In view of the overall positive experience with the application of that Regulation, which expires on 31 May 2010, and taking into account further experience acquired since its adoption, it is appropriate to adopt a new block exemption regulation.

(3) The category of agreements which can be regarded as normally satisfying the conditions laid down in Article 101(3) of the Treaty includes vertical agreements for the purchase or sale of goods or services where those agreements are concluded between non-competing undertakings, between certain competitors or by certain associations of retailers of goods. It also includes vertical agreements containing ancillary provisions on the assignment or use of intellectual property rights. The term 'vertical agreements' should include the corresponding concerted practices.

(4) For the application of Article 101(3) of the Treaty by regulation, it is not necessary to define those vertical agreements which are capable of falling within Article 101(1) of the Treaty. In the individual assessment of agreements under Article 101(1) of the Treaty, account has to be taken of several factors, and in particular the market structure on the supply and purchase side.

(5) The benefit of the block exemption established by this Regulation should be limited to vertical agreements for which it can be assumed with sufficient certainty that they satisfy the conditions of Article 101(3) of the Treaty.

(6) Certain types of vertical agreements can improve economic efficiency within a chain of production or distribution by facilitating better coordination between the participating undertakings. In particular, they can lead to a reduction in the transaction and distribution costs of the parties and to an optimisation of their sales and investment levels.

(7) The likelihood that such efficiency-enhancing effects will outweigh any anti-competitive effects due to restrictions contained in vertical agreements depends on the degree of market power of the parties to the agreement and, therefore, on the extent to which those undertakings face competition from other suppliers of goods or services

regarded by their customers as interchangeable or substitutable for one another, by reason of the products' characteristics, their prices and their intended use.

(8) It can be presumed that, where the market share held by each of the undertakings party to the agreement on the relevant market does not exceed 30%, vertical agreements which do not contain certain types of severe restrictions of competition generally lead to an improvement in production or distribution and allow consumers a fair share of the resulting benefits.

(9) Above the market share threshold of 30%, there can be no presumption that vertical agreements falling within the scope of Article 101(1) of the Treaty will usually give rise to objective advantages of such a character and size as to compensate for the disadvantages which they create for competition. At the same time, there is no presumption that those vertical agreements are either caught by Article 101(1) of the Treaty or that they fail to satisfy the conditions of Article 101(3) of the Treaty.

(10) This Regulation should not exempt vertical agreements containing restrictions which are likely to restrict competition and harm consumers or which are not indispensable to the attainment of the efficiency-enhancing effects. In particular, vertical agreements containing certain types of severe restrictions of competition such as minimum and fixed resale-prices, as well as certain types of territorial protection, should be excluded from the benefit of the block exemption established by this Regulation irrespective of the market share of the undertakings concerned.

(11) In order to ensure access to or to prevent collusion on the relevant market, certain conditions should be attached to the block exemption. To this end, the exemption of non-compete obligations should be limited to obligations which do not exceed a defined duration. For the same reasons, any direct or indirect obligation causing the members of a selective distribution system not to sell the brands of particular competing suppliers should be excluded from the benefit of this Regulation.

(12) The market-share limitation, the non-exemption of certain vertical agreements and the conditions provided for in this Regulation normally ensure that the agreements to which the block exemption applies do not enable the participating undertakings to eliminate competition in respect of a substantial part of the products in question.

(13) The Commission may withdraw the benefit of this Regulation, pursuant to Article 29(1) of Council Regulation (EC) No 1/2003 of 16 December 2002 on the implementation of the rules on competition laid down in Articles 81 and 82 of the Treaty, where it finds in a particular case that an agreement to which the exemption provided for in this Regulation applies nevertheless has effects which are incompatible with Article 101(3) of the Treaty.

(14) The competition authority of a Member State may withdraw the benefit of this Regulation pursuant to Article 29(2) of Regulation (EC) No 1/2003 in respect of the territory of that Member State, or a part thereof where, in a particular case, an agreement to which the exemption provided for in this Regulation applies nevertheless has effects which are incompatible with Article 101(3) of the Treaty in the territory of that Member State, or in a part thereof, and where such territory has all the characteristics of a distinct geographic market.

(15) In determining whether the benefit of this Regulation should be withdrawn pursuant to Article 29 of Regulation (EC) No 1/2003, the anti-competitive effects that may derive from the existence of parallel networks of vertical agreements that have similar effects which significantly restrict access to a relevant market or competition therein are of particular importance. Such cumulative effects may for example arise in the case of selective distribution or non compete obligations.

(16) In order to strengthen supervision of parallel networks of vertical agreements which have similar anti-competitive effects and which cover more than 50% of a given market, the Commission may by regulation declare this Regulation inapplicable to vertical

agreements containing specific restraints relating to the market concerned, thereby restoring the full application of Article 101 of the Treaty to such agreements,

HAS ADOPTED THIS REGULATION:

Article 1 Definitions

1. For the purposes of this Regulation, the following definitions shall apply:
   (a) 'vertical agreement' means an agreement or concerted practice entered into between two or more undertakings each of which operates, for the purposes of the agreement or the concerted practice, at a different level of the production or distribution chain, and relating to the conditions under which the parties may purchase, sell or resell certain goods or services;
   (b) 'vertical restraint' means a restriction of competition in a vertical agreement falling within the scope of Article 101(1) of the Treaty;
   (c) 'competing undertaking' means an actual or potential competitor; 'actual competitor' means an undertaking that is active on the same relevant market; 'potential competitor' means an undertaking that, in the absence of the vertical agreement, would, on realistic grounds and not just as a mere theoretical possibility, in case of a small but permanent increase in relative prices be likely to undertake, within a short period of time, the necessary additional investments or other necessary switching costs to enter the relevant market;
   (d) 'non-compete obligation' means any direct or indirect obligation causing the buyer not to manufacture, purchase, sell or resell goods or services which compete with the contract goods or services, or any direct or indirect obligation on the buyer to purchase from the supplier or from another undertaking designated by the supplier more than 80% of the buyer's total purchases of the contract goods or services and their substitutes on the relevant market, calculated on the basis of the value or, where such is standard industry practice, the volume of its purchases in the preceding calendar year;
   (e) 'selective distribution system' means a distribution system where the supplier undertakes to sell the contract goods or services, either directly or indirectly, only to distributors selected on the basis of specified criteria and where these distributors undertake not to sell such goods or services to unauthorised distributors within the territory reserved by the supplier to operate that system;
   (f) 'intellectual property rights' includes industrial property rights, know how, copyright and neighbouring rights;
   (g) 'know-how' means a package of non-patented practical information, resulting from experience and testing by the supplier, which is secret, substantial and identified: in this context, 'secret' means that the know-how is not generally known or easily accessible; 'substantial' means that the know-how is significant and useful to the buyer for the use, sale or resale of the contract goods or services; 'identified' means that the know-how is described in a sufficiently comprehensive manner so as to make it possible to verify that it fulfils the criteria of secrecy and substantiality;
   (h) 'buyer' includes an undertaking which, under an agreement falling within Article 101(1) of the Treaty, sells goods or services on behalf of another undertaking;
   (i) 'customer of the buyer' means an undertaking not party to the agreement which purchases the contract goods or services from a buyer which is party to the agreement.
2. For the purposes of this Regulation, the terms 'undertaking', 'supplier' and 'buyer' shall include their respective connected undertakings.

   'Connected undertakings' means:

(a) undertakings in which a party to the agreement, directly or indirectly:

(i) has the power to exercise more than half the voting rights, or

(ii) has the power to appoint more than half the members of the supervisory board, board of management or bodies legally representing the undertaking, or

(iii) has the right to manage the undertaking's affairs;

(b) undertakings which directly or indirectly have, over a party to the agreement, the rights or powers listed in point (a);

(c) undertakings in which an undertaking referred to in point (b) has, directly or indirectly, the rights or powers listed in point (a);

(d) undertakings in which a party to the agreement together with one or more of the undertakings referred to in points (a), (b) or (c), or in which two or more of the latter undertakings, jointly have the rights or powers listed in point (a);

(e) undertakings in which the rights or the powers listed in point (a) are jointly held by:

(i) parties to the agreement or their respective connected undertakings referred to in points (a) to (d), or

(ii) one or more of the parties to the agreement or one or more of their connected undertakings referred to in points (a) to (d) and one or more third parties.

Article 2 Exemption

1. Pursuant to Article 101(3) of the Treaty and subject to the provisions of this Regulation, it is hereby declared that Article 101(1) of the Treaty shall not apply to vertical agreements.

This exemption shall apply to the extent that such agreements contain vertical restraints.

2. The exemption provided for in paragraph 1 shall apply to vertical agreements entered into between an association of undertakings and its members, or between such an association and its suppliers, only if all its members are retailers of goods and if no individual member of the association, together with its connected undertakings, has a total annual turnover exceeding EUR 50 million. Vertical agreements entered into by such associations shall be covered by this Regulation without prejudice to the application of Article 101 of the Treaty to horizontal agreements concluded between the members of the association or decisions adopted by the association.

3. The exemption provided for in paragraph 1 shall apply to vertical agreements containing provisions which relate to the assignment to the buyer or use by the buyer of intellectual property rights, provided that those provisions do not constitute the primary object of such agreements and are directly related to the use, sale or resale of goods or services by the buyer or its customers. The exemption applies on condition that, in relation to the contract goods or services, those provisions do not contain restrictions of competition having the same object as vertical restraints which are not exempted under this Regulation.

4. The exemption provided for in paragraph 1 shall not apply to vertical agreements entered into between competing undertakings. However, it shall apply where competing undertakings enter into a non-reciprocal vertical agreement and:

(a) the supplier is a manufacturer and a distributor of goods, while the buyer is a distributor and not a competing undertaking at the manufacturing level; or

(b) the supplier is a provider of services at several levels of trade, while the buyer provides its goods or services at the retail level and is not a competing undertaking at the level of trade where it purchases the contract services.

5. This Regulation shall not apply to vertical agreements the subject matter of which falls within the scope of any other block exemption regulation, unless otherwise provided for in such a regulation.

Article 3 Market share threshold

1. The exemption provided for in Article 2 shall apply on condition that the market share held by the supplier does not exceed 30% of the relevant market on which it sells the contract goods or services and the market share held by the buyer does not exceed 30% of the relevant market on which it purchases the contract goods or services.
2. For the purposes of paragraph 1, where in a multi party agreement an undertaking buys the contract goods or services from one undertaking party to the agreement and sells the contract goods or services to another undertaking party to the agreement, the market share of the first undertaking must respect the market share threshold provided for in that paragraph both as a buyer and a supplier in order for the exemption provided for in Article 2 to apply.

Article 4 Restrictions that remove the benefit of the block exemption — hardcore restrictions

The exemption provided for in Article 2 shall not apply to vertical agreements which, directly or indirectly, in isolation or in combination with other factors under the control of the parties, have as their object:

(a) the restriction of the buyer's ability to determine its sale price, without prejudice to the possibility of the supplier to impose a maximum sale price or recommend a sale price, provided that they do not amount to a fixed or minimum sale price as a result of pressure from, or incentives offered by, any of the parties;

(b) the restriction of the territory into which, or of the customers to whom, a buyer party to the agreement, without prejudice to a restriction on its place of establishment, may sell the contract goods or services, except:

    (i) the restriction of active sales into the exclusive territory or to an exclusive customer group reserved to the supplier or allocated by the supplier to another buyer, where such a restriction does not limit sales by the customers of the buyer,

    (ii) the restriction of sales to end users by a buyer operating at the wholesale level of trade,

    (iii) the restriction of sales by the members of a selective distribution system to unauthorised distributors within the territory reserved by the supplier to operate that system, and

    (iv) the restriction of the buyer's ability to sell components, supplied for the purposes of incorporation, to customers who would use them to manufacture the same type of goods as those produced by the supplier;

(c) the restriction of active or passive sales to end users by members of a selective distribution system operating at the retail level of trade, without prejudice to the possibility of prohibiting a member of the system from operating out of an unauthorised place of establishment;

(d) the restriction of cross-supplies between distributors within a selective distribution system, including between distributors operating at different level of trade;

(e) the restriction, agreed between a supplier of components and a buyer who incorporates those components, of the supplier's ability to sell the components as spare parts to end-users or to repairers or other service providers not entrusted by the buyer with the repair or servicing of its goods.

Article 5 Excluded restrictions

1. The exemption provided for in Article 2 shall not apply to the following obligations contained in vertical agreements:
   (a) any direct or indirect non-compete obligation, the duration of which is indefinite or exceeds five years;
   (b) any direct or indirect obligation causing the buyer, after termination of the agreement, not to manufacture, purchase, sell or resell goods or services;
   (c) any direct or indirect obligation causing the members of a selective distribution system not to sell the brands of particular competing suppliers.

   For the purposes of point (a) of the first subparagraph, a non- compete obligation which is tacitly renewable beyond a period of five years shall be deemed to have been concluded for an indefinite duration.
2. By way of derogation from paragraph 1(a), the time limi- tation of five years shall not apply where the contract goods or services are sold by the buyer from premises and land owned by the supplier or leased by the supplier from third parties not connected with the buyer, provided that the duration of the non-compete obligation does not exceed the period of occupancy of the premises and land by the buyer.
3. By way of derogation from paragraph 1(b), the exemption provided for in Article 2 shall apply to any direct or indirect obligation causing the buyer, after termination of the agreement, not to manufacture, purchase, sell or resell goods or services where the following conditions are fulfilled:
   (a) the obligation relates to goods or services which compete with the contract goods or services;
   (b) the obligation is limited to the premises and land from which the buyer has operated during the contract period;
   (c) the obligation is indispensable to protect know-how transferred by the supplier to the buyer;
   (d) the duration of the obligation is limited to a period of one year after termination of the agreement.

   Paragraph 1(b) is without prejudice to the possibility of imposing a restriction which is unlimited in time on the use and disclosure of know-how which has not entered the public domain.

Article 6 Non-application of this Regulation

Pursuant to Article 1a of Regulation No 19/65/EEC, the Commission may by regulation declare that, where parallel networks of similar vertical restraints cover more than 50% of a relevant market, this Regulation shall not apply to vertical agreements containing specific restraints relating to that market.

Article 7 Application of the market share threshold

For the purposes of applying the market share thresholds provided for in Article 3 the following rules shall apply:

(a) the market share of the supplier shall be calculated on the basis of market sales value data and the market share of the buyer shall be calculated on the basis of market purchase value data. If market sales value or market purchase value data are not available, estimates based on other reliable market information, including market sales and purchase volumes, may be used to establish the market share of the undertaking concerned;

(b) the market shares shall be calculated on the basis of data relating to the preceding calendar year;

(c) the market share of the supplier shall include any goods or services supplied to vertically integrated distributors for the purposes of sale;

(d) if a market share is initially not more than 30% but subsequently rises above that level without exceeding 35%, the exemption provided for in Article 2 shall continue to apply for a period of two consecutive calendar years following the year in which the 30% market share threshold was first exceeded;

(e) if a market share is initially not more than 30% but subsequently rises above 35%, the exemption provided for in Article 2 shall continue to apply for one calendar year following the year in which the level of 3 5% was first exceeded;

(f) the benefit of points (d) and (e) may not be combined so as to exceed a period of two calendar years;

(g) the market share held by the undertakings referred to in point (e) of the second subparagraph of Article 1(2) shall be apportioned equally to each undertaking having the rights or the powers listed in point (a) of the second subparagraph of Article 1(2).

Article 8 Application of the turnover threshold

1. For the purpose of calculating total annual turnover within the meaning of Article 2(2), the turnover achieved during the previous financial year by the relevant party to the vertical agreement and the turnover achieved by its connected undertakings in respect of all goods and services, excluding all taxes and other duties, shall be added together. For this purpose, no account shall be taken of dealings between the party to the vertical agreement and its connected undertakings or between its connected undertakings.
2. The exemption provided for in Article 2 shall remain applicable where, for any period of two consecutive financial years, the total annual turnover threshold is exceeded by no more than 10%.

Article 9 Transitional period

The prohibition laid down in Article 101(1) of the Treaty shall not apply during the period from 1 June 2010 to 31 May 2011 in respect of agreements already in force on 31 May 2010 which do not satisfy the conditions for exemption provided for in this Regulation but which, on 31 May 2010, satisfied the conditions for exemption provided for in Regulation (EC) No 2790/1999.

Article 10 Period of validity

This Regulation shall enter into force on 1 June 2010.

It shall expire on 31 May 2022.

This Regulation shall be binding in its entirety and directly applicable in all Member States.

Guidelines on Vertical Restraints

Part II
Vertical Agreements Which Generally Fall Outside Article 101(1)

2. Agency agreements

2.1 Definition of agency agreements

(12) An agent is a legal or physical person vested with the power to negotiate and/or conclude contracts on behalf of another person (the principal), either in the agent's own name or in the name of the principal, for the:

- purchase of goods or services by the principal, or
- sale of goods or services supplied by the principal.

(13) The determining factor in defining an agency agreement for the application of Article 101(1) is the financial or commercial risk borne by the agent in relation to the activities for which he has been appointed as an agent by the principal. In this respect it is not material for the assessment whether the agent acts for one or several principals. Neither is material for this assessment the qualification given to their agreement by the parties or national legislation.

(14) There are three types of financial or commercial risk that are material to the definition of an agency agreement for the application of Article 101(1). First there are the contract-specific risks which are directly related to the contracts concluded and/or negotiated by the agent on behalf of the principal, such as financing of stocks. Secondly, there are the risks related to market-specific investments. These are investments specifically required for the type of activity for which the agent has been appointed by the principal, i.e. which are required to enable the agent to conclude and/or negotiate this type of contract. Such investments are usually sunk, which means that upon leaving that particular field of activity the investment cannot be used for other activities or sold other than at a significant loss. Thirdly, there are the risks related to other activities undertaken in the same product market, to the extent that the principal requires the agent to undertake such activities, but not as an agent on behalf of the principal but for its own risk.

(15) For the purposes of applying Article 101(1) the agreement will be qualified as an agency agreement if the agent does not bear any, or bears only insignificant, risks in relation to the contracts concluded and/or negotiated on behalf of the principal, in relation to market-specific investments for that field of activity, and in relation to other activities required by the principal to be undertaken in the same product market. However, risks that are related to the activity of providing agency services in general, such as the risk of the agent's income being dependent upon his success as an agent or general investments in for instance premises or personnel, are not material to this assessment.

(16) For the purpose of applying Article 101(1) an agreement will thus generally be considered an agency agreement where property in the contract goods bought or sold does not vest in the agent, or the agent does not himself supply the contract services and where the agent:

(a) does not contribute to the costs relating to the supply/purchase of the contract goods or services, including the costs of transporting the goods. This does not preclude the agent from carrying out the transport service, provided that the costs are covered by the principal;

(b) does not maintain at his own cost or risk stocks of the contract goods, including the costs of financing the stocks and the costs of loss of stocks and can return unsold goods to the principal without charge, unless the agent is liable for fault (for example, by failing to comply with reasonable security measures to avoid loss of stocks);

(c) does not undertake responsibility towards third parties for damage caused by the product sold (product liability), unless, as agent, he is liable for fault in this respect;

(d) does not take responsibility for customers' non-performance of the contract, with the exception of the loss of the agent's commission, unless the agent is liable for fault (for example, by failing to comply with reasonable security or anti-theft measures or failing to comply with reasonable measures to report theft to the principal or police or to communicate to the principal all necessary information available to him on the customer's financial reliability);

(e) is not, directly or indirectly, obliged to invest in sales promotion, such as contributions to the advertising budgets of the principal;

(f) does not make market-specific investments in equipment, premises or training of personnel, such as for example the petrol storage tank in the case of petrol retailing or specific software to sell insurance policies in case of insurance agents, unless these costs are fully reimbursed by the principal;

(g) does not undertake other activities within the same product market required by the principal, unless these activities are fully reimbursed by the principal.

(17) This list is not exhaustive. However, where the agent incurs one or more of the above risks or costs, the agreement between agent and principal will not be qualified as an agency agreement. The question of risk must be assessed on a case-by-case basis, and with regard to the economic reality of the situation rather than the legal form. For practical reasons, the risk analysis may start with the assessment of the contract-specific risks. If contract-specific risks are incurred by the agent, this will be enough to conclude that the agent is an independent distributor. On the contrary, if the agent does not incur contract-specific risks, then it will be necessary to continue further the analysis by assessing the risks related to market-specific investments. Finally, if the agent does not incur any contract-specific risks and risks related to market-specific investments, the risks related to other required activities within the same product market may have to be considered.

2.2 *The application of Article 101(1) to agency agreements*

(18) In the case of agency agreements as defined above, the selling or purchasing function of the agent forms part of the principal's activities. Since the principal bears the commercial and financial risks related to the selling and purchasing of the contract goods and services all obligations imposed on the agent in relation to the contracts concluded and/or negotiated on behalf of the principal fall outside Article 101(1). The following obligations on the agent's part will be considered to form an inherent part of an agency agreement, as each of them relates to the ability of the principal to fix the scope of activity of the agent in relation to the contract goods or services, which is essential if the principal is to take the risks and therefore to be in a position to determine the commercial strategy:

(a) limitations on the territory in which the agent may sell these goods or services;

(b) limitations on the customers to whom the agent may sell these goods or services;

(c) the prices and conditions at which the agent must sell or purchase these goods or services.

(19) In addition to governing the conditions of sale or purchase of the contract goods or services by the agent on behalf of the principal, agency agreements often contain provisions which concern the relationship between the agent and the principal. In particular, they may contain a provision preventing the principal from appointing other agents in respect of a given type of transaction, customer or territory (exclusive agency provisions) and/or a provision preventing the agent from acting as an agent or distributor of undertakings which compete with the principal (single branding provisions). Since the agent is a separate undertaking from the principal, the provisions

which concern the relationship between the agent and the principal may infringe Article 101(1). Exclusive agency provisions will in general not lead to anti-competitive effects. However, single branding provisions and post-term non-compete provisions, which concern inter-brand competition, may infringe Article 101(1) if they lead to or contribute to a (cumulative) foreclosure effect on the relevant market where the contract goods or services are sold or purchased (see in particular Section VI.2.1). Such provisions may benefit from the Block Exemption Regulation, in particular when the conditions provided in Article 5 thereof are fulfilled. They can also be individually justified by efficiencies under Article 101(3) as for instance described below in paragraphs (144) to (148).

(20) An agency agreement may also fall within the scope of Article 101(1), even if the principal bears all the relevant financial and commercial risks, where it facilitates collusion. This could for instance be the case when a number of principals use the same agents while collectively excluding others from using these agents, or when they use the agents to collude on marketing strategy or to exchange sensitive market information between the principals.

(21) Where the agent bears one or more of the relevant risks as described in paragraph 16, the agreement between agent and principal does not constitute an agency agreement for the purpose of applying Article 101(1). In that situation the agent will be treated as an independent undertaking and the agreement between agent and principal will be subject to Article 101(1) as any other vertical agreement.

Part III
Application of the Block Exemption Regulation

3. Hardcore restrictions under the Block Exemption Regulation

(50) The hardcore restriction set out in Article 4(b) of the Block Exemption Regulation concerns agreements or concerted practices that have as their direct or indirect object the restriction of sales by a buyer party to the agreement or its customers, in as far as those restrictions relate to the territory into which or the customers to whom the buyer or its customers may sell the contract goods or services. This hardcore restriction relates to market partitioning by territory or by customer group. That may be the result of direct obligations, such as the obligation not to sell to certain customers or to customers in certain territories or the obligation to refer orders from these customers to other distributors. It may also result from indirect measures aimed at inducing the distributor not to sell to such customers, such as refusal or reduction of bonuses or discounts, termination of supply, reduction of supplied volumes or limitation of supplied volumes to the demand within the allocated territory or customer group, threat of contract termination, requiring a higher price for products to be exported, limiting the proportion of sales that can be exported or profit pass-over obligations. It may further result from the supplier not providing a Union-wide guarantee service under which normally all distributors are obliged to provide the guarantee service and are reimbursed for this service by the supplier, even in relation to products sold by other distributors into their territory. These practices are even more likely to be viewed as a restriction of the buyer's sales when used in conjunction with the implementation by the supplier of a monitoring system aimed at verifying the effective destination of the supplied goods, eg the use of differentiated labels or serial numbers. However, obligations on the reseller relating to the display of the supplier's brand name are not classified as hardcore. As Article 4(b) only concerns restrictions of sales by the buyer or its customers, this implies that restrictions of the supplier's sales are also not a hardcore restriction, subject to what is said below regarding sales of spare parts in the context of Article 4(e) of the Block Exemption Regulation. Article 4(b) applies without prejudice to a restriction on the buyer's place of establishment. Thus, the benefit of the Block

Exemption Regulation is not lost if it is agreed that the buyer will restrict its distribution outlet(s) and warehouse(s) to a particular address, place or territory.

(51) There are four exceptions to the hardcore restriction in Article 4(b) of the Block Exemption Regulation. The first exception in Article 4(b)(i) allows a supplier to restrict active sales by a buyer party to the agreement to a territory or a customer group which has been allocated exclusively to another buyer or which the supplier has reserved to itself. A territory or customer group is exclusively allocated when the supplier agrees to sell his product only to one distributor for distribution in a particular territory or to a particular customer group and the exclusive distributor is protected against active selling into his territory or to his customer group by all the other buyers of the supplier inside the Union, irrespective of sales by the supplier. The supplier is allowed to combine the allocation of an exclusive territory and an exclusive customer group by for instance appointing an exclusive distributor for a particular customer group in a certain territory. This protection of exclusively allocated territories or customer groups must, however, permit passive sales to such territories or customer groups. For the application of Article 4(b) of the Block Exemption Regulation, the Commission interprets 'active' and 'passive' sales as follows:

- 'Active' sales mean actively approaching individual customers by for instance direct mail, including the sending of unsolicited e-mails, or visits; or actively approaching a specific customer group or customers in a specific territory through advertisement in media, on the internet or other promotions specifically targeted at that customer group or targeted at customers in that territory. Advertisement or promotion that is only attractive for the buyer if it (also) reaches a specific group of customers or customers in a specific territory, is considered active selling to that customer group or customers in that territory.
- 'Passive' sales mean responding to unsolicited requests from individual customers including delivery of goods or services to such customers. General advertising or promotion that reaches customers in other distributors' (exclusive) territories or customer groups but which is a reasonable way to reach customers outside those territories or customer groups, for instance to reach customers in one's own territory, are passive sales. General advertising or promotion is considered a reasonable way to reach such customers if it would be attractive for the buyer to undertake these investments also if they would not reach customers in other distributors' (exclusive) territories or customer groups.

Commission Notice
on agreements of minor importance which do not appreciably restrict competition under Article 81(1) of the Treaty establishing the European Community (*de minimis*)
(2001/C 368/07)

I

1. Article 81(1) prohibits agreements between undertakings which may affect trade between Member States and which have as their object or effect the prevention, restriction or distortion of competition within the common market. The Court of Justice of the European Communities has clarified that this provision is not applicable where the impact of the agreement on intra-Community trade or on competition is not appreciable.
2. In this notice the Commission quantifies, with the help of market share thresholds, what is not an appreciable restriction of competition under Article 81 of the EC Treaty. This negative definition of appreciability does not imply that agreements between undertakings which exceed the thresholds set out in this notice appreciably restrict competition. Such agreements may still have only a negligible effect on competition and may therefore not be prohibited by Article 81(1).
3. Agreements may in addition not fall under Article 81(1) because they are not capable of appreciably affecting trade between Member States. This notice does not deal with this issue. It does not quantify what does not constitute an appreciable effect on trade. It is however acknowledged that agreements between small and medium-sized undertakings, as defined in the Annex to Commission Recommendation 96/280/EC, are rarely capable of appreciably affecting trade between Member States. Small and medium-sized undertakings are currently defined in that recommendation as undertakings which have fewer than 250 employees and have either an annual turnover not exceeding EUR 40 million or an annual balance-sheet total not exceeding EUR 27 million.
4. In cases covered by this notice the Commission will not institute proceedings either upon application or on its own initiative. Where undertakings assume in good faith that an agreement is covered by this notice, the Commission will not impose fines. Although not binding on them, this notice also intends to give guidance to the courts and authorities of the Member States in their application of Article 81.
5. This notice also applies to decisions by associations of undertakings and to concerted practices.
6. This notice is without prejudice to any interpretation of Article 81 which may be given by the Court of Justice or the Court of First Instance of the European Communities.

II

7. The Commission holds the view that agreements between undertakings which affect trade between Member States do not appreciably restrict competition within the meaning of Article 81(1):
   (a) if the aggregate market share held by the parties to the agreement does not exceed 10% on any of the relevant markets affected by the agreement, where the agreement is made between undertakings which are actual or potential competitors on any of these markets (agreements between competitors); or
   (b) if the market share held by each of the parties to the agreement does not exceed 15% on any of the relevant markets affected by the agreement, where the agreement is made between undertakings which are not actual or potential competitors on any of these markets (agreements between non-competitors).

In cases where it is difficult to classify the agreement as either an agreement between competitors or an agreement between non-competitors the 10% threshold is applicable.

8. Where in a relevant market competition is restricted by the cumulative effect of agreements for the sale of goods or services entered into by different suppliers or distributors (cumulative foreclosure effect of parallel networks of agreements having similar effects on the market), the market share thresholds under point 7 are reduced to 5%, both for agreements between competitors and for agreements between non-competitors. Individual suppliers or distributors with a market share not exceeding 5% are in general not considered to contribute significantly to a cumulative foreclosure effect (1). A cumulative foreclosure effect is unlikely to exist if less than 30% of the relevant market is covered by parallel (networks of) agreements having similar effects.

9. The Commission also holds the view that agreements are not restrictive of competition if the market shares do not exceed the thresholds of respectively 10%, 15% and 5% set out in point 7 and 8 during two successive calendar years by more than 2 percentage points.

10. In order to calculate the market share, it is necessary to determine the relevant market. This consists of the relevant product market and the relevant geographic market. When defining the relevant market, reference should be had to the notice on the definition of the relevant market for the purposes of Community competition law. The market shares are to be calculated on the basis of sales value data or, where appropriate, purchase value data. If value data are not available, estimates based on other reliable market information, including volume data, may be used.

11. Points 7, 8 and 9 do not apply to agreements containing any of the following hardcore restrictions:

(1) as regards agreements between competitors as defined in point 7, restrictions which, directly or indirectly, in isolation or in combination with other factors under the control of the parties, have as their object:

(a) the fixing of prices when selling the products to third parties;

(b) the limitation of output or sales;

(c) the allocation of markets or customers;

(2) as regards agreements between non-competitors as defined in point 7, restrictions which, directly or indirectly, in isolation or in combination with other factors under the control of the parties, have as their object:

(a) the restriction of the buyer's ability to determine its sale price, without prejudice to the possibility of the supplier imposing a maximum sale price or recommending a sale price, provided that they do not amount to a fixed or minimum sale price as a result of pressure from, or incentives offered by, any of the parties;

(b) the restriction of the territory into which, or of the customers to whom, the buyer may sell the contract goods or services, except the following restrictions which are not hardcore:

— the restriction of active sales into the exclusive territory or to an exclusive customer group reserved to the supplier or allocated by the supplier to another buyer, where such a restriction does not limit sales by the customers of the buyer,

— the restriction of sales to end users by a buyer operating at the wholesale level of trade,

— the restriction of sales to unauthorised distributors by the members of a selective distribution system, and

— the restriction of the buyer's ability to sell components, supplied for the purposes of incorporation, to customers who would use them to manufacture the same type of goods as those produced by the supplier;

(c) the restriction of active or passive sales to end users by members of a selective distribution system operating at the retail level of trade, without prejudice to the possibility of prohibiting a member of the system from operating out of an unauthorised place of establishment;

(d) the restriction of cross-supplies between distributors within a selective distribution system, including between distributors operating at different levels of trade;

(e) the restriction agreed between a supplier of components and a buyer who incorporates those components, which limits the supplier's ability to sell the components as spare parts to end users or to repairers or other service providers not entrusted by the buyer with the repair or servicing of its goods;

(3) as regards agreements between competitors as defined in point 7, where the competitors operate, for the purposes of the agreement, at a different level of the production or distribution chain, any of the hardcore restrictions listed in paragraph (1) and (2) above.

12. (1) For the purposes of this notice, the terms "undertaking", "party to the agreement", "distributor", "supplier" and "buyer" shall include their respective connected undertakings.

(2) "Connected undertakings" are:

(a) undertakings in which a party to the agreement, directly or indirectly:

— has the power to exercise more than half the voting rights, or

— has the power to appoint more than half the members of the supervisory board, board of management or bodies legally representing the undertaking, or

— has the right to manage the undertaking's affairs;

(b) undertakings which directly or indirectly have, over a party to the agreement, the rights or powers listed in (a);

(c) undertakings in which an undertaking referred to in (b) has, directly or indirectly, the rights or powers listed in (a);

(d) undertakings in which a party to the agreement together with one or more of the undertakings referred to in (a), (b) or (c), or in which two or more of the latter undertakings, jointly have the rights or powers listed in (a);

(e) undertakings in which the rights or the powers listed in (a) are jointly held by:

— parties to the agreement or their respective connected undertakings referred to in (a) to (d), or

— one or more of the parties to the agreement or one or more of their connected undertakings referred to in (a) to (d) and one or more third parties.

(3) For the purposes of paragraph 2(e), the market share held by these jointly held undertakings shall be apportioned equally to each undertaking having the rights or the powers listed in paragraph 2(a).

Index